Thomas Keith Tindale
Chicago, 1945.

CURRICULUM
DEVELOPMENT

HOLLIS L. CASWELL
PROFESSOR OF EDUCATION
GEORGE PEABODY COLLEGE

AND

DOAK S. CAMPBELL
PROFESSOR OF EDUCATION
GEORGE PEABODY COLLEGE

AMERICAN BOOK COMPANY
NEW YORK CINCINNATI CHICAGO BOSTON ATLANTA

EDITOR'S INTRODUCTION

There has been much discussion of the need for revision of the curricula of our schools during the past ten years. There is common agreement that the traditional program suited to the needs of an earlier social and economic order is not suited to present-day conditions.

Schools in which reading, writing, and arithmetic were taught to young children a hundred years ago could not possibly be accepted as meeting the requirements of the situation today. School education in those earlier days was supplementary to a much more significant education carried on by the family and in local community enterprises. Children worked with their fathers and mothers and with their older brothers and sisters. They were inducted into their responsibilities as citizens through co-operation with their elders in providing the labor necessary for many community enterprises and in actual participation in those discussions which resulted in local governmental action. In this earlier period, with the difficulties of transportation and communication which then existed, each family, or at least each local community, was for the most part self-sustaining.

Any attempt to propose the program of education which the state is obligated to provide today must take into account the contrast between that earlier society and our modern, inter-dependent, industrial, urbanized society. An earlier generation lived in an age of scarcity; we live in an age of plenty. They depended upon the use of power from human beings and from farm animals; we derive our power from the burning of coal and oil and from the harnessing of great rivers. They were compelled to work long hours in order to provide food, clothing, and shelter; we live in a period in which the hours of labor must be restricted in order to provide employment for all of our people.

They lived in communities in which it was possible to discuss the issues of local government in town meetings. They had so little to distract them by way of commercialized entertainment that it was customary for them to spend such little leisure time as was available in the discussion of political and governmental problems which concerned the state and the nation. We live in communities so large and so complex that we find it difficult to act intelligently or effectively in the development of efficient local government. We are provided with so many opportunities for the use, or the waste, of our free time that the great majority of us pay little or no attention to our responsibilities as citizens of the state or nation. The only hope that we have for the maintenance of liberty and the perpetuation of our democracy is to be found in a more adequate program of public education.

The authors of this book have brought together the best of current thought with respect to the aims and purposes of education as they function in the perpetuation and the improvement of democratic ideals. They have analyzed the objectives to be achieved and have presented the techniques essential in the development of curricula. The discussion is sound in theory and based upon a wide experience in the development of curricula in co-operation with state and city superintendents of schools, supervisors, and teachers. One who reads the book cannot fail to be impressed with the vision and the constructive suggestions with which it is filled.

GEORGE D. STRAYER

PREFACE

This volume is based on extended field experience in curriculum programs and on the intensive study of specific problems in the curriculum laboratory of George Peabody College for Teachers. The authors have served as consultants for state, city, and institutional curriculum programs, and have directed studies of teacher training curricula. Out of this experience and study have developed considerations, conclusions, and practices differing in various respects from those generally held and followed. It is the purpose of this book to present in organized form the considerations and practices which have come to hold a place of importance in the point of view of the authors toward curriculum development. It is believed that this presentation will be found of value to those concerned with curriculum problems. Throughout the treatment consideration is given both to the theoretical and practical aspects of the various phases of curriculum development.

Grateful acknowledgment is made to Mary Louise McGlothlin who rendered valuable aid in preparing the manuscript for publication; to Dr. J. E. Brewton and Dr. Floyd Jordan who made suggestions on certain portions of the manuscript and assisted in preparation of tabular and bibliographical materials; and to Dr. W. T. Rowland who read and criticized certain portions of the manuscript.

Development of the point of view toward the curriculum expressed in the book would have been impossible without the opportunities afforded by working with Dr. M. R. Hinson, Dr. D. W. Peters, Mr. Ed McCuistion, and Dr. Frank Jenkins, directors of state curriculum programs in Florida, Virginia, Arkansas, and Mississippi, respectively, and the committees under their supervision.

HOLLIS L. CASWELL
DOAK S. CAMPBELL

CONTENTS

LIST OF CHARTS

LIST OF TABLES

CHAPTER I

CHALLENGE OF CONTEMPORARY LIFE
TO THE SCHOOL

The extent of the need for organized education is largely determined by the complexity of social life. In relatively simple and primitive conditions where a family or a community is largely self-contained, the controls of conduct needed by members of a group for satisfactory adjustment of relationships are much fewer in number and simpler in type than in complex conditions where the family is dependent in a major way on the community, the community on the state and nation, and the nation on other nations. Life today is of this latter type, being extremely complex in most of its aspects. Ease and rapidity of transportation and communication have especially contributed to this condition. Man has become the master of distance. He secures products from afar. He multiplies his points of personal contact. In so doing, he has greatly increased his dependence on others, and likewise the dependence of others on him.

Interdependence of this type influences human activity in two important ways: first, results of individual acts reach beyond immediate association, influencing in vital ways persons far removed in time and space, and, second, the consequences of an individual's acts are removed from his immediate observation. It is these far-reaching influences that make necessary the development, through careful study and training, of an acute discernment and a sensitive understanding of human relationships.

Thus, the rapid development of interdependence in contemporary life has intensified the need for education. New conditions require the development of new controls of conduct and fre-

1

quently make useless those that tradition sanctions. In fact, present educative efforts often run counter to present needs. This condition has not been recognized consistently by educative agencies, with the result that the present educational program fails to meet at many points the needs of present living. Reconstruction of the general educational program of society is therefore essential. Such reconstruction must be based on consideration of the present need for education if significant results are to be achieved.

The development of conditions leading to a need for reconstruction of the educational program has been recognized for some time by students of society. Schools especially have given attention to such demands during the past decade. This attention has resulted in significant scattered efforts to develop an educational program for schools that takes account of the conditions and needs of contemporary life. "America has witnessed in the last decade more activity in curriculum and course of study construction than in all its previous history," states Bruner.[1] This activity, no doubt, has been actuated by many motives, not all of which have been laudable. Much of the work has been piecemeal and poorly conceived. But the persistence of such endeavors, often with limitations of inadequate time, training, and finances, is an indication that schools have been honestly seeking to develop educational programs that meet society's enlarging need for education. Even so, considering the entire school program, attention and change have been desultory at best.

Many objections have been raised to these efforts to reconstruct the program of the school. Much criticism could justly be given. But in recent years the operation of forces that increase the need for education has become intensified until the results may now be seen even by the casual observer. Many of the very people who previously objected to change in social programs are now clamoring for overthrow of the existing order. In some

---

[1] H. B. Bruner, "Present Status of Curriculum," *Curriculum Making in Current Practice,* Conference Report, School of Education, Northwestern University, Evanston, Illinois, 1932, p. 11.

cases the demand is to discard everything and start anew, while in others it is to return to the status of fifty years ago. This lack of critical evaluation makes it imperative that in attempting to improve the work of the school, care be exercised to see that values secured through long struggle are not cast aside lightly, and that at the same time the requirement of society for a program to care for additional educational needs be met.

Developments that create new demands for education are suggested here by brief consideration of a few aspects of contemporary life which have pronounced implications for education.

OPPORTUNITY FOR GAINFUL EMPLOYMENT

Several phases of employment—or perhaps we should say unemployment—are of special importance to education. In the first place, there is a decided tendency for children to be displaced from gainful employment. In 1900, 18.2 per cent of all children from ten to fifteen years of age were gainfully employed. By 1920 the rate had dropped to 8.5 per cent and by 1930 to 4.7 per cent. Also, during the past decade, there has been a steadily decreasing proportion of persons, fifteen to twenty years of age, gainfully employed. In 1920, 39.5 per cent of all persons in the population sixteen years of age were gainfully employed. By 1930, the proportion had dropped to 24.8 per cent. The proportion of persons in the population seventeen years of age employed in 1920 was 50.3 per cent and in 1930, 38.8 per cent, while the proportion of persons eighteen and nineteen years of age employed in 1920 was 60 per cent, and in 1930, 55.3 per cent. During the same period, 1920 to 1930, there has been a tendency for the proportion of the total population gainfully employed to increase. For example, the proportion of persons twenty to twenty-four years of age who were gainfully employed increased during the period from 63.9 per cent to 65.7 per cent. As the demand for employment becomes more and more pressing from the mature age groups, the opportunities for young people fifteen to twenty years of age to enter industry or business will decrease.

Trends in unemployment for all workers make it appear that the pressure from more mature groups will continue, very probably with increasing emphasis.

Conditions in a particular community are shown by studies made in the Minneapolis Public Schools. Follow-up studies have been made of graduates of Minneapolis high schools at three-year intervals since 1926. Data are now available on the classes of 1926, 1929, and 1932. The report of these studies issued in 1934 includes the following statement concerning the status of employment for these high school graduates:

The difficult plight of the pupil who is unfortunate enough to finish school during these years of depression is indicated in the fact that less than one out of five of the high-school graduates had found work when this survey was taken. The study of 1926 graduates showed 38 per cent at work; the study of 1929 graduates made in 1930 when it was expected that the depression would have influenced these figures, showed 45 per cent at work. This class studied in 1933 shows only 18.8 per cent able to find jobs. The boys fared better than the girls, for 21.9 per cent of the boys were at work as compared with 16 per cent of the girls. In 1926 and 1929 practically the same percentage of boys as girls were at work.

The difficulty is further emphasized in the fact that almost one out of three of these young people was unemployed and seeking work a year after they had completed school. Over 1,100 such young people from just two graduating classes makes us realize the seriousness of the social problem that faces the community in the enforced idleness of its older adolescents. The percentage of unemployed jumped from 8.4 per cent reported in 1929 to 30.9 per cent. Thirty-five per cent of the girls have failed to find work, as against 25 per cent of the boys. Either boys are more enterprising, or in a period like this the tendency is for girls to be pushed back to the home life of an earlier decade, while the men and boys are given whatever jobs there are. There was no significant sex difference in the percentage unemployed either in 1926 or 1929.[2]

Society dare not leave this young adult group, which is being displaced from gainful employment, without opportunity to en-

[2] Minneapolis Public Schools, *Vocational Guidance Bulletin*, January, 1934. Quoted in "Educational News and Editorial Comment," *The School Review*, 42:171, March, 1934.

gage in some challenging worth-while undertaking. The possibility of several years of idleness during a period of life so important in developing character is appalling in the possibilities for developing traits inimical to the pursuance later of worth-while activities and for developing qualities that are definitely anti-social. It is true that increases in school attendance during the past decades suggest that many members of this group are continuing in school as the desirable alternative to idleness. The proportion of the total population attending school increased steadily from 16.6 per cent in 1870 to 22.7 per cent in 1930. The increase from 1920 to 1930 was 2.1 per cent. Recently, the proportionate increase in school enrollments on the high school and junior college levels has been much greater than on the elementary level. Both public secondary school and college enrollments more than doubled from 1920 to 1930. Public and private junior college enrollments increased from 16,121 in 1922 to 107,807 in 1934.

Increases in school enrollments, however, by no means account for all boys and girls of school age who are not employed. The Children's Bureau of the United States Department of Labor estimated in 1933 that 200,000 boys were drifting over the country with home ties broken and no visible means of support. The seriousness of this situation was mentioned in a statement presented by a group of educators to President Roosevelt.

For the first time in our history hordes of youths, thousands upon thousands, wander over the country, living as best they can, cut off from the stable supports of society. At the same time, graduates of schools and colleges in immense numbers search vainly for employment. Though highly trained they wait vacantly in dangerous idleness, feeling that society has no place for them and seemingly does not want them.

Thus, the tendency for the age to increase at which young men and women become gainfully employed increases the demand and need for education. The crucial problem facing the school in this connection is whether or not the present offerings of formal education provide profitable activities for an increasing number of students with an expanding range of interests, capacities, and needs. The extent to which this factor may operate in the future is suggested by the fact that even now only one-fourth of the persons seventeen to twenty years of age in the total population are in school. Factors such as financial ability of the family and current non-promotion practices cause this group to be rather highly selected. As these selective factors become less operative, the present program of secondary education will become less adapted to needs of prospective students. The relation of secondary education to the needs of society requires redefinition if the school is to meet this increased need for education.

Two other phases of the employment situation yield important implications for education. One is the trend towards a shorter working day with fewer working days per week. The other is the persistence, and probable increase during the past decade, of periodic unemployment resulting from technological advance and seasonal influences on production. Reduction in the hours of work has been a persistent tendency, until, at the present time, many industrial workers spend fewer hours on their jobs than do the members of some professions. Evidence on the later point is difficult to evaluate. However, after careful study Wolman and Peck state:

The striking increase in the output of labor following the recovery from the depression of 1921 would warrant the inference that displacement leading to technological unemployment has been greater in this last decade than in earlier periods. Seasonal unemployment, likewise, under the influence of competitive business conditions which depend for sales upon frequent changes in styles and fashions may be said to have grown during the past years.[3]

Data on the extent of unemployment indicate that even in so-called normal times a significant percentage of workers will probably be without employment so long as we operate on our

[3] Leo Wolman and Gustav Peck, "Labor Groups in the Social Structure," *Recent Social Trends*, McGraw-Hill Book Company, 1933, Vol. II, Chapter XVI, p. 808.

present plan of economic organization. The national census of unemployment in 1930 showed that 6.6 per cent of persons previously gainfully employed were without employment. Of course, depression periods make this percentage greater than it otherwise would be.

Whatever the actual number of unemployed may be, it is evident that shorter working hours and periodic unemployment raise a myriad of problems. By no means the least of these problems is the one of education. Some social agency must provide for the continuous guidance of the education of adults who find increasing amounts of time available for their own direction. Chance cannot be relied upon to assure the wise use of this time. The development of standards of value which make for the good of both the individual and society requires the guiding hand of a group of workers prepared to give special study to the problem.

CHANGING STATUS OF THE HOME

The home and school are the major social institutions for educating the young. Part of the educational program needed by society is unprovided for if the activity of either home or school is restricted. Recent changes in home life have tended to limit the educational opportunities provided by the home.

One significant change in home life has been caused by the large scale manufacture of goods used in the home. No longer, in as large a proportion of American homes as in times past, does the child have duties to perform that entail important responsibilities. No longer does the child gain much first-hand experience with the processes of producing the goods consumed. Even in sections farthest removed from centers of population there is a great tendency to depend on factory and shop for a multitude of things previously produced in the home, while in urban homes the most rudimentary of activities, such as baking bread and doing laundry, have been largely taken over by specialized agencies in the community. The extent to which this trend has developed is reflected by a significant increase in the production of goods and services by such agencies as bakeries, laundries, canneries, the clothing trades, packing houses, and dairies. This rapid shift of production activities from the home has operated to limit both the advantageous employment of the child in the home and the development of his knowledge and understanding of important aspects of life.

At the same time, as pointed out earlier, each family has become increasingly dependent on numerous persons and agencies far removed from the immediate community. This interdependence necessitates greater rather than less knowledge and understanding of the source and production of goods and services used in the home. In short, large scale manufacture of goods has operated to increase the need for education in two ways: first, by limiting the educative activities in the home, and second, by increasing interdependence.

Another significant development in home life is the tendency for an increasing proportion of married women to enter gainful employment. In 1900 there were 769,000 married women gainfully employed, while in 1930 the number had increased to 3,071,000. Between 1920 and 1930 the number of married women gainfully employed increased 60 per cent. During the same decade the increase in the employment of all women was 29 per cent. The increase in the percentage of women over sixteen years of age in the population during this decade was practically the same as the increase in the percentage of married women. Thus, the rate of gainful employment of married women is increasing more rapidly than employment of unmarried women.

This tendency for women to spend the working day out of the home exerts a profound influence on home life. Time spent in the home tends to be reduced to a few hours, and hence a relatively small number of activities can be carried forward there. Under such circumstances the home cannot form so effective a center for a child's activities as it did formerly. Hence, there is little provision made for many educational needs once cared for by the home.

Still another development that reduces the potency of the home as a constructive educational agency is the gradual increase in the proportion of broken homes. Increasing divorce rates account for this condition to a large extent. The percentage of divorces has increased regularly for several decades, the rate of increase being approximately 3 per cent a year. It is estimated by a reliable source that one in six of the marriages in 1930 will probably end in divorce.[4] Lack of stability in such a large proportion of homes exerts great influence on the effectiveness of the home as a center for the activities, interests, and care of children. This may account for the tendency for other social agencies to take over functions heretofore discharged by the home.

Other phases of family life tend to reduce the stability of the home and to limit its educative function. Greater mobility of population, decrease in the proportion of one-family houses and increase in the number of apartments, decrease in the amount of space available for families, increase in commercialized recreation, as well as other factors, have been important influences in directing the course of family life. All have tended to reduce the strength of the home as a social institution and to lessen the educational opportunities and guidance afforded children in the home.

NEED OF THE CONSUMER

Production of goods and services, as mentioned earlier, has become a less and less important part of home life. Slowly at first directly after the passing of the frontier, and then with increasing rapidity, mass production became accelerated, taking from home to factory the manufacture of an increasing number of products. Impossible as it would have seemed a few years ago, breadmaking has now become a lost art in millions of homes and "wash day" a forgotten drudgery. In many cases the production of the goods and services necessary for the functioning

[4] William F. Ogburn, "The Family and Its Functions," *Recent Social Trends,* Vol. I, Chapter XIII, p. 693.

of the home are provided almost wholly by agencies organized for mass production.

Numerous educational problems have arisen from this development. The homemaker who previously was required to know how to produce goods, now must be able to estimate, by examining the finished product, the quality of goods produced perhaps thousands of miles away. This becomes an extremely difficult problem, especially when complicated by the development of clever ways of adulterating goods or of lowering quality without changing the external appearance of the final product. Harap gives a number of illustrations of such practices. For example:

Cowhide and sheepskin are often embossed with an artificial grain to resemble fancy leathers, such as seal, walrus, alligator, tortoise, and fishskin, and are sold as such. Sheepskin makes an inferior bag, but it is often given a pigskin grain and sold as such without a blush. Leather bags marked "genuine leather" or "genuine cowhide" are often but a thin layer from the flesh side of the hide of the cow mounted on paper. The imitation leather industry has succeeded in reproducing the grains of alligator, pigskin, or box calf, and morocco on pyroxylin-coated cloth with sufficient similarity to deceive the average person. The unscrupulous retailer sells these imitations as the real articles.

Silk is a superior fabric because of its excellence in lustre, strength, softness, elasticity, and affinity for dyes. Because of its value, silk has been misrepresented by cellulose, collodion, or gelatin threads woven into a fabric; by mixtures of silk and cotton; by silk weighted with mineral salts; by cotton soaked in a solution of pure silk; by mercerized cotton. These imitations of silk are either brazenly sold as the genuine commodity or palmed off under a misleading name.

Linen is cleaner, stronger, glossier, and costlier than cotton. Besides, it launders more easily than cotton and does not shrink when laundered. The unscrupulous merchant sells towels and handkerchiefs as linen that in reality are mercerized cotton or a specially treated mixture of cotton and linen. Sometimes he sells the false or adulterated product under a misleading name.[5]

In all respects except one, producers and middlemen have generally been little concerned with the consumer, and that one

---

[5] Henry Harap, *Economic Life and the Curriculum*, pp. 12–13. By permission of The Macmillan Company, publishers.

is to devise means of securing the greatest use of their goods with the greatest profit to themselves. Problems of price, competition, and quality are often one-sided, the consumer being left out of the picture. Consider, for example, the pledges of a business association in its 1933 meeting:

1. To end destructive competition and demoralization of price.
2. To prevent overproduction.
3. To maintain fair profits for all.

Chain merchandising and similar systems for distribution of goods have tended to remove further the distributor from the consumer, often resulting in less consideration to the wishes and needs of the consumer. The seriousness of the problems involved is evidenced by efforts of the government to protect consumers from harmful drugs and foods and to maintain competition. The Anti-Trust and Pure Food and Drug Acts marked the beginning of government activity. The Department of Agriculture within recent years has engaged in many activities to assist the consumer to purchase wisely. Private non-profit organizations also have provided valuable services to consumers.

As yet, however, little real progress has been made in teaching the American people to be wise consumers. Every year witnesses the purchase of millions of dollars worth of useless goods. Inferior or even harmful goods often are selected when high quality products could be secured at the same cost. Ability to judge the quality of competing clothing, machines, toilet articles, etc., is extremely limited. The result is that the consumer gets less for his money and the producer is encouraged to make goods of inferior quality.

At the same time, campaigns to induce people to buy are developed on an ever-widening scale. The result is increased pressure on the consumer. The fact that expenditures for advertising exceeded one and three quarters billions of dollars in 1929 indicates the proportions of the drive to influence consumers.

Advertising conceivably might be of real assistance to the prospective purchaser, but in the way it is operated it is more apt to be detrimental. Often the appeals have nothing whatever to do with the product and many times are directly misleading. It is a well-known fact that the claims of many of the most highly advertised products are utterly false. Yet, admonitions to buy product A or product B, or any one of a thousand other products, hammer at the consumer from billboards, magazines, newspapers, and the radio in a never-ending stream. The knowledge of the average consumer is entirely inadequate to cope with such pressure. The result is that both quality of product and protection of health are frequently sacrificed. Here is a great need for an organized educational program for the consumer. The schools have taken some steps in this direction but as yet the provision for education of this kind is far from adequate or satisfactory.

The situation for the consumer is further complicated by intricate developments of the credit system. The form that most directly affects the consumer is installment selling. Business not only urges the purchase of a vast array of goods, but makes it possible to secure such goods with small down payments followed by periodic payments. This method of extending credit may be desirable when used with due care. However, it has been very much abused by a great many companies to the decided disadvantage of the consumer. Thousands of persons have been encouraged to adopt even more desultory methods of personal finance than they previously employed. In many cases there has been established the ill-founded belief that goods may be purchased on "easy payment plans." It has materially increased the cost of goods to the consumer. In some cases the goods are consumed before payments are completed. The least that can be said is that installment selling is a method of extending credit which necessitates great care on the part of the consumer in making his purchases. The problem of employing available purchasing power most wisely is thus further complicated and the need for education is increased.

CRIME AND EDUCATION

Universal education is generally believed to be a necessity for the safe development and preservation of a democratic society. Knowledge of the good of the entire body politic and willingness to forego personal desires for that good—outcomes which should be derived from education—contrast with ignorance and a willingness to exploit the group for personal advantage. One measure of the extent to which outcomes expected are actually achieved is the prevalence of crime.

It is rather generally believed that the post-war period has witnessed a phenomenal increase in crime. Newspaper and magazine articles have done much to give currency to this impression. For example, an article in a leading magazine—issue of May, 1933—begins thus:

Crime casts a bigger, uglier shadow over the lives and property of the law-abiding every day. Undiminished by the forces combating it, crime recruits yearly more and more weaklings under its sinister leadership until, at last, fear-stricken society has wakened to the need for a diagnosis.[6]

As a matter of fact, available data are inadequate to maintain successfully that crime has increased at a materially greater speed since 1920 than before. Nevertheless, its present proportions are most distressing.

There are a variety of measures that may be used to estimate the extent of crime. Conclusions based on different measures often are at variance. A research bulletin of the National Education Association lists in order of probable value the measures that follow:

1. The total number of law violations
2. The number of offenses known to the police
3. The number of persons arrested
4. The number of persons brought to trial

[6] Augusta W. Hinshaw, "Crime and the Cortex," *Harper's Magazine*, 166:709, May, 1933.

5. The number of persons convicted
6. The number of persons committed to penal institutions annually
7. The population of penal institutions in any specific year [7]

Since 1930 the United States Bureau of Investigation has issued Uniform Crime Reports for cities which now have an aggregate population exceeding fifty-three millions. These reports provide a more adequate basis than previously existed to judge the extent of criminal acts. The fourth quarterly bulletin of 1932 reports crime rates (offenses known to police) per 100,000 population as follows: murder 7.0, manslaughter 4.3, rape 6.1, robbery 110.2, assault 45.9, burglary 387.5, theft 715.0, and auto theft 369.1. It is pointed out that "crime rates are higher in the larger cities than the smaller ones."

As the Uniform Crime Reports have been prepared only since 1930, it is difficult to secure comparable data that indicate clearly whether or not crime has been increasing. In dealing with this point Bagley takes the position that crime rates have increased greatly.[8] In support of this position he presents data on the homicide rate (in the registered area of 1900) for a period of years. His data are for a period up to 1926. Adding data for years up to 1930, we have homicide rates as follows:

1900—1.2	1926—5.1
1910—3.9	1927—5.0
1920—4.2	1928—4.8
1924—5.1	1929—5.0
1925—5.0	1930—5.1

Employing homicides as an index, it appears that there was a rapid increase in crime from 1900 to 1925 when a plateau was reached. Since that time the rate has fluctuated within narrow limits.

[7] "Crime Prevention Through Education," *Research Bulletin of the National Education Association*, 10:140, September, 1932.
[8] William C. Bagley, *Education, Crime, and Social Progress,* The Macmillan Company, 1931, p. 21.

It is pointed out, however, by Sutherland and Gehlke that "the number of arrests and of court cases per 100,000 population has increased moderately from 1900 to 1930, with a tendency to increase more rapidly after 1920 than before." [9] Since the number of arrests and persons brought to trial are generally considered more adequate measures of the amount of crime than homicide rates, the soundest conclusion appears to be that there has been a gradual and continuous increase in the total number of crimes.

This gradual, continuous increase in lawlessness is a direct challenge to educational forces. It is evidence that ignorance and willingness to exploit the group for personal advantage have been gaining on knowledge of the good of the entire people, and willingness to forego personal desires for that good.

Another significant aspect of the crime situation is the fact that America has higher rates of crime than other nations. Bagley says, "There can be no doubt that our crime ratios are much higher than any other comparable nation . . ." [10] In support of this statement he presents data on the homicide rates in Great Britain and Canada. In Great Britain the rate in 1900 was .98 per 100,000 population and in 1928 it had dropped to .5. In Canada the rate in 1918 was 2.7 and in 1928 it had dropped to 1.7. When these rates are contrasted with the rate in the United States, which rose steadily until 1924 when it stabilized around 5.0, the condition in the United States stands out conspicuously. Again these differences may be explained in a variety of ways, but the pertinent question for the educational agencies of society is whether or not they have built an educational program that takes into account the situation revealed by such an analysis.

A further significant aspect of the situation is found in the number of young adults involved in criminal activity. The Uniform Crime Reports (*Fourth Quarterly Bulletin,* 1932) show

[9] Edwin H. Sutherland and C. E. Gehlke, "Crime and Punishment," *Recent Social Trends,* Vol. II, Chapter XXII, p. 1165.
[10] *Op. cit.,* p. 21.

arrests for criminal charges by age groups up to twenty-one years of age as follows:

Age	Percentage
Under 15	.26
15	.35
16	1.70
17	3.24
18	4.76
19	5.23
20	4.53
Total	20.07

One-fifth of all arrests are of age groups within the secondary school period, the largest age group arrested for criminal charges being the nineteen-year-old group. Data are not available to determine definitely whether or not the average age of those committing crimes is decreasing. At all events, it is clear that crime is recruiting a significant number of young adults of secondary school age.

Various efforts have been made to establish a relationship between the extent of crime and the provision of educational opportunities. Certain persons, on the one hand, have endeavored to indict modern education as a causal factor in crime. They have pointed to increasing crime rates and increasing school costs. On the other hand, persons interested in education have endeavored to show that education reduces the amount of crime. They have cited as evidence the prevalence of persons with limited school opportunities in criminal populations.[11] Neither has met with success. The causal factors in the crime situation are so complicated that they have not been successfully isolated. Even so, the condition is of greatest concern to the

[11] For example, Warden Lewis E. Lawes of Sing Sing Prison, from a study of 500 consecutive prisoners, found that 225 had left school before the sixth grade and 111 more before completion of the eighth grade. Of the entire group only five had graduated from college.

school as well as to all other educational agencies in the community. Crime indicates a need for a more adequate educational program. Whether or not existing educational agencies can care for the need is another question.

SOCIAL CONFUSION

America has depended for direction of development on broad generalizations in which we profess belief. Action, however, often has tended to be based on desires and opportunities provided by particular situations rather than by application of the generalizations to which we have subscribed. This opportunism has led to some startling contradictions in our social life. Time and again our actions and avowals have been irreconcilable. Yet this has seemed to concern us little, for we have continued to hold to both.

The relationship of government and business is a case in point. As a people, we have held that the government should not engage in enterprises that compete with private business. We have gone further and opposed, in theory, the regulation of private business by government. Those who have stood for such regulation often have been spoken of disparagingly as socialists or communists who are promoting doctrines contrary to "good Americanism." While we have been giving lip service to the principle that the government should have as little as possible to do with private business and have branded as undesirable comprehensive programs to dictate governmental relationships to business, our action in dealing with specific problems has been in the opposite direction. The government has continually extended its control over various aspects of business. Regulation of trusts and monopolies was only the beginning. The end is by no means in sight.

A strange contradiction to this opposition of business to governmental regulation is the demand on the part of business for help from the government in times of stress, even to the point of extreme regulation. Thus, business welcomed the intervention of the government in the critical banking situation in 1933 even though the closing of all banks was involved. But suppose, on the other hand, that as business expanded beyond reason in 1929 the government had stepped in with such severe regulation. It is highly improbable that intervention and regulation at that time would have been welcomed. In like manner, during the boom period preceding 1929 governmental regulation of transactions in securities would have been resented. However, when malpractice had so shaken the confidence of the people as to endanger the financial structure, the demand for governmental action was strong.

This conflict of avowal and action has left the educative agencies of society in a bad muddle. The school has not dared make even a fair analysis of the direction in which society has been moving, much less to help point the way. Had it done so, there would be those persons so blind to the real situation as to accuse the school of teaching doctrines contrary to Americanism, and this would serve for condemnation in the eyes of many people. Facing this situation, the school has remained silent on vital problems, dealing with the relation of government and business in such academic terms as to throw little if any light on the real situation. It has tended to teach the avowal and to ignore practice. In so doing, the school not only has failed to clarify social problems and needs, but actually has contributed to confusion.

Confusion is further confounded by the tendency for various educative agencies to direct their activities toward different ends. The school, for example, has been endeavoring to develop an appreciation of a type of literature that meets generally accepted standards of high quality. At the same time, magazines and motion pictures have encouraged consumption of literature that does not meet the lowest of such standards. Similarly, the schools have developed concepts of an idealistic democracy operating as visioned by the founders and idealists of our nation. Political organization has trained people in a system of "ring" and "boss" control, political "pull," and favoritism. The church, school, and home continue to emphasize traditional standards of morality; while advertising, magazines, newspapers, and motion pictures often educate away from such standards. To illustrate, it was found by Mill and McGarraghy that 45 per cent of 1932 motion pictures in which characters violated monogamy, approved such violations, while approval by magazines of various types ranged from 16 to 31 per cent.[12]

Such diversity in practices and ideals among various educative agencies confuses individuals and tends to nullify the returns of education. A person subjected to such a confused educational program seldom develops a real scale of values by which he can direct his everyday living. He is more apt, in self-defense, to move in whatever direction appears the least troublesome and the most satisfying for the moment. This seems to be inevitable until a scale of values is evolved for our society to which all of our educative agencies—the school, church, home, newspapers, magazines, motion pictures, advertising, clubs, etc.—can and will subscribe; a scale of values that such agencies will consciously help evolve and which they will continuously redefine and expand. That such a condition may be reached may seem visionary, but it is essential nevertheless to the effective development of an educational program for our society, both the part of such a program carried on by the school and the part carried on by other agencies.

Confusion is contributed to by a third condition which is discussed at some length by Bode. It is the tendency of the American people to compartmentalize beliefs. This willingness for an individual to hold to a belief that fits a given occasion most advantageously results in much contradictory action. Bode illustrates the situation as follows:

A business man, for example, who has become thoroughly grounded in the notion of business as based on competition and as being incompatible with sentiment, joins the Rotary Club, where he absorbs the idea that business should be conducted in the spirit of service. How these different conceptions harmonize with one another is not

[12] Hornell Hart, "Changing Social Attitudes and Interests," *Recent Social Trends,* Vol. I, Chapter VIII, p. 419.

immediately apparent to the unaided eye, but they seem to dwell together in the same bosom without causing any disturbance. Or a person brought up with traditional religious beliefs may also adopt the scientific belief that even the most trifling details of this universe of ours are determined by natural law; yet he may remain completely untouched by what is commonly called the conflict between science and religion. Or again, we insist that people must regulate their conduct in accordance with their best insight and conscience, but we grow indignant when pacifists undertake to put our teachings into practice. The belief in anything is apparently not regarded as a bar to the belief in its opposite.[13]

The work of the school, especially, has been so organized as to encourage contradictions. Being concerned largely with the mastery of knowledge and the development of certain specific habits, training in school has considered conflicts that may develop in the realm of conduct as being out of the field of formal education. In some cases where such conflicts become pronounced and involve social issues of controversial nature, schools have studiously avoided any effort to guide the individual to develop a consistent basis for action. This procedure has further limited the possibility of the school's contributing to the development of a way out of social confusion and leaves as a pressing educational need the provision of such direction.

OTHER ASPECTS OF CONTEMPORARY LIFE

Many other aspects of contemporary life, some of which are suggested by the previous discussion, have further increased the need for education. Concentration of population, mobility of population, advances in scientific knowledge, increasing machine production, improved means of communication and transportation, concentration of wealth, narrow nationalism and sectionalism, exploitation of natural resources and workers, an inadequate credit and monetary system, the undue influence of organized

[13] From *The Educational Frontier*, p. 7. By William H. Kilpatrick and others. Used by permission of D. Appleton-Century Company, Publishers, New York, N. Y.

minorities—these and other phases of our life involve relationships of such general importance and of a nature so intricate that only careful education can develop individuals capable of dealing with the resultant problems.

Confusion in American life can be accounted for largely by the fact that our material development has created social problems more rapidly than regulatory and educative agencies have been able to provide solutions. Some lag in social adjustment to new material developments is inevitable, for the varied consequences of material expansion cannot be anticipated with assurance. At the present time, however, material development and possibilities are so far beyond our ability to use them wisely that we are paying a terrific price in life, health, and happiness for the resulting social maladjustment. Salter says, ". . . our material resources, technical knowledge, and industrial skill, are enough to afford every man of the world's teeming population physical comfort, adequate leisure, and access to everything in our rich heritage of civilization that he has the personal quality to enjoy. We need but the regulative wisdom to control our . . . activities. . . ."[14] Inability of our people to grapple successfully with the social problems that face us, indicates fundamental inadequacies in the work of educative and regulatory agencies. Continuation of these inadequacies carries with it consequences of increasing seriousness. The road of cumulative social maladjustment may well lead to the point where our particular social experiment will meet the insurmountable difficulty.

The alternative to cumulative maladjustment is for regulatory and educative agencies to take a more aggressive and intelligent part in dealing with social problems. A comprehensive educational program must be developed which encompasses the pressing issues of present living. Change must be anticipated and

[14] From *Recovery,* p. 347. By Sir Arthur Salter. Used by permission of D. Appleton-Century Company, Publishers, New York, N. Y.

educative agencies must take a greater part in directing new developments. The forces of business and politics must not be permitted alone to determine the direction in which our society shall move. To achieve this, leaders and workers must enlarge their vision of the function of education in a democracy, and resolve to make education real social engineering.

This supreme task for all educative and regulatory agencies provides an especially direct challenge to the school, democracy's chief educative agency. To develop an educational program in the school that will serve such a function requires both vision and courage. It is possible that a school that endeavors to do more than conserve the social heritage, one that deals with the vital concerns of people and attempts to influence social development, cannot secure the continued support of the people. Even recognizing this possibility, however, acceptance of the challenge is encouraged by three considerations. In the first place, the pressing nature of the need and the dire consequences that appear most certain to follow continued failure to meet it, make it impossible for the schools to choose with equanimity the easy safe procedure of restricting teaching to matters of little social significance. In the second place, failure to accept such a fundamental challenge must lead in the direction of impotence and insignificance, a condition most strongly to be avoided by a public school system. In the third place, no opportunity has been offered the public to appraise such an educational program. Consequently, it is quite possible that such a program in actual operation would receive wide approval.

This challenge to the school is of primary significance in curriculum making, for it is through curriculum development that the challenge must be largely met. The responsibility of curriculum workers is, consequently, great indeed. Upon them rests the task of evaluating the situation and of transforming philosophy into educational practices which move forward with steps measured, on the one hand, to the ability of teachers to instruct, and, on the other hand, to the willingness of the public to follow.

SELECTED REFERENCES

Bagley, William C., *Education, Crime and Social Progress*, The Macmillan Company, New York, 1931.

Chase, Stuart, *Men and Machines*, The Macmillan Company, New York, 1929.

Counts, George S., *American Road to Culture*, John Day Company Inc., New York, 1930.

Engelbrecht, H. C. and Hanighen, F. C., *Merchants of Death*, Dodd, Mead and Company, Inc., New York, 1934.

Forman, Henry J., *Our Movie Made Children*, The Macmillan Company, New York, 1933.

Harap, Henry, *Education of the Consumer*, The Macmillan Company, New York, 1924.

Kallet, Arthur, and Schlink, F. J., *100,000,000 Guinea Pigs*, The Vanguard Press, New York, 1933.

Kilpatrick, William H., *Education for a Changing Civilization*, The Macmillan Company, New York, 1927.

Kilpatrick, William H. and others, *The Educational Frontier*, D. Appleton-Century Co., New York, 1933.

Lynd, Robert S. and Helen M., *Middletown*, Harcourt, Brace & Company, New York, 1929.

Minehan, Thomas, *Boy and Girl Tramps of America*, Farrar and Rinehart, Inc., New York, 1934.

Recent Social Trends in the United States, Report of the President's Research Committee on Social Trends, McGraw-Hill Book Company, New York, 1933.

Rugg, Harold, *The Great Technology*, John Day Company Inc., New York, 1933.

Steffens, Lincoln, *Autobiography of Lincoln Steffens*, Harcourt, Brace and Company, Inc., New York, 1931.

CHAPTER II

THE SOCIAL RESPONSIBILITY OF THE SCHOOL

In projecting an educational program which undertakes to contribute significantly to social development, there is a fundamental social principle that requires special consideration. This principle defines the relationship which exists between the school and the maintaining society. We shall consider it as a general guide for projecting educational programs in all their aspects, and more particularly as it aids in defining the responsibility of schools for social guidance in a democracy.

THE SCHOOL AN AGENCY IN ACHIEVING SOCIAL IDEALS

Schools have been established and maintained by a variety of social groups. Examination of the relationship between maintaining societies and schools reveals a common element. In each case the school is designed, established, and supported to assist in perpetuating and improving the type of society which maintains it. Many examples of this essential relationship might be given. The educational system of Athens conformed to the class basis of society in which the system functioned. The schools of Sparta supported the ideal of service to the state upon which the social organization rested. Turkey, under Suleiman the Magnificent, devised a unique educational program to carry forward the type of social organization desired. When the church became the most significant determinant of social ideals, it in turn developed an educational program designed to achieve its ends.

The rise of nationalism served to emphasize this relationship between school and society. Leaders of nationalistic states, seeing the advantages of a state-controlled school system, challenged the part the church had come to play in education and began the development of school systems especially designed to further nationalistic purposes. One of the most carefully developed of these programs of education was projected by Napoleon. He stated his position thus: "Of all political questions, that (of education) is perhaps the most important. There cannot be a firmly established political state unless there is a teaching body with definitely recognized principles." Prussia developed an educational system composed of two groups of schools, one to train the leaders and the other to train the followers considered necessary for development of the Prussian ideal of life. Likewise, other nationalistic states devised educational programs to prepare individuals to participate in the particular type of life which their social systems presented. As the power of the school was strengthened by nationalistic states, the obligation to assist in achieving the social ideals of the maintaining society became more firmly established.

Cataclysmic changes during recent years in the purposes and organization of national groups illustrate this relationship and further indicate it to be of fundamental significance for the school's program. In each case major changes in social purposes were followed by reorganization of the program of the school. Changes in the schools of Russia, Bulgaria, Italy, and Germany all illustrate this point.

Democracy also emphasizes the dependence of the maintaining society upon schools to help achieve desired social ideals. Wherever, throughout the world, efforts have been made to develop a democratic society the need for training in democratic methods through education has been emphasized. The emphasis placed on education in American development serves as a good illustration of the point. Education occupied an important place in the thoughts and plans of leaders of the Revolutionary period, as is witnessed by frequent references in speeches and papers. The

oft-quoted statement from Washington's Farewell Address illustrates the attitude of most leaders of the period.

> Promote, then, as an object of primary importance, institutions for
> the general diffusion of knowledge. In proportion as the structure of
> government gives force to public opinion, it is essential that public
> opinion should be enlightened.

The well-known statement from Jefferson shows the same vision
for education:

> If a nation expects to be ignorant and free in a state of civilization
> it expects what never was and never will be . . . There is no safe
> deposit (for the functions of government) but with the people them-
> selves; nor can they be safe with them without information.

In the Ordinance of 1787 schools were mentioned specifically:
"Religion, morality, and knowledge being necessary to good government and the happiness of mankind, schools and the means
of education shall be forever encouraged." Obviously, education provided by schools was looked upon as a means of achieving democratic ideals and educational programs were expected
to be projected to that end.

Schools continue to be considered a primary means of progress
toward realization of democratic ideals. President Roosevelt
recently said, "We have faith in education as the foundation of
democratic government . . . Our schools need the appreciation
and co-operation of all those who depend upon them for the education of youth—the state's most valuable asset."

Thus, while nationalism and democracy have increased the
importance of the school, they have at the same time operated
to fix more firmly its obligation to help achieve the ideals of the
maintaining society. This relationship establishes a major control for an educational program. "An educational system,"
states William F. Russell, "is successful only when in all its aspects it contributes to the ends of the society in which it lives and
has its being." [1] A school, then, can be only as wise as it is per-

[1] School Administration and Conflicting American Ideals," *Teachers
College Record*, 31:17, October, 1929.

mitted to be by the society which maintains it. A program of formal education can reach only as far as the purposes of the society in which the program is developed will permit it to go. It is on this basis that a program of formal education must be projected.

This relationship may seem to limit unduly the influence the school may exert on the direction of social development, but to see the inevitableness of the relationship one has only to examine actual school situations. Imagine teaching in pre-war Russia that the divine right of kings was a myth; or in pre-war Germany that all men should have equal political rights; or in Soviet Russia that private ownership contributes to a desirable economic system; or in Fascist Italy that democracy is the most satisfactory method of government. Such teaching would be anti-social and would not be tolerated. "It is inconceivable," as is stated editorially in the *Elementary School Journal*, "that any society should support a system of schools with the avowed purpose of destroying the fundamental principles upon which that society was organized." [2]

HOW THEN CAN THE SCHOOL FULFILL A DYNAMIC ROLE

But, it may well be asked, if the school is so tied to the maintaining society, and so restricted by the social ideals of that society, how can the dynamic function described in the preceding chapter be discharged? How can the school possibly play a vital part in social guidance and development under such limitations?

The extent to which the school can provide direction for social development depends upon the methods and ideals of the particular society which is being served. In other words, the role the school may play in social development is directly determined by the type of society which maintains the school. For example, schools that are maintained by dictatorships have little if any part in determining the direction of social development. The dictatorial power outlines a social program in detail. The school

[2] Editorial, *Elementary School Journal*, 33:85, October, 1932.

is assigned a part to play in the realization of this program and it is reorganized until it will contribute to the desired ends. In Germany the Commissar for Education, Rust, announced his educational principles, saying that "Unprejudiced, objective, scientific teaching, which is blind to the spiritual changes within the nation, will no longer be tolerated. The revolutionary transformation within the intellectual classes must find its expression in the professorial study and in the lecture hall." [3]   We may consider a social organization which so restricts the school very undesirable. That is a matter of opinion upon which we may express ourselves, but it does not alter the fact that schools in a dictatorship cannot provide direction for social development.

On the other hand, the methods and ideals of democracy provide quite a different role for the school. The question, consequently, which we must consider is not whether schools in general can assume a significant part in social guidance and development, but whether schools in a democracy can do so. The answer must be found in analysis of the responsibilities of schools in a democracy.

RESPONSIBILITY FOR DEFINING SOCIAL IDEALS

Obviously, if the school is to discharge its function of helping to achieve social ideals, there must be a reasonably clear concept of the nature of these ideals. The clarity and fixity of social ideals and purposes vary markedly in different types of social life. As pointed out before, in a planned society autocratically controlled, definite goals are available, usually in objective form, toward which the energies of the entire social group are directed. This makes it possible for the school to proceed directly in planning a program which will contribute to desired social ends. By this very procedure, however, it becomes impossible for the school to modify social ideals to a noticeable degree and thus assist in directing social development. In a democratic social order, on

[3] Quoted in "The Plight of the German Intellectuals," by Alice Hamilton, *Harper's Magazine,* 168:160, January, 1933.

the other hand, there is no central agency to impose a planned program. Plans for action are presumed to evolve through the interaction of various groups and individuals until a majority favor a particular procedure. In this process, it is hoped that democratic ideals will work themselves into practice. Thus, a democracy, by its very nature, tends to have neither a clear, fixed statement of its ideals, nor a planned course of action to achieve its purposes. Instead, it has a relatively vague concept of social ideals stated in general terms, such as, equality, liberty, and justice, and a continuously evolving program of action. The resulting emphasis on a planning rather than a planned social order places a responsibility on the schools in a democracy not required in other types of social organizations. The schools cannot sit by and wait for other agencies to discover and define democratic ideals in usable terms, but must undertake this task in co-operation with other social institutions. In fact, there is no other institution for which it is so essential to have a careful analysis of social ideals. Without such a source of guidance, an educational program is at loose ends; it is rudderless. Consequently, it is a major responsibility of the school to prepare a statement of these ideals in usable form for directing the educational program. In discharging this responsibility the school will inevitably exert significant influence on the direction of social development.

In general, schools have failed to recognize the full implications of this responsibility. This has been due in part to failure to recognize the obligation and in part to the difficulty of the task. Whatever the reason may be for not discharging this obligation, failure to do so has led to fundamental criticism of our educational program and the way in which schools are fulfilling their function. "Education," says James Truslow Adams, "by which we thought to keep the electorate competent for self-government, was breaking down because we had no scale of values and no real objective in our educational system. For the masses, at its best, it had become a confused jumble of 'book learning' that gave them neither values to strive for nor that knowledge and intellectual training which might have been of help in understanding the complexity of the forces with which they had to deal intelligently." [4]

Counts states in the same connection: "A major task which these changes are forcing upon us is the reformulation of the purposes of American life. And until we face this problem we shall find our educational theories unreal and sterile." [5]

More serious attention has been given recently to clarifying social ideals for educational guidance. Two especially noteworthy attempts have been made in this direction, the one a statement by the Commission on the Social Studies of the American Historical Association entitled *A Charter for the Social Sciences in the Schools,*[6] and the other a statement by the National Education Association's Committee on Social-Economic Goals of America.[7] There is also evidence in the statements of aims of education in connection with some curriculum programs that the importance of democratic ideals as a control of the school program is being more fully recognized.

PROVISION FOR CONTINUOUS RE-DEFINITION OF SOCIAL IDEALS

A second responsibility of the school in a democracy is to provide for the continuous re-definition and re-interpretation of social ideals. This is made necessary, first, by economic, political, and social change; and second, by the inherent quality of an ideal.

The importance of social change as an influence on education has been emphasized perhaps as much as any other factor during recent years. It has been pointed out frequently that in America material change has been readily accepted, while changes in social institutions, regulations, and customs necessitated thereby

[4] James Truslow Adams, *The Epic of America,* Little, Brown and Company, 1931, p. 349.
[5] George S. Counts, "Culture and Educational Theory," *Teachers College Record,* 33:586, April, 1932.
[6] Charles A. Beard, *A Charter for the Social Sciences in the Schools,* Scribner's, 1932.
[7] *Journal of the National Education Association,* 23:5–11, January, 1934.

have been slow to develop. There is a further point not so generally recognized at which change strikes; that is, the social
ideals held by a people. Change may remold a social setting so
rapidly as to make impractical interpretations of ideals previously held. An agrarian society may have as an interpretation
of its ideals individual ownership of homes and land. But let us
suppose that a rapid change from an agrarian to an industrial
order takes place. Mobility and concentration of population
are then demanded and the concept of individual home ownership is inappropriate. Likewise, an agrarian society might have
as an acceptable ideal individual competition and success. But
if the society becomes industrialized, an ideal of co-operation and
group success must be substituted.

Henry Pratt Fairchild gives an excellent illustration of this
point:

> It is a strange and awesome fact that whole societies can become
> imbued with false beliefs, and consequently build up institutions and
> mores which are diametrically opposed to their own welfare. This is
> particularly true because certain beliefs may have high utility at one
> stage in human affairs and yet be a positive hindrance at a later point
> of development. An excellent illustration of this truth is furnished by
> the egalitarian doctrines of the late eighteenth and early nineteenth
> centuries—the dogmas that all men are born free and equal, and
> endowed with certain natural and inalienable rights and liberties.
> These doctrines were evolved as a protest against the favoritism,
> privilege, and partiality that characterized the social gradation, politi-
> cal and religious affiliation, and judicial administration of the day. They
> were useful, indeed indispensable, to the attainment of democratic prog-
> ress and, therefore, in the pragmatic sense, they were true. But having
> achieved their purpose, and helped to usher in an era of greater
> equality, they have now become a drag and a handicap to further
> advance.[8]

But even if social change did not require reconstruction of
social ideals, the inherent nature of an ideal would do so. Ideals
serve as guides to action and as we engage in each new activity

[8] Henry Pratt Fairchild, "The Great Economic Paradox," *Harper's Magazine,* 164:642, May, 1932.

directed toward the realization of an ideal, the ideal itself is somewhat changed. Each step forward reveals possibilities that were not evident before, so that the ideal, as efforts are made to achieve it, is continuously modified. For example, the seventeenth-century American, demanding liberty, was inclined to be content with freedom in religion; the eighteenth-century American extended the ideal to emphasize political liberty; the nineteenth- and twentieth-century American has extended the ideal to include economic liberty. As time passes, liberty will continue to take on new meanings so that the present concept will seem highly inadequate to future generations.

Social progress is conditioned in a major way by the extent to which the demands of changed conditions for reconstructed social ideals are recognized and employed as a basis for re-formulation of ideals. This is especially important for those agencies charged with the responsibility of aiding in social development, for a program perfectly suited to a setting at one time may be carried over to later periods for which it is entirely inadequate. This is particularly a danger with formal educational programs. It is easy for the school to drift in the wake of social development. This makes it an essential responsibility of the school in a democracy to study and analyze social developments continuously so that modifications of social ideals may be anticipated and appropriate adjustments be made in the educational program.

In this process of re-interpretation of social ideals the school may exert significant influence on the direction of social development. This does not mean necessarily that the school may see major trends in one direction and change them to another. As Beard states, "Jefferson's America of free and upstanding farmers ruling the country in liberty has been turned upside down by steam and machinery. Ten million teachers singing the praises of agriculture would have been powerless to block that inexorable march. . . ." [9] But by the very fact of antici-

---

[9] *A Charter for the Social Sciences in the Schools,* p. 24. Scribner's.

pating such trends and their requirements for re-interpretation of ideals of liberty and justice and equality, the schools could have contributed to social direction and movement. For a situation which now involves great injustice and inequality might thereby have been brought to exemplify in these new relationships extensions of the democratic concepts. In other words, justice and liberty and equality might well be far greater realities if the school and other social agencies had seen in the shift from an agrarian to an industrial order the need for re-interpretation of these ideals. Thus, this second major responsibility of the school in a democracy provides opportunity for contributing to the direction of social development.

PROVISION OF AN EQUALIZED MINIMUM EDUCATIONAL OPPORTUNITY

The third major responsibility of the school in a democracy is to provide for all boys and girls an equalized minimum educational opportunity. This responsibility is based on the need in a democracy for education of all citizens. It found expression early in the development of our nation in demands for universal education. These demands were the basis of the great struggle for free public schools during the nineteenth century. By the latter part of the century the concept was thoroughly imbedded in American thought, even though its extension to secondary education remained in the large yet to be made. A statement by Lester F. Ward on the point in 1880 shows the position of a leading student of society during this period.

Just as poverty in the midst of wealth aggravates its evils, so ignorance in the midst of intelligence is intensified by the contrast. A generally low state of intelligence is comparatively harmless, since there is a normal degree of correspondence among all the parts of the social fabric. But a stolid and vicious class in the midst of science, learning, and culture, like a "bull in a china-shop," presents such a complete state of inharmony and unfitness that the effect is out of proportion to the cause. . . .

There is even a worse consequence. So long as society has this burden on its shoulders it can not progress in refinement. It must cling to a large part of its old crudeness, as a protection against its un-assimilated membership. It must be perpetually hampered by a heavy coat of mail in consequence of the perpetual dangers that beset it. This tends powerfully to neutralize the progressive agencies within and to equilibrate the rhythm of its motion. In a word, while the state of civilization around them has no tendency to raise the uncivilized classes up toward its level, but rather aggravates the contrast, the presence of these classes in the midst of civilization tends powerfully to lower the condition of the latter and clog its advance. The need of ridding itself of these classes, therefore, becomes twofold, and, since they can-not be annihilated, and will not civilize themselves, the importance of undertaking their artificial civilization is doubly great.

It is evident, therefore, that any system of education which falls short, even in the least particular, of absolute universality, can not proceed from any true conception of what education is for, or of what it is capable of accomplishing.[10]

During the nineteenth century it became evident that uni-versal education and equality of educational opportunity were not necessarily synonymous terms. Equality of educational op-portunity, although implying universal education, was a larger, more compelling concept. Steps were taken to define other im-plications of the concept. The Educational Finance Inquiry stated in definite form in 1921 the application of this concept to finance and employed it as a guiding principle.

The state should insure equal educational facilities to every child within its borders at a uniform effort throughout the state in terms of the burden of taxation; the tax burden of education should throughout the state be uniform in relation to tax-paying ability, and the provision for schools should be uniform in relation to the educable population desiring education.[11]

Gradually the concept has been extended to the instructional program. It has been recognized that equality of opportunity is

[10] Lester F. Ward, *Dynamic Sociology*, Vol. II, pp. 595–96. Used by permission of D. Appleton-Century Co., Publishers, New York, N. Y.

[11] George D. Strayer and Robert Murray Haig, *The Financing of Edu-cation in the State of New York*, 1923, p. 173. By permission of The Macmillan Company, publishers.

not provided when all children must take precisely the same work, that what may be a significant opportunity for one child is a relatively valueless opportunity for another. Rather, the term has come to mean that every child should have equal opportunity to develop his particular abilities and aptitudes for successful and happy living in a democratic order. It is under the pressure of this demand that the curriculum has been broadened, special classes formed, varied types of materials introduced, and flexibility of school organization increased.

This responsibility of the school to provide an equalized minimum educational opportunity also offers greater opportunity than in some types of social organization for the school to provide direction for social development. The mere fact that the school has under its care all the people for a period of years gives the educational program the possibility of great potency. When the educational program can be adjusted to individual needs and capacities the possibilities of molding the developing social order are even greater.

But does not the foregoing point of view leave out of consideration the individual? it may be asked. Is not he the one primarily concerned with education and does not this approach look upon him merely as a means to an end, when his welfare should be the end?

The point of view developed does not imply that the characteristics of the individual and the nature of learning are unimportant. We would be among the first to contend that they be given full consideration. The point simply is that the nature of the individual does not provide an initial point of orientation for curriculum development. There are too many illustrations of individuals developing widely different traits and characteristics apparently with equal facility, and living according to varying customs and mores with self-assurance and satisfaction, to permit us to believe that the nature of the individual accounts for the direction of the development that is taken. We do recognize that there are certain principles of development which operate regardless of the direction in which the individual moves, or the customs by which he lives. Therefore, although we seek our initial point of orientation in social ideals, we endeavor in attacking the problems of curriculum making to observe fundamental principles which govern human development. Briefly, we might say that society, the group operating through its recognized agencies, determines the direction of development for which the school shall strive; while the individual, his characteristics, and growth processes determine how this development shall be attained. It follows that the extent to which the individual is considered a means or an end—that is, the extent to which social ideals embody individual welfare—is determined by the type of society in which the individual finds himself. It so happens that the democratic ideal conceives the function of organized social life as that of freeing the individual, of making it possible for him to live a fuller, richer life than he otherwise would live. Consequently, the school program in a democracy must give major attention to development of the capacities of each individual for happy and successful living. But we reiterate, this is a merit of democracy, rather than a merit of the school as a social institution.

RESPONSIBILITIES OF THE SCHOOL AND CURRICULUM MAKING

The foregoing analysis of the responsibilities of the school not only indicates that schools in a democracy have an obligation to assist in providing direction for social development, but it also provides an important point for orientation in curriculum making. Each of these responsibilities has important implications for the curriculum. As we turn to the more specific tasks of curriculum making it will be seen that the effectiveness with which the curriculum is developed determines in a large way the success or failure of the school in discharging its major social responsibilities.

SELECTED REFERENCES

Briggs, T. H., *The Great Investment*, Inglis Lecture, Harvard University Press, Cambridge, Massachusetts, 1930.

Caswell, Hollis L., "The Schools and Social Progress," *School Executive's Magazine*, 51: 435–437, June, 1932.

Committee of the Progressive Education Association on Social and Economic Problems, *A Call to the Teachers of the Nation*, John Day Company, New York, 1933.

Counts, George S., *The Social Foundations of Education*, Charles Scribner's Sons, New York, 1934.

Hand, Harold C., "Social Reconstruction: Its Implications for Secondary Education," *Teachers College Record*, 34: 587ff., April, 1933.

Kandel, I. L., "Education and Social Disorder," *Teachers College Record*, 34: 359–367, February, 1933.

Kandel, I. L., "Mobilizing the Teacher," *Teachers College Record*, 35: 473–479, March, 1934.

Peffer, Nathaniel, "Educators Groping for the Stars," *Harper's Magazine*, 168: 230–238, January, 1934.

Reisner, Edward H., *Nationalism and Education Since 1789*, The Macmillan Company, New York, 1922, Preface.

Russell, William F., "Federal Aid—Boon or Bane," *School and Society*, 39: 289–296, March 10, 1934.

Russell, William F., "School Administration and Conflicting American Ideals," *Teachers College Record*, 31: 17, October, 1929.

Strayer, George D., Director, *Report of the Survey of the Schools of Chicago, Illinois*, Vol. III, Bureau of Publications, Teachers College, Columbia University, New York, 1933.

Strayer, George D., "The Ability and the Obligation of the State to Support Education," *Teachers College Record*, 35: 580–591, April, 1934.

CHAPTER III

SIGNIFICANT INFLUENCES ON CURRICULUM DEVELOPMENT

When curriculum development is considered a means which the school should employ to discharge more effectively its fundamental social responsibilities, a different source of orientation is required than has generally been made the basis for changes in the curriculum. Influences apart from these responsibilities have been potent sources of curriculum change, or lack of change, in the past. Development of an educational program which contributes more significantly to directing and achieving social advancement will require full recognition of the force of these influences and the ways in which they operate. In many cases they act in opposition to development of a curriculum which makes such a contribution. Consequently, consideration is given in this chapter to four especially important influences that have conditioned and continue to condition development of the curriculum. They are: (1) the influence of logically organized subject matter, (2) the influence of the textbook, (3) the influence of organized minority groups, and (4) the influence of quantitative standards.

INFLUENCE OF LOGICALLY ORGANIZED SUBJECT MATTER

However far we may have advanced in stating a philosophy of education which takes into account social needs and change, both courses of study and classroom practices still reflect the dominant position of logically organized subject matter. Logical relationship of subject matter even now determines largely the character and scope of the work of the schools. It conditions the method of stating objectives, and the manner in which they are supposed to function. It determines the basis for organizing instruction and the means of evaluating the results. It lends itself readily to the scientific method in education and the traditional assumption that knowledge of organized bodies of subject matter, properly selected and faithfully acquired, will achieve the desired personal and social ends. This has resulted in the division and subdivision of the broad fields or areas of logically organized knowledge into smaller and smaller units, each allocated to its carefully scheduled place in the respectable family of knowledge. Thus is engendered a kind of specialization in the various subjects that is common in the secondary school and reaches even into the elementary grades.

"Minimum essentials" are stated in terms of subject matter that the individual must know if he is to be educated. Other desirable educational values, usually stated as attitudes and appreciations, are considered concomitants of the learning process and are subordinated to the facts, principles, and skills which represent the organization of subjects. Evaluations of the results of instruction, whether by means of the occasional or periodic tests administered during the school term, or the longer "comprehensive" or "final" examinations at the end of the semester or term, are tests primarily of the memory of facts and mastery of skills considered essential in the subject.

Efforts to reduce the domination of logically organized subject matter have taken form in the development of fusion courses in the social studies, in organizing courses around specific objectives, in organizing activity curricula, and in basing courses of study on the unit organization. When the schools of the nation are considered as a whole, however, it is apparent that these developments have not made much headway. For example, Harap and Bayne analyzed 317 courses of study from seventy-two school organizations for the period 1929–31.[1] With

---

[1] Henry Harap and Alice J. Bayne, "A Critical Survey of Public School Courses of Study Published 1929–1931," *Journal of Educational Research*, 26:48, September, 1932.

regard to fusion courses in the social studies they found that separate courses in history and geography outnumbered social studies courses. They further found that courses of study labeled social studies, in the majority of cases, were not fusion courses in history and geography. These findings are supported by a study by Lindahl,[2] who examined fifty-seven courses of study in history for grades four, five, and six, for the period 1928–31. He concludes that in actual practice the fusion of history and geography does not exist to any appreciable extent. Only 7 per cent of the fifty-seven courses examined were fusion courses.

Although many courses of study have been organized in terms of specific objectives, there is little evidence that the domination of the curriculum by the logical relationships of subject matter has been lessened thereby. A conclusion by Beauchamp, who examined 160 courses of study in science, appears to present the condition very fairly.

> Some of the methods of stating the objectives are "to comprehend," "to understand," "to become familiar with." . . . If the infinitives are written on one side of the page and the subject matter on the other, we have on one side a series of infinitives and on the other a topical outline. It may be taken for granted that the teacher wishes pupils to obtain a knowledge of the topics in an outline and it is, therefore, questionable whether the addition of the infinitives is any contribution.[3]

Harap and Bayne gave consideration to the number of activity curricula developed. Out of the 317 courses of study which they examined, only seventeen were found which could be classified as activity curricula; and only ten of these were integrated. Except in three cases the activity curricula were limited to the primary grades.

These authors gave consideration as well to the organiza-

[2] H. M. Lindahl, "History in the Intermediate Grades," *Elementary School Journal*, 32:257–265, December, 1931.
[3] Wilbur L. Beauchamp, *Instruction in Science*, National Survey of Secondary Education, Bulletin No. 17, Monograph No. 22, 1932, p. 18.

tion of courses of study in units. They found that this organization did not imply any radical change from logical relationships in the organization of subject matter. They state in this regard:

In our analysis, we took the view that a unit was a clearly defined subdivision of a course which had unity or completeness, although its unity may have been based upon any of the following factors: a child or adult experience, a center of interest, a theme, a principle, a topic, or a graded step. From this viewpoint, 78 per cent of the courses were subdivided into units of work. Of these courses of study, 80 per cent of the units were based on graded steps or processes such as *percentage* (arithmetic), *machines* (physics), *circulatory system* (health), the *halogens* (chemistry), etc. This does not represent a radical change in organization or treatment of formal courses . . .[4]

Beauchamp finds the same to be true of the 160 courses in science which he examined. He states that, "An analysis of the courses divided into units indicates that the term 'unit' has been taken over as a convenient term to replace the word 'topic,' rather than as a principle of organization."[5]

Thus, it appears that these departures from traditional organization in most cases have little real significance. When this is considered in conjunction with the fact that even such departures as these are far in the minority, the extent of the domination of logically organized subject matter becomes apparent. Of the 160 courses in science which Beauchamp examined, ninety-three simply presented a topical outline of subject matter. This is probably a fair representation of the practice in most fields. He concludes:

Examination of the studies which have been made discloses that the sole emphasis has been upon the determination of the principles or subject matter which should be included in our science courses. Apparently, no studies have been made of the difficulty of these materials. Placement of the topics or principles in the various courses is de-

[4] *Op. cit.*, p. 52.
[5] *Op. cit.*, pp. 15–16.

termined by the logical demands of the subject rather than by the psychological characteristics of the learner.[6]

This consideration is especially significant in light of the fact that since the beginning of the present century there has been a constantly increasing amount of criticism of the practice of permitting the demands of logically organized subjects to dominate the curriculum. Educational philosophers have pointed to the undesirable consequences of such a procedure and national committees have emphasized the importance of giving primary consideration to social needs and problems in organizing the curriculum. For example, the Commission on Character Education of the Department of Superintendence made this relevant observation:

It is entirely conceivable that if schools insist upon limiting their function to attempting to teach pupils only in matters so academic as to have little or no direct bearing on the real social problems which people have to meet in some way or another, the public confidence and support which schools have thus far enjoyed to a remarkable degree may be lost.[7]

Evidence of the domination of logically organized subject matter is also provided by the way in which new materials have been forced to find entrance into the curriculum. Traditional subjects, as a practice, have not been subjected to a continuous process of reorganization in terms of social situations and needs. Rather, they have rested for acceptance on tradition. The result is that when society has demanded the inclusion in the curriculum of new materials, a new *subject* or *course* is introduced, allied as closely as possible with one of the established fields, and given a place in the program of studies. Thus, the offerings of the schools have been multiplied within a generation. The extent of this sort of curriculum revision is indicated in

[6] *Ibid.*, p. 38.
[7] *Tenth Yearbook, Department of Superintendence,* National Education Association, 1932, p. 191.

the following observation in the National Survey of Secondary Education.

The most significant changes over the full period are shown in the tendency to provide a much wider range of materials of instruction, and these of a richer and more practical nature. Between 1860 and 1895, the number of units offered by the average school changed very little; between 1895 and 1918, the average school shows an increment of approximately one unit per year; and between 1918 and 1930, an increment of approximately two units per year is shown for the average school. The number of *different* courses offered increased 475 per cent between 1906 and 1930, while the total number offered more than doubled. These increments are far greater in the nonacademic than in the academic fields, but in each the tendency is to make the offering more immediately significant.[8]

This procedure shows the inflexibility of a curriculum dominated by logically organized subject matter and the difficulty encountered in meeting social needs. This is not the only consequence of the procedure, however. As course has been added to course, a body of materials has developed with untold overlappings and complexities. The result is a state of confusion which makes it difficult to plan for the rounded development of a given pupil with a minimum of wasted time and effort. Bode describes the situation as follows:

If we note next how the schools adapted themselves to this rising tide of demands, we are in a position to see both how our educational system has become needlessly cumbersome and how it has become involved in a sorry confusion of purposes or aims. The cumbersomeness is a natural result of the tendency to meet new demands by the simple process of adding new courses without engaging in any basic reconstruction of the curriculum. If, for example, the pressure for a new subject, like music or art or commercial geography, became sufficiently strong, the situation was met by the expedient of adding new courses and special teachers . . .

The result of this general tendency has naturally been to produce a curriculum containing a bewildering variety of more or less unrelated

[8] A. K. Loomis, Edwin S. Lide, and B. Lamar Johnson, *Program of Studies*, National Survey of Secondary Education, Bulletin No. 17, Monograph No. 19, 1932, p. 167.

"subjects." New subjects were added as occasion arose, without disturbing those which were already in the curriculum, except to require them to move up so that the newcomer might have a seat along with the rest.[9]

Many conditions have operated to make logical subject relationships exert such a potent influence on the educational program. Not the least of these is tradition. The use of logically organized subject matter as the center around which the work of the school is organized has been the prevailing practice for centuries. The assumption that the acquisition of knowledge constitutes effective learning, and the resultant problem of selecting that "knowledge which is of most worth" are matters of ancient origin. These questions were especially pertinent so long as education was considered a means of raising a person above the masses. The result of accepting this as the chief purpose for education was emphasis on erudition. This, consequently, became a fundamental objective of education which persisted down through the ages. As Morrison points out:

From time immemorial, that man whose mind was fullest stored with the erudition of the ages had been conceived to be the best educated, and so education and erudition were thought to be one and the same. The curriculum was formulated with that principle in mind, and teachers were held to be best prepared who knew most about the subjects which they proposed to teach in the sense of being best informed about them.[10]

Thus tradition has sanctioned the idea of education as a pursuit for the elite with a consequent emphasis on erudition. The inevitable result has been emphasis on knowledge of subjects rather than social effectiveness. American schools still labor under this eruditional concept of education. As steps are taken to make education serve its real function in a democratic social order, this concept will be changed and the logical rela-

[9] From *The Educational Frontier*, by William H. Kilpatrick and others, pp. 3–4. Used by permission of D. Appleton-Century Company, Publishers, New York, N. Y.
[10] Henry C. Morrison, *The Practice of Teaching in the Secondary School*, p. 16. Reprinted by permission of the University of Chicago Press.

tionship of subject matter assigned its appropriate place in organization of the curriculum of schools in a democracy. What
this place should be is given consideration in a later chapter.

INFLUENCE OF THE TEXTBOOK

Another influence of great significance in curriculum development is the textbook. The general place it holds in educational
thought, the dependence of teachers—especially of poorly trained
teachers—on it, and methods of selecting textbooks for use are
all important aspects of this influence.

The important place which the textbook holds in American
education is especially noticeable to European observers. Hylla,
in discussing American education in comparison with German
education, says, "It is very significant that in place of our word
'instruction-hour,' almost always the term, 'recitation-period,'
is used.[11]   Uher says of American education, "As far as methods
are concerned, we can see the spreading of new tendencies, but
this is far from being so general as many believe. The American
school in this respect is rather below the average. A badly prepared teacher is dependent upon the textbook. This explains
the long-windedness of many American textbooks and the array
of details contained there . . ."[12]

The great dependence of American teachers on textbooks is,
of course, generally recognized by American educators. Ed-
mondson[13] says that the textbook in thousands of classrooms
determines not only the content of instruction but also the teaching procedures. Suzzalo, in the introduction to Fuller's *Scientific
Evaluation of Textbooks*, says:

The textbook is the most important of the teacher's tools. In determining the subject matter of the child's experience, it is more de-

[11] Erich Hylla, *Die Schule der Demokratie,* Langensalza, Julius Betz,
1929, pp. 141ff.
[12] Jan Uher, *On American Education,* The English-Speaking World
Series, No. 3, Politka, Prague, 1930, p. 64.
[13] *Thirtieth Yearbook, National Society for the Study of Education,*
Part II, Introduction, 1931, p. 1.

cisive in day-to-day affairs than is the course of study outlined by the school system. In determining teaching procedure the text is more influential from hour to hour than a manual of methods. In fact the total series of textbooks in use by students and teachers are the real course of study and manual of teaching. This is not the usual theory, but it is actual fact.[14]

Kimmel concludes in the National Survey of Secondary Education that: "The most influential factor in the determination of the content in courses of study, based on internal evidence and the testimony of teachers, seems to be the representative textbooks." [15]

Such opinions are supported by quantitative studies which indicate in general the dominance of the textbook in American education. Jensen asked 172 city superintendents of schools, "Do you build a course of study and then select a textbook, or, do you select a textbook and then build your course of study?" [16] Eighty-four and nine-tenths per cent of these superintendents replied that they built a course of study and then selected a textbook, while 22.1 per cent of them reported that they selected a textbook and then built a course of study. This would indicate that practically one-fourth of the city courses of study reported were directly dictated by textbooks. The extent to which the other courses of study were influenced by textbooks cannot be determined, but examination of courses of study reveal very few indeed that do not reflect to a marked degree the organization of textbooks customarily used. Statements from some of the city superintendents queried by Jensen throw interesting light on the problem. One superintendent, for example, stated: "Both ways have been done. I am under the impression that textbooks are selected first, as a rule." Another said, "Select textbooks to meet the need of the community. Then build

[14] Florence D. Fuller, *Scientific Evaluation of Textbooks,* 1928, p. iii. Used by permission of and special arrangement with Houghton Mifflin Company.

[15] William G. Kimmel, *Instruction in the Social Studies,* National Survey of Secondary Education, Bulletin No. 17, Monograph No. 21, 1932, p. 75.

[16] Frank A. Jensen, *Current Procedure in Selecting Textbooks,* J. B. Lippincott Company, 1931, p. 122.

a course around it." A third stated, "Sometimes a course is built with a textbook in mind; at other times not." Still another said, "Our course of study is invariably the textbooks." [17]

Bagley studied evidences of the dominance of the textbook in the classroom presented in reports of school surveys. The following are typical of the statements which he found of the observations and opinions of survey staffs:

Texts were followed almost slavishly; the curiosity of the pupils was seldom aroused; rarely was an inquiring spirit stimulated by the teacher.

In M——— schools, as in most American schools, textbooks are an important part of the machinery of instruction. To a considerable extent they determine both the content and the method of instruction. This is of necessity true when teachers are not well trained; when competent professional supervision is generally lacking; and when reference materials are scarce, unsuitable, and inadequate. In practice the textbook is the course of study in most M——— schools.

Methods of instruction used . . . represent too frequently a slavish memorization of the textbooks.

The teachers in the small rural schools are very deficient in training and educational outlook. The blind dependence of the teachers upon textbooks is generally evident.[18]

Bagley also studied the problem through observers' reports of 539 classroom exercises. These exercises were, presumably, a random sampling, representing elementary and high schools in cities, towns, villages, and the open country in thirty states. The results of this study indicate somewhat less dependence on the textbook than do the foregoing comments. They show that "one or another form of the socialized recitation and project methods appeared approximately as frequently in these lessons as did the 'straight' recitation from the single textbook." It

[17] *Ibid.*, pp. 123–124.
[18] William C. Bagley, "The Textbook and Methods of Teaching," *Thirtieth Yearbook, National Society for the Study of Education*, Part II, 1931, pp. 7–26.

was revealed that non-textbook methods were used in the city elementary schools in more than one-third of all the lessons observed. It was found that in the high schools the textbook-recitation method is much more common, this method being noted in 42.8 per cent of the lessons observed.

The extent to which teachers restrict their teaching to textbook assignments and recitations appears to be closely related to training and experience. Bagley found that teachers with long periods of training tend to use non-textbook methods to a greater extent than teachers with short periods of training. He also found that the beginning teacher, whatever his training, tends to depend upon formal textbook methods more than teachers with from two to five years' experience. Teachers with more than five years' experience revealed the least dependence upon textbook methods.

These findings suggest that further implications as to the extent of textbook teaching may be secured from consideration of the training and experience of teachers. According to Bachman, "In three-fourths of all the states, probably 50 per cent of all elementary teachers in service have had two years or more of preparation beyond high school, and in one-fourth, 50 per cent have had less than two years of preparation on the college level." [19] Although the experience is apparently increasing, the same author finds that from 20 to 47 per cent of all elementary teachers round out their careers as elementary teachers in less than four years. Thus, it appears that a considerable proportion of elementary teachers have both the training and experience which tends to make them rely largely on textbooks. The same is probably true to a considerable extent of high school teachers.

However, the dominance of the textbook probably rests on foundations even more secure than the ignorance or helplessness of teachers. Bode suggests that a fundamental misconception

[19] Frank P. Bachman, *The Education and Certification of Elementary Teachers,* Field Study No. 5, Division of Surveys and Field Studies, George Peabody College, Nashville, Tenn., 1933, p. 8.

of the purpose of education, a misconception previously discussed, contributes to the slavish following of textbooks. He
states:

> In part, at least, this predilection may spring from misdirected piety.
> The business of the schools is supposed to be limited to the preservation
> or perpetuation of our civilization. Consequently, we should teach the
> subjects in the curriculum as we teach the catechism, not to encourage
> a spirit of independence and inquiry, but to insure a set of correct
> responses . . .
> It is a fine thing for a teacher to have a rich intellectual background,
> provided that he makes no use of it. The disposition to engage in
> exploration beyond the limits of the textbooks is regarded as evidence
> of intellectual frivolity, if not of irreverence or bolshevism . . .
> Our worship of the textbook, then, appears to be a joint product of
> plain ignorance and an ignorant veneration of tradition. A combina-
> tion of this sort can scarcely fail to make the world safe for the
> textbook.[20]

The superiority of the American textbook is advanced by some
as a reason for its continued place of prominence in educational
practices. Cubberley [21] speaks of the textbook as a distinctive
American achievement. Winship extols the textbook as developed in the United States. He says, "Nowhere in the world
have they (textbooks) improved as in the United States. There
is not a nation on earth in which the schoolbooks approach even
faintly those of America." [22]

The most potent factor insuring textbook dominance of American education, and the one with most implications for the curriculum, is the uniform prescription of textbooks by legislatures.

The significant aspect of textbook uniformity under the laws now
prevailing in the different states is the fact that in twenty-five states
the uniform use of the books selected is prescribed for the state as a

[20] Boyd H. Bode, "On the Use of Textbooks," *Educational Research
Bulletin,* Ohio State University, 7:10, January 11, 1928.
[21] Ellwood P. Cubberley, "A Distinctive American Achievement," *Educational Progress,* 5:4–5, January, 1926.
[22] A. E. Winship, "Textbooks—Educationally, Commercially, and Politi-
cally," *Addresses and Proceedings,* National Education Association, Department of Superintendence, February, 1915, p. 274.

whole, whereas the laws of twenty-three states prescribe or permit the establishment of uniformity regulations over smaller units of school organization within the state.[23]

There are, it is true, differences in the scope and the meaning of the uniformity regulations in the different state-adoption states. In three states the adopting body does not have authority to prescribe textbooks beyond the elementary grades, while in three other states the adopting agency may, but is not required to, select the books which are to be used in the high schools. Fifteen of the twenty-five uniformity states limit the books prescribed to a single text for each grade or subject, while the other ten allow the adopting agency to select two or more texts for each subject. From this latter multiple list, local school authorities may then select and prescribe the books to be used in the schools under their jurisdiction. Another difference in regulations is found in the extent to which they apply to different types of local units within the state. Nine of the state-uniformity units exempt by law either cities or school districts of a specified class from the uniformity rule which in general applies to the schools of that state. The reason given for this apparent discrimination is that some communities tend to maintain higher educational standards.

Historically [24] the trend has been toward state-uniformity of textbooks. By 1890 textbooks were selected and prescribed on a state-wide basis in fourteen states. Fifteen years later, eleven additional states had adopted uniformity while two had discontinued it, leaving a net total of twenty-three states requiring uniformity by 1905. Since then there have been few changes. There are now twenty-five states requiring some type of textbook uniformity.

The political aspects of this problem are of such importance that the issue is kept almost constantly before the voting public.

[23] Nelson B. Henry, "Value of State Textbook Adoption is Debatable," *The Nation's Schools*, 12:19, December, 1933.
[24] Nelson B. Henry, "How the Various States Prescribe Textbooks on a Uniform Basis," *The Nation's Schools*, 12:53–56, November, 1933.

Frequent efforts are made to induce additional states to adopt state uniformity, or to modify or repeal textbook laws in states where uniformity is prescribed. The layman, as a rule, "favors long-period adoptions, uniformity of adoptions over wide political units, the adoption of a single rather than several texts, free textbooks, and is readily tempted by State publication and local authorship without stopping to consider the disadvantages." [25]

The result is emphasis upon textbook teaching. Laymen assume that this is the type of instructional program that should be carried on. Continual emphasis on textbook adoptions not only encourages them to hold to this belief, but also emphasizes to the teacher the need of covering certain textbook materials and gives the impression that it is the primary function of the teacher to see that this is done. Thus, the practice of uniform prescription of textbooks provides a basis upon which textbook domination rests with considerable security.

THE INFLUENCE OF ORGANIZED MINORITY GROUPS

Another restraining influence upon the instructional program of the school is the pressure exerted by organized minority groups. These groups frequently attempt to thwart independent efforts on the part of the school to deal with vital problems and often try to force the school to teach specific solutions to problems. Pressure is made operative in two ways; first, through control of school legislation, and second, through control of teaching personnel.

Control of school legislation has been possible because of the constitutional provision that legislatures have the power and duty of providing free public schools and the "means of education." The constitutional theory is that public opinion regarding the function of the schools should be represented in constitutions and in legislative enactments. Constitutions, because of their nature, deal less with details and therefore respond

[25] C. R. Maxwell, *The Selection of Textbooks,* Houghton Mifflin Co., 1921, p. vi.

less readily to change than do statutes. They cannot be molded so easily by the machinations of special interests and minority groups. Couched in general terms, they provide the basic law of the state, leaving details to be provided by specific legislative enactments.

In recognizing the constitutional rights of the people to determine the general nature of their schools, however, the way is left open for organized minority groups to enforce restrictions upon the offerings of the school or to dictate specific teachings that do not represent the majority. Often these teachings are detrimental to society and are real deterrents to social progress.

Clothed with indisputable constitutional power, legislatures in all the states have found in school legislation a means of satisfying the demands of various groups, groups frequently consisting of small but vigorous minorities. Whether it be sound procedure or not, the general public allows legislative action inspired by special group interests to determine what shall or shall not be taught in the schools. Not all school legislation has its inception in the selfish desires of interested groups, but it is significant that much of it does, thereby giving official sanction to their demands. An example of the effectiveness of the organized effort of a minority group to control what is taught in the schools may be cited from the legislation that followed the activities of the various temperance groups:

In 1923 all but five states made mandatory the teaching of these subjects (physiology and hygiene), the statutes generally requiring instruction in "the effects of alcoholic drinks and narcotics upon the 'human system.'" By 1929 every state was said to have upon its statute books some law which prescribed temperance instruction, either directly or through the observance of Temperance Day.[26]

Such organizations frequently attempt to carry on their work on a national scale, conducting campaigns of propaganda in the various states preceding and during the sessions of the legisla-

[26] Bessie Louise Pierce, *Citizens' Organizations and the Civic Training of Youth,* Part III, Report of the Commission on the Social Studies, Scribner's, 1933, p. 300.

ture. Such was the plan of the "fundamentalists" a few years ago who succeeded in securing the passage of "monkey bills." Referring to this type of legislation, Flanders says:

There are agencies, entirely apart from the government and therefore not subject to popular control, which are definitely working to induce legislatures to enact specific laws directing that certain subjects be taught. One cannot read the laws of the several states without being impressed by the frequent recurrence of the same phraseology.[27]

Wholesale assumption of control of the curriculum by legislatures is due almost wholly to pressure brought to bear upon these bodies by organized minority groups. It is not a question of whether these things should or should not be included in the school curricula, but rather a question as to who should prescribe them, politicians and lobbying groups, or educators.

The extent to which legislatures have engaged in curriculum making is shown in comparatively recent studies. For example, Nixon[28] shows that legislative prescriptions for elementary and high schools in Ohio range from the statutory requirement of the three R's in 1825 to the compulsory teaching of the state and federal constitutions in 1923. He also shows that legislative acts affecting the curriculum have increased materially since 1900. Similarly, Flanders[29] finds that the number of legislative prescriptions increased 65 per cent during the twenty-year interval, 1903-1923.

The present extent of legislative prescription of high school curricula is indicated in the following table taken from the National Survey of Secondary Education:[30]

[27] Jesse K. Flanders, *Legislative Control of the Elementary Curriculum,* Teachers College, Columbia University, Contributions to Education No. 195, 1925, p. 182.

[28] O. Floyd Nixon, *A Critical Study of Curriculum Legislation with Special Reference to Ohio from 1803 to 1901,* Abstracts of Doctors' Dissertations, No. 9, Ohio State University Press, 1932.

[29] *Op. cit.,* p. 174.

[30] Ward W. Keesecker, *Legal and Regulatory Provisions Affecting Secondary Education,* National Survey of Secondary Education, Bulletin No. 17, Monograph No. 9, 1932, p. 77.

TABLE I

CHARACTER AND EXTENT OF LEGISLATIVE CONTROL OF PUBLIC-SCHOOL AND COMMON-SCHOOL CURRICULA, 1930

SUBJECT	NUMBER OF STATES	SUBJECT	NUMBER OF STATES
Nature of alcoholic drinks .	48	Drawing	13
Physiology and hygiene . .	39	Bible	13
History (United States) . .	38	Prevention of communi-	
Constitution (United States)	38	cable diseases	12
Reading	36	Composition	12
Arithmetic	36	Language	11
Geography	35	Music	9
Writing	34	Manual training . . .	7
Spelling	34	Domestic science . . .	7
Grammar	32	Thrift	5
Physical training	29	Safety	4
Citizenship	26	Hygiene and sanitation .	4
History (State)	22	Elementary science . .	4
Civil government	22	Algebra	3
Morals	21	Preservation of birds and	
Humane treatment of		game	2
animals	20	Industrial work	2
Health	17	Spanish	1
Agriculture	14	Forestry	1

Doubtless, much minority group legislation regarding the curriculum is enacted because of the conservatism of teachers and leaders in education. Inertia, complacency, and indifference of teachers have also played an important part. In other words, when a need has arisen for modifying the curriculum, teachers, instead of assuming their prerogative of leadership, have by their complacency either forced outside groups to demand the inclusion of needed instructional materials; or, if they made any efforts toward change, have allowed the opposition of minority groups to thwart them. Consequently, too frequently, the *status quo* has been changed or maintained at the will of forces outside the schools themselves.

The other principal means through which the pressure of minority groups is exerted on the curriculum is through direct relationship with the teaching personnel. This takes the form of making certain materials available for the use of teachers or of holding teaching positions and advancement in jeopardy through local boards of education.

Many of the materials prepared by minority groups are of fundamental educational value. On the other hand, many times they are prepared with the deliberate purpose of propagandizing the nation through the schools for certain special interests. For example, the purpose of one organization cited by Pierce is as follows:

To put into the hands of school children a book conforming to the theories held by the utilities became one of the problems of the Public Relations Committee. This was considered necessary in order that "future generations of Americans will be staunch friends of the public utilities . . ." [31]

The control over teaching positions and advancement through local boards of education is often a subtle but nevertheless a real influence. Since the men who control our schools as a rule also control the social and financial affairs of the community, they are in position to dominate the work of the schools. Beale points out that:

They (minority groups) see that certain subjects are tabooed: government control of railroads in a railroad town; conditions in the mines in a mining town; labor questions and company police in a steel town; criticism of the mill owners in a textile town; the fact that a particular local business is not paying its share of school taxes.[32]

The creation of a better social order involves change. Therefore, many powerful minority groups which benefit from the present order inevitably will oppose any social progress. It is these groups that exert pressure upon the schools to accept conditions as they are. They insist, to be sure, that the schools develop character, instill respect for law and order, make good citizens, and teach patriotism. However, when interpreted from

[31] *Op. cit.*, p. 251.
[32] Howard K. Beale, "Forces that Control the Schools," *Harper's Magazine*, 169:609, October, 1934.

the point of view of the interested groups, this means simply the acceptance of things as they are.

Obviously, so long as organized minority groups are allowed to exert such a controlling influence upon education, schools will be unable to exert a positive influence on social progress. Our schools will remain impotent and helpless so long as they are complacent and indifferent to the vital issues of the present, or else deal with them in such a way as to present specific solutions dictated by some special interest or minority group. To free the schools from these influences calls for both courage and vision on the part of teachers and educational leaders. It also demands an awakened public opinion as to the true function and potential influence of the school in a democratic society.

INFLUENCE OF QUANTITATIVE STANDARDS

A third significant influence which must be accorded consideration in curriculum development finds expression in quantitative standards. These standards have taken various forms and have influenced the educational program at various points. Their development has been a part of the scientific movement in education which has held such an important place in educational work and thought during the present century. While many highly desirable results have accrued from the use of quantitative standards, in many cases they have now reached a stage of inflexibility which results in a limiting influence on curriculum development. Consequently, they are accorded consideration as one of the major influences which must be given special consideration in the development of a curriculum which meets social needs more adequately.

Quantitative standards which have developed in connection with tests of intelligence and achievement, and in connection with college entrance and institutional accreditment, have exerted the most important influence on the curriculum. Brief consideration will be given to each of these.

The development of intelligence tests may be said to have begun about 1905, the year Alfred Binet, a noted French psychologist, devised the first scientifically constructed test. He had been given the task of selecting candidates for special schools for subnormals in Paris. To accomplish this he devised a technique for measuring intelligence. Psychologists generally were much interested. This interest resulted in many refinements of Binet's techniques. By 1915 many series of tests had been developed and statistical techniques were perfected to the point where tests were required to meet definite standards with respect to validity and reliability. Several important revisions and adaptations of the Binet scale had been made by that time.

During the World War, 1,700,000 soldiers and officers of the United States Army were given intelligence tests. After the War there was a great interest and enthusiasm in the use of intelligence tests in schools. The National Intelligence Test was constructed by a committee of psychologists who had been concerned with the development of the army tests, and was given wide use. Within less than a year after publication, over 575,000 copies were sold, and during 1922–23, 800,000 copies were distributed. It is estimated that by 1923, 20,000,000 intelligence tests of various kinds had been sold.

The achievement test movement may be said to have begun with the report in 1897 of Rice's test of the spelling ability of 33,000 school children. Stone's *Reasoning Test in Arithmetic* appeared in 1908 and Thorndike's *Scale for Measuring the Quality of Handwriting* in 1910.

From these beginnings, mental and educational tests developed in great numbers and came to occupy an important place in educational practices. A review of test literature made in 1922 revealed fifty functions tests had performed. Authors of tests themselves set forth sixteen different functions.[33]

The standards thus evolved exerted great influence on curriculum development. The influence has been in two directions. On the one hand there has been a tendency to recognize more

---

[33] A. G. Capps, "The Functions of Tests and Scales as Found in Recent Educational Literature," *Journal of Educational Research,* 6:204–208, October, 1922.

fully the nature and extent of individual differences among pupils. This has resulted in the development of the curriculum in such ways as to permit adjustment to individual needs. Rigidity of offering has thus been lessened through test development. The other direction of influence, however, has been in direct opposition to this broadening influence. The availability of grade standards and norms as supplied by tests has encouraged the practice of defining minimum essentials for the respective grades, thus increasing the inflexibility of the curriculum. This has been especially significant, inasmuch as the tendency has been to state the minimum essentials in terms of abilities measured by standard tests. The result has been emphasis throughout the instructional program and the development of the curriculum upon the objectively measurable aspects of the learning process. Facts and skills, as a result, have been accorded far more than their equitable share of attention, without regard for attitudes and appreciations; and drill, memorization, and recitation have too generally dominated instruction.

This tendency is suggested by the almost complete emphasis in courses of study on measurement of skills and facts to the exclusion of other types of outcomes. Harap and Bayne appraised the tests suggested in the courses of study which they examined as follows:

They do not test for expression and creative ability; they do not test for the ability to organize parts into a coherent product; they test for reasoning only to a limited degree; they do not test for the ability to apply facts, skills, or generalizations; they do not test for the accomplishment of child or adult objectives. Beyond the basic discovery of the brief answer and objective scoring, ingenuity in test making has run out. It is of fundamental importance that the test should be based on the objectives of the given course and that the test items should elicit lifelike responses.[34]

Other points of influence, many of them favorable, of standardized tests on curriculum development might be mentioned, but the principal point for our purpose should be clear. The de-

[34] *Op. cit.*, p. 55.

mand for uniformity, the undue emphasis on objective measurement and statistical treatment, and the encouragement of a type of instructional program which emphasizes drill, memorization, and recitation forms an influence that must be recognized as limiting the development of a curriculum of major social significance.

Quantitative standards have also exerted great influence on the secondary school curriculum through the development of college entrance requirements. The demand for uniform college entrance requirements, which began to appear late in the nineteenth century, resulted in the rapid growth and power of regional standardizing agencies. Such terms as hours, credits, points, courses, majors, units, and semester hours came to have meaning in terms of quantity. These were applied with varying meanings until the "Carnegie Unit" brought a semblance of order out of the confusion. This unit was heralded as a quantitative means of checking up on the quality of education.

From the definition of the Carnegie Unit many other aspects of standardization developed until the curriculum of the high school especially was dictated in many particulars by standardizing agencies. Deviations from average practice were discouraged and unthinking observance of detailed requirements came to be a general practice. This was especially true in curriculum development. The first question usually asked in connection with a proposal for curriculum development in the secondary school was concerning the attitude of the accrediting agency toward such an undertaking.

As the defects of such standardization became increasingly clear, criticism was leveled at the procedure. Illustrative is a comment made by White in a 1930 issue of the *High School Quarterly*. He states:

Standardization, at best, is a counsel of mediocrity. Mediocrity is normal, but it is not excellence. To encourage deviation from it in the right direction is the duty of every standardizing agency.[35]

[35] Howard D. White, "Beyond Standardization," *The High School Quarterly*, 18:136, April, 1930.

Gradually more and more educational leaders demanded changes in accrediting practices. In 1932 Jessup stated in an address to the North Central Association of Colleges and Secondary Schools:

> We have standardized school years, school months, school weeks, school days, school hours and school minutes in terms of units, credits, points, majors. At the rate we have been going in recent years, we will soon interpret education in terms of split seconds.[36]

The most significant development at the present time is the attack on the problem being made by the North Central Association. A committee has been working for a considerable period of time to devise procedures for accreditment that will eliminate the bad effects of the quantitative standards of the type now employed. The general approach to the problem made by this committee marks the development of a most significant point of view. They state:

> As a first step in the consideration of this program it seems desirable to discard the word standard from our thinking. This is not proposed on the ground that standards are of no importance or that the word has not served a useful purpose in the past. It is because the concept of standard in the old sense is foreign both to the spirit and to the method of the new plan. . . .
> Then, too, in its long history as an accrediting term the word has gathered its own meanings. It implies minimal conditions of acceptability, uniformity of pattern, and, too often, mediocrity of status. Connotations like these interfere with thinking about a program shaped to permit variety and individuality. Our task is to create a plan of accrediting through which will flow the spirit of freedom and the urge of institutional growth. This is not easy in any case, and one of the hampering influences is the vocabulary to which we are accustomed. Hours, credits, points, courses, majors, units, semesters, degrees, standards are symbols of status and not of processes. Their wide employment tends to mechanize our thinking about education. It would be fortunate if we could discard all of them and form a fresh vocabulary that would more adequately signify the vital character of education.[37]

[36] Walter A. Jessup, "Standardization and Achievement," *Educational Record,* 13:115, April, 1932.

[37] M. E. Haggerty, "Accrediting Institutions of Higher Education," *The North Central Association Quarterly,* 9:179, October, 1934.

Inasmuch as the Carnegie Foundation was instrumental in developing the Carnegie Unit officers of the Foundation were asked their opinion on developments in the field of standardization of colleges. The following statement was made in the 1933 Annual Report of the Foundation in answer to this query:

Today, none recognizes more clearly than the Foundation that these standards have served their purpose. With changed conditions and sharper and more wieldy tools, such expedients become obsolete. They should undoubtedly give place to more flexible,. more individual, more exact and revealing standards of performance as rapidly as these may be achieved. The Carnegie Foundation for the Advancement of Teaching looks with favor upon any and all means of judging qualifications for college admission which recent widespread experiment, scientifically and practically appraised, reveals as distinctly better than previous methods. A system of continuous individual records, including information about every phase of student interest and accomplishment, represents a decided advance over any basis for college admission previously in use. Certainly it is a marked improvement upon the "unit" system which in the early years of the present century began to bring order into the much confused situation respecting admission to college.[38]

Thus far, only the North Central Association has moved to revise its procedures in a significant way and the work in this Association has been restricted to college accreditment. But the general recognition of the problems developed by the rigid use of quantitative standards in accreditment and the nature of the attack on the problem at the college level provide ample grounds to believe that curriculum development will be rapidly freed from undesirable elements in accreditment and standardization.

IMPLICATIONS FOR CURRICULUM PROGRAMS

In developing a practical program of curriculum making, influences such as the ones discussed in this chapter must be given due consideration. They represent potent forces with which the

[38] *Twenty-eighth Annual Report,* The Carnegie Foundation for the Advancement of Teaching, 1933, p. 38.

curriculum worker must deal. Two points of view may result from such consideration. These points of view are reflected in educational literature. It is generally recognized that many changes needed in the curriculum would bring conflict with some of the interests which make operative such influences as those discussed, and would involve encounters with many trying and difficult problems. According to one point of view, these influences are so well intrenched and the teaching force of the nation is so inadequate in training and ability that no fundamental attack on the problem of curriculum development dare be made. Proponents of this point of view counsel continued "shuffling of courses and topics" as the only *practical* procedure that can be followed. In brief, they recognize the need for a fundamental attack on the problems, but hold that we are not in position to make such an attack.

According to the other point of view, the only way in which to achieve fundamental change and to develop the ability to deal with the problems involved is to cease palliative measures and halfway steps and to attack such phases of the problems as we do treat in a fundamental way. Better a little activity which strikes at a fundamental point than a great deal which merely skirts the edges of the real problems. It is further held that these influences which block fundamental curriculum development are not so intrenched that they can prevent real progress.

The issue which the curriculum worker must face, consequently, is whether, in view of the influences which operate to maintain existing conditions and practices, comprehensive and fundamental curriculum programs should be projected to meet the challenge for education discussed in the preceding chapter. If such a program is projected, it seems evident that major consideration must be given to the problems of educating laymen, influencing the pre-service training of teachers, and providing comprehensive in-service training opportunities. Only as all of these factors are included in a program of curriculum development can important issues and problems be attacked with assurance that changes found desirable may be effected.

SELECTED REFERENCES

Beauchamp, Wilbur L., *Instruction in Science*, National Survey of Secondary Education, Bulletin No. 17, Monograph No. 22, Government Printing Office, Washington, D. C., 1932.

Bode, Boyd H., "On the Use of Textbooks," *Educational Research Bulletin*, Ohio State University, Columbus, Ohio, 7:10–11, January 11, 1928.

Flanders, Jesse K., *Legislative Control of the Elementary Curriculum*, Contributions to Education No. 195, Bureau of Publications, Teachers College, Columbia University, New York, 1925.

Haggerty, M. E., "Accrediting Institutions of Higher Education," *The North Central Association Quarterly*, 9:177–188, October, 1934.

Hamilton, O. T., *The Courts and the Curriculum*, Contributions to Education No. 250, Bureau of Publications, Teachers College, Columbia University, New York, 1927.

Harap, Henry, and Bayne, Alice J., "A Critical Survey of Public School Courses of Study Published 1929–31," *Journal of Educational Research*, 26:48, September, 1932.

Jessup, Walter A., "Standardization and Achievement," *Educational Record*, 13:115, April, 1932.

Keesecker, Ward W., *Legal and Regulatory Provisions Affecting Secondary Education*, National Survey of Secondary Education, Bulletin No. 17, Monograph No. 9, Government Printing Office, Washington, D. C., 1932.

National Society for the Study of Education, Thirtieth Yearbook, Part II, Introduction, Public School Publishing Co., Bloomington, Illinois, 1931.

Pierce, Bessie Louise, *Citizens' Organizations and the Civic Training of Youth*, Part III, Report of the Commission on Social Studies, Charles Scribner's Sons, New York, 1933.

White, Howard D., "Beyond Standardization," *The High School Quarterly*, 18:136, April, 1930.

CHAPTER IV

CONCEPTS OF THE CURRICULUM

The scope and character of any enterprise are controlled in the main by the meanings ascribed certain basic terms and the relationships that are assumed to exist between the various elements involved in the enterprise. This is but another way of saying that the nature of an enterprise is determined largely by the definitions and principles that are accepted for guidance. This is especially applicable in curriculum development, inasmuch as there are widely varying concepts in these regards. Consequently, early in the projection of a curriculum program it becomes important to give consideration to basic concepts and relationships that are to control the work. Such consideration will lessen to an appreciable extent misunderstandings and confusion as work progresses.

In this chapter consideration is given to concepts of the nature of the curriculum and in the following chapter to principles that are basic to curriculum development.

DEFINITIONS OF THE CURRICULUM

There are many concepts of great importance in curriculum development, but perhaps the one which exerts the most far-reaching influence on programs as they actually develop is in connection with the nature of the curriculum itself. The purposes of curriculum programs, the steps in their development, and the means employed to achieve the purposes are all conditioned in important ways by this concept. This is especially noticeable inasmuch as there are widely different ideas of the curriculum, and, consequently, of what is involved in curriculum making.

Definitions of the curriculum fall into three general groups. The first group includes uses of the term in a very restricted sense, that is, to indicate a group of subjects or fields of study arranged in a particular sequence. This definition is employed especially in secondary schools and colleges. The terms, classical curriculum, college preparatory curriculum, and general curriculum, for example, refer to the subjects and sequence of subjects required of given groups of pupils for graduation. When this meaning is employed, the plural form is often used, reference being made to the various curricula of a school. Specification of time units and sequences of large segments of subject matter are the principal tasks of curriculum making when this definition of the curriculum is accepted.

This concept of the curriculum was held in the original phases of the work of the North Central Association's Committee on Standards for use in the reorganization of secondary school curricula. The report of the committee states: "The term *curricula* was obviously intended to mean a sequence of units organized as four-year programs for two or more groups of secondary school students."[1]

Some writers on educational problems hold this general concept of the curriculum. For example, Puckett employs the definition which follows:

Curriculum is the selection, organization, and administration of a body of subject matter designed to lead the pupil on to some definite life objective. Examples are the college preparatory, the industrial arts, and general curricula.[2]

The second group of definitions of curriculum is based on the concept that the curriculum is the subject matter or content that is to be employed in instruction. This concept extends the mean-

[1] *High School Curriculum Reorganization,* North Central Association of Colleges and Secondary Schools, 1933, p. 2.
[2] Roswell C. Puckett, *Making a High School Schedule of Recitations,* Longmans, Green and Company, 1931, p. 6.

ing just discussed to include, in addition to the selection and arrangement of subjects, the selection and arrangement of the content in these subjects. Curriculum making from this point of view consists largely in selecting and arranging the topics that are to be taught in the various subjects. This meaning is subscribed to by a number of students of educational problems. For example, Briggs implies this meaning when he states:

> Although the importance of the curriculum has always been recognized, it is only at long intervals that material changes are made in it. One would not go far wrong in asserting that the history of education is written in terms of these changes in subject matter.[3]

The third group of definitions is much broader than the concepts of the curriculum expressed by the foregoing groups. The definitions in this latter group are based on the experience of the learner. The curriculum under this concept involves all elements of experience rather than one only, that is, the content or subject matter that may be employed in experience. The task of curriculum making is very complex under this concept. Pupil interests and activities, aims, method, content, in fact everything that influences the experience of the learner must be considered during the process of curriculum making.

Numerous writers subscribe to this latter concept. The statements which follow serve for illustration.

> The curriculum should be a series of guided experiences so related and so arranged that what is learned in one experience serves to enrich and make more valuable the experiences that follow.[4]

> The curriculum represents the experiences in which pupils are expected to engage in school, and the general order of sequence in which these experiences are to come.[5]

> The word *curriculum* is Latin for *race-course*, or the *race* itself,—a place of deeds, or a series of deeds. As applied to education it is *that*

---

[3] Thomas H. Briggs, *Curriculum Problems,* 1926, p. 1. By permission of The Macmillan Company, publishers, 1926.
[4] *Report of the Survey of the Schools of Chicago, Illinois,* George D. Strayer, Director, 3:19, 1932.
[5] Frederick G. Bonser, *The Elementary School Curriculum,* p. 1. By permission of The Macmillan Company, publishers, 1920.

series of things which children and youth must do and experience by way of developing ability to do the things well that make up the affairs of adult life . . .[6]

A canvass of writers on curriculum problems indicates that most of them deal with the curriculum from the experience point of view. They treat topics and problems in research and discussion which deal with many aspects of the learner's experience in addition to the content employed. For example, Hopkins deals specifically with aims, content, method, and outcomes. He discusses, as well, certain administrative problems as they relate to curriculum making.[7]

Harap discusses, among other topics, aims, activities, teaching units, repetition to assure permanence of learning, formulating tests and practice materials, and grade placement.[8]

The bibliography on curriculum materials of the Society for Curriculum Study includes in its major classification the following topics: objectives, learning activities, time allotment, grade placement, providing for mastery, and learning equipment and supplies. As is suggested by this classification, it is general practice for students of the curriculum to include in their writing and research, topics and problems that relate to all the varied forces that condition experience.

Cocking secured an indication of the meaning employed in directing recognized practice by means of statements from twelve selected cities engaged in outstanding curriculum making programs. He concludes, ". . . it would seem clear that the term is being used to include all that has to do with the instructional work of the school." [9]

Items included in courses of study also suggest the tendency

[6] Franklin Bobbitt, *The Curriculum*, p. 42. Used by permission of and special arrangement with Houghton Mifflin Company, 1918.

[7] L. Thomas Hopkins, *Curriculum Principles and Practices,* Benjamin H. Sanborn and Company, 1929.

[8] Henry Harap, *The Technique of Curriculum Making,* The Macmillan Company, 1928.

[9] Walter D. Cocking, *Administrative Procedures in Curriculum Making for Public Schools,* Teachers College, Columbia University, Contributions to Education No. 329, 1928, p. 43.

to employ the inclusive definition to direct practice. An analysis
of the contents of thirty-five state courses of study shows that
among other items the following occur frequently: guiding principles, time allotments, general educational objectives, subject
objectives, grade objectives, outline of content, teaching methods
and procedures, pupil activities, pupil attainments, reference materials for both teacher and pupil, illustrative lessons, and units
of work. This shows that the general work of curriculum making includes more than the allocation of time units, the arrangement of subjects, and the selection of content; and that the more
inclusive definition, the latter one presented heretofore, has
been employed in the curriculum program from which these
courses of study developed.

This conclusion is further supported by the items suggested
in the Stratemeyer-Bruner *Rating Scale for Elementary Courses
of Study* as being strong points in the courses of study which
they examined. The items follow:

1. Clear statement of objectives.
2. Provisions for individual differences.
3. Suggestions under each subject gives teacher insight into
   value of subject matter and methods of teaching it.
4. Illustrative lessons given.
5. Material based on present conditions.
6. Well-selected references.[10]

The tendency for both theory and practice to support the
broader interpretation of the curriculum very probably has been
encouraged by restrictions imposed on curriculum making by
the more limited definitions. In employing either of the more
limited ones, the curriculum tends to become static and mechanistic, while the experience concept gives it vitality and life. The
limited concepts relate to the classroom at only one point, the
latter concept at all points. The limited concepts imply a curriculum apart from the learner, the larger concept sees the cur-

---

[10] Florence B. Stratemeyer and Herbert B. Bruner, *Rating Elementary
School Courses of Study*, Bureau of Publications, Teachers College, Columbia University, 1926, p. 7.

riculum only through the learner. Taba points out the importance of this contrast. "The curriculum," she states, "cannot be regarded as a dead and summative body of all the materials, experiences, and activities contained in the educational process. It is a living whole, composed of experience actually going on in school. As such it is what it becomes in practice. Its content is identical to the content of the actual experience of the learners." [11]

The vital element in the broader concept of the curriculum and the direct relationship to work in the classroom have no doubt contributed much to the general acceptance of this concept among curriculum workers. This broad concept is accepted in the development of the discussion presented in this book. Stated specifically, the school curriculum is held to be composed of all the experiences children have under the guidance of teachers.

THE CURRICULUM AND CURRICULUM DEVELOPMENT

When the curriculum is defined to include all elements of experience, curriculum development becomes a complicated process. It is not sufficient, in making the curriculum, to shuffle courses, add or eliminate subject matter, or rearrange topics. Each of these activities may contribute at some point to the development of a well-conceived curriculum; but alone or in chance relationship they more often than not lead to confusion. An adequate curriculum can be developed only when all elements in the experience of the learner are considered, and when an orderly program is provided to assist the teacher in bringing these varied elements into suitable relationships.

This is the task of curriculum development. It can be accomplished only through assistance from many workers and many fields of study. Philosophy, sociology, psychology, and the subject matter fields must all be called upon for help. The ma-

[11] Hilda Taba, *The Dynamics of Education,* Harcourt, Brace and Company, 1932, pp. 243–44.

terials from these fields, however, cannot be employed by an additive method. Each field contributes its share of materials— raw materials for curriculum making—but mere compilation by no means represents the process of curriculum development. Materials must be so selected and arranged as to become a unity in the experience of the learner. The process is one of synthesis rather than compilation. In providing for this synthesis lies the peculiar task of curriculum development. This task is in clear contrast to the work in most fields of study where the major emphasis is given to organization or development of materials within particular cultural limitations. Thus, curriculum considered as a field of study represents no strictly limited body of content, but rather a process or procedure.

THE CURRICULUM AND THE PROGRAM OF STUDIES

"Program of studies" is a term that is used in connection with the secondary school curriculum. The term as generally accepted refers to the subjects of study offered by a given school and the arrangement or sequence of these subjects. Tryon, Smith, and Rood made a study of a large number of programs of study. They include in their study lists of subjects for which the number of periods per week was specified and constants and variables were indicated. They give a composite program of studies for the junior high school that is presented in Table II for illustration.

When the definition of the program of studies is compared with the most limited concept of the curriculum, it is found that the terms are employed with essentially the same meanings. Use of the term program of studies, however, to indicate the arrangement and specification of subjects, tends to eliminate confusion in dealing with curriculum problems. When so employed, the term curriculum may be used consistently with the broad meaning suggested heretofore. Preparing the program of studies then becomes one of the specific tasks to be accomplished in a curriculum program.

TABLE II

A PROGRAM OF STUDIES FOR THE JUNIOR HIGH SCHOOL BASED ON PRACTICES
IN SEVENTY-EIGHT CENTERS [12]

	Average Number Periods Per Week		Average Number Periods Per Week		Average Number Periods Per Week
Seventh Grade:		Eighth Grade:		Ninth Grade:	
English* . . .	7	English . .	5	English . .	5
Social studies*	6	Social studies	5	Social studies	5
Mathematics .	5	Mathematics	5	Mathematics	5
Industrial arts .	4	Home		Health . . .	2
Home economics	3	economics .	4	Foreign	
Health	3	Industrial arts	3	language† .	5
Music	2	Health . . .	2½	Industrial	
Art	2	Science . .	3	arts† . .	5
		Music . . .	2	Home	
		Art	2	economics†	5
		Foreign		Commercial	
		language† .	5	subjects† .	5
		Commercial		Science† . .	5
		subjects† .	4	Music† . .	3
				Art† . . .	3

* Each of these subject groups has more than five periods a week because it comprehends two or more branches.

† Variables.

THE CURRICULUM AND THE COURSE OF STUDY

The relationship between the curriculum and the course of study is an important one for clear understanding of curriculum programs. Curriculum and course of study are sometimes used synonymously. For example, Davis states: "The curriculum is the course of study." [13] This has, in fact, been quite a generally accepted concept. Not infrequently curriculum programs have

[12] R. M. Tryon, H. L. Smith and Allan F. Rood, "The Program of Studies in Seventy-eight Junior High School Centers," *School Review*, 35:107, February, 1927.

[13] Sheldon E. Davis, *Teaching the Elementary Curriculum*, The Macmillan Company, 1931, p. 2.

had as their one goal revision of courses of study, thus indicating by action at least that the concept expressed above served to guide the programs.

When the curriculum is looked upon as being composed of the actual experiences children have under the direction of teachers, it obviously is impossible to consider it as synonymous with the course of study. In this case, the course of study becomes a printed manual or guide which has been prepared to assist teachers to direct satisfactorily the development of the curriculum. This contrast is well drawn in the section on curriculum of the Arithmetic Yearbook of the National Society for the Study of Education. "The *curriculum*," it is stated, "may be defined as the totality of subject matter, activities, and experiences which constitute a pupil's school life. A *course of study* is the material, usually in pamphlet form, which sets forth for the teacher such items as the objectives and content of a given subject, and the activities and books to be used to accomplish desired results." [14]

The course of study may be likened to the plans and specifications for a building. Both are carefully developed suggestions for directing a process; the one a construction process with building materials, the other a growth process with human abilities. Just as the plans and specifications are not the building, neither is the course of study the curriculum, even though in both cases there should be an intimate relationship between the two. Obviously, a good course of study is a valuable aid to the development of a good curriculum. However, it is entirely possible for a school to have a superior course of study and a poor curriculum, or a poor course of study and a superior curriculum. If this concept of the course of study is held clearly in mind it will eliminate much confusion in the process of curriculum development. It will be noted in the following discussion how the distinction in the meaning of these two terms is an essential basis for proceeding with work on the curriculum.

[14] *Twenty-ninth Yearbook, National Society for the Study of Education,* 1930, p. 65.

WHO MAKES THE CURRICULUM

Much discussion has been given to the problem of who should make the curriculum. Especially has the question of the responsibility of teachers in this regard been a point of dispute. It has been maintained by some that only specialists can perform the intricate tasks involved in curriculum making. Others have contended that, since the teacher is closer to classroom situations than the specialist, he should have a major part in curriculum development. Bagley especially emphasizes the former point of view and ridicules the latter one, as well as those workers in the field of curriculum development who project comprehensive programs of curriculum making. He states in a recent discussion of the matter that the tendency for certain individuals to undertake study of the total curriculum problem has resulted in a state of confusion. He holds that study of the curriculum in city school systems by committees of teachers has become an educational fashion which is based on the "silly" and "tragic" idea that each community should have a curriculum of its own.[15]

Whipple takes the same position. He states:

Too much of present-day curriculum making is amateurish trifling and a sheer waste of time—nay, worse than that, an injection of pernicious confusion in what should be orderly progress. The let-everybody-pitch-in-and-help method is ludicrous when applied to curriculum-building. It is too much like inviting a group of practical electricians to redesign a modern power plant.[16]

The other point of view is expressed in an answer to Whipple's article:

Some of this work is doubtless amateurish; . . . but all of it has helped to focus the attention of teachers and school officials on the faults of the past scheme and on the present needs of the pupils and school.

[15] William C. Bagley, *Education and Emergent Man,* Thomas Nelson and Sons, 1934, pp. 144–45.
[16] Guy M. Whipple, "What Price Curriculum-Making," *School and Society,* 31:367, March 15, 1930.

No, curriculum making by the teachers, at its worst, has not torn down the educational structure; neither has it brought about the disorganization which the "viewers with alarm" would have us see as the sole result. . . . (It) has served to turn the spot-light of scrutiny on the old methods and materials which were formerly used without questioning; it has motivated study in the field of the curriculum and has helped to reveal to teachers some idea of what the new may accomplish. . . .

Rather than wrecking the machine, the teachers, in the process of curriculum making, are able to become acquainted with the mechanism which they are called upon to operate, to keep in repair and to improve.[17]

Unquestionably there will always be many fundamental disagreements about the objectives and procedures of curriculum development, but much disagreement of the type just illustrated arises out of different concepts of the curriculum and its meaning.

Shall teachers participate in curriculum making? If so, in what ways? These questions can be answered only in light of the definition accepted for the curriculum. If the curriculum and the program of studies are considered synonymous the answer may be one thing. On the other hand, if reference is to the preparation of a course of study, the answer may be entirely different. When the curriculum is held to be composed of the experiences children have under the guidance of teachers, it becomes obvious that teachers must participate in curriculum development. It is under their direction that the curriculum actually takes form and they engage in curriculum development regardless of the formal recognition given the process. They do so, poorly or well, according to their previous training, their ability, and the assistance that is rendered them.

But what of the participation of teachers in various phases of curriculum development, especially in writing courses of study? This is the problem to which attention is next briefly turned.

[17] Howard K. Bauernfeind, "What Value Curriculum Making," *School and Society,* 31:710–12, May 24, 1930.

WHO MAKES THE COURSE OF STUDY

This problem will be considered in detail in Chapter XVI. It is treated in this chapter only in so far as is necessary to make clear the general point of view held toward this phase of curriculum development.

Mass participation in course of study writing provides the basis of many criticisms of curriculum development and is possibly what Bagley and Whipple consider undesirable. This procedure for preparing courses of study, in most cases, probably grows out of the point of view that the course of study and the curriculum are synonymous, and consequently that general participation in curriculum making means general participation in course of study writing. Yet it seems doubtful that anyone who has had wide experience in preparing courses of study would look on it as a task that could be performed satisfactorily by large groups of teachers. As a matter of fact, it is a highly technical task requiring much intensive work. It involves the selection and organization of contributions from technical studies by specialists, from the general experience of teachers, and from the work of special committees in such form that they can be employed easily by teachers to direct instruction. It is the rare teacher indeed who can participate with effectiveness directly in this phase of curriculum making. Such specialized tasks should be undertaken by individuals or committees specially prepared to do them.

However, those who do the actual writing of courses of study, in order to do an efficient job, must build their work on general teacher experience if the courses are to serve their purpose satisfactorily. As is pointed out in Chapter XVI, a course of study should serve to consolidate and organize the advance or improvement made in curriculum development up to a given time and should prepare the way for further improvement. Thus, much of the work of curriculum improvement takes place ahead of course of study preparation and independently of it. In brief, a well-conceived program of curriculum improvement is so much larger than the mere task of preparing courses of study that, although select groups do this specialized task, there are still many phases of the program to be carried forward in which the general participation of teachers is needed. A curriculum program should represent an organization of all available means of improving the curriculum in such a way that each will supplement the others. When this is done, writing the course of study will assume proper relationship to the larger program of curriculum making. It will be considered neither a task to be carried out by a select group working entirely apart from the general teaching force, nor an undertaking to be achieved alone through general work and discussion by all teachers. Rather, a select group will assume the direct responsibility for bringing into organized form contributions from the general experience of teachers and from technical studies by specialists in the various fields.

Writing a course of study, then, is but one phase of a well-conceived curriculum program, and when so considered, assumes proper relationship to the larger program of curriculum making in which specialist, administrator, supervisor, and teacher must work co-operatively, each making his particular contribution to the development of an improved curriculum.

RELATION OF CURRICULUM DEVELOPMENT TO ADMINISTRATION

The major function of administration is to see that boys and girls are provided optimum educational opportunities. The adequacy of educational opportunities is conditioned by a variety of factors, such as finance, physical plant, supplies and equipment, and the teaching personnel. Among these many factors, one of the most potent is the procedure for synthesizing the various forces that directly influence the experiences of children. Administration, to be effective, must concern itself vitally with this procedure, which is curriculum development.

The importance of curriculum development as an administrative responsibility has been recognized to varying degrees. In a great many cases, this task is left almost wholly to the undirected and unaided efforts of teachers. This may be accounted for to a considerable extent by the fact that the period from 1900 to 1930 was a time of rapid material expansion in public education. Phenomenal increases in enrollments, resulting from both an increasing population and a tendency for children to spend more years in school, defined the problems to which the school administrator gave a major part of his time and attention. The construction and maintenance of school buildings, supply management, janitorial service, budgetary procedures, insurance, accounting, organization of classes and schools—these and similar problems persistently pushed to the fore. The resulting emphasis on the material and management side of school administration finds expression not only in the work of administrators, but also in the training offered them by higher institutions. If the time spent on the study of a particular subject is used as a criterion of emphasis, we might fairly conclude in many cases that it is more important for a school administrator to know how to wash windows and sweep floors, or what records and forms to employ in supply management, than it is for him to know how to determine and employ aims of education, or for him to understand and appreciate the place of public schools in American life and to have a clear concept of their responsibility. Thus, problems encountered in the field and training in school administration provided by schools of education have often encouraged administrators to overlook responsibilities related directly to the instructional program.

However, there has been an increasing tendency to recognize that the material and technical aspects of the educational program are only means to an end, and that the end is the growth of boys and girls toward the realization of acceptable ideals. Concerning the training provided for administrators by schools of education, Hill states:

No longer, in our best schools of education, is it possible for one to obtain an advanced degree in school administration without having acquired a sufficiently comprehensive knowledge of education in general, its history, its aims, its agents, its organization, its techniques, to make clear the functions of administrative procedures.[18]

Administrators are giving greater emphasis to the instructional aspects of administration, as is evidenced by the large number of supervisory and curriculum programs carried on in public schools. The idea gains in currency that an administrator who lives up to his full responsibility will interpret his entire program in terms of the growth of the boys and girls in his school system, and will accept as his principal responsibility and greatest opportunity the development of an instructional program that will achieve this end.

Unfortunately, however, in many "so-called" curriculum programs, administrators are concerned almost wholly with the development of courses of study. The methods employed in such programs often leave the curriculum little changed. Although this emphasis may be a necessary step toward the development of comprehensive curriculum programs, there is pressing need in American education for administrators to become more concerned with the larger task of curriculum making.

RELATION OF CURRICULUM DEVELOPMENT TO SUPERVISION

The activities involved in operating a school may be classified under three major heads: administration, supervision, and instruction. As Knudsen [19] points out in his treatment of supervision, it is impossible to draw a clear line of distinction between administrative and supervisory activities. For the purposes of his treatment, he includes in supervision those activities that are involved in studying classroom teaching by actual contact with the teacher at work. He further points out that this is a more restricted concept than often is applied to supervision. Yet it gives a clearness of meaning not provided by general uses

---

[18] Clyde M. Hill, "Trends in the Teaching of School Administration," *School and Society*, 38:34, July 8, 1933.

[19] Charles W. Knudsen, *Evaluation and Improvement of Teaching*, Doubleday, Doran Co., 1932, pp. 1–3.

of the term. This restricted definition also appears to indicate those activities that are generally thought of as constituting supervision. Hence, this definition is accepted in this discussion.

Supervision depends for full effectiveness upon the existence between teachers and supervisor of a common ground of agreement as to the essentials of the educational program. Such agreement may be reached by individual teachers and the supervisor through a trial and error process based on personal relationships. This method is uncertain in outcomes and is time consuming. Agreement may be reached, as well, by means of orderly group consideration of the issues involved. This latter method may be carried forward in organized form with thoroughgoing analysis and study, and is distinctly superior in most respects to dependence on personal relationships. This latter procedure is a part of a comprehensive curriculum program. Thus, curriculum making, rightly conceived, is of importance to supervision because it provides teachers and supervisors a common ground of agreement from which to approach their work.

Curriculum making can render a further service to supervision because supervisory programs frequently tend to scatter efforts and to make the instructional program appear to be composed of a number of somewhat unrelated parts. For example, during one year work may be concentrated on remedial instruction in reading, the next year on units of work in social studies, the next year on non-promotion, and the next on aims of education. The tendency is to attack each problem as a separate, distinct phase of instruction. Thus, desirable relationships between various aspects of instruction are not developed and teaching tends increasingly to become divided into separate compartments. A comprehensive curriculum program provides a complete, related view of the problems of instruction. Each phase of work is seen in relationship to the other phases. With such a basis, supervision can relate the specific problems more adequately to other phases of instruction. Steps in a supervisory program may be planned to grow logically out of preceding steps and to lead on to other steps. Supervision may thus be provided with direction and coherence when based on a comprehensive curriculum program.

Supervision is further aided by curriculum making through the courses of study that are developed in a curriculum program. A good course of study can materially increase a supervisor's effectiveness, and decrease the amount of direct assistance required by individual teachers. Its value lies in the availability to all teachers of such materials as a statement of the aims of education, an outline of the scope of work for the grade or subject, suggested lists of activities and references, and descriptions of good teaching procedures. Obviously, it is more economical for a supervisor to refer a teacher for suggestions to a given teaching procedure or suggestive activities or references in the course of study than it is to describe these materials in detail. If carefully prepared, the written materials provided in a course of study are usually more adequate than the oral directions.

When all these points are considered, it is apparent that supervision can be most effective when it is based on a comprehensive curriculum program. Since the effectiveness of supervision does depend to a considerable extent on a comprehensive curriculum program, supervisors should be specially trained to engage in curriculum work and should assume large responsibilities in curriculum development.

CURRICULUM DEVELOPMENT A CO-OPERATIVE ENTERPRISE

Curriculum development, then, is a co-operative enterprise. Teacher, research worker, subject matter specialist, psychologist, sociologist, philosopher, educator, administrator, and supervisor must all make contributions. Some make available basic materials, others provide for the synthesis of these materials, while others are concerned directly with the use of these materials in enriching and guiding the experiences of boys and girls. Efficient production at each of these points eventuates in a good curriculum. Deficiency at any point, either in quality of work or co-operation, results ultimately in a weakened curriculum. A common purpose binds this varied group of workers together.

ELEMENTS IN THE CURRICULUM

A curriculum program, we have seen, should assist teachers to guide boys and girls in fruitful experiences. Administratively, assistance may be rendered through the preparation of good courses of study and through the provision of opportunities for discussion, study, observation, and demonstration. Lines of attack in developing such sources of help are suggested by analyzing the elements of experience and their ways of reacting.

In undertaking such an analysis, however, it should be held clearly in mind that experience is not a thing or a state of being. It is not something objective that may be isolated and examined. Experience is a process; it is the living through of actual situations. This process of living through situations involves the reaction of a variety of elements. The presence of these elements in different proportions and relationships determines the type and strength of the reaction or experience. It is possible through analysis to determine what these elements are and to examine evidences of each, but when they come into relationship and reaction takes place it becomes impossible to distinguish clearly one from the other, or to discover in the outcome the characteristics of the elements involved. The observable characteristics of the situation are a process and an outcome, different in character from any of the elements in the process. Thus, the process of experiencing results in changes in an individual which are unities different from any of the elements which went to make up the experience. The situation is not unlike the action of physical elements. A number of physical elements, each with its own peculiar characteristics and qualities, when placed in given relationships react upon each other, resulting in the formation of a substance with characteristics and qualities unlike those of any of the elements involved.

Consequently, the elements of experience and the process of

interaction suggest points at which the problem of curriculum development may be attacked. Following consideration of principles basic to curriculum development attention is turned to these points.

SELECTED REFERENCES

Bagley, William C., *Education and Emergent Man*, Thomas Nelson and Sons, New York, 1934, pp. 140–149.

Bauernfeind, Howard K., "What Value Curriculum Making?" *School and Society*, 31: 710–712, May 24, 1930.

Brewer, John M., *Education As Guidance*, The Macmillan Company, New York, 1933, Chapter I.

Cocking, Walter D., *Administrative Procedures in Curriculum Making for Public Schools*, Contributions to Education No. 329, Bureau of Publications, Teachers College, Columbia University, New York, 1928, Chapters IV and V.

Dewey, John, *Art As Experience*, Minton, Balch & Co., New York, 1934, Chapter III.

Fletcher, John M., *Psychology in Education*, Doubleday, Doran & Co., Garden City, New York, 1934, Chapter VII.

High School Curriculum Reorganization, North Central Association of Colleges and Secondary Schools, Ann Arbor, Michigan, 1933.

Strayer, George D., director, *Report of the Survey of the Schools of Chicago, Illinois*, Vol. III, Bureau of Publications, Teachers College, Columbia University, New York, 1932.

Taba, Hilda, *The Dynamics of Education*, Harcourt, Brace & Co., New York, 1932, Chapter VII.

Whipple, Guy M., "What Price Curriculum-Making?" *School and Society*, 31: 367, March 15, 1930.

CHAPTER V

PRINCIPLES BASIC TO CURRICULUM DEVELOPMENT

The relationships assumed to exist between the various elements in an enterprise must be compatible if a consistent program is developed. Lacking such compatibility the action in developing the program frequently becomes diffuse and contradictory. This is especially true in a program of curriculum development because of the widely varied elements involved and the many ways in which the several aspects of the work may be carried forward. For this reason, many programs of curriculum development contain highly conflicting assumptions and procedures.

It has been common practice in curriculum programs to endeavor to provide for consistency of action through a statement of principles to guide the work. Preparation of such statements is customarily looked upon as one of the first tasks in the development of a curriculum program. An analysis by David [1] of thirty-four city courses of study shows that most of the curriculum organizations involved drew up such statements. Similarly, a majority of recent state courses of study or bulletins for guiding curriculum workers contain statements of principles, point of view, or philosophy. Educational surveys, in dealing with curriculum problems, emphasize the importance of such statements. Survey reports frequently "present educational theories and offer suggestions for the practical application of basic

[1] Flavius L. David, *The Selection and Organization of Personnel for Curriculum Revision*, Bulletin No. 30, Curriculum Laboratory, Western Reserve University, October, 1932, p. 15.

educational principles to the construction of the curriculum." [2]

Examination of courses of study, however, reveals inconsistencies within given curriculum programs which indicate that very frequently the process of developing statements of principles is an academic task which exerts little real influence on the procedures of curriculum development. It is the purpose of this chapter to suggest ways and means of facilitating the effective use of principles in developing programs which possess consistency and unity.

DIVERSE PRACTICE IN STATEMENTS OF PRINCIPLES

Statements of principles presumed to guide the development of various curriculum programs differ most radically in form, content, and number of items included in the statements. This diversity suggests a lack of common agreement as to the function principles should serve and as to the form in which statements of principles are most suitable for use in guiding curriculum development.

It is the practice in some programs to define principles to be followed in each step of curriculum development. For example, principles are stated to guide development of the administrative organization, the statement of aims, the selection of subject matter and activities, and evaluation of outcomes. In such cases the number of so-called principles becomes very large. Sometimes fifteen to twenty principles are stated as guides for a single phase of the work. For example, the following statement of principles was developed to serve as a guide in the statement of aims in a city program.

1. Self-activity is fundamental to learning.
2. While transfer of training may take place under certain conditions, it is neither automatic nor inevitable.
3. There is no desirable "discipline" in doing what is merely difficult and distasteful.

[2] Mina M. Langvick, *Current Practices in the Construction of State Courses of Study,* United States Office of Education Bulletin No. 4, 1931. p. 22.

4. Education serves both proximate and ultimate ends.

5. The universal interdependence of man is basic for education.

6. The welfare of society demands the optimal development of the individual.

7. Education represents an investment by society to promote the common welfare.

8. The school is only one of the educative agencies established by society, and the inevitable overlapping in duties and responsibilities necessitates mutual co-operation.

9. Schools serve two interests: those of the individual and those of society. Wherever the two come into conflict, those of society take precedence.

10. It is the duty of the school to adjust itself to social progress.

11. The school should endeavor to give to all a common integrating body of functional knowledge, of habits, of ideals, and of appreciation.

12. It is the duty of the school to adapt the means of education to the needs of the individual, whatever may be the mental, physical, moral, or environmental conditions.

13. The need of the individual for two co-ordinate types of ability is recognized: unspecialized, to discharge common personal, domestic, and civic duties; specialized, to render expert service to society.

14. The fact of individual differences conditions the results that may be expected from the educative process.

15. Education includes teaching the individual to do better the desirable things of life that he would do anyhow.

16. Culture, as a desirable outcome of education, consists in the all-round development of those capacities and ideals which make for human progress; it includes social service, many-sidedness, democracy, physical well-being, development of spiritual life, aesthetic appreciation, well-mannered expression, insight, force, and idealism; it is altruistic, dynamic, and creative.[3]

In contrast to this type of procedure some programs list only a few principles to serve as fundamental or basic guides. A good example of this procedure is seen in the Los Angeles County schools. The heading for the section of the course of study dealing with principles is suggestive: "Some Principles of Teaching and of Learning." The material is presented in descriptive form. It includes this direct statement concerning principles:

[3] Walter D. Cocking, "The St. Louis Program of Curriculum-Revision," *Twenty-sixth Yearbook, National Society for the Study of Education,* Part I, 1927, pp. 242-43.

The three principles which we are attempting to stress are: first, that *learnings never come singly;* that is, *acquisition of a skill or a knowledge is always accompanied by an attitude of mind* toward the thing which is being done; second, that *each experience provides a background for future experiences,* and an attitude of receptivity or non-receptivity for the new experience to come—an attitude of readiness, if you will; third, that *we learn as we associate old experiences and new experiences.* These things being true, it is incumbent upon the teacher to evaluate proposed enterprises or experiences with exceeding care.[4]

Discussion of this statement is followed by a brief outline and statement under the heading, "Our Basic Philosophy of Education."

In addition to these forms in which long lists of formal statements are developed in outline to guide each phase of curriculum development and in which a few basic guides are presented in discussion form, a procedure is sometimes employed in which statements of principles are presumed to be evolved by the various committees as needed. The practice in the Denver program is perhaps the best illustration of this use of principles. The position is shown by the following statement:

If certain principles of education are sound, it is not at all necessary to present them in a ready-made form to those who are about to go to work on the problem of curriculum making. If the entire program is based on the best available research, it may be taken as a certainty that those principles which are sound will tend to emerge.[5]

An illustration of the type of statement evolved is provided by material from the junior high school mathematics committee. This committee stated certain principles to guide in the selection of subject matter, as follows:

Each subject and each item in the subject must justify itself.
Each year of the junior high school should give emphasis to the

[4] *Teachers' Guide Intermediate Unit, Courses of Study,* Los Angeles County Board of Education, 1931, p. 31.
[5] *Denver Program of Curriculum Revision,* Bulletin No. 12, Denver Public Schools, 1927, p. 19.

subject matter that is most valuable for the pupil at that period of his work with little consideration for later courses.

The content of each course must be selected to meet the social needs of the children.

The course shall enable the child to compare mentally with a fair degree of accuracy quantities, sizes, distances, and forms.

The idea of relationship or of the dependence of one quantity upon another should be emphasized throughout.[6]

It is impossible to examine these diverse uses of principles without seriously questioning just what function principles should serve in curriculum development and in what form they are most useful. It would seem reasonable to presume that if principles are as important as they are generally held to be in curriculum development, practice would have at least some uniformity. The fact is that, in general, inadequate critical consideration has been given to these issues by curriculum committees, and that the extreme diversity of practice is, in part, a result of this condition. Consequently, in projecting a curriculum program, it is highly necessary to give special consideration and study to these issues. It becomes evident upon brief study that the term itself is used in a variety of ways. Consequently, it is desirable first of all to consider the nature of a principle.

THE NATURE OF A PRINCIPLE

The term "principle" is used with a variety of meanings. At one extreme is a very narrow and restricted use of the term applied in its generic sense to indicate a primary truth or law. At the other extreme may be found statements, frequently called "guiding principles," that take the form of theses, opinions, or rules. Either of these uses is acceptable in so far as the meaning of the word itself is concerned. However, the two concepts permit principles to hold distinctly different places in curriculum development, or for that matter, in the development of any type of undertaking.

[6] Denver, *op. cit.,* p. 36.

The restricted use of the term is common practice in the sciences. That is, there is a tendency to consider a principle as an underlying generalization which has been substantiated by controlled observation and experimentation. The scientist proceeds from theories or hypotheses which partake of the nature of principles. His observations prove that his hypothesis is either correct or incorrect. If he believes the results of his investigation to be conclusive, he restates his hypothesis in the form of a generalization which, if very widely applicable, is sometimes called a principle or law; such as, Boyle's Law, the law of gravitation, and the principle of Archimedes. There are relatively few such fundamental, generally applicable, and demonstrable truths as these. This is especially true in the fields of the social sciences with which education is primarily concerned. Nevertheless, experience provides a basis for certain generalizations concerning social life which cause them to partake, in general at least, of the qualities of principles as used in the way the term is commonly employed in the exact sciences. Psychology has tended to adopt the scientific use of the term and thus provides certain principles or laws for use in education directly comparable to scientific principles.

The significance of social principles has been questioned frequently because of their lack of exactness and objectivity. However, the general concept of a principle has been somewhat modified in recent years inasmuch as the finality and exactness of the most basic principles in the exact sciences have been shown to be open to modification and question. New facts and relationships have greatly changed concepts of basic principles in the sciences in recent years, requiring, upon occasion, reorganization of whole schools of thought. Unfortunately for curriculum development, this influence has not been felt in psychology and has not modified as greatly the outlook in psychology as in the pure sciences according to Ragsdale, who states:

There persists in psychology an attitude toward "laws" and "principles" which has disappeared from the natural sciences. In the natural sciences laws or principles are recognized as being the statement merely of *probabilities,* rather than of *absolute uniformities.* They are merely theories which fit a finite number of facts.[7]

Even so, however, certain basic concepts must be assumed to be true in order to develop a science, and these concepts, although more readily subject to change than believed in the past, represent the principles of the science as the term is generally used.

Similarly, in education there are certain basic concepts, which are assumed to be true, upon which educational programs are developed. These basic concepts are of the nature of principles as referred to in science and may be so used with all appropriateness. This is, in fact, the way in which the term is frequently used in educational literature.

In contrast with the restricted concept of a principle, there is the concept that a principle is a specific rule of action. Used in this latter sense a principle may be an opinion or belief which gives specific direction to behavior. In educational literature, particularly in courses of study, the term is often used with even less restriction than is indicated by this definition. In fact, the term is frequently used to designate desirable ends to be achieved or procedures for achieving those ends. Often such "principles" might more appropriately be designated as theses used to justify a given course of action. In some cases they might be more accurately defined as criteria by which procedures or objectives are judged. In developing long lists of principles such as those mentioned previously the term is employed to mean specific rules for action. This accounts for the large number of statements and preparation of separate lists of principles for each step in curriculum development.

The difference between these concepts of principles may be illustrated by an example from the realm of the sciences. The air brake is a mechanical device the purpose of which is to reduce the speed of a train or trolley car. Principles might be set up for operating air brakes that would serve as specific rules of action.

[7] Clarence E. Ragsdale, *Modern Psychologies and Education,* 1932, p. 233. By permission of The Macmillan Company, publishers.

On the other hand, the air brake is based on fundamental and widely applicable principles, such as the principles of inertia and friction. In this case the air brake is merely looked upon as a mechanical means of achieving certain results in conformity with basic laws or principles.

While specific guides to serve as rules of action may be helpful in developing the details of an undertaking, it is the fundamental generalizations of wide applicability upon which these guides are based that give the undertaking consistency. Consequently, the type of principle which is of primary concern in curriculum development is the one which is fundamental and general, rather than derived and specific. To know *why* to do or not to do a thing insures more intelligent compliance with specific directions than otherwise is possible. Certainly, in the complicated process of curriculum development, an understanding of the basic principles involved is necessary for developing a unified program.

SOURCE OF PRINCIPLES

Statements of principles are often made in connection with curriculum programs in such a way as to suggest that there are principles peculiar to curriculum making just as there are principles of physics. This is not the case if principle is used to indicate a basic truth or generalization. Generalizations of wide applicability that are significant in curriculum development are derived from basic fields of study. Important principles are provided by the fields of biology, psychology, and sociology. It is to such fields, in the final analysis, that the curriculum worker must look for principles basic to curriculum development.

Assistance is provided in discovering what principles are applicable to curriculum development from two sources. In the first place, educational philosophy, upon the basis of the findings of such fields as the foregoing and observation and study of the nature of human experience, presents comprehensive, unified, and systematized points of view concerning education which set forth the basic principles upon which the points of view rest. These principles are generally applicable to curriculum development.

To illustrate, Rugg sums up the basic concepts of pragmatic instrumentalism as follows:

First: Human experience is unified and continuous; there are no separate instincts; ends and means, character and conduct, motive and act, will and deed—all are continuous; hence all dualistic interpretations of experience are fallacious.

Second: Knowing comes only through active response; meaning arises only through reaction; a concept is synonymous with corresponding operations.

Third: Knowing arises through testing consequences. This is Dewey's concept of "the experimental method of knowing" and the contemporary physicists' "operational" definition of thinking.

Fourth: Experience consists primarily in the adjustment and interaction of individuals; both individual and group understanding and behavior are the product of the social human environment; the social environment "consists of all the activities of fellow beings that are bound up in the carrying on of the activities of any one of its members."

Fifth: Society is conceived as a democracy, built on the foregoing principles; that is, on the experimental method of knowing, the unity and continuity of experience, "numerous and varied points of shared common interest."

Sixth: An educational system, also based on the foregoing concepts, which will give "individuals a personal interest in social relationships and control and the habits of mind which secure social changes without introducing disorder." [8]

The principles given in the first four statements are of great significance in curriculum development.

Another illustration of the contribution philosophy makes to curriculum development by bringing to light fundamental principles is provided by Finney's emphasis on the implications of social life for education. He points out certain basic or fundamental principles upon which his point of view is based. The

---

[8] Harold Rugg, *Culture and Education in America,* Harcourt, Brace & Company, 1931, pp. 123–124.

implications for curriculum development are most significant.

For example, he describes the principle of social parallelism as one of these basic concepts. This principle relates to the parallelism between a given civilization and the educational system that functions in it. He concludes that, ". . . in civilized societies the curriculum normally corresponds to the culture." [9] This principle is of utmost significance in planning a program of curriculum development. It conditions materially the concept of the function of the school and source from which aims of education should be derived. The discussion in Chapter II of the social responsibility of the school is based to a considerable extent on this principle of social parallelism.

The second source of assistance in discovering principles of significance in curriculum development is educational literature as it deals generally with problems of instructional organization. Much of this literature shows the application of principles derived from the various fundamental fields to educational problems. For example, principles derived from consideration of the nature of society are illustrated by two principles stated by Inglis as follows:

1. The character and purpose of secondary education at any time and in any society must conform to the dominant ideals and to the form of social organization of that society.
2. The dynamic character of the social process requires the constant readjustment of secondary education to the changing demands of society.[10]

The principle of equalization of educational opportunity has been mentioned in Chapter II. Application of the principle to various aspects of curriculum development will be found in a number of treatments of educational problems. Treatments of teaching methods and of principles of education contain much material that is suggestive of fundamental concepts. In general,

[9] Ross L. Finney, *A Sociological Philosophy of Education,* 1928, p. 97. By permission of The Macmillan Company, publishers.
[10] Alexander Inglis, *Principles of Secondary Education,* p. 341. Used by permission of and special arrangement with Houghton Mifflin Company, 1918.

however, these sources require especially critical consideration in that the term principle is used in the non-restrictive sense. Psychology abounds in statements of principles and laws, many of them, as proposed by various schools of psychology, being contradictory. Consequently, considerable difficulty is usually experienced in determining which ones are most acceptable for guiding curriculum development.

Frequently in curriculum development the need for a unified point of view based on fundamental principles is not recognized. The statement of principles in such cases is done in a perfunctory manner and the principles do not function in giving the program consistency. In such cases, it becomes an important task to make clear the need for such a statement.

This need can be felt only as the workers in the program become conscious of conflicts in procedures and of need for a fundamental basis upon which issues may be decided. Conflicts and needs for a fundamental basis upon which choices are to be made may be brought to attention by various means, all of which should be employed.

One of the most effective ways is to set forth issues that must be decided and to secure statements of position on these various issues. Inconsistencies and conflicts in such positions may be brought to light and a gradual process of reconciliation undertaken. This process may grow into development of a unified point of view and the setting forth of fundamental principles to serve in guidance of all phases of the work.

An illustration of the type of issue used in this procedure is supplied by the statements which follow. After a year of general study and cultivation of the teachers in a school system, these issues were presented to a select committee which was assigned the responsibility of preparing a statement of point of view and principles to submit to the entire group as a basis for guiding the various steps in the program.

Issues for Consideration of the Committee

The following issues must be faced very soon in developing the curriculum program. The way in which they are decided will exert far-reaching influence on the program. The committee is requested to prepare statements of position in regard to each issue and a unified report indicating the basis of decision in order that the administration of other phases of the program may be consistent with the basic point of view.

1. Should steps be taken toward the development of an integrated educational program? If so, what steps should be taken?

2. Should steps be taken to give the educational program a fundamental social orientation?

3. Should steps be taken to organize the educational program on a functional basis?

4. Should steps be taken to eliminate specialization from the elementary school and the high school and to make this a period of general education?

5. Should provision be made for the psychological organization of subject matter rather than the logical organization of subject matter?

FORM OF STATEMENTS OF PRINCIPLES

Statements which set forth the principles accepted as basic to development of the curriculum may be presented in a variety of forms. The most formal and probably the most frequently used type of statement is a list of principles briefly stated. This form is illustrated by the statement in the Alabama course of study:

Principles Relating to Society

1. Society is necessary for the full expression of individual life.
2. The school is an agent of society.
3. The school is established for the purposes of society.

Principles Relating to the Individual

1. Learning results from activity.
2. Activities should be related to the past experiences of the learner.
3. The aim of an activity should be accepted by the learner as his own.
4. The learner should experience satisfaction from engaging in activities.[11]

[11] *Course of Study for Elementary Schools,* State of Alabama Department of Education, 1930, p. 22.

Mere listing of principles is varied somewhat in some cases by the presentation of brief discussions of each principle as it is listed. An illustration of this form of presentation is provided by the report of the Principles Committee in Virginia:

Here are proposed the broad underlying principles agreed upon by the Principles Committee. These principles should be accepted by all committees as guides for their work.

Principles Governing Educational Aims and Processes

I. The school is an agency of society for its perpetuation and re-creation.

A democratic society is a dynamic, stimulating, and co-operative agency created by individual and group action for discovering higher values and more effective ways of attaining them. It is not an end product to be perpetuated in static form through indoctrination of individuals with a fixed system of values.

In function society has evolved many special institutions. Some are primarily protective, conservative, and regulatory, seeking so to control individual and collective behavior as to realize recognized values of the present. Other institutions are primarily creative in that their function is to promote developmental, evolutionary and growth processes in individuals and the social body as a whole. The school has emerged in our society as its chief creative institution. In its processes the school should:

1. Discover and define the ideals of a democratic society.

2. Provide for the continuous re-definition and re-interpretation of the social ideals in light of economic, political and social changes.

3. Provide experiences for boys and girls which make possible their greatest contribution to the realization of the social ideals. From the social point of view this involves:

   a. The definition of understandings, attitudes, appreciations and automatic responses that are necessary for the realization of the social ideals.

   b. The selection from the group culture of materials which will assist most effectively in the realization of the social ideals.

II. Growth processes in individuals and in society are resultants of continuing interaction between individuals and society.

Individuals are influenced by changing social groups. They must, on occasion, respond with adjustment to the social group; with acceptance of group ideals; with adoption of approved ways of doing. On other occasions individuals can and do change and control social groups as they do the physical environment. Profound social changes in ideals as a result of social interaction with individuals are easily seen when we consider such cases as, "Ye have heard it hath been said, an eye for an eye, and a tooth for a tooth; but I say unto you, . . . love your enemies." Profound social changes in ways of doing are seen in such cases as adoption of the telephone as a means of communication. Just as the present social environment in the United States forces an individual to specialization in occupation with its attendant profound influence on the whole life of the individual, so unique concepts and ways of doing by individuals produce the rapid and profound changes in the social order which are everywhere manifest. Because such interaction is the law of individual and social evolution and growth, society is concerned with individualizing individuals for the creation of new values and with socializing individuals with a view to the conservation and use of existing values.

III. Individuals differ in interests, abilities, attitudes, appreciations and understandings, habits and skills, and in capacity to learn.

Since individuals are born with very different endowments they develop at very different rates. In adult life individuals will live on very different levels of intellect, character and skill. The school then must provide differentiated education for a variety of capacities and needs.

IV. Growth is continuous.

Education must be a continuous development produced by progressive reorganization of experiences on increasingly higher and more complex levels:

1. The school system should be a series of intimately connected links without a break.

2. There should be a smooth and natural issue from the school into the life of society.

The value of school education is determined by the extent to which it creates a desire for continued growth and supplies the means whereby it may be realized.

V. All learning comes through experience.

Mere activity does not constitute experience. Experience is both trying or doing and undergoing. When we experience something we act upon it, then we undergo the consequences. Experience as trying or doing involves change, but change is meaningless transition unless it is consciously connected with the resultant consequences. It is only when an activity is continued into the undergoing of experience that the activity has significance for the learner. "It is not experience when a child merely sticks his finger into a flame, it is experience when the movement is connected with the pain which he undergoes in consequence. Being burned is a mere physical change, like the burning of a stick of wood if it is not perceived as a consequence of some other action" (John Dewey, *Democracy and Education*). When we have had an experience we gain something which may be carried over to enable us to foresee what is likely to happen next, and to gain ability to adjust ourselves to what is coming.

VI. An individual tends to avoid experiences which annoy and to seek experiences which satisfy.

From the very beginning of life an individual gives evidence of a set of desires and aversions which lead him to seek certain experiences and to avoid others. All of the senses respond pleasurably to certain stimuli and unpleasantly to others. A baby with the most limited control over his environment endeavors to satisfy his desires and to avoid his aversions. As rapidly as an individual's control over his environment increases, his efforts are extended to meet stimuli which satisfy his desires and to avoid those which involve his aversions. This has great significance for teachers. It assures us that the teacher who associates school work with punishment is teaching the child to avoid further experiences of that kind. It gives us an understanding of how teachers who have used the memorization of poetry to punish children have developed a thorough going dislike for poetry. In brief, from this principle may be discovered the reason that many things which children are taught to do in school are not continued when school days are over.

Sometimes this principle is interpreted to mean that only easy things will be undertaken in school. This is an unsound conclusion, for very often the highest degree of satisfaction is realized from achieving an extremely difficult task. Observance of this principle in teaching leads almost always to more intensive, intelligent activity on the part of pupils.[12]

Another form of presentation is to state an educational creed. In this case a position is taken in regard to fundamental issues. The principles upon which the position rests are not stated formally, but are employed in the preparation of the statement of belief to give it consistency. An illustration of this form of

[12] *Procedures for Virginia State Curriculum Program,* State Board of Education, 1932, pp. 11–13.

statement is provided by the Ann Arbor, Michigan, course of study in social studies:

Our Educational Creed

We believe:

That EDUCATION is living.

That living implies growing.

That growing means the continuous re-creation of the individual through experience.

That the method of education is experiencing.

That experience which is educative in the best sense of the word produces at each stage of life a more completely integrated personality.

That the end of education is found in the present as well as in the future.

We believe:

That the SCHOOL is society's agency for furnishing a selected environment in which directed growth during certain periods of life may more effectively take place.

That this environment should stimulate the child to grow through experiences which have a high degree of personal worth.

That through these intrinsically worth-while experiences the child should grow in his power to interpret the physical world and the society in which he lives.

That the experiences which the school furnishes should make possible active participation in group life on increasingly higher levels by giving opportunities for the practice of those habits and attitudes which are necessary for physical and mental health and for wholesome group life.

That the school is only one of many agencies for developing character and personality and should co-ordinate its program with that of the home and other agencies of society.

We believe:

That the ELEMENTARY SCHOOL should be concerned with stimulating growth in personality by providing in the main, opportunities for experiences which are basic race experiences. That through these experiences the child should grow in his power to understand the simpler facts of the physical world around him and the more elementary basic problems of the group life in which he finds himself.

That through these experiences the child should gain dynamic control over the skills and information which are the necessary tools in meeting the common needs of life.

That it should provide for the practice of the desirable personal and social habits which are being built in the home and should in addition provide for the beginning of other habits of a positive social type.

We believe:

That the CURRICULUM should be organized in terms of experiences.

That these experiences integrate subject-matter and eliminate sharply drawn distinctions between the conventional school subjects.

That such a curriculum is based upon the assumption that subjects of study, as organized bodies of information, should be the end point and not the beginning of an educative experience.

That within certain limits teachers and pupils should be given a large degree of freedom in choosing and organizing the particular unit experiences which they will enter into in any grade.

That these experiences should be so chosen and arranged that participation in life on increasingly higher levels of achievement is possible.

We believe:

That while such a curriculum is highly desirable, it is hardly expedient at the present time for the public schools to depart entirely from the generally accepted school organization.

That it is both desirable and expedient in the Elementary School to bring into closer relationship the materials of history, geography, and industrial arts through the organization of a unified course in the social studies.

We believe:

That an INTEGRATED COURSE in the SOCIAL STUDIES in the Elementary School will further the aim of education.

That it will bring about a freer, more flexible organization of the Elementary School.

That it will furnish a core of rich life-experiences which will make meaningful many of the other school activities.

That it will make possible a more significant and unified interpretation of the problems of social life which the child meets from day to day.

That it will make more probable an intense and a lasting learning of many of the skills and facts which are considered tools for the successful solution of individual and group problems.

That it will give greater opportunity for the growth in the child of the power to think independently and for mastery of the technique of problem solution.

That it will give greater opportunity for the development of individuality.[13]

Statements may also be presented as a point of view or platform. In this form a discussion is presented which involves a somewhat systematic consideration of the various aspects of education with which curriculum development is concerned. The principles upon which this point of view is based are either woven into the discussion or deduced at the conclusion of the discussion. An illustration of this type of statement is provided by the Los Angeles County course of study for the intermediate grades:

Some Principles of Teaching and of Learning

Education, or growth, is conditioned by that inner thing which we are, and by those outer environmental experiences which tend to modify it. It is with these modifications that the schools are concerned. After all, we must take each individual as we find him, with whatever abilities and tendencies he has, and strive to develop these abilities or modify these tendencies in such a way that he will be an acceptable, contributing member of a social group. About the only thing we can hope to do, since individual instruction in public schools is practically impossible, is to provide an environment and a succession of worthwhile experiences which will help children progressively to improve their behavior, and which will help them to acquire the knowledges and skills which we feel they must have. We must remember that the school is only one factor in education, if education is the thing we say it is, and that the experiences which children have in schools should help them to engage in more desirable and more meaningful experiences outside of schools.

Education is a continuous succession of one experience after another which make and remake our ways of thinking, of feeling, or acting. Each new experience contributes something to the process. In other words, learning proceeds through a gradual accumulation of assimilated experiences, by which we interpret, or think we interpret, life about us. We learn as we associate new experiences and old experiences, and the greater the intensity or vividness of the experience the greater its effect upon us. "The royal road to learning," says the California Curriculum Commission, "is through these four stages of a typical life experience: purposing, planning, executing, evaluating. No step can be

---

[13] *Social Studies in the Public Schools of Ann Arbor, Michigan, Grades Three to Six,* Board of Education, 1929, pp. 1–2.

omitted, and the child must take each step himself actively. No one, not even the teacher, can short-circuit the process for him. The teacher may guide at each step, but the learner must experience. . . . The work of the teacher can be completely summarized in two aims: to help children set up ever more worthy purposes, and to help them to achieve those better purposes in more desirable ways."

Experiences naturally will vary in kind, in vividness, in effect, in value. We may have the experience of driving an automobile in the rain on slippery streets, of shopping in a Christmas rush, of having a molar extracted, of learning to use decimal fractions, of balancing a bank account, of writing a letter, of meeting an artist, of traveling abroad, of threading a needle, and what not. We have little experiences, and big experiences. We repeat that they vary in kind, in vividness, and in effect. Each meaningful experience, however, aside from whatever specific knowledge or skill it may provide, either changes our attitude or strengthens the feeling we have already built toward the thing which is brought to our consciousness. For example, a new experience develops or strengthens certain feelings which we have, let us say, concerning driving in the rain—not only the technique of driving in the rain, but the attitude of pleasure or fear which comes from the activity. A new experience with a painful molar develops or strengthens certain feelings which we already have, perhaps, concerning teeth and toothbrushes, dentists and pain. Each new experience in reading has some effect on our attitudes toward reading. And so on.

. . . .

You will recall that the laws of learning are *readiness, exercise,* and *effect*. We cannot begin to give you even elementary comments on psychology and the principles of learning. All of you have had courses in psychology and numbers of courses in education. We shall only try to recall to your attention in naïve fashion certain things which are usually couched in scientific language. *The first law of learning,* you remember, is that of mind-set, or readiness of the learner, which only means, after all, that the learner should have had experiences which have caused a favorable attitude toward the new experience or an eagerness for it which will make him wish to engage wholeheartedly in its pursuit. The greater the readiness, the less stimulation will be needed. Interest is favorable mindset and, in general, we can say the stronger the interest on the part of the learner the greater his effort. We have emphasized all through the courses of study the necessity of first of all creating an eagerness on the part of children for experiences before proceeding with the experience.

The second law of learning is that of exercise, which, in simple terms, means something like this: we tend to remember things we use and to forget things which we do not use. We tend, also, to recall things which have been satisfying or pleasant to us and to forget, or to try to forget, experiences which have been unpleasant. Abilities to use tools and techniques are developed by exercise—repetition, drill, experiences of recurring frequency, whatever you wish to call them. Knowledges are fixed by use. Habits are formed by use. Habits may be either good or bad. The more fixed by use is a knowledge or a habit, or a skill, the more difficult it is to change. In planning experiences with your children, be sure that the facts or skills which you endeavor to establish, sometimes with difficulty, are useful ones, which will not be promptly forgotten because of disuse. Avoid a waste of energy and concentrate on helping the learner establish the things which are sufficiently worth while to merit establishing. Let your emphasis be on doing this well.

The last law of learning is that of effect; that of satisfaction or annoyance. We tend to repeat experiences which give us satisfaction; to avoid those which give us annoyance. Do you see the tremendous significance in providing the child with experiences whose outcomes are satisfying, if you would help him to grow normally and keep him eager for further enterprises? You will find excellent discussions of this deep subject which we have touched so lightly in Thorndike's *Psychology of Learning* and in Kilpatrick's simpler discussion in his *Foundations of Method*. We believe you will enjoy reading *Psychology for Teachers*, by Collings and Wilson, a very recent book.

Do you remember the characteristics of learning which are considered secondary in importance to the laws of learning: multiple response to the same external reaction (varied response), attitude adjustment (determination of the learner), assimilation or analogy, and associative shifting? Kilpatrick's famous four steps in learning: purposing, planning, executing, evaluating?

Our Basic Philosophy of Education

The basic philosophy as expressed in the prescribed courses of study for all grades may be summed up somewhat in this fashion:

(1) The efforts of the teacher shall be directed toward providing the learner with rich and varied experiences, appropriate to his individual needs, present and future.

(2) These experiences shall be chosen to the end that the child shall show progressive improvement (growth) in his ability to attain personal and social excellence as he learns

    (*a*) To adjust to a changing world, and

    (*b*) To control its forces.

(3) We believe that this growth must be accomplished by means of a mastery of those procedures which the race has found to be indispensable.

These include:

(a) The fundamental manual and mental skills, such as speaking, writing, computing;

(b) Basic vocational skills, such as the use of common tools appropriate to the learner's sex, interest, and ability;

(c) Such avocational skills as the learner can master in the fields of the crafts and in the fine arts;

(d) A knowledge of the world and its life, past and present, with reference to the future;

(e) The establishment by each learner of a body of socially desirable habits and attitudes;

(f) The appreciation of the best thought, action, and material creation which have been preserved in the world.

All these experiences and attainments shall be a part of our deliberate and planned cultivation of the good life for each learner.

We believe that the transitional outcome of the educational process as outlined shall be the learner's developing abilities to make worthy contributions to the higher social values, as he becomes an increasingly co-operative member of a stable and happy community life. The ultimate outcome shall be the ability of our whole people as individuals and as a nation to live in a spirit of sympathetic international understanding, permitting each national group to preserve and develop its racial spirit, and encouraging each such group to make a worthy contribution to world life.[14]

There is still another form of statement which differs considerably in method of development from the other forms. Whereas the other forms serve specifically in directing curriculum work, this last form is a comprehensive and systematic statement of point of view to guide development of all phases of an educational program. It is developed by some group within a school system concerned with all aspects of the educational program. Such a statement, when developed in a comprehensive, consistent, and systematic form may appropriately be referred to as a philosophy of education to direct development of an educational program. From such a statement guidance may be derived to

[14] Los Angeles, *op. cit.*, pp. 30–33.

decide the issues in a consistent manner which arise in curriculum development. Such a statement was prepared by the Teacher Training Council of Wisconsin. It is presented here for illustration:

This philosophy is offered with the sincere conviction that it points the way to necessary readjustments in educational emphases. Despite tumultuous challenges hurled at education and the conflict on objectives, we have tried to set forth purposes and means whereby the school can become more potent in modern life.

The entire statement has been submitted to various professional groups for review and many suggestions received have been incorporated. The general approval given by educators of Wisconsin and other states encourages us to hope for its influence upon our schools. Translation of the philosophy into school practice is obviously out of the hands of the Council. It is hoped, therefore, that teachers will take a few points which appeal to them and develop techniques by which they may be carried out. Adoption of the entire program by one teacher or school for experimental purposes, would, in our opinion, be unwise.

Your committee will appreciate reports from teachers upon any classroom methods developed upon the basis of this philosophy.

—*Teacher Training Council*

Educational Objectives

The character of any educational system is determined by its objectives. The most acceptable idea underlying educational objectives is the growth of the individual so that he will act as wisely as possible in the social groups of which he is or may become a member. Acting wisely in this connection is to be interpreted as acting in such a way that he will make the greatest possible contribution to society and at the same time receive the greatest possible personal satisfaction. These two ends are not regarded as essentially in conflict.

Democracy

The essential idea in democracy is that of respect for personality—the consideration of people as persons and not as things. If we are to develop in America a democratic society, the school cannot escape partial responsibility. All the relations of the school must conform to this principle in practice as well as in theory. The idea of growth through critical thinking fits in with democracy since it conditions human action upon wise self-expression. The teacher-dominated school does not allow for the freedom necessary for growth through self-expression in a typically social environment. The teacher should make every effort to make the pupils responsible to social forces within and without the school rather than center responsibility in himself. The traditional school is a teacher-dominated autocracy rather than a democracy. The teacher or some force still further removed from the learner sets the tasks, the standards of learning and conduct, and the teacher appropriates all judicial and executive authority. By the term democratic school is not meant that the school should be administered by the pupils without due respect for society and its institutions, but the school set-up should be such that the pupils can assume all responsibility consistent with other social interests that are in any way connected with the school, and respect for these interests should be recognized through reason and understanding rather than through authoritative control. Only beginnings have been made in the reorganization of the traditional autocratic school to make it more democratic. These are found chiefly in the modern kindergarten and primary grades. We should not preach democracy and continue to practice its opposite in our educational institutions.

Individual Differences

There is a wide range of difference in the rates at which individuals develop, intellectually and emotionally. For the same individual also, the rate of growth is neither constant in any one line nor uniform in different lines of educational endeavor. Since an individual develops best when his environment tends neither to accelerate nor to retard his growth beyond the present limits of his native capacity, constant vigilance must be exercised by the teacher in the adjustment of the pupil's educational surroundings. The purpose of differentiating the curriculum is to provide for different child interests and not for different levels of ability. Provision should be made in each curriculum for different ability levels.

The Attitude of Inquiry

One of the basic principles involved in the growth of the human mind is that of critical inquiry. This means open-mindedness, toleration of others' views, deferring judgment, and a willingness to alter beliefs in the light of new evidence. School procedures should be controlled by this scientific attitude. In cases where the evidence is sufficiently conclusive to warrant independent action, educational practice should stimulate the individual to act according to his convictions even though they may run counter to tradition or to usually accepted social practice. Present practice, however, should be accepted as the guide until there is a reasonable doubt established as to its superiority to the proposed change. The teacher's attitude, therefore, should be that of inquiry, of problem-solving, rather than that of ready acceptance or of uncritical rejection of new ideas.

Controversial Questions

The principle of free inquiry is often in conflict with the personal interests and opinions of individuals and groups. The problem of how far the school can go in the study and discussion of controversial questions is a difficult one. Personal beliefs must be respected but on the other hand we can only find the best solution of our most difficult political, social, and economic problems through both intensive and extensive study and discussion of them. Partisanship has no place in the school but opportunity for free inquiry must be protected.

Interests as Educational Objectives

The principle of growth emphasizes the present life of the child rather than preparation for adulthood. Both the direction and rate of the pupil's growth are closely related to the present interests. These act both as cause and as effect. Habits are not consciously formed except on the basis of desire and interest. The school can scarcely serve the child better than by helping him to acquire an assortment of interests which are in line with his native capacities. These interests should multiply and strengthen his social relations as well as his personal satisfactions. They represent, therefore, the basis of his moral life and they furnish the drive that carries him through difficulties to the realization of his desires.

Some Essential Factors of Learning

Interest, satisfaction, and success are closely related factors of learning. The motive power of self-directed activity is purpose and interest. When activity is successful, that is, when conscious progress is being made toward a goal, the activity is accompanied by interest and followed by satisfaction. The reverse is also true. The driving power of purpose, the stimulation of interest, and the satisfaction resulting from successful effort are essential factors of learning. Attitudes are, therefore, all important in education. It has been demonstrated that learning takes place more rapidly when the learner knows how well he is succeeding.

It is evident from the preceding statement that only beginnings in learning can be forced from without. Purposes which are self-initiated or freely appropriated create true learning situations. Coercion may and often does produce an attitude of opposition. One of the chief defects of the traditional school is its emphasis on coercion rather than on purpose. Unless outward compulsion is soon replaced by the inner drive of purpose, learning is thwarted and opposing attitudes are developed. These are cardinal principles of the Wisconsin Philosophy of Education.

Self-Direction Necessary in Learning

Artificial or external stimuli may and often do set up the goals and methods of approach, but no critical learning takes place until the individual has accepted the goal as his own and his interest in reaching the goal is constantly stimulated by an understanding of his progress toward the goal. Outside forces may stimulate inside forces to action, but critical learning takes place only in so far as the inside forces become self-directing in their interplay with outside forces in the quest for the objective. Though artificial stimuli, or stimuli not inherent in the goal or the progress toward the goal, may be accepted in a critical educational set-up, the inherent danger in the abuse of these stimuli is so great that extreme care must be exercised to limit their use, especially coercive stimuli, to individual cases where a careful analysis indicates that such stimuli are necessary to obtain a critical educational set-up. Since the method of problem attack is the dominant objective, no educational process can be justified under the above philosophy where the coercive elements are consistently dominant, or where coercion is used when the objective can be obtained through critical practice. Under this philosophy, an educational set-up must be judged solely from the amount of self-directed activity it stimulates in the contemplation of worth-while problems.

Growth and "The Child-Centered School"

The philosophy of growth is consistent with the child-centered school if by that term is meant educating the child so to understand his social and natural environment as to make it possible for him to get the highest degree of satisfaction out of his social relations. It is not consistent with the child-centered school if such a school means developing an individual so that he receives satisfaction only when he can make everything in his environment yield to his own desires no matter how unsocial these may be. It is consistent with the society-centered school if this means that the individual is to be brought to understand his relations with his environment in such a way that he lives most fully as an individual when he is living most completely for society. It is not in agreement with the society-centered school if it means to develop in the child a blind indoctrinated slavish adherence to the accepted social customs irrespective of his individual well being.

The characteristics of a child-centered school as conceived in this philosophy are freedom, initiative, activity, interest, and self-expression for every pupil. These qualities are in contrast with those of the traditional teacher-centered school. These new ideas and ideals for the school have grown out of the new educational philosophy and psychology here advocated and are in harmony with them. They have already revolutionized practice in the kindergarten and primary grades and have modified the administration of university graduate schools. It is of the greatest importance that every teacher should study the advantages of the new child-centered school as well as its dangers.

Education as Adjustment

Adjustment is regarded by many educators as the chief aim of education. The institutions of society become the dominant educational objectives rather than individual freedom. There is direct opposition between the ideas of education as adjustment and education as growth through problem-solving. The character of instruction and of the curriculum under one of these aims differs widely from that under the other. The nature of these two concepts is such, however, that they represent the opposite ends of a scale along which human relations move, sometimes approaching one extreme and sometimes the other. The school must continually seek the most satisfactory solution of this age-old problem of individual freedom versus institutional control, the relation of the wolf to the pack, and must fashion its organization and instruction accordingly.

The Problem of Drill

The educational principles here accepted imply that a large part of education consists of problem-solving activities. There is also in the curriculum, however, a considerable amount of skills, habits and informational data useful as tools and means rather than as ends in themselves. In general these tools and skills are best acquired incidentally in connection with their use in reaching some end desired by the pupil rather than by formal drill apart from such use. The difficulty in the latter procedure is to secure, when needed, the transfer or application desired. Common experience indicates, however, that for the sake of economy of time and without too great a violation of the principle of interest, these tools and skills may possibly be taught through formal drill. Such a course is justified only when suitable follow-up tests indicate that the power to use the tool in a new problematic situation has actually been achieved.

Transfer of Training

The nature and possible extent of transfer together with the conditions under which it may be secured must be carefully considered in formulating an educational program. The solution of this problem belongs to psychology which up to the present time has given only a partial answer. It is generally agreed among psychologists, however, (1) that transfer is possible, but not automatic; (2) that the amount of transfer depends on the intelligence of the child, the nature of the learning experience, and the technique of the teacher. This statement throws a tremendous responsibility on the teacher and her helpers who must now determine where expected transfer is lacking and how it may be achieved.

The School as One Educational Agency among Many

The public school is but one of the educational institutions of society. Its functions are limited by its nature and its organization. Constant study should be made to determine what can and should be taught in the school, and what cannot. Much of the present failure ascribed to the school is probably due to the fact that it is attempting to secure educational outcomes beyond its power to teach. The school cannot compete, but must fully co-operate with the other educational agencies of the community.

These limitations necessitate a careful selection of the educational factors to be emphasized in the school. Only a limited part of a child's education is directly or indirectly the result of formal school education. The great school of life of which the formal school is only a factor is responsible for the child's education. The school should not try to assume the responsibility for all phases of child education, but that part of it which is vital, transferable, and is not furnished in the desirable degree by any other agency. For instance, the school, on account of the above limitations, can at best be a small factor in the health education of the child. In this education it is limited to assisting rather than taking the lead. On the other hand, in the case of beginning reading, the school must accept leadership because society has no other educational force that will accomplish this very desirable part of the child's education. An analysis of the school's function in the general educational objectives is necessary to selection of the subject matter and activities in an effective program of school education.[15]

[15] "A Philosophy of Education for the State of Wisconsin," Publication of the Council on Education of the Wisconsin Teachers Association.

The particular form of statement that may be employed with greatest advantage depends somewhat upon the particular situation for which the statement is being prepared. In general, however, the value of the various forms is in inverse order from that given in the foregoing discussion. Mere listing of principles is of very doubtful value. In such cases they very possibly exert influence on development of the curriculum through the guidance of certain individuals, but there is little help provided by such a statement for other individuals who may have a limited outlook. The addition of paragraphs of discussion helps somewhat but still leaves the average curriculum worker pretty much at sea. The statement of creed is a definite advance and undoubtedly has a great deal more significance to most curriculum workers than the foregoing forms. Statement in the form of a unified point of view appears still better, in that systematic organization is required and the principles upon which the point of view rests may be indicated. The last form mentioned is highly desirable in that it presumes direction and organization of all aspects of the educational program according to the same basic point of view.

CONSTANT REVISION NECESSARY

Whatever form of statement is employed it will be found necessary to revise it constantly. As the program progresses insight will deepen and inconsistencies will arise not anticipated at the beginning. Consequently, provision should be made for the development initially of a statement which will make operative a consistent point of view based on sound principles and for the continuous development of this statement as experience indicates a need. When this procedure is followed a sense of unity and direction is injected into a program of curriculum making which is lacking when guiding principles are not considered or when they are stated in academic terms. At the same time, growth in concept and interpretation is required by the process of constant revision to which the statement must be subjected if it is to prove effective.

SELECTED REFERENCES

Bode, Boyd H., *Modern Educational Theories,* The Macmillan Co., New York, 1927.

Bode, Boyd H., "Where Does One Go for Fundamental Assumptions in Education?" *Educational Administration and Supervision,* 14: 361–70, September, 1928.

Childs, John L., *Education and the Philosophy of Experimentalism,* The Century Co., New York, 1931.

Denver Public Schools, *Denver Program of Curriculum Revision,* Bulletin No. 12, Denver, Colorado, 1927.

Dewey, John, *My Pedagogic Creed,* The Progressive Education Association, Washington, D.C., 1929.

Finney, Ross L., *A Sociological Philosophy of Education,* The Macmillan Company, New York, 1928.

Freeman, Frank N., "Psychology as the Source of Fundamental Assumptions in Education," *Educational Administration and Supervision,* 14:371–77, September, 1928.

Morrison, Henry C., *Basic Principles in Education,* Houghton Mifflin Company, Boston, 1934, Chapter I.

Peters, Charles C., "Educational Sociology as a Source of Fundamental Assumptions in Education," *Educational Administration and Supervision,* 14:385–92, September, 1928.

Ragsdale, Clarence E., *Modern Psychologies and Education,* The Macmillan Company, New York, 1932.

Reisner, Edward H., "The History of Education as a Source of Fundamental Assumptions in Education," *Educational Administration and Supervision,* 14:378–84, September, 1928.

South Dakota, *Preliminary Reports on Approaches to and Theories Regarding Curriculum Construction,* General Aims and Guiding Principles of Education for the State of South Dakota, Bulletin No. 1, Pierre, South Dakota, 1930.

CHAPTER VI

AIMS OF EDUCATION

The way in which the aims of the educational system should operate in connection with the educative process is at present a matter of considerable uncertainty. The reasons for this situation may be seen from a brief review of the development of procedures for stating and using aims and from consideration of certain recent developments in educational theory.

Students of social progress and development in all ages have given consideration to the aims that education should achieve. Plato set forth a general aim of education in the exposition of his concept of an ideal society in *The Republic*. He held that education should fashion the life of the individual in an all-round manner and "give to the body and to the soul all the beauty and all perfection of which they are capable." Other outstanding scholars in turn stated aims for education. Those stated by Aristotle, Comenius, Locke, Rousseau, Pestalozzi, Herbart, and Spencer, are frequently quoted. All of these statements have one common characteristic. They are very general in nature. What they may mean when employed for developing an educational program is subject to widely varied interpretations.

During modern times statements of the aims for education have continued to be made. Philosophers, psychologists, administrators, and teachers have participated in this activity, both individually and through committees. For a time the statements continued to be of a highly generalized nature. Expressions such as "good citizenship," "ethical character," and "maximum child growth," found a prominent place in the statements. Such expressions provided a basis for philosophical discussion

112

and served as a means of arriving at agreements, but when the problem was faced as to how the statements could be made operative in directing the learning process difficulty was encountered. What is ethical character and how can it be used as an aim to guide in selecting content and activities? How will the aim of maximum growth help a given teacher to organize his instruction? Questions of this type were asked. As a result, general statements of aims came into disfavor and a demand was made for an organization and statement that would exert real influence on the development of the instructional program. This would be achieved, it was held, when aims were so stated and arranged that they could actually be used by classroom teachers to direct day-by-day instruction. This criticism is illustrated by a statement from Monroe. In speaking of general statements of aims, he says:

Certain difficulties become apparent when one attempts to apply such formulations of educational objectives in devising and selecting learning exercises. Phrases such as "ethical character," "health," "right habits of conduct," "appreciations," "life activities," and "citizenship" do not express concepts that the high-school teacher is able to apply directly in deciding what learning exercises he should ask his students to do. In so far as such "high-sounding terms" have meaning, they describe the conduct of "educated" persons rather than the particular abilities or controls of conduct they possess. Hence "character," "culture," "social efficiency," "a well-disciplined mind," and the like refer to ultimate and general educational objectives rather than the immediate goals to be attained by students in first-year algebra, civics, Latin, home economics, English literature, etc.[1]

Since this criticism of general statements of aims was pronounced at the time that the scientific method in education was receiving great emphasis, it is not surprising that curriculum workers, who must face the practical problem of preparing statements of aims for use, turned to the method of analysis to meet the difficulty.

For a period, detailed analyses of aims were made. Step by

[1] From *Directing Learning in the High School* by Walter S. Monroe, pp. 52–53. Copyright Doubleday Doran & Co., Inc. Used by permission.

step the supposed component parts of general aims were analyzed into specifics, until the statements were such that the aim would dictate the instruction required. These analyses usually took the form of lists of specific abilities to be developed. Such lists could be used to direct in considerable detail the organization of instruction. For example, the ability to count from one to ten, the ability to wash the teeth, the ability to spell given words, and so forth, could control the selection of learning activities of pupils and the selection of content.

Extended studies were made to determine comprehensive lists of abilities and activities that function in life. These were employed by curriculum committees to assist them in setting up long lists of aims to be achieved by school divisions, grades, and sometimes by month and week within grades.

This is the procedure which has been most generally accepted in curriculum making during the past decade. It has in fact been accepted by curriculum committees almost as a truism that the procedure for curriculum making is selection of aims and organization of instruction to achieve them. In this way aims have been looked upon as the primary criterion by which to evaluate all succeeding steps in curriculum making.

However, certain developments have occurred which lay open to grave question this process of analysis and the function assumed by it for aims. The result, as pointed out in the beginning, is great uncertainty as to just what part aims should play in directing instruction and, consequently, in curriculum making. For the most part, curriculum committees are adopting what may be described as a compromise position. They are departing from the detailed processes of defining aims characteristic of many programs of the past decade, yet they continue to state aims in some form for many parts or phases of the instructional program. In some cases the conclusion has been reached that aims, other than a few general statements, have no place in curriculum making, and thus aims are again assuming their original position, the position held before the scientific movement in education had exerted influence upon them.

TERMINOLOGY

Analytical procedures for developing statements of aims led to the use of certain terms in specialized ways. Some of these terms must be employed in discussing the problems which are treated in this chapter. Consequently, before proceeding further, we shall consider the meanings of these terms and the way they are used in this discussion.

Three classifications of aims have received rather wide use: in the first case, aims are distinguished from objectives; in the second case, a distinction is made between ultimate and immediate objectives; and, in the third case, the classification is in terms of general and specific objectives. All of these classifications represent efforts to distinguish between inclusive statements from which analysis starts, and derived particularized statements which serve to direct individual phases of instruction.

Hopkins draws a distinction between aims and objectives. This distinction is based on scope and time. According to his definition, the ends striven for in education in general and in given subjects for particular grades are aims, whereas the ends defined within the grade for time units less than the year or semester are objectives.[2] Thus, reference is made to the aims of a subject and the objectives of an instructional unit.

The distinction between ultimate and immediate objectives is essentially the same as the distinction made by Hopkins between aims and objectives. An ultimate objective is held to be a generalized statement. It does not indicate specifically what activities pupils should engage in or what content should be used. The immediate objective, on the other hand, does. It provides the teacher immediate goals to be reached and around which instruction can be directly organized.

The distinction between general objectives and specific objectives is not drawn as clearly as in the other classifications.

[2] L. Thomas Hopkins, *Curriculum Principles and Practices,* Benjamin H. Sanborn & Co., 1929, p. 81.

Usually general objectives are held to be those which are stated for education in general, for a school division, or for a subject in general; while specific objectives are those which are stated for given grades or parts of grades. Thus, according to these classifications, aim, ultimate objective, and general objective refer to highly generalized statements of aims; while objective, immediate objective, and specific objective, refer to particularized statements.

As a matter of fact, all of these distinctions are based on the relationship of statements of aims or objectives on one level of analysis to those on other levels. That is, some statements as compared with other statements, are more or less general in nature. There is, consequently, nothing absolute about any of the terms. Arbitrary definition is the basis upon which they all rest and consequently one may be as acceptable as another if the meanings assigned the terms are clear and mutually understood.

In so far as the treatment in this book is concerned, no distinction will be made between aims and objectives, and therefore the two terms will be used synonymously. This is based on experience which shows that teachers and curriculum workers are unduly confused by use of the terms with different meanings, and are apt to seek and to expect a distinction between the two which is more significant than any that can be made. The terms *ultimate* and *immediate* will be avoided because of certain unfortunate implications of the terms for instructional organization, as is pointed out in a later section of the chapter. The terms *general* and *specific* will be employed occasionally. They will be used entirely in a relative manner, however. That is, the more inclusive statements of aims will be referred to as the general aims of education, whereas all statements resulting from analysis of these general statements will be referred to as specific aims. When reference is made to the aims on a particular level, the level referred to will be specified definitely, *e.g.*, subject aims and grade aims. In this way it should be clear to what aims reference is made at any time.

DIFFICULTIES ENCOUNTERED IN ANALYTICAL PROCEDURES

Four especially noticeable difficulties have been encountered in employing analytical procedures in dealing with aims. Dictation of the instructional program by specific aims assumes that in and of themselves specific aims provide an adequate basis for selecting pupil activities and subject matter. In other words, it is held that the steps of analysis from the most general statement of aims to the most specific are necessarily sequential, that each step paves the way for the next, making the specific aims the more or less inevitable outcome of the general aim or aims. The work of curriculum committees based on this procedure shows that this is not a sound assumption. There is always a point, as an analysis proceeds, when arbitrary decisions must be made; a step is reached which does not necessarily grow out of preceding ones. This point is marked by the injection of subject matter into the aim. Whenever this point is reached it will be noted that the tendency is to insert into the statement of aims what has customarily been taught. The result is that the long process of analysis usually leads to the curriculum organization and subject matter sanctioned by tradition. The procedure fails, as a rule, either to cause old materials to be eliminated from the curriculum or new ones to be added, and it fails also to influence significantly the organization of materials. This is a shortcoming of great significance. The one thing that the procedure does accomplish is to call the attention of teachers to aims that may be realized through the materials they ordinarily teach. It has essentially the same effect as if teachers were to start with the subject matter they customarily teach and seek the aims that should be realized through it. A realistic picture of the procedure in most cases would probably show certain general committees analyzing aims to the point where subject matter is required to make them sufficiently specific to direct instruction. At this point the assistance of committees in various subjects is enlisted. They take the statements of aims prepared by the general committees and find those which can be used to justify the content which they believe should be taught. These then become the specific aims.

By tending in this way to direct the attention of teachers to what should be realized through the subject matter that is customarily taught, this procedure performs valuable service. However, it must be recognised, as is pointed out in the preceding chapters, that the demands are so great on education at the present time that new curriculum organization and new subject matter must be introduced in many cases. This need is not met by the analysis procedure described. As a means of achieving fundamental and thoroughgoing revision of the curriculum, it is largely useless because of the tendency to perpetuate the subject matter that is being taught without adequate appraisal of its value or of the method of organization.

Charters pointed out this shortcoming during the period that the procedure was being developed. He stated in 1923:

> While writers on the curriculum have begun with the statement of aim, none has been able to derive a curriculum logically from his statement of aim. In every case he has made an arbitrary mental leap from the *aim* to the *subject matter,* without providing us with adequate principles such as would bridge the gap—without presenting steps which irresistibly lead us from aim to selection of material. This may seem to be a sweeping statement, but a few illustrations will demonstrate its accuracy.[3]

A second difficulty became evident from observation that children might achieve the specific aims and still not achieve the general aims. In fact, it was observed that this was a common rather than an uncommon occurrence. For example, children might achieve the specific aims defined for English—reading the selections indicated, mastering the facts and skills required— and come out of the experience without the love or appreciation for good literature which was the general aim. Thus, it became clear from practical situations that the achievement of specific aims does not lead necessarily to specified generalized outcomes.

[3] W. W. Charters, *Curriculum Construction,* pp. 6–7. By permission of The Macmillan Company, publishers.

The same specific abilities may contribute to honesty or dishonesty, to a scientific attitude or a non-scientific attitude, to tolerance or intolerance.

In the meantime, this fact was explained theoretically by certain developments in psychology. It was pointed out that the significance of a particular activity or object is determined by the other activities and objects to which it is related. For example, a golf club in a corner of a bedroom in which a person has just had a half dollar roll under the bed has one meaning and significance, while it has an entirely different meaning on a golf course with a particular shot to be executed. In other words, the significance of the detailed skills, items of knowledge, and activities upon which specific objectives are based is determined by the situation in which they are placed. When they are dissociated from particular situations, it becomes impossible to predict what meaning or significance they have. Thus, as specific aims were made the basis for instruction without regard for the related elements, the meaning and significance taken on by the abilities required for the achievement of these aims by pupils could not be predicted.

A third difficulty arose from the extent of the detail the procedure developed. Each general aim, it seemed, could be analyzed into an almost infinite number of specific aims. The scientific impetus to the procedure led to further and further analysis in an effort to include all desirable specific aims and to make them as definite as possible. Pendleton lists 1581 social objectives for English.[4] Guiler[5] lists more than 300 aims for arithmetic in grades one to six. Billings[6] found 888 generalizations which were important in the social studies.

This plethora of detail is shown in courses of study. The committee on social studies of the National Survey of Secondary

[4] Charles S. Pendleton, *The Social Objectives of School English,* The Author, Nashville, Tennessee, 1924.
[5] Walter S. Guiler, *Objectives and Activities in Arithmetic,* Rand McNally & Co., 1926.
[6] Neal Billings, *A Determination of Generalizations Basic to the Social Studies Curriculum,* Warwick and York, 1929.

Education pointed out this condition. One course of study for seventh grade social studies lists 135 objectives. A course in another subject contains 85 objectives. One course for junior high school contains 47 mimeographed pages of objectives.

As a result, the teacher is overwhelmed with aims. The lists are so extensive and complex that no reasonable instructional program can be developed around them. It is found by teachers that they limit work unduly, making it impossible to consider adequately individual pupil needs and interests.

A further difficulty was encountered because of an impression this concept of specific aims frequently gives teachers concerning the way in which general aims are achieved. This impression is strengthened by the terms immediate and ultimate. It is because of this fact that the writers avoid their use. The implication is that after a series of specific (or immediate) aims have been realized, a general (or ultimate) aim will be achieved. That is, if certain specific aims are achieved each day of the semester, the general aim will be realized at the close of the semester. This led teachers to give attention to specific aims in their day-by-day instruction and to wait until the end of the semester or year to consider whether or not general aims had been achieved. This is contrary to the way learning progresses.

The attitudes, character traits, and other general abilities in terms of which general aims are stated, develop continuously. Every situation in which the individual is placed involves growth in such abilities. Consequently, during daily school work, as children develop or fail to develop the abilities indicated as specific aims, they also develop or fail to develop those abilities indicated as general aims. Whether or not desired general aims are achieved depends upon the relationships established between the various specific factors in the day-by-day situations. The emphasis on specific aims as the direct control of learning situations encouraged teachers to overlook this fact and thus to ignore the really important ends which education should achieve.

The use of specific aims, then, as the major determinant in

organizing the curriculum, is of questionable soundness because (1) the procedure emphasizes one or at least a very few abilities in learning situations, whereas many abilities of significance are involved in every situation; (2) achievement of specific aims does not necessarily lead to achievement of general aims; (3) the procedure results in such long lists of aims that they can be employed in instruction only with difficulty; and (4) the procedure gives an erroneous impression of the way abilities classified as general aims are developed. These difficulties necessitate a re-thinking of the use that should be made of aims in curriculum making and the development of procedures which facilitate such use. It is the purpose of the following discussion to suggest certain points that should receive consideration in this regard and to indicate in so far as possible procedures that contribute to the effective development of the point of view expressed.

THE NATURE AND FUNCTION OF AIMS

In attacking the problem thus raised, the curriculum worker advisedly may give greater attention to the nature and function of aims than has been customary in the past. Aim is a term of general significance. It is by no means peculiar to education, even though it has been used so widely in this connection that we are apt to think such is the case. Every line of planned or conscious activity has in it an aim, for this is merely the term used to describe the end or condition the individual is striving to achieve. This end or condition has a number of characteristics. In the first place it serves as a real force in directing activity. It is not some mystical far-away condition that the individual vaguely considers might be desirable, but toward the realization of which there is no possibility of directing activity. To be classified as an aim the desired condition or end must be such that something can be and is done about it. In the second place, an aim is peculiar to a given individual or group of individuals. One person cannot have an aim for another person. The first person may have an aim which involves the second person, but it does not become the second person's aim until he accepts it as a desirable end to achieve and begins consciously to plan his activities to achieve it. In the third place, aims are dynamic and changing. When they are formulated at a given time they represent the extent of vision operative at that time, but as progress is made toward their realization possibilities are seen more clearly, and the aim may change.

It will be noted from the nature of aims that they exert a general directive influence on experience. That is, a person wishes to accomplish a certain end. He maps out a line of action that seems to be appropriate to achieving the end. Thus, aims exert influence on the selection of activities. As these activities are carried forward they do not, as a rule, result in precisely the outcomes anticipated and so modifications of activities are required in order to reach the aim. Here again the aim serves to direct the experience. Finally, as the aim is achieved, new aims evolve from the experience by which it was reached and the directive influence of the aim continues.

In education, there are two groups of aims that must receive consideration. On the one hand, there are the aims of the adults who establish, maintain, and operate the educational system. These are referred to usually as the aims of education. On the other hand, there are the aims of the pupils who are taught in the school system. These are frequently referred to as pupil purposes. These two groups of aims may, upon occasion, coincide, but generally they do so only as the pupil approaches maturity. It is seldom that the child knows or cares what the aim of the teacher may be. All too frequently the teacher has taken the same attitude toward the aim or purpose of the pupil. This has had unfortunate results, as is pointed out in Chapter VIII. Only as the teacher guides the child in the formulation of aims or purposes that are compatible with the aims of education can the aims of education be realized. The fact that aims of education are adult aims is of great importance in considering the function of such aims. These aims are originated by adults and may appropriately serve to direct the activities of adults who are guiding children. They are or should be the teacher's aims. They should guide him in selecting his activities; they should condition the further development of his aims.

This is sharply in contrast with the function assumed for aims of education in analytical procedures. In such cases, aims of education are assumed to be pupil aims as well as teacher aims. It is considered the function of the teacher to get the pupil to organize his activities around the aims of education. Consequently, aims of education are assumed to provide a suitable basis upon which the child can select activities, organize them, and evolve new aims. This means imposition of adult aims on children. It is not a successful procedure because, in the first place, the nature of aims makes their imposition by one person on another impossible, and, in the second place, children cannot comprehend adult aims, no matter how willing or submissive they may be. The result is that teachers have assumed that pupil aims coincide with theirs because pupils engage in certain activities, when, as a matter of fact, the real aim of the pupil may be something entirely foreign to the thinking of the teacher.

In brief, from the one point of view, aims of education serve to direct the activities of the teacher and through the activities of the teacher to influence the aims and activities of the pupils. They are not looked upon as sources that may serve appropriately for the organizing center and actuating force of the child's activities. From the other point of view, they are supposed to serve as the organizing center and actuating force of the activities of both pupils and teachers.

When aims of education are looked upon as the directive force in the activities of the teacher and not as suitable centers about which pupil activities may be organized, it becomes necessary to make an entirely different provision for their use than has been generally followed. A statement of aims of education may be considered a checking source to be employed by the teacher in directing his own activities. As he touches each phase of the experience of the child from the development of the child's aim, through the selection and organization of activities for its realization, and evaluation of outcomes, he checks against the aims of education to see that he is guiding the child in such a way as to provide greatest opportunity for growth in the direction desired by those who maintain the educational system. Aims of education thus exert a direct influence on the experience of the teacher in serving as the basis for selecting and organizing his activities, and an indirect influence on the pupil through the effect the teacher exerts on the pupil's aims and activities.

SOURCE OF AIMS OF EDUCATION

Aims of education are essentially social in origin. They represent the principal means through which the society which establishes and maintains an educational system indicates the ends which the system should serve. In every case, as is pointed out in Chapter II, these demands of society on the educational system are made, although the form of expression may differ. Consequently, the direct source of aims of education is the ideals of the society which maintains the educational system. Hence, the source of aims of education for American schools is the democratic ideal.

It follows that the first step which must be taken in determining a valid statement of aims of education is to study the democratic ideal and to discover in so far as possible its many implications. This must be accomplished largely through consideration of the work and reflections of leading students of society. However, the well pondered thoughts of others are not alone sufficient. The curriculum worker must ponder deeply himself. He must come to see democracy in all its achievements and failures, in all its promises and shortcomings. He must appreciate the experience of mankind which led to acceptance of the democratic way of living as the ideal form of life. He must understand how changing conditions and deepening insight necessitate new interpretations of the ideal. When he commences to understand these things he is ready to undertake the task of defining suitable aims for education in a democracy.

DEFINING DESIRABLE TYPES OF CONDUCT

Social ideals are realized only as the individual members of the social group generally develop certain types of conduct which lead to their realization. Consequently, in preparing a statement of aims the types of conduct needed to realize the particular social ideals must be defined. Such a definition may take the form either of definite solutions to specific problems or of means of solving problems of all types according to certain standards of value. In the former case, the social ideals are such that unvarying responses to situations are desired. Consequently, the individual is trained intensively in the desired responses. He is not encouraged to think or to evaluate. He is given the solution. In the latter case, the individual is guided in the development of generalized procedures and standards of value. The purpose is not to train him to meet certain situations with unvarying responses, but to meet all situations, new as well as old, according to certain standards of value. Means of solving problems are thus emphasized in contrast to solutions to problems.

Whether conduct considered necessary for the realization of social ideals is defined in terms of solutions to problems or in terms of the ability to develop solutions that are consistent with certain standards of value, depends on the social ideals themselves. In a democracy the intelligent participation of all members in the solution of problems is required. This means that individuals must have command of the means of solving problems rather than of ready-made solutions. The rapid development of new problems further emphasizes this need. Consequently, aims of education for American schools must be defined in terms of certain generalized controls of conduct which, if developed, will lead to the realization of the democratic ideal.

The nature of these generalized controls of conduct will perhaps be better understood when we consider that it is common practice to recognize certain general types of conduct. That is, certain activities performed in a variety of situations meet the same general standards. We say a man is honest, or thoughtful, or open-minded, or has the scientific attitude. These terms suggest that he engages in the various activities of life in such a way as to conform to certain standards, and to observe certain relationships. There is some difference of opinion concerning these standards and relationships. Nevertheless, certain general characteristics are agreed upon well enough to define the general nature of a person who is honest and sincere, or who lacks these qualities. These general aspects of behavior are frequently called emotionalized attitudes, generalized controls of conduct, and character traits. As indicated before, they are referred to in this discussion as generalized controls of conduct.

Generalized controls of conduct are appropriate aims for education because achievement of the social ideals of a particular group depends directly upon the nature of the generalized controls developed by the individual members of the group. If the members of the group have widely developed the generalized control of conduct described by the term *considerateness*, it may be expected that the democratic ideal of respect for individual rights will be rather fully realized. But if people generally lack this generalized control of conduct, or if it is not generalized to a high degree, the inevitable outcome is that the ideal is largely impossible of realization.

This suggests the second step in developing a statement of aims of education. This consists of the indication of the generalized controls of conduct which, if widely developed by the individual members of the social group, will lead progressively to greater realization and effective interpretation of the ideals stated in the first step. In developing this statement, the philosophical method must be relied upon. Two techniques may be employed to aid the reflective process. One is controlled observation. Analytical studies of conduct actually observed may be made to determine what activities people engage in and what are the characteristics, procedures, and outcomes of various types of activities. Such an analysis may suggest desirable and undesirable types of conduct. The consensus of opinion technique may also be used. A select group of competent persons may be asked to indicate types of conduct deemed necessary and contributory to the realization of the democratic ideal of life. With such assistance as can be secured from these methods, a conprehensive statement of the desired generalized controls should be prepared. Suggestions for development of such a statement may be secured from *The Commonwealth Teacher-Training Study.* A list of desirable traits of teachers was prepared as a part of this study. Separate lists were prepared for senior high school, junior high school, intermediate grades, and kindergarten and primary grade teachers. However, many of the traits have general significance as controls of conduct. The list for senior high school teachers follows:

1. Adaptability
2. Appreciativeness
3. Attractive personal appearance (cleanliness, neatness)
4. Breadth of interest (interest in pupils, interest in community, interest in profession)
5. Considerateness (courtesy, kindliness, refinement, sympathy, tact, unselfishness)
6. Co-operation (helpfulness, loyalty)
7. Definiteness
8. Dependability (consistency)
9. Diligence (industry, patience, perseverance)
10. Enthusiasm (alertness, animation, inspiration)
11. Exactness (accuracy, carefulness, thoroughness)
12. Fluency
13. Forcefulness (courage, decisiveness, firmness, purposefulness)
14. Good judgment (discretion, foresight, insight, intelligence)
15. Good taste
16. Health
17. Honesty (fairness, frankness)
18. Leadership (independence, initiative, originality, resourcefulness, self-confidence)
19. Magnetism (approachability, cheerfulness, optimism, pleasantness, pleasing voice, sense of humor, sociability)
20. Open-mindedness
21. Progressiveness (ambition)
22. Promptness (punctuality, dispatch)
23. Propriety (conventionality, morality)

24. Scholarship
25. Self-possession (dignity, modesty, poise, self-control, sobriety, reserve)
26. Thrift [7]

PROVISION FOR EFFECTIVE USE OF STATEMENTS OF AIMS

Statements of aims of education in terms of generalized controls of conduct are very general in nature. Consequently, if teachers are expected to employ them effectively in directing their activities, certain steps may advisedly be taken to assist in this regard.

In the first place, it must be recognized that prolonged detailed study should be devoted by teachers to statements of aims of education. Provision for such study should be a part of a curriculum program. The aims to be realized by an educational program in a democracy must inevitably be complex in nature and sufficiently flexible to provide for continuous reinterpretation. So long as they possess these qualities they will require careful study and reflection for their interpretation. Teachers, as participants in an enterprise of social significance, may reasonably be expected to give serious, continuous study to the aims to be realized through the work of the school. If this is done as a part of curriculum making the meaning and significance of various generalized controls of conduct for teachers is greatly increased.

In the second place, the meaning of such terms may be clarified a great deal if their outstanding characteristics are indicated in concise statements. Development of such statements should form a part of the procedure of stating aims. An illustration of such clarification is provided by the aims of education stated in connection with the Arkansas State Curriculum Program. Twenty-two generalized controls of conduct are indicated as the aims of education. Each one is elaborated in the following form:

[7] W. W. Charters and Douglas Waples, *The Commonwealth Teacher-Training Study*, The University of Chicago Press, 1929, p. 67.

APPRECIATIVENESS: The quality of recognizing or feeling the value or worth of accomplishments of others; race heritage; good workmanship; intelligent thought.

Suggested Dispositions, Tendencies, or Inclinations

The recognition of the value of the contributions to the social heritage of the philosophers and scientific thinkers.

A feeling of respect toward the forebears for their spirit of determination and sacrifice that produced the social heritage.

The feeling of the value of the achievement of people and groups in the school and community.

The feeling of the worth of the scientific method in solving social and civic problems.

A high regard for the spirit of science.

Sensitivity to artistic merit.

CAREFULNESS: The quality marked by the performance of activities with attention and concern; attentiveness; precision; caution; pains, vigilance when guarding against evil and providing for safety.

A. *Accuracy:* The state or quality of being accurate; freedom from mistake when this exemption arises from carefulness; conformity to a rule or model; precision; exactness; correctness; carefulness.

B. *Definiteness:* The quality of having an exact signification or positive meaning; the quality of being clear, precise, determinate, unqualified.

C. *Thoroughness:* The quality of position marked by careful attention throughout, leaving nothing undone; not superficial; searching; hence, completeness.

D. *Orderliness:* The quality or state characterized by keeping things in order; tidiness; regulation.

Suggested Dispositions, Tendencies, or Inclinations

The disposition to be accurate in thought and execution.

The tendency to avoid superficiality.

The inclination to do well whatever is undertaken.

The disposition to be precise and definite in thought and action.

The tendency to follow a definite plan of action.

CONSIDERATENESS: Thoughtful regard for another's circumstances or feelings.

A. *Courtesy:* Politeness; courtliness; graciousness; civility.

B. *Kindliness:* The quality or habit of having a friendly, benevolent disposition; kind-heartedness; good-naturedness.

C. Sympathy: The quality or state of being affected with feelings correspondent in kind or correlative with those of another person; fellow-feeling; specifically, a feeling of compassion for another's sufferings or evils; pity; commiseration; an agreement of affections, tastes, or inclinations, or a conformity of natural temperament, which makes persons agreeable to one another; harmony; accord.

D. Tact: A quick or intuitive appreciation of what is fit, proper, right; fine or ready mental discernment shown in saying or doing the proper thing, or especially in avoiding what would offend or disturb; skill or facility in dealing with men or emergencies; adroitness, address; cleverness.

E. Unselfishness: The characteristic or state of being unselfish; generosity; thoughtfulness of others. Regard for others' interests, gratifications, advantages, or the like.

Suggested Dispositions, Tendencies, or Inclinations

The tendency to have consideration for the welfare of others.

The disposition to make concessions for the maintenance of pleasant relations.

An inclination to respect the point of view of others.

The disposition to be courteous in all contacts with people.

A sensitiveness to the wishes of other people.

A feeling of kindness toward others.

CO-OPERATION: The act of working together to one end or of combining for a certain purpose; joint operation or endeavor; concurrent effort or labor.

A. Helpfulness: The quality or state of affording aid or assistance, of being beneficial, useful.

B. Loyalty: The quality or state of being loyal; hearty service in friendship or love, to a cause, or duty; devoted allegiance to an organization or a superior; *intelligent followership.*

Suggested Dispositions, Tendencies, or Inclinations

The inclination to engage in group activity based upon desirable interests.

The disposition to engage without friction in work, play, and social intercourse with others.

The tendency to adapt oneself to the thought, feeling, and action of one's associates.

The disposition to disagree with another's point of view without personal antagonism.

The tendency to subordinate personal desire to the public good.

DEPENDABILITY: The quality of being worthy of being depended upon; trustworthiness; reliability.

A. Consistency: Agreement or harmony of the elements of a person's life or conduct (*e.g.*, of his profession and practice, of his statements at one time and at another); constant adherence to the same principles of thought and action.

Suggested Dispositions, Tendencies, or Inclinations

The urge to do all work efficiently and honestly.
The tendency to do one's full duty.
The desire to be faithful to promises.
The disposition to maintain emotional balance in face of difficulty or defeat.

THE SCIENTIFIC ATTITUDE: The tendency to, or the habit of being, precise and accurate, impartial, objective, and open-minded.

Suggested Dispositions, Tendencies, or Inclinations

The disposition to respect and to use the experimental method.
The inclination to believe in universal cause and effect relations.
The disposition to be free from superstitious beliefs.
The tendency to give careful attention to all details which are relevant to the solution of problems.
The tendency to take an objective view of basis.[8]

The third step in facilitating the effective use of generalized controls of conduct as aims is to suggest various elements which are frequently involved in them. This requires consideration of the composition of generalized controls of conduct.

COMPOSITION OF GENERALIZED CONTROLS OF CONDUCT

Observation of the flow of activities which we describe as conduct reveals that responses possess three noticeable characteristics. In the first place, there are responses that are made uniformly and quickly to certain stimuli. These are usually referred to as specific habits and motor skills. They make possible such activities as walking, talking, and the use of dates,

[8] *Study Program,* The Arkansas Co-operative Program to Improve Instruction, Bulletin No. 1, State Department of Education, 1933, pp. 107–112, 123–124.

names, and number facts. Second, there are responses to novel
situations. Such situations possess a problem element and require the individual to organize or select an appropriate response. This is generally referred to as knowledge. Included
are ideas which take the form of generalizations and principles.
Third, there are various emotional reactions. These are frequently referred to as attitudes or appreciations. They ac-
company all conscious activity and depend to a considerable extent upon the outcomes of previous experience related to that
which is in progress at the given time. All three of these characteristics are important attributes of a generalized control of
conduct. No such control can conceivably be developed without
many specific habits and motor skills as a basis. Neither can it
be developed without knowledge or the means of meeting new
situations, and if these two elements are present without the
proper emotional response, the generalized control of conduct
is as far from functioning as before. Thus, generalized controls
of conduct can be developed only as specific habits, motor skills,
and knowledge are associated with certain emotional responses.
In brief, a generalized control of conduct is represented by the operation of a pattern of specific habits, motor skills, and knowledge
with a certain emotional response. Specific habits, motor skills,
and knowledge are the framework on which such controls must
be built by associating with them proper emotional responses.

Conduct, considered at any particular time, usually involves
all three of these elements. That is, a person depends continuously on specific habits and motor skills; there are elements
of the new or novel, to greater or lesser degree, which must be
met; and there is always some type of emotional response.
Consequently, it is impossible in actual experience to have one
of these elements present without the others. Nevertheless,
some abilities involve specific habits and motor skills to a large
extent; and certain ideas, in the form of generalizations and
principles, are found especially useful in meeting new situations. Therefore, stating aims in terms of generalized controls
of conduct does not mean, as has sometimes been assumed, ignor-

ing habits and knowledge. It means, rather, seeing that the habits and knowledge are used in particular situations which make operative the desired generalized controls of conduct. It requires that habits and knowledge be considered the means of meeting situations in certain desirable ways rather than as ends in themselves.

It becomes necessary, nevertheless, for the teacher to give direct attention to the habits and knowledge which the child possesses. If the child lacks the ability with numbers required for him to be honest and accurate in the various situations in which he finds himself, this lack should be of immediate concern to the teacher. If his work habits and knowledge of scientific concepts are such that he cannot exhibit the scientific attitude in various situations, this should receive the teacher's attention. When a particular generalized control of conduct fails to operate, the first question that may well be asked is whether the individual possesses the essential habits and knowledge for its operation in the given situation. If not, he must be guided in their development.

Consequently, the effectiveness with which the teacher translates the aims stated in terms of generalized controls of conduct into classroom experiences depends to a large extent on his ability to recognize the habits and knowledge essential for their operation in given situations. The habits and knowledge required by particular situations cannot be defined apart from the situations, thus the teacher has to make the final analysis and interpretation. But this analysis may be facilitated if a suggestive list of such habits and knowledge is available. Preparation of such a list is the third way in which curriculum making may aid teachers in the effective use of aims.

A number of sources will be found helpful in developing such a list. Analysis of abilities involving specific habits to a large extent has been carried out rather completely in researches in the various subjects. These abilities should be indicated in the terms in which they function. That is, ability to read is an ability which functions as a unit. It involves many specific habits, such as, eye movement, word meaning, and word recognition. These specific habits do not function in and of themselves but as a part of the larger whole we describe as reading. So long as these abilities which actually function are made the unit of consideration, teachers will not be encouraged to teach a series of specific habits with the idea that added together they represent the whole ability as it functions. This is an error frequently made. Representative abilities of this type are:

Ability to read
Ability to write
Ability to speak
Ability to maintain correct posture
Ability to study
Ability to operate mechanical appliances
Ability to use number facts and combinations
Ability to represent things graphically
Ability to express oneself musically

Generalizations and principles of significance are also suggested by researches in various subjects. Science, mathematics, and social studies have especially emphasized such knowledge. In preparing an illustrative list of such generalizations and principles, no effort should be made to make the list comprehensive. This is an almost impossible task because such statements are so numerous and are presented on so many different levels. Moreover, there are no generalizations and principles that are absolutely essential for the development of particular generalized controls of conduct. The experience of the individual determines what ones may be required. Thus, this list should be just what the term "suggestive" implies. It suggests to the teacher knowledge that frequently is used in effective generalized controls of conduct. In so far as possible the list should include those generalizations and principles most commonly used.

These suggestive lists of abilities involving to a large extent specific habits or motor skills and generalizations and principles may be presented in a variety of ways. The particular form chosen should depend to a considerable extent upon the training and experience of the teachers who must use the aims. The form chosen should also be subject to revision as teachers broaden their experience in use of such statements.

The statement of aims in the Virginia state course of study provides an illustration of one form in which these materials may be presented. The generalized controls of conduct are given in one classification; suggestive generalizations and principles, classified under major headings, are given in another classification; and special abilities involving to a large extent specific habits and motor skills are given in a third. Twenty-four classifications of generalizations are given with about 150 illustrative generalizations. Seventeen special abilities are listed. The classifications are coded so that ready reference may be made to them. The following is illustrative of the form of presentation:

Generalized Controls of Conduct

104. The Attitude of Self-Integrity
    The disposition to accept responsibility for the consequences of one's acts.
    Freedom from fear, worry, and the sense of inferiority.
    The disposition to maintain emotional balance in the face of difficulty or defeat.
    The belief in the worth of one's personality.
    The tendency to face reality squarely.
    The desire to be faithful to promises.
    The tendency to accept criticism cheerfully.
    Willingness to assume the obligations of leadership.
    The urge to do all work efficiently and honestly.
    The tendency to do one's full duty.
    The determination to be happy.
105. The Attitude of Respect for Personality
    The inclination to believe in the integrity and worth of other persons.
    The tendency to admire fine qualities in other people.
    Willingness to let others develop their own personalities.
    The disposition to insist upon fair play in all situations.
    The disposition to make concessions for the maintenance of of pleasant relations.

The belief in equality of opportunity.

The tendency to have consideration for the welfare and convenience of others.

The desire to co-operate with others.

The inclination to believe that personality indicates the nature of the creative force of the universe and the ultimate meaning of creation.

The disposition to regard personality as the key to the individual's success.

106. The Attitude of Critical Mindedness.

The tendency to seek explanations, causes, and consequences of social and natural conditions.

The disposition to consult reliable authorities.

The inclination to distinguish between belief and proof.

The tendency to question authority constructively.

The disposition to discriminate and to evaluate and verify statements heard and read or things seen.

117. The Attitude of Respect for Constituted Authority.

Willingness to surrender personal independence in the proportion that social justice is extended to all persons.

The determination to promote the extension to all persons of those rights stated in the preamble and bill of rights of the Constitution; namely, justice, liberty, freedom of religion, etc.

Active and intelligent obedience to all laws while reserving the right to advocate modification of any that prove unjust.

Loyalty to the government, the school, and other social institutions.

The desire to make success within the social group possible to all as an antidote for anti-social conduct.

The disposition to respect the property rights of others.

The tendency to obey parents.

Generalizations and Principles

201. The Understanding of the Interdependence of All Forms of Life.

Individuals are dependent upon other individuals and have responsibilities to them.

Individuals are dependent upon social groups and have responsibilities to social groups.

All types of groups are dependent upon one another and have responsibilities to each other.

Man's thinking grows out of his experience with individuals, groups, and nature.

People are dependent upon the wise use of plants and animals.

Personal liberty is decreased as man increases his control of nature and society.

Opportunities for exploitation increase as interdependence grows.

202. The Understanding of the Necessity of Man's Adaptation to Changing Conditions.

Nature and social life are in a constant state of change.

Man's conception of the truth changes.

Man's survival and happiness depend upon his ability to adapt himself to changed ways of doing things.

Much knowledge yet remains to be revealed.

Man's success depends upon his ability to adapt himself to those aspects of nature that he has not yet learned to control.

Man's concepts are limited by the customs, ideas, and knowledge of his time.

Man resists change of ideas, ideals, and concepts.

203. The Understanding of Man's Increasing Control of Nature.

Man has modified the nature of plant and animal forms through application of the knowledge of the laws of heredity.

Man has increased the quantity and improved the quality of raw materials of food, clothing, and shelter.

Man has increased the power available for his use.

Man has increased the distance that he can cover in a given length of time.

Man has increased his ability to transport materials long distances with speed.

Man has increased the distance over which he can transmit messages in a given length of time.

Man has increased his means of using power to satisfy his wants.

Man has increased his supply of useful plants and animals by their domestication, wise use, and protection.

204. The Understanding of the Influence of Nature upon the Devolopment of Plants, Animals, and Civilization.

All organisms must be adjusted to climate, natural resources, topography, and other environmental factors in order to survive in the struggle for existence.

Reproduction, the struggle for existence, variation, natural selection, and heredity constitute the basis of the physical development of life.

Food, oxygen, certain conditions of temperature, moisture, and light are essential to the life of most living things.

Micro-organisms are the cause of some diseases.

Heredity largely determines the differences and resemblances between parents and offspring.

There are processes that go on within an organism that are vital to its continued existence.

Types of civilization have been largely determined by climate, natural resources, and topography.

Man's customs, occupations, habits of work, and modes of living have been affected by climate, natural resources, and topography.

Density of population is influenced by climate, topography, and availability of natural resources.

Abilities Involving Specific Habits and Motor Skills to a Marked Degree

301. The Ability to Read.

The ability to use the mechanics needed in reading.

The ability to analyze, interpret, and evaluate reading materials.

The ability to use reference books.

The ability to interpret thought in oral reading.

The ability to use silent reading as recreation.

303. The Ability to Write.

The ability to express one's thoughts clearly, forcibly, and correctly in all forms of written discourse.

The ability to spell needed words.

The ability to use handwriting.

305. The Ability to Study.

The ability to begin work promptly.

The ability to ignore both internal and external distractions.

The ability to get a clear insight into the meaning of the material to be learned.

The ability to concentrate on the important elements of a discussion.

The ability to review in spare moments material which has been learned.

The ability to apply newly acquired principles in wider fields.

The ability to take notes which will insure ready availability of material or ready reference to sources.

The ability to concentrate on a problem until it is completed.

The ability to make skillful use of such aids to study as tables of content, indexes, card catalogs, reader's guides, etc.

The ability to keep in mind that work is not being done for teachers.

The ability to provide external conditions of work—light, temperature, humidity, chair, desk, etc.—favorable to study.

The ability to provide the tools of study.

The ability to form a place-study and time-study habit.

306. The Ability to Use Quantitative Symbols and Procedures.

The ability to use integers.

The ability to use measures and measurements.

The ability to use fractions.

The ability to use graphs.

The ability to check answers.

The ability to think through the solution of a problem before computation.

The ability to make computations accurately.

The ability to work with reasonable speed.

The ability to interpret problems carefully.

The ability to estimate quantities.

The ability to become sensitive to the uses and values of the quantitative aspects of life of whatever sort.[9]

FINAL STEP IN USE OF AIMS MUST BE TAKEN BY INDIVIDUAL TEACHERS

The steps outlined thus far in developing a statement of aims will provide a master check list for the use of teachers in planning and directing instruction. This final step must be taken by individual teachers for it is impossible to predict just what combinations of abilities will operate to make the generalized controls of conduct function in given situations. As each teacher plans instruction and guides pupils, he should check his activities constantly against the statement of aims. Only in this way will aims of education actually provide direction for the educational program. This places a greater responsibility on teachers than customarily has been considered necessary. However, it is a procedure consistent with the growing recognition of the fact that in the final analysis effectiveness of instruction depends on the ability of individual teachers to recognize and meet the needs of individual children under given conditions. The procedure here suggested provides flexibility in the use of aims that permits

[9] *Tentative Course of Study for Virginia Elementary Schools, Grades I–VII,* State Board of Education, 1934, pp. 3–5, 7–8, 13.

teachers to base instruction on the needs of children. The points at which definite checks should be made against the statement of aims are indicated in succeeding chapters.

SELECTED REFERENCES

Billings, Neal, *A Determination of Generalizations Basic to the Social Studies Curriculum,* Warwick and York, Baltimore, Maryland, 1929.

Brewer, John M., *Education as Guidance,* The Macmillan Company, New York, 1932, Chapter II.

Briggs, Thomas H., *Secondary Education,* The Macmillan Company, New York, 1933, Chapters XVIII–XXI.

Charters, W. W., *The Teaching of Ideals,* The Macmillan Company, New York, 1927.

Charters, W. W., and Waples, Douglas, *The Commonwealth Teacher-Training Study,* The University of Chicago Press, Chicago, Illinois, 1929.

Craig, Gerald, S., *Certain Techniques Used in Developing a Course of Study of Science,* Contributions to Education, No. 276, Bureau of Publications, Teachers College, Columbia University, New York, 1927.

Dewey, John, *Democracy and Education,* The Macmillan Company, New York, 1916, Chapter VIII.

Finney, Ross L., *A Sociological Philosophy of Education,* The Macmillan Company, New York, 1928, Chapter IV.

Pendleton, Charles S., *The Social Objectives of School English,* The Author, Nashville, Tennessee, 1924.

Peters, Charles C., *Objectives and Procedures in Civic Education,* Longmans, Green and Co., New York, 1930, Chapters IV and V.

Taba, Hilda, *The Dynamics of Education,* Harcourt, Brace and Company, New York, 1932, Chapter VI.

CHAPTER VII

SCOPE OF THE CURRICULUM

When the desired direction of growth has been defined by the aims of education, the next problem encountered in curriculum development is to provide limitations for the various phases of the curriculum which stimulate regular, consecutive movement of the experience of the learner in the desired direction. This requires that the curriculum be so arranged that each experience of children grows normally out of past experience and leads on to other experiences of increasing significance. The problem, in brief, is that of defining the general limitations of the curriculum in such a way as to provide for a flow of experiences throughout the school life of the child that will possess maximum breadth and depth of meaning and significance.

Flow of experience may be likened in certain respects to the flow of a river. It is continuous and unbroken, each phase moving imperceptibly into the next; yet it may possess widely varying characteristics at different times. Just as streams differ in type so may experiences differ. Some streams have poorly defined banks, and many obstructions in their beds. Such streams tend to wander and overflow, and to be divided into many diverse currents and eddies. Other streams have well-defined banks and few obstructions in their beds. In such streams the water gathers increasing momentum and the stream gains both depth and breadth as it moves forward.

Similarly, experience may be of the type that wanders here and there with no clearly marked course of development. It may encounter obstructions and form diverse currents and eddies which take the form of personality conflicts and inconsistent

action. Or experience may possess unity, wholeness, and consistency. A continuous reconstruction of ideas, beliefs, and
modes of action may occur with the forward movement. In this
case cross currents are reduced to a minimum for conflicts are
resolved as they develop and experience moves forward with
increasing depth and breadth of meaning.

Organization of the curriculum to provide for this latter type
of experience is one of the most important phases of curriculum
development. Consideration must be given to it throughout
curriculum development, but its successful achievement depends
first of all on an adequate definition of the general boundaries
within which the curriculum should develop. Definition of these
boundaries is a problem which generally has not been analyzed
with care. It is an especially important problem because of the
many obstructions in the curriculum which block the flow of the
experience of the learner. Unrelated subjects and breaks in the
curriculum at each administrative division of the school are
especially noticeable obstructions.

TEXTBOOK PROCEDURE

Traditionally, scope of work in American schools is determined by the organization and content of textbooks. When a
school system adopts a text the tendency is to assume that the
organization and materials of the text represent the work that
given classes should cover. The traditional concept of teaching—covering a specified number of pages in the text—is a part
of this general attitude of reverence for textbook materials and
organization. With this point of view functioning, the task of
curriculum making in connection with scope of the curriculum
has been largely a matter of indicating the number of pages to
be covered during specified periods of time. Twenty years ago
Moore described this procedure as follows:

That it (knowledge) may be passed on easily, it must be prepared
in little carefully molded cubes or accurately weighed doses. That is
the work of textbook makers and of manufacturers of methods. . . .
Courses of study are written chiefly, in many cases, to indicate the

quantity which every good retailer of knowledge must succeed in lodging in the memory of the child.[1]

There are a number of reasons why this procedure has persisted so long. The dominant one, perhaps, is that the procedure is logical and may be easily applied. It simplifies and objectifies the task of the curriculum worker, the teacher, and the administrator. The least capable teacher can assign pages in a textbook and hear pupils recite the facts involved. He can give evidence that he has done his part by covering a given number of pages. Thus he has an alibi for failure because he can place the blame for low achievement on his pupils. From the administrator's point of view, it is easy to divide the work of the school, to tell precisely where every child should be in his work, and to have a systematic organization that appears to operate smoothly. Even though educational theory has been challenging, with increasing emphasis, the basic assumptions of the procedure for three decades, it is probably still the dominant means of determining the scope of work in American schools.

There are many illustrations in courses of study of the application of this procedure. A good one is found in the 1927 Kansas state course of study. The introductory statement to arithmetic in the third grade, for example, is, "The work of this grade is based on S——'s *Primary Arithmetic* and covers pages 1 to 152, inclusive, with the text in the hands of the pupils."[2] The work is then divided by months. Pages 1 through 19 are to be covered the first month; pages 20 through 38 the second month; pages 39 through 57 the third month; and so on for each succeeding month. The 1929 Georgia state course of study provides another illustration. The form in different subjects varies somewhat. The scope of fifth-grade history is outlined as follows:

Texts:
Evans' *First Lessons in American History*
Evans' *First Lessons in Georgia History*

[1] Ernest C. Moore, *What is Education,* Ginn and Company, 1915, pp. 19–20.
[2] *New Course of Study, 1927, for the Elementary Schools of Kansas,* Kansas State Board of Education, p. 12.

Chap. 1. Discoverers and Explorers:

   A. Christopher Columbus.
   B. John Cabot.
   C. Americus Vespucius.
   D. Balboa.
   E. Magellan.
   F. Ponce de Leon.
   G. Cortez.
   H. Narvaez.
   I. De Soto.
   J. Coronado.
   K. Verrazano.
   L. Cartier.
   M. Champlain.

Chap. 2. The English Colonists:

   A. Sir Walter Raleigh.
   B. The Settlement of Jamestown.
   C. The Settlement of Plymouth.
   D. Other Colonies in New England.
   E. The Dutch Come to the New World.
   F. Lord Baltimore and the Colony of Maryland.
   G. William Penn and the Colony of Pennsylvania.
   H. The Carolina Colonies.
   I. James Oglethorpe and the Colony of Georgia.
   J. The Original Thirteen Colonies.

Chap. 3. How the French Lost America:

   A. Marquette Explores the Mississippi.
   B. The French Claim Louisiana.
   C. The Young George Washington.
   D. Braddock's Defeat.
   E. The Capture of Quebec.
   F. Life in the Colonies:
         (1) Customs and Beliefs.
         (2) Travel.
         (3) Servants and Slaves.[3]

(The entire year's work is outlined in this manner.)

[3] *Course of Study for Elementary Schools,* Georgia State Department of Education, 1929, pp. 180–181.

The slavish following of textbooks, which results from this procedure of defining scope, has been strongly condemned by the progressive education movement because of the limitation thus placed on the opportunity to provide children rich and varied experiences. Such a restriction, it is held, encourages memorizing at the expense of understanding fundamental meanings, and makes education a process of administering to the child certain prescribed doses of subject matter regardless of his particular needs and abilities.

In the revolt against the extreme restriction imposed by following textbooks page by page, many progressive schools have gone to the opposite extreme. In such cases, no guidance at all is provided teachers for determining desirable scope of work. Each teacher is left to his own devices to discover what will be most fruitful for the group of children he is teaching. In some cases the teacher is even encouraged to limit the direction given children. He is told that the teacher should be in the background and that the children should decide what they wish to do.

This extreme position, often referred to as the "planless curriculum," has been severely criticized. School administrators have held it to be an impractical procedure for public school systems. They have pointed out that transferring pupils from school to school becomes an impossible administrative problem under this plan. The children, as well, are subjected to the whims of individual teachers. Educational theorists have objected to the procedure on various grounds. Some have held that there are definite phases of the group culture with which a child must be familiar and that this procedure does not provide for contacts with all these desirable phases. They point out that a child may deal intensively with a few phases and entirely ignore numerous other important ones. They further hold that this procedure makes it extremely difficult to assist the teacher to improve his instruction.

Some of the closest friends of progressive education have considered this entire lack of organization undesirable. Rugg states,

"I am convinced that the outstanding weakness of laboratory schools is . . . lack of outlines planned-in-advance." [4] Dewey states in connection with this point:

Organization and administration are words associated together in the traditional scheme, hence organization conveys the idea of something external and set. But reaction from this sort of organization only creates a demand for another sort. Any genuine intellectual organization is flexible and moving, but it does not lack its own internal principles of order and continuity. An experimental school is under the temptation to improvise its subject-matter. It must take advantage of unexpected events and turn to account unexpected questions and interests. Yet if it permits improvisation to dictate its course, the result is a jerky, discontinuous movement which works against the possibility of making any important contribution to educational subject-matter. Incidents are momentary, but the use made of them should not be momentary or short-lived. They are to be brought within the scope of a developing whole of content and purpose, which is a whole because it has continuity and consecutiveness in its parts.[5]

As the inadequacies of the textbook and extreme freedom procedures have become increasingly evident, efforts have been made to develop more satisfactory ways of defining the scope of the curriculum.

SUBJECT MATTER PROCEDURE [6]

Some curriculum programs have made a short step from the traditional textbook procedure for defining scope to a method which we shall designate as the subject matter procedure. In this procedure, the definition of scope is not restricted to the materials presented in a particular textbook. Instead, all the

[4] Harold Rugg, "Curriculum Making: Points of Emphasis," *Twenty-sixth Yearbook, National Society for the Study of Education,* Part II, 1927, p. 159.

[5] John Dewey, "Progressive Education and the Science of Education," *Progressive Education,* 5:201, July, August, September, 1928.

[6] It should be clearly understood that the procedures discussed in the following pages refer specifically to determining the scope of the curriculum and not to general approaches to curriculum making.

content in a particular subject field is canvassed. What is considered desirable for children is selected and organized for logical development. This content is then divided by grades and by instruction periods. When so divided, it serves to indicate the scope of work for each grade. An illustration of the careful use of this procedure is provided by the Long Beach, California, *Course of Study in Nature Study and Elementary Science*. The introduction opens with the following statement: "This course is based on the nature materials with which the pupils come in contact at home, at school, and on their week-end trips." The organization is given in Chart I. An examination of this chart will reveal that the usual subject lines and progressions form the basis of organization; that the major divisions correspond to zoology, botany, and physiography; and that the classifications under the major headings follow usual subject classifications.

The New Orleans course of study in geography outlines the work on the same basis, although a somewhat different form is used. The outline of work for the fifth grade follows:

Outline Work:
    I. The Earth as a Whole.
        1. Continents and Oceans.
        2. Directions, Latitude, Longitude.
        3. Size.
        4. Motions.
        5. Climate Belts.
            A. United States' Possessions in Torrid Zone.
                a. Philippines.
                b. Hawaii.
                c. Puerto Rico and Virgin Islands.
                d. Panama Canal.
            B. United States' Possessions in Frigid Zone.
                a. Alaska.

   II. Other Countries of North America.
        1. Canada and Newfoundland.
        2. Mexico and Central America.
        3. West Indies.

CHART I

LONG BEACH, CALIFORNIA, COURSE OF STUDY IN NATURE STUDY AND ELEMENTARY SCIENCE*

		NATURE ATTITUDE	NATURE ACTIVITY	NATURE KNOWLEDGE	EMOTIONAL ATTITUDE	CIVIC ATTITUDES AND ACTIVITIES
		1. To stimulate the child's interest in the out-of-doors and his curiosity concerning cause and effect.	2. To stimulate the child's careful observation of nature in order that he may draw truthful conclusions concerning it and also that he may be able to relate clearly his nature experiences and thus share them with his associates.	3. To increase his knowledge concerning the interrelation of the various types of life with one another and with physical nature.	4. To increase the child's sympathy with nature and to help him overcome his superstition, prejudice, needless fear, and desire to hurt or kill unnecessarily.	5. To impress the child with the need for civic recognition of nature's contribution to city welfare; to secure his interest in city beautification and . . . protection of parks and public buildings; to secure his co-operation in matters concerning individuals and public health, and to obtain his willing obedience . . . to laws protecting . . . natural resources.
GRADE I	First Semester	I. Interesting butter-flies, moths, and caterpillars II. Birds III. Trees	II. Birds: judgments through observation, class reports		I. Interesting butter-flies, moths, and their caterpillars	III. Trees
	Second Semester	I. Shore life II. Flowers III. Clouds	I. Shore life: solution of problems through observation IV. Pets: observation and judgment as to care needed. . . .		IV. Pets: rough play, neglect	II. Flowers, wild flower conservation
GRADE II	First Semester	I. Insect homes II. Spider homes III. Bird homes and nurseries IV. Gopher and squirrel homes		V. Children's homes, nature material for homes	II. Spiders: homes and young III. Pets: rough play, neglect	V. Children's homes
	Second Semester	I. Ocean homes II. Plant homes III. Wild flowers		II. Potting plants, moisture, sunshine, soil, etc.		

Grade / Semester					
Grade III First Semester	III. Sun, moon, rain, wind		III. Wind, rain, etc.	I. Pets; white rats, rough play, neglect	
Grade III Second Semester	I. Shell collections II. Fresh water collection III. Dry land animal collection IV. Bird . . . collection	I. Pets . . . collections; II. Seed . . . collections; judgment as to advantages of types of seed in distribution		II. Crayfish, salamanders in aquarium III. Collection of lizards, horned toads, land turtles	
Grade IV First Semester	II. Poinsettias	I. Birds: observation assignments. Reports in class on observation	I. Bird friends; A. B. C.	II. City animal friends	I. Birds, conservation of II. Christmas plants
Grade IV Second Semester					I. City plants II. City animals III. City health
Grade V First Semester	I. Soil and garden	I. Insects: observation assignments. Reports in class on observation	I. Insects in home and garden II. Living plants		
Grade V Second Semester			IV. Gopher	II. Toads	V. Value of gardening and the healthful preparation of garden food; Problem II, III
Grade VI First Semester	III. The earth and the moon		I. The stars II. The earth and the sun		
Grade VI Second Semester	I. The seasons and plant life II. The seasons and animal life				II. Laws concerning migrating game birds

* Columns 6, 7, and 8, Economic Attitude and Activity, Cultural Attitude and Activity, and Spiritual Attitude, respectively, are omitted. Adapted from Long Beach Course of Study, *op. cit.*

III. South America.
    1. As a Whole.
        A. Location with regard to: oceans, latitude and longitude, zones, and hemispheres,
            Other countries,
            Large world ports,
            New Orleans.
    2. Size.
        Relative; as compared with other continents.
        Actual.
    3. Form.
        General shape, coast irregularities.
    4. Surfaces.
        Highlands and lowlands.
        Drainage.
    5. Climate, as determined by:
        Latitude, altitude, winds, currents.
    6. Life.
        Native plants, animals, humans.
    7. Resources.
        Plant, animal, mineral.
    8. People.
        Race, industries and trade routes, cities.
    9. Political Divisions:
        In general:
        In regard to eight topics given above.
        B. Argentine.
        C. Brazil.
        D. Chile.[7]

(The entire year's work is outlined in this manner.)

Other illustrations might be given but these two serve our purpose, for, although the form of presentation may vary, the general basis is the same. In most cases it is probable that particular textbooks and textbook organizations have exerted an important influence on the outline of subject matter to be covered, even though a text is not referred to definitely. National committees have also exerted great influence on the scope of work when outlined by this procedure.

[7] *Course of Study New Orleans Public Schools, Elementary Schools,* 1927, pp. 265–267.

This procedure is subject to most of the criticisms applicable to the textbook procedure. It does have the advantage of not being restricted to the ideas of a particular author, and it permits classroom teachers and curriculum workers to add their contributions. So far as teaching procedure is concerned, however, the basic assumption is that the task of the teacher is to teach predetermined, limited phases of subject matter; and to proceed through them in a particular order. There appears to be nothing inherent in this procedure to encourage the organization of instruction in a manner differing from that employed with the textbook procedure.

From one point of view this procedure may be inferior to the textbook procedure. If logical arrangements of subject matter are to define the scope of work, it is possible that the textbook writer can provide these arrangements in better form than committees of teachers and general curriculum workers. Especially does this point merit consideration as textbook writers come more and more to base their work on actual experience with children.

AIMS PROCEDURE

Probably the most widely used method of indicating scope of work in curriculum programs during recent years has been the aims procedure or some adaptation of it. Use of aims to define the scope of the curriculum rests on analysis of aims as discussed in the preceding chapter. Consequently, it is necessary here to reconsider certain aspects of analysis of aims as they relate specifically to the problem of defining the scope of the curriculum. Although aims have been used widely to define scope, only rarely has the procedure been applied with consistency on a comprehensive basis. Consequently, many variations of the procedure are to be found.

The "activity analysis approach" to curriculum making as developed by Bobbitt, depends on aims to define desirable scope of work. The general steps as they relate to scope are: (1) divide human activities into major fields, (2) state specific abilities needed in each major field, (3) eliminate the abilities which should be developed by general processes of living, (4) determine the abilities which should be achieved in the various school divisions (Bobbitt uses the terms, early grades, middle grades, and later grades), (5) derive subject objectives from the foregoing lists. The work to be covered in each grade is indicated by the objectives so derived. This particular approach was followed in detail in the Los Angeles curriculum program of 1922.

The aims procedure has been employed more frequently on another general plan. This plan is based on the following general steps or a variation of them. First, a general, all-inclusive aim of education is stated. Second, this all-inclusive statement is broken up into a small number of highly generalized statements. Third, the statement of a small number of aims is divided to suit the administrative organization of the school. For example, with a junior high school organization, the phases of these aims to be achieved by the elementary school are stated as the divisional aims for the elementary school; those to be achieved by the junior high school are stated as the aims for the junior high school; and those to be achieved by the senior high school are stated as the aims for the senior high school. Fourth, the aims for each division are further broken up by stating the objectives to be achieved by each subject. Fifth, the general objectives for the subjects in each division are analyzed into specific objectives for the several grades; that is, statements in as specific terms as possible are made of the part of the subject objectives to be achieved in each grade. The specific objectives for all the subjects in each grade represent the work to be carried forward in the respective grades and indicate the scope of work for the grades.

In the St. Louis, Missouri, curriculum program of 1924–25 this method was followed with unusual thoroughness. Hence, the St. Louis plan is presented for illustration. The "General Aim of Public Education in St. Louis," which serves as the basis from which other aims presumably are derived, is as follows:

To develop the individual to the end that he may effectively direct his life toward his own self-realization and toward his participation in the creation and realization of the ideals of society. . . .

This general aim is divided into seven phases which serve as a classification for more detailed statements of aims.

A. Health and Physical Development.
B. Discovery, Communication, and Expression.
C. Worthy Home Membership.
D. Vocation.
E. Worthy Citizenship.
F. Worthy Use of Leisure.
G. Ethical Character.[8]

Divisional aims are derived from the foregoing classification. For example, the divisional aims falling under *Health and Physical Development* are as follows:

KINDERGARTEN–PRIMARY

A. *Health and Physical Development.*

I. Knowledge:
   1. Necessity for personal cleanliness.
   2. Sanitary care of personal belongings.
   3. Clean and safe surroundings.
   4. Simple everyday safety precautions.
   5. Healthful food and drink.
   6. Clothing suited to weather conditions.
   7. Need for favorable conditions for rest.
   8. Healthful conditions for work and play.

II. Habits:
   1. Cleanliness: face, hands, teeth.
   2. Cleanliness of personal belongings.
   3. Choice of healthful food and drink.
   4. Choice of clean and safe surroundings.
   5. Rest when tired.
   6. Protection against rain, heat, and cold, with proper clothing.
   7. Observance of simple safety and health rules such as, looking both ways when crossing a street, proper use of sharp instruments, covering cough and sneeze, etc.

[8] *General and Divisional Aims,* Curriculum Bulletin No. 1, Board of Education of the City of St. Louis, September, 1926, pp. 10–12.

154 SCOPE OF THE CURRICULUM

8. Cheerfulness.
9. Exercise through suitable play and work.

III. Ideals:
Desire to grow strong and happy like certain persons in whom their interests center.

IV. Appreciations:
Strength and happiness gained through observing simple physical and mental health practices.

ELEMENTARY

A. *Health and Physical Development*

I. Knowledge:
1. Hygienic practices suited to later childhood.
2. Precautions necessary to safeguard life and health.
3. Proper physical exercise to promote and maintain health.
4. Appropriate and comfortable clothing.
5. Right kind and amount of rest.
6. Favorable home, school, and neighborhood conditions.
7. Wholesome food and drink.
8. School and neighborhood health agencies.
9. Social and economic value of health.

II. Habits:
1. Assistance in the sanitation and cleanliness of the home, school, and community.
2. Observance of rules concerning fresh air, rest, cleanliness, proper eating, appropriate clothing, recreation, and the special sense organs.
3. Carefulness pertaining to the physical safety of self and others.
4. Caution in regard to contagion and infection incident to later childhood.
5. Cheerfulness and self-control.
6. Mental cleanliness.

III. Ideals:
1. Cleanliness, of person, home, school, and neighborhood.
2. Athletic attainments.
3. An outdoor boy and girl.

IV. Appreciations:
1. Personal cleanliness.
2. Sanitary and restful home and school.
3. Fresh air and wholesome exercise.
4. The out-of-doors.
5. Strong healthy body.
6. Effective response in emergency.

INTERMEDIATE

A. *Health and Physical Development*

I. Knowledge:
1. Physiological and dietary facts concerning nutrition.
2. Hygienic dress.
3. Principles underlying heating, lighting, and ventilation.
4. Facts fundamental to personal, domestic, and public sanitation.
5. Hygienic and biologic information suited to the early adolescent.
6. Care of the younger children suited to the early adolescent.
7. First aid and public safety.
8. Occupational hygiene.
9. Health agencies.
10. Physical standards for early adolescents.
11. Relation of physical fitness to good citizenship.

II. Habits:
1. Skillful participation in wholesome and appropriate physical activities.
2. Skillful participation in creative activity.
3. Diet and table etiquette appropriate to the early adolescent.
4. Avoidance of infection.
5. Correct posture.
6. General sanitation.
7. Sufficient sleep under proper conditions.
8. Optimism.

III. Ideals:
1. Fitness, mentally and physically.
2. Personal, school, and community cleanliness.
3. Mental composure.
4. Good appearance in relation to health.

5. Wholesome enjoyment of work and play.
6. Moderation in all physical activities.

IV. Appreciations:

1. Health as an asset and sickness as a liability to the individual and community.
2. Value of a normal healthy body.
3. Great natural out-of-doors.
4. Possibilities of overcoming physical handicaps.

HIGH SCHOOL

A. *Health and Physical Development*

I. Knowledge:

1. Physical standards of successive stages of adolescent development.
2. Hygienic and biologic information suited to the adolescent, such as will function in adult life.
3. Important development in the body and in the functions of its organs during adolescence, such as the heart, glands, etc.
4. Race preservation and heredity.
5. Interpretation of common symptoms of bodily irregularities or disturbances.
6. Suitable forms of physical recreation with some attention to those which may carry over to adult life.
7. Influence of emotions on the health of adolescents.
8. Scientific interpretation of environment.
9. Current development in science concerning health preservation.
10. Dietary and nutritive value of foods.

II. Habits:

1. Personal hygienic practices on the adolescent level.
2. Periodical physical examination.
3. Diet, clothing, exercise, posture, and sleep appropriate to maturing youth.
4. Skillful practice of first aid.
5. Cultivation of healthful emotions.

III. Ideals:

1. Proper emotional attitude toward health, personal, domestic, public.

   2. Importance of being a good ancestor.

   3. A healthy mind in a healthy body.

IV. Appreciations:

   1. Desirability of physical excellence for life pursuits.

   2. Dependence of health upon scientific understanding of environment.

   3. Importance of moderation in all things.

   4. Value of scientific health methods.

   5. Need for organized effort in promoting community health.

   6. Importance of outdoor activities.[9]

This arrangement of aims provides the general outline of scope of work. All subject committees derive their objectives from this basic outline. Subject objectives, so derived, are stated as *General Objectives* for the subject, *Divisional Objectives,* and *Specific Objectives* for the respective grades. The specific objectives provide the basis for organizing instruction. For each specific objective in each subject on each grade level, activities, procedures, and desirable outcomes are suggested. Thus, specific objectives, derived by logical steps from a single inclusive aim of education, indicate the work allotted to each grade.

In most cases where the aims procedure is employed, the logical steps of deduction have been less thoroughly followed than in St. Louis. Sometimes the general aims for each subject are stated independently as the beginning point and grade aims are derived from these. In other cases, general aims of education are stated and subject aims are derived directly from them. A brief examination of courses of study reveals a number of other variations of the method.

The aims procedure for defining scope has the advantage of being highly logical. It appears perfectly reasonable and desirable to evolve specific objectives from the all-inclusive aim of education. It seems sound to expect all educational efforts to be directed toward achieving this aim. For this reason it has wide appeal. However, inasmuch as the procedure rests on the process of analyzing general statements of aims into specific

[9] *Ibid.,* pp. 14, 20, 26, 34.

statements around which instruction may be organized, it is subject to the difficulties of analysis of aims pointed out in the preceding chapter. Especially important for defining the scope of the curriculum is the concept of learning involved. It may be implied from the procedure that we might expect on the first day of school, specific objective I to be achieved; on the second day, specific objective II; on the third day, specific objective III; etc. When II is added to I, and III to II and I, and so on with the other specific objectives, the ultimate result is the achievement of the general objective for the year. Year after year this additive process continues until the objectives of each division are realized, and finally the general aim of education is presumed to be accomplished.

As is pointed out in Chapter VI, this appears to be an inadequate concept of learning. The child does not develop one fragment of an ability or trait today, another tomorrow, and another next year; and thus finally come out with the whole ability or trait developed at the completion of the elementary school, the junior high school, or the senior high school. Rather he is a growing whole like any growing thing, and although his characteristics may be modified from day to day, this modification occurs as a total process, affecting the whole individual. Thus, nearly every learning situation involves a complex pattern rather than a simple relationship. One situation may involve abilities a-b-c-d, the next abilities a-b-x-y-d, and the next abilities m-n-o-x-a. Ability *a* must be developed in situations with such varieties of relationships. Special attention may be given *a*, but it cannot safely be given exclusive attention. To do so ignores the complex nature of behavior. This complexity, Hollingworth points out as follows:

The fact is . . . that nearly any event in our experience and nearly every act in our behavior is complex. It is in itself analyzable and is a more or less elaborate *pattern* of related parts or items, in definite *organization*.[10]

---

[10] From *Educational Psychology,* by H. L. Hollingworth, p. 35. Used by permission of D. Appleton–Century Company, Publishers, New York, N. Y.

The additive concept of development has been subjected to most severe attack by biologists who hold the organismic point of view and by psychologists who hold the configuration point of view. Wheeler expresses the point of view of these groups toward piecemeal learning.

The inductive bias assumes knowledge to be built up piecemeal from so much experience here and so much there. The bits are put together. The school curriculum is based upon this thesis from the kindergarden to the graduate school. Separate courses; separate skills. Now we know that knowledge accumulates in no such fashion and that, for the most part, individuals become educated, in spite of, rather than because of, formal efforts to integrate these isolated scraps of knowledge into a single whole, the individual mind.[11]

Thus, when the teacher undertakes to achieve a small part of an aim in the first grade, which is to be added to specifically in the second and so on, he overlooks many elements in the learning situation. Seeing the growth of the child as a simple process of addition, he overlooks a multitude of important factors in the intricate integrative process of modifying continuously the whole individual. He sees only ability a in a given learning situation, and only ability b in another learning situation, when abilities a and b and many others may all be involved. He deals with activities and subject matter as though abilities a and b only were involved. In brief, he strives to develop abilities in isolation when they develop in intricate relationships.

Thus, it is on the validity of this basic assumption of piecemeal learning that the aims procedure rests. If this assumption is accepted, the procedure may be considered essentially sound. If it is not accepted, the procedure will not stand.

UNIT OF WORK PROCEDURE

The method of defining the scope of the curriculum to which attention is now turned is referred to as the unit of work pro-

[11] Raymond H. Wheeler, "The Crisis in Education," *School and Society*, 38:756–59, December 9, 1933.

cedure. This procedure has been developed by public schools in an effort to follow the lead of experimental schools which have developed unit of work curricula. Whereas experimental schools generally permit the teacher to decide what units of work are appropriate in light of the particular situation he finds in his classroom, most public schools have been unwilling to trust their teachers to this extent. Yet they have wished to organize a unit of work curriculum. In an effort to do this and still provide continuity, they have outlined in advance units of work to be taught, indicating the order and grades in which units are to be developed. A good illustration of this procedure is provided by the Denver course of study in *General Science and Earth Science,* grades seven, eight, and nine.

GENERAL SCIENCE

Grade 7B
(3 periods per week)

Unit   I. Air and Water.   36 lessons
Unit   II. Weather and Climate.   18 lessons

Grade 7A
(2 periods per week)

Unit III. The Heavens.   18 lessons
Unit IV. Movement of the Earth.   6 lessons
Unit   V. Changes in the Earth's Surface.   6 lessons
Unit VI. Geology of Denver and Vicinity.   6 lessons

Grade 8A
(5 periods per week)

Unit VII. Adaptation of Plants and Animals.   35 lessons
Unit VIII. Health.   20 lessons
Unit   IX. Energy and Machines } 35 lessons
Unit   X. Magnetism and Electricity }

EARTH SCIENCE

Grade 9B
(3 periods per week)

Unit   I. The Planet Earth and Its Evolution
Unit   II. The Earth's Surface

Grade 9A
(3 periods per week)

Unit II. The Earth's Surface—Continued
Unit III. Earth Materials and Their Service to Man [12]

The California state course of study in social studies for the elementary school also illustrates this procedure.

Social Studies in the Primary Grades
Unit I. The Home
Unit II. The Farm
Unit III. Community Life

Social Studies in the Fourth Grade

First Semester—Our California Home
Unit I. Water in California
Unit II. The First White Men Come to California
Unit III. Indians—The People the White Men Found Living in California
Unit IV. The Gold Rush
Unit V. California Today

Second Semester—Journeys in Distant Lands
Unit I. Travel by Men: The Jungle Region of the Congo
Unit II. Travel by Beasts
A. The Desert Regions of the Tigris, Euphrates, Nile
B. Grasslands of Tigris, Euphrates, Nile: The Oasis, The River Farming Region
C. Cold Regions of the Northland by the Sea: Northern Norway, Lapland
Unit III. Travel by Train: The Po Valley, The Alpine Region
Unit IV. Travel by Boats
A. Through Mediterranean Lands
B. Through the Lowland of the Rhine
Unit V. Travel by Automobile: The Plain of France
Unit VI. Travel by Airplane: Seeing the Polar Regions
A. The South Pole
B. The North Pole
C. The Story of Byrd's Flight

[12] *General Science and Earth Science,* Course of Study Monograph No. 2, Public Schools, Denver, 1931, pp. 19–20.

Social Studies in the Fifth Grade

Unit   I. How the Old World Came to Find the New
Unit   II. Peopling the New World
Unit   III. A New Nation in the New World
Unit   IV. How the Pathfinders Opened the Way Westward to the Pacific
Unit   V. How Invention Has Changed Our Way of Living
Unit   VI. How the Nation Was Nearly Destroyed
Unit   VII. How the United States Became Really United in Spirit
Unit   VIII. Why Our Country Is a Good Place in Which to Live
Unit   IX. Our Neighbors, North and South

Social Studies in the Sixth Grade

Unit   I. What We Owe to Southeastern Asia, the Cradle of the Race
Unit   II. What We Learn from the Excavations of Egypt
Unit   III. What Heritage the "Glory that Was Greece" Has Given Us
Unit   IV. What the People Who Lived in Italy Have Done for Us
Unit   V. What the Orient (China, Japan, and India) Has Contributed to the Occident
Unit   VI. How the People Lived in the Middle Ages and How the Nations of Central and Southern Europe Rose
Unit   VII. United Kingdom, Our Motherland—England, Scotland, Wales, and Ireland
Unit   VIII. The Sea-going Norsemen—Norway, Sweden, Denmark
Unit   IX. The Thrifty "Low Countries"—Holland and Belgium
Unit   X. Russia, the Land of Travail.[13]

An examination of both courses of study and textbooks, which outline the scope of work in terms of pre-selected units of work, shows that they represent a reorganization of subject matter. The center of organization is broadened to major topics. These topics may or may not represent definite segments of a recognized logically organized subject field. The Industrial Revolution, for example, is a topic generally treated in logically organized history and continues to find a place in scope of work as a prescribed unit of work. On the other hand, it would be

[13] *Suggested Course of Study in the Social Studies for Elementary Schools,* Department of Education Bulletin No. 13, State of California, 1933, p. vii.

difficult to find some units included by this method represented in organized subject fields. Often, however, there is striking similarity between the major topics treated by better texts organized in the traditional way and the units of work in texts organized on the unit basis. For example, the following titles are from a text organized by units of work and from another text not organized by units.

Units of Work in Text *A*

1. Europeans Find the Red Man's Continent.
2. Europeans Settle in the New World.
3. The Struggle for the Red Man's Continent.
4. America's First Steps Toward Democracy.
5. Life in the New States and the Great Westward Movement.
6. The Industrial Revolution in America.
7. The Northern Industrial Zone Versus the Cotton Kingdom.
8. The Age of Big Business: 1865–1914.
9. The Industrial Revolution and the Worker.
10. American Foreign Expansion and the Era of Prosperity.

Parts of Text *B*

1. The Colonial Period.
2. Conflict and Independence.
3. The Union and National Life.
4. The West and Jacksonian Democracy.
5. Democracy and Conflict.
6. National Growth and World Politics.
7. Progressive Democracy and Foreign Relations.

The unit of work procedure is like the subject matter procedure in that scope of work is outlined in terms of phases of the group culture to be treated. It differs from the subject matter procedure in three particulars. First, the phases of culture are larger than in the subject matter procedure; second, pupils' interests may be considered in selecting units of work; third, logically organized subject matter is not required. These differences provide greatly increased flexibility for the teacher. Since it becomes necessary for the teacher to deal with larger topics than is required by the subject matter or textbook procedure, he must organize for particular teaching situations the materials related to these topics. It gives opportunity to employ materials from various subjects and various chronological periods. Thus, although the prescribed unit does indicate bodies of subject matter or culture areas with which the teacher must deal, it permits considerable freedom within these areas.

There is, however, nothing in prescribed units to necessitate a materially different type of classroom instruction than is required by the textbook procedure. For example, a popular unit of work of the prescribed type is one on Holland. It seems probable that it would make relatively little difference to many teachers whether they are told to teach Holland as a unit of work or as a major topic in geography and history.

To summarize, the organization of scope around prescribed units of work may be characterized as a development of a larger topical organization of subject matter which may be very much more flexible than the textbook procedure, but which has in it possibilities of becoming just as rigid as the previously employed smaller units of subject matter.

THEME PROCEDURE

The general plan of the theme procedure is to organize the curriculum around certain of the most important generalizations employed by adults in interpreting contemporary life. This procedure has been employed exclusively in defining the scope of the social studies curriculum. It is based on work by Billings who studied the generalizations basic to the social studies. He suggests that the numerous generalizations in social studies may be classified under certain broad concepts which he refers to as themes. He suggests also that the subject matter of social studies can be conveniently centered and organized around these themes and that the themes thus will greatly aid the curriculum maker "in perfecting the organization and bringing about the unity of the courses he prepares." [14] This suggestion has been

[14] Neal Billings, *A Determination of Generalizations Basic to the Social Studies Curriculum,* Warwick and York, 1929, p. 211.

followed in certain curriculum work and the scope of the curriculum in social studies has been determined by themes.

The general procedure is to select themes, usually a rather limited number, which are to control the social studies program. This is followed by indicating on each grade level the aspects of the various themes that are to be treated. These aspects are then made the major point of reference in selecting activities and subject matter.

An illustration of the way in which the theme procedure operates is provided by the South Dakota course of study in social studies, in which the procedure is applied with care. Concerning the themes basic to the program, the following statement is made:

Themes Basic to the Program

The themes or generalizations used in this program are few in number but they represent those most fundamental ones that the adult mind uses constantly in interpreting contemporary life. Because these themes are abstract and difficult they are presented through a definite body of material that is adapted to the pupil's level of interest and experience and is considered suitable for the development of the theme idea. These ideas or themes need to be presented many times but always through new and fresh materials. For this reason only a limited number can be developed in the elementary school. This program groups all the materials of the social studies around the following five themes, each of which is variously stated to represent its different aspects and each of which is developed through different units written on different grade levels. The themes used are as follows:

> The Interdependence Theme
> Man's Increasing Control Over Nature Theme
> The Adaptation Theme
> The Population Theme
> The Democracy Theme [15]

The way in which these themes are allocated to grade levels is shown in Chart II.

After aspects of themes are stated for the grade, instructional

[15] *Social Studies Course of Study for Primary Grades,* South Dakota Department of Education, 1931, pp. 12–14.

CHART II

SCOPE OF THE SOUTH DAKOTA STATE PROGRAM IN SOCIAL STUDIES

Themes Controlling the Social Studies Program	Grade I	Grade II	Grade III	Grade IV	Grade V	Grade VI	Grade VII	Grade VIII
	Aspects of the Theme to be Developed	Aspects of the Theme to be Developed	Aspects of the Theme to be Developed	Aspects of the Theme to be Developed	Aspects of the Theme to be Developed	Aspects of the Theme to be Developed	Aspects of the Theme to be Developed	Aspects of the Theme to be Developed
The Increasing Interdependence of Groups of People	The Interdependence of the Members of a Family Group. The Interdependence of the Family and Farm Workers.	The Interdependence of the Family and Community Workers. A. A Study of the Rural Family. B. A Study of the Town Family.	The Increasing Interdependence of Different Groups of the Community.	The Increasing Interdependence of Communities and the World at Large.	The Increasing Interdependence of the Family and Local Community.	The Increasing Interdependence of Communities and the World at Large.	The Increasing Interdependence of Communities and the World at Large.	The Increasing Interdependence of Communities and the World at Large.
The Necessity of Man's Adaptation to Meet the Requirements of Subsistence, the Pressure of Competing Groups and the Conditions Implicit in Change			The Physical Environment Tends to Determine the Modes of Living. Pioneers Adapt Themselves to Conditions.	The Tendency of the Physical Environment to Determine Modes of Living and Man's Relation to the Sun. Land Forms. Surface Features.	The Tendency of the Physical Environment to Determine Industries of the People.	The Tendency of the Physical Environment to Determine the Industries of the People.	The Pressure of Competing Nations Brings Adaptation to Changing Conditions. Failure to Adapt Themselves to Changing Conditions Results in Conquests, Absorption or Transformation of People or Nations.	The Pressure of Competing Nations Brings Adaptation to Changing Conditions. The Pressure of Competing Groups Brings the Necessity for Change.

Man's Increasing Control over Nature	Man's Early Control of the Soil. How Man has Learned to Control Nature through Use of the Sea. Control over Nature Gives Leisure for Culture.	Making the Available Natural Resources of the Earth. Man's Control over Nature through the Application of Scientific Knowledge and Method.	Improving the Standard of Living by Making Available the Resources of the Earth. Man's Control over Nature through the Application of Scientific Knowledge and Method.	Controlling Nature through Use of Fire, Water, Metals, Animals, and the Soil. Man's Control over Nature through the Application of Scientific Knowledge and Method.	Man has Increased His Control over Nature by the Application of Scientific Knowledge and Method. The Control of Nature through the Application of Scientific Knowledge and Method.
Man's Tendency to Move From Place to Place in Quest of a Higher Standard of Living	The Tendency of Simple Independent People to Wander About without Definite Destination.	The Tendency of Established People to Migrate with Definite Destinations in Mind. The Tendency of People to Migrate with Definite Destinations in Mind.	The Tendency of People to Migrate with Definite Destinations in Mind.	The Tendency of Nations to Expand Their Boundaries.	The Tendency of Nations to Expand Their Boundaries.
The Inevitable Progress of Democracy		The Tendency of People to Demand Political Democracy.	The Tendency of People to Strive to Keep Political Democracy.	The Tendency of People to Demand Political Democracy.	

materials are canvassed to discover those suitable for developing the several aspects of themes. On the basis of this canvass, units of work are prescribed for each grade. The prescribed units are referred to as course of study units and teachers are directed to develop their own teaching units. This overcomes, in part at least, the objections to prescribed units. In some programs other than South Dakota the units prescribed to develop particular themes appear to be intended as teaching units. In these latter cases, of course, the theme procedure is subject to the same criticisms as the prescribed unit procedure.

There are a number of points about this procedure which merit attention. In the first place, there appears to be some confusion between themes and aims of education. In some cases the same generalization is stated both as an aim and as a theme. For example, one general objective stated in the South Dakota course of study is "To Develop an Understanding of Interdependence Plus a Feeling of Membership in the World Community." One of the themes, it will be noted, is "The Increasing Interdependence of Groups of People." This makes it appear that themes and objectives are essentially the same. Yet, both themes and objectives are given. When the units of work are organized, the heading includes the *theme, theme aspect, generalizations,* and *objectives.*

A further problem is encountered in the allocation of themes to the respective grades. Grades one and two, for example, are supposed to deal only with one theme, while grade three deals only with two themes. The assumption is that in the South Dakota social studies course the entire work of grades one and two is for the purpose of developing the theme, "The Increasing Interdependence of Groups of People." Yet examination of the work outlined for the first and second grades indicates that the beginning of the development of a number of basic generalizations would be required in addition to the one on interdependence. When units of work are prescribed to develop particular themes this becomes clearer. For example, in the scope of the curriculum of the Houston, Texas, schools, which is developed on the theme procedure, a unit of work in grade four—Life in Ancient Greece and Rome—is to develop the "Control over Nature" theme.[16] This unit is assigned six weeks. It seems obvious that generalizations not related to this theme and of equal or greater importance than those related to it would be required to develop this unit of work.

This plan assumes that work can be organized to develop directly particular basic generalizations or classified groups of generalizations, and that one particular basic generalization can dominate work for long periods of time. This is extremely doubtful. In fact, it has become increasingly clear that it is a mistake to permit a particular aim, whether it be a generalization or a specific ability, to pre-empt the attention of the teacher for a long period of time. Every learning situation involves so many abilities that it is only for short periods of time, and then in relationship to a larger general context, that instruction may safely be devoted to particular abilities, whether they be important generalizations or specific habits. Learning situations which result in the development of a significant generalization may more appropriately be related to a pattern of abilities than to a single one. In brief, the theme approach falls into the same difficulty that is inherent in the aims procedure. It assumes the overwhelming predominance in instruction of a major generalization or aim for long periods of time.

A further difficulty is evidenced by the lack of relationship between the various aspects of themes in a particular grade. Consider for example, the material in grade four of the South Dakota outline. The first aspect of the work of the grade deals with "The Increasing Interdependence of Communities and the World at Large." The second aspect is "The Tendency of the Physical Environment to Determine Modes of Living and Man's Relation to the Sun," "Land Forms," and "Surface Features"; third, "Man's Early Control of the Soil," and "Control Over Nature Gives Leisure for Culture"; and fourth, "The Tendency

[16] *The Scope of the Curriculum,* Curriculum Bulletin No. 2, Houston Public Schools, 1933–34.

of Simple People to Wander About Without Definite Destination." Definite time allotments to these four divisions of the work of the grade are made. The first one is allotted six weeks, the second eighteen weeks, the third nine weeks, and the fourth three weeks; yet, if there is any tendency for one of these divisions to grow into the subsequent division, this tendency is extremely difficult to discover. In fact, it appears that this vertical relationship does not receive consideration. Yet it cannot be denied that provision for this relationship is one of the very important requirements for the smooth, continuous movement of pupils through their work.

Another difficulty is encountered when the units of work based on these aspects of themes are examined. Even when course of study units only are prescribed and the teacher is directed to feel free to develop teaching units within course of study units in terms of the needs of particular situations, frequently the limitations are rather narrow. For example, consider the Houston fourth-grade outline of units:

Low Fourth Grade
Unit   I. Living in Temperate Lowland—Holland
Unit II. Living in Mountainous Region—Switzerland
Unit III. Living in an Insular Region—Japan

High Fourth Grade
Unit   I. Life in Ancient Egypt and Mesopotamia
Unit II. Life in Ancient Phoenicia and Palestine
Unit III. Life in Ancient Greece and Rome [17]

These unit titles are not dissimilar to the usual list of topics that might be encountered in the grade if the textbook method of outlining scope were employed. Topics in the South Dakota course, such as, "Colonial Life," "The English Colonies of America Demand Political Democracy—The American Revolution," "South Dakota History and Geography," "The Economic and Political Development of the People of the United States," also sound very much like the scope of work provided by the subject

[17] Houston, Texas, *op. cit.*

matter procedure. There appears to be nothing in this procedure which necessitates the inclusion in the curriculum of new industrial, scientific, economic, political, and social materials. It seems possible to apply the procedure with care and thoroughness without noticeably influencing the scope of work. Either the traditional curriculum organization is much less faulty than is currently held or this procedure is an inadequate means of discovering needed changes.

CENTER OF INTEREST PROCEDURE

The center of interest procedure places the emphasis on the interests of children. An effort is made through study of child interests to discover within what large phases of culture their interests tend to lead them. Interests, as is pointed out in the following chapter, may be indicated in terms of objects or activi· ties. Both objects and activities tend to group themselves in terms of various classifications of the group culture. Grouping may be in terms of social institutions, functions, ideals, or personal or group undertakings. These groupings may be called culture areas and, being areas which include activities and objects in which certain individuals are interested, they become for those individuals *centers of interest*. Thus, a center of interest is a phase of the group culture within which a variety of activities or objects of interest may be classified.

As the centers of interest of children on various levels are discovered, these phases of the group culture are allocated to grades. On the respective grade levels they serve to delimit the work of the grades.

This procedure is seldom applied alone but is usually combined in some way with another procedure. Even when an effort is made to apply it strictly, a great deal of difficulty is encountered in discovering enough data on which to develop a comprehensive outline of scope. As a result there is a tendency to fall back on traditional organizations, especially in the upper grades.

The San Antonio course of study in social studies illustrates this procedure in the lower grades. One of the principles set forth in this course is as follows:

Child Interest as the Basis for the New Educational Program

The school is setting up a program of work which has a personal connection with the immediate life of the child. It starts from his needs and interests and organizes its program around centers of interest rather than around academic subjects, except where life needs coincide with the school subjects.[18]

The scope of work follows:

Low First
   The child's games, pets, and toys.
High First
   Home life in the city and on the farm.
Low Second
   The community in relation to the home.
High Second
   Child life in other lands.
Low Third
   Primitive life.
High Third
   San Antonio, past and present.
Low Fourth
   Geography and history of Texas.
High Fourth
   World explorers connected with United States history, and geography of the countries that sent explorers and of the countries explored.
Low Fifth
   Geography of the United States and history of the United States, beginning with colonization.
High Fifth
   Interdependence of the nations of the world in trade, health, and culture.[19]

[18] *Social Studies,* Course of Study Monographs, Elementary Schools, San Antonio, Texas, 1929, p. x. Permission of Elma A. Neal.
[19] *Ibid.,* pp. xi, xii.

Whether one is willing to employ this procedure for outlining scope of work depends upon the emphasis given to pupil interest. If pupil interest is considered the one and only requirement for the study of a phase of culture, this procedure may be considered satisfactory.

SOCIAL FUNCTIONS PROCEDURE

A recently developed means of defining the scope of the curriculum may be referred to as the social functions procedure. This procedure is based on the assumption that the activities of children in school should be organized in such a way as to carry over with greatest ease to real life situations. This concept of organization of the instructional program suggests that the school program should provide in so far as possible for children to gain an increasing understanding of the issues and problems encountered outside the school, should aid them in developing desirable controls of conduct that operate in meeting such issues and problems, and should give them opportunity to participate extensively in such real situations. This procedure further assumes that an adequate program of education will provide for the introduction of the child to all of the important areas of activity in real life and will provide for his gradual induction into participation in these activities.

Study of group life shows that there are certain major centers about which the activities of individuals and the plans and problems of the group tend to cluster. These centers, which may be referred to as social functions, tend to persist and to be common for all organized groups. For example, certain of the activities of primitive tribes tended to center around protection of the lives and property of the members of the group. In group life today protection of life and property continues to be an important function about which many activities cluster and from which a group of related problems and issues arise. Since these centers or social functions represent points about which real life activities tend to gather and organize, it is considered reasonable that a curriculum which is concerned with guiding chil-

dren into effective participation in the activities of real life
may appropriately use these social functions as points for emphasis and orientation in outlining the curriculum. As the individual develops an understanding of the efforts to discharge
these functions in the past, and of the problems of the present;
as he develops ability to anticipate somewhat the problems of
the future, and actually participates in the discharge of the
functions in the present; he will become an effective member of
the social group, participating intelligently in the many activities required of him. It is concluded, therefore, that the curriculum should be organized so as to emphasize the major functions
of group life. It is believed that mere contact or acquaintance
with phases of culture will not provide this emphasis. The relationship of knowledge, facts, and principles to social functions must be established by the school rather than left to
chance.

The procedure is also based on the assumption that work in
all subjects should contribute to the development of an integrated
program of education. This does not mean that abilities organized for effective use into subject fields should not be so
organized, but it does mean that a core should be provided for
the curriculum so that all subjects may contribute to integrating
experiences of children. It follows from this assumption that
there will not be different scopes of work for the various subjects, for example, one scope of work in science, another unrelated one in geography, another in history, and another in language arts; but one scope of work to which materials from all
fields may contribute. It is also assumed that this core should
extend throughout the school life of the child. Administrative
organization, departmentalization and methods of promotion
should not be permitted to interfere with the development of
such a unifying core.

A further assumption upon which the procedure rests is that
the scope of work for given groups of children should be planned
so that the work will grow out of their interests. This, it is
held, guarantees effective and economical learning. It follows

from this assumption that pupil interest should be one determinant of the scope of work on the respective grade levels.

Use of this procedure requires three analyses. First, the
various functions of social life are canvassed. From this list
functions that serve in a major way as unifying forces of action
in group life are selected to serve as points of emphasis in outlining the scope of the curriculum.

Functions vary in one respect that may at first thought appear to condition their importance and influence selection, but
which upon further reflection is seen not to do so. Some functions require a great deal more organized group action for their
discharge than do others. The one mentioned previously, for example, the protection of life and property, requires elaborate
social organization in the form of fire and police departments,
courts, hospitals, and other such agencies. The activities of
these organized agencies are outstanding in discharge of the
function, while the self-directed activities of individuals appear
to play a much less important part. On the other hand, some
functions require a predominate proportion of self-directed activities by individuals rather than organized group activity.
For example, the expression and enjoyment of aesthetic impulses
are such fundamental human needs that practically all organized social groups have made some provision for such enjoyment and expression. To make such provision and to prepare
individuals to participate effectively in the activities involved
may be considered a fundamental function of society. Activities
involved in discharge of this function are generally self-directed
activities of individuals. This does not detract, however, from
the importance of making social provision for members of the
group to enjoy and express themselves aesthetically. Thus,
the term, social, is used in a broad sense to include those functions
recognized as important by the group, whether they be discharged
largely through organized action of society or by self-directed
individual action.

The major social functions, as selected, are employed to determine desirable points of emphasis for work throughout the

curriculum. A list of the functions selected in one curriculum program may be found in the first column of Chart III.

The second analysis is to discover what forces influence the discharge of social functions. It is through consideration of these forces that the child will come really to understand a particular social function; for example, how such forces as the westward movement, the development of machine technology, and social change have operated to condition materially the way in which society discharges its respective functions. Growth in understanding of contemporary life and in ability to contribute to social development depends upon the individual's ability to discover and understand how such forces influence the discharge of the functions of group living.

The third analysis relates to the interests, abilities, and needs of children on the respective grade levels. This is for the purpose of discovering upon what grade levels the various forces, indicated in the analysis described above, may be dealt with appropriately. Careful study is required of the characteristics of children on the various grade levels to determine the phases of group culture in which their interests may lead them and which their abilities make them able to deal with advantageously.

With the data from the third analysis in hand, the major forces discovered in the second analysis are allocated to grade levels as general limitations for the grade. They may be referred to appropriately as "centers of interest" since interests of children are employed to place them on grade levels. These major limitations are then applied to the functional phases of social life. The resulting statements are called aspects of the center of interest. The aspects to be emphasized on the respective grade levels are then selected. In making this selection care is exercised to see that:

(a) Growth in understanding of the functional phases of social life is planned from grade to grade;

(b) Materials are available for use of the children in dealing with the aspect of the center of interest;

(c) Children on the given level are of sufficient maturity to grasp the concepts required to deal with the aspect.

An illustration of the use of this procedure is provided by the Virginia state course of study as shown in Chart III. It will be noted that provision is made for both horizontal and vertical relationships; that is, points for emphasis within a grade are related to each other because they all develop from the same center of interest, and the work from grade to grade is related through the social functions.

It will be noted further that if particular social functions are omitted, the omission is intentional. Frequently this has not been true in the past. For example, little attention has been given to education as a social function in a democracy. Treatment of this social function has been accidental and no provision has been made for a growing understanding and appreciation of the place of education in group living. The shaken faith of America in education no doubt is due to considerable extent to this lack of attention. With the social functions procedure of outlining scope, such functions cannot unintentionally be omitted.

It will also be observed that this method requires the organization of instruction around points of contemporary significance. The plans and methods of improving group living become the core of the educational program. This is in direct contrast to certain methods in which the assumption appears to be that mere contact with phases of the group culture is sufficient guarantee of an understanding of contemporary life. The dynamic quality of the organization provided by this procedure necessitates the use of newer social, scientific, economic, and political materials, as well as the older basic materials. This difference becomes especially obvious as the work beyond grades one and two is considered. For example, traditional topics, such as, Indian life, Eskimo life, American Revolution, and the Industrial Revolution, have been supplanted by issues of direct relationship to contemporary life. Many of these issues, of course, require for satisfactory treatment the subject matter suggested by the fore-

CHART III

MAJOR FUNCTIONS OF SOCIAL LIFE *	GRADE I HOME AND SCHOOL LIFE (Center of Interest) Aspects Selected for Emphasis
Protection and Conservation of Life, Property, and Natural Resources	How do we protect and maintain life and health in our home and school?
Production of Goods and Services and Distribution of the Returns of Production	How do the things we make and grow help us?
Consumption of Goods and Services	How does our family provide itself with food, clothing, and shelter?
Communication and Transportation of Goods and People	How do members of our family travel from place to place?
Recreation	How can we have an enjoyable time at home and school?
Expression of Aesthetic Impulses	What can we do to make our home and school more beautiful and pleasant?
Expression of Religious Impulses	
Education	
Extension of Freedom	
Integration of the Individual	
Exploration	

* The order in which the major social functions and the aspects of the centers of interest for each grade are presented has no particular significance.

178

CHART III (*Continued*)

GRADE II COMMUNITY LIFE (Center of Interest)	GRADE III ADAPTATION OF LIFE TO ENVIRONMENTAL FORCES OF NATURE (Center of Interest)
Aspects Selected for Emphasis	Aspects Selected for Emphasis
How do we in the community protect our life, health, and property? How do animal and plant life help people in our community and how are they protected?	How do people, plants, and animals in communities with physical environment markedly different from ours protect themselves from forces of nature?
What do we do in our community to produce goods and services?	How do environmental forces of nature affect the goods produced in different communities?
How do we use the goods and services provided in our community?	Why can communities markedly different from ours furnish us with goods we cannot produce?
How does our community provide for transportation and communication?	How does physical environment affect transportation and communication?
How does our community provide for recreation?	How does the physical environment influence types of recreation?
What do we do to make our community attractive?	How do people in communities markedly different from ours express their artistic impulses?
	How do people in different communities express their religious tendencies?
	How do people in different communities provide education?

CHART III (*Continued*)

GRADE IV ADAPTATION OF LIFE TO ADVANCING PHYSICAL FRONTIERS (Center of Interest)	GRADE V EFFECTS OF INVENTIONS AND DISCOVERIES UPON OUR LIVING (Center of Interest)
Aspects Selected for Emphasis	Aspects Selected for Emphasis
How does frontier living affect the protection of life, property, and natural resources?	How do inventions and discoveries alter our ways of protecting and conserving life, property, and natural resources?
How does frontier living modify and how has it been modified by the production and distribution of goods and services?	How do inventions and discoveries affect the variety and availability of goods?
How does frontier living restrict the consumption of goods and services?	How is the consumption of goods and services influenced by discoveries and inventions?
How do ways of transportation and communication serve to advance frontiers?	How do inventions and discoveries improve our means of transportation and communication?
How is recreation influenced by frontier living?	How do inventions and discoveries influence recreation?
How are music, literature, and art affected by frontier living?	How do inventions and discoveries affect our art, music, and literature?
How is religion affected by frontier living?	How do discoveries influence the spread of religion?
How is education influenced by frontier living?	How do inventions and discoveries influence education?

CHART III *(Continued)*

GRADE VI EFFECTS OF MACHINE PRODUCTION UPON OUR LIVING (Center of Interest)	GRADE VII SOCIAL PROVISION FOR CO-OPERATIVE LIVING (Center of Interest)
Aspects Selected for Emphasis	Aspects Selected for Emphasis
How does machine production lead to the conservation and to the waste of life, property, and natural resources?	How do social and governmental agencies protect and conserve life, property, and natural resources?
How does machine production increase the quantity and variety and change the quality of goods?	Why are governmental monopolies established for the provision of certain services?
How does machine production of standardized goods influence the choice and use of goods?	How do social agencies influence the consumer in his choice and use of goods?
How does machine production affect transportation and communication?	How do methods of transportation and communication affect co-operative living?
How does machine production influence recreation?	How are social and governmental organizations extending opportunities for the wise use of leisure time?
How does machine production modify art, literature, music, and architecture?	How do social organizations provide opportunities for expression of aesthetic impulses?
How does machine production influence the developmentof the church?	How does the church function as a means of social control?
How does machine production influence education?	How does education function as a means of social control?

CHART III (*Continued*)

GRADE VIII ADAPTATION OF OUR LIVING THROUGH NATURE, SOCIAL AND MECHANICAL INVENTIONS, AND DISCOVERIES (Center of Interest)	GRADE IX AGRARIANISM AND INDUSTRIALISM, AND THEIR EFFECTS UPON OUR LIVING (Center of Interest)
Aspects Selected for Emphasis	Aspects Selected for Emphasis
How and why do nature and agencies resulting from invention and discovery affect the protection and conservation of life and property?	How and why does the change from an agrarian to an industrial order affect the use and conservation of natural resources?
How does man depend upon plant life, animal life, and minerals, and how do inventions and biological discoveries increase man's use and control of nature?	How does the change from an agrarian to an industrial society affect the production and distribution of goods and services?
How do inventions and discoveries affect the well-being of the consumer?	How and why do standards of living vary in agrarian and industrialized societies?
How do improved means of communication influence the behavior of individuals and groups?	How does the application of power and modern business enterprise to transportation modify our living and thinking?
How does man adapt his play to the character of the society in which he lives?	How can recreation lend significance and beauty to the common activities of life in modern society?
How do man's natural environment and his inventions provide worth-while opportunities for the cultivation of aesthetic appreciation?	How do agrarianism and industrialism influence the development of our artistic resources and the adjustment of all individuals to their use?
How does man manifest his religious impulses through social inventions?	How do religious organizations influence living in agrarian and industrial societies?
How does the home utilize social invention in the early development of standards of value in the child?	How does the American system of education contribute to the development of the ideals of democracy in our industrialized life?
How and why are men denied the freedom which social and mechanical inventions make possible?	How and why does the struggle for attaining the democratic ideal modify industrialism and agrarianism?
How can physical development and social controls promote the integration of the individual and avoid conflicts?	How can an industrialized society provide for realization of individual ideals and ambitions?
How does man's conquest of nature aided by the spirit of adventure lead to geographic exploration and commercial expansion?	How does the spirit of pioneering influence the development of equality of opportunity both in an agrarian and in an industrial setting?

CHART III (*Continued*)

GRADE X EFFECTS OF CHANGING CULTURE AND CHANGING SOCIAL INSTITUTIONS UPON OUR LIVING (Center of Interest)	GRADE XI EFFECTS OF A CONTINUOUSLY PLANNING SOCIAL ORDER UPON OUR LIVING (Center of Interest)
Aspects Selected for Emphasis	Aspects Selected for Emphasis
Why is advancement in the protection and conservation of life and property essential in a changing society and how can it be achieved?	How can nations through social planning guarantee to all the protection of life, property, and natural resources?
How can we improve production, establish an economic balance between production and consumption, and provide for a more equitable distribution of the returns of production?	How can nations plan for the establishment of proper economic interdependence by apportioning the production of goods and services and by distributing these more equitably to the consumer?
How does the advancement of science affect the thinking and the welfare of the consumer?	Used above
How do improved means of transportation and communication influence changing cultures and affect relations between nations and people?	How can modern means of transportation and communication be utilized to enhance the social welfare of nations and people?
How may changing ideas lead to the elimination of undesirable phases of commercialized recreation and promote creative recreation?	How can a planning society utilize increasing leisure time to develop recreation as a creative agency for everybody?
How do culture areas and changing social institutions influence the development of the fine arts?	How can a planning society improve the quality of living for all by utilizing man's desire for beauty?
How does a changing culture affect the church as an agency of social control?	How can religion in a planning society give stability to personality, and foster ethical business practices?
How and why does individual and social adaptation to a changing culture make necessary constantly changing emphasis in education?	How shall social groups plan to provide for their preservation and reconstruction through education?
How do changing culture and social institutions make necessary a changing concept of freedom?	How can a planning society extend political, economic, intellectual, and social freedom to all people?
How can the individual maintain mental poise in a rapidly changing culture?	How can opportunity for the integration of the individual in a modern social order be provided through organized means?
How do changes in culture result from social and intellectual pioneering?	How can we plan to advance human welfare and eliminate the defects of the present social order by scientific modes of thought?

Tentative Course of Study for Virginia Elementary Schools, Grades I–VIII, State Board of Education, 1934, pp. 16–19.

going topics, but this subject matter becomes a means to the end of understanding the plans and methods of our own group life.

This procedure encounters the difficulty of not having adequate materials available for the use of children to carry forward the study of a number of the aspects of centers of interest selected for emphasis. Until such materials are made available, work dealing with these aspects will of necessity be limited. Also, much greater familiarity with contemporary life is required than most teachers possess. Furthermore, many teachers, as now trained, do not have adequate background in the content subjects to deal with many aspects of centers of interest included in an outline such as the one in the Virginia course of study.

This procedure is also subject to the criticism that it places too much emphasis on the social phases of education and too little on the individual appreciative and creative phases. It may have this result unless the term social is used in the broad sense of group living, and purposes realized either through organized or unorganized social means are included in the analyses. When this interpretation is made, this criticism is less valid.

CRITERIA FOR EVALUATING PROCEDURES FOR DEFINING SCOPE

Evaluation of procedures for defining scope of work is complicated by the controversial issues involved. No criteria can be set up to which general agreement can be secured. However, the writers present four criteria that appear to them to be sound.

1. *Provision should be made for the consecutive, cumulative movement of children through the curriculum.* In the statement by Dewey, presented at the opening of the chapter, the point is clearly made that it is unwise to permit chance incidents to dictate the general movement of pupil activities. Such incidents may be of value from time to time, but the general course cannot rest upon chance, for such a basis is apt to result in disconnected and disjointed movement rather than in smooth, cumu-

lative growth. A satisfactory method of outlining the scope of
the curriculum must assure smoothness of movement and relationship of activities. This requires that general areas be indicated through which the growth of children may advisedly proceed.

Statement of the problem implied by this criterion in question
form may help clarify its application: Within what areas may
children of various levels of maturity and with various general
backgrounds most profitably be guided? When experiences of
children have been principally within certain culture areas, what
new areas will probably yield richest experiences? These questions suggest that the consecutive, cumulative movement required
by this criterion will be found through study of the growth of
children rather than through independent study of phases of
culture.

2. *Freedom should be allowed for the teacher to organize instruction around purposeful experiences of children of varying
capacities and abilities.* In the following chapter the importance of pupil purpose is discussed. One of the major responsibilities of teachers in directing instruction is to guide pupils in
the formulation of worthy purposes. Scope of work can be so
restrictive that a teacher finds this an impossible task.

This criterion guards against narrow limitations which restrict
unduly the development of children with various types of abilities. Educational outcomes depend to such a large extent on
the richness of activities in which children have opportunity to
engage, and progressive development so depends on interests fostered, that any plan of organization which unduly restricts individual pupil adjustments defeats the ends of education.

In application, the criterion requires that the culture areas
which serve to delimit the work of a particular group of children be so broad that their interests will touch a sufficient number of points to provide a variety of activities and a basis for
developing worthy purposes. It requires that the teacher have
opportunity to select subject matter that will serve as a means
to ends desirable for the particular pupils. Failure to observe

this criterion leads to the organization of instruction around some point other than the needs and purposes of the learner, admits mechanical teaching, and encourages learning by memorization rather than by association.

3. *The individual should be oriented to the aspects of the social life in which he must participate.* In *The Educational Frontier* emphasis is given to the importance of seeking in the operation of social life the fundamental basis for orienting the education of an individual. Three statements are presented which bear on this point.

> . . . conditions of the present social-economic situation . . . compel a course of study that uses as centers of orientation those aspects of the social life . . . in which the student must inevitably participate.

> What is now needed is . . . an orientation of the individual which cuts deeper than the surface of life. . . . The immediate point of departure for the school is that host of activities which bring to the family, and thus to the individual, food, shelter, clothing, recreational opportunities, and the like.

> In a planning society, the plans and methods of maintaining and furthering the life of the community would form the natural core of the course of study.[20]

The same general point was emphasized by Glenn Frank in an address given at a conference at the Century of Progress Exposition, in which he considered the needs and future of education. He stated:

> *First,* from one end of our school system to the other, we must rebuild our curricula around a spinal column of political, social, and economic studies which reduce to utter simplicity and intelligibility the plain principles of organization and operation that must govern the work of an age of science and technology if its magnificent mechanism for producing abundance is to serve instead of sink us. These studies must be organized, not in terms of traditional academic ob-

[20] From *The Educational Frontier,* by William H. Kilpatrick and others, pp. 67, 165, 170. Used by permission of D. Appleton-Century Company, Publishers, New York, N. Y.

jectives, but for the avowed social purpose of training a generation of citizens to play a productive role in the creation, comprehension, and control of a workable social and economic order in an age of plenty.

Application of this criterion requires that scope of work provide an organization which contributes in a fundamental way to the understanding of contemporary life and to effective participation in its many activities. It holds as unsound the assumption, so often dominant when the scope of the curriculum is outlined, that specialization in particular subjects is the primary concern in common school education. It implies rather that first consideration should be given to relationships of activities and subject matter to plans, problems, and methods of carrying on and improving the functions served by group living.

4. *A core around which materials from the various subjects may be organized should be provided for the entire period of school attendance.* Usually the scope of the curriculum is so organized that work in a large number of subjects is pursued independently. Materials in one course in no way supplement materials in other courses. This failure to establish relationships between the various subjects limits the fundamental understandings developed by the child. The result tends to be the acquisition of facts in relative isolation. An adequate definition of scope of work provides a core organization to which the various subjects can contribute. It eliminates the procedure whereby each subject is a wholly independent entity. It makes possible the development of an educational program for the child in which facts and principles from all fields may be related and brought to bear as need arises on problems and issues.

Not only would real integration of subject matter thus be achieved, but by defining scope for the entire period of the school life of the child without regard to various phases of administrative organization, the disintegrating influence of particular types of school organization would be obviated. In other words, the entire body of culture, the growing child, and aspects of social life in which the individual must participate should be the elements involved in determining the scope of the curriculum.

EFFECTS OF PROCEDURES FOR DEFINING SCOPE ON THE
INSTRUCTIONAL PROGRAM

The test, of course, of various procedures for determining scope of work is the way in which they influence the instructional program. In a great many cases, curriculum programs have set up elaborate procedures and have come out in the end with essentially the same curriculum organization and materials with which they started. This is especially true of the definition of scope of work. In numerous curriculum programs, much oratory and many heated discussions have been devoted to the new demands on education and to the inadequacies of the present instructional program. But when the curriculum program is over, more often than not, essentially the same instructional program remains. Examination of curriculum materials leads one to believe that it is not an uncommon practice for curriculum committees to work backwards from the answer they now have through the new procedure rather than to follow a procedure considered sound to its logical conclusion. In dealing with scope of work, this appears to be equally true of both "so-called" traditionalists and progressives. As curriculum committees meet, the one asks, "Where are Old World Background and Colonial Life coming in?" and the other asks, "Where can we include Indian Life and Transportation?"

There is pressing need for curriculum making programs to canvass carefully all methods of determining the scope of the curriculum, adopt the method which appears to be soundest, and follow it consistently. Then there will be less of a tendency for educational orators to get the table set for a new dish in education only to turn up in the end with the same old food slightly rehashed and warmed over.

All things considered, there is no phase of curriculum making that has received less careful attention than the matter of defining scope of work. Individual curriculum programs often do not follow a uniform method. Even within a particular subject variations occur. Careful study of this phase of curriculum making by curriculum committees and agreement on an acceptable procedure will do a great deal to eliminate confusion in the development of curriculum programs.

SELECTED REFERENCES

Bagley, William C., "The Task of Education in a Period of Rapid Social Change," *Educational Administration and Supervision*, 19:651–71, November, 1933.

Dewey, John, "Progressive Education and the Science of Education," *Progressive Education*, 5:197–204, July, August, September, 1928.

Houston, *The Scope of the Curriculum*, Curriculum Bulletins One, Two, and Three, Houston Public Schools, Houston, Texas, 1933–34.

Kilpatrick, William H. and others, *The Educational Frontier*, The Century Co., New York, 1933, Chapters V, VI, VII.

Morrison, Henry C., *The Evolving Common School*, Harvard University Press, Cambridge, Massachusetts, 1933.

Newlon, Jesse H., "Principles of Articulation and Functions of Units," *Ninth Yearbook of the Department of Superintendence*, Part V, 1931.

South Dakota, *Social Studies Course of Study for Primary Grades*, Department of Education, Pierre, South Dakota, 1931.

St. Louis, *General and Divisional Aims*, Curriculum Bulletin No. 1, Board of Education of the City of St. Louis, Missouri, September, 1926.

Virginia, *Tentative Course of Study for Virginia Elementary Schools*, State Board of Education, Richmond, Virginia, 1934.

CHAPTER VIII

PUPIL PURPOSES

Three phases of the procedure of curriculum development have been treated thus far: the discovery and clarification of principles basic to curriculum development, the statement of aims of education, and the determination of the scope of the curriculum. The statement of principles provides general guides to be followed in subsequent phases of the work in order that a consistent program may be developed. The statement of aims of education indicates the direction in which it is socially desirable for the growth of children to proceed. The outline of scope indicates general areas of culture through which growth of children may advisedly be guided from year to year. Attention is turned in this chapter to the purposes of pupils and the consideration these purposes should receive in curriculum development.

Brief reference was made to the purposes of pupils in Chapter VI, in which the relationship to aims of education was pointed out. It will be recalled that there are two types of aims which must receive consideration in curriculum development—the aims of adults who plan the educational program and the aims of pupils. It was indicated that the terms aim and purpose may be used synonymously and that the second type of aims, that is, those of pupils, would be referred to as pupil purposes. The brief discussion of the general nature of aims in Chapter VI applies both to the aims of education and to pupil purposes.

DOMINANT PHILOSOPHY OF EDUCATION EMPHASIZES PURPOSE

The importance of purpose in learning has been emphasized by the philosophy of experimentalism, the school of thought that has influenced to a far greater extent than any other the development of American education during the present century. Purpose is looked upon as that characteristic of experience which serves the general function of organizing, vitalizing, and relating the activities in which people engage and the objects with which they deal. It is the operation of purpose through activities which makes the difference between a mere series or sequence of acts and a "progressive co-ordination" of acts as means to an end. Activities and objects take on unity and meaning as they are related to particular ends or purposes an individual is endeavoring to realize. "The developing course of action," states Dewey, "whose end and conditions are perceived, is the unity which holds together what are often divided into an independent mind on one side and an independent world of objects and facts on the other." [1] This fundamental characteristic which purposes impart to experience makes them of utmost importance in the educative process, inasmuch as the meanings and ideas that children develop are thus significantly conditioned by the purposes which actuate activity.

When pupil purposes are ignored and the fundamental quality which good purposes impart to activities are lacking, highly mechanical procedures in instruction result. In such cases children do not have an intrinsic reason or purpose for engaging in many of the activities required of them. Activities are thus separated from purpose, and, as Dewey points out ". . . isolation of an act from a purpose . . . makes it mechanical." [2] The child in this case has no adequate basis upon which to judge the appropriateness of activities and can engage in them only as he is specifically directed to do. He is not permitted to grow in ability to make decisions and choices and the principal aims of education are thus not realized.

The point of view of experimentalism on purpose is summarized by Childs as follows:

---

[1] John Dewey, *Democracy and Education,* 1930, p. 162. By permission of The Macmillan Company, publishers.
[2] *Ibid.,* p. 167.

. . . man lives in a world in which the character of existence is such that intelligent, purposeful activity is demanded if he is to achieve a satisfying experience. In the second place, the experimentalist also believes that the nature of experience is such that the necessary condition for learning to behave intelligently is the freedom to engage in purposeful activity. By purposeful activity is not meant mere random activity in response to fleeting impulse. Purposeful activity is controlled, experimental activity. But the primary controls inhere in the subject matter of the situation of concern rather than in externally imposed influences. Purposeful activity is activity freely initiated by the agent in response to a situation whose difficulties have a challenging grip in his present experience. He frames his ends in the light of the resources and difficulties found in the actual problematical situation.[3]

PSYCHOLOGICAL BASIS OF PURPOSE

Psychologists have given a great deal of attention to the nature and function of purpose in behavior. On this matter there has been radical disagreement. Some psychologists have considered purpose the key to all behavior of the type usually described as conscious. Others, who have sought explanations for all aspects of behavior in physical structure, have rejected the concept in its entirety. For a time this latter group tended to dominate psychology. The result is described by Kilpatrick as

. . . a psychology better fitted to describe the movement of rats than to guide the richer lives of men. Under its influence education—unless otherwise counteracted—has tended to reduce itself to such mechanical processes as habits, skills and other assignable procedures. More recently measurement as the willing handmaiden of the movement has attracted many, particularly in the United States, by its promise of more efficient results. The actual result has been an even more desiccated dryness . . .[4]

Recently, however, there has been a renewed interest on the part of psychologists in that type of behavior described by the term purposive. This has been encouraged by further analysis

[3] From *Education and the Philosophy of Experimentalism,* by John L. Childs, p. 81. Used by permission of D. Appleton-Century Company, Publishers, New York, N. Y.
[4] Hilda Taba, *The Dynamics of Education,* Harcourt, Brace and Company, New York, 1932, Preface, p. xv.

of laboratory findings and the resulting evidence of the inadequacy of the wholly mechanistic explanation of behavior, even in animals. The result is that psychologists are giving considerable attention again to studies of complete units of behavior rather than to isolated activities alone. This development has been emphasized by Gestalt psychology which stresses the importance of "wholes" and that "parts" derive their characteristics from "wholes" rather than "wholes" being a summation of their various "parts." This point of view also emphasizes the concept of "insight" which involves the ability of an individual to select and organize activities in terms of an anticipated end or condition. This concept has much in common with the concept of purpose as described from the point of view of experimentalism.

The result is that the concept of purpose is now accorded much more consideration by psychologists than was given when the wholly mechanistic point of view tended to dominate the field. Fletcher, in a recent consideration of the concept as developed from the point of view of experimentalism, states:

Normally learning is incidental to the pursuit of purpose. This accounts, doubtless, for the fact that mere curriculum-stuffing is so barren of educational results. That learning is a process concomitant with purposive activities is one of the keynotes of progressive education. The psychology of it is unquestionably sound.[5]

Perhaps one of the most critical considerations of purpose in relation to behavior is presented by Troland in an extended analysis of motivation, an aspect of behavior to which purpose is intimately related. "Purpose," he states, "as it is understood by the man-in-the-street, is undeniably a factor in life, and no amount of introspection or physiological research can rule it out. A psychology which eliminates purpose cannot possibly correspond with the facts."[6]

[5] From *Psychology in Education*, by John M. Fletcher, p. 219. Copyright Doubleday, Doran and Company, Inc., 1934. Used by permission.
[6] Leonard T. Troland, *The Fundamentals of Human Motivation*, D. Van Nostrand Co., 1928, p. 346.

NATURE OF PURPOSE

Although psychologists rather generally agree at the present time that a significant aspect of behavior is suggested by the concept of purpose, they by no means agree as to the nature of this aspect. The minute distinctions which are drawn are of little concern to the curriculum worker. Yet it is necessary to have at least a general understanding of the psychological basis of the concept.

All behavior is initiated by a disturbance or irritation to an organism. This is equally true of the lowest and highest forms of life. There are a variety of disturbing forces that may bear on an organism. The most obvious source of disturbance is found in physical needs, although man is subject to a wide range of mental and emotional disturbances as well.

The sources of these disturbances to organisms are generally referred to psychologically as *motives*. It is often the practice, however, to use the term motive in a more restricted sense. When so restricted, disturbances which organisms experience are of two general types. "It is general custom," says Hollingworth, "to call brief and transitory irritants 'stimuli' or 'incentives' and to refer to the more persistent ones as 'motives' or 'drives.' " [7]

When an organism is disturbed or irritated, methods of various kinds may be employed to change the disturbed condition into a condition of equilibrium. Book states:

On the lowest level responses are crude physical and chemical affairs. On the somewhat higher levels the development of adaptive response is unsystematic and often very wasteful. On still higher levels the steps in developing a response are taken in a more efficient manner, not only because higher capacities are possessed and employed but also because better use can be made of the habits and skills that the learner already has acquired.[8]

[7] From *Educational Psychology*, by H. L. Hollingworth, p. 63. Used by permission of D. Appleton-Century Company, Publishers, New York, N. Y.
[8] William F. Book, *Economy and Technique of Learning*. Reprinted by special permission of D. C. Heath and Company, 1932, p. 36.

Dodge and Kahn describe the highest form of behavior as that which "invokes the conscious striving for purposes and values." [9]

The level on which an organism is able to respond so as to eliminate disturbances or to change conditions that annoy it, depends upon its ability to forecast the condition that will result in equilibrium, and to arrive readily at ways of producing this condition. As the levels of response become higher, the organism calls to a greater and greater extent on past experience to suggest what condition would provide equilibrium and the means by which such a condition could be achieved most readily. On the highest levels of response, past experience is called on consciously. The situation is examined and consideration is given to means of achieving the desired change. These various means are tried out intellectually, the ones that promise successful outcomes are retained, and those that hold no promise are discarded. Thus a plan is evolved to achieve the desired change most expeditiously. Carrying on the trial and error process intellectually rather than overtly shortens the road to successful reduction of the disturbance. Not only does it shorten the road, but it guarantees greater possibility of success. This mapping out of a course of action that promises most immediate and expeditious reduction of a disturbance is the element of behavior that introduces purpose.

Purpose, then, evolves from the disturbance or irritation of an organism that can recognize in advance what change in condition will result in equilibrium, that can predict the consequences of given activities, and that can organize a given group of activities so that a desired change will be accomplished. Thus, purpose involves two elements, *motive* and *plan of action*.

Psychologists have long recognized the importance of motivation in learning, and that different sources of motivation have varying degrees of potency in inducing behavior of a desired type. The importance in this connection of a plan of action, and its close relationship to the motive has not been so clearly

[9] Raymond Dodge and Eugen Kahn, *The Craving for Superiority,* Yale University Press, 1931, p. 16.

pointed out. Consideration of motive alone encourages unintelligent piecemeal action, while development of a plan of action without a motive is an impossibility. Hóllingworth makes this relationship between motive and plan of action clear in his recent treatment of the learning process. He states:

> When . . . a plan occurs in connection with a motive, the two together constitute a *purpose*. A purpose then is the symbolic representation of a mode of eliminating a motive. It is a technique of relief, a plan of salvation, tentatively mapped out and considered before its execution. Since purposes play so large a part in human life, it is important to be clear about their character. A plan without a motive is inert. But a motive without a plan is likely to be futile. A purpose requires the point of occurrence and synergy of a motive and a plan.[10]

PURPOSE NOT A DISCRETE PHASE OF EXPERIENCE

While the general characteristic of behavior described by the term purpose may be analyzed in the foregoing manner, it should not be assumed therefrom that the formulation of purpose forms a discrete, clearly marked step in experience, and similarly, that the other characteristics of experience represent separate phases or steps in development of experience.

In the various undertakings of life, a specific series of activities is not devoted to the development of purpose, then another series to the realization of the purpose, and still another series to the evaluation of the outcomes, even though these are all important characteristics of experience. Purpose starts in a small way and matures as activities directed toward realization are carried forward. It is subject to modification up to the very completion of an undertaking. Activities for realization of the purpose are engaged in from first to last. The outcomes of activities are continuously evaluated. In other words, these aspects do not represent parts of experience that may be added together to make

[10] From *Educational Psychology*, by H. L. Hollingworth, p. 72. Used by permission of D. Appleton-Century Company, Publishers, New York, N. Y.

up the whole. Rather, they indicate important characteristics of the whole. One characteristic may be much in evidence for a time and then another may become pronounced. The development of purpose is the dominant characteristic for the initial stage of experience. The pursuit of activities to achieve the desired end then tends to become dominant. And finally, there is a tendency to react to the total series of activities, or, in other words, to evaluate them. Thus, purpose may be considered one element of experience which interacts continuously with other elements to make experience what it is, but which is especially pronounced during the initial stages of an experience.

IMPORTANCE OF PUPIL PURPOSE

The influence of pupil purpose on learning has often been ignored by teachers and curriculum workers. Attention has been devoted so completely to getting children to engage in certain specified activities or to employ certain subject matter that little attention has been given to what the children were endeavoring to achieve by means of the activities and subject matter. This emphasis has often led to the use of sources of motivation ordinarily extraneous to the activities and subject matter involved, and to procedures that allow the child little opportunity to plan a course of action in order to achieve an end that he desires to reach. Apparently it is a common belief that any stimulus which causes children to engage in desired activities is a satisfactory one. In other words, the activity alone is considered sufficient to produce the desired outcome, and planning of his course of action by the pupil seems to be considered in many cases a useless complication of the educative process.

There is no more fatal misconception in education than this one. Not only does the pupil's purpose materially condition his present experience, but it also determines to a considerable extent the way present experience will serve as a guide to future conduct.

The type of behavior exhibited by an individual in a particular situation depends upon connections he is able to make between the disturbance he is experiencing and activities that may reduce it. If the disturbance involves stimuli to which the individual has reacted in such a way previously as to secure a satisfactory reduction of the disturbance, he will tend to react that way in the new situation or to develop a new response based on the previous one. Thus, particular ways of behaving depend for recurrence on the presence in new situations of stimuli or "cues" to the stimuli, previously reacted to. If the school secures particular types of behavior by means of stimuli that the child is unable to identify in out-of-school experiences, these types of behavior will not operate generally in life situations.

This relationship of particular stimuli to particular ways of behaving is of special importance in meeting new situations. Meeting new situations satisfactorily requires that the individual be able to discover in the stimulus of the situation elements or "cues" of previously experienced stimuli. Having discovered these "cues" he is in position to devise a satisfactory way of behaving in the new situation. Obviously, if the school employs stimuli that the child will not find in the new situations he meets in life, his behavior in the new situations cannot be modified by experiences he has had in school. Furthermore, unless the school provides him opportunity to meet many new situations under guidance, the possibility is small that he will be able to recognize in new relationships the elements or "cues" of stimuli previously experienced, with sufficient clarity to plan a satisfactory method of acting.

There are numerous examples of the tendency for teachers to overlook this point. Pupils present neat, well-written papers to the English teacher, but prepare poorly written papers for other teachers, and in out-of-school situations. In this case, the element which stimulates the production of a well-written English paper is extraneous to writing papers in general. It may be fear of a low grade in English, fear of the teacher, or some other extrinsic element, but since it is not present in other writing situations, it cannot stimulate the desired response of well-written papers in all situations. Similarly, a student may, through sheer fear of the teacher, respect the property of others at school, but fail to exhibit such respect in out-of-school situations. Not finding in out-of-school situations the stimulus of teacher fear, the child does not make the desired response. Fear of low grades is often employed almost exclusively to motivate work in the school. Often the result is that as soon as the student leaves school and the fear of low grades is no longer found in the stimuli to action, he ceases to engage in the activities learned at school. This accounts in no small way for the fact that many desirable activities carried on at school are not continued in life situations.

Studies of motivation suggest the importance of the end which the individual is endeavoring to achieve. These studies show how changes in anticipated results materially modify the performance of required activities.

Knight and Remmers conducted an experiment at the University of Iowa in which a group of freshmen and juniors were given a series of addition problems and similar exercises.[11] The juniors did the work under usual classroom conditions. The freshmen were told that the results would have a bearing on their fraternity standing. The freshmen averaged twenty-one columns of addition for each five-minute period of work, while the juniors averaged eleven columns.

Peterson had the members of a class copy twenty words from the blackboard.[12] They believed that these words were to be used later in an experiment. After the students checked the words, they were directed unexpectedly to turn the page and to write as many of the words as they could recall. The class was then given another list of words of equal difficulty and warned that they would be required to reproduce the words. Equal op-

[11] F. B. Knight and H. H. Remmers, "Fluctuations in Mental Production When Motivation Is the Main Variable," *Journal of Applied Psychology*, 7:223, September, 1923.
[12] Joseph Peterson, "Effect of Attitude on Immediate and Delayed Reproduction: A Class Experiment," *Journal of Educational Psychology*, 7:523-32, November, 1916.

portunity was afforded for studying the lists. On the second trial the students' recall was on the average about 22 per cent better than on the first, and after forty-eight hours, recall of the words used in the second trial was about 50 per cent better.

Kitson made a study of the output of journeymen printers. They were given a bonus for work above the norm previously maintained. During a five-month period these workers increased their output on the average 78 per cent. Every man increased his output somewhat and some increased it as much as 289 per cent.[13]

When such relatively minor changes in the ends to be accomplished influence so vitally the performance of activities, it seems that educational outcomes might be influenced in most fundamental ways by changes from a classroom procedure in which pupils tend to engage in isolated activities, each under the direction of the teacher, to a procedure in which they select activities and organize them because of their appropriateness for achieving a certain purpose.

GUIDANCE INVOLVES THE DEVELOPMENT OF WORTHY PURPOSES

The implication in the foregoing discussion is not that pupils have purposes in some situations and not in others; or that they have purposes under good instruction and not under poor instruction. Pupils have purposes in every situation where conscious behavior is involved. The difference is to be found in the quality of the purposes. From the standpoint of education, some are good, some are mediocre, and some are bad. The task of teacher and curriculum worker is to see that children are guided in the formulation of worthy purposes. To provide such guidance, a basis must be available for judging the quality of purpose. The following criteria may serve as such a basis.

The purpose should be one that requires behavior compatible with the aims of education. It is sometimes held that the ends

[13] H. D. Kitson, "A Study of the Output of Workers under a Particular Wage Incentive," *University Journal of Business,* 1:54–68.

of education will be realized if children develop strong purposes and engage actively in efforts to achieve them. There is strong reason to believe that this is an inadequate concept. There is nothing inherent in the nature of children or of their environments that leads them to develop only socially desirable ways of behaving. Social and anti-social traits are developed in precisely the same way. Strong purpose and intense activity may lead with equal facility to the development of either type of trait. The trait developed depends to a major extent on the *kind of purpose* held. Socially desirable traits will be developed if pupil purposes are compatible with the aims of education. This, then, is one of the distinguishing qualities of a desirable purpose.

This criterion may be applied by checking against the aims of education the behavior that most probably will be required to realize the child's purpose. If the behavior is the type required by the aims of education, one may have greater confidence that the experience involved will be educationally valuable.

The purpose should be one for which the plan of action can be based on past experiences. This second requirement recognizes that present experience is a reconstruction of past experience and that it can be rich and meaningful only to the extent that essential elements may be adapted from past experience. Thus, if a purpose is to lead to fruitful activity, it must be closely related to rich and vital past experiences. Lacking this relationship the pupil is not in position to make adequate plans to meet the new situation. His learning tends to be reduced to the trial and error basis, with small chance of a satisfactory outcome.

This criterion rules out the passing fancies of children. It indicates that desire alone to engage in a particular undertaking is not an adequate assurance that the experience will be educationally worth while.

Moreover, this criterion indicates the essential weakness of the type of teaching which strongly emphasizes the importance of securing vocal requests from children as an indication of their readiness to engage in particular undertakings. Vocal request at most is but an incident in the development of a worthy purpose. The teacher should look below such immediate incidental happenings to discover what substantial foundation there is in the experience of the children upon which to build further experience. Request and assent should be grounded in the experience of the children. Both should be dynamic, alive, constantly enlarging in scope and increasing in intensity as the experience develops.

This criterion also lays bare the fallacy in the statement frequently made that children can be interested in anything and, hence, that instruction may just as well be organized about one thing as another. Perhaps it is true that children can be brought to give vocal assent to almost any undertaking. But, as was just pointed out, vocal assent or passing desire to engage in an undertaking has little to do with the fundamental type of assent which has as a basis meanings, facts, and principles developed in previous experience. Even though it may be possible for the clever teacher to get pupils to request a particular undertaking, it does not follow necessarily, according to this criterion, that they are ready to engage in the undertaking. Thus, both passing fancies of children and requests extrinsically motivated by teachers are inadequate bases for developing desirable pupil purposes.

The purpose should be one that the pupil believes is worth while for him to achieve. Among the readily observable characteristics of behavior are the intensity, regularity, and persistence with which an individual carries forward activities. These characteristics are generally admitted as desirable, and, in fact, essential qualities of learning activity. Consequently, much attention has been given to the way in which these characteristics may be secured. The most satisfactory and only really effective means of achieving this end is to have pupils striving for something they really want to achieve and which they see requires the activities engaged in for success. The more keenly pupils desire to achieve a given end and the more clearly they see the relation of their activities to this end, the more intense, regular, and persistent will be their efforts. Bode states: " . . . there must be an aim or purpose that is 'internal' to the learning process instead of being imposed from without." [14]   It is this "internal" element of purpose to which this criterion applies.

The importance of this criterion is generally recognized. For example, one of the statements accepted by the committee that prepared the curriculum yearbook of the National Society for the Study of Education included the following sentence: "Learning takes place most effectively and economically in the matrix of a situation which grips the learner, which to him is vital— worth while." [15]   However, the extent to which the criterion can be applied in formal education is often questioned.   Counts holds a position subscribed to by many.

Learning is prosecuted most effectively when the individual identifies himself most completely with the thing to be learned. Only under these conditions is there neither dispersion of attention, nor dissipation of energy. Yet, that the purposes of education can be achieved wholly through interest of this type is a fatuous deception. A fair measure of the work of the world must be performed under the conditions of derived interest.[16]

Application of the criterion is complicated by the fact that the teacher has to deal with twenty-five to fifty individuals at a time.   The interests and abilities of the group are often so varied that situations rarely arise that stimulate the thoroughgoing concern of all members of the group.   Certainly their concern cannot be brought to a uniform stage of intensity.   Consequently, under the best of conditions, this criterion is more fully met in dealing with some children in a group than with others.

It must be recognized also that the extent to which this criterion can be applied with a given group of pupils is materially conditioned by the type of purposes the pupils have held previously.   If children have been stimulated by the fear motive

[14] Boyd H. Bode, *Conflicting Psychologies of Learning*. Reprinted by special permission of D. C. Heath & Co., 1929, p. 273.
[15] "The Foundations of Curriculum-Making," *Twenty-sixth Yearbook of the National Society for the Study of Education*, Part II, 1927, p. 18.
[16] George S. Counts, "Some Notes on the Foundations of Curriculum-Making," *Twenty-sixth Yearbook of the National Society for the Study of Education*, Part II, 1927, p. 79.

to carry on their school work, an immediate, precipitous about-face cannot be made. Sudden release from this motive results in pandemonium. This is inevitable because the children have no basis in experience for organized responses to stimuli based on other motives. Change must be gradual so that a basis in experience can be developed. That is, stimuli based on the fear motive must be gradually supplanted by other stimuli which involve purposes that meet this criterion. Failure of teachers to recognize the need for building gradually in the experience of the child the basis for observance of this criterion has led to unfortunate results and to conclusions that the practical application of the criterion is impossible.

In spite of the difficulties encountered in applying this criterion, it represents a most important characteristic of a worthy purpose and every teacher should strive to meet its requirements to the highest possible degree. Its application makes teaching a live, vital, exciting undertaking. Failure to observe it tends to make teaching a meaningless routine.

The purpose should be one that arises from stimuli of a kind the pupil will meet in out-of-school experiences. As has been pointed out previously, particular ways of behaving depend for recurrence on the presence in new situations of stimuli or "cues" to stimuli previously experienced. This is the basis of the criterion to which consideration is now turned. This criterion is especially important because the regimen of school makes it possible to motivate children in several ways not possible in life situations. Schools tend to under-emphasize the importance of stimuli which the child will find in other life situations. From time to time the school will find it necessary to employ methods of motivation that are to be found only in school situations, but the ideal should be to grow from this type to those that are encountered in many types of life situations.

Motives consistently overworked in school are fear of punishment, fear of ridicule, fear of teacher or parent disapproval, and desire for individual acclaim. For motives of this type others must be substituted, such as fundamental desire for achievement for the sake of achievement, concern for the good of the group, or desire to improve one's effectiveness as a member of the group. Motives of this latter type may be expected to operate in other life situations to bring about behavior of the type desired in a democracy.

The purpose should be one for which the pupil has mastered or can master in reasonable time the requisite abilities to carry on the activities required for successful realization. Nothing is more inimical to desirable educational outcomes than failure. Various studies have shown that past success and belief in the possibility of success in the undertaking at hand determine to a marked extent whether or not success is finally achieved. Book states:

> Nothing is more important in any instance of learning than to develop in the learner the habit of succeeding with every task that he is asked to perform. For a pupil to succeed, he must first of all believe that he can succeed and that it is worth while for him to do so. This belief is born of previous successes and is in direct proportion, so far as its strength and persistence are concerned, to the habit of success that has already been established in school and in life.[17]

Every purpose depends for successful realization upon possession of certain abilities by those engaged in the undertaking. The abilities required vary with each undertaking. They may range from specific habits such as ability to pronounce words, to knowledge such as ability to apply scientific principles. Whatever the abilities required to realize a particular purpose, unless the child masters or has mastered these abilities, his chances of success in the undertaking are small. Thus, it is important in guiding pupils in the formulation of purposes to see that purposes are not developed which lead to undertakings that require for successful completion abilities which the children do not possess or cannot master in a reasonable time. If undue time is required for the mastery of such abilities the force of the purpose will be impaired.

[17] William F. Book, *Economy and Technique of Learning*, pp. 95–96. Reprinted by special permission of D. C. Heath and Company.

The purpose should be one which requires behavior on a higher level than the pupil has exhibited before. When children are not adequately guided they may fail to see in experience the basis for developing more challenging and worth-while undertakings. Like the Irishman's mule, they may run too long in one spot. In evaluating pupil purposes and considering the possibility of their development, the teacher should canvass the activities that may be required to realize the purpose. Unless these activities promise opportunity for behavior on a higher level than has been experienced up to that time, the teacher should guide the children toward other undertakings.

Evidence that this criterion is being met may be found in the tendency for pupils to work increasingly for deferred values. One of the desirable characteristics of adult purposes is that they give attention to long-time consequences of acts and that the individual be willing to forego passing pleasures for outcomes of more permanent worth. In formulating their purposes children should be so guided as to develop an appreciation of the importance of such deferred values. If this criterion is applied, willingness to work increasingly for the future will be inevitable.

CURRICULUM DEVELOPMENT SHOULD PROVIDE FLEXIBILITY

The purposes that various groups of children formulate differ as their past experience, abilities, and environment vary. If a teacher is to guide children in the formulation of worthy purposes he must have freedom to take account of these variable factors.

Too often, curriculum making has been considered as merely a means of defining narrow boundaries within which teachers must work and specific ends that they should achieve. Courses of study, for example, occasionally go so far as to divide work to be covered into small time units. Review, examinations, and other details of this type are sometimes indicated. Other courses, with slightly less rigid restrictions, define rather narrow limitations of subject matter and prescribe sequences with which the teacher must deal. Such narrow restrictions make it extremely difficult to develop worthy pupil purposes.

Curriculum making can help correct this situation by developing a more flexible program and by providing many suggestions for teachers out of which they are permitted to select those that are appropriate for given situations. Much can also be done to direct the teacher's attention to the pupil as the central factor in the instructional program. The ideal for curriculum development should be to provide a wealth of suggestions for teachers at all points without undue restrictions at any point.

Although teachers should be permitted freedom to guide children so as to meet individual needs, materials should be provided to encourage the intelligent use of this freedom. The provision of such materials is a major task in curriculum development. We now turn to materials that can be provided to assist the teacher to guide children in the formulation of worthy purposes.

AIMS OF EDUCATION AND WORTHY PURPOSES

A definite, clear-cut statement of aims of education provides the teacher with the first essential material for evaluating pupil purposes. If the statement is so arranged that aims can readily be particularized, the process of evaluation is made relatively easy.

The use teachers make of aims in evaluating purposes is also conditioned by the accepted function of aims. We have already seen that one concept of aims is that they are definite ends to be reached. When so conceived, the teacher first of all decides what aim should be realized and then seeks means of achieving it. On the other hand, aims may be conceived as indicators for direction of growth. They tell not how far to go, or where to go, but in what direction to go. "How far?" and "Where?" are left to be answered in terms of the particular individuals who are doing the traveling. When this point of view is held, the teacher's attention is first directed to the pupils. He considers the various elements in the situation that will stimulate growth in the direction indicated by the aims of education. He seeks maximum growth rather than development to a specified point. If aims are considered as relatively fixed goals to be reached one after another, an element of inflexibility is introduced. If they are considered as indices of the direction in which growth should go, progress being as rapid as possible, the teacher's attention is directed first of all to the pupils to be taught.

ORGANIZATION OF THE COURSE OF STUDY AND WORTHY PURPOSES

A teacher may be assisted or hampered in guiding pupils in the formulation of worthy purposes by the form in which courses of study are organized. Two basic plans may be used. In the first, a definite instructional arrangement is presupposed. For example, it may be assumed that the teacher will teach a given textbook, covering it sequentially with individual recitations as the instructional unit. Or, it may be assumed that certain specified units of work will be taught in a particular sequence. Whether on the basis of class recitations, units of work, or some other unit, the course of study provides a definite instructional arrangement around which materials are organized. This arrangement restricts the teacher to a relatively small area at a given time in the development of the instructional program. It tempts teachers to resort to undesirable levels of motivation if need be to get pupils to work in the restricted areas.

The other plan for organizing a course of study is based on the assumption that each teacher will develop instructional plans especially suited to the group of children taught. Materials in the course of study are considered as sources from which the teacher will select that which is appropriate to develop a particular instructional plan. Thus, a plan of organizing materials in the course of study for ready reference supplants organization around pre-determined instructional units. Course of study materials serve to supplement teacher planning of instructional units rather than to eliminate the need for it by providing pre-digested materials. In this case the materials in the course of study are organized somewhat as a source book or encyclopedia. The aim is to make a wealth of materials readily available for general use, regardless of the specific enterprise with which various individuals may use them.

With a course of study of this latter type, teachers find it possible to organize the materials in the course of study into an instructional program based on the purposes of their particular groups of children. Thus, such a course of study is a definite aid to teacher consideration of pupil purpose.

PUPIL INTERESTS AND WORTHY PURPOSES

The most fruitful point at which curriculum making can assist teachers to guide pupils in developing worthy purposes is in connection with pupil interests. Just how this assistance should be provided, however, is an open question because of differences in belief as to the place pupil interest should hold in the educative procedure. This question has been discussed from many angles. Extreme interpretations of various points of view have many times obscured fundamental considerations. In addition, the use of "interest" with a variety of meanings has led to confusion. This makes it necessary for us to give consideration, first of all, to the meaning ascribed the term in our discussion.

DEFINING INTEREST

We shall employ "interest" to indicate the attitude developed through a pleasant or satisfying experience. Opposed to "interest" is the attitude termed "aversion." There are two evidences of interest: persistence of efforts to realize an end, and a tendency to continue to seek experiences of similar type. Conversely, "aversion" is evidenced by a tendency for an undertaking to be dropped as quickly as possible and by efforts to avoid future experiences of the same type. These attitudes are associated with either objects or activities involved in experiences. Hence, interests may be indicated either in terms of the objects or the activities that stimulate the individual. Fryer calls these objects or activities "interests." He states:

For this designation of interests as stimulating objects and activities in the individual's environment there is precedent from the measurement of abilities. The measurement of abilities consists in the measurement of ability expressions. The abilities receive their name, as do the interests, from the stimulating objects and activities. Interests are the objects and activities that stimulate pleasant feeling in an individual.[18]

To illustrate, when we observe a boy who seeks opportunities to play football and who plays with great vigor, we say he is interested in football or in playing football. If we observe him frequently working with diligence on arithmetic problems, we say he is interested in arithmetic or in working arithmetic problems. Of course, conclusions of this type are often misleading, for we may associate the activity with the wrong stimulus. The boy playing football so energetically may be doing so in order to get his picture in the paper or to even a grudge with a boy on the opposing team. The boy working arithmetic may be doing so to avoid the restraint of staying in after school. In these cases we would say the boys are interested in popular approval and freedom from physical restraint, rather than football and arithmetic. The fact that this type of misinterpretation is possible on the part of an observer, however, in no way changes the nature of the attitude in the one who is "interested," and, hence, does not affect our definition.

Interest, according to this concept, is closely related to pupil purpose and is fundamental to it. Upon this foundation, purposes are developed which the learner holds to be worth while for him to realize. Lacking a basis of interest, there is nothing in past experience on which to develop worth-while present experience. Under such circumstances present experience becomes largely meaningless or an imposed task. In either case, the ends of education are being defeated since the learner does not engage

[18] Douglas Fryer, *The Measurement of Interests,* Henry Holt & Co., 1931, p. 15.

in the undertaking at hand with persistence and continuity of effort, nor does he continue his activities when relieved from the pressure of the extraneous motivating force.

The place of interest in education has often been confused by superficial interpretations of the concept. Emphasis has been placed on getting pupils to state orally that they are interested in particular things and on the unusual things in the environment which may attract a child's attention. Things indicated as interests by these means may be interests of the shallowest sort. They may involve things with which the child has had no adequate background of experience, or materials with which he is entirely incapable of dealing. Pupil interests with which educational procedures should be concerned should not be thus lacking in depth. They must represent favorable attitudes based on ever-enriching experience. They must be discovered more by careful study and analysis of the experience and environment of the child than by the chance objects which attract his attention.

Interests, then, do not represent passing fancies or whims. They are deep-lying attitudes, developed through experience, which largely determine the intensity and consecutiveness of efforts and the tendency to engage in particular activities in the future. They are, when so conceived, a most important element in the educative process. As previously stated, worthy pupil purposes must grow out of pupil interests. Consequently, one of the first steps a teacher should take in guiding pupils in the formulation of purposes is to discover in what they are already interested.

DISCOVERING AND MEASURING INTERESTS

Considerable attention has been given recently, especially on the secondary school level, to means of discovering and measuring interests. Referring to this development during the past ten years, Fryer states, ". . . the measurement of interests has gone forward at a rapid pace. A decade ago there were no inventories and tests of interests. The early forms of many of those that we have today were just being given an experimental trial." [19]

The most commonly used method of discovering interests is that of having an individual give an estimate of his feelings. He is asked to record in written form or to state orally whether or not he is interested in certain objects or activities. This method has certain obvious limitations. Novel objects or activities may appeal to an individual merely because of the novelty, or the manner of describing the activity or object may exert undue influence. Moreover, an interest may be associated with a variety of objects and activities. This method depends upon the selection of a key object or activity from which the individual estimates his reaction. The reaction will be conditioned by the object or activity selected as the key for reaction.

These limitations may be made clearer by an illustration. Essentially the same interest might be implied by any one of the following terms: (a) rocks, (b) studying rocks, (c) analyzing rocks, (d) geology. A child might indicate an interest in *geology* because the term was novel to him, deny an interest in *studying rocks* because of unfavorable reactions to the word *studying*, indicate an interest in *analyzing rocks* because of the implication of experimental activities, and indicate no reaction to *rocks* because of the failure of the term to suggest activities to him.

Fryer concludes, however, that in spite of limitations on estimates of interests, such estimates are as valid as estimates of any trait. [20]

In an effort to improve the validity of interest estimates, various types of interest questionnaires and inventories have been developed. A list of such instruments is presented in Table XII. These instruments have been developed principally to assist in guidance, both educational and vocational, on the college level and in business and industry. They provide a stimulus to the individual to canvass his interests thoroughly, an easy means of recording reactions, and a basis for comparison. The Gar-

[19] *Ibid.*, Preface, p. v.
[20] *Ibid.*, p. 22.

retson-Symonds *Interest Questionnaire for the Guidance of High School Boys* is such an instrument for use on the high school level.[21]

Interests may also be discovered by observing the activities in which children engage voluntarily. This is one of the most satisfactory methods for the use of teachers. Interests so dis-covered are usually sufficiently well-developed to provide an adequate basis for developing worthy pupil purposes.

Eginton suggests seven ways in which teachers in practical school situations can discover interests:

1. Create situations in school where potential capacities and in-terests . . . may be discovered and given opportunity for self-ex-pression.
2. Analyze topics pupils choose for essays.
3. Observe pupil conversation in halls and on the playground.
4. Study out-of-school activities.
5. Interview the pupils to find how they spend their leisure time, what they read, and what they like to do.
6. Consult studies of pupil interests.
7. Provide a question box or designate a space on the blackboard for pupils to indicate what they would like to do.[22]

The Florida State Course of Study for Elementary Schools reports several methods successfully used by teachers.

1. Ask the members of the class to answer questions somewhat similar to these: Why do you want to come to school? What do you want to learn this year? Have you seen something lately about which you have wondered but about which you could not find the answer? What do you like to do at school, at home? . . .
2. Watch the children while they are playing or working during their free time. The books which the children use voluntarily, the objects which they make, the playthings which they choose, the groups which they join, and the free discussions—all give to the teacher an excellent idea of the things about which the children are concerned.
3. Talk casually to individuals and to small groups letting them take

[21] Published by the Bureau of Publications, Teachers College, Columbia University, New York.
[22] Daniel P. Eginton, "Discovering Pupil Interest," *Journal of Education,* 116:281–82, June 5, 1933.

the lead in the conversation. Occasionally when questions are asked, the teacher may make mental notes without comment. As soon as possible these notes should be recorded for future reference.

4. Give the children an opportunity to tell the others about good times they have enjoyed, about the interesting things they are doing or have done, and about the things they would like to do . . .

5. Ask the children to collect pictures which appeal to them or which they think would appeal to some member of the group. (These pictures may be brought to school and classified by the teacher for her own guidance. Other objects of interest may be used in a similar manner.)

6. Distribute to small groups of children catalogs from . . . mail-order houses and give the pupils directions for using the index. The teacher may watch to see what the children look for . . .

7. Talk to the parents to find out how the child spends his free time at home and the interests which his parents know about.[23]

Helseth makes the following suggestions about discovering and developing interests:

I. We may seek a well-rounded picture of the child.

   1. Find his physical, mental, and social status.

   2. Study his record at school. Analyze weaknesses and strengths. Trace back to causes.

   3. Enter into his playground hours and his free minutes at school as definitely as into his class hours.

   4. Know his home hours and his community hours by direct participation or by conferences with an understanding mother.

   5. Observe analytically the child's ways of responding—his methods of studying, of playing, and of reacting to comrades, situations, and materials.

   6. Discover what child reads, what games he plays, what responsibilities he carries, what he thinks about, with whom he converses seriously, what he does with scraps of time that he controls, etc.

   7. Observe mischievous or pernicious tendencies; study their instinctive basis; see if some happy expression of basic impulse may not be substituted.

   8. Read analyses of children made by others and consider their truth with regard to the child we are studying.

[23] *The Course of Study for Florida Elementary Schools, Grades I-VI,* State Department of Public Instruction, 1933, p. 13.

II. We may make *school setting* such that it will tend to bring actions connected with child's interests. We may then see and strengthen these interests.

    1. What child sees of classroom when he enters, should express *ideas* to him.

    2. Opportunity for *doing* in many different ways should be evident to child from classroom itself.

    3. What goes on in class hours, in auditorium, in library, in walks, in playground, in lunch room and corridors, should make a total meaningful experience to child, into which own planning and evaluating enter.

    4. Child should *see relationships* between his activities in the home, community, and school, and be free to express ideas he sees.

III. We may find *something to do* in which child and teacher can both be active in developing new interests and strengthening old interests of child.

    1. Should have connection with the particular child's past vivid experiences. (This does not refer to his past attempts at learning lessons assigned him.)

    2. Should arouse his particular tendencies to plan, to investigate, to make, and to enjoy.

    3. Should arouse imaginative and creative impulses of this child and not merely arouse habits of repeating or copying.

IV. We may buy, gather, borrow, . . . or make whatever is needed by child in order for him to investigate, to experiment, to express ideas and feelings, and to perfect skill. His reactions to a rich variety of materials will reveal and develop interests.

    1. Books.

    2. Visual materials.

    3. Practice materials.

    4. Tools.

    5. Raw materials.

V. We may find ways of individualizing our contacts with the child.

    1. *Many printed materials* may be used so that each child can have an "audience situation" with teacher and comrades when he brings forward ideas and facts.

    2. A big enough job may be undertaken by the class so that every child can find *something unique to do* within that job for class and himself.

    3. Enough reading and formal written response can be assigned at one time for children to have something formal to do when-

ever their personal plans or materials or abilities fail to permit further work on the more free activities. Teacher's time is thus released for *individual conferences*.

4. *Objective practice* materials with keys and charts of progress, usable again and again by same child or many children, may be bought and prepared. Child drills himself and teacher's time is freed for finding and developing his interests.

5. *Talents of every child* may be consciously sought and developed. Teacher may begin by listing at least one for each child, with plans on how to use in classroom, and note of material needed. (Conception of "talents" must be wide to include abilities with regard to: beautiful penmanship, water coloring, drawing, making illustrations with paper, woodworking, map making, modeling, dramatizing, imagining stories, hunting materials, school-housekeeping, keeping records, using reference books, making outlines, experimenting, leading in games, arguing, singing, reading aloud, checking upon results, planning for class, summarizing results, seeking better forms, etc.)

6. Specific help in removing causes or counteracting results should be given each child who has a serious weakness.

7. The *child's particular methods* of working should be *analyzed*.

8. Much of the teaching may be in small groups with ever shifting membership, each membership brought together for a very specific job.

9. Records on individual children may be kept constantly developing. In a folder for each child may be gathered data on forms, samples of work, bits of analyses by the teacher, and plans for helping the child.[24]

STUDIES OF INTERESTS

A large number of studies of interests have been made. Studies that may be used for curriculum development may be classified under the following heads:

A. Preferences of pupils for school subjects.

B. Preferences for various topics or objects included in a school subject.

[24] Outline of a chapter in an unpublished manuscript by Inga Olla Helseth, College of William and Mary, Williamsburg, Virginia.

C. Preferences of children and adults for various types of reading materials; *e.g.*, magazines, books, literary selections, poems, newspaper contents.

D. Preferences for colors, forms, and various types of pictures.

E. Preferences for various play and recreational activities.

F. Choice of vocation.

A. *School subjects.* Studies of the preferences of pupils for various subjects have contributed little of value to curriculum development. The fact that there appears to be no uniformity of preferences in different schools indicates that factors other than the nature of the subject tend to determine differences. Probably the teacher factor is of overwhelming importance. Without this factor controlled, studies of the problem are of little value. In fact, it is doubtful if they would be of much value under any circumstances. They are so broad in scope that no real indication is provided of what objects or activities are associated particularly with the interest. Hence, there is no indication of what type of curriculum development should be undertaken. At best, a general area may be suggested in which study is required more urgently than in other areas.

B. *Topics and objects in subjects.* Some studies have particularized the attack on pupil interests by studying pupil preference for certain topics or objects with which a particular subject deals. Thorndike [25] employed this method to try to discover what type of algebra problem pupils prefer. Curtis [26] studied the topics of science in which pupils are interested. He employed his analysis as a basis for developing a reading program in science materials.

Studies of this type are of considerable value in curriculum development. They suggest areas in which teachers may discover interests of children and in which materials may be provided. They are subject, however, to a limitation of technique

[25] Edward L. Thorndike and others, *The Psychology of Algebra,* The Macmillan Company, 1923, Chapter XVI.

[26] F. D. Curtis, *Some Values Derived from Extensive Reading of General Science,* Teachers College, Columbia University Contributions to Education No. 163, 1924.

discussed previously. Dependence is placed on the ability of the individual to associate his interests with key objects or activities. As pointed out, recognition is conditioned by the particular object or activity selected, and novelty may play a large part in selections. Even with the limitation of technique, however, study of the objects or activities children believe they are interested in is suggestive and valuable.

C. Reading materials. Interest in various types of reading materials is considered in Chapter X as an aspect of the problem of selecting subject matter. As is pointed out there, as early as 1902, Abbott [27] made a study of pupils' preferences for various classics. Since that time a large number of studies have been made of the reading interests of both adults and children. Studies have been made of preferences for literary selections of all types, magazines, books for recreational reading, and the sections of newspapers. Gray points out that "more studies have been made of the reading interests and preferences of children and adults during the last few years than of any other reading problem." [28] A survey of studies of reading interests up to 1930, is presented in a bulletin of the Catholic University of America. [29] Forty studies are recorded.

Recently the American Library Association and the Carnegie Corporation have sponsored some extensive studies of reading preferences. *What Children Like to Read* is one of these studies. [30] A list is given of recommended books for children of various grade levels of reading ability. Waples and Tyler made an extensive study of adult reading preferences. [31] Studies of this type not only exert a desirable influence on the content

[27] Allan Abbott, "Reading Tastes of High School Pupils," *School Review,* 10:585–600, October, 1902.
[28] William S. Gray, "Psychology of the School Subjects," *Review of Educational Research,* 1:333, December, 1931.
[29] Sister May Celestine, *A Survey of the Literature on the Reading Interests of Children of the Elementary School Grades,* Catholic University of America, Education Research Bulletin 5:114, 1930.
[30] Carleton Washburne and Mabel Vovel, *What Children Like to Read,* Rand McNally & Co., 1926.
[31] Douglas Waples and Ralph W. Tyler, *What People Want to Read About,* University of Chicago Press, 1931.

of the curriculum, but suggest types of interests that predominate during various periods of life.

D. *Colors, forms, and pictures.* Studies of preferences of children for various colors and forms have been made in an effort to secure evidence as to what types of art materials are of greatest interest to pupils. These studies have revealed the colors children prefer, the influence of saturation and brightness of color on preferences, the forms which children are most interested in drawing, and pictures children prefer. Gale's study [32] is one of the most suggestive for curriculum making. However, these studies as yet have exerted relatively little influence on practical curriculum programs.

E. *Play and recreational activities.* Considerable attention has been given to play activities which pupils prefer. Workers interested in both extra-curricular activities and physical education have dealt with the problem. One of the most helpful studies was made by Lehman.[33] He studied the play activities of several thousand persons of different ages. Activities preferred by boys and girls and persons of different ages were discovered. Lehman and Witty present a list of activities that pupils like, which also are of value in curriculum making.[34]

F. *Choice of vocation.* Careful and extensive studies have been made of vocational interests. These studies have as their principal objective provision of a more adequate basis for pupil guidance in the secondary school. Attention has been given largely to two problems: first, to the permanence of vocational interests; and, second, to means of securing the most accurate indication of interests. As a result of studies of these problems a variety of rating scales and interest questionnaires have been developed. Data that can be collected with such instruments may be employed effectively in curriculum development. How-

[32] Ann Van Nice Gale, *Children's Preferences for Colors, Color Combinations and Color Arrangements,* University of Chicago Press, 1933.

[33] Harvey C. Lehman, "The Play Activities of Persons of Different Ages," *Pedagogical Seminary,* 33:250–72, June, 1926.

[34] Harvey C. Lehman and Paul A. Witty, *The Psychology of Play Activities,* A. S. Barnes & Co., 1927.

ever, Koos and Kefauver, who present a critical analysis of these scales and questionnaires, give the following warning:

These interest scores supplement the results of the exploratory courses and other evidences of interest and capacity of students . . . These measures of interest should not replace other data but should be used only in supplementary relationships. The evaluative data are so inadequate and the extent of their use so limited that the present writers are disposed to urge both critical care and caution in their interpretation and use of these indications.[35]

THE COURSE OF STUDY AND INTERESTS

Materials may be presented in the course of study that will help the teacher to use interests effectively in guiding pupils in the formulation of worthy purposes. One means is through suggestions of things that tend to be of general interest to children of the particular age or grade to be taught, and, hence, to stimulate activity. These may be indicated either in terms of the object or the activity which is associated with the interest. That is, it might be said that a child is interested in reading or in books, in cooking or in food. In either case the meaning is the same. In the one case, the complete statement would be: Children of this age or grade, general background, and ability tend to have a mind set which leads them to engage wholeheartedly in undertakings involving reading. In the other case, the statement would be: Children of this age, general background, and ability tend to have a mind set which leads them to engage wholeheartedly in undertakings involving books.

Such suggestions may be made available for teachers in a variety of ways. An illustration of one way follows:

Grade One

Center of Interest: *Home and School Life*

1. If your pupils become interested in any of the following items, it will provide opportunity to initiate work that deals

[35] Leonard V. Koos and Grayson N. Kefauver, *Guidance in Secondary Schools*, 1932, p. 347. By permission of The Macmillan Company, publishers.

with *protecting and maintaining life and health in our home and school:* fire, toy fire engines, water, food, work of the school nurse, a doctor, a policeman, or a fireman, traffic signals and regulations, traffic accidents or accidents on the playground.

2. If your pupils become interested in any of the following items, it will provide opportunity to initiate work that deals with *providing the family with food, clothing, and shelter:* cafeteria, parties, school lunch, milk, pets, fruits, garden, play house, cooking, the work of the milkman or vegetable man, construction of a house.

3. If your pupils become interested in any of the following items, it will provide opportunity to initiate work that deals with *having an enjoyable time at home and school:* visitors, dancing, parties, radio, pets, play house, movies, songs, circus, birds, flowers, pictures, toys, musical instruments.

4. If your pupils become interested in any of the following items, it will provide opportunity to initiate work that deals with *making our home and school more pleasant and beautiful:* flowers, pictures, music, goldfish, furniture, curtains, bedtime stories, radio.

5. If your pupils become interested in any of the following items, it will provide opportunity to initiate work that deals with *ways our family travels from place to place:* boats, trains, work of trainmen, or street car men, automobiles, busses, street cars, airplanes, horses, wagons.

Suggestions of this type have the advantage of being very flexible. There is no suggestion that a teacher should force a particular phase of work. On the other hand, it is assumed that a teacher is able to study his own group of children and deal with them as a particular group. More careful inventories than those usually employed of the abilities and interests of the children taught would be required by this procedure.

Another way of assisting teachers to guide pupils in the formulation of purposes is to suggest various approaches to the units of instruction. The following suggested approaches to a unit of work on Holland illustrate the procedure.

Suggested Ways to Approach This Unit

1. Through a discussion of the sea wall at Galveston; why it was built, the manner of its construction, materials used, etc., which should gradually lead into the study of the dikes in Holland and the differences in their purpose, mode of construction, materials used, appearance, etc.

2. Through the study of some phase of art or literature that treats of life in Holland, such as: "The Windmill," by Ruysdael; the poem, "The Leak in the Dike," or Longfellow's poem, "The Windmill."

3. Through the use of lantern slides or stereoscopes which will cause the children to ask questions about the dikes, the wooden shoes, etc.

4. Through reading to the children one of the many interesting books about child life in Holland, such as, "Hans Brinker," "Marta in Holland," "Our Dutch Cousins," or "Holland Stories," that give vivid and accurate pictures of the land and the people.

5. Through placing pictures of the Dutch people in their quaint costumes about the room, or pictures of windmills, storks, tulips, etc., to call forth questions on the part of the children.

6. Through the discussion of modern problems such as those which follow.

Conservation through Careful Planning (Thrift)

This concept might be developed around the introduction of such problems in *arithmetic* as deal with the child's use of his own personal belongings and their cost as:

The average school child of your age wears out a pair of shoes costing about $6.00, every three months. Suppose that you plan to make every pair of your shoes last four months instead of three, how much could you save at the end of the year? This money might be used to start a savings account, or be used for something that you desire to have.

Other problems dealing with the breaking of dishes, or of discarding things that are still useful, might serve the same purpose.

The same principle might apply to the people of a whole nation in saving the things that nature has stored in the earth for us, which cannot be replaced when used up, by trying to plan for the production of just such things as will be used by the people without the waste of any. Do you know anything about the regulation as to the amount of oil that is permitted to be produced from our Texas oil fields? Should our government regulate the amount of things of this kind that may be produced within a given time? This is a question that is before the people today.

Let us try to find out whether Holland has used her resources wisely.

Through discussion of the location of the Mississippi delta lands and the opportunity that we have to reclaim some of it for useful agricultural lands, by:

Map locations of the region and the building up of concepts of the dangers of overflow that threaten this region at certain seasons. *Map interpretations* of the probable climate of a region that lies so far south, bordering a warm inlet of the sea, in a level region, and finding out what crops that type of region might produce if made available for continuous cultivation.

Discussion as to how the price of sugar might be affected if all this delta land were used for this crop.

We would not consider the expense of reclaiming this land unless it were profitable to us to do so. How could we decide whether it would be profitable? Does the United States Government have a department that could furnish information on such things?

Let us see whether the little country of Holland has done anything along the line of reclaiming lands in delta regions. Why has it seemed so advantageous to them to do as they have about it?

Individual Responsibility for Community Welfare

Through a discussion as to whether we are responsible for the traffic regulations; whether we are responsible in matters of preventing unnecessary waste from fires that might have been prevented; whether we are responsible for observing the regulations of the city and school health departments in observing the requirements that they set for us in the matters of vaccination, quarantine, etc. Let us see to what extent the people of Holland have a feeling of their personal responsibility in community welfare, by the way in which they live, and through interpretation of the poem, "The Leak in the Dike."

Government Responsibility in Social Welfare

Through a discussion as to why we have compulsory education in our country; why there are laws regulating young children's working in factories, etc.; why there should be a system of taxation. Compare with these the consideration that these problems have been given in Holland, through use of the materials in the content of this unit.[36]

This procedure has one outstanding difficulty. It necessitates the development of the child's purpose within a relatively re-

[36] *Living in a Temperate Lowland: Holland,* Unit IV, High Fourth Grade, Curriculum Bulletin No. 125, Houston Public Schools, 1930–31, pp. 2–3.

stricted field. It is obvious from an examination of the fore-going material that the children are going to study Holland, regardless of whether or not they are interested in the matter. The problem, then, is for the teacher to find a means of interesting them in a predetermined body of subject matter. In all probability the same difficulty will be encountered that has been met in organizing instruction around logical arrangement of subject matter. The most worthy and educationally valuable pupil purpose may cut across a predetermined body of subject matter. It may not be restricted to Holland or to any other single phase of subject matter, however valuable in itself. To force it into such a limitation reduces the possibility of developing a pupil purpose which the child himself believes is worth while and with which he is really concerned.

CLASS INVENTORY OF INTERESTS

Whatever provision may be made through development of curriculum materials for aid in organizing an instructional program based on fundamental pupil interests, the satisfactory use of such materials must culminate in the planning and execution of a type of instruction based on worthy pupil purposes.

To assist in the wise use of materials and information on pupil interests, each teacher should keep an inventory record of the interests of his class. Group and individual interests, passing and fundamental interests, should be noted. All available means of discovering and measuring interests should be employed to develop the inventory. The inventory should be cumulative and, when possible, information on the interests of individuals and groups should be summarized at the completion of a school year and made available for the next teacher. Such an inventory, along with measures of ability and capacity, may be considered the basic specifications for instruction arising from the nature of the child, just as the aims of education are the specifications arising from the nature of society.

SELECTED REFERENCES

Bode, Boyd H., *Conflicting Psychologies of Learning*, D. C. Heath & Co., Boston, 1929, Chapters XI–XV.

Book, William F., *Economy and Technique of Learning*, D. C. Heath & Co., Boston, 1932, Chapters XX and XXIV.

Burnham, William H., *The Normal Mind*, D. Appleton & Co., New York, 1926, Chapter XV.

Dewey, John, *Interest and Effort in Education*, Houghton Mifflin Co., Boston, 1913.

Fryer, Douglas, *The Measurement of Interests*, Henry Holt & Co., New York, 1931.

Hildreth, Gertrude, "An Interest Inventory for High School Personnel Work," *Journal of Educational Research*, 27: 11–19, September, 1933.

Hollingworth, H. L., *Educational Psychology*, D. Appleton-Century Co., New York, 1933, Chapters IV–V.

Koos, Leonard V. and Kefauver, Grayson N., *Guidance in Secondary Schools*, Part II, The Macmillan Company, New York, 1932.

Lehman, Harvey C. and Witty, Paul A., *The Psychology of Play Activities*, A. S. Barnes & Co., New York, 1927.

Monroe, Walter S. and Engelhart, Max D., *Stimulating Learning Activity*, University of Illinois Bulletin, Vol. XXVIII, No. 1, September 2, 1930.

Raup, R. B., *Complacency; the Foundation of Human Behavior*, The Macmillan Company, New York, 1925.

Troland, Leonard T., *The Fundamentals of Human Motivation*, D. Van Nostrand Co., New York, 1928.

CHAPTER IX

ACTIVITIES FOR REALIZATION OF PURPOSES

Purpose, as previously shown, involves a plan of action to bring about some end or condition an individual desires to achieve. A plan of action is merely a proposed series of activities so related that the individual believes they will result in the desired outcome. The appropriateness of the activities selected and the way they are carried forward determine the success or failure of an undertaking. Similarly, the educational value of the experiences depends upon the activities employed for realizing the individual's purposes. This being the case, curriculum making should assist teachers to guide children in the selection and prosecution of activities designed to realize their purposes.

VARIOUS INTERPRETATIONS OF ACTIVITY

The progressive movement in education has given the term activity wide currency in educational discussions during recent years. The term is used, however, with different meanings. On the one hand, it is used to indicate a particular way of organizing instruction. With this meaning, activity, unit of work, and center of interest are used synonymously. The term is generalized by reference to an "activity curriculum." Activity is defined in this way in the California *Teachers' Guide to Child Development*.

An "activity" is any large learning situation brought about by the strong purpose of a child or group of children to achieve a worthy end desirable to themselves, which, like those situations in life through which we are most truly educated, draws upon a large number of different kinds of experiences and many fields of knowledge.[1]

Carey, Hanna, and Meriam apparently found this a commonly used meaning, for in their *Catalog* they place in the same category, *Unit of Work, Activity,* and *Project.*[2]

The term, however, is often given a quite different connotation. It is employed in the psychological sense to refer to efforts of an organism to adjust to various conditions. When used in this way activity becomes of general significance to learning. This is recognized in statements frequently made to the effect that there is no learning without activity.

Many references to activities in the curriculum appear to use the term with a meaning that more nearly approaches this latter concept. Rugg and Shumaker refer to the "component activities" of a unit of work. They state: "The difference in range of activities, therefore, is only an obvious surface distinction between the unit of work and the school subject."[3] Numerous courses of study refer to activities that may be included in units of work. The Long Beach, California, courses of study, for example, which are organized around units of work, include lists of activities among the materials suggested for the units. The Virginia state course of study lists suggestive activities suitable for use in units of work. The Maryland state course of study in science in the elementary school gives in connection with each unit, "Things to Do and Talk About."

When activity is used with this more specific meaning it includes such activities as: reading stories, reading for information, making maps, making booklets, constructing playhouses, making rugs, carrying on specific experiments, such as making

[1] *Teachers' Guide to Child Development, Manual for Kindergarten and Primary Teachers,* California State Board of Education, 1930, p. 17.

[2] Alice E. Carey, Paul R. Hanna, and J. L. Meriam, *Catalog: Units of Work, Activities, Projects, etc., to 1932,* Bureau of Publications, Teachers College, Columbia University, 1932.

[3] From Rugg-Shumaker's *The Child-Centered School.* Copyright 1928 by World Book Company, Yonkers-on-Hudson, New York, p. 99.

oxygen, growing bacteria, observing plants develop, and keeping an aquarium. Obviously, the meanings of activity in the two instances are quite different. Using the term in the first sense, some schools may have activities and others may not. That is, some schools may employ the particular method of organizing instruction indicated by the terms "unit of work" or "center of interest" while others may not. On the other hand, activity used in the second sense is found in all schools regardless of the particular type of instructional organization employed.

Confusion has often arisen in curriculum work because of failure to make clear the way in which the term activity is used. In some cases it is used in one way part of the time and in another way part of the time. Lane says, for example, "The activity and the large unit of work are obviously the same thing, . . ." At another point he states: "In nearly every unit of work there are a few activities in which the whole class is interested; others which appeal to small groups of children and still others which have little appeal except to some individualist who does not care to work with the group." [4] Obviously, *the activity* is one thing and *activities* another.

Meanings are sometimes confused in discussions of the "activity curriculum." It appears that this term refers sometimes to the organization of instruction around dominant purposes of children and other times to the predominance of overt physical activity. For example, the California *Teachers' Guide to Child Development* states:

By the term "activity program" is meant a school curriculum which provides a series of well-selected activities for different levels of growth; which offers opportunities to children to engage in worth while, satisfying experiences while carrying out their most worthy and most challenging purposes. [5]

Stevens, on the other hand, indicates that the determining characteristic of an activity curriculum is emphasis on first-

[4] Robert Hill Lane, *A Teacher's Guide Book to the Activity Program,* 1932, pp. 5, 37. By permission of The Macmillan Company, publishers.
[5] *Op. cit.,* p. 18.

hand experience with people, things, and materials.[6] Freeman considers this emphasis the earmark of the activity curriculum for he states: "A program which involves a large measure of . . . overt activities is called an activity program."[7] Such diverse implications of the term activity when employed in conjunction with the curriculum make it especially important to use the term consistently.

In considering the foregoing interpretations of activity, it must be recognized that activities may be indicated on a variety of levels of complexity. One activity so flows into another and is so integrated with others that any breaking up of the whole appears more or less artificial. For example, suppose a group of children develop the purpose of beautifying the school grounds. This undertaking would be broken up into a number of more specific undertakings.

They might decide that the front yard should be leveled, that a sidewalk should be built from the door to the street, that trees and flowers should be planted, that containers for waste should be built for the school grounds, and that a garden should be planted in the rear of the school. Each of these undertakings may be considered an activity. Yet each may be broken up into a large number of more specific activities. For example, leveling the front yard depends on securing necessary tools, digging and carrying dirt, devising a means of telling when the ground is level, and smoothing and rolling newly filled-in dirt. Each of these activities might be broken up into still more minute muscular or intellectual actions needed for performance.

The possibility of indicating activities on such a variety of levels accounts for the use of the term in different ways. Nevertheless, it is important to avoid confusion in use of the term. In our discussion, the term does not refer to a method of organizing instruction. It is not used synonymously with unit

[6] Marion Payne Stevens, *The Activities Curriculum in the Primary Grades*, D. C. Heath & Co., 1931, p. 16.
[7] Frank N. Freeman, "Major Issues with Reference to Proposed Reforms," *Department of Superintendence Official Report*, 1933, p. 65.

of work. It refers to the efforts expended by an individual to modify conditions. Used in this way a unit of work, or for that matter any instructional unit, involves a number of activities. Considering our previous illustration then, the term activity is used to refer to leveling the front yard, planting trees and flowers, building a sidewalk, making containers for waste, planting and keeping a garden; in other words, to the several undertakings in which the pupils engaged to realize their purpose of beautifying the school grounds.

RELATION OF ACTIVITIES TO LEARNING

Activities have been so much emphasized in curriculum making that it is well to consider briefly the relation of activity to learning. Accurately speaking, life is but a continuous flow of activities, one activity setting the stage for the next. Education is achieved by participation in activities. There is no such occurrence as passive learning. Monroe indicates the relation of activity and learning thus: "It is only through engaging in . . . activities that the child learns. The teacher cannot communicate skills, ideas, facts, principles, and ideals directly to the student; knowledge is not transferred from a textbook to the learner's mind." [8]

Considered from the standpoint of learning, activities occur on various levels. On the lowest level they are physiological. They have to do with the growth of the body, bones, muscles, etc. A more advanced level includes activities described as reflexes, such as coughing and yawning. A somewhat higher level may be referred to as the observational level, while a still higher stage may be called the ideational level.

With this concept of the relation of activities to learning before us, we may consider a point about which there is often confusion. Active and passive schools have been so discussed as to give the impression that in some schools pupils en-

[8] Walter S. Monroe, *Directing Learning in the High School*, p. 2. Copyright 1927 Doubleday Doran & Co. Used by permission.

gage in activities while in others they do not. As a matter of fact there is activity in the most traditional classroom. Reading, reciting, listening to lectures, working problems, writing themes, taking examinations, and throwing erasers are activities as surely as building a play house or churning cream. This is true, although it must be recognized that the traditional concept limits very much the type and variety of activities in which pupils may engage in school, as well as their control over these activities. Melvin states the point thus:

This conception of the school activity of children as being chiefly listening and occasionally participating by answering of questions pertinent to the teacher's organization of the lesson, has had an enormous influence upon discussions of teaching procedures. Listening is an activity which is comparatively passive. The listener exerts no control over the form his conduct takes in listening. He contributes nothing to the organization of the elements of the situation. He only demands that the lesson which is being taught him be presented by the teacher with the maximum of clarity and effectiveness. He exerts no positive control over the activity in which he is engaged, but allows the teacher full freedom of organization and presentation.[9]

It is not a case then, of one situation having activities and another not having them. Rather it is a difference in the kind and variety of activities. The question is, Are the activities in which children in a particular classroom engage good ones, or are there others in which they could engage more profitably?

A further impression given by many discussions of activities is that overt physical activities are of predominant educational worth. As a result, hammering, sawing, building things, taking trips, making booklets, cooking, making rugs and furniture, and other observable activities have been emphasized. At the same time, there has been a tendency to hold that activities of a predominantly intellectual type are of questionable value. The fallacious reasoning that leads to this emphasis is indicated by psychologists as follows:

[9] A. Gordon Melvin, *The Technique of Progressive Teaching,* John Day Co., 1932, p. 227.

Psychology teaches that the mind functions through bodily activity; . . . in school, children should be moving about and doing things with their hands.[10]

Overt physical activities have no monopoly on educational worth. Intellectual activities which involve vicarious experiencing have an equal claim to consideration. The limitations of time and space make activities of this type an essential part of educational procedure. They should not be relegated to a minor position. It is true that overt physical activities may quite appropriately hold a large place in the education of the young child, but to assume that this type of activity should hold the same predominance in education as maturity progresses is fallacious. In all probability such activities gradually diminish in educational importance from childhood to adulthood and activities that are primarily intellectual become increasingly important. Probably by the latter part of the elementary school period the intellectual type of activity should become predominant. It is possible that failure to recognize the importance of intellectual activities accounts in part for the difficulty experienced in introducing progressive practices into higher grades. The effort to introduce into higher grades the same kind of activities that are suitable for lower grades and to evaluate work in higher grades in terms of the presence or absence of activities commonly considered desirable in lower grades has been unfortunate from whatever point of view it is considered.

In summary, the oft-quoted statement, "We learn to do by doing," is fundamentally sound. It suggests a truth generally recognized by psychologists. But, it does not follow, as is sometimes concluded, that some children are active and others are not, or that overt physical activities are of superior educational worth to intellectual activities. Rather, some children are more active than others, some schools emphasize certain types of activity and other schools other types, and the edu-

[10] E. H. Cameron, "Psychology and Recent Movements in Education," *University of Illinois Bulletin,* 28:14, February 24, 1931.

cational worth of activities is determined by the characteristics of the individual and the nature of the outcomes desired.

A VARIETY OF ACTIVITIES DESIRABLE

Schools have often fostered activities that are relatively value-less or actually detrimental. In traditional schools, the activities in which pupils are permitted to engage are often so restricted that educational possibilities are severely limited. Reading textbooks, preparing notebooks, memorizing facts, reciting, and performing routine experiments cover the range of activities in many schools. This gives the child little opportunity for direct first-hand experience and thus omits from the educational program an important vitalizing force. Such restriction also overlooks fundamental biological needs of children. For example, it cannot be denied that the young child needs opportunity for movement. When activities involving movement are limited unduly a real hardship may be imposed on the child and a general physiological condition inimical to effective learning may be developed.

On the other hand, schools often have children engage in overt physical activities without recognizing the educational value of such activities. Not infrequently, schoolrooms are encountered in which a heterogeneous group of unrelated activities is being carried on under the name of education, when it is obvious that the teacher does not see the educational value in these activities. Activity for the sake of activity appears to be the motto. There is in such a procedure little educational merit, for as Mursell states, " . . . *it is not the activities themselves which produce learning; it is their quality, their content, their aim, their meaningfulness.*" [11]

In practice, the effort should be to guide children in a wide variety of activities. Points of concern to the child should be approached from many angles. He should read, construct,

[11] James L. Mursell, *The Psychology of Secondary School Teaching,* W. W. Norton and Company, 1932, p. 62.

discuss, interview, write, model, survey, experiment, visit, paint, draw, build, dance, play, sing, observe, listen—use whatever types of activities are appropriate to deal with the situation with which he may be concerned. In brief, education should be liberated from the traditional concept of school activities and the curriculum should be enriched by employing any and all activities that will help realize those purposes of the child which are compatible with the aims of education.

APPROPRIATE ACTIVITIES

We have implied that some activities are desirable and others undesirable. Three points require consideration in determining the appropriateness of an activity.

In the first place, an activity in which children engage should be one that they can recognize will help them achieve an end they desire to accomplish. Unless the child can see the relationship of his activity to a purpose he wishes to realize, the activity is largely meaningless and the child will engage in it only under compulsion. As Dewey points out, ". . . action done under external constraint or dictation . . . has no significance for the mind of him who performs it." [12]   But if the child sees the relationship of an activity to his purpose and is able to estimate his progress toward realization of the purpose, he will tend to work persistently and to learn quickly.

In the second place, an activity should contribute to the realization of the aims of education. Many activities are not educationally valuable. These may be eliminated by testing their contribution to the aims of education. It is also important that a teacher recognize the particular contribution each activity in which pupils engage may make toward realization of the aims of education. With this relationship clearly in mind the teacher is in position to direct activities effectively. On the other hand, failure to recognize the educational worth of activities

[12] John Dewey, *Interest and Effort in Education,* Houghton Mifflin Co., 1913, p. 66.

may lead to their performance in such a way that they are largely valueless.

In the third place, activities should be suited to the physical, mental, and emotional characteristics of the individuals who engage in them. Little children should not be required to sit quietly for long periods of time, when their physical development is such that they require frequent opportunity for movement. Nor should they be expected to profit a great deal from activities involving vicarious experiences when they lack the background of first-hand experience which provides a foundation for interpretation. Similarly, it should not be considered necessary to provide a preponderance of physical activities when maturity has changed the biological structure, or a preponderance of first-hand experience when a broad background has been developed to make vicarious experience meaningful.

It is equally important in selecting activities to give consideration to the attitudes children have already developed. For example, failure is almost assured for given children if activities are selected in which they have failed consistently at other times. Selection of activities which children dislike because of previous experience leads to efforts to evade the undertaking of which these activities are a part. Belief in the possibility of performing the activity successfully and a real desire to succeed are essential prerequisites for undertaking an activity.

AVAILABLE ACTIVITIES FOR EDUCATIONAL USE

There are many classifications of activities. We have already mentioned one, that is, division according to the physical or intellectual predominance in the activities.

Another classification, sometimes used in curriculum making, is *approach activities, developmental activities,* and *culminating activities.* This classification groups activities in terms of the relationship they hold to undertakings of the children. A particular activity may fall under any one of these headings in different situations. For example, dramatizing a story might be an activity which stimulates children to find out a great many things about some point raised in the story and thus serve to initiate an undertaking; or it might be an activity employed to develop a plan the children had formulated after being stimulated from some other source; or it might be the means of bringing together in organized and culminating form a great many details brought out during efforts to realize a purpose. This classification is of value when the organization of instruction is considered, but a more detailed classification is of greater assistance in considering the availability, variety, and appropriateness of various activities for achieving pupil purposes.

There are a number of more detailed classifications of activities which have been employed in curriculum making. In studying such classifications it is found that the various headings are not mutually exclusive, that is, activities listed under one heading sometimes may be classed almost equally well under another. This, however, does not detract from the value of the classification, since these classifications provide only a general means of checking the range of activities.

The classification as presented hereinafter gives a good indication of the major types of activities available for the use of the teacher. As in other classifications, it will be found that the groupings are not mutually exclusive. However, they do indicate the dominant characteristic of the various activities.

Activities Primarily to Secure Information. A great many of the activities engaged in, both in school and in other life situations, are for the purpose of securing information. In the traditional school, activities of this type have received major emphasis. However, the variety of such activities has been much more limited than is necessary. Reading textbooks and listening to lectures have been predominant means of securing information. In the illustrative list which follows other activities of real value are given.

    A. Reading for information
    B. Listening to lectures
    C. Participating in conferences and interviews

D. Participating in discussions
E. Studying maps, charts, graphs, cartoons, pictures
F. Seeing slides, motion pictures
G. Conducting experiments
H. Taking field trips and excursions
I. Making surveys
J. Observing with regularity and care various phenomena
K. Collecting specimens

Activities Primarily to Organize and Present Information. As information is collected, it often becomes important to organize and present it to others so that it will be clear and understandable. These activities, of course, are carried on in close relationship with those to secure information. There are, in this group, a number of activities which merit greater attention than has been given them traditionally. Some, such as writing papers and making outlines, have no doubt been overworked.

A. Making charts, graphs, maps, cartoons, posters, friezes
B. Making booklets
C. Giving programs
D. Giving exhibits
E. Writing papers, articles
F. Making speeches and oral reports
G. Making outlines
H. Dramatizing
I. Debating

Activities Primarily to Facilitate Mastery of Skills. Activities to facilitate mastery of skills have received a large share of teachers' attention. Very often these activities are selected with inadequate consideration for economical learning. Much reliable information has been written about the wise use of this type of activities. In using them it is especially important that they be meaningful to the child. Activities of this type are more limited in number than certain other types.

A. Reciting
B. Memorizing
C. Working practice exercises
D. Taking examinations and tests

Activities Primarily for Construction or Production of Material Objects. A great deal of emphasis has been placed in recent years on the importance of construction activities. The passing of much of the work of production from the home has emphasized the need for formal education to give children acquaintance with production processes. Also the needs of younger children for first-hand experience and for physical movement have led to emphasis in the lower grades on activities of this type.

A. Constructing play houses, play towns, play stores, play post offices, bird houses, insect cages
B. Making furniture and toys
C. Making cloth, rugs, dishes
D. Making clothing
E. Preparing and serving food
F. Gardening

Activities Primarily for Creative Expression. It is held by many students of American education that our schools have provided entirely inadequate opportunities for creative expression. The excessive routine and strict regimen of schools have resulted in inflexibility that suppresses the desire of children to express themselves creatively. One of the significant contributions of progressive schools has been to show the great possibilities for work of this type. Mearns, Coleman, and others have shown that children can produce things of creative value if they have the opportunity and sympathetic guidance. Efforts have been made in many public schools to introduce creative activities. As yet, however, relatively little progress has been made in this direction. The weight of formalism tends to perpetuate the mere reproduction of assigned material. Activities in this classification undoubtedly should receive increased attention.

A. Writing poems, stories, essays
B. Drawing and painting
C. Modeling, sculpturing, carving
D. Singing, and playing musical instruments

E. Composing music
F. Dancing
G. Giving plays and recitals

Activities Primarily for Recreation. The increase in leisure
time and unemployment has led to a strong emphasis in education on activities for recreation. Consequently, numerous activities in this classification have been added to the curriculum in
recent years. Even so, it is still difficult for many teachers to
realize that the primary purpose of such activities is enjoyment.
Failure to realize this oftentimes causes these activities to be
so directed that boredom rather than enjoyment results for the
children. Activities in this classification will, no doubt, have
an increasing place in the curriculum.

A. Playing games
B. Having parties
C. Listening to music
D. Looking at pictures
E. Reading stories, plays, and novels
F. Going to the theatre
G. Telling or listening to stories
H. Singing
I. Having clubs

CURRICULUM DEVELOPMENT AND PUPIL ACTIVITIES

Successful curriculum development depends to a marked degree
on the guidance provided pupils in the activities they employ
to achieve their purposes. Examination of courses of study
suggests that often curriculum making has given little attention
to this point. Traditionally, courses of study have tended to
ignore almost wholly pupil activities, centering attention on required subject matter and reference lists. Some recent courses
of study, however, include many helpful suggestions on pupil
activities. Such suggestions provide a valuable source of assistance for the teacher and indicate increased consideration of
this problem as a part of curriculum development.

It is important that the activities suggested in courses of

study be so arranged that the teacher can readily associate them with undertakings in which children may engage. A heterogeneous list too often encourages teachers to have their pupils engage in unrelated activities. On the other hand, it is highly undesirable for the organization to be such that the teacher is inclined to use all of the activities suggested with a particular group of children in the particular sequence in which they are given.

The precise way in which suggested activities are organized and the points to which they are related depend upon the method used to define the scope of the curriculum. If the unit of work procedure is employed, activities, of course, are suggested for the units of work. On the other hand, in the social functions procedure, activities are related to the aspects of the centers of interest selected for emphasis. In any case the arrangement should be such as to encourage the teacher to select from the lists of activities given those which will help his pupils to achieve their purpose, or which will suggest to him other more appropriate activities.

An illustration of the unit of work organization is provided by material from the Long Beach, California, *Social Studies Course of Study for Junior High Schools*. The following is the list of principal types of suggested student activities for the unit, *The Westward Movement and the Growth of Transportation and Communication:*

1. Reading
2. Class discussion
3. Special reports
4. Committee work
5. Maps, graphs, and charts
6. Bulletin board
7. Debates
8. Illustrated projects
9. Dramatization
10. Slides

Special activities suggested for use in connection with various problems in the unit follow:

PROBLEM I

What movements and developments in Europe aided and encouraged discovery and exploration?

Activities:

1. Show on a wall map of the Eastern Hemisphere the extent of the Mohammedan empire. . . .
2. Be able to discuss two Crusades.
3. List the motives of the Crusaders.
4. Show on a wall map the crusading routes.
5. List the results of the Crusades with reference to the following:

    a. Ruling of the Holy Land
    b. Learning in Europe
    c. Trade and travel in distant lands
    d. Feudalism
    e. Effect upon the life of the wealthy.

6. Johannes Gutenberg and the printing press. . . .
7. Make a sketch of the world as we know it today. Show how the early map makers pictured the world.
8. Bring to class a compass and demonstrate its use.
9. Make an illustrated chart to show the relation between invention and exploration in the fourteenth and fifteenth centuries. . . .
10. Indicate on an outline map the type of regions which the trade routes traversed. . . .
11. List the products which were obtained from the East and show on an outline map the region from which each is obtained.
12. List the products which were returned from the West to the East.
13. Contrast by means of sketches, models, or cut-outs, the trading vessels of today with those of the Venetians in the Middle Ages.
14. Imagine that you are a Pilgrim who has just returned from the Holy Land. You have returned on a Venetian boat. Describe to the class the voyage from time of embarkation. . . .

PROBLEM II

What were the steps that led to the discovery of America?

Activities:

1. Reports on Columbus and Prince Henry the Navigator.
2. List the characteristics of Columbus which led to his success.

3. Sketch to scale or model in approximate proportion the *Santa Maria* and the *Leviathan*.

4. Dramatize "Columbus at the Spanish Court" before and after the first voyage.

5. Make an illustrated map showing the results of exploration up to the close of the fifteenth century.

6. Students write imaginary letters of Columbus or members of his crew telling of the voyage.

7. Motion picture "Columbus."

PROBLEM III

What other important explorations and discoveries closely followed the discovery of the New World?

Activities:

1. List the motives of the Spanish, Portuguese, French, English, Dutch in coming to the New World.

2. Make a list of the names of cities in the United States which bear Spanish, French, English, and Dutch names.

3. Make a time line showing the period of exploration. . . .

4. Make an illustrated map to show what the early explorers and discoverers accomplished.

5. Collect pictures to show the influence of the Spanish on the architecture in the southwestern part of the United States.

6. Make a map of the New World showing the territorial claims of each of the European nations who engaged in explorations during the fifteenth, sixteenth, and seventeenth centuries.

7. Show by a series of maps the gradual unfolding of knowledge of the world from the period of the Crusades to the year 1700.

8. Reports on the following:

    a. Voyage of Magellan
    b. Cortez in Mexico
    c. Conquests of Pizarro.

. . . .

9. Show on a globe the line of demarcation and the routes of Magellan and Drake in circumnavigating the globe.

10. Describe the experiences of Marquette and Joliet as they explored the Mississippi regions.

11. Dramatize

    a. The planting of the English flag
    b. Hudson entertaining the Indians on board ship
    c. Balboa discovering the Pacific.

PROBLEM IV

What dangers and difficulties stood in the way of the settlement of North America?

Activities:

1. Reports
    a. Seafaring today compared with seafaring in colonial times
    b. How Uncle Sam provides for the Indians.

. . . .

2. Make a map showing the early tribe locations of Indians in the territory now included in the United States. . . .
3. Sketches, cut-outs, or models showing the development of seafaring crafts up to the time of the Mayflower.
4. Students may select for developing an Indian project, either a single tribe or the combined tribes of one section. . . . Each student should prepare some form of class presentation of his project. . . .
5. Students may bring to the classroom for an exhibit a collection of any Indian articles which they happen to own.
6. Collect for the bulletin board clippings from magazines and newspapers on the Indian, past and present.
7. Make a collection of Indian pictures for classroom display.

PROBLEM V

Why did the English begin to settle in North America?

Activities:

1. Reports
    a. The Reformation
    b. Oliver Cromwell
    c. Life in England at the beginning of the seventeenth century.

2. List the reasons for colonization by England.[13]

Illustration of the activities suggested by the social functions approach is provided by the Virginia course of study for elementary schools. Activities suggested for only one aspect of a center of interest are given. Similar lists are given for other aspects in the course of study.

[13] *Social Studies Course of Study for Junior High Schools,* Long Beach, California, 1927, pp. 80–100.

CENTER OF INTEREST: *Effects of Machine Production upon Our Living*

Aspect of Center of Interest: How does machine production increase the quantity and variety and change the quality of goods?

SUGGESTIVE ACTIVITIES:

Reading about and discussing leaders of American industry

Writing biographies of men responsible for changes in manufacturing

Reading about, discussing, and reporting on the development of the factory system of producing goods

Making a motion picture showing the change from the domestic to the factory system

Discussing and making reports on the work of the master craftsmen, as goldsmiths, lace makers, and weavers

Reading about and discussing the growth of cities

Making individual bar graphs to show the increase in population from 1890 to 1930 of a large industrial city of the United States

Experimenting with and discussing the six simple machines that help control natural forces: lever, inclined plane, wedge, screw, wheel and axle, and pulley

Discussing the physiological differences between hand and machine labor

Making a time line showing the evolution of the machine

Reading about and discussing "sweat shops," where they are located, who works in them, how they affect the lives of workers, and the price of commodities they manufacture

Taking excursions to museum, factory, railroad shop, steamship line, where old and modern types of machines may be seen

Reading about, discussing, and reporting on the ways that human labor co-operates with the machine in modern industrial plants to assemble finished articles

Making reports on visits to industrial plants

Reading about, discussing, and reporting on the sun, moon, planets, and stars as revealed by the use of the machine

Visiting available experiment stations, such as those dealing with seed, fertilizer, feed, soils, and crops

Inviting county demonstration agent to demonstrate modern methods of canning goods and to discuss canning budgets for families

Inviting the county agent to visit the school and give a talk on "Why Rotate Crops?"

Reading about and discussing the effects of machines on preserving and canning goods

Reading about and reporting on the history of tools and machines used in the production of foodstuffs

Making a graph showing by ten-year periods from 1900 to 1930, inclusive, the increased production of agricultural products resulting from the use of machinery

Making a pictorial map of the leading agricultural products of the United States

Making horizontal bar graphs to show the use of land in the community

Reading about and discussing the development of farm machinery

Making a series of large paintings illustrating the evolution of methods of agriculture

Reading about and discussing the changes in rural life as a result of the machine

Collecting and exhibiting pictures to show how machines have influenced dress in the past century

Reading about, discussing, and reporting on processes used in making cloth

Testing and washing cloth

Dyeing cloth by primitive and commercial methods and comparing results

Reading about and discussing the life history of the silkworm

Making hand looms and weaving bags and rugs to demonstrate changes that have been brought about by the machine

Visiting an industrial plant such as hosiery mill, textile mill, and shoe or furniture factory to see how rapidly and cheaply articles for home consumption can be produced

Making a map of the United States, locating the leading textile mills and discussing the reasons for their location

Reading about and discussing the effects of the machine upon the production and consumption of synthetic goods (rayon)

Writing to industrial companies for exhibits and information on rayon

Writing and presenting a pageant about the development of the textile industry

Visiting antique shops, museums, and department stores to observe old glassware and standardized reproductions

Discussing the reasons for the increased quantities, standardized colors, and patterns of glassware

Exhibiting antique glassware and pottery with modern designs and reproductions to show the contrast and the similarity of design effected by the machine

Collecting pictures showing the development of the glass industry

Making tile or pottery utensils to contrast them with standardized production of the ceramic industry

Reading about and discussing the processes involved in the lumber industry

Making a chart showing the place Virginia occupies in the production of lumber and other raw materials

Collecting pictures and data on the "houses of tomorrow"

Discussing and reporting on the contributions of Bessemer and others to the steel industry

Reading about, reporting on, and discussing the principles of heat expansion and contraction in connection with modern steel construction

Collecting samples of machine-made building materials for homes and discussing their merits

Making sketches to show evolution of homes from cave days to modern times

Exhibiting pictures and samples of floor coverings, presenting the advantages of types illustrated

Reading about and discussing mass production of materials and designs in paper, cloth, furniture, etc.

Examining pictures of the beautiful crafts of earlier times, as the Mexican handicrafts, Greek vases, tapestries of the Middle Ages, gesso decorations of the Renaissance, jewelry of the Egyptians, etc., to appreciate the beauty of handmade things

Reading to find what health conveniences have been made more available as a result of the machine

Reading about and discussing the factors other than the machine that have assisted in mass production

Interviewing a chemist to get information on how petroleum is converted into various products

Reading about, reporting on, and discussing the origin and uses of electricity

Visiting an electric plant to see how electricity is made

Examining an electric dry cell to learn the use of chemical materials in the production of power

Making a shocking machine to show how the strength of electric current may be increased.[14]

CAREFUL EVALUATION OF ACTIVITIES NEEDED

Examination of the activities suggested in courses of study and observation of the work of curriculum committees lead to the belief that activities are often suggested without an adequate

[14] *Tentative Course of Study for Virginia Elementary Schools,* Grades I–VII, 1934, pp. 222–228.

basis of trial. Many activities are trivial and some are actually undesirable. Others of considerable educational value are often overlooked. There is need for more careful evaluation and trial of activities before teachers are generally encouraged to use them. This is one of the tasks to which greater attention should be given in curriculum development.

SELECTED REFERENCES

Borgeson, F. C., *Elementary School Life Activities*, Vol. I, *Group-Interest Activities*, Vol. II, A. S. Barnes & Co., New York, 1931.

Cameron, E. H., *Psychology and Recent Movements in Education*, University of Illinois Bulletin, No. 26, 28:12–17, November 20, 1930.

Carey, Alice; Hanna, Paul R.; and Meriam, J. L., *Catalog: Units of Work, Activities, Projects, etc., to 1932*, Bureau of Publications, Teachers College, Columbia University, New York City, 1932.

Freeman, Frank N., "Major Issues with Reference to Proposed Reforms," *Department of Superintendence Official Report*, 1933, pp. 59–68.

Knox, Rose B., *School Activities and Equipment*, Houghton Mifflin Co., Boston, 1927.

National Society for the Study of Education, Thirty-third Yearbook, Part II, Public School Publishing Co., Bloomington, Illinois, 1934.

CHAPTER X

SELECTION OF SUBJECT MATTER

Perhaps no other point has been an issue of so much dispute in educational theory as the treatment which should be accorded subject matter in instructional organization. Consequently, as the curriculum worker approaches the problem of dealing with subject matter he is projected into an area of conflict in which he must make choices with the full realization that whatever his position there will be those who hold that the decision is wrong. The point that should receive primary consideration, however, is the development of an approach to subject matter that is consistent with procedures employed in other phases of curriculum development. All too often workers enter courageously upon the task of reorganizing the curriculum in fundamental ways only to deal with subject matter in a manner obviously incompatible with procedures in other phases of the program. This is due to the fact that traditional practices of dealing with subject matter are thoroughly entrenched and that vested interests have a considerable stake involved. The subject matter specialist and the textbook maker are sometimes loath to see basic changes made in the organization of subject matter. Many times this is from fear that values of fundamental worth will be lost, but often it seems to be because of the intellectual effort and the material cost that such change involves.

The curriculum worker who is to deal successfully with the problems centering around subject matter must have a clear understanding of certain basic concepts which explain the nature, function, source, and use of subject matter. Only through mastery of these concepts will he be able to project a program of curriculum development that is consistent and thorough-going.

NATURE OF SUBJECT MATTER

Subject matter is popularly looked upon by teachers as being the facts, generalizations, and information contained in text-books. The subject matter of American history, for example, is, to many teachers, merely the material in the American history text; the subject matter of algebra, the material in the algebra text; and similarly in other subjects. A slightly broader concept, sometimes held, is that subject matter is composed of all the facts, generalizations, and information in a particular subject or in all subjects. According to this concept, facts about American history would be subject matter of American history even though not included in the textbook, and similarly with other fields. Usually this latter point of view is about as far as teachers go in breadth of concept of subject matter. Yet neither of these concepts presents an adequate notion of the nature of subject matter.

The philosophical view of subject matter is presented by Dewey as follows: "It (subject matter) consists of the facts observed, recalled, read, and talked about, and the ideas suggested, in course of a development of a situation having a purpose." [1]

This concept is elaborated by the following discussion:

In the traditional schemes of education, subject matter means so much material to be studied. Various branches of study represent so many independent branches, each having its principles of arrangement complete within itself. . . .

Later on a chapter is devoted to the special consideration of the meaning of the subject matter of instruction. At this point we need only to say that, in contrast with the traditional theory, anything which intelligence studies represents things in the part which they play in the carrying forward of active lines of interest. Just as one "studies" his typewriter as part of the operation of putting it to use to effect

[1] John Dewey, *Democracy and Education,* By permission of The Macmillan Co., 1916, p. 212.

results, so with any fact or truth. It becomes an object of study—that is, of inquiry and reflection—when it figures as a factor to be reckoned with in the completion of a course of events in which one is engaged and by whose outcome one is affected. Numbers are not objects of study just because they are numbers already constituting a branch of learning called mathematics, but because they represent qualities and relations of the world in which our action goes on, because they are factors upon which the accomplishment of our purposes depends. Stated thus broadly, the formula may appear abstract. Translated into details, it means that the act of learning or studying is artificial and ineffective in the degree in which pupils are merely presented with a lesson to be learned. Study is effectual in the degree in which the pupil realizes the place of the numerical truth he is dealing with in carrying to fruition activities in which he is concerned.[2]

This concept of subject matter is obviously quite different from the traditional one. From this point of view what is or is not subject matter can be determined only in terms of specified individuals at specified times. The facts, generalizations, information, or objects an individual uses in activities to promote a purpose which he is endeavoring to realize compose his subject matter. When applied to classroom situations we see that a given fact or item of information such as the sum of two and six may be subject matter to some children in a class and not to others. Use and understanding determine what is subject matter for a learner rather than memory. Thus, classes that memorize a great many facts may not be gaining control of subject matter at all.

If this concept of subject matter is accepted, there is of course a body of material which a given person does not use but which, nevertheless, is available for use if the need arises. This body of material is composed of facts, information, principles, and generalizations which are organized into fields of knowledge. When so organized they represent the content of subjects and are the subject matter of adult specialists. These specialists have found such materials significant and useful, and

[2] John Dewey, *Democracy and Education*, pp. 157–158. By permission of The Macmillan Company, publishers.

because the materials possess these qualities they can be designated as subject matter. Thus, when reference is made to the subject matter or content of a particular field, the allusion is to the subject matter of adult specialists in that field. Such subject matter represents a storehouse or source of supply upon which the child may call for subject matter suitable for his use. Thus, from the standpoint of the teacher interested in directing the growth of children, the subject matter of the adult specialist is potential subject matter for the child. That is, it may be used by the child if need arises and, if used with meaning and significance, will become the child's subject matter.

A further point should be made clear. In the preceding paragraphs we have spoken of the subject matter in an organized field or subject. This may suggest that only materials included in an organized field may rightly be considered subject matter. In fact, many curriculum workers appear to operate on this assumption. The fact is that whatever in the way of facts, information, generalizations, or materials are employed to forward a desired end is subject matter for the person using it. Organization of these materials into logical relationships does not modify the inherent nature of the materials.

SOURCE OF SUBJECT MATTER

Consideration of the source of subject matter often clarifies thinking about its nature and function. If we look at subject matter from a long-time point of view we find that its source is the accumulation of solutions to problems and means of adjustment developed by man down through the ages to deal with difficulties which he has encountered. In the beginning these solutions were simple in nature. An imaginary account of the way in which these beginnings were made is given in a recent bulletin:

A shaggy man crept from his cave and blinked in the morning sunlight, as he had done almost every morning of his life.
But this morning his eye caught a cluster of luscious fruit, dangling

252 SELECTION OF SUBJECT MATTER

from the bough above his head. He wanted that fruit for breakfast, so he licked his lips and stretched out his long hairy arm to get it.

But the distance from the ground to the fruit was greater than the distance from the ground to the tips of his upstretched fingers. In other words, his arm wasn't long enough to reach it. So he crouched and jumped, but the fruit dangled higher than he could leap.

Next he threw a stone; it missed and went crashing through the branches.

Then an historic event occurred. His hand happened to grasp a stick. As he lifted it up to hurl it, the far end grazed the branch. A new idea began to take shape in his groping brain. He lifted the stick again and the same thing happened. He felt it touch the branch he couldn't reach. Fascinated, he wavered the stick in air till it touched the fruit, and down dropped his breakfast.

And thus, thousands of years before recorded history, a primitive ancestor of the human race found out that he could use a club to increase the length of his arm.[3]

Solutions to problems in many cases were doubtless reached in the manner described here; but as time went on and solutions were passed from generation to generation, man gained the idea that conscious effort could be employed to resolve his difficulties. The result was an increase in the variety, and an improvement in the quality of solutions to problems devised by man. These solutions consequently became quite complex in nature. They now are extremely intricate and complicated. Looked on as a body or composite, they are frequently referred to as our group culture or race heritage. The group culture or race heritage may take a variety of forms. It may take the form of accounts, descriptions, aesthetic expressions, customs, laws, principles, techniques, formulas, doctrines, and social institutions. These forms of the group culture, it will be noted, include intellectual and emotional adjustments to social problems. There is another large and important phase of race experience that takes the form of material objects such as a typewriter, a baseball, an automobile, an ax, or a radio. This part of the group culture is often referred to as the material aspect.

[3] *Research—An Eye to the Future,* General Motors Research Division. Detroit, Michigan, 1934, p. 1.

This classification serves to indicate the breadth of the group culture. That is, all means of adjustment developed by the race, whether intellectual or material in nature, are a part of the group culture.

The importance of the group culture can hardly be over-emphasized. It is the race's storehouse; it is the working capital of the present. As such it is the source of all subject matter. Whenever any phase of the group culture is used by an individual that phase becomes his subject matter. Frequently, we fail to realize how completely we depend on subject matter so conceived. On the other hand, we often fail to profit as much as we might from consideration of race experience.

Education has a major responsibility for developing dispositions and techniques that lead the individual to select and to use subject matter wisely. This end is far from realized at present. Very few people would undertake a flight to the stratosphere without thoroughly studying the experiences of others in such an enterprise. Yet every day people engage in social undertakings of great consequence to our group life without first studying the experiences of others in similar undertakings. Boards of education seldom base their activities on a careful study of the past experience of boards and superintendents in operating schools. Many high school teachers and faculty members of higher institutions are content to undertake the task of teaching without a study of past experience in teaching. Yet it should be obvious that study of these experiences of others and the solutions to difficulties which they encountered would be of as much assistance and are just as indispensable to intelligent action as study of past experience in making flights to the stratosphere. Thus, the use of race experience as a guide for present action of all types is a phase of the application of intelligence to our living. It should not be overlooked, however, that race experience becomes meaningful and significant only in terms of our present undertakings. Race experience then, although indispensable for intelligent action, contributes to education only as it aids the individual to meet his needs.

The task of selecting subject matter for use in the instructional program is a difficult one. Clearly, a child during the course of his school life can use only an infinitesimal part of the race experience. Even in case of the most broadly and thoroughly educated adult there are great fields of knowledge about which he is ignorant. It is also quite evident that he who attempts to gain thorough mastery and·use of a given phase of the group culture must limit that phase very strictly and be content to know little outside of his chosen speciality. Thus is raised the problem that has plagued men interested in education for many generations: What knowledge is of most worth? Out of all the valuable things that could be learned, what shall I choose? And, even more pertinent, what shall be chosen for the immature person under the guidance of the school? This is the problem upon which those responsible for curriculum making have expended more effort and thought, perhaps, than any other.

Before considering the bases available for selecting subject matter, it may be well to emphasize in this connection the implications of concepts of subject matter developed heretofore. From the discussion of the nature of subject matter it should be clear that it is impossible to determine what will be the subject matter for a particular child or group of children until the actual experiences are carried forward. Consequently, the curriculum worker can only select from the great mass of material in the race heritage that part which he believes may appropriately become subject matter for the child. That is, he selects from the subject matter of the adult specialist potential subject matter for pupils. We now turn to a consideration of the bases on which this selection may be made.

The control that should be exerted on the selection of content by the aims of education and by the scope of the curriculum has already been considered in Chapters VI and VII. Whatever the specific basis or bases for selecting potential subject matter, their use should be consistent with the procedures accepted for defining aims and scope in so far as these procedures relate to content.

There are four principal bases upon which the selection of potential subject matter may be made: (1) significance to an organized field of knowledge; (2) significance to an understanding of contemporary life; (3) adult use; and (4) child interest and use. The first two of these bases rest largely on tradition and judgment. The last two may be determined by scientific procedures.

The significance of particular items of content to an organized field of knowledge has been, and still is, the most generally used basis for selecting potential subject matter. This procedure assumes at the outset, of course, that the curriculum shall be constricted within the recognized logically organized fields of knowledge. Consequently, the first step is to define these fields. Each field is treated independently. The means of selection may vary somewhat. The total content in an organized field of knowledge may be used as a starting point. A person who knows this field and understands the relationships involved— a subject specialist—selects from the field a portion of organized subject matter to be assigned to the particular phase of the educational program under consideration. The selection may be in terms of the most important materials in the entire field, *e.g.*, in the case of world history; or it may be by selection of of the most important material in segments of the subject, which segments may be arranged in a logical sequence, *e.g.*, in the case of ancient history, medieval history, and modern history. In either case the criterion for including a particular item of material is its importance to an understanding of the subject. Certain events and developments are retained because historically they are more important than other events and developments. This method of selecting subject matter is the one generally employed by subject specialists in preparing textbooks and syllabuses.

The second basis for selecting subject matter is the significance of the material to contemporary life. As in the case of the foregoing basis of selection, this basis rests largely on judgment. It is employed much more generally in the selection of materials for some courses than for others. For example, the course introduced in comparatively recent years in Problems of American Democracy selects subject matter with reference to significant contemporary problems. Some general science courses emphasize the relation of science to significant problems, and consequently materials selected for such courses are chosen on the basis of their significance to contemporary life. On the other hand, the idea of a survey of science, which dominates other general science courses, leads to selection of materials in terms of their significance to the fields of science.

The third basis of selecting subject matter is adult use. This basis has been widely studied, numerous researches having been made to facilitate its application. There are some three or four specialized techniques by means of which this basis is employed. It has been used especially in selecting facts and skills which should receive emphasis. Consequently its application has been largely in relation to subjects such as spelling, arithmetic, and reading.

The principle of selection upon which this procedure rests was employed in a study as early as 1582. In that year a list of words was published that had been prepared by Richard Mulcaster, an English schoolmaster. His list was for the purpose of standardizing English spelling. It contained over 8000 words. Words most commonly used were selected for inclusion in the list.[4] In 1904 a study of this type was made a definite basis for curriculum development. At that time Knowles, by analyzing passages from the English Bible and from various authors, prepared a list of 353 most commonly used words. This list was employed by him in developing a system of reading for the blind. In 1911 Eldridge made an analysis of the vocabularies

[4] This list is described by H. G. Good in "Three Lists of English Words," *Educational Research Bulletin*, 7:273–274, October 3, 1928. *See also* E. T. Campagnac, editor, *Mulcaster's Elementarie*, Oxford University Press, 1925.

of 250 different articles taken from four issues of four Sunday newspapers published in Buffalo. On the basis of this analysis he prepared and published a list of 6000 common English words. In 1915 Ayres [5] reported a study of the spelling vocabularies of personal and business letters. The study involved tabulation of the words used in 200 short letters written by 200 people. The total vocabulary used was found to be 2001 words. Other studies of this type followed with increased frequency and broadened scope. The influence such studies might exert on selection of content for the curriculum was shown by a scale developed by Ayres for measuring spelling ability. He used a number of studies of most frequently used words to develop his word list. It is estimated that these studies through similar sources of influence reduced the spelling vocabularies required of children by 25 to 50 per cent.

Studies of adult use of arithmetical abilities followed shortly after the initial work in spelling. One of the earliest of these was made by Wilson in 1917.[6] Children in the sixth, seventh, and eighth grades collected during a period of two weeks the arithmetic problems which their parents solved. These problems were classified and studied with reference to the content of the school program in arithmetic. In 1919 Wilson [7] followed this study by another of similar type but of much more extended scope. Problems encountered by 4068 persons were analyzed. In 1922 he applied his method of determining the arithmetic needed for social and business use to the development of a course of study. This was done in the Connersville, Indiana, schools.

This technique is readily applicable to the field of language

---

[5] Leonard P. Ayres, *A Measuring Scale for Ability in Spelling,* Division of Education. Russell Sage Foundation, 1915.

[6] G. M. Wilson, "A Survey of the Social and Business Use of Arithmetic," Second Report of the Committee on Minimal Essentials in Elementary School Subjects, *Sixteenth Yearbook of the National Society for the Study of Education* Part I, 1917, pp. 128–42.

[7] G. M. Wilson, *A Survey of the Social and Business Usage of Arithmetic,* Teachers College, Columbia University Contributions to Education No. 100, 1919.

and consequently there have been a number of studies of language activities of adults. In 1921 Searson [8] reported a study of the language needs of 3600 persons in twelve different occupations. This study shows the relative emphasis placed in writing, reading, and speaking, in transacting the affairs of life. In 1924 he [9] reported a more extended investigation relating to the language skills necessary for ordinary success in life. He listed twenty-seven language skills and consulted 7752 persons in forty-two states engaged in a variety of occupations concerning their need for these skills. His findings indicate the several skills persons in various occupations and trades found essential in their work.

In 1926 a committee of the National Council of Teachers of English, under the chairmanship of Clapp, made an even more extended study of adult needs in language. A survey was made of the types of language activity most used and most important in daily life, and the degrees of difficulty found in various activities. Two thousand six hundred and fifteen persons in 300 towns in thirty-five states were included in the survey. Results are reported by education groups, thus showing what differences, if any, exist between college graduates, high school graduates, and grammar school graduates.

Studies of this type are numerous. Several of the more significant ones are summarized in Table III. Those reported in the foregoing illustrations serve only to indicate the way in which the use made by adults of certain skills and information is secured as a basis for determining the content of the curriculum.

Another technique by which adult practices are made the basis for developing the curriculum is known as "activity analysis." This technique, developed by Bobbitt, seeks to base the selection of content of the curriculum on a comprehensive analysis of the activities performed by adults. It is assumed

[8] J. W. Searson, "Meeting the Public Demand," *English Journal,* 10:327–31, June, 1921.
[9] J. W. Searson, "Determining the Language Program," *English Journal,* 13:99–114, February, 1924.

that a study of the activities in which adults actually engage will indicate what activities children should be taught to perform. For example, it may readily be seen that adults engage in a wide variety of activities, such as, reading newspapers, writing letters, walking, caring for the teeth, and avoiding accidents. A comprehensive list of such activities, according to this technique, determines the objectives of education. Stated in such specific terms the objectives determine to a large measure the content or subject matter to be used. This technique was developed most completely in the Los Angeles curriculum program some ten years ago. Since that time application has been more limited, the findings of activity analyses being used in conjunction with other procedures.

The "job analysis" technique is another procedure which implies the selection of subject matter by reference to adult needs. This technique is in fact closely related to "activity analysis." It is employed in developing curricula to prepare students to engage in particular occupations or professions. The activities involved in carrying on a particular occupation or profession are analyzed in detail and the student is trained in the performance of these activities. This, of course, determines in large measure the subject matter or content to be employed. The most extensive application of this technique is in connection with the *Commonwealth Teacher-Training Study* in which the activities of teachers are analyzed in detail and proposed as a basis for developing a suitable curriculum to train prospective teachers.

Checking the subject matter employed in school programs against that used in adult life has in many cases resulted in desirable outcomes. Much relatively useless material has been eliminated by this means. It must be recognized, however, that this by no means provides a solution to the problem of selecting content. There always remains the basic and really fundamental issue as to whether the activities performed by adults are desirable. Adults engage in many undesirable as well as desirable activities. Bode points this out very clearly:

TABLE III

SELECTED STUDIES OF ADULT USE WHICH SUGGEST A BASIS FOR THE SELECTION OF SUBJECT MATTER *

SUBJECT	AUTHOR	SOURCE	PROBLEM	TECHNIQUE OF STUDY	FINDINGS
Arithmetic	Bowden, A. O.	*Consumers Uses of Arithmetic*, Contribution to Education No. 340, Teachers College, Columbia University, 1929.	To determine the actual uses made of arithmetic in adult social life, exclusive of vocational uses.	"Answeraires" containing problems adults might use outside of their vocations were submitted to a representative group of adults to check the ones used.	It was concluded that 85 per cent of the arithmetic now taught is unnecessary. This conclusion rests upon three assumptions: that present practice is desirable; that adults are conscious of all the arithmetic they use; and that all types of arithmetic are equally well remembered.
Arithmetic	Dale, Edgar	"An Unsolved Problem," *Educational Research Bulletin* 8: 355-57, November 6, 1929.	To determine the arithmetic necessary to the lay reader of investment materials.	An analysis was made of 310,000 running words of investment literature. Two-thirds of the materials related to stocks and bonds and one-third to banking, insurance, and real estate. A comparison was made with four arithmetic textbooks.	Textbooks fail to emphasize sufficiently certain words appearing with high frequency in investment materials. Likewise, words appearing frequently in textbooks rarely or not at all were mentioned in investment materials.
Social Science	Bagley, W. C.	"The Determination of Minimum Essentials in Elementary Geography and History," *Fourteenth Yearbook*, N. S. S. E., Part I, pp. 131-9, 1915.	To find the types of references to geographical materials in certain printed materials.	Samplings were taken from such magazines as the *Outlook* and the *Literary Digest*.	The most frequently mentioned countries, continents, rivers, gulfs, seas, and straits were given. The reference to presidents, wars, etc., were listed. References to wars were more frequent than any other type of historical events.
Social Science	Branom, M. E. and Reavis, W. C.	"The Determination and Measurement of the Minimum Essentials in Elementary School Geography," *Seventeenth Yearbook*, N. S. S. E., Part I, 1918. pp. 27-39.	To select a list of minimum essentials in geography.	Fifty countries selected from the Statistical Abstracts, 1915, were ranked according to certain criteria.	According to these analyses the relative importance of these countries are listed. The United States, Great Britain, Germany, France, India, Austria-Hungary, Russia, Canada and Italy are most important.

* Certain studies are included in the table because of their historic interest.

		To determine a list of minimal essentials in elementary geography.	An analysis was made of newspapers to determine the geographical allusions made in them.	The analysis of 88 pages of such printed matter revealed 5,027 geographical references. Cities, countries, and continents are listed according to frequency.
Social Science	Thomas, J. B.	*A Study in Minimum Essentials of Geography for the Elementary Schools,* M.A. Thesis, Indiana University, 1919.		
Social Science	Alderman, G. H.	"What an Iowa Layman should Know about Courts and Law," *School Review,* 30: 360–364, May, 1922.	To determine the knowledge of courts and law valuable to the layman.	The records of one court from 1907–1909 were examined to determine the charges that bring the layman to court.	Instruments involving the principles of contract, writs or decrees from the court, and principles of torts were the main items that brought the layman into court.
Social Science	Cocking, W. D.	*The Attitude of the Public to the Teaching of Citizenship.* M. A. Thesis, Univ. of Iowa, 1923.	To determine what laymen regard as important topics in citizenship.	Representative citizens in various occupational groups were asked to submit topics for a citizenship course.	Some 593 people suggested 4,728 topics which were divided into 247 distinct classifications.
Social Science	Washburne, C. W.	"Basic Facts Needed in History and Geography. A Statistical Investigation," *Twenty-Second Yearbook,* N. S. S. E., Part II, 1923, pp. 216–33.	To find what facts children must know in order to be reasonably intelligent concerning the persons, places, and events to which allusions are frequently made.	Analyzed four literary periodicals, five popular fiction periodicals, and four newspapers. Samples of each were made periodically between 1905–1922 so that no period would be missed. Every allusion to a person, place, date, or event was recorded.	Over 81,000 allusions were recorded and arranged in frequency order. The relative importance forms an objective basis for a fact course in history and geography, according to the author.
Social Science	Rugg, Harold, and Hockett, John	*Objective Studies in Map Location,* Social Science Monograph No. I, Lincoln School of Teachers College, 1924.	To determine the relative importance in contemporary life of map locations of all kinds.	Eight criteria were employed to determine rank order lists of cities, regions, rivers, mountains, countries, islands, etc.	The first 30 cities in importance in the United States and the first 50 foreign cities are listed. The 30 most important countries and the 40 most important regions of the World are listed. Likewise the most important rivers, mountains, bodies of water, and islands are given.

TABLE III—*Continued*

SELECTED STUDIES OF ADULT USE WHICH SUGGEST A BASIS FOR THE SELECTION OF SUBJECT MATTER

Subject	Author	Source	Problem	Technique of Study	Findings
General Science	Washburne, C. W.	*Scientific Method in the Construction of School Textbooks,* World Book Co., 1924.	One phase of the study was to determine what applications of science are commonly made in everyday life.	Experiences were collected from adults involving practical applications of science. These were added to a list of children's questions to formulate a master list.	The curricular elements found were: gravitation, molecular attraction, heat, conservation of energy, radiant heat and light, sound, magnetism, and electricity, mingling of molecular, chemical change and energy, and solution and chemical action.
Biology	Finley, Chas. W. and Caldwell, Otis W.	*Biology in the Public Press,* Lincoln School, Teachers College, 1923.	To determine the types of biology now going through the public press.	Complete issues of 11 newspapers for June, 1921, and 3 of the same and 3 others for November, 1921, were analyzed for reference to biological materials. The 17 full months' issues gave a total of 492 different papers with an estimated 13,796 pages.	Some 3,061 biological articles with a total length of 25,506 inches, or an average of 8.3 inches were found. The classification according to space was in the order of health, animals, plants, food, organization of producers, nature, evolution, and fiction.
General Science	Curtis, F. D.	*Some Values Derived from Extensive Reading of General Science,* Contribution to Education No. 163, Teachers College, 1924, pp. 10–27.	To determine what sort of scientific knowledge is demanded for an intelligent reading of the public press.	Six hundred thirty articles from 6 representative newspapers were added to Finley and Caldwell's list and all were analyzed according to function, method of treatment, and content.	The results indicate a need for the broadest possible training in general science to understand the science in the press, and a need for a course to train for newspaper science reading. The scientific terms indicate an enormous range of vocabulary found in the press.
Language	Clapp, John M.	"Place and Function of English in American Life," *School and Society,* 23: 424–5, April 3, 1926.	To determine the language activities used in American life.	A survey was made of the language activities of 2,615 persons in 300 towns in 35 states which were used and most important in their daily life.	The activities are summarized under the following heads: conversation, public speaking, writing, reading, and listening.

262

Language	Johnson, Roy I.	"Determining Standards in English Composition," *School Review*, 36: 757-67; Dec. 1928, and 37: 44-48, January, 1929.	To determine the expressional situations in ordinary experience both in school and out.	A detailed cataloguing was made of experiences to discover the functional character of such activities as group discussions, formal and informal talks, keeping personal memoranda, giving directions, etc. Interviews, questionnaires, selected readings, and individual difficulties were used in determining the final list of traits.	A list of 54 traits is given which is supposed to describe a good conversationalist. Difficulties found by 35 experienced persons in round-table discussion are listed and a final list offered.
Language	Matravers, C. H.	"A Corrective Language Program," *The English Journal*, 18: 564-570, September, 1929.	To determine the comparative usefulness of conventional forms from the standpoint of social utility.	Senior high school pupils doing stenographic work made reports of conversation they heard both in school and out. From these 107,000 words, both right and wrong, were tabulated. Social usefulness indexes were established and errors weighted.	It was found that accuracy in 18 forms of usage would eliminate 63.8 per cent of the actual errors. The indexes of social utility ranged from 30.7 per cent for *ain't* to 0 per cent for the past tense of the verb *lie*.
Spelling	Knowles, J.	*The London Point System of Reading for the Blind*, privately published in pamphlet form, London, 1904.	To develop a list of words for blind students.	Analyzed passages from the English Bible and various authors containing 100,000 words and tabulated them on a basis of frequency.	The result was the establishment of a list of 353 words which with their repetitions accounted for three-fourths of the total number.
Spelling	Eldridge, R. C.	*Six Thousand Common English Words*, privately published in pamphlet form in Niagara Falls New York.	To determine the words used in the press.	Analyzed 250 articles from 2 pages each of four Buffalo newspapers and made a frequency distribution of the words used.	The author found 43,989 running words and 6,002 different words, excluding proper nouns and numerals. The first 250 constitute the chief English sentence forming words and the first 750 including the repetitions constitute three-fourths of all words tabulated.

TABLE III—*Continued*

SELECTED STUDIES OF ADULT USE WHICH SUGGEST A BASIS FOR THE SELECTION OF SUBJECT MATTER

SUBJECT	AUTHOR	SOURCE	PROBLEM	TECHNIQUE OF STUDY	FINDINGS
Spelling	Thorndike, E. L.	"Word Knowledge in the Elementary School," *Teachers College Record*, 22: 334-370, September, 1921.	To determine the words most needed for instructional purposes.	Forty-one different sources were used in compiling the list, among which were children's literature; the Bible and English classics, books about cooking, farming, trades, and the like; newspapers; correspondence, etc. The composite list was graded for frequency, range, etc.	Following this technique a list of 10,000 words was chosen. The list is keyed to show the position of each word. The list aids the teacher in telling how important a word is and the relative difficulty.
Spelling	Horn, Ernest	"A Basic Writing Vocabulary," University of Iowa, Monographs in Education, First Series, No. 4.	One of the four purposes is to make available a list of the 10,000 words most often used in writing done in the United States outside of the school.	A compilation was made of available word studies. A very elaborate set of rules was drawn up to serve as a standard in weighting each word in the list. The number of different sources was 65 producing 5,136,816 running words.	The list of 10,000 words is given, together with a key for reading the weight assigned. The value to teachers of spelling is pointed out as furnishing a basis for selecting words to be taught, for grading the course of study, for aid in method and to serve as a basis for testing.
Home Economics	Arnquist, Inez F. and Roberts, Evelyn H.	"The Present Use of Work Time of Farm Homemakers," State College of Washington, Agriculture Experiment Station, *Bulletin*, No. 234, July, 1929.	To determine the time spent and the conditions of work of Washington farm homemakers.	Detailed records kept by homemakers for seven consecutive days during a week which they considered typical of the winter and summer season.	Most of the homemakers do all the cooking and baking, laundering, cleaning, etc. Homemaking calls for managing ability and a fund of information and skill in workmanship in different kinds of work.
Home Economics	Kugel, Daisy Alice	"The Opinion of Parents Regarding the Teaching of Family Relationships," *Journal of Home Economics*, 21: 1-6, Jan., 1929.	To determine the family relationship topics to be included in home economics.	A questionnaire containing 53 items divided into 5 categories was submitted to parents in 14 states.	Twenty-seven per cent approved every topic, 10 per cent disapproved of only one and 46 per cent favored the inclusion of 50 of the 53 topics. The 2 most objectionable topics were companionate marriage and limiting the size of the family.

No scientific analysis known to man can determine the desirability or the need of anything. Statistical investigation, for example, may show that a certain number of burglaries occur annually in a given community, but it does not show whether the community needs a larger police force or more burglars. That is altogether a question of what sort of community we may happen to want. Or to take Bobbitt's own illustration, a scientific analysis would doubtless show that a reading ability is necessary for the conduct of many of the complicated operations in civilized society. But whether it is desirable that these operations should be carried on the deponent saith not. Old Governor Berkeley of Virginia—God rest his soul!—was of a negative opinion. The notion that ideals can be evolved from a process of collecting environmental facts is just another of the many delusions to which our sinful human flesh is heir.[10]

Adult use as a criterion for selecting content also overlooks the influence of changing conditions. The activities in which adults engage may not be suitable at all for children when they become adults. These basic weaknesses of adult use as the basis for selecting subject matter to be included in the curriculum have been emphasized in a number of sources.

The fourth basis upon which content may be selected is children's interest or use. Studies of pupil interest have already been mentioned in Chapter VIII. It was pointed out there that numerous efforts have been made to discover what type of reading material children are interested in, what subjects and topics are of interest to them, children's preferences for colors and types of pictures, and their preferences for play and recreational activities. These studies have significance for the selection of content, since they give at least a general indication to the curriculum worker of the materials children use with interest. A tabulation of some of the more important studies of this type is given in Table IV.

Some studies have been made to determine the type of material children use voluntarily. These have been made principally in connection with the language usage of children. For

[10] Boyd H. Bode, *Modern Educational Theories*, 1927, pp. 80–81. By permission of The Macmillan Company, publishers.

TABLE IV

SELECTED STUDIES OF CHILD INTEREST WHICH SUGGEST A BASIS FOR THE SELECTION OF SUBJECT MATTER *

SUBJECT	AUTHOR	SOURCE	PROBLEM	TECHNIQUE OF STUDY	FINDINGS
Reading	True, M. B. C.	"What My Pupils Read," *Education*, 10: 42–45, September, 1889.	To determine the books read by the pupils in school.	A record was kept of the books checked out for home use that had not been assigned.	The following books were used most frequently: *Little Women, Eight Cousins, An Old Fashioned Girl, Story of a Bad Boy, Soldiers and Patriots,* and *Under the Lilacs.*
Reading	Vostrovsky, Clara	"A Study of Children's Reading Tastes," *Pedagogical Seminary*, 6: 523–35, December, 1899.	To ascertain the general reading taste of school children before any organized effort has been made to direct it.	A questionnaire was given to children including the following questions: Do you take books from the public library? If so, how often? What was the name of your last book? Why did you take it? How did you like it?	The percentage of pupils taking books increases from 10 per cent at 9 years of age to 80 per cent at 19. The books most frequently drawn were juvenile fiction, general literature, and history. Certain sex differences are pointed out.
Reading	Abbott, Allan	"Reading Tastes of High-School Pupils," *School Review*, 10: 585–600. October, 1902.	To determine the books liked by high school pupils.	Books that appeared on the Harvard and the National Education Association Committee on College Entrance Requirements lists were rated by high school pupils on a three point scale and omissions of interest to the pupils were added by them.	Twenty-seven titles representing 16 authors were ranked highest and 33 titles representing 28 authors were lowest. The authors concluded: "It is our business as teachers to study the lines of normal growth and to lead our pupils naturally from one interest to the next higher. . . ."
Reading	King, Cora E.	"Favorite Poems for Children of Elementary School Age," *Teachers College Record*, 23: 255–273, May, 1922.	To find the poems in which the elementary school pupils were most interested.	Four thousand eight hundred children in ten cities were asked to select two poems they liked the very best.	A list of 100 poems is given that were mentioned ten times or more. A table showing children's reasons for their selection suggests fields of interest.

* Certain studies are included in the table because of their historic interest.

Subject	Author	Reference	Purpose	Method	Findings
Reading	Eckert, Molly H.	"Children's Choices of Poems," *Elementary English Review*, 5: 182–5, June, 1928.	To determine whether children in grades 1 to 3 enjoy reading or learning to read poems in text-books.	Selection was made of three groups of poems, each group being composed of four poems from a textbook and one from another source. These were read to the children who stated their preferences.	Approximately 89 per cent of the non-textbook poems had a rating of first choice.
Reading	Lancaster, T. J.	"A Study of the Voluntary Reading of Pupils in Grades Four to Eight," *Elementary School Journal*, 28: 525–37, March, 1928.	To determine the reading interests of pupils in grades 4 to 8, inclusive.	The pupils in six city schools in Illinois filled out a questionnaire listing books read and their interest in them. Books were listed according to frequency in order to determine the type of material to include in children's books.	Ninety-eight per cent of the books read were prose. They were usually fiction. Children's tastes in literature may be satisfied by reputable books by reputable authors.
Reading	Elder, V and Carpenter, H. S.	"Reading Interests of High-School Children," *Journal of Educational Research* 19: 276–82, April, 1929.	To determine the out-of-school reading of senior high-school girls.	Questionnaire addressed to 487 senior high-school girls.	Fiction was more generally read and better liked than any other type of literature. Quality of materials improves term to term. Physical make-up of book is not a factor in choice.
Reading	Jennings, Joe	"Leisure Reading of Junior High School Boys and Girls," *Peabody Journal of Education*, 6: 333–348, May, 1929.	To determine the leisure reading of junior high-school boys and girls.	Pupils were asked to record for one week their reading not related to school work.	Practically all pupils read newspapers. A very large number of magazines were read. A total of 1084 books were read. Continued stories were read by 106 pupils. A wide variety and high quality of reading is shown.
Reading	Gates, Arthur I.	*Interest and Ability in Reading*, Macmillan Co., New York, 1930, Chapter II.	To determine general characteristics of reading materials of interest to primary children.	Thirty selections were made of children's literature by experts. The criteria used in making the selection were familiar family experience, unusual experience, humor, fancy, information, and heroism.	The frequency given the literary selections was as follows: humor, fancy, heroism, familiar experience, unusual experience, and information.

TABLE IV—*Continued*

SELECTED STUDIES OF CHILD INTEREST WHICH SUGGEST A BASIS FOR THE SELECTION OF SUBJECT MATTER.

SUBJECT	AUTHOR	SOURCE	PROBLEM	TECHNIQUE OF STUDY	FINDINGS
Reading	Beinhart, Frieda	"My Leisure Time," *Training School Bulletin*, 27: 161–66, February, 1931.	To discover the type of stories and poems interesting to pupils of low intellectual capacity.	Each pupil was questioned individually concerning his favorite poem and story and a record was kept of his answers.	The stories and poems in which these pupils were interested were decidedly lower in literary merit than the stories and poems in which normal pupils are interested.
Reading	Dowell, Pattie S. and Garrison, K. C.	"A Study of Reading Interests of Third Grade Subjects," *Peabody Journal of Education*, 8: 202–6, January, 1931.	To determine children's interest in reading content.	One hundred nine pupils from the third grade in Raleigh, N. C., were given a questionnaire by which to record their choice of reading materials. The choices of the pupils were analyzed to determine the elements of the selections preferred.	The results of the questionnaire revealed the most interesting elements to be kindness, bravery, happiness, beauty, humor, animals, story quality, achievement, love, Bible stories, and wisdom.
Reading	Gates, A. I., Peardon, Celeste C., and Sartorius, Ina C.	"Studies of Children's Interests in Reading," *Elementary School Journal*, 31: 656–70, May, 1931.	To determine the interest of children in informative and narrative reading materials.	Selections of narrative and informative literature were made by competent teachers and specialists. Records were kept of the children's choices.	The percentage of choices for narratives selections was 72.3 per cent and the percentage favoring informative selections was 23.7.
Reading	Cain, Wm. R., and Brown, Francis J.	"An Evaluation of the Outside Reading Interests of a Group of Senior High School Pupils," *Journal of Educational Sociology*, 5: 437–442, March, 1932.	To evaluate the outside reading interests of adolescent children.	The sophomore and senior groups in a high school in northern New Jersey were asked to list the books read during the summer and the first three months of school, exclusive of school assignments.	Findings showed that more than half the books read by seniors had some literary merit. The percentage of harmful books was very small. Those having no special merit were mystery, detective, murder, and light love stories.

268

General Science	Finley, Chas. W.	"Some Studies of Children's Interests in Science Materials," *School Science and Mathematics*, 21: 1-24, Jan. 1921	To secure data on children's interest in animals.	A "water dog" was exhibited to 1716 pupils in grades 1-8. For three minutes the children were permitted to ask questions orally, after which written questions were collected. The written questions were tabulated and classified. After 40 days a composition was written about the animal and the elements mentioned in the composition were compared to the questions that had been asked.	The phases in the compositions compared closely with the questions asked. There was considerable change in the emphasis of phases according to the age and grade of the pupils. For example, interest in life history and adaptation to environment increased from grade to grade.
General Science	Palmer, E. L.	"How to Meet Some of Children's Nature Interests," *The Nature Study Review*, 18: 23-30, Jan., Feb., 1922.	To determine the nature interests of rural children as revealed by their questions.	Teachers were asked to send to the investigator the nature study questions which had been asked by their pupils. The first 500 received were analyzed.	Questions of a zoological nature were first of importance according to the percentage of all questions asked. Biology, botany, ecology, were next in importance.
General Science	Curtis, F. D.	*Some Values Derived from Extensive Reading of General Science*, Contribution to Education No. 163, Teachers College, 1924, pp. 27-40.	One phase of the study was to determine the scientific interests of children.	A questionnaire was addressed to pupils asking them to list five topics in science about which they would like to know. A total of 3,330 were returned.	Both boys and girls were much more interested in the physical sciences than in the biological sciences. Boys were more interested in technical processes than girls. There is a shift from the physical to the biological sciences as maturity is reached.
General Science	Pollock, C. A.	"Children's Interests as a Basis of What to Teach in General Science," *Educational Research Bulletin*, 3: 3-6, Jan. 9, 1934.	To determine the interest of children in general science topics.	A questionnaire was addressed to pupils asking them to list topics of scientific interest.	Topics with a frequency of mention exceeding 100 are electricity, stars, radio, heat lightning, planets, and the moon. Much more emphasis is given physical science than biological science.

TABLE IV — *Continued*

SELECTED STUDIES OF CHILD INTEREST WHICH SUGGEST A BASIS FOR THE SELECTION OF SUBJECT MATTER.

SUBJECT	AUTHOR	SOURCE	PROBLEM	TECHNIQUE OF STUDY	FINDINGS
General Science	Downing, E. R.	"Children's Interests in Nature Materials," *Third Yearbook*, Department of Superintendence of the National Education Association, p. 299, 1925.	To determine whether children are more interested in animal, plant, or physical materials and in what phases they are most interested.	An analysis was made of questions written voluntarily by 742 children to a magazine inviting them to ask any questions they would like to have answered.	Sixty-one per cent of the questions concerned animals, 20.6 per cent plants, and 1.8 per cent miscellaneous materials. Most of the animal questions concerned wild animals.
General Science	Trafton, G. H.	"Children's Interests in Nature Materials," *Third Yearbook*, Department of Superintendence, National Education Association, 1925, pp. 299-300.	To test children's knowledge of animals and plants to find what natural interest they have in nature.	Approximately 1000 children in grades 4-7 answered questions about birds, plants, and animals, such as, which animal do you like best?	The average number of animals named was 18; trees, 10; and flowers, 9. In adapting subject matter of nature study to children the interest of the children must be approached through the life activities, of animals, plants, and birds.
General Science	Peters, Chas. C., and Himes, H. E.	"What Biology Functions Most Largely in Giving Pleasures of Recognition?" *Second Yearbook*, National Society for Study of Education, 1929, pp. 118-128.	To determine an index of relative utility for each item in biology according to the pleasure received by the pupil in studying it.	An analysis of 90 questionnaires received from pupils who had studied biology earlier in their high school course was made. The measure of value of each phase of biology studied was determined according to pleasure indicated by the questionnaires.	Means of locomotion, economic importance, external structure, reproduction, were rated highly.
General Science	Nulton, Lucy	"Science Interests and Questions of a Second Grade," *Peabody Journal of Education*, 7: 224-30, January, 1930.	To record the various science interests of a second grade over a nine-months' term.	The questions relating to science that developed naturally during a nine-months' period were recorded by the teacher.	The range and variety were wide. Many questions pertained to the earth, moon, moss, insects, flowers, plants, milk, fish, deserts, shells, paper, and printing.

General Science	Nettels, Chas. H.	"Science Interests of Junior High School Pupils," *Science Education*, 15: 219–225, May, 1931.	To determine the interests of pupils of the junior high school in science.	From 1,067 papers returned, 178 different scientific interests were found. Differences in sex, and the mental ability of the pupils, were shown.
Social Studies	Kyte, Geo. C.	"Experimentation in the Development of a Book to Meet a Book to Meet," *Educational Administration and Supervision*, 14: 86–100, February, 1928.	To determine the content for a book to be used by the fourth grade in the social studies.	Selections were made of social science materials by the author. They were mimeographed and given to the children, who recorded their reactions to them.
Vocational Occupations	Sheldon, Donald R.	"Children's Interests," *Elementary School Journal*, 33: 205–14, November, 1932.	To determine the likes and dislikes of children in certain occupational and recreational choices.	A five-point scale was devised for the rating of various occupational and recreational choices. The results of ratings of the topics were studied and ranked according to frequency.	Aviator, mechanic, and engineer were highest choices among the boys; teacher, actress, and nurse were highest among the girls.

example, more recent studies in spelling have included word counts of children's compositions. These studies have been used as a check on the words included in spelling lists.

General studies of child interest and use are subject to severe limitations. Interest and use cannot be dissociated from individuals and retain a great deal of meaning. Children under one set of environmental conditions may be interested in one type of thing and children under other conditions in something totally different. Likewise, children under varying conditions will use widely different content. For example, there may well be a considerable margin of words used in spelling by children in an industrial area which differ significantly from those used by children in a mountainous rural area. When the individual and his environmental surroundings are removed from consideration and averages are taken, much of the value of interest and child use disappears. That is, interest and use are of greatest significance to the teacher in actually organizing instruction for a given group of children. There they are of primary importance.

But even with these limitations, there are certain general findings of such studies that are of value to the curriculum worker in selecting potential subject matter. It has been shown, for example, that there is a tendency for children to like reading materials which possess certain general qualities and to dislike materials which have other general qualities. Findings of this type provide a basis for selecting potential subject matter which simplifies the task of the teacher in dealing with a particular group of children. That is, if the curriculum worker suggests only potential subject matter that has been found interesting and useful to some children at the general stage of development of the children for which the curriculum is planned, the teacher will have a much easier task selecting from these suggestions what is suitable for a given group than would be the case if the curriculum worker did not make the check against general interest and use.

One type of study, frequently used, is not included under

any of the foregoing bases. This type is concerned with analyses of the material treated in textbooks and courses of study. Omission under the foregoing bases is caused by the fact that the basis of selecting content cannot be determined with accuracy in the case of such studies. This will be seen from a consideration of the procedure employed. If a course is to be prepared in a given subject, American history for example, a study is made of the topics treated in a representative group of American history textbooks or courses of study. Those topics which have high frequency are then selected for inclusion in the course under preparation.

Inasmuch as the writers of different texts or the committees that prepare different courses of study may use entirely different bases of selecting the materials they include, analyses of texts and courses of study merely indicate the materials that are most generally considered worthy of inclusion without regard to basis of selection. The traditional practice, for example, of a particular school or the opinion of a single person is accorded equal weight by this procedure with the results of careful reflection, extended analyses, and experimentation. Items of low frequency may really have a far sounder basis for being included in a course than those with a high frequency. Even so, this procedure is of value to those who wish to pursue a middle-of-the-road course. It makes it possible to be neither the first to adopt the new nor the last to discard the old.

Studies are occasionally made which combine two or more of the bases for selecting subject matter. Robertson's [11] study of content in science is a recent one of this type. He defines a basis for selecting content in terms of scientific principles, subject matter topics, and children's interests. A collection of scientific principles was made and submitted to a jury of three science teachers. The resulting list was refined and submitted to a group of subject matter specialists. A list of **243** principles

---

[11] Martin Robertson, *A Basis for the Selection of Course Content in Elementary Science,* Unpublished Doctor's Dissertation, University of Michigan, 1934.

resulted. A list of subject matter topics was prepared in much the same way. Children's interests were checked by reference to questions asked. These principles, topics, and interests may be employed as a basis for checking the potential value of content. Thus, significance to the subject field and children's interests are used as a basis of selection of subject matter in this case.

The practical curriculum worker will find it unwise to employ exclusively any single basis for selecting potential subject matter. Fundamentally, a question of values is involved. Given an opportunity to have A or B, but not both, which shall I take? More specifically, which phase of the race heritage, A or B, promises to be of greatest worth to the child? Since this choice of values is the root of the problem, the answer must be approached from the philosophical point of view. But this does not mean that the evidence from quantitative studies should be ignored. Such evidence is in fact a vital means of clarifying the respective values and characteristics of A and B. Consequently, we may be wholly consistent in applying all four of the bases of selection. Although inadequate when taken separately, they provide a valuable check when all are employed. For example, although the significance of a given phase of subject matter to the organized field of knowledge of which it is a part is by no means an adequate basis in and of itself for selecting potential subject matter, yet if subject matter does have such significance, assurance is increased as to its general importance and value. Similarly, the significance of subject matter to contemporary life is a worth while criterion of value. Although adult use may not advisedly be employed as the sole determinant of the content that is included in the curriculum, yet it does add assurance that the material selected is significant. The fact that adults use some particular items of subject matter may be just as strong an indication that they should not be used by children as that they should be used. Yet studies of adult usage provide valuable data for determining what is socially significant. Consequently, when quantitative studies of adult use are employed in conjunction with the philosophical estimate of the social significance of the material, this basis makes a real contribution to the selection of subject matter. Likewise, general indications of the type of material in which children are interested and the type of material that they use provide a suggestive list of content of much greater value to the teacher as he actually begins the organization of instruction with children than otherwise would be available.

Our conclusion, therefore, is that no single basis of selecting potential subject matter is adequate in practical programs of curriculum development. Rather, attention may well be given to each basis. Assurance of the value of the proposed material will be increased as it is seen to be (1) significant to the organized field of knowledge, (2) significant to contemporary life, (3) commonly used by adults, and (4) of general interest to children.

PLACE OF SUBJECT ORGANIZATION

It has already been pointed out in Chapter III that the logical arrangement of subject matter is the traditional method of organization. Ever since man became concerned with learning as such he has tended to organize knowledge in terms of relationships inherent between the facts and principles involved. Down through the centuries this organization has been elaborated. Steps lacking for the complete development of the organization have been filled in from time to time and are being continuously elaborated. Frequently new discoveries have invalidated the logic of certain organizations and have required complete reorganization. Also as knowledge has increased, new divisions and organizations of subject matter have developed. The result is an ever-increasing array of logically organized areas of knowledge, each area or subject possessing increased complexity. Consequently, whereas the seven liberal arts were considered an adequate classification and organization of knowledge for many centuries, we now have a great multiplicity of subjects and divisions of subjects. As knowledge increases, this complexity of subject organization must of necessity continue to increase.

Reference has been made to the malefic influence of the logical arrangement of subject matter on instructional organization. That this is the case is agreed to by many careful students of the instructional program. Whitehead, for example, in discussing shortcomings of the educational program states:

> The solution which I am urging, is to eradicate the fatal disconnection of subjects which kills the vitality of our modern curriculum. There is only one subject-matter for education, and that is Life in all its manifestations. Instead of this single unity, we offer children—algebra, from which nothing follows; geometry, from which nothing follows; science, from which nothing follows; history, from which nothing follows; a couple of languages, never mastered; and lastly, most dreary of all, literature, represented by plays of Shakespeare, with philological notes and short analyses of plot and character to be in substance committed to memory. Can such a list be said to represent Life, as it is known in the midst of the living of it? The best that can be said of it is, that it is a rapid table of contents which a deity might run over in his mind while he was thinking of creating a world, and had not yet determined how to put it together.[12]

James Harvey Robinson writes on the same point:

> At present vital knowledge is broken up into fragments; shuffled into large piles labelled history, philosophy, psychology, philology, anthropology, ethics, politics, economics, astronomy, physics, chemistry, biology, geology, geography, botany. . . .
>
> These departments of knowledge, great and small, correspond to a necessary division of labor, and have, of course, a great significance in *research,* but they form one of the most effective barriers to the cultivation of a really scientific frame of mind in the young and the public at large.[13]

Dewey ascribes much of our present educational confusion to our too strict adherence to the logical organization of subject matter. "In a situation," he says, "where the skills or arts and the subject matter of knowledge have become interwoven and

---

[12] A. N. Whitehead, *The Aims of Education and Other Essays,* 1929, pp. 10–11. By permission of The Macmillan Company, publishers.
[13] From *The Humanizing of Knowledge,* by James Harvey Robinson, p. 63. Copyright 1926, Doubleday, Doran & Co., Inc. Used by permission.

interdependent, adherence to the policy forming the studies of secondary and collegiate instruction on the basis of many isolated and independent subjects is bound to result in precisely the kind of confusion we have at present." [14]

We should not conclude, however, from criticisms of the undesirable ways in which logically organized subject matter has been employed that this organization has no place in an instructional program. This is not the case. Although the logical organization of subject matter has been employed in curriculum making and instructional organization so as to have many bad results, it does, nevertheless, hold an indispensable place in the educative process. The question which the curriculum worker needs to consider is not whether logically organized subject matter has a function or place in education, but rather what that function or place should be.

The logical organization of subject matter is primarily significant to education by reason of two services it renders. First in importance, perhaps, is its relationship to the advancement of knowledge and the discovery of truth. It is in fact an indispensable basis upon which workers who strive to achieve these ends must build. Areas in which knowledge is lacking or is of doubtful accuracy are revealed by this organization. A basis is also provided for checking the reliability and implications of new findings. Suggestions are available as well for methods of discovering truth. In the second place, the logical organization of subject matter is significant in that it serves to systematize and arrange the race's knowledge somewhat as a cataloguing system serves to arrange and systematize the books in a library. Rarely would we want to study or use the books in the order in which they are arranged on the library shelves; yet having them arranged in a definite order and knowing the general plan of arrangement aids in getting the books we need with least delay. Knowledge of the arrangement of subject matter aids in the same way by furthering effective use. Thus, the person who

[14] John Dewey, *The Way Out of Educational Confusion*, Harvard University Press, 1931, pp. 17–18.

knows the chronological and causal relationships of certain events and facts in history will be able to use those events and facts with greater effectiveness in dealing with specific problems and issues than one who does not understand these relationships.

A difficult issue arises for the curriculum worker when consideration is given to the provision that should be made in the educational program for establishing these logical relationships. In the past, as has been shown in Chapter III, it has been assumed that establishing these relationships is the primary purpose of education, and that this purpose should be achieved by direct and intensive study of the materials as logically organized. Work has been organized from the intermediate grades on through the educational program in this way. This practice is now severely criticized. In dealing with the issue thus raised, we will consider first the training required for the specialist who will advance the frontiers of knowledge.

Recognizing the need such a specialist has for thorough mastery of the logical relationships in the field in which he is working, when should direct training start for such mastery? What provision should be made previous to such training for experience in dealing with logically organized subjects so that wise selection of fields of specialization may be made? Of primary importance in dealing with the first of these questions are the characteristics of the individual at various stages of intellectual growth. It is generally recognized that there are certain stages of mental growth just as there are of physical growth, and that certain stages of development are essential for achieving certain types of understanding and behavior. Stage of growth or degree of development is in fact probably the most important factor in accomplishing undertakings of practically all kinds. Little can be done in the way of direct training to develop particular abilities before the stage of development essential for their mastery is reached. For example, premature attempts to train babies to walk or climb have little influence on the time at which they become able to engage in these activities. Likewise, attempts to train children in reading techniques before they attain a mental age of at least six years does little to lower the age at which they can read successfully. In fact such training may leave no increment when the child has been reading for a time, and the effects of the training may be detrimental. It is somewhat like feeding a baby solid foods before his organism is ready for them. There is similarly a stage of development at which the individual is ready for intellectual specialization. To use methods of specialization before that time is a waste of effort just as in the case of the foregoing illustrations. The part that logically organized subject matter should play in preparing the specialist who will advance the frontiers of knowledge must be determined first of all by discovering the stage of growth at which the individual is ready to engage in specializing activities.

Dewey points out in this regard that there are three discernible stages of mental development.

In its first estate, knowledge exists as the content of intelligent ability—power to do. This kind of subject matter, or known material, is expressed in familiarity or acquaintance with things. Then this material gradually is surcharged and deepened through communicated knowledge or information. Finally, it is enlarged and worked over into rationally or logically organized material—that of the one who, relatively speaking, is expert in the subject.[15]

The latter stage mentioned is the one at which intellectual specialization is undertaken. At just what period of life this development is attained differs, of course, greatly among individuals. Little has been done experimentally to determine what ages represent most accurately various stages of intellectual growth. Opinion seems to agree generally, however, that individuals are not ready for specialization, especially in highly intellectual areas, before late adolescence. In line with this opinion there is a general movement in practice to designate the major responsibility of the secondary school through the first two years of college as that of providing general education. Training of specialists in the several fields of knowledge as well

[15] John Dewey, *Democracy and Education*, 1916, pp. 216–17. By permission of The Macmillan Company, publishers.

as in the professions is assigned as a special function of the university which is composed of the senior college and graduate school. This division of function is well illustrated by the report of the Carnegie Foundation on State Higher Education in California. Whatever else may be said of this report, it represents what is probably the most concise and clear-cut statement available on the function of various phases of the educational system.

It is the primary and fundamental function of the common school system extending from the earliest years of schooling, through kindergarten, elementary school, junior and senior high school, and the junior college, to educate the citizen for effective participation in all those common understandings and co-operations which are necessary to sustain the best in our complex contemporaneous civilization which is American. . . .

It is the main function of the university system, which includes the upper divisions of colleges, the graduate schools, and the professional schools, to educate specialists for the strategically important social services which modern civilization requires, and to do this with full regard to the number of such specialists that society can utilize.[16]

In elaborating the function of the common school system the report has the following to say about the secondary school program in which the logical arrangement of subjects has been especially dominant.

Much of the current criticism of the behavior of citizens as the product of schools is based on the fact that the common schools, above the elementary school are not really utilized by the student nor fully managed by teachers and administrators for this fundamental civilizing purpose. When this ideal is realized, subject boundaries will be less sharply defined. New and more practical groupings of materials will be devised, and the process of learning will be reorganized, much as is now being done in comprehensive courses at some 160 institutions in the United States. Problems will become more important than topics, libraries than textbooks. . . .

[16] *State Higher Education in California,* Report of the Carnegie Foundation for the Advancement of Teaching, California State Printing Office, June 24, 1932, pp. 17–18, 20.

The reconstruction of secondary education . . . will involve several marked changes from the traditional outlook and method.

In the first place, secondary education will be not less intellectual but more social and adaptive. It will be directed toward giving the student an understanding of the natural and social world in which he lives. The mastery of the academic letters, arts, and sciences will be no longer the end of his school mastery, but the educational means of understanding life. Whatever other resources of experience lie outside of the traditional disciplines, such as industrial arts and fine arts, will be utilized with full scholastic respectability as valued aids in realizing the new and broader conception of the human and social purposes of the common schools.

In the second place, secondary education will focus its attention more steadily on contemporaneous life, with its oncoming problems. The lag between what the school teacher and what present and impending citizenship requires will be decreased. Scholarship, once chiefly related to the past, will now be related to the present, with study of the past still highly valued to the extent that the contributions of the past inevitably persist in the present.

Thirdly, schooling will not be thought of as practically the end of education or learning, now too commonly and so fatally the case. Education will be regarded as a continuous process, coterminous with life, to which schools merely give impetus for further and continuous personal inquiry and growth. An education at school will be regarded as preparatory to continuous adult learning. How much academic ground is covered in the school building under a licensed or accredited teacher, will no longer be so important as it has been. What one learns anywhere in life, and the degree to which one has the impulse and power to continue to learn and think accurately will be far more important to all concerned—to the world, to the university, and, most of all, to the student himself.[17]

The position on specialization stated in this report appears to be gaining ground rapidly in professional schools and university departments. The qualifications asked of students entering this phase of training are, to an increasing degree, breadth of background, good work habits, and desirable attitudes. There is relatively little concern as to the proficiency which the entering student may have gained in lower schools in his chosen field of specialization. Thus, specialization, according to leading

[17] *Ibid.,* pp. 18–19.

thought, may appropriately make few specific demands for mastery of prescribed logically organized fields below the senior college level.

However, there still remains the question as to what provision should be made previous to specialization for experience in dealing with logically organized fields so that wise choice of a field of specialization may be made. It must be recognized that growth processes are gradual. The boy or girl does not suddenly gain insight upon entering senior college adequate to assure wise choice of a field of specialization. The student needs to know rather definitely what he is undertaking. He should have reasonable assurance that his abilities and interests will find opportunity for expression and growth in the field of specialization chosen. Thus the common school does have the responsibility, in addition to providing a general education, of making it possible for the individual to develop specialized interests and to become well acquainted with the demands in various fields of specialization. If this is done, the individual will have a real foundation for entering a chosen field of specialization. If it is not done, selection is largely the result of chance.

This development of interest and of adequate understanding to enable wise choice of a field of specialization probably proceeds through a gradual process of differentiation. That is, the child's interests, being at first extremely general and highly utilitarian, tend gradually to become more specialized and intellectual. Out of these general situations comes some particular element which attracts the child's attention. This may then become a point for study in and of itself. If encouraged, the individual may expand these special interests over a period of years, and ultimately choose his field of specialization on the basis of the experience thus gained.

The common school should so plan its program as to lay this foundation for wise entrance into specialization. This means that opportunity must be provided for pupils to follow and develop special interests of all types. It is not known specifically at what age such special interests are developed with sufficient

Chart IV

A Representation of Major Points of Emphasis in the Curriculum at Various Levels of the School System

PRE-SCHOOL		COMMON SCHOOL SYSTEM					UNIVERSITY SYSTEM	
Nursery School	Kindergarten	Primary Grades	Intermediate Grades	Junior High School	Senior High School	Junior College	Senior College	Graduate School

GENERAL EDUCATION

This phase of the curriculum should be concerned primarily with developing competency to assume the social obligations of membership in American democracy. The primary point of reference in its organization should be the social life in which the individual participates. It should be directed specifically to developing understanding of social life and to achieving effective participation in its activities.

SPECIAL INTERESTS AND APTITUDES

General courses should be provided for cultivation of special interests. Opportunity should be given to develop interests in a wide variety of fields, such as the languages, art, music, and mechanics. Choice of individual courses in the junior high school should lead to choice of fields of concentration in the junior college. Avocational interests should be developed and the basis laid for wise choice of vocation.

SPECIALIZATION

Choice of a field of specialization should be made on or before entrance to senior college. The requirements of specialization should be the chief determinant in making the curriculum in this phase of the educational program.

ADULT EDUCATION PROGRAM

At the close of the period of general education the individual should have developed adequate work habits to continue general education on a self-directive basis. Provision should be made for group activities through a program of adult education. Such a program should provide as well for those who drop out of school before completion of the program of general education.

283

intensity to be employed in a major way in shaping the educational program, but general opinion and practice suggest that it is during early adolescence. It may reasonably be expected then that some differentiation in curriculum should start in the junior high school. From this point on through the period of general education probably the opportunity to work on special interests should be gradually increased. On the junior college level the individual may select fields of concentration within which to work. In following out and developing special interests in this way the individual will frequently engage in undertakings that involve segments of logically organized subject matter. By so doing he gains a good idea of the demands the various fields make for specialization.

To summarize the point of view, the period of general education should include in its program opportunity for developing and following special interests. This may lead in the closing years of general education to selection of fields of concentration in which a major portion of the student's energies are spent. Such opportunities during the period of general education provide a basis for making a wise choice in specialization. The general concept is shown by Chart IV.

Now let us consider the relationship of study of logically organized subjects in the elementary and secondary school to effective use of the race heritage. We have already stressed the importance of gaining some understanding of the logical arrangement of subject matter in order to use it most effectively. How shall this be done in such a way as to accomplish the purposes of general education? In instruction of the better type developed primarily around logically organized subject matter, segments of logically arranged content are studied and then possible applications of these materials in life situations are sought. For example, in history the facts about a certain period are learned and then the significance of these facts for contemporary life is sought. In geography, generalizations and facts about various areas of the earth are memorized and then, when possible, relationships to things the child knows and considers important are pointed out. In arithmetic, processes are taught and then the types of situations in which these processes may be used are illustrated.

For effective general education there must be a shift in emphasis in this procedure. Subject matter must first be used, it must have significance for the learner. Then its internal relationships and logic of organization may be considered intelligently. In this case the learner's end or purpose to be realized is the primary point of orientation. Logical organization is secondary and is looked upon as a tool or means of achieving more effective use in the future. This does not mean, however, that the secondary orientation is unimportant or is to be slighted. It means simply that concepts of the organized fields of knowledge grow gradually in the mind of the student as he develops understanding of life and the world about him, and sees that logical organization of knowledge aids in understanding the factors with which he must deal. He generalizes before he states the generalization in formal terms. He knows before he defines.

When the facts and principles included in a logically organized subject have such a background of meaning and use, direct emphasis in the form of instruction and drill may appropriately be given to their mastery and to developing an understanding of the logical relationships involved. Gaps in the logical relationship may also be filled in by direct emphasis if the child's experience permits deduction of the intervening steps in meaningful terms to him. As the child approaches maturity the opportunity to do this increases. For example, the child from the first grade engages in experiences that involve facts and interpretations of historical significance. At first these facts have only limited meaning in terms of immediate situations. But as the child's experience broadens he becomes able to see more abstract relationships. For example, he commences to develop a concept of time relationships. As he proceeds from one undertaking to another the wise teacher will point out and emphasize time relationships. How is this event we are dealing with today related to the one we considered yesterday or last week? Did this occur before or after the undertaking we found out about in our work at the beginning of the year? Gradually the concept of relationship in time grows. And as it grows it is charged with meaning and significance. It is not mere memory. Eventually the child himself will come to appreciate the significance of this relationship in time to such an extent that he will engage directly in the enterprise of broadening his grasp of this relationship with understanding and of filling in gaps which he has not fully mastered. The illustration in Chart V may serve to emphasize the contrast in emphasis.

Thus, we have before us the possibility of organizing instruction so that the first and primary point of orientation is the end to be achieved or the purpose of the learner. Subject matter is selected first of all from this point of reference. A second point of orientation is the logical relationship that exists between the facts, information, principles, and formulas used, and those used previously. Development of an understanding of these relationships increases the significance of the material for the situation at hand. As situation is added to situation and more and more logical relationships established as a background, the material which is used by the individual in dealing with subsequent situations becomes increasingly significant.

ASSISTANCE IN SELECTING SUBJECT MATTER PROVIDED IN CURRICULUM DEVELOPMENT

We have already seen how studies of adult use and child interest and use contribute to the wise selection of subject matter. Attention is now turned to certain more general ways in which curriculum development influences the selection of subject matter. Consideration of these more general influences requires emphasis again on the point that what does or does not become the actual subject matter of the pupils is determined by specific learning situations. Teachers cannot make pupils master certain subject matter. They can only guide them in situations that require subject matter and help them to select and use sub-

Chart V

Illustration with Time Relationship in American History of the Way in which Logical Relationships of Subject Matter may Grow Out of the Meaningful Experiences of Children

Years of School

Concept of

Time Line
1500   1600   1700   1800   1900

XII — Twelfth Grade Child →

XI — This phase of the curriculum is composed of experiences which are of primary social significance. — Eleventh Grade Child →

X — The purposes which the children endeavor to achieve provide the basic relationship of subject — Tenth Grade Child →

IX — matter. Here is where the subject matter takes on social significance for the learner. Understanding of — Ninth Grade Child →

VIII — logical relationships of subject matter should grow out of this experience. Facts, events, and — Eighth Grade Child →

VII — principles should continuously be incorporated in a logical organization. For example, facts and events — Seventh Grade Child →

VI — in American History should be used continuously from grade to grade to develop understanding — Sixth Grade Child →

V — of the time relationship involved. Facts and events used at a particular time should flow into re- — Fifth Grade Child →

IV — lationship with other facts and events so that knowledge of time relationship grows from grade to — Fourth Grade Child →

III — grade. Concepts of this relationship might evolve as suggested on the right hand section of the chart. — Third Grade Child →

II — Second Grade Child →

I — First Grade Child →

Note: The dots suggest areas in which facts and events may be located in time. The number and specific location of dots have no particular significance inasmuch as the concept of time relationship developed by each child in a group will differ markedly.

ject matter wisely. The function of curriculum making is to place the teacher in the best possible position to give such guidance.

This desired end may be achieved by making available to the teacher a wide selection of carefully chosen potential subject matter. To illustrate the point, we may assume that a given individual decides to undertake exploration of certain Antarctic areas. He has the assistance in planning his expedition of one who has had some experience in such exploration and who has studied the matter extensively. The assistant may suggest a great variety of materials and equipment that should be taken. But this list will not be followed in all details. Discoveries in science and improved means of transportation and communication will modify the equipment chosen. The particular purpose of the expedition will exert a similar influence. Consequently, the person engaged in the undertaking will make a selection from the suggestions of the one who has had previous experience in such exploration in terms of the newly developed materials and the specific outcome he has in mind. A further selection is made as the expedition gets under way. Unexpected conditions and events make some materials useless and make desirable other materials not originally chosen. In other words, the developing course of action, being different from that experienced in previous expeditions, causes variation in the materials used and the extent of their use.

The curriculum worker can take the preliminary step in selecting subject matter. He can canvass available subject matter for educational ventures in certain areas as defined by the scope of the curriculum. He can see that the most valuable and worth while materials, in terms of past experience, are included in the suggestive list. He can see that the list is carefully selected in terms of the area to be dealt with. He can see that it is reasonably inclusive. He can suggest possible relationships to child purposes and outline the logical relationships that will most probably be involved. But this is as far as he can go. He cannot make the actual selection for the child any more than the one aiding the would-be explorer can determine previous to the exploration just what will be used.

These suggestions of potential subject matter may be in terms of pertinent generalizations, principles, laws, facts, events, formulas, and techniques; or in the form of objective materials, such as maps, charts, graphs, or construction materials. The more complete and carefully selected such suggestive lists are, the greater the possibility that appropriate subject matter will be found for given groups of children. Magazines, newspapers, pamphlets, bulletins, specimens, environmental materials, and similar items should find a large place in such suggestions. Much free material of real value is available for teacher and pupil use.

This procedure of suggesting a great variety of potential subject matter is contrary to much practice in which a very limited amount is suggested, but in which that little is prescribed. Such a procedure encourages, in fact almost requires, mere memorization. It looks on the acquisition of facts and skills as the end of education rather than the development of dispositions, attitudes, and methods of work. It overlooks, in brief, the essential relationship of race experience to the education of the individual. In contrast we hold that the school should provide extended and varied opportunities for the individual to make wide and discriminating selection of materials from the race experience that will help him achieve the worthy purposes for which he strives.

SELECTED REFERENCES

Adams, Sir John, "The Teacher as Integralist," *The Kadelphian Review*, 14: 5–10, November, 1934.
Bode, Boyd H., *Modern Educational Theories*, The Macmillan Company, New York, 1927, Chapter III.
Demiashkevich, M. J., "Integrated Instruction," *The Peabody Reflector and Alumni News*, 6: 133–34, May, 1933.
Dewey, John, *Democracy and Education*, The Macmillan Company, New York, 1916, Chapter XIV.
Dewey, John, *The Way Out of Educational Confusion*, Harvard University Press, Cambridge, Massachusetts, 1931.

Finney, Ross L., *A Sociological Philosophy of Education*, The Macmillan Company, New York, 1928, Chapter II.

Robinson, James Harvey, *The Humanizing of Knowledge*, George H. Doran Company, New York, 1926.

Wallas, Graham, *Our Social Heritage*, Yale University Press, New Haven, Connecticut, 1921.

Wesley, Edgar B., "Techniques for the Selection of Curricular Materials in the Social Studies," The Social-Studies Curriculum, *Fourth Yearbook of the National Council for the Social Studies*, 1934, pp. 32–44.

Whitehead, A. N., *The Aims of Education and Other Essays*, The Macmillan Company, New York, 1929, Chapter I.

CHAPTER XI

GRADE PLACEMENT AND TIME ALLOTMENT

The selection of subject matter was treated in the foregoing chapter as a general problem. Consideration is given in this chapter to the closely related problems of determining suitable grade placement and time allotment for various items of subject matter. These problems have received a great deal of consideration both from general curriculum committees and research workers. Courses of study present the work of curriculum committees and studies of widely varied types present pertinent research findings.

The chapter is organized in four main divisions. First, consideration is given to sources from which recommendations and standards for grade placement and time allotment are currently derived. Second, the bases upon which various recommendations and standards rest are treated. Third, certain factors of great importance in grade placement and time allotment, which are frequently overlooked, are discussed. Fourth, suggestions are made for dealing with grade placement and time allotment in practical programs of curriculum making. Before turning to consideration of the first of these, two preliminary points will be briefly discussed.

GRADE ORGANIZATION BASIC TO THE PROBLEM

Organization of our school system into grades is basic to the problems, as currently attacked, of placement of content and time allotment. In the early history of elementary education in America children of all ages were taught together in one room.

As attendance increased, additional rooms were provided but heterogeneous grouping was continued. The division of pupils among teachers was generally by subjects. Gradually, however, as numbers increased the school came to be divided into primary and grammar divisions. In some cases the terms higher and lower schools were used. Organization of the school into primary and grammar divisions was followed in turn by organization into classes. The master or teacher had the assistance of "ushers" who heard the various classes recite in small recitation rooms off the main room. Out of this practice grew grade organization with individual classrooms. Each group of students entering during a year formed a grade. There was consequently a grade for each year of attendance. Soon the idea developed that each year of school or each grade should represent a certain amount or level of achievement and steps were taken to define grade standards. The standards in turn became the chief determinants in regulating the progress of pupils, the subject matter which they studied, and the amount of time devoted to various types of undertakings. Consequently, the problems of grade placement and time allotment in the present school organization relate to the placement of content on grade levels and to the allocation of specified periods of time to the various items of content.

RELATION TO METHOD OF DEFINING SCOPE OF THE CURRICULUM

The first step in grade placement and time allotment is taken when the scope of the curriculum is defined. The method employed to define scope determines the terms in which grade placement and time allotment may be made, and very largely conditions the flexibility or rigidity, and the generality or minuteness of placement and time allotment. For example, if the textbook method of defining scope is employed, it becomes necessary automatically to define grade placement and time allotment quite rigidly in terms of text materials to be covered. The center of interest procedure, on the other hand, places hardly any restrictions on the materials that may be treated and the time to be alloted to various phases of work. The basis employed in a given program for defining grade placement and time allotment should be consistent with the particular method used to define the scope of the curriculum. As the sources of recommendations and standards for grade placement and time allotment and their bases are discussed it should become clear which may be employed consistently with various methods of defining the scope of the curriculum.

SOURCES OF RECOMMENDATIONS AND STANDARDS

There are four available sources of recommendations and standards for grade placement and time allotment. They are as follows: (1) current practice, (2) judgment of specialists, (3) experimentation, and (4) practices in experimental schools. These sources are not mutually exclusive as to the particular basis upon which the recommendations or standards rest. Difficulty of content may be the basis of recommendations from any one of the sources. The difference is that in one case the findings on difficulty may represent experimentation; in another, they may represent what specialists believe to be the order of difficulty; in another, what practitioners generally think about the matter; and in another, what experimental school practice may show. It is sometimes difficult to tell what the basis is in a particular case. The recommendations and standards derived from one source also influence those presented by other sources. For example, current practice has no doubt been influenced by the judgment of specialists, while the judgment of specialists has in turn been influenced by current practice. Consequently, certain relationships will be noted between the sources as the discussion proceeds.

CURRENT PRACTICE

Current practice is the most widely employed source of standards for both grade placement and time allotment. In grade placement this basis is used in determining what subjects should be taught in particular grades; how topics within subjects should be divided between grades; and what specific materials, such as poems, stories, and plays, should be assigned to the respective grades. Current practice may be determined by analysis of courses of study, of programs of study, and of textbooks. A number of such analyses to facilitate the development of standards have been made. Certain representative ones have been selected for illustration.

Kyte [1] made an extensive study of practice in placing the subject matter of history in the elementary grades. Fifty-three courses of study, none of which were more than seven years old and all of which were in use in the public schools, were used in collecting the data. He found in regard to the grade organization of subject matter that twenty-two courses of study make no provision for history in the first two grades, that sixteen of the twenty-two courses omit it in the third grade, that eleven of the sixteen omit it in the fourth grade, and that four of the eleven omit it in all grades below the seventh. He found also that six broad topics are given for the second grade in the thirty-one courses of study which outlined work for that grade. The number of topics increases to twenty in the fifth grade and decreases to seventeen in the sixth grade. In the second grade, community and primitive life is listed in ten courses of study and primitive life is listed in eight additional courses. In the third grade, primitive life, city, county, and community life, local history and pioneer life are listed in twenty of the thirty-seven courses of study offering history in this grade. There is considerable agreement on subject matter in twenty courses, although there is general disagreement as to the terms used to describe it. In regard to the repetition of the various topics of American history it was found that three of the courses of study omit topics that are covered four times by three other courses. The number

[1] George C. Kyte, "Variations in the Organization of the Elementary Courses of Study in History," *Educational Administration and Supervision*, 13:361-376, September, 1927.

of courses that repeat the materials of American history two times range from twenty-two to thirty-four, while the range is from one to nine that repeat materials three times. The range of dates indicated by the courses shows that some of the pupils in the seventh year cover 2700 years of history while other pupils cover only seventy years. Even more extreme differences were noted in other grades. The author concludes that "we find comparatively little guidance regarding the grade-placement of subject matter," and "when we compare the recommendations emanating from the deliberations of the various committees we are forced to conclude that the proposals of any one committee constitute guesses which may or may not be any better than those of any other committee." [2]

The Superintendents' and Principals' Association of Northern Illinois appointed a Committee of Seven to make an investigation to determine when to teach the topics of arithmetic. This committee,[3] as a preliminary step, gathered data as to the grades in which different topics are now being taught. In doing this they analyzed current practice in 125 Middle West school systems. A study of the data reveals that there are wide differences among the schools as to the time topics are introduced and almost as great variation in the time indicated for completion of instruction on the topics. For example, addition facts are introduced in the first grade in seventy schools, in the second grade in fifty-two schools, and in the third grade in three schools. It is indicated that instruction on this topic should be completed in the second grade in thirty-six schools, in the third grade in forty-seven schools, in the fourth grade in twenty-four schools, in the fifth grade in four schools, in the sixth grade in one school, and in the seventh and eighth grades in two schools each. Subtraction facts have about the same distribution. Multiplication is introduced from the first to the fourth grade and is to be completed from the third to the eighth grade.

[2] *Ibid.*, 375.
[3] Carleton W. Washburne, "When Should We Teach Arithmetic?" *Elementary School Journal,* 28:659–665, May, 1928.

A study of grade placement of topics in oral English was made by Pribble.[4] He analyzed five series of language books to determine in which grades certain forms are introduced for drill. The number of points of usage on which the books provide drill in the third grade range from eleven to twenty-seven. There is agreement of all the books on just two items; namely, "saw" and the elimination of "ain't." Four of the five agree on the use of "came" and the proper distinction between "is" and "are," while three agree on six other items. In the fourth grade there is even less agreement and in the fifth grade there is agreement on only one point. The distribution indicated in Table V shows the grade in which the five series of language textbooks

TABLE V

GRADE PLACEMENT OF TOPICS IN ORAL ENGLISH [5]

FORM	NUMBER OF SERIES WHICH INTRODUCE FORMS IN THIRD GRADE	NUMBER OF SERIES WHICH INTRODUCE FORMS IN FOURTH GRADE	NUMBER OF SERIES WHICH INTRODUCE FORMS IN FIFTH GRADE	NUMBER OF SERIES WHICH INTRODUCE FORMS IN SIXTH GRADE	NUMBER OF SERIES WHICH DO NOT PROVIDE FOR DRILL ON FORM
ate	2	1	1	0	1
sit	1	2	1	1	0
lie	0	2	2	1	0
ran, run . . .	2	1	1	0	1
broken	1	3	0	1	0
well, good . . .	1	2	1	1	0

first introduce certain forms for drill. From these data it will be seen that there is very little agreement among the series of language textbooks concerning the introduction of drill in language forms.

Conrad and Hickok [6] studied the grade placement of literary selections in junior and senior high schools. Their source of

[4] Evalin Pribble, "Grade Placement of Topics in Oral English," *Elementary School Journal*, 29:437–438, February, 1929.
[5] *Ibid*, p. 438.
[6] Erna B. Conrad and Katherine Hickok, "Placement of Literary Selections," *The English Journal*, 19:477–484, May, 1930.

data was fifty-four courses of study. They found that twenty-five selections appeared in twenty-three of the courses of study. Ten of these selections had a grade range of six; four, a grade range of five; four, a grade range of four; and seven, a grade range of three. In other words, 40 per cent of the selections were assigned to every grade in the junior and senior high school.

A study of the grade placement of poems that are commonly used in the grades was made by Dyer.[7] Three sources of data were employed. The first source consisted of sixty-one courses of study that contained lists of poems for the various grades of the elementary school and the junior high school. The second source consisted of twenty-one series of elementary school readers. The third source consisted of 201 books written by specialists in the teaching of English. Thirteen of these books listed poems for the separate grades. A list of 161 poems was compiled from these sources. The poems ranged in frequency of mention from twenty to 164. Nearly a fourth of them are suggested for a range of six or more grades.

A number of studies of practices in grade placement were made in connection with the National Survey of Secondary Education. Smith made a study of the placement of literary selections in English courses. She concluded:

As You Like It is taught in every grade in junior and senior high schools except one. The same is true of recent poetry, the Rime of the Ancient Mariner, and Ivanhoe. The Lady of the Lake appears in grades 8 through 11. So also do the Vision of Sir Launfal, the Tale of Two Cities, and Julius Caesar. The mode for Julius Caesar is grade 9, the year for which Irion's study proves it too difficult except for pupils with an intelligence quotient of 110 or higher.[8]

Hilpert studied fifty-six courses of study ranging in size from a single typed page to a bound volume of 262 printed pages to de-

---

[7] Clara A. Dyer, "The Placement of Poems in the Grades," Curriculum Investigations, Franklin Bobbitt, editor, Supplementary Educational Monographs No. 31, University of Chicago Press, 1926, pp. 181–202.

[8] Dora V. Smith, Instruction in English, National Survey of Secondary Education, Bulletin No. 17, Monograph No. 20, 1932, p. 52.

termine the grade placement of topics in art. Eighteen per cent were too brief or indefinite to give an indication of grade placement. Of the remaining courses of study he says:

There is a general spread of all art topics through every grade in the secondary school. Most of the art work offered in the seventh and eighth grades is required, while art offered above the ninth grade is chiefly elective. With the exception of stage design, clay modeling, and metal craft, all topics were found as low as grade 7 up through grade 12. Certain topics are taught in every grade in a comparatively large number of schools. For example, the topics, art appreciation, design, and drawing are organized into separate courses and taught (1) chiefly as required work in grades 7 and 8, (2) either as a required or an elective course in grades 9 and 10, and (3) as an elective course in grades 11 and 12. Other topics tend to be grouped at certain grade levels. For example, costume design, interior decoration, figure drawing, and fabric design are more frequently taught in grades 10 and 11 than in the lower grades. Metal craft is found in grades 10, 11, 12, although it is taught in comparatively few schools. The courses of study offer no clue as to the manner of determining the grade placement of topics in art. Some traditional placements are still adhered to because no educational research has been made to determine the proper level for the different topics in art.[9]

Other studies of current practice in grade placement might be given but these are sufficient to show what current practice standards have to offer on the problem. There is no evident tendency for topics in any of the subjects to gravitate to particular grade levels. The same materials in the case of every study are found to be placed in several grades. Consequently, the guidance in grade placement provided by current practice is of little value. At best it suggests a range of grades in which certain content is generally held to be satisfactory.

Current practice has dominated standards of time allotment even more than standards of grade placement. As early as 1905 a study of time allotment was made by Payne,[10] who studied

[9] Anne E. Pierce and Robert S. Hilpert, *Instruction in Music and Art*, National Survey of Secondary Education, Bulletin No. 17, Monograph No. 25, 1932, pp. 49–50.
[10] Bruce R. Payne, *Public Elementary School Curricula*, Silver, Burdett and Company, 1905.

the curricular offerings and time allotted to them in ten cities. This was followed by a study by Holmes [11] in which the number of cities from which data were gathered on time allotment was increased to fifty. More recent studies have been made by Ayer,[12] Kyte,[13] Mann,[14] and Covert.[15]

These several studies vary little in significant findings and implications. This is shown, for example, by comparison of the time found by Ayer, Mann, and Covert, to be devoted to the three R's, the content subjects, and special subjects. These comparisons may be made from the data in Table VI. It will

TABLE VI

COMPARISON OF TIME ALLOTMENT AS SHOWN IN VARIOUS STUDIES

SUBJECTS	49 CITIES (Ayer)	444 CITIES (Mann)	80 CONSOLI-DATED SCHOOLS (Covert)	15 STATES (Mann)
Threee R's	50.6	51.7	50.9	48.9
Content	15.5	11.8	22.7	13.8
Special	33.9	36.5	26.4	37.3

be seen that the three R's receive very nearly the same proportionate allotment of time in every case. Content subjects and special subjects receive very much the same proportionate allotment in the cities and states. The consolidated schools give more time proportionately to the content subjects and less to special subjects.

Perhaps the most significant fact brought out by studies of cur-

[11] Henry W. Holmes, "Time Distribution by Subjects and Grades in Representative Cities," *Fourteenth Yearbook, National Society for the Study of Education,* 1915.

[12] Fred C. Ayer, "Time Allotments in the Elementary School Subjects," *City School Leaflet No. 19,* Bureau of Education, Washington, D. C., 1925.

[13] George C. Kyte, *A Study of Time Allotments in the Elementary School Subjects,* California Curriculum Study, Bulletin No. 1, University of California Press, 1925.

[14] Carleton H. Mann, *How Schools Use Their Time,* Teachers College, Columbia University Contributions to Education No. 333, 1928.

[15] Timon Covert, *Time Allotment in Selected Consolidated Schools,* Rural School Leaflets, No. 49, United States Office of Education, 1930.

rent practice is the extreme variation in the amount of time allotted to various subjects. Mann, whose study is the most extensive of the more recent ones, emphasizes this point especially. He presents for each subject the maximum and minimum allotments in the cities which he studied. He shows that allotment to grades one to six in reading varies in the 444 cities studied from 600 minutes per week to 2,475 minutes per week. In arithmetic, the variation is from 405 minutes per week to 1,797 minutes per week. When considered in terms of ratios the study shows that in one subject the city giving the maximum time allotment devoted 144 times as much time as the city with the smallest allotment. The smallest difference found is in arithmetic where the largest allotment is 4.4 times greater than the smallest allotment. Table VII, showing all of the variations, is reproduced from Mann's study. From the findings of this investigation the author concludes that "standardization in time allotment practice in the school systems of the United States is totally lacking." [16] These results reveal how little agreement there is as to what constitutes the amount of time essential for instruction in a given subject.

The weakness of current practice as a basis for grade placement and time allotment should be obvious. It represents the average of many divergent judgments and divergent practices under varying conditions, based upon widely different ideas of what education is and what it should attempt to accomplish. In the particular cases used to make up the average, each item of content and time allotment is associated with a complete plan of curriculum organization. When these cases are averaged, a result is secured which is entirely dissociated from a given type of curriculum or instructional program and, therefore affords little guidance for time allotment in a given curriculum program. Average practice in time allotment merely assigns a given amount of time to a school subject but does not indicate what the objectives or materials of instruction should be during that time. With this relationship lacking, there is danger that schools using

[16] *Op. cit.*, p. 141.

TABLE VII

BY POPULATION GROUP

SUBJECT	444 CITIES, ALL GROUPS COMBINED	POPULATION GROUP					
		100,000 or over	30,000–100,000	10,000–30,000	5,000–10,000	2,500–5,000	Less Than 2,500
Reading	11.8	4.1	5.6	4.2	10.3	5.5	4.8
Phonics	35.8	11.4	31.3	14.0	10.0	12.4	8.0
Literature	109.0	4.4	8.8	13.3	31.2	22.5	82.5
Language	14.1	3.6	14.1	7.5	5.5	7.4	3.3
Arithmetic	4.4	2.7	3.2	3.8	3.0	2.9	4.0
Penmanship	12.0	2.8	6.3	3.6	2.2	6.4	8.3
Spelling	48.0	5.7	2.8	3.9	3.0	38.0	6.8
Geography	5.4	4.2	4.3	3.9	3.1	5.1	4.0
History	22.9	12.9	6.8	17.9	15.5	17.1	12.0
Social Science	33.8	4.8	6.8	25.6	—	1.4	—
Citizenship and Civics .	107.1	5.0	14.3	46.7	40.0	107.1	18.5
Nature Study and Elementary Science . .	144.0	6.4	8.4	31.3	43.3	108.0	19.0
Art and Drawing . . .	47.6	6.1	17.0	12.0	18.0	40.8	37.4
Music	18.0	2.5	2.5	3.1	3.4	11.0	14.8
Household and Manual Arts	41.4	20.2	41.4	22.0	9.0	13.3	4.4
Handwork	83.0	2.9	31.0	83.0	23.5	27.5	14.0
Projects and Activities .	422.5	3.3	422.5	13.3	30.0	20.4	10.0
Health Education . .	42.0	6.1	21.0	36.0	11.6	19.4	8.7
Physical Training . . .	66.0	5.2	18.7	66.0	12.2	51.0	24.8
Recess	31.9	4.4	18.0	9.6	26.0	8.0	16.0
Opening Exercises . .	19.7	6.0	7.1	13.3	13.8	8.0	16.1
Supervised Study . . .	174.0	5.0	108.3	49.5	60.0	154.0	139.2
Unassigned and Free Time	696.7	142.8	293.3	283.3	189.5	117.5	326.6
Miscellaneous	490.7	22.5	66.0	116.7	28.4	59.2	184.0

Table VII should be read as follows: Among 444 cities of all population groups the city which allots the greatest amount of total time in grades 1–6 to reading gives 11.8 times as much time as the city making the smallest total allotment. Among cities having a population of 100,000 or over, one city allots 4.1 times as much time to reading as another city of the same group. Of those cities belonging to the 30,000–100,000 population group one city allots 5.6 times as much time for reading as another. Data are to be read similarly for other groups and for other subjects.

[17] Mann, *How Schools Use Their Time*, p. 142.

this average standard will set up allotments to cover widely different courses of study. The merits and shortcomings of average current practice as a basis for standards are well summarized in a research bulletin of the National Education Association.

Is such present practice a safe guide to those charged with the drafting of courses of study? This question cannot be answered with certainty. The opinion and experience of a considerable number of persons is generally more reliable than that of a few. On the other hand *the prevailing practice* is not necessarily *the best practice*. An average of the practice resulting from many discordant ideals may be worthless. Most people would agree, however, that considerable deviation from common practice is justified only for carefully thought out reasons. If for some good reason a city wished to lift the ability of its children considerably above the average standard in a particular subject such as handwriting, an allotment of time to handwriting above that of common practice might be defended. Such an allotment might also be defensible as a part of a scientific experiment. On the other hand, it would be indefensible to deviate significantly from general practice on no other basis than the vigorously expressed opinion of a few individuals.[18]

Practically, however, it must be recognized that current practice is the only source from which data can be secured for all the subjects and activities included in the offerings of a majority of public schools. Consequently, even in cases where certain other standards are adopted for given subjects or phases of the curriculum, present practice is frequently resorted to in dealing with the remaining phases or subjects. At least current practice can serve as a check on extreme practices that are not carefully considered in light of the educational needs of the child. It is reasonable to expect the school or teacher who departs widely therefrom to have carefully analyzed reasons for so doing. On the other hand, progress undoubtedly will be made only through departure from current practice, and consequently well-conceived variations should be encouraged.

[18] "Keeping Pace with the Advancing Curriculum," *Research Bulletin of the National Education Association,* 3:127–28, September and November, 1925.

JUDGMENT OF SPECIALISTS

Judgment of specialists has exerted influence on grade placement and time allotment through a variety of sources. Yearbooks and special studies of professional societies, prepared by committees that are national in scope, have been an especially important source of such influence. Rugg says of this influence that, "curriculum making by national committees was so vigorous that by 1900 the prestige of these committees, made up of subject-matter specialists, was unquestioned." [19]

The first important national committee, the Committee of Ten, indicated the pattern of work for succeeding committees. This committee organized nine separate conferences on a subject basis. Members of the conferences were predominantly college faculty members. All committees made efforts to extend their subject further down into the high school and six of the committees specifically sought a greater time allotment. A great deal of attention was given to standardization of content and to time allotment.

The report of the Committee of Ten was followed immediately by the appointment of the Committee of Fifteen. This committee had the specific responsibility of investigating the length of elementary education. The major outcome of its work was the recommendation of the earlier introduction of certain academic studies such as Latin and algebra.

Work of these committees led in turn to the appointment of various committees in subject fields. The influence of these later committees was especially far-reaching in English and history. The placement of materials in these fields in various grades was dominated almost wholly by such committees, and the organization of the subject matter of English and history in the present school program is largely the result of their influence.

The activities and influence of such committees have continued up to the present time and most of them have persisted in fol-

[19] Harold Rugg, "Three Decades of Mental Discipline: Curriculum-Making via National Committees," *Twenty-sixth Yearbook of the National Society for the Study of Education*, Part I, 1927, p. 39.

lowing the general pattern set by the conferences of the Committee of Ten. The importance of the subject under consideration and the need for consideration of it in the curriculum as a separate field from all other work are emphasized. Recommendations are usually made which would extend the subject further down into the grades or would increase the time allotment, or both. Recent committees of importance include the Classical Investigation (1924), the Modern Language Study (1930), the Committee on Arithmetic of the National Society for the Study of Education (1930), the Committee on Science of the National Society for the Study of Education (1932), the Committee on Geography of the National Society for the Study of Education (1933), and the Commission on the Social Studies of the American Historical Association (1934).

The last of the aforementioned committees represents a hopeful departure in committee procedure and vision. In so far as grade placement and time allotment are concerned it is held that the social studies curriculum should be developed as an integral part of the entire instructional program. The position of the committee is shown by the following statement:

> The program of social science instruction should not be organized as a separate and isolated division of the curriculum but rather should be closely integrated with other activities and subjects so that the entire curriculum of the school may constitute a unified attack upon the complicated problem of life in contemporary society.[20]

Whereas specialists have made operative general limitations on grade placement and time allotment through national committees, they have exerted a more specific influence through textbooks. Due to the textbook domination of the curriculum, discussed in Chapter III, the topics included by subject specialists in textbooks and the comparative emphasis given them have served as important determinants of grade placement and time allotment.

[20] *Conclusions and Recommendations of the Commission,* Report of the Commission on the Social Studies, American Historical Association, Charles Scribner's Sons, 1934, p. 48.

It is extremely difficult to evaluate the recommendations of specialists for grade placement and time allotment. Their recommendations, because of their specialized interests, all too frequently emphasize a particular subject unduly. It is the rare specialist who does not feel that his subject should receive more time than it is accorded. The result is a tendency to pit subjects against subjects rather than to look at the educational program as a whole in marking out general time and grade guide lines. This encourages the development of a piecemeal, unrelated instructional program.

There is also a further difficulty encountered when the judgments of specialists are expressed through national committees. The basis of this difficulty is well described by Kelley.[21] When a group of specialists are involved the majority of the group tends to be traditional in point of view. Decisions consequently do not represent the forward-looking point of view in the field, but tend to represent the intrenched position. The result is that few reports of national committees have been liberal or progressive in nature. The point is emphasized by the statement sometimes made that the minority reports of national committees are generally the ones which suggest the direction of progress and development.

Analysis of the sources in which the judgments of specialists as to desirable grade placement and time allotment are presented indicates a tendency to avoid specific recommendations. Reports of national committees appear to be increasing in generality. Consequently, curriculum committees will find few specific statements by specialists upon which to base practice. Recent yearbooks, mentioned previously, and professional books discuss the issues involved and make general recommendations. In a few cases, as for example the recommended time allotments by the Arithmetic Committee of the National Society for the Study of Education,[22] specific suggestions are made.

[21] Truman L. Kelley, *Scientific Method,* The Macmillan Company, 1932, pp. 153ff.
[22] *Twenty-ninth Yearbook of the National Society for the Study of Education,* "Report of the Society's Committee on Arithmetic," 1930, p. 77.

EXPERIMENTATION

The number of experimental studies that bear on grade placement and time allotment is surprisingly small when considered in light of the emphasis that has been placed in the past quarter of a century on scientific procedures. There have been several limited studies dealing largely with skills and a very few that are more comprehensive in nature. When considered as a whole, however, investigations in any subject cover such a small part of the subject that they throw relatively little light on the problems of time allotment and grade placement in the large.

The scarcity of experimental evidence on these problems is made especially obvious in the report of the Committee on Arithmetic of the National Society for the Study of Education, a subject in which a large amount of such evidence might be expected. The time allotments recommended are not supported by a single experimental study. The only supporting data are from current practice in public school systems.

A number of studies have been made of the grade in which work in various subjects should begin. Taylor[23] conducted an experimental study bearing on this problem in arithmetic in 1916. He omitted formal work in arithmetic in the first grade for the experimental group. He found that by the time these children completed the third grade they were as capable in arithmetic as children in the control group who had formal work in the first grade. Haggerty[24] studied arithmetic results in schools in Indiana with this point in mind. He concluded that the second grade was the best place to begin formal arithmetic work.

Since these two early studies of the problem, little has been done that even approaches experimental procedures. Studies have been made of the situations in which young children need and use numbers and number concepts, and of ways of teaching

[23] Joseph S. Taylor, "Omitting Arithmetic in the First Year," *Educational Administration and Supervision*, 2:87–93, February, 1916.
[24] M. E. Haggerty, *Arithmetic: A Co-operative Study in Educational Measurements*, Indiana University Bulletin No. 18, 12:385–507, 1915.

primary number. But the problem is still one that must be determined by judgment based largely on general experience. When attention is turned to the placement of arithmetical topics after formal work is introduced there is even less evidence of an experimental nature. A committee of the Superintendents' and Principals' Association of Northern Illinois reports a study of the placement of certain topics in arithmetic according to mental age.[25] The committee introduced a series of topics at different grade levels in an effort to discover at what mental age children learn most effectively certain phases of arithmetic and what mastery of more elementary facts is necessary for the effective learning of various phases. Certain minimal mental-age levels and achievement scores in arithmetic are specified which the findings indicate are necessary for effective mastery of various phases of arithmetic.

In considering the grade placement of topics in arithmetic, Buswell and Judd point out the wide divergence of practice and indicate the general lack of evidence with which to solve the difficulty. They state: ". . . there is the widest possible divergence regarding the distribution of topics throughout the grades. . . . What has been done up to this time opens the way to analytical study but can hardly be said to have determined, with anything like completeness, the proper content and arrangement of the topics of the course."[26]

The situation is revealed even more strikingly by Brownell's analysis of research in arithmetic. He does not report a single controlled-group experiment on grade placement or time allotment.[27] In fact, all of the studies on grade placement use the "consensus technique" or "analysis of school records and marks." The same is true of studies of time allotment, with one exception, in which case the "special training technique" is used. One can only conclude that the extent of experimentally verified evidence

[25] *Twenty-ninth Yearbook, op. cit.*, pp. 641–670.

[26] Guy T. Buswell and Charles H. Judd, *Summary of Educational Investigations Relating to Arithmetic*, Supplementary Educational Monographs, University of Chicago Press, 1925, pp. 19, 21.

[27] *Twenty-ninth Yearbook, op. cit.*, pp. 423ff.

on the problems of grade placement and time allotment in arithmetic is practically *nil*.

Arithmetic is selected for rather extended consideration on this point because in this field especially it might be expected to find experimentally verified evidence. The condition found is typical of other fields. For example, Mann states of the situation in reading: "A search through the literature on reading fails to show any conclusive experimental evidence bearing on the amount of time necessary for instruction in reading." [28]   In fact, in no field has the optimum grade placement, sequence, or time allotment of topics been verified experimentally. Arrangement rests almost wholly on current practice and judgment of specialists.

When all available evidence that has experimental verification is considered, it seems necessary to conclude that there is practically no help provided for treating the problems of grade placement and time allotment. This matter is given further consideration in a discussion, later in this chapter, of difficulty as a basis for determining standards of grade placement and time allotment.

PRACTICE IN EXPERIMENTAL SCHOOLS

Practice in experimental schools of the progressive type has exerted a marked influence on grade placement and time allotment. This practice differs markedly from most public school practice. This is due largely to emphasis on different bases of placement and allotment. Whereas the other sources of recommendations and standards rest largely on difficulty of content and logical relationships of subject matter, experimental schools have emphasized the importance of pupil interests, aptitudes, and needs. As a result, the tendency has been for experimental schools to depart from the rigidity characteristic of public school grade placement and time allotment.

The position of the progressive group of experimental schools on time allotment and grade placement is rather well indicated

[28] *Op. cit.*, p. 66.

by Rugg and Shumaker's contrast of the daily program in a traditional and a progressive school.

> The first difference is one of flexibility. The program of the formal school is rigid, permanent; that of the child-centered school is very flexible, tentative. The former is a scheme of narrow pigeonholes: spelling from 9:20 to 9:35, penmanship from 9:35 to 9:45, oral or written composition from 9:45 to 10:00, and so forth.
>
> A day in a child-centered school, however, is a much more flexible affair. . . . It is, indeed, merely a provisional plan for the work of the class. Certain intervals in the day must be arranged for in advance—those, for example, that make use of special teachers in shop, laboratory, gymnasium, music room, and library. But the preponderance of the day in a child-centered school is left relatively unprogrammed. . . .
>
> Flexibility! Schedules so tentative that educative units may be developed, "rich in group and individual activity; in opportunity for developing responsibility, initiative co-operation, and scientific attitude; in the need for information and skill; and in social meaning."
>
> A daily program planned in part by the pupils themselves; partially evolving from the newly discovered interests and needs of pupils, and partly planned, in skeleton only, in advance by the teacher. Finality in scheduled details is incompatible, therefore, with both the aims and the content of the new education.[29]

Grade placement and time allotment according to this point of view obviously cannot be set up in final form in advance, nor can they be made by subjects. Rather, grade placement tends to be in terms of large centers of interest or units of work, and time allotment in terms of major divisions of the school day for types of activities. These are held as general guides and the details are developed as the work with a particular class progresses. But even the general guides may be modified if the teacher feels that some other plan of work would be more valuable for the pupils. The daily program presented on the following page illustrates these general characteristics.

The influence of experimental schools, therefore, on grade placement and time allotment has been in the direction of in-

[29] From Rugg-Shumaker's *The Child-Centered School*, Copyright 1928 by World Book Company, Yonkers-on-Hudson, New York, pp. 72–73.

DAILY PROGRAM IN THE CHILD–CENTERED SCHOOL [30]

TIME	MONDAY	TUESDAY	WEDNESDAY	THURSDAY	FRIDAY
9: 00	Informal greetings, reports, observations, rhymes, music, events of current interest, informal activities designed to create a mental set conducive to a happy profitable day.				
9: 15	**ARITHMETICAL ENTERPRISES** Play stores, banking activities, handling of school supplies, etc. Although rich in arithmetical content through which the child is trained in skills and abilities, such units also yield abundantly in group and individual situations which develop initiative, responsibility and co-operation. The flexible period provides opportunity for individual instruction.				
10: 00	**HEALTHFUL LIVING ENTERPRISES** Physical education enterprises, free play, the nutrition program, and adequate relief periods are provided for daily; units of work, such as: "the study of milk," "a balanced meal," etc., provide enterprises which have healthful living as a center of interest but provide situations developmental of social and civic attitudes as well.				
10: 50	**LANGUAGE ARTS*** Oral and written composition, spelling and writing developed from activities rich in opportunities for expression, as the writing of a play to be presented in the auditorium period, puppet shows, the school newspaper, etc. The period should provide opportunity for literary discrimination and original expression; the long period provides for concentration of effort and attention according to individual interest and need.				

* In one-teacher schools, the program during this period should include special activities for the younger children abundant in reading experiences. Much interesting and profitable material for self-directed activities for the younger children is indispensable.

[30] *Teacher's Guide to Child Development*, Ruth Manning Hockett, Ed., California State Department of Education, 1930, pp. 355–56.

TIME	MONDAY	TUESDAY	WEDNESDAY	THURSDAY	FRIDAY
12 : 00	Lunch, Rest, and Directed Playground Activities				
1: 00	Music: Activities, music appreciation, rhythm, harmonica, band, orchestra, etc.	Avocational Activities			
		Nature Club, school museum, aquarium, gardens, terrarium.	Creative Art and constructive activities in pottery, weaving, painting, drawing.	Use of auditorium for music, dancing, dramatics, projects, stagecraft, related to class activities.	Civics Club. Committees responsible for various phases of school life.
1: 50	Recreation and Rest				
2: 00	READING GROUPS: LIBRARY ACTIVITIES Group organization on the basis of reading ability provides opportunity for remedial work with children having reading deficiencies and library guidance to superior readers. The quiet reading period may contribute to the development of information needed in the class activities related to social science, avocational, or health or other interests.				
2: 50	Recreation and Rest				
3: 00	Social studies activities	Social studies activities	Free creative work period	Social studies activities	Shop enterprises

creasing flexibility. This influence, while not so widespread as sometimes believed, judging from present courses of study, unquestionably has done much to liberalize public school practice on these points. The administrator who demands that above all else the teacher devote to each subject the precise number of minutes assigned it and to each topic its exact proportion of time is undoubtedly more rare than in former years. This may be accounted for to a considerable extent by the impact of experimental school practices on public schools.

It is difficult to know just how far experimental school practices provide a safe guide for public schools. Manifestly it is the purpose of such schools to try new and unverified procedures. Consequently, it is important that the experience of the experimental school be of such type and duration as to show the procedure to be a good one before it is adopted elsewhere. The situation is complicated also by the fact that experimental schools frequently deal with highly selected pupils and have especially well-prepared and capable teachers. They can, consequently, secure a higher quality of work from the pupils than in ordinary cases and place larger responsibilities on teachers than could be assumed successfully by the average teacher. Nevertheless, those practices in regard to time allotment and grade placement which prove successful in experimental schools may advisedly be given gradual trial in public school systems.

BASES OF RECOMMENDATIONS AND STANDARDS FOR GRADE PLACEMENT AND TIME ALLOTMENT

The sources of recommendations and standards for grade placement and time allotment rest on certain bases. That is, standards recommended by specialists may be based on judgment of the difficulty of the materials to be taught; practices in experimental schools may rest largely on the interests of the children taught; and so with the other sources of recommendations and standards. There are, in fact, three bases upon which these various sources of recommendations and standards may rest. They are: (1) logical relationship of subject matter, (2) difficulty of subject matter, and (3) interests of pupils.

LOGICAL RELATIONSHIP OF SUBJECT MATTER

The relation of logically organized subject matter to the selection of content has been discussed at some length in the preceding chapter. This relationship may exert considerable influence on grade placement and time allotment. This is especially true if the "subject matter" procedure of defining the scope of the curriculum is employed. For example, if a particular subject is to be taught in a particular grade, the logical relationships in the subject may be permitted to dictate what the content of the course will be and the order in which it will be treated. This automatically determines grade placement of topics and influences in a vital way the time that may be devoted to each.

For example, if ancient history is to be taught in a particular grade, there are certain facts, events, and generalizations which mark essential steps in the development of ancient civilizations. These facts, events, and generalizations, are automatically placed in sequence in the grade to which ancient history is allocated. It is the relationship of one to the other and the need of one for an understanding of the other that dictates their inclusion. Or it is frequently contended that the child must develop arithmetical abilities in a prescribed order. He must move through a series of number processes because of the logic of the series. Division, for example, must follow addition and subtraction.

This position has a certain amount of validity but it may lead to gross violations of conditions for effective learning. There are, undoubtedly, certain stages of growth and development which have discernible characteristics which are significant for education. But that the minute classification of abilities and their development according to their logical antecedent is desirable is another matter. It is to be doubted, for example, that a child does in fact first learn addition, and then subtraction, and then division. He most probably learns them all together. That is, as a three-year old he begins to ask for two pieces of candy and half a banana. The concept of division does not wait for the concept of addition to reach a specified stage and then begin development. It has its beginning apparently along with addition in a large, general, indistinct concept of number.

Whitehead discusses the relationship of the necessary antecedence of subjects to the basis of organizing subject matter.

It is impossible to read *Hamlet* until you can read; and the study of integers must precede the study of fractions. And yet even this firm principle dissolves under scrutiny. It is certainly true, but it is only true if you give an artificial limitation to the concept of a subject for study. The danger of the principle is that it is accepted in one sense, for which it is almost a necessary truth, and that it is applied in another sense for which it is false. You cannot read Homer before you can read; but many a child, and in ages past many a man, has sailed with Odysseus over the seas of Romance by the help of the spoken word of a mother, or of some wandering bard. The uncritical application of the principle of the necessary antecedence of some subjects to others has, in the hands of dull people with a turn for organization, produced in education the dryness of the Sahara.[31]

A second factor requires consideration in the use of the logical arrangement of subject matter as the basis of grade placement. What the essential facts, events, and generalizations are in a particular subject is usually left to the judgment of specialists. We sometimes assume a considerable unanimity in their judgments on this point. That is, ancient history is ancient history no matter who deals with it and algebra is algebra regardless of personalities. Analyses of topics and materials included in textbooks, however, indicate that judgments vary widely as to just what is essential for mastery of most subjects. These considerations should lead the curriculum worker to question critically any content which for the reason alone of logical relationship with other content is held to require particular grade placement or time allotment.

[31] A. N. Whitehead, *The Aims of Education and Other Essays*, 1929, p. 26. By permission of The Macmillan Company, publishers.

DIFFICULTY OF SUBJECT MATTER

Difficulty of subject matter is probably the most generally favored basis for grade placement and time allotment. The work of educational psychologists and of specialists in elementary school subjects especially emphasizes this basis. The general procedure is to determine first of all the relative difficulty of various items of subject matter in the particular subject. Logical analysis and studies of the ability of pupils to learn the various items are the techniques most frequently employed. Consensus of opinion, case studies, and other techniques are used occasionally. The various items are next arranged in sequence from the most easily mastered item to the one most difficult to master. This sequence determines the grade placement of materials once the beginning grade is set. Traditional practice and judgment exert the greatest influence on determining the grade at which the subject is introduced. Length of time assigned to each item of subject matter under present practice is largely determined by the number of items that must be covered by each grade in order to complete the material included in the subject.

This basis is emphasized in several subjects. A number of studies have been made that are designed to determine difficulty and thus make grade placement and time allotment on this basis possible. Brownell reports eleven such studies in arithmetic.[32] One of these is based on the consensus technique and the remaining ten on logical analysis. Thus logical analysis is employed almost exclusively in determining steps of difficulty in arithmetic. This means, of course, that what is known about difficulty in arithmetic rests largely on judgment. More adequate studies have been made of the difficulty of number combinations, but even here conclusions are highly tentative. Knight points out that data are inadequate to determine difficulty with assurance in the case of most arithmetical processes. He states:

[32] *Twenty-ninth Yearbook, op. cit.,* p. 432.

Perhaps of greater damage than our relative ignorance of interference factors is our relative ignorance of the learning difficulty of many of the important items to be learned. Amounts of practice needed to learn most items are yet to be determined or even approximated.[33]

In geography difficulty is also emphasized as a basis for grade placement. The National Society for the Study of Education Yearbook Committee on Geography states: "Materials should be carefully graded on the basis of their relative difficulty."[34] They define seven levels of difficulty in geographical materials. These levels were determined by logical analysis and error studies. Each level of difficulty is made the basis of the work of one grade. Current practice is followed in recommending that geography start in grade four. Thus, grade four is assigned materials of difficulty level I, grade five of level II, and so on.

Webb[35] endeavored to determine the difficulty of various materials in science. He analyzed eighteen textbooks to discover the amount of space devoted to certain major divisions. He devised tests upon the material and tested from one thousand to two thousand pupils in each grade of the elementary school. Success in the items of the tests is used as the basis of determining difficulty. He concludes that physiology and physiography are suitable in the sixth grade; biology in the seventh; and physics in the eighth. Chemistry is of doubtful value in any of the grammar grades.

Mathews'[36] study of the extent to which pupils in the public school in grades four to twelve inclusive comprehend various types of social studies materials involves consideration of difficulty. The measure of difficulty employed is the percentage of objective questions dealing with the various types of material

[33] *Ibid.*, p. 156. Quoted by permission of the Society.

[34] *Thirty-second Yearbook, National Society for the Study of Education,* 1933, p. 204.

[35] Hanor A. Webb, *General Science Instruction in the Grades,* Contribution to Education No. 4, George Peabody College for Teachers, Nashville, Tennessee, 1921.

[36] C. O. Mathews, *Grade Placement of Curriculum Materials in the Social Studies,* Teachers College, Columbia University Contributions to Education No. 241, 1926.

correctly answered by the median of each group of pupils. A sample of each type of material was tried in three grades. The types of materials included in the samples were: episodes; descriptions; newspaper articles; expositions; bar, line, and circular graphs; time lines; pictograms; and maps. The conclusions reached were: (1) ability to comprehend and interpret graphic selections increased gradually from the fourth to the twelfth year; (2) episodes are comprehended better than other types of material in all grades except the sixth and the ninth; (3) the circular graph is the easiest and the line is the most difficult to comprehend, while the bar graph is midway between.

Cavins [37] made a study in which he assigned various poems to grade levels he found to be most appropriate. Difficulty was the primary basis of assignment. His procedure was to ask a group of experts what they considered the most important factors involved in determining the place of a particular poem in the course of study. The factors in the placement of a poem most frequently mentioned by the experts were experience required for interpreting the poem, factual background, abstractness of theme, diction and style of language, meter, imagery, and narrative thread. The majority of these, it will be noted, relate to difficulty. With these factors as a guide he prepared tests to measure pupil understanding of selected poems in grades five to eight. Each test item was decided upon according to whether it represented the difficulties of the particular poem and whether it tested the ability of the pupil to understand the difficulties. Upon the basis of the results of the test, poems were assigned to the various grades.

A number of efforts have been made to determine the relative difficulty of reading materials. Kyte [38] reports such a study that was made as a basis for developing a series of readers. Fifty-four selections were chosen arbitrarily. Tests were then devised to measure the difficulty of the selections. These tests were ad-

[37] Lorimer V. Cavins, *Standardization of American Poetry for School Purposes*, University of Chicago Press, 1928.

[38] George C. Kyte, "Calibrating Reading Material," *Elementary School Journal*, 25:553–546, March, 1925.

ministered to the second, third, and fourth grades. Selections that were too easy for more than 80 per cent of the pupils were considered inappropriate. It was concluded that 40 per cent of the reading materials selected upon the basis of individual opinion would be ill-adapted to the grade assigned and that arrangement of materials on the same basis in a text would be chaotic.

Mullins, Stone, and Reed attempted to devise a statistical procedure whereby French selections could be rated for difficulty. They studied the relationships of vocabulary, sentence structure, and idioms. A refined statistical technique was employed in an effort to discover a basis upon which the difficulty of selections might be determined. They conclude: ". . . it seems that the determination of the difficulty of a selection of literature is such a complex problem that it cannot be attained by statistical computation." [39]

Other studies might be mentioned, but the foregoing provide a reasonably representative list. When all subjects are considered this basis has probably exerted greater influence than any other on recommendations and standards of time allotment and grade placement. Although it is a basis looked upon with considerable favor, it rests upon a basic assumption which is open to question. This assumption is that intellectual growth proceeds most effectively by advancing from simple to more difficult learnings. There is some evidence which leads to the questioning of the soundness of this assumption as applied to all situations and cases. In the first place, it is doubtful if learning as a rule actually proceeds in this way. Many times complex learnings precede simple learnings. Whitehead states this matter forcefully:

It is not true that the easier subjects should precede the harder. On the contrary, some of the hardest must come first because nature so dictates, and because they are essential to life. The first intellectual task which confronts an infant is the acquirement of spoken lauguage.

[39] Marjorie Mullins, Margaret B. Stone, and Georgia B. Reed, "A Consideration of Some Criteria for Textbook Selection," *The French Review,* 7:480, May, 1934.

What an appalling task, the correlation of meanings with sounds! It requires an analysis of ideas and an analysis of sounds. We all know that the infant does it, and that the miracle of his achievement is explicable. But so are all miracles, and yet to the wise they remain miracles. All I ask is that with this example staring us in the face we should cease talking nonsense about postponing the harder subjects.

What is the next subject in the education of the infant minds? The acquirement of written language; that is to say, the correlation of sounds with shapes. Great heavens! Have our educationists gone mad? They are setting babbling mites of six years old to tasks which might daunt a sage after lifelong toil. Again, the hardest task in mathematics is the study of the elements of algebra, and yet this stage must precede the comparative simplicity of the differential calculus.[40]

In the second place, there are some grounds to believe that the initial attack on a problem or step in an undertaking or development of an idea must by the very nature of the situation be the most difficult one in so far as learning is concerned. That is, the individual must first of all get a general idea of what the problem or undertaking or idea is about. He must test it here and there trying to find out what its general characteristics are and what elements are involved in it. This is a most trying, slow, and frequently tedious process. But as the elements of the situation begin to clarify or to become differentiated, attack may be made on more specific aspects of the situation and learning may increase in speed as it becomes more simple in nature. The further the individual proceeds with the endeavor the more simple do things learned frequently tend to become. The child, for example, beginning work with addition has the overwhelming task of finding out the characteristics of addition. To him, at most, it is a very general idea. Addition facts must be associated with a wealth of content. They must be treated slowly. But as he moves forward and the idea of addition grows he can deal with increasing readiness with the specific facts involved in addition. Addition consequently becomes easier rather than more difficult as he progresses.

[40] A. N. Whitehead, *The Aims of Education and Other Essays*. By permission of The Macmillan Company, publishers, 1929, pp. 25–26.

Obviously this concept of addition is in direct opposition to the concept that memory of addition facts represents effective knowledge of addition. Addition facts are merely the means of arriving at a convenient common practice and a way of thinking. Of the two, the way of thinking is the important thing. Consequently, if difficulty is related to understanding, to ideas, to problems, rather than to mere memory, there is reason to believe that in many cases we tend to proceed from the difficult to the less difficult.

In the third place, difficulty as a basis for grade placement and time allotment is open to question because of the fact that intensity of stimulus may make a difficult thing easier. For example, given processes x and y to be learned, y may be learned much more readily than x even though more difficult if the learner has a strong stimulus to learn y and a weak stimulus to learn x.

In the fourth place, grade placement and allotment of time in terms of comparative difficulty overlooks the wide variability of achievement and ability within a group of children on a given grade level. When children in the same grade vary, as they do, three, four, and five grades in achievement in the several subjects and fifty to sixty points in intelligence, it is impossible for them as a grade to study material of uniform difficulty.

These considerations lead to the conclusion that difficulty merits much more critical evaluation as a basis for grade placement and time allotment than it is usually accorded. Undoubtedly it is of some significance, but it is highly questionable that the analytical studies that propose to reduce the steps in learning to scientific accuracy and the materials used to statistical certainty of fitness can be followed safely. Evidence on this point will have to be much more conclusive than it now is to warrant the minute following of the requirements of difficulty in grade placement and time allotment when even an individual teacher's or supervisor's judgment indicates something else to be better for a child.

INTERESTS OF PUPILS

In the preceding chapter interests of pupils were considered as a general basis for selecting subject matter. As a basis for grade placement interests may be used in two ways. First, the interests of a particular group of children may be permitted to determine the placement of subject matter. That is, what a given group of children are interested in at a given time and the duration of their interest may determine what books they read, what references they use, what facts they employ, what they write about, and so on. Time allotment may be determined in the same way. The children may be permitted to spend as much time on a particular phase of subject matter as they care to spend. This procedure places the entire burden of determining desirable grade placement and time allotment on the teacher.

Second, interests that tend to be common to the respective grades may be made the basis for placing subject matter on grade levels. For example, if it is found that pupils generally in the fourth grade are interested in airplanes, then material about airplanes is considered appropriate for the fourth grade. If pupils in the fifth grade generally are found to like a particular poem or story, then that poem or story is considered appropriate for that grade.

When interest is used in this second way, studies of the characteristics of interests common to pupils on the several grade levels are necessary. A limited number of such studies have been made. One of the first of such studies was made by King.[41] She enlisted the aid of the school superintendents and supervisors in ten representative cities. A day or two before the experiment the children in all the grades were asked to think over poems which they had learned or read and to select at least two that they liked best. They were also asked, but not compelled, to state why they liked them. Using the results thus obtained, the poems with the highest frequency of mention in each grade

[41] Cora E. King, "Favorite Poems for Children of Elementary School Age," *Teachers College Record*, 23:255–273, May, 1922.

were listed in a suggested course of study. From the reasons given by the children as to why they liked them, lists were also made around centers of interest. Typical of these interests are: poems about nature, poems about life, poems appealing to the emotions, story-telling poems, social poems, patriotic poems, and humorous poems.

Another study of the poems to be included in the various grades using interest as a basis was made by Huber, Bruner, and Curry.[42] They conducted an extensive experiment lasting two years to determine the poetry most suitable for children in the elementary and junior high schools.

The first step taken in this study was to determine present practice. This was done in two ways. First, they considered the subjective opinion of expert teachers of poetry. Second, they examined 900 courses of study and practically all of the most used textbooks and made a minute analysis of thirty of each of the books used in grades one to nine. From these analyses preliminary lists of poems were prepared to be submitted to the children.

The experimental list, which consisted of approximately one hundred poems for each grade, was published in experimental booklets and put into the hands of about fifty thousand children in experimental centers. The administrative organization was so developed that each booklet was used in five different grades. The plan of experimentation consisted in having the pupils come in contact with a certain number of poems and asking the pupils to check which they liked best and which they liked least. During a study of sixty poems twelve definite reactions from each child were recorded. Out of 573 poems used in the experiment, only fifty-nine or 10.3 per cent of the entire list rank among the upper fifty poems of three or more grades. Results of this experiment show that present practice is only 39 per cent right.

These authors also suggested centers of interest in sequence of the various grades: animals and play, lullabies, fairy poems,

[42] Miriam B. Huber, "Children's Interest in Poetry," *Teachers College Record*, 28:93–104, October, 1926.

humor and nonsense, heroes, home and danger, satire, romance and tragedy, and seeking the causes of things.

An extended study of the grade placement of books suitable for the independent reading of children on various grade levels has been made under the general direction of Washburne. This study was carried forward initially in the research department of the Winnetka, Illinois public schools. The result was the preparation of the *Winnetka Graded Book List*. Later the study was extended in co-operation with the Children's Committee of the American Library Association and a list of books suitable for pre-school children, children in each grade of the elementary school, and in junior high school was prepared for the guidance of parents, teachers, and librarians. This list is entitled *The Right Book for the Right Child*.[43]

The technique employed in preparing this list involves both pupil interest and difficulty. The ultimate criterion, however, is pupil interest and for this reason the study is classified under this heading. The general procedure was to secure a list of books which children of known age, sex, and reading ability had read and enjoyed. In the primary grades a selected group of experienced primary teachers listed the book which they found most interesting to children and indicated the grade for which each book was most appropriate. In the remaining grades a large number of pupils indicated how well they liked various books. This list of books in terms of preference shown for them by children on various grade levels formed the basis for developing a procedure by means of which books of unknown qualities might be allocated to grades. The procedure for allocation is highly technical. The statistical result implies that it is possible to place books for which the degree of pupil interest or preference is not known on grade levels where pupils have expressed a preference for books of similar characteristics.

The place of pupil interest in organizing instruction has already been considered at some length in Chapter VIII. Little need

[43] Carleton Washburne, Vivian Weedon, and Mary S. Wilkinson, *The Right Book for the Right Child,* John Day Company, 1933.

be added here to that discussion. As pointed out there, spontaneous, unguided interests of children do not provide a sound basis for organizing instruction and consequently for selecting subject matter for grade levels. On the other hand, fundamental interest which rests upon experiences that provide a basis of understanding is essential to learning. Consequently, studies of interests commonly found in various stages of the child's development may provide valuable data for grade placement.

FACTORS FREQUENTLY OVERLOOKED IN GRADE PLACEMENT AND TIME ALLOTMENT

There are a number of important factors that influence grade placement and time allotment which are frequently overlooked. Most of these factors have been suggested in discussing the various bases of grade placement and time allotment. It is the purpose here to call attention specifically to them.

Whatever the method of regulating their progress may be, pupils in a given grade vary widely in achievement of all kinds as well as in capacity to learn. This is a fact of utmost significance to any plan of grade placement and time allotment. Frequently, the fact that a given group of children approximate, on the average, the standard for their grade is permitted to blind the curriculum worker to the fact that the average may represent children of most diverse abilities. For example, the tabulation in Table VIII presents the number of questions in the Thorndike-McCall Reading Test that were answered correctly by children in various half grades of a city school system. Although each succeeding half grade tends to answer more questions correctly than preceding grades, the distribution of questions answered correctly by each grade covers a large portion of the same range.

The situation is the same when measurement is in terms of more specific abilities. Consider, for example, the data in Table IX on achievement of lower fifth and seventh grade pupils in paragraph meaning, sentence meaning, and word meaning.

TABLE VIII

A SUMMARY OF THE RESULTS ON THE THORNDIKE-MCCALL READING TEST PRESENTED BY GRADES AND DISREGARDING AGE AND INTELLIGENCE FACTORS [44]

QUESTIONS CORRECT	GRADE							
	4L	4H	5L	5H	6L	6H	7L	7H
1	1							
2								
3	1	1						
4	2							
5	2		1					
6	1	1					1	
7	4		1					1
8	4	1	1					
9	1					1		
10	4	3	1					
11	4	5	2					
12	7	5	2			2		
13	7	1	4	1				
14	10	4	1	3	1			1
15	10	3	6		4			1
16	6	6	5	7	4	1		3
17	9	10	7	4	4	1	1	1
18	12	13	7	1	6	1	4	2
19	12	7	10	8	3	8	6	3
20	8	6	11	9	6˙	10	6	5
21	9	10	10	6	11	13	6	10
22	7	2	6	8	9	9	9	17
23	4	5	4	6	8	5	10	10
24		2	1	6	7	7	12	10
25	2	3		5	6	3	10	14
26		3	1	5	4	4	11	9
27			1	1	5	1	16	2
28			1	1	4	1	6	2
29					2	1	3	1
30							3	2
31					1			
32							1	
33								
34								
35								
Number of Cases	127	91	83	71	85	68	105	94

[44] Adapted from *Survey of the Schools of Port Arthur, Texas, 1925-1926*, Bureau of Publications, Teachers College, Columbia University, New York. 1926, p. 132.

TABLE IX

SUMMARY OF THE RESULTS ON THE STANFORD ACHIEVEMENT TESTS
IN READING [45]

GRADE SCORE IN 7-YEAR ELEMENTARY SCHOOL	5L			7L		
	Para-graph Meaning	Sentence Meaning	Word Meaning	Para-graph Meaning	Sentence Meaning	Word Meaning
			2			
	1	1				
	1	2				1
2.8 –2.9	2	3	2	1		
3.0 –3.1	2	2	5			2
3.2 –3.3	2	5	5			
3.35–3.5	5	8	6		4	
3.6	3	8	4		3	
3.7 –3.9	7	16	9		4	3
4.0	10	12	8	4	3	
4.05–4.2	15	8	9	1	4	2
4.3 –4.5	13	14	18	11	9	6
4.6 –4.75	10	9	8	2	6	6
4.8 –5.0	3	8	12	2	8	12
5.1 –5.2	15	1	7	12	3	6
5.3 –5.45	5	5	5	5	9	5
5.5 –5.7	3	1	6	4	4	6
5.8 –5.9	7	7	6	5	4	7
6.0 –6.25	2		2	7	4	6
6.3 –6.4	1	2	1	3	3	3
6.5 –6.6				1	3	5
6.7 –6.8	4	2	2	5	5	4
6.9 –7.0	3	1		8	1	2
7.1					1	
7.2 –7.3	1	1	1	4		2
7.5					2	1
7.6 –7.65	3	2	2	5		2
7.8 –7.9	2		1	2	4	3
8.0 –8.2	1	3		6	3	2
8.3		1			3	2
8.4 –8.7	1			2	1	4
8.8 –9.0			1	1		
+		1	1	1	1	2
+	1			4		1
+				1	2	1
+				1	2	2
+						
+					2	
Number of Cases	123	123	123	98	98	98

[45] Adapted from *Survey of the Schools of Port Arthur, Texas, 1925–1926,* p. 134.

Even though the average of the seventh grade is above that of the fifth, much of the range covered by scores is the same.

This variability results in the possibility that any instruction group may have in it pupils of widely varying achievement. For example, one instruction group selected at random in a city school system in grade 6A had the following variability: One pupil had a mental age of nine years three months; and another, a mental age of thirteen years three months. The differences in achievement in the school subjects were even greater than the difference in mental age. In reading, one pupil achieved only as well as an average beginning grade four pupil; another achieved considerably better than an average grade ten pupil. In spelling, one pupil achieved only as well as an average pupil two-thirds through grade three; another achieved almost as well as an average beginning grade nine pupil. In English, the variation was from half way through grade two to the beginning of grade ten, and in arithmetic from half way through grade three to above grade ten. In chronological age, the variation was also great. To find children of all capacities in intelligence in each grade of the public school system is to be expected. It seems, then, rather fantastic to expect to find definite distinctions between grades in suitability of materials and in time required for their mastery. Variability in achievement and capacity of the pupils suggests the need for widely varied subject matter and materials on each grade level rather than uniformity.

A second factor frequently overlooked is that individual pupils vary greatly in different abilities. As a rule it is true that level of ability in one field tends to be associated with a similar ability in other fields. Consequently, the child who is good in one subject or type of activity tends to be good in others. But there are enough exceptions to the rule to complicate the matter of grade placement and time allotment. For example, a child may equal the sixth grade standard in arithmetic, the fifth grade standard in spelling, and the fourth grade standard in reading. If he is in the fourth grade, it is obvious that much of the material selected for a grade four average would not suit .

him at all. He needs materials of one type in reading, another type in spelling, and still another type in arithmetic. This leads again to a need, not for standardized subject matter, but for varied subject matter to meet the needs of each particular child in a given field.

A third factor that is overlooked by certain approaches to the problems of grade placement and time allotment is that certain stages of growth or development are essential for effective participation in certain types of activities. As discussed in the preceding chapter, the fact that specialization with its requirement for mastery of logically organized fields of knowledge is characteristic of maturity has been particularly ignored in connection with grade placement. Specialization is a stage of growth or development which is reached through other stages of growth that have their own peculiar characteristics. But the curriculum has been organized as though it was something that had to be prepared for specifically for many years, and has forced into the lower grades of the schools undue emphasis on logical relationships.

Difficulties are encountered in giving consideration to this factor because of the inadequacy of knowledge about various stages of growth. Such work as has been done is largely with infants and young children. This work, of course, suggests the importance of the problem and possible methods of attack, but throws no particular light on the problem in the period of common school education. Beauchamp points out the need for studies of this type in order to attack the problem of grade placement satisfactorily. He states in connection with a study of grade placement and organization of materials in science that ". . . the problem of how pupils progress in the development of the ability to use science as a method of thinking should be investigated and should be made a major factor in determining the content and organization of the materials of instruction." [46] In the meantime, until studies are made available to provide

[46] Wilbur L. Beauchamp, *Instruction in Science*, National Survey of Secondary Education, Bulletin No. 17, Monograph No. 22, 1932, p. 39.

exact information concerning the characteristics of various stages of growth and their implications for grade placement and time allotment, judgment, as critical as possible when based on uncontrolled observation, should be used to give this factor consideration in dealing with grade placement and time allotment.

GRADE PLACEMENT AND TIME ALLOTMENT IN PRACTICAL PROGRAMS OF CURRICULUM MAKING

The practical curriculum worker usually seeks a procedure whereby subject matter can be arranged on grade levels and the time required to master it stated with some finality. Optimum arrangement and time allotment are goals long striven for, but as conditions now stand there is little hope of attaining these. So many variable elements are involved in grade placement and time allotment that fixed relationships and quantities cannot be defined as absolutes. It must be recognized that there are few "specifics" in subject matter to influence mental development in a particular predetermined way. That is, the same desirable way of behaving can be induced through a variety of subject matter, and subject matter that will induce it with one person may not do so with another. Consequently, so long as children differ radically in their capacities, abilities, aptitudes, and temperaments; so long as environmental conditions vary as they now do; so long as the ability and methods of teachers vary; so long as our lack of experimentally verified evidence is anything like as great on these problems as it now is; the much sought for optimum arrangement of subject matter and optimum allotment of time will not be attained except as the individual teacher has the insight and judgment to provide it for the individual pupils under his guidance. In brief, grade placement and time allotment are ultimately resolved into the questions of what is best for a given pupil in a given situation, and how much of his time he can afford to devote to it. This individual basis is clearly implied by the principles enunciated by Thorndike and Gates to determine the optimum placement of facts or principles. They state:

1. Other things being equal, introduce a fact or skill at the time or just before the time when it can be used in some serviceable way. This is the criterion of *need*.

2. Other things being equal, introduce a fact or skill at the time when the learner is conscious of the need for it as a means of satisfying some useful purpose. This may be called the criterion of *felt need*.

3. Other things being equal, introduce a fact or skill when it is most suited in difficulty to the ability of the learner. The optimum degree of difficulty is one which challenges the learner to enlist his best efforts but which is not so hard as to lead to failure or serious errors. A person's ability will depend both upon the level of maturity reached through inner growth and upon the facts and skills acquired by means of previous experience. This is the criterion of *difficulty*.

4. Other things being equal, introduce a fact or skill when it will harmonize most fully with the level and type of emotions, tastes, instinctive and volitional dispositions most active at the time. This may be called the criterion of *temperamental compatibility*.

5. Other things being equal, introduce a fact or skill when it is most fully facilitated by immediately preceding learnings and when it will most fully facilitate learnings which are to follow shortly. This is the criterion of *facilitation*.[47]

What then can the curriculum worker do in regard to the matter, if the ultimate responsibility must be the teacher's? In practical programs of curriculum making several things can be done to aid teachers in accomplishing this desirable end. In the first place, general guides can be set up. That is, general limitations for the work of grades with suggested points of emphasis and major time divisions may be given. In doing this the demands of the particular situation for which the curriculum is being developed should be given special consideration. Teachers with one type of training, working with children in one type of school and in a particular social setting will find one type of general guides helpful, while to teachers in other situations the same guides would be largely worthless. In making the necessary adjustments, it will be found desirable to use various sources of recommendations for grade placement and time allotment.

[47] Edward L. Thorndike and Arthur I. Gates, *Elementary Principles of Education*. By permission of The Macmillan Company, publishers, 1929, pp. 209–210.

The Florida State committees, for example, studied current practice, recommendations of specialists, experimental school practices, practices in their own schools, the type of training of their teachers, the demands of the administrative organization of the schools, practices in use of textbooks, and other items relating to the state situation, and then on the basis of judgment set up general guides that appeared to be most satisfactory for Florida schools. Frequently, special studies of the factors that condition grade placement and time allotment in the given school system may advisedly be undertaken. Studies of prevailing practice, pupil interests, environmental conditions, and materials found most useful by teachers may be found valuable.

In the second place, a variety of suitable subject matter and possible points of emphasis may be suggested. So long as conditions make it necessary for the teacher to make the ultimate adjustment in grade placement and time allotment in terms of individual pupil needs, this adjustment will be most adequately made if the curriculum worker suggests to the teacher a wide variety of possibilities. The effort should not be to suggest subject matter of one level of difficulty on a given grade level, but rather of many levels of difficulty, not to suggest books that deal with a limited group of interests but that deal with a wide group of interests. Similarly, varied ways of arranging emphasis in terms of time should be suggested rather than one only.

Closely related to the foregoing point is the provision for flexibility. Curriculum making can aid in achieving wise grade placement and time allotment if the individual teacher is permitted flexibility to adjust subject matter and time allotment to pupil needs, interests, and abilities. If limitations are made in general terms and a variety of suggestions are given, the intelligent teacher, if permitted flexibility in developing his program, will make a much wiser grade placement and time allotment for a given group of children than the curriculum worker considering children in general can possibly make. The poorer teacher can still be guided in the selection of one particular plan and be no worse off than previously.

In the fourth place, more effective time allotment and grade placement can be achieved if specific help is given teachers to develop programs of work. Most teachers have worked so long under rather severe restrictions in grade placement and time allotment that they require considerable help in organizing programs of work that meet adequately the needs of particular groups of children and school situations. Consequently, if desirable flexibility is provided in grade placement and time allotment, teachers must have a great deal of help and guidance in its wise use. Frequently, the mistake is made of trying to shift suddenly and completely from one type of program of work to another type. A curriculum program should provide opportunity for teachers to grow gradually from the particular point where they are toward more effective programs. Provision of opportunity to do this and guidance in its accomplishment is one of the ways in which effective grade placement and time allotment may be achieved through curriculum making.

In practical programs of curriculum making then, it will be found possible to aid in achieving optimum grade placement and time allotment (1) by providing general guides for the work of the several grades, (2) by suggesting a variety of suitable subject matter and points of emphasis, (3) by providing for flexibility, and (4) by providing aids for teachers to develop programs of work that fit their particular situations. In doing these things it will be found necessary to employ a variety of sources of recommendations and standards, to study the various bases of these, to study the particular situation at hand, and finally to make a judgment as to what is most appropriate.

SELECTED REFERENCES

American Historical Association, *Conclusions and Recommendations*, Report of the Commission on the Social Studies, Charles Scribner's Sons, New York, 1934.

Beauchamp, Wilbur L., *Instruction in Science*, National Survey of Secondary Education, Bulletin No. 17, Monograph No. 22, Government Printing Office, Washington, D. C., 1932.

Bagley, W. C. and Kyte, G. C., *The California Curriculum Study*, University of California Press, Berkeley, California, 1926.

Caswell, Hollis L., *Program Making in Small Elementary Schools*, Revised edition, Field Study No. 1, Division of Surveys and Field Studies, George Peabody College for Teachers, Nashville, Tennessee, 1932.

Dyer, A. R., *The Placement of Home Economics Content in Junior and Senior High Schools*, Home Economics Curriculum Study No. 1, Bureau of Publications, Teachers College, Columbia University, New York, 1927.

Mann, Carleton H., *How Schools Use Their Time*, Contributions to Education No. 333, Bureau of Publications, Teachers College, Columbia University, New York, 1928.

Mathews, Chester O., *The Grade Placement of Curriculum Materials in the Social Studies*, Contributions to Education No. 241, Bureau of Publications, Teachers College, Columbia University, New York, 1926.

National Society for the Study of Education, Twenty-ninth Yearbook, Public School Publishing Company, Bloomington, Illinois, 1930.

National Society for the Study of Education, Thirty-first Yearbook, Part I, Public School Publishing Company, Bloomington, Illinois, 1932.

National Society for the Study of Education, Thirty-second Yearbook, Public School Publishing Company, Bloomington, Illinois, 1933.

Pierce, Anne E. and Hilpert, Robert S., *Instruction in Music and Art*, National Survey of Secondary Education, Bulletin No. 17, Monograph No. 25, Government Printing Office, Washington, D. C., 1932.

Rugg, Harold O. and Shumaker, Ann, *The Child-Centered School*, World Book Company, Yonkers-on-Hudson, New York, 1928, Chapter VI.

Smith, Dora V., *Instruction in English*, National Survey of Secondary Education, Bulletin No. 17, Monograph No. 20, Government Printing Office, Washington, D. C., 1932.

Thorndike, Edward L. and Gates, Arthur I., *Elementary Principles of Education*, The Macmillan Company, New York, 1929, Chapter IX.

Washburne, Carleton; Weedon, Vivian; and Wilkinson, Mary S., *The Right Book for the Right Child*, John Day Company, New York, 1933.

Whitehead, A. N., *The Aims of Education and Other Essays*, The Macmillan Company, New York, 1929, Chapter II.

CHAPTER XII

TEACHING PROCEDURES

Thus far our discussion has centered on the one hand around the elements of the curriculum that relate to the aims and purposes of society and the means of achieving them through the schools, and, on the other hand, around the interests, purposes, and activities of children. Activity on the part of the teacher as the immediate agent of society has been implied throughout the discussion.

We turn now to consideration of the activities in which the teacher engages in order to carry forward the educative process. The number and variety of such activities may be extended almost without limit. Even when reduced to types of activities they constitute a list of such proportions as to be both confusing and discouraging. Charters and Waples,[1] from a number of sources, compiled a list of approximately twelve thousand duties or activities engaged in by teachers. These they classified by types under seven main divisions which contain one thousand and one different statements of teacher activities. Out of such a maze of possible activities there arises the necessity of providing some means of selecting and organizing teacher activities appropriate to the teacher's immediate task. Such selection and organization of teacher activities we designate as teaching procedures.

CONCEPTS OF TEACHING PROCEDURES

A distinction should be made between the use of the terms teaching method and teaching procedure. Method is commonly

[1] W. W. Charters and Douglas Waples, *The Commonwealth Teacher-Training Study,* The University of Chicago Press, 1929.

thought of as an adopted pattern or a special or definite system of procedure. Thus, we refer to the inductive or the deductive method of reasoning, the lecture method, or the question-and-answer method of teaching a lesson. In either case a general pattern or plan determines the manner of selecting and organizing the specific activities engaged in. In other words, it determines the teaching procedure. In the traditional organization of instruction, activities tend to become stereotyped and routinized so that the teaching procedure becomes in fact a special method. Thus, we refer to a special method of teaching subtraction or reading or the use of the comma. Each of these methods requires certain teacher activities often developed in great detail. This concept of teaching procedures as a series of special methods admits the possibility of setting forth an entire course of action in detail in advance. On the contrary, the concept of teaching procedures here employed is that specific things to be done by the teacher cannot be determined in advance, but that guides or procedures may be provided that will make possible suitable choice and organization of teacher activities as they may be dictated by the situation in which they are to be used.

It is not suggested that the teacher must eschew teaching methods. On the contrary, if the teacher is to choose his activities wisely an even wider acquaintance with various methods of instruction is necessary than would be required if his way were charted in detail in advance. Such a concept of teaching procedure requires an evolving method rather than a predetermined one. In order to develop effective procedures to meet day-to-day situations as they arise, it is necessary that teachers not merely know a method but that they know many methods, and that they be able to choose activities appropriate to pupil needs at the moment.

Implications for general method are considered in Chapter XIV under the general question of organizing instruction. We turn, therefore, to consideration of teaching procedures implied by such a plan of organization and in accord with the concept pointed out above.

TEACHER ACTIVITIES INVOLVE A PLAN OF ACTION

The selection and organization of teacher activities involve a plan of action. A plan of action is merely a proposed series of activities so related that the individual may reasonably expect that they will result in the desired outcomes. In accord with the concept of the curriculum held by the writers, teacher activities may be conveniently divided into four general classes which indicate major steps of teaching procedure. It is recognized that other classifications might be just as appropriate as those here used. It is further recognized that this classification holds no particular implication for the organization of instruction although it is in accord with the organization suggested in the succeeding chapter. The classifications here treated are: (1) teacher activities that have to do with the study of the environment; (2) teacher activities that have to do with the study of the pupils; (3) teacher activities that have to do with the limitations of the curriculum; and (4) teacher activities that have to do with the direction of pupil activities.

TEACHER ACTIVITIES THAT HAVE TO DO WITH THE STUDY OF THE ENVIRONMENT

The general environment of children exerts a marked influence upon the nature of the activities engaged in and the results obtained in the schools. Information concerning various elements in the environment is, therefore, essential to proper organization of the teacher's work. Rankin says:

The school dare not work independently of these factors, but should make periodically a survey of the general conditions in the community. On the basis of the findings various steps may be taken. Gaps in requisite governmental service may be brought to the attention of the proper authorities and when necessary a campaign for extension may be launched. Specific activities may be instituted in the school program to develop in children the power to select intelligently among the many possibilities offered by commercial agencies such as the radio and the motion pictures. When general community influences are impossible to change, the school may need to introduce new activities calculated to take the place of desired facilities that are lacking, or to compensate for harmful influences.[2]

Information concerning the environment may be obtained by means of a continuing community survey. In some school systems provision is made for a central agency to gather such information and to make it available to the teachers. However, in the absence of such provision, the teacher will find it necessary to make an independent study of environmental factors as far as possible. The following items are usually included in a community survey:

Types of homes in the community
Types of industries
Occupations of parents
Community organizations
Natural resources
Public buildings
Community attitudes
Recreations
Items of unusual historic or scientific interest
Newspapers
Public records
Traditions and customs peculiar to the community.

In order to secure such information a number of specific activities on the part of the teacher are necessary. Among these are:

Visiting homes
Visiting places of business
Talking with public officials, ministers, laborers, business men, social leaders, housewives, physicians, etc.
Tabulating materials gathered by observation, interview, reading, and from records
Making graphs, charts, etc., to show graphically the results of the survey
Developing plans for cumulative inventory.

[2] Paul T. Rankin, "Environmental Factors Contributing to Learning," *Thirty-fourth Yearbook of the National Society for the Study of Education*, 1935, pp. 91–92.

Numerous sources of help are available to the teacher in discovering and organizing environmental data. For example, Symonds [3] devotes a chapter to a discussion of "measures of the environment" under the following major heads: measures of occupational level; measures of the home; measures of socio-economic level; and testing for cultural background. Under each of these heads the author describes and illustrates the various attempts to measure "(a) occupation level, (b) home background, and (c) certain combinations of the two, and (d) attempts to get at the cultural background through the cultural responses of the children." [4] Table X describes a number of tests, scales, and score cards that have been devised for measuring various environmental factors. A study of such measuring instruments should be helpful to teachers.

In order for environmental data to have significance, observations must be made continuously and the results recorded and interpreted. A single snapshot of an environmental condition is of little value. It may even be positively misleading. Such information becomes valuable to the teacher only when it serves to make the total environmental picture more nearly complete. Thus there is need for consistent use of a cumulative inventory of environmental data. The form on the facing page suggests a simple means of providing such an inventory.

TEACHER ACTIVITIES THAT HAVE TO DO WITH THE STUDY OF PUPILS

The importance of securing information about pupils is generally recognized. The teacher activities necessary to secure such information fall into two general classes: those that relate to the characteristics of pupils as a group, and those that relate to the characteristics of the different individuals in the group.

The study of characteristics of children of a given age group requires reference to various studies from the field of psychology. Data may also be derived from the teacher's own observation.

[3] Percival M. Symonds, *Diagnosing Personality and Conduct*, Century Co., 1931, Chapter XV.
[4] *Ibid.*, pp. 536–37.

GENERAL CUMULATIVE INVENTORY

Only information which significantly influences instruction should be recorded. This inventory should assist teachers in selecting interests suitable for developing units of work. It should be checked each time a unit is initiated and additional interests recorded. This inventory should be carefully kept and a copy passed on from year to year to the teacher of the group. Additional copies of these sheets can be secured from the State Department of Education.

School_____City or County_____

Grade or Grades_____Year_____Teacher_____

ENVIRONMENTAL DATA FOR INSTRUCTIONAL PURPOSES

Types of Homes: (Permanent, tenant, etc.)	Industries: (Lumber, dairying, etc.)
Public Buildings: (Courthouse, churches, schools, etc.)	Occupations: (Farmers, merchants, etc.)
Community Services: (Fire department, banks, nurses, etc.)	Community Organizations: (Music clubs, community leagues, etc.)
Public Officials: (Judge, policemen, etc.)	Recreational Facilities: (Parks, movies, etc.)
Historical Materials: (Markers, homes, etc.)	Attitudes: (Interested in education, etc.)
Natural Materials: (Caves, quarries, wild flowers, etc.)	

NEEDS OF SCHOOL AND COMMUNITY

NEEDS OF THE SCHOOL AND COMMUNITY (Record as observed in light of data)	IMPROVEMENTS THROUGH PUPIL PARTICIPATION

[5] *Tentative Course of Study for Virginia Elementary Schools, Grades I–VII,* State Board of Education, 1934, pp. 213–14.

339

TABLE X [6]

INSTRUMENTS FOR MEASURING FACTORS OF THE ENVIRONMENT

AUTHOR	SOURCE	TYPE	DESIGNED FOR	PURPOSE OF THE TEST	CONTENT OF THE TEST
Burdick, Edith	*Appreciation Test*, The Association Press, 347 Madison Avenue, New York, 1928.	Environment Test	Grades 5 to 8	Designed to measure the social level of the home background.	There are 11 parts dealing with such items as naming furniture, duties in the home and who performs them, situations and outcomes, vocational expectations, associations, etc.
Chapin, F. Stuart	*A Scale for Rating Living-Room Equipment*, Institute of Child Welfare, University of Minnesota, Minneapolis, Minnesota, 1930.	Environment Scale	Any home	To measure the socio-economic status of the home.	Contains 53 items relating to living-room furniture, which items are divided into four divisions: fixtures, built-in features, standard furniture and furnishings, and cultural resources.
Clark, W. W. and Williams, J. H.	*Whittier Scale for Grading Neighborhood Conditions*, California Bureau of Juvenile Research, Whittier, California, 1919.	Environment Scale	Any community	To measure the social adequacy of neighborhood conditions.	There are five scales, namely: (1) neatness, sanitation, improvements; (2) recreational facilities; (3) institutions and establishments; (4) social status of residents; (5) average quality of home.
McCormick, Mary J.	*Social Adequacy Measuring Scale*, C. H. Stoelting Co., Chicago, Illinois, 1931.	Environment Scale	Any family	To measure the social adequacy of families.	The items, most of which are answered by yes or no, are in four groups: (1) quality of neighborhood; (2) education, occupation, and civic status; (3) material status of home; (4) cultural and social influences.

[6] Compiled from catalogues of tests, from Percival M. Symonds, *Psychological Diagnosis in Social Adjustment*, and from Henry E. Garrett and Mathew R. Schneck, *Psychological Tests, Methods, and Results*.

Sims, Verner M.	*Score Card for Socio-Economic Status*, Public School Publishing Company, Bloomington, Illinois, 1927.	Environment Score Card	Grades 4 to 12.	For ascertaining and recording the general cultural, social, and economic background.	Consists of 25 items regarding the home to be answered by the pupils. Most answers are of the yes or no type.
Wallin, John E. W.	*Home Conditions and Personal and Family History*, C. H. Stoelting Co., Chicago, Illinois, 1914.	Environmental and Heredity Record Form.	Children up to 20 years.	For recording home conditions and personal and family history.	The blank consists of three sections, namely: home and environmental conditions, child's developmental history, and hereditary factors.
Williams, J. Harold	*Whittier Scale for Grading Home Conditions*, California Bureau of Juvenile Research, Whittier, California, 1918.	Environment Scale	Any home containing minor children	For measuring the social adequacy of any home containing minor children.	Five factors are considered in the scale: (1) necessities, (2) neatness, (3) size, (4) parental conditions, and (5) parental supervision.
Williams, J. Harold	*Whittier Home Rating Scale*, Whittier State School, Whittier, California, 1916.	Environment Scale	All levels	To study the cultural and economic level of the home.	Contains a score card with directions for grading each of the five different items: necessities, neatness, size of home, parental conditions, and parental supervision.

Information of particular value to the teacher at this point should include significant facts concerning physical condition and mental growth of children; the characteristic attitudes, activities, social traits, and interests, of children at various levels of maturity.   In order to secure such information the teacher will find it desirable to engage in activities, such as studying the results of research with specific reference to all these points; studying psychologies that deal with information applicable to the group under consideration; reading reports of observations of successful teachers; making, recording, and organizing observations from personal contacts with pupils.

Having studied the various characteristics of pupils as a group, the teacher is in better position to study individual pupils within his particular group.   While special attention should be given to this phase of the teacher's activity early in his experience with his group, it involves continuing attention so long as teacher and pupil are associated together in the school.   Items of special importance in studying the individual pupil may be classed under the physical, mental, and social characteristics of the pupils. Many subdivisions of these areas and many ways of gaining the desired information have been proposed.   One curriculum bulletin states that adequate knowledge of all the following factors is necessary in order to understand the needs of pupils:

1. Physical condition of child.
2. His chronological age.
3. His home environment.
4. His previous training.
5. Nationality and language difficulties of child.
6. Social attitudes and habits of child.
7. Work attitudes and habits.
8. His emotional development.
9. His characteristic interests.
10. His special abilities.
11. His mental age.
12. His intelligence quotient.[7]

[7] *Teachers' Guide to Child Development,* California State Department of Education, 1930, p. 436.

This bulletin adds that "it is important that a study of the child be made from the very beginning of his first school year, and that the record of this study be supplemented during each year of his life in school with all the relevant facts which can be accumulated. Only by access to such complete records may teachers hope to form accurate judgments of children's needs." [8]

To gain such information the teacher should interview the pupil, the parents, the former teacher, the public health nurse, the school nurse, the physician, the principal, and the truant officer. He should administer diagnostic tests, study the pupil's record, observe the pupil in various situations, secure estimates of other pupils, and visit the pupil's home. Activities involved in conducting interviews and in administering and interpreting various instruments of diagnosis merit special consideration.

CONDUCTING INTERVIEWS

Conducting an interview is a highly important activity of the teacher and involves a number of rather definite procedures. While the nature of the person to be interviewed and the purpose of the interview call for variations in procedure, a number of general helps have been suggested. Bingham and Moore [9] present a comprehensive list of suggestions for "intelligent direction and control of interviews." The following items selected from this list should prove helpful to teachers in planning and conducting interviews:

A. General Suggestions:

   1. Use interviews discriminatingly.
   2. Use interviews to obtain opportunity for observation.
   3. Use interviews to determine opinions, attitudes, or trends of belief.
   4. Avoid use of the interview for compiling data of uncertain value.
   5. Avoid use of the interview for getting general information or common facts.

[8] *Idem.*
[9] Walter Van Dyke Bingham and Bruce Victor Moore, *How to Interview*, Harper and Brothers, 1931, Chapter III, pp. 40–55.

B. Preparing for the Interview:
6. Formulate your problem.
7. Prepare a schedule or list of questions.
8. Know your field.
9. Know your interviewee.
10. Provide for privacy.
11. Practice taking the interviewee's point of view.

C. Interviewing:
12. Gain and deserve the interviewee's confidence.
13. Establish pleasant associations.
14. Render your interviewee a real service.
15. Help the interviewee to feel at ease and ready to talk.
16. Do not ask questions directly until you think the interviewee is ready to give the desired information and to give it accurately.
17. Listen.
18. Let the interviewee tell his story; then help him to supplement it.
19. Keep on the subject.
20. Be straightforward and frank rather than shrewd or clever.
21. Avoid the role of teacher.
22. Take pains to phrase your questions so that they are easily understood.
23. Avoid implying the answer to your own question.
24. Avoid impertinence.
25. Give the interviewee opportunity to qualify his answers.
26. Check answers whenever possible.
27. Record all data at once, or at the very earliest opportunity.
28. Practice separating facts from inferences.
29. Allow time enough.
30. Do not dawdle.
31. Keep control of the interview.

ADMINISTERING AND INTERPRETING INSTRUMENTS OF DIAGNOSIS

Gathering information about pupils has been facilitated in recent years by the development of quantitative means of obtaining information concerning intelligence, interests, attitudes, behavior, adjustment, and physical condition. The validity of such means of securing information is often questionable, but when used discreetly they provide valuable assistance to the teacher in studying the individual pupil. These devices for gathering information about pupils should not only be helpful to teachers in studying the pupil, but should also be suggestive of ways of devising their own means of securing valuable information. A summary of representative tests, rating scales, and questionnaires that have been developed for the purpose of studying various phases of the individual pupil is presented in Tables XI, XII, and XIII. In addition to such instruments for studying the pupils, numerous less formal procedures have been suggested. For example, illustrative informal procedures for studying pupil interests are presented in Chapter VIII.

In order that information about the pupils may be used effectively it should be recorded as gathered. As previously stated regarding environmental data, this record should be made cumulative. General cumulative records or inventory sheets applicable to the peculiar needs of a given school should be devised. The following example illustrates the type of inventory sheets developed in one school system:

GENERAL CUMULATIVE INVENTORY [10]

INTERESTS OF CHILDREN
(Record as observed)

ATTITUDES, ABILITIES, AND NEEDS

ATTITUDES (Record as observed)	HABITS (Record as observed)	NEEDS (Record as observed)	CHECK IN THIS COLUMN NEEDS MET

[10] Virginia, *Op. cit.*, p. 35.

TABLE XI

INSTRUMENTS FOR MEASURING FACTORS OF PERSONALITY [11]

AUTHOR	SOURCE	TYPE	DESIGNED FOR	PURPOSE OF THE TEST	CONTENT OF THE TEST
Allport, F. H.	*North Carolina Rating Scale for Fundamental Traits*, C. H. Stoelting Co., Chicago, 1924.	Rating Scale	Any age group	To rate persons on twenty-four traits.	Consists of 24 paired statements expressing the extremes of a given trait. A nine-point scale is provided for the use of the rater.
American Council on Education	*Personality Rating Scale*, American Council on Education, 744 Jackson Place, Washington, D. C., 1928.	Rating Scale	College freshmen	To rate students on five traits.	Consists of five traits to be rated on a graphic scale. The five traits are appearance and manner, industry, ability to control others, emotional control, and distribution of time and energy.
Brown, Edwin J.	*Character-Conduct Self-Rating Scale for Students*, Bureau of Educational Measurements, Kansas State Teachers College, Emporia, Kan., 1931.	Rating Scale	Elementary and junior high school	To be used by pupils as an instrument of self-analysis.	The test consists of ten sections: (1) fidelity, (2) obedience, (3) insight, (4) courtesy, (5) co-operation, (6) industry, (7) fair play, (8) good health, (9) self-control, (10) service.
Chassell, Laura M.; Upton, Siegfried M.; and Chassell, Clara F.	*Short Scales for Measuring Habits of Good Citizenship*, Bureau of Publications, Teachers College, Columbia University, New York, 1922.	Rating Scale	Elementary and high school	To measure habits of good citizenship.	There are eight scales of 24 items each. Each item is weighted and is rated on a scale from 0 to 3.

[11] Instruments are grouped alphabetically by types.

Compiled from catalogues of tests, from Percival N. Symonds, *Psychological Diagnosis in Social Adjustment*, and from Henry E. Garrett and Matthew R. Schneck, *Psychological Tests, Methods, and Results*.

Author	Title	Type	Population	Purpose	Description
Clark, Willis W.	*Whittier Scale for Grading Juvenile Offenses*, California Bureau of Juvenile Research, Whittier, Cal., 1922.	Rating Scale	Elementary and high school	To evaluate the seriousness of juvenile offenses.	One hundred and twenty-two statements classified under 14 headings have been scaled from 1 to 7 according to their social consequences from the least serious to most serious.
Cornell, Ethel L.; Coxe, W. W.; and Orleans, J. S.	*New York Rating Scale for School Habits*, World Book Co., Yonkers, N.Y., 1927.	Rating Scale	Third grade through high school	To obtain ratings on school habits and attitudes which are important outcomes of education.	Consists of nine qualities on a graphic rating scale with a brief phrase at each end and in the middle of the scale.
Hacker, L. W.	*A Character Scale*, McKnight and McKnight, Normal, Ill.	Rating Scale	Elementary and high school	To rate the character traits of school pupils.	The scale consists of 40 items grouped in six sections: physical, intellectual, working, personal, social, and emotional character.
Haggerty, M. L.; Olson, W. C.; and Wickman, E. K.	*Behavior Rating Schedules*, World Book Co., Yonkers, N. Y., 1930.	Rating Scale	Elementary school children	To measure problem tendencies in children.	Consists of two forms, the first consisting of 15 behavior problems and the second consisting of 35 graphic ratings of mental, physical, social, and emotional aspects of character.
Hayes, Margaret L.	*A Scale for Evaluating the School Behavior of Children Ten to Fifteen*, Psychological Corporation, 522 Fifth Ave., New York, 1933.	Rating Scale	Children 10 to 15	To show the habit patterns of adolescents in terms of desirable and undesirable personality development.	One hundred habit patterns are listed to be checked as true, false, or uncertain. Ratings are given on items grouped into eight sections.
O'Reilly, F. L.; Dougherty, B. L.; and Mannix, Mary E.	*Character Analysis Chart*, Public School Publishing Co., Bloomington, Ill., 1931.	Rating Scale	Elementary and high school	To stimulate pupils to examine or analyze their own character.	Ten traits are to be rated, namely: health, honesty, loyalty, cheerfulness, courtesy, co-operation, moral courage, industry, self-control, and leadership.

TABLE XI—*Continued*

INSTRUMENTS FOR MEASURING FACTORS OF PERSONALITY

AUTHOR	SOURCE	TYPE	DESIGNED FOR	PURPOSE OF THE TEST	CONTENT OF THE TEST
Watson, Goodwin B.	*Rating Scales*, The Association Press, 347 Madison Ave., New York, 1928.	Rating Scale	Elementary and high school	To be used for rating various phases of character.	Form B is a behavior rating scale; Form F is a fundamentals of character scale; Form S is a situation scale; and Form T is a trait rating scale.
Yepsen, Lloyd M.	*Adjustment Score Card*, Extension Department, The Training School, Vineland, N. J., 1928.	Rating Scale	Children all ages	To obtain a measure of a child's social adjustment.	Seventy items grouped into 14 categories, each dealing with some phase of the adjustment of the individual to his environment.
Allport, G. W. and Allport, F. H.	*A Scale for Measuring Ascendance-Submission in Personality*, Houghton Mifflin Co., Boston, 1928.	Personality Adjustment Questionnaire	Adult men, adult women	To "discover the disposition of an individual to dominate his fellows (or to be dominated by them) in various face-to-face relationships of every-day life."	Consists of situations or problems with from two to five alternative responses given. Some situations appear in a form for women, others appear on forms for both men and women.
Bernreuter, R. G.	*Personality Inventory*, Stanford University Press, Stanford, Cal., 1931.	Personality Inventory Questionnaire	High school and college students, also adults	To measure neurotic tendencies, self-sufficiency, introversion-extroversion, and dominance-submission.	Includes 125 questions taken from Allport, Thurston, and others; and rated by yes, no, and ?.
Chassell, J. O.	"*Experience Variables*" *Record*, by author, University of Rochester Medical School, Rochester, N. Y., 1928.	Personality Adjustment Questionnaire	Adults	To provide a systematic survey of an individual's attitudes toward his family, sex and religious standards, social and emotional adjustments, intellectual and vocational interests and aptitudes.	Consists of twelve sections. Within each section questions are classified into four groups, in accordance with the kind of behavior investigated.

348

Furfey, Paul H.	*Developmental Age Test*, C. H. Stoelting Co., Chicago, 1930.	Personality Adjustment Questionnaire	Children 7 to 17	To study the changing volitional life of the growing child.	Six sub-tests containing 196 items on things to do; things to be when grown up; books to read; things to have, see, and think about.
Mathews, Ellen	*Revision of the Woodworth Personal Data Sheet*, C. H. Stoelting Co., Chicago, 1923.	Personality Adjustment Questionnaire	Children 8 and above	To measure the emotional stability of children.	Form A contains 60 questions; Form B, 40 questions. Each question is followed by yes and no. The two forms were later combined into a single form of 75 items.
Morris, Elizabeth H.	*Trait Index L*, Public School Publishing Co., Bloomington, Ill., 1929.	Personality Adjustment Questionnaire	High school graduates	To test for qualities of leadership.	Consists of 137 items arranged in six divisions. Presents typical situations to secure the general trend of an individual's reactions.
Pressey, S. L.	*X–O Tests for Investigating the Emotions*, C. H. Stoelting Co., Chicago, 1920.	Personality Adjustment Questionnaire	Adults and children	To find individual differences in moral, emotional, and affective tendencies.	The test consists of four sub-tests each containing 25 sets of five words each.
Symonds, P. M.	*Adjustment Questionnaire*, Psychological Corporation, 522 Fifth Ave., New York, 1934.	Personality Adjustment Questionnaire	Grades 9 and 10	To measure pupil adjustment.	Pupils express their likes and dislikes of 180 items arranged into seven categories.
Thurstone, L. L. and Thurstone, T. G.	*Personality Schedule*, University of Chicago Press, Chicago, 1929.	Personality Adjustment Questionnaire	Adults, college students	To detect personal and social maladjustments.	Consists of 223 questions followed by yes, no, and ?, the last meaning not sure or undecided.
Watson, Goodwin B.	*Self-Estimate of Happiness*, The Association Press, 347 Madison Ave., New York, 1931.	Personality Adjustment Questionnaire	High school and college	Designed to give a measure of personal happiness.	Two graphic rating scales are used to get a self-estimate of general happiness and variability of mood.

349

TABLE XI—*Continued*

INSTRUMENTS FOR MEASURING FACTORS OF PERSONALITY

AUTHOR	SOURCE	TYPE	DESIGNED FOR	PURPOSE OF THE TEST	CONTENT OF THE TEST
Woodworth, R. S.	*Personal Data Sheet,* C. H. Stoelting Co., Chicago, 1917.	Personality Adjustment Questionnaire	Adults	To estimate an individual's psychoneurotic tendencies.	Consists of 116 questions to be answered by yes and no. Examples are: Were you shy with other boys? Do you feel tired most of the time? Do your interests change quickly?
Willoughby, R. R.	*Emotional Maturity Scale,* Stanford University Press, Stanford, Cal. 1931.	Personality Adjustment Questionnaire	College students and adults	To estimate emotional maturity as shown by a subject's willingness to accept responsibility, etc.	Sixty items, "each of which describes in terms of a hypothetical subject (S) a type of situation and a reaction to it."
Downey, June	*Group Will-Temperament Test,* World Book Co., Yonkers, N. Y., 1922.	Personality Test	Children and adults	To evaluate certain temperamental traits in individuals through a study of simple motor reactions.	Consists of twelve tests arranged in three groups of four tests each. Subject marks one of a series of pairs of contrasted adjectives that best describes himself, practices copying a model, writes with eyes closed, etc.
Kohs, S. C.	*Ethical Discrimination Test,* C. H. Stoelting Co., Chicago, 1922.	Personality Test	Children, adolescents, and adults	To measure knowledge of ethical and moral principles.	Contains six divisions as follows: social relations, moral judgment, proverbs, definition of moral terms, offense evaluation, and moral problems.

350

TEACHER ACTIVITIES THAT HAVE TO DO WITH THE LIMITATIONS OF THE CURRICULUM

In planning procedures for directing the activities of pupils, the teacher is confronted by a number of conditions which definitely limit the manner in which the curriculum is to be developed. An important task for the teacher is to discover the character and extent of such limitations, and to provide for planning and carrying on activities in such a manner as will tend to reduce to a minimum the undesirable effects of such limitations. Limiting factors commonly found in school programs are usually due to the manner in which the curriculum is organized, or to external causes. Among such limiting factors are:

Rigid prescription of textbooks
Scope of work for grade
Rigid time allotment
Promotion and grading
Material equipment
Non-teaching duties expected of teachers
Extra school duties expected of teachers
Program of studies required
Rules and regulations of the school system
Prescription of use of the course of study
Character of supervision
Disciplinary requirements in the school.

Upon careful investigation the teacher often finds that what he has considered a limiting factor does not really operate to limit his work. For example, one of the common excuses offered by teachers for carrying on a narrow uninteresting program of work is that the adopted textbooks must be taught. While, in order to comply with state laws, this is frequently true, the limitation implied does not often exist in aggravated form. In other words, while the teacher must use the adopted texts, he is usually free to go as far beyond the text as his inclination and ability may dictate. Similarly, other limiting factors may exist only for the teacher who is not resourceful and energetic. In any case, however, all possible limitations should be canvassed, since aware-

TABLE XII

INSTRUMENTS FOR MEASURING FACTORS OF INTEREST [12]

AUTHOR	SOURCE	TYPE	DESIGNED FOR	PURPOSE OF THE TEST	CONTENT OF THE TEST
Freyd, Max	*Occupational Interest Blank,* C. H. Stoelting Co., Chicago, 1922.	Interest Questionnaire	Men and women	To measure occupational interest.	Contains a list of 80 occupations opposite each of which are five symbols rating the attitude of the subject toward the occupation.
Freyd, Max	*Minnesota Interest Analysis,* Marietta Apparatus Co., Marietta, O., 1928.	Interest Questionnaire	Junior high school	To determine the interest that accompanies mechanical ability.	One part consists of 115 items about occupations, another consists of 73 items on activities and school subjects.
Garretson, O. K. and Symonds, P. M.	*Interest Questionnaire for High-School Students,* Bureau of Publications, Teachers College, Columbia University, New York, 1930.	Interest Questionnaire	High school boys	To measure the inclinations of pupils entering high school toward the academic, commercial, and technical curricula.	Consists of eight tests dealing with occupations, sports, student school activities, school subjects, things desired, magazines read, etc.
Hepner, Harry W.	*Vocational Interest Quotient Booklet,* Psychological Corporation, 522 Fifth Ave., New York, 1931.	Interest Questionnaire	Ages 15 or above	To determine the agreement of an individual's interest preferences with those of other occupations.	One hundred and sixty-seven items are to be marked by L, ?, or D, indicating a liking for, an indifference, or a dislike for the occupation.
Lehman, H. C.	*Play Quiz,* The Association Press, 347 Madison Ave., New York, 1926.	Interest Questionnaire	Ages 8 to 22	A check list for discovering a pupil's interests.	The questionnaire lists 200 play activities. Pupils are asked to check the activities they have engaged in the previous week.

352

[12] Instruments are grouped alphabetically by types.

Lehman, H. C.	*Vocational Attitude Quiz*, School of Education, University of Kansas, Lawrence, Kan., 1925.	Interest Questionnaire	Ages 8 to 18	To study the persistence of vocational interests.	Seven groups of occupations are given, such as occupations best for money-making, those most likely to be followed, those liked best, and those liked least.
Manson, Grace E.	*Occupational Interest Blank for Women*, School of Business Administration, University of Michigan, Ann Arbor, Mich., 1931.	Interest Questionnaire	Women	To determine whether a given woman's interests serve to identify her with a well-defined occupational group.	The test consists of 160 occupations open to women arranged alphabetically. Symbols are provided to determine the degree of liking or dislike for the occupations.
Miner, James B.	*Analysis of Work Interest Blank*, C. H. Stoelting Co., Chicago, 1922.	Interest Questionnaire	High school	To aid in finding special interests and abilities that are related to different types of work.	Consists of 28 paired items representing divergent interests. Provides also a record for various social and vocational interests.
Stewart, Frances J. and Brainard, Paul	*Specific Interest Inventory*, Form W, Psychological Corporation, 522 Fifth Ave., New York, 1932.	Interest Questionnaire	Boys, girls, men, and women	To aid in the discovery and analysis of interests, with a view toward vocational guidance.	Contains 20 groups of questions and an inventory of likes and dislikes.
Strong, E. K.	*Vocational Interest Blank*, Stanford University Press, Stanford, Cal., 1927.	Interest Questionnaire	High school and adults	To discover whether an individual's interests are closely identified with those of some well-defined occupational group.	Contains eight parts, five of which deal with occupations, amusements, school subjects, activities, and peculiarities of people; and three parts dealing with preferences for various activities as typified by well-known men, comparisons of interests, abilities, and characteristics.

TABLE XII—Continued

INSTRUMENTS FOR MEASURING FACTORS OF INTEREST

AUTHOR	SOURCE	TYPE	DESIGNED FOR	PURPOSE OF THE TEST	CONTENT OF THE TEST
Terman, Lewis M.	*Plays, Games, and Amusements Test,* Stanford University Gifted Child Research, Stanford University, Stanford, Cal., 1921.	Interest Questionnaire	Children	To discover children's play interests, their play activities and their knowledge of play.	Parts I, II, and III consist of a list of games to be checked. Part IV is a list of 45 questions to determine whether the child has participated in certain play activities. Parts V, VI, and VII contain information about play and games.
Benge, E. J.	*Stenogauge Test,* Stenogauge Company, Philadelphia, 1923.	Vocational Aptitude	All ages	To measure aptitude for stenography.	Contain four parts, namely: dictation, transcription rate, transcription accuracy, and spelling.
Elwell, F. H. and Fowlkes, J. G.	*Bookkeeping Test,* World Book Co., Yonkers, N. Y., 1928.	Vocational Aptitude	High School	To measure achievement in bookkeeping in high schools and business colleges.	Consists of two forms, each of which is divided into five divisions: general theory, journalizing, classification, adjusting entries and closing the ledger, and statements.
Engle, Edna M. and Stenquist, John L.	*Home Economics Test,* World Book Co., Yonkers, N. Y., 1931.	Vocational Knowledge	Grades 5 to 10	To measure pupil's knowledge in various fields of home economics.	Three separate tests are included in the complete test: (1) Foods and Cookery, (2) Clothing and Textiles, and (3) Household Management.

354

Author	Publication	Category	Population	Purpose	Description
Frear, Florence D. and Coxe, Warren. W	*Clothing Test*, Public School Publishing Co., Bloomington, Ill., 1929.	Vocational Knowledge	High school girls	To measure the knowledge girls have concerning the quality of clothing.	The test contains five parts: fundamentals of construction, care and repair of clothing, hygiene of clothing, appropriateness of clothing, and economics of clothing.
Thurstone, L. L.	*Examination in Clerical Work*, World Book Co., Yonkers, N. Y., 1922.	Vocational Aptitude	Clerks of all types	To measure aptitude for clerical and general office work.	This is a group test consisting of eight sub-tests as follows: (1) checking arithmetic errors, (2) locating misspelled words, (3) cancellation, (4) code learning, (5) alphabetizing, (6) directions, (7) arithmetic problems, and (8) matching proverbs.
Thurstone, L. L.	*Vocational Guidance Tests for Engineers*, World Book Co., Yonkers, N. Y., 1922.	Vocational Guidance or Aptitude	High school and college freshmen	To determine probable success in an engineering course.	Consists of five tests, one in each of the following subjects: arithmetic, algebra, geometry, and physics. The fifth part contains 100 questions on technical information.

TABLE XIII

INSTRUMENTS FOR MEASURING FACTORS OF ATTITUDES

AUTHOR	SOURCE	TYPE	DESIGNED FOR	PURPOSE OF THE TEST	CONTENT OF THE TEST
Burdick, Edith	*Apperception Test*, Association Press, 347 Madison Ave., New York, 1927.	Attitude Questionnaire	Elementary school children	To measure the cultural background and social status of the child in light of his attitudes and connections.	One scale contains eleven sections to be answered by the child as a group. Another scale of five sections to be answered by the child at home deals with his knowledge of social usage, things liked and disliked, play activities, books read, etc.
Case, Adelaide T. and Limbert, Paul M.	*Around the World*, Association Press, 347 Madison Ave., New York, 1932.	Attitude Questionnaire	Grades 6 to 10	To discover how young people feel concerning certain international problems.	One part is a yes-no test of opinion, another concerns information about great leaders, and a third is a multiple choice test on "What do you think about it?"
Hart, Hornell	*Test for Social Attitudes and Interest*, University of Iowa City, Ia., 1923.	Attitude Questionnaire	Adults and children over 12	To indicate predominant attitudes toward a number of social and economic situations and to show likes and dislikes toward a variety of activities.	Chart I is a practice list; Chart II gives four lists of activities: emotional, social, religious, and economic, for which a preference or lack of it is to be expressed; Chart III contains two lists of economic and social reforms upon which the subject expresses an opinion.
Hill, Howard C.	*Test of Civic Information and Attitudes*, Public School Publishing Co., Bloomington, Ill., 1926.	Attitude Questionnaire	Grades 6 to 12	To test civic information and attitudes	Consists of a series of multiple choice questions concerning civic information and civic attitudes.
Lewerenz, Alfred S.	*Orientation Test*, Southern California Book Depository, Hollywood, Cal., 1931.	Attitude Questionnaire	High school and college students and adults	To measure beliefs in a number of fields.	Consists of nine divisions with from 25 to 75 items in each division. The seven cardinal objectives form the basis of the divisions.

Author	Title / Publication	Type	Audience	Purpose	Description
Newman, G. B.; Kulp, D. H.; and Davidson, Helen	*Test of International Attitudes,* Bureau of Publications, Teachers College, Columbia University, New York, 1926.	Attitude Questionnaire	Young people and adults	To discover international and interracial attitudes.	A test of four sections dealing with attitudes toward international questions, beliefs, and convictions regarding other races and nations.
Thurstone, L. L., Editor	*The Measurement of Social Attitudes,* University of Chicago Press, Chicago, 1929–1934.	Attitude Questionnaire and Tests	High school, college students, and adults	To measure individual or group attitudes toward certain social institutions.	A series of 35 scales, each containing approximately 20 statements. The scales are designed to measure attitudes toward such things as divorce, war, foreign missions, public office, free trade, patriotism, free speech, etc.
Watson, Goodwin B., compiler	*A Test of Public Opinion,* Bureau of Publications, Teachers College, Columbia University, New York, 1923.	Attitude Questionnaire	High school seniors and adults	To show the extent and strength of an individual's prejudices as exhibited in extreme opinions upon moral, religious, and economic questions.	Contains six parts concerned with opinions upon social, religious, and economic questions; the certainty of opinions in these same fields; the extent to which the subject is willing to commit himself on most questions; and the subject's willingness to generalize his opinions upon controversial issues.
Watson, Goodwin B., compiler	*Opinions on International Questions,* The Association Press, 347 Madison Ave., New York.	Attitude Questionnaire	High school, college, or adults	To measure attitudes on international questions.	The test consists of 100 statements covering disputed issues, such as, war, imperialism, true patriotism, international dangers, public opinion, and immigration.
Watson, Goodwin B.	*Opinions on Race Relations,* The Association Press, 347 Madison Ave., New York.	Attitude Questionnaire	High school students and adults	To obtain a measure of liberalism towards questions of race relations.	A questionnaire of 35 items from the white Gentile point of view. Arranged so that a prejudice score may be obtained.

ness of limitations is necessary if the teacher is to plan and engage in a course of action effectively.   The teacher may find the following suggested activities helpful: reading carefully the course of study and the rules and regulations of the school system; familiarizing oneself with the teaching schedules; examining textbooks, prescribed or recommended; checking the library carefully for available materials; making an inventory of the physical equipment available; and discovering the general program of supervision.

TEACHER ACTIVITIES THAT HAVE TO DO WITH THE DIRECTION OF PUPIL ACTIVITIES

Teacher activities considered up to this point are, in a sense, preliminary to the main task, the immediate direction of the activities of pupils.   However, they are none the less important. Moreover, we should not assume that the preceding consideration of the various types of activities necessarily indicates a rigid sequence to be followed.   As has been previously stated, the appropriate time for engaging in a given activity will be determined by the method of organizing instruction and the particular situation in which the teacher finds himself.

The procedures to be followed by the teacher in directing pupil activities will be dictated by the nature of the activities engaged in by the pupils.   In Chapter IX it has been pointed out that there is a wide variety of possible pupil activities involving many situations that may be utilized.   Regardless of the particular method of organizing instruction that may be in use in a given school or school system, many of these pupil activities will appear, and the procedures for directing them will be essentially the same.   A list of such activities has been included in a state course of study as follows:

Making books
Publishing periodicals
Exhibiting
Developing a school museum
Arranging a bulletin board

Making decorative maps and wall hangings
Making posters
Diagramming and charting
Making graphs
Modeling
Making plaster of Paris plaques and molds
Constructing
Making friezes
Making motion and talking pictures
Constructing peep shows and miniature scenes
Giving shadow plays, puppet shows, and marionette performances
Dramatizing
Developing hobbies
Conducting clubs
Developing programs
Playing
Making surveys
Taking excursions or field trips
Beautifying home and school environment [13]

In order that teachers may have guidance in directing these activities, the course of study referred to has included a section on general teaching procedures which includes suggested procedures for directing each type of activity. For example, making posters is an activity engaged in quite generally by pupils at various grade levels. Through experience successful teachers have discovered satisfactory ways of directing pupils engaged in this type of activity. The procedures developed from these experiences have been tested and revised and have been made available to other teachers for their guidance in the following form:

Activity: Making posters

Suggested Procedure: A poster is a means of presenting one idea in a clear and convincing manner. It should be arranged so that it will attract the attention of a disinterested person, and be clear in its message. The poster should not be crowded with many illustrations and much lettering, but the whole effect should be clear and to the point.

[13] Virginia, *op. cit.,* p. 471.

Illustrations for a poster may be free-hand drawings or representations cut or torn from colored paper. Letters may be drawn on the poster or cut from paper and pasted thereon. They should harmonize in color with the illustration. Strong contrasts should be used, the amount of light and dark balancing in the lettering and illustrations. Before beginning work on the poster paper, margins should be placed on newsprint or wrapping paper the size of the poster desired. In measuring for margins, the top and sides of the poster should be equal while the bottom margin should be slightly wider than these. Strips of paper representing the words, or small blocks of paper the size of letters, should be arranged on newsprint or wrapping paper. The position should be changed until the best effect is discovered. The whole should form a rectangle.

When blocking in the letters the space between the lines should be less than the height of the letters; the space between words should equal the width of the letters; and space between the letters should appear equal. Straight up and down strokes in lettering, careful spacing of horizontal lines, and correct spacing of letters, words, lines, and margins are important points to be observed. Careful measurements for accurate subdivisions of spaces are necessary in poster making.

Such activities as presenting plays, conducting exhibits, and reviewing books present numerous opportunities for the use of effective posters.

References:

Mathias, *Art in the Elementary School*, Scribner.
Lemos, *Modern Art Portfolio on Posters*, Davis Press.[14]

TEACHING PROCEDURES AND CURRICULUM DEVELOPMENT

One of the most important phases of a curriculum program is that of providing suggestions to teachers for directing pupil activities, providing suitable means for reporting concisely procedures that have been followed in a given situation, and for presenting them in such form as may be suggestive to other teachers in planning their work. Procedures developed along the lines here indicated call for the inclusion in courses of study of procedures somewhat different from the usual practice. Just

[14] *Ibid.*, p. 477.

as there must be offered a variety of materials that may be helpful to the teacher in planning and organizing a series of activities, so there must be suggested procedures from which to choose. Thus the course of study, instead of designating a specific activity to be engaged in and a specific procedure to be followed, provides a number of suggested possible activities and descriptions of procedures which have been found suitable by teachers who have directed similar activities. This is consistent with the point of view that the course of study is a source of raw materials to which the teacher can go for assistance in developing the curriculum. The suggested teaching procedures should be classified and indexed so that the teacher will be able to find them readily.

In this way programs of curriculum making may contribute significantly to the improvement of teaching procedures. The critical appraisal required by the individual teacher of his own procedures, and the opportunity to become acquainted with procedures found effective by other teachers provide the basis for this improvement.

SELECTED REFERENCES

Bingham, Walter Van Dyke and Moore, Bruce V., *How To Interview,* Harper and Brothers, New York, 1931.
California State Department of Education, *Teachers Guide to Child Development,* California State Printing Office, Sacramento, California, 1930.
Charters, W. W., and Waples, Douglas, *The Commonwealth Teacher Training Study,* University of Chicago Press, Chicago, Illinois, 1929.
Rankin, Paul T., "Environmental Factors Contributing to Learning," *Thirty-fourth Yearbook of the National Society for the Study of Education,* Public School Publishing Company, Bloomington, Illinois, 1935.
Symonds, Percival M., *Diagnosing Personality and Conduct,* Century Company, New York, 1931, Chapter XV.

CHAPTER XIII

EVALUATING THE OUTCOMES OF INSTRUCTION

Attention to evaluation of the outcomes of instruction has been a characteristic of education in every epoch. The necessity of checking the results accomplished against the work undertaken has usually been accepted as a matter of course. Probably no more definite index to the philosophy of a given educational program can be found than that shown in the means used for evaluation. The procedures followed, the purposes and functions implied, the interpretation and use of the results obtained, all reflect the general point of view upon which a curriculum is developed. Practices in evaluation vary from that of the direct and exact imitation characteristic of oriental systems of education, to the highly specialized techniques of the modern objective testing movement, or to the less formal type of evaluation based upon observation of conduct.

THE NATURE OF OUTCOMES

The term outcome is interpreted in a variety of ways. During recent years it has been frequently construed as synonymous with aim or objective. Thus, in certain courses of study specific aims are stated; specific procedures for achieving these aims are indicated; and specific outcomes, identical with the aims or practically so, are listed. This use of the term is confusing since outcomes thus set up in advance become merely more specific statements of the aims. This confusion may be clearly seen in courses of study which employ the term outcome in the sense here indicated. Frequently they contain the statement that the outcomes are the teaching ends which the pupils actually reach, rather than those they are expected to reach, thus indicating that they cannot be determined in advance. However, in suggesting procedures for organizing instruction they imply the necessity of stating the outcomes definitely in advance. As a rule, this use of outcomes in courses of study consists of the translation of the stated aims into specific knowledge and skills to be acquired by the pupils. For example, an aim is stated: "To know how to use chisels," and the correlative desirable outcome, "Ability to use chisels properly." [1]

A general concept of outcome, implied in the example referred to and often reflected in educational literature and in practice, is that the outcome is a specific isolated aspect of behavior. This concept doubtless has been stimulated by the scientific movement in education. It has resulted in the minute analysis of human conduct and of ideals for the purpose of stating aims or objectives. It has lent itself to the objective means of evaluating the results of instruction. It has encouraged, if not demanded, uniformity of materials and procedures. It lends itself to a simplicity and directness of procedure that may easily be reduced to a formula. This concept, however, places an undue restriction upon evaluation as a function of the educative process.

Another concept of outcomes is that they are the result—not necessarily the result desired or expected—but the actual result as represented in the changes brought about in the behavior of pupils. Ideally, the outcomes of instruction should be in accord with or should approximate the aims of education. The means of identifying and of evaluating them should, therefore, be in accord with the nature of the aims and the manner in which they function. The aims of education, as stated in Chapter VI, involve more than specific items of knowledge to be learned and skills to be acquired. Since, as previously stated, the activities engaged in by pupils do not result in precisely the outcomes an-

---

[1] *Manual Arts for Grades Seven, Eight, and Nine,* Revision of Curriculum Bulletin No. 20, *Public School Messenger,* St. Louis, 28:8, September, 1930.

ticipated, constant modification and reinterpretation of the various elements of the educative process are required as progress is made toward the realization of aims. If, instead of representing merely specific abilities to be acquired, aims are conceived as a means of giving direction to the educative process, then outcomes observed in a given situation should reflect the extent and the direction in which a given experience or series of experiences has led the individual taught. Any evaluation of observed outcomes, therefore, must be in terms of the aims. In other words, evaluation does not consist merely in checking a completed process but in continuously appraising progress in the direction indicated by the accepted aims.

The aims of education as stated in terms of generalized controls of conduct form the basis for the concept of the function of evaluation in the curriculum. The composition of generalized controls of conduct is referred to in Chapter VI as specific habits and motor skills, knowledge, and attitudes and appreciations. Although these are designated as components of generalized controls of conduct, as previously stated, it is impossible in actual experience for one of these elements of conduct to be present without the others. Moreover, there seem to be no generalizations and principles that are absolutely essential for particular controls of conduct. This implies that there are no specifics that will determine whether a given control of conduct has been satisfactorily developed. Just as it is important to know the characteristics of the generalizations and abilities largely involving specific habits at various stages of growth, so it is necessary in evaluating outcomes to employ varying interpretations of standards appropriate to the particular stage of growth. Therefore, progress toward the achievement of these standards cannot always be stated in quantitative terms. It will vary in degree and in kind with different individuals and in different situations. In the case of the specific habits, motor skills, and knowledge requisite to a desired generalized control of conduct, however, evaluation consists in applying such measures as will determine whether the desired response is habitually given, or the extent to which the desired habit has been acquired. Such measures serve to indicate also what additional application may be necessary in order to bring achievement up to an accepted standard.

EVALUATION A FUNCTION OF THE CURRICULUM

Such a concept of outcomes requires that evaluation not be considered as a procedure separate from the curriculum, introduced from time to time to perform a specific function; nor even as a step in developing the curriculum if by that we mean that it appears in a rigid sequence of procedures in the learning process. Instead, it is a function of the curriculum, interacting with each element of it at all points. Thus considered, evaluation occurs continuously as the curriculum develops and is concerned with every aspect of it. There are, however, three important aspects of a program of evaluation that require special attention: (1) It should provide pupils the means of evaluating their own activities; (2) it should provide the teacher a basis for planning the activities of pupils and for continuous evaluation of the results; and (3) it should provide a basis for constant revision of the curriculum.

As is pointed out in Chapter IX, as the pupil undergoes an experience he is constantly evaluating that experience in terms of his own purposes. The various elements that go to make up the experience are subordinated to the experience itself, although a given element may be in the focus of his interest at a given time. The relationship to his dominating purpose, however, is constantly before him. He plans and engages in a series of activities to achieve his purpose, and revises and improves his plan of action from time to time as his own evaluation of progress toward the achievement of his purpose may dictate. This constant process of evaluation develops an awareness of his need for more adequate mastery of certain abilities and thus brings about the inclusion of steps to secure such mastery in his plan of action. As a course of action matures or comes to a conclusion evaluation includes a view of the enterprise as a whole in the light of the pupil's purpose. It should result in the consideration of improvements that might have been made and should stimulate interest that may result in purposeful activity in some other related enterprise.

Similarly, the teacher directing the activities of a group of pupils should be constantly evaluating in terms of his own purpose as it is dictated by the aims of education, the progress that is being made toward the achievement of that purpose. By whatever means may be at hand, the teacher determines whether suitable progress is being made in a desired direction and continues a given course of action or modifies it accordingly. Thus, if the outcomes at any step in the progress of a series of learning activities indicate that changes should be made, the program should be so flexible that changes can be made without apparent abruptness. This may operate in a number of directions. For example, a teacher may plan a series of activities extending over a period of time during which he believes the desired results may be achieved. However, if for any reason the interest of the group cannot be normally sustained for that time, the program should be changed. If, on the other hand, the purposes of a given series of activities have not been achieved when the allotted time has been spent, the time should be extended. This calls for constant appraisal by the teacher of pupil purpose, of the activities engaged in by teacher and pupils, of the materials used, and of the evaluations that pupils make of their own experiences.

Similarly, evaluation as a function of the curriculum provides a check upon the aims, the selection and organization of materials, the teaching procedures, and the means of evaluation itself. In other words, the revision of the curriculum takes place properly through constant evaluation of its various elements as they are observed in action.

PROVISION FOR EVALUATION IN COURSES OF STUDY

According to this point of view courses of study for the use of teachers in developing the curriculum should provide suggestions that will assist them in the various phases of evaluation. Many courses of study contain provisions for assisting teachers in evaluating the results of their instruction. These usually consist of suggested procedures for administering standard tests or for constructing and applying tests developed in a given curriculum program.

Objective tests and examinations have been used more widely than any other means for evaluating the results of instruction. This may be due, to a large extent, to the ease with which they are administered and scored, and to the uniformity with which the results may be treated. Therefore, this method of evaluation is either stated or implied in a majority of courses of study. In some instances tests are included in the course of study. When included they are usually given for illustration, although in some cases they are suggested or even prescribed for actual use. The inclusion of tests in courses of study is a relatively new element that has been introduced into course of study making. Harap [2] found in his analysis of courses of study in 1930 that only 8 per cent of the courses examined included tests. A similar analysis by Harap and Bayne [3] in 1932 showed that 18 per cent included tests. Although the results of these studies show an increase of only 10 per cent for the two-year period, they indicate an increasing emphasis upon provision in courses of study for some means of evaluation.

As a rule, the tests included in courses of study are designed for testing specific habits and knowledge. The tests usually found may be classed as, completion, direct recall, multiple choice, true-false, reason, enumeration question, thought question, classification or association, multiple choice-recall-recognition, and matching. While most courses of study state that certain attitudes, appreciations, and dispositions are desirable

[2] Henry Harap, "A Critique of Public School Courses of Study, 1928–1929." *Journal of Educational Research*, 21:109–119, February, 1930.

[3] Henry Harap and Alice J. Bayne, "A Critical Survey of Public Schools Courses of Study Published 1929–1931," *Journal of Educational Research*, 26:46–55, September, 1932.

outcomes, the testing procedures usually included provide no means for evaluating them.[4] There is little doubt, however, that the use of objective tests has improved the evaluation of those educational results concerned with specific knowledge and skills. However, two outstanding defects of such tests as commonly used should be noted.

The first of these defects is their doubtful validity. Tyler observes that "in general, it may be said that valid and reliable tests of these types (objective achievement) are much more difficult to construct than is commonly realized."[5] The tests usually call for specific information in a given field, and are so constructed that they test the pupils' knowledge of the specific items included. However, we have no assurance that knowledge of specific facts in a given field is a valid measure of pupil growth or of the ability to use the knowledge in its proper relationship. In a recent investigation to determine the relation between the ability to secure facts and the ability to do inferential thinking regarding the material read, Joseph C. Dewey concludes that "we can no longer assume that, by making factual tests of reading, we have at the same time measured true understanding of what is read."[6] Even when aims are stated in terms of the acquisition of specific information a number of factors operate to reduce the validity of the test used. By isolating each testing device and the particular elements in behavior it is supposed to test, the reliability of the test as an adequate measure of educational results has been improved at the expense of its validity.

[4] The use of objective tests to evaluate certain elements of general patterns of conduct, such as attitudes and appreciations, has been much less extensive than in evaluating specific knowledge and skills. A recent summary of such tests published between 1916 and 1931, *Psychological Tests, Methods and Results,* by Henry E. Garrett and Matthew R. Schneck, includes tests of six general types. These are rating scales for certain character traits, personality adjustment questionnaire, introversion-extroversion questionnaire, attitudes questionnaire, interest questionnaire, and personality test. It is significant that only thirty-seven such tests were produced and of that number, eighteen were primarily for adults.

[5] Ralph W. Tyler, "The Master-List as a Device," *Educational Research Bulletin,* 10:1, January 7, 1931.

[6] Joseph C. Dewey, "The Acquisition of Facts as a Measure of Reading Comprehension," *Elementary School Journal,* 35:346–348, January, 1935.

Tyler[7] also points out that the chief defects are that we have limited our means of observing behavior. He suggests that validity requires that tests should be made in normal situations; that they should provide a means of control over extraneous factors; and that they should represent an adequate sample of behavior. Thus, we may raise the question: Which of the many objectives that education seeks can be measured directly by such tests? May not indirect measures be properly employed? The primary consideration at this point, however, is the extent to which achievement and similar tests really indicate the results of instruction, or, in other words, are a valid means of evaluation.

There is a tendency in the development and use of objective tests and examinations to overlook the fact that evaluation is a function of the learning process. Because tests are objective there is the inclination to treat them as something separate and apart from the rest of the process. As a matter of fact, their validity may be determined largely by the extent to which they become a part of the normal experience of the individual being tested. Tyler says: ". . . the criterion of a valid test should be the reaction of students in a variety of situations appropriate to the objectives of the subject."[8] In other words, the test should take its place along with the other elements in the process of instruction.

A second defect in the use of tests is the variety of uses made of test results. Test results have been made to serve a number of purposes that are only remotely related to the immediate purposes for which they are devised. While many of these uses are meritorious they tend to exercise an undue influence upon numerous phases of the educational program. For example, standard achievement tests serve to show the comparative achievement of pupils in various divisions of a particular school system, as well as to compare the average achievement with national norms. This use of tests may possess value provided it

[7] Ralph W. Tyler, "Techniques for Evaluating Behavior," *Educational Research Bulletin,* 13:1-2, January 17, 1934.

[8] Ralph W. Tyler, "Assumptions Involved in Achievement-Test Construction," *Educational Research Bulletin,* 12:31, February 8, 1933.

does not become the sole or principal means and purpose of evaluation. However, in some school systems the results of such tests determine to a large extent the grade placement and promotion of pupils, the promotion or retention of teachers, the salaries of teachers, and the organization of instruction. Working under such external pressures, teachers are often influenced to modify their instructional programs even when their better judgment is against such modification. Harap says: "The use of standard tests may have the effect of diverting instruction from the attainment of carefully determined objectives of a course to preparing pupils to pass standard tests." [9]

Tests are also used as a means of motivation, of stimulating the pupil to greater application. Knudsen states that "A teacher may effectively use the results of tests to motivate the learning activity of a class," but adds "A teacher may overwork a device of the kind just described, and one who is careless of the adequacy of the tests he gives may actually discourage effort on the part of a class." [10] Finney warns "that testing, *as a device for motivating the learner*, is more likely to be an obstacle than an aid to teaching." [11] Frequently, tests and examinations are used for regulatory or punitive purposes, in which case the results are almost certain to be positively harmful. This practice of using tests as a means of enforcing desired conduct not only tends to invalidate the results of the particular test, but also tends to create a resistance to tests in general. Moreover, it tends to destroy the effect of what otherwise might have been stimulating teaching.

When the aims of education are stated only in terms of specific knowledge or habits, the types of tests usually found in courses of study may be considered a reasonably satisfactory means of evaluating instruction. However, when generalized

[9] Henry Harap, *The Technique of Curriculum Making,* The Macmillan Company, 1928, p. 216.
[10] Charles W. Knudsen, *Evaluation and Improvement of Teaching,* Doubleday, Doran & Company, 1932, pp. 367–368.
[11] Ross Finney, *A Sociological Philosophy of Education,* The Macmillan Company, 1928, p. 371.

controls of conduct are expected as outcomes, other means of evaluation must be provided.

Most courses of study, either directly or by implication, recognize the importance of evaluating generalized controls of conduct. However, provision for such evaluation is rarely made. Certain courses of study organized largely from the social point of view contain suggestions for observing certain attributes of general patterns of conduct.

A recent state course of study suggests the following procedure:

Both *attitudes and fixed associations* will have to be measured almost entirely by observational tests, that is, by observation by the teacher of the every day activities of the children.

. . . .

Observational tests are much more important than teachers usually realize. More can be told about the complete development of a child by observing him from day to day than in any other way. Important attitudes, appreciations, and methods of work may be tested by securing from observation of a pupil answers to such questions as the following:

Does he work well with a group?
Does he get along with other children?
Is he on time?
Is he pleasant and cheerful?
Does he read good books during leisure time?
Does he get books from the public library?
Does he raise interesting and stimulating questions?
Is he increasingly effective in his use of references?
Does he stick to a task until it is finished?
Does he give undivided attention to the undertaking at hand?
Does he listen courteously to others?
Is he thoughtful of smaller children?
Does he enjoy hearing good music? [12]

An example of the application of observational tests in the various subjects is found in the course of study in arithmetic as follows:

[12] *The Course of Study for Florida Elementary Schools, Grades I to VI,* 1933, pp. 766–770.

The teacher should also observe carefully the general methods of work and attitudes that children display in arithmetic work. The following questions may be suggestive of what to look for:

1. Self-reliance.

   Does the child rely upon himself for the solution and checking of arithmetic problems? Does he willingly attack a problem and see it through?

2. Accuracy.

   Does he feel responsible for the accuracy of his own results? Does he check his own reasoning for accuracy? Does he have a sense of satisfaction in the acquisition of accuracy?

3. Satisfaction with completed work.

   Do inaccurate and vague results annoy him? Is he proud of completed work? Does he express himself with precision?

4. Discrimination.

   Does he discriminate between relevant and irrelevant data? Does he see relative values?

5. Interest.

   Is he interested in the perfection of his own technique? Does he practice of his own volition for skill? Does he seek after knowledge of number? Does he "tinker" with numbers, make up problems and imagine mathematical problems?

6. Application.

   Does he tend to apply mathematics honestly to solution of the problems he meets in his daily life? Is he measuring, "figuring out," "stepping off"? Does he practice making figures like a surveyor, a bookkeeper, or like his father does?

7. Analysis.

   Does he break up complex situations into their component parts? Does he seek causes for certain results and situations? Does he feel relationships? Is he acquiring the habit of selecting?

8. Generalization.

   Does he see that problems group themselves into large classes? "That this one is like that one." Does he see that the same method of solution will apply to similar problems?

9. Neatness of work.

   Is he satisfied with an erased paper? Does he arrange his work in a succession of steps or is it "jumbled"? Is he careful of statement, margins, formation of figures and diagrams?

10. Love of the truth.

    Does he weigh evidence on both sides? Does he cling to his

result and surrender upon conviction? Does he search after the truth? Does a wrong answer irritate him and is he eager to give the correct one or search for it? [13]

Such courses of study not only suggest procedures for observing behavior, but frequently provide illustrative inventory or check sheets. In such check sheets the specific items of behavior to be observed are listed under proper headings. After each item space is provided for such evaluation as the teachers may choose to make. If a situation arises in which a pupil's behavior presents a special problem, or if it is exceptional in any respect, notation is made in a proper column. Such a record is cumulative and becomes a part of the pupil's permanent record.

SUGGESTED PROVISIONS FOR EVALUATING OUTCOMES IN A CURRICULUM PROGRAM

In planning and carrying forward a curriculum program, provision should be made for each element to function in its proper relation to the whole process of instruction. In order that the evaluation of outcomes may be effective, a curriculum program should possess certain characteristics. These are here suggested for the guidance of curriculum workers.

1. *The curriculum should provide for continuous evaluation.* Evaluation is a continuous process. It is not merely one of a series of separate acts. However important it may be to think of learning as involving such steps as planning, purposing, executing, and judging, we must keep in mind that these elements of the learning process are constantly interacting at every point. This applies both with respect to the pupil's evaluation of the results of his own activities and the teacher's evaluation of the results of instruction. And, while there may be special emphasis upon evaluation at the culmination of a series of activities, to reserve it for that occasion alone, or even principally, would tend to defeat the purposes of instruction.

[13] *Ibid.,* pp. 773–774.

2. *Provision must be made for evaluating individual progress.* The use of the results of evaluation, particularly of standardized tests, frequently tends to emphasize group rather than individual progress. Test scores, however valuable they may be, may have little meaning for evaluating the progress of a given individual except when studied in relation to numerous other factors that influence his behavior. A personal continuous record of every observation that may indicate growth of the individual should be provided with suggested means for its use.

3. *Evaluation should stimulate rather than retard.* The discouraging effects of examinations or tests upon pupils are too well known to require treatment here. If evaluation functions properly as an intrinsic part of the total learning process, it becomes a co-operative task of pupils and teacher. The reasonableness of the means used, then, will be apparent both to teacher and pupils. When the pupil understands his own share of responsibility for the continuous evaluation of his progress, testing ceases to be a cause for discouragement and becomes rather a stimulus.

4. *Evaluation should be in terms of the aims of education.* Observation of behavior should be made primarily in terms of the particular aim or aims selected for specific emphasis in a given situation. However, observations should not be limited to these aims alone. As has been stated previously, the experience of the individual pupil is extremely complex. Often other factors than those we are able to observe have the most potent influence on the one whose activities we would direct.

5. *The course of study should contain suggestions for evaluation.* Specific means of evaluation may be properly included in courses of study as illustrative tests for specific knowledge and skills. Suggestions as to general procedures in evaluation may be helpful both with respect to objective and subjective means of evaluation. References to sources of information on the construction and administration of tests should be included in the references provided for teachers. The principal means of evaluation should be indicated by the materials of instruction and the

suggestive activities that are provided as raw materials to aid the teacher in developing the curriculum.

6. *Provision should be made for the results of evaluation to be utilized in continuous revision of the curriculum.* Evaluation should be concerned with the progress of pupils in the direction indicated by the stated aims of education. Moreover, every phase of the curriculum should be under constant evaluation in the light of the major purpose which it is to serve. Therefore, provision should be made for the teacher to report consistently upon the success of the instructional program and to suggest ways of improving it. The program should be so flexible that the teacher will feel free to change a course of action at any point where the results observed indicate that a change is desirable.

SELECTED REFERENCES

Dewey, Joseph C., "The Acquisition of Facts as a Measure of Reading Comprehension," *Elementary School Journal*, 35:346–48, January, 1935.

Garrett, Henry E. and Schneck, Matthew R., *Psychological Tests, Methods and Results,* Harper and Brothers, New York, 1933, Chapter III.

Harap, Henry and Bayne, Alice J., "A Critical Survey of Public School Courses of Study Published 1929–1931," *Journal of Educational Research*, 26:46–55, September, 1932.

Knudsen, Charles W., *Evaluation and Improvement of Teaching*, Doubleday, Doran & Company, Garden City, New York, 1932.

Tyler, Ralph W., "Assumptions Involved in Achievement-Test Construction," *Educational Research Bulletin*, 12:31, February 8, 1933.

Tyler, Ralph W., "The Master-List as a Device," *Educational Research Bulletin*, 10:1, January 7, 1931.

CHAPTER XIV

ORGANIZING INSTRUCTION

Consideration is given in preceding chapters to various elements that enter into the experience of children at school and condition development of the curriculum. It was pointed out in Chapter IV that these elements do not enter into experience in additive fashion, but rather on a reaction basis. A process moves forward and an outcome results entirely different from any of the elements involved, although the outcome is the result of their interaction. Consequently, although much light is thrown on the issues and problems involved in curriculum development by consideration of the various elements involved, there remains the difficult problem of providing for their interaction in desirable ways. This task may be referred to as organizing instruction. The task is the ultimate one to which teachers must devote attention and its achievement depends upon their skill and ability. The procedure of curriculum development, however, should assist teachers to discharge the task well.

BASIS FOR ORGANIZING INSTRUCTION

Many methods have been employed to organize instruction. Most of these have come into prominence for a time, only to pass off the scene as popular fancy has turned to a new procedure. The recitation, traditional basis for organizing instruction, is probably still the major determinant in most instructional organization, although projects, type studies, problems, and units have been popularized from time to time. The variety of these methods presents a problem in the organization and development of a practical program of curriculum making. It must be decided whether a particular type of organization shall be adopted and all work be required to conform to the type, whether various types of organization shall be employed, or whether a general form of organization shall be used with limitations derived from the general concepts accepted as guides for the particular curriculum program. The problem has been solved in various ways in different curriculum programs. In some cases, programs have been projected from the very beginning to develop an activity curriculum, a project curriculum, a mastery unit curriculum, or a curriculum based on daily recitations. In other cases, general limitations have been defined which permit the use of various types of organization as they seem most appropriate for particular classroom situations.

All of these ways of organizing instruction have both merits and shortcomings. Certain ones seem to contribute to one phase of an instructional program and others to another. Instruction, for example, to achieve one type of outcome may partake more of the qualities of the recitation method, while to achieve another outcome the organization may have the characteristics of a project or unit of work. Consequently, when developing a practical curriculum program, it would seem wise to look beyond any single method of organizing instruction and to seek a basis broad enough to include the advantages of various methods. It may be further emphasized that this basis of organization should be found in the guiding principles and theories accepted for a particular curriculum program. If the controlling concepts are fundamental in nature, the type of instructional organization which results will be sound. If, on the other hand, the curriculum program has not been conceived as a comprehensive, related program, the basis for organizing instruction will be inadequate and the adoption of a particular method that is fully developed and illustrated may save confusion.

If a general basis of organizing instruction is sought from the implications of principles and procedures accepted for given programs, instructional organization will vary in different pro-

grams as principles and procedures and interpretations of them
vary. The suggestions for instructional organization presented
in this chapter are an outgrowth of the point of view presented
in the preceding chapters.

The concept that is held of aims of education is especially
significant in implications for organizing instruction. One concept will suggest one type of instructional organization and another concept an entirely different type. The consistency of a
program of curriculum development depends to a considerable
extent on the adequacy of the interpretation of the implications
for instructional organization of the concept of aims held in the
program.

The concept of aims of education as generalized controls of
conduct, as presented in Chapter VI, involves two points that
are suggestive for organizing instruction; namely, generalized
controls of conduct are integrations of specific habits and knowledge, and the degree of generalization depends principally upon
the number of specific habits and the extent of knowledge involved. These points suggest two requirements for the organization of instruction.

First, opportunity must be provided for the child to develop
the desired integrations of habits and knowledge. This seems
a perfectly obvious conclusion. Yet it is a requirement for instructional organization frequently overlooked. Integrations of
habits and knowledge which represent desired types of conduct
can be developed only by guiding the child in situations which
require such conduct. In other words, there is only one way to
learn to be honest, and that is to be honest; or to learn to be
scientific-minded, and that is to be scientific-minded. The role
of the teacher starts in securing one act that exemplifies the
desired type of conduct. Having secured one such act the
chances are slightly better than before that situations requiring
the same type of conduct will be met as desired. As other situ-

ations arise, and the pupil is guided in these so that he responds with the desired conduct, more and more habits and knowledge become a part of the control of conduct and the chances increase that in all new situations he will exhibit the desired trait. Thus, it is required in organizing instruction that many situations be provided in which the pupil can exhibit the desired types of conduct.

Not only should many opportunities be provided to exhibit the desired type of behavior, but also the learner should experience a wide variety of such situations. Similar situations require similar integrations of habits and knowledge to deal with them successfully. Meeting essentially the same situation again and again contributes comparatively little to the development of generalized controls of conduct. But if varied situations are encountered, new relationships are established and habits and knowledge not previously mastered are required. This aids the process of generalizing and adds assurance that the desired pattern of conduct will function in new situations.

The possibility that controls of conduct will be successfully generalized is further enhanced if the situations in which guidance is provided have lifelike qualities. In other words, behavior of the type exhibited in school will most certainly be exhibited in situations out of school, if school experiences have characteristics similar to out-of-school experiences. This is true because we can deal with new situations only in terms of past experience. Given a new type of machine to operate, for example, we may select something from an experience with a Model T Ford, a motor boat, a tractor, and an experiment in chemistry, from which to construct a satisfactory mode of operation. We make such selections because elements in the new-machine situation suggest the appropriateness of certain habits or knowledge employed in other situations. Obviously, the more similar in character these situations are, the greater the chance is that we will develop a satisfactory mode of behavior.

The school has too frequently provided an instructional organization with such artificial characteristics as to limit to a large measure the possibility of developing generalized controls of conduct. School situations have been over-simplified. The intricacy of relationships characteristic of life situations outside of school has been eliminated. The result is that when the pupil meets complex life situations he fails to carry over the mode of behavior the school endeavored to develop. Consequently, it is of utmost importance that there be included in the school life of the child complex situations which require that the appropriateness of a particular mode of behavior be deduced from a continuous flow of varied events.

Instructional organization, then, should have as a primary point of emphasis the provision of a large number of varied situations with lifelike qualities in which the child is guided in behavior of the desired type. Such instructional organization provides opportunities for establishing relationships for achieving rich associative learning, and thus for developing generalized controls of conduct. The desired attitudes have opportunity to function under a variety of conditions and with a variety of relationships. They have opportunity to function under circumstances similar to those encountered out of school and to influence ends of vital concern to the pupil, thus paving the way for even more effective exemplification of the attitudes in succeeding undertakings.

A second point of emphasis is suggested by the fact that ability to use effectively appropriate habits and knowledge makes it possible for an individual to employ a particular generalized control of conduct. Lack of facility in their use reduces the possibility that the individual will employ in a satisfactory manner the desired generalized control of conduct. The use of habits and knowledge may be facilitated both by a high degree of mastery and by organization in terms of inherent relationships. Activities to achieve mastery of habits and knowledge are frequently referred to as the drill phase of instruction. Effective organization of habits and knowledge implies establishing the relationships which indicate subject fields. The two are directly related and both frequently require direct, concentrated effort and guidance, as well as continuous checking.

If either of these points of emphasis is overlooked in organizing the instructional program, the child receives a one-sided education. Lacking the basic experiences, the child does not formulate out of his habits and knowledge generalized controls of conduct. They remain unrelated, relatively meaningless bits. Lacking, on the other hand, effective control of habits and knowledge, there is nothing from which to build generalized controls of conduct and consequently little increase in ability to meet new situations in desirable ways.

IMPLICATIONS OF THE NATURE OF LEARNING FOR ORGANIZING INSTRUCTION

The concept held of the nature of learning also has significant implications for organizing instruction. The central point of reference in organizing instruction from the standpoint of the learner may be either the knowledge and specific habits it is considered desirable to master, or the purpose of the learner. In other words, either potential subject matter or the experience of the learner may be the point about which instruction is organized. If subject matter is made the central point of reference, the purpose of the learner must be forced to correspond to predetermined content. If the experience of the learner is made the central point of reference, subject matter is selected to help achieve ends about which the learner is concerned and which he believes are worth while. The importance of making the purposes and needs of the learner the primary point of orientation in selecting activities and subject matter has been emphasized in foregoing chapters. Consequently, in so far as the point of view presented in this book is concerned, we turn to consideration of types of purposes for implications as to organizing instruction.

Purposes fall into two general types which are suggestive for organizing instruction. These types are suggested by essential differences in stimuli which give rise to purposes. Stimuli vary greatly in intensity and persistency. Some may be easily eliminated and equilibrium quickly established. Others persist for long periods of time and require a complex series of activities to eliminate them. Hollingworth describes the differences as follows:

Transient stimuli lead on the whole to brief responses, and these, as we have seen, are often nicely calculated to eliminate the stimulus. Persistent stimuli, or motives, in the narrow sense, must lead to long-continued activity . . .

. . . .

The motive, in other words, brings into play a certain general set of responses, of a certain general sort and in a certain general direction; responses which on the whole may in the past have succeeded in the effective relief from such an irritant. All that the motive can account for is the occurrence of the activity and its general character and persistence. Just what acts come, from moment to moment, is likely to be due to the contributing effect of *other stimuli,* occurring from moment to moment.

. . . .

A hunting dog, intent upon the pursuit of another animal, will serve as a simple example. So long as the prey is in sight, or in sound, or in smell, but out of reach, it constitutes a persisting stimulus. It sets up, in the animal hunting it, varied activities and changes, of a general character. We recognize the dog to be excited, rather than sleepy; he is animated, rather than at ease; it is the fore part of his body, his eyes and jaws and ears that are especially animated, not his tail; moreover his movements of locomotion are all in a given *direction,* he is after the prey. So the persistent irritant, the fleeing prey, sets up a general set or repertoire of activity which we call the attitude of attack.

But *precisely* what the dog will do from moment to moment will be determined by *transitory* stimuli encountered on the way. Coming to a fence, he crawls through it; reaching a ditch or a wall, he springs over it; grabbed at by a passerby, he snaps at the extended hand; joined by another dog, he yelps, and so on. It is true that such a dog is likely to show limited scope for the present situation. If he injures his foot, he "pays no attention"; if his master whistles, he seems oblivious to this stimulus. He may, in fact, seriously injure himself because of the lack of sagacity which characterizes him in this moment of excitement.[1]

[1] From *Educational Psychology,* by H. L. Hollingworth. Used by permission of D. Appleton-Century Company, publishers, New York, N. Y., 1933, pp. 65–67.

This distinction suggests two general types of situations in which the teacher must direct learning. The first arises from the action of persisting stimuli. The purposes evolved from such stimuli project well into the future. They require careful initial planning, continuous readjustment of plans to secure progress toward the desired outcome, working for deferred values, persistence; and they involve a great complexity of activities. Such purposes may be described by the term dominating.

The second general type of situation arises from the action of transient stimuli. There are two general sources of such stimuli. The first source develops from efforts to realize a dominating purpose of the kind described above. Such efforts often make necessary the use of specific habits and knowledge of which the child does not have adequate mastery. When such a condition develops, activity may for a time appropriately be directed toward the mastery of the requisite abilities. Then it is that the teacher may safely direct attention almost exclusively to a specific ability. But having gained the necessary mastery, efforts are again made directly toward realization of the dominating purpose. The second source is from the general course of life activities. Much of life is on a habit level and consists of habitual adjustments to simple stimuli. Eating, dressing, protecting ourselves from accidents, driving a car, are illustrations. Upon occasion situations involving more than usual difficulty arise and special attention must be given temporarily to development of specific habits that serve as satisfactory means of adjustment. The school program should assist in developing this habituated basis for carrying forward the regular course of life activity. To achieve this end the teacher finds it necessary from time to time to give direct attention to specific habits that the child has not mastered sufficiently well to carry on routine life activities effectively. Thus, the action of transient stimuli frequently leads to situations in which attention must be given directly to the mastery of specific habits and knowledge. It should be noted especially, however, that these stimuli arise out of larger, more commanding situations and have meaning only as they are related to these situations.

This analysis suggests, as did consideration of the implications of aims, two types of instructional situations that should be provided in organizing instruction: first, situations developed from dominating purposes of children; and, second, situations developed from the need for organization and mastery for effective use of specific habits or knowledge as a means of realizing dominating purposes and of carrying on routine life activities. It will be noted that the points of emphasis in the two analyses suggest types of learning situations with essentially the same qualities. The requirement from consideration of aims that provision be made for a large number of varied situations with lifelike qualities coincides with the organization of instruction around dominating purposes of children. The need for mastery of specific habits and knowledge suggested by study of aims coincides with the type of instruction required by operation of transient stimuli. Consequently, so far as the implications of the general point of view of curriculum making presented in this book are concerned, there appear to be required two points of emphasis in organizing instruction. For convenience we shall refer to the first of these as the major experiential phase of the instructional program, and to the second as the direct teaching phase of the instructional program.

THE MAJOR EXPERIENTIAL PHASE OF THE INSTRUCTIONAL PROGRAM

Development of an adequate instructional organization requires careful observance of the characteristics of the two phases of the instructional program just discussed. Instructional organization that provides the major experiential phase of the program should have three characteristics. These characteristics may be deduced from preceding discussions.

The children have a dominating purpose which they consider worth while and which is compatible with the aims of education.

This is the first and most indispensable characteristic of instruction designed to broaden and enrich the experiences of children. It is the dominating purpose which ties the various activities together and gives them meaning for the child. The discussion in Chapter VIII of the general significance of purpose indicates further the importance of this characteristic. The preceding discussion in this chapter presents the basis upon which the modifier *dominating* is added. The purpose must be considered worth while by the pupils or the drive for continued, persistent action is lacking. It must be compatible with the aims of education or the resulting activity will not be educationally worth while. The importance of this characteristic can hardly be over-emphasized. In organizing instruction it should receive first consideration.

The children, under the guidance of the teacher engage in a series of activities, which they consider a means of realizing their purpose. A dominating purpose requires many activities for realization. If these activities are carried forward by the children with the recognition of the relationship of each to the outcome they hope to realize, real unity will be achieved. Lacking such understanding, the integrating force of experience is eliminated and the activities tend to become mere movements. The careful guidance of the teacher is considered essential because activities of varying worth, as measured by the desired outcomes of education, are always suggested by children. The teacher must estimate the value of each activity that is proposed and either encourage or discourage its use. Also, there is nothing in the mere performance of an activity to guarantee achievement of desirable outcomes. In other words, the same activity may be performed in such a manner as to result in significant educational outcomes or to be of negative value. The teacher must be on the alert continually to see that pupils perform the various activities in which they engage so as to realize educationally desirable outcomes. The careful guidance of the teacher is also required because pupils frequently need help in performing necessary activities. Failure to recognize the need for assistance and to provide it tends to encourage slipshod methods of work and low standards of achievement. A discussion of the various types of activities that may be employed to help realize purposes is given in Chapter IX.

The children evaluate the outcomes of the activities in which they engage. The importance of evaluation of the outcomes of activities is discussed in Chapter XIII. There is required a relatively continuous evaluation of outcomes of activities as they are carried forward. Maximum value will be derived from experience only if there is also a more comprehensive review and evaluation of a total series of activities after a purpose has been realized. Such a summarizing evaluation develops attitudes that facilitate the achievement of purposes involving similar elements.

OTHER CONSIDERATIONS

Many rather specific requirements are set up for certain methods of instructional organization which provide broadening experiences for children. For example, in organizing certain types of units of work the length of time required for completion of the unit is emphasized. In some cases, units are uniformly planned for eighteen or thirty-six weeks. Frequently, instructional organization involving markedly shorter periods is looked upon askance.

Length alone is not a determining characteristic of instructional organization designed to provide children with broad, meaningful, experience. Such experience, it is true, evolves from a purpose which requires a relatively complex series of activities for realization, but this series of activities may consume widely varying amounts of time. In one case two or three weeks may suffice to achieve the purpose, while in other cases eighteen or twenty weeks may be required. Realization of purpose should be the sole determinant of length.

Length of an instructional unit is definitely conditioned by the maturity of the learner. As maturity approaches purposes tend to involve more and more deferred values. Hence, it is reasonable to expect that due consideration for the experience of children would lead to comparatively short instructional units with young children and to longer ones with older children. Strangely enough exactly the opposite practice is commonly followed. The first grade child has units that cover an entire semester or year and the junior high school pupil has units two to six weeks in length.

Another point that merits attention is the relationship which must exist between instruction organized as described heretofore and subject fields. In developing such instructional organization no effort is made to restrict activities and content to one subject field or to include material from all subject fields. Freedom must be provided to go to any source from which help may be secured in realizing the pupils' purpose. Teachers, of course, guide development so that the most worth-while subject matter is used. But subject matter is selected because it helps the child solve a problem rather than because it happens to be in a textbook or in a particular subject field. Often purposes will be developed that require materials almost wholly from one subject field, and again, materials from many fields may be needed. As adulthood approaches it is entirely possible that purposes may be formed which require thorough-going study and mastery of certain relatively narrow, logically organized fields of subject matter. If such a purpose develops, it should receive as careful attention as purposes which involve materials from several fields. The development of a sound instructional unit is just as possible as in the lower grades where a purpose requires materials from many fields without regard for the logical arrangement of the subject matter. In brief, the learner's purpose is the *unifying* force in all cases. As such it may require materials from a single logically organized subject field or it may make necessary disregard of all conventional arrangements of subject fields.

A basis for evaluating the extent to which a given instructional unit possesses the foregoing characteristics is provided by criteria and suggestions set forth in preceding chapters. A check list of the type given in Chart VI assists in evaluation.

CHART VI

CHECK LIST TO ASSIST IN EVALUATING INSTRUCTIONAL UNITS

QUESTIONS FOR GUIDANCE	COMMENT
1. Do the pupils have a dominating purpose?	1.
a. Is the type of behavior required compatible with the aims of education?	a.
b. Is the plan of action to realize the purpose based on the past experience of the pupils?	b.
c. Do the pupils believe the purpose is worth while?	c.
d. Did the purpose arise from stimuli of a kind the pupils will meet in out-of-school experiences?	d.
e. Have the pupils mastery of the abilities needed to carry out the plan successfully or can they master them in reasonable time?	e.
f. Does the purpose require behavior on a higher level than the pupils have exhibited before?	f.
2. Have the pupils engaged in a series of activities planned by them and the teacher to realize their purpose?	2.

a. Do the children recognize the part the various activities in which they engage are to play in realization of the purpose?

a.

b. Do the various activities contribute to realization of the aims of education?

b.

c. Are the activities suited to the mental, physical, and emotional characteristics of the individuals who engage in them?

c.

3. Have the children evaluated their activities in terms of the purpose they set out to achieve?

3.

a. Has the plan of action been continuously revised and improved as steps have been taken in its development?

a.

b. Have the children recognized the need for more adequate mastery of certain abilities and have steps been taken to achieve such mastery?

b.

c. Have the children considered the enterprise as a whole when completed to see what improvements could have been made?

c.

d. Have the children canvassed other related enterprises in which they would like to engage?

d.

e. Did the enterprise develop conduct of the desired type?

e.

THE DIRECT TEACHING PHASE OF THE INSTRUCTIONAL PROGRAM

The point of emphasis in the instructional program which we have referred to as the direct teaching phase involves, as pointed out before, a twofold task. Essential knowledge and specific habits must be mastered and organized for most effective use in new situations. This phase of instruction has been subjected to much careful study. Extended analyses have been made to determine what facts, generalizations, and principles are used frequently. Numerous experimental studies have been made to discover the most efficient methods of mastery. From these analyses and experiments many valuable data are available. These data should be employed in curriculum making to provide for a wise selection of abilities to be given attention in the direct teaching program and for selecting the most effective means for their mastery.

Even with the large amount of scientific evidence available for developing this phase of instruction, much time is wasted and a great deal of ineffective instruction given. This results perhaps more from an unwise selection of abilities to be given direct emphasis separate from the major experiential phase of instruction than from any other cause. At least it is of utmost importance that very careful selection be made. The following criteria appear to the writers to provide a sound basis for choice of abilities to receive direct emphasis.

The child uses or can use the ability now in meaningful school or out-of-school experiences. Very frequently abilities are given direct, intensive cultivation when the child has no meaningful situations in which he can use the abilities. This leads to learning by memory and contributes nothing to the child's understanding. This tendency has been furthered by studies of grade placement which emphasize placement of content in the lowest grade at which a child can remember a fact or perform a skill rather than at the stage of development at which optimum mastery and understanding can be achieved. The tendency is also furthered by tests that emphasize ability to reproduce facts or to perform specific habits in isolation rather than use of the ability in situations when it is needed.

The importance of this criterion has been recognized to a considerable extent in developing curriculum materials for primary grade children. For example, Brueckner, after considering the findings of studies which show that children in the primary grades acquire through informal activities much larger arithmetical backgrounds than is ordinarily believed possible, concludes: "The curriculum maker in the primary grades should recognize this important fact, reduce the emphasis on formal arithmetic in these grades, and provide rich units of instruction in which number may function in meaningful ways." [2]

There has been hesitance, however, to give merited consideration to the same point in intermediate and high school grades. Nevertheless, the principle of learning involved operates regardless of grades, and the criterion is as applicable to one level of learning as to another. Its more careful observance would inject some of the vitality characteristic of good primary grade work into other levels of work.

The ability can be mastered economically by the child at his present level of development. There is reason to believe that certain stages of the growth process are particularly adapted to development of certain types of abilities. The infant, for example, goes through a period of motor adjustments. Major development centers around gaining mastery of large movements. Later, he reaches a stage of growth when language ability begins to develop in a marked way. No doubt, throughout the period of immaturity there are similar stages of growth conducive to optimum development of certain types of abilities. It is an important task in teaching to provide for the mastery of various types of abilities at the stage of growth best suited to their mastery. Failure in this regard makes teaching a difficult, trying, and often, to all appearances, hopeless task.

---

[2] Leo J. Brueckner, "Curriculum Investigations at the Elementary- and Secondary-School Levels: C. Arithmetic," *Review of Educational Research,* 4:141, April, 1934.

Yet, it is a very general tendency to fail to observe this criterion. Two children may enter a first grade together. One may have started talking at eighteen months, the other at thirty months, yet they are presumed to be equally ready to begin development of another language ability, reading. If the second child is inept in developing the ability he is apt to be called a failure by the school while a year of broadening experiences and maturation might place him where he could as easily gain command of the reading ability as he did of the speaking ability. This same principle applies with particular force to study of specialized fields in the secondary school. There are, no doubt, numerous "school failures" in high school who are really children who simply have not reached the stage of maturation required to develop effectively and economically the type of ability required.

When one considers numerous abilities now taught in various grades, the questions arise: Why spend hours of drudgery developing this ability now when a little later it may be developed more effectively in a half or a third of the time? Why drill and drill when a broadened background of basic experience which gives the ability meaning will make possible its mastery with little drill?

The problem then is to find the general stage of growth at which particular types of abilities are mastered most economically and to guide individual children in mastery of these abilities as they enter the respective growth stages. This means that the development of specific abilities cannot be assigned to arbitrary time divisions such as grades, but rather that general periods of emphasis must be indicated. It means also that the youngest age at which a child can achieve a particular ability is not necessarily the optimum age for such development. Both of these assumptions are frequently made in curriculum work.

The ability cannot be mastered adequately without special emphasis not possible in ordinary use. This criterion guards against developing a program of instruction which requires drill for the mastery of abilities whether the child needs the drill or not. Much time is wasted in schools by children studying and spelling words they already know, working problems they already can work, developing skill in writing significantly above a point that it can be maintained in ordinary use, and in similar ways. This emphasizes the point that abilities to receive direct emphasis should be those of which the child evidently lacks sufficient mastery for effective use.

THE DIRECT TEACHING PROGRAM AND SUBJECT FIELDS

There is a close relationship between the direct teaching phase of instruction and subject fields. Principles, generalizations, facts, and specific habits are organized in subject fields to establish the relationships between them. These relationships add meaning and increase materially the possibility of effective use of various abilities. Consequently, subject fields may appropriately play a part in this phase of the instructional program. The child should be made conscious of the relationships suggested by subject fields and should be guided in understanding and appreciating these relationships. He should, in brief, be brought to see that subject organization is a useful tool which the race has developed and which he can use to advantage in attacking his problems. The teacher should recognize at all times, however, that the extent to which given children can use this tool varies greatly and that in this regard constant adjustment is needed to the capacity, needs, and maturity of the learner.

INSTRUCTIONAL PROGRAM SHOULD NOT BE DIVIDED INTO DISCRETE PARTS

It will be noted that throughout the foregoing discussion, the phrase, "points of emphasis for instructional organization," has been used. This phrase was selected because it suggests that the instructional program should be considered a unit. One of the major faults of curriculum programs in organizing instruction is the tendency to set up various parts of the instructional program without relationship to other parts. First, subject divisions are usually made in such a way that there are no fundamental relationships between work in the various fields. Then divisions are made within the subjects which further make for separateness. For example, English is separated from the other content fields; then literature and composition are divided; then within each of these divisions more minute divisions are made. All of this contributes difficulties in establishing relationships and in developing a fundamental educational program.

Ideally, the instructional program should move along much as life out of school moves. General time and place guides, such as a time for getting up, going to work, and for meals, should be employed, but within these guides the demands of the particular situation should determine the kind of activity engaged in and the time devoted to it. To realize this ideal will require a more flexible program of work than has generally been employed in both elementary and secondary schools.

THE TEACHER'S PROGRAM OF WORK

The traditional program of work in the elementary school consists of uniformly short periods, followed with absolute regularity. Such a program cannot be employed to develop the type of instructional organization suggested by the foregoing discussion. In the secondary school the program is characterized by strict adherence to subject matter lines, the exclusive use of the recitation method, and general lack of concern on the part of teachers of different subjects for the work in other subjects. These conditions stand in the way of effective instructional organization in the secondary school. In the place of these rigid programs of work must be substituted flexible programs that serve as general guides within which instructional organization may be adjusted as need arises. The amount of flexibility that should be permitted in a program of work depends on several factors, the most important of which is the ability of the teacher to plan his work in light of the demands of a developing situation. Even though a given teacher may be very much limited in this ability, a curriculum program should nevertheless so present materials as to encourage growth in that direction.

A program of work in an elementary school, in order to provide for an instructional organization of the kind described here, should have two general divisions. One division should provide for the major experiential phase of the instructional program and the other for mastery and organization of specific habits and knowledge for effective use. It will be necessary, of course, to provide as well for the routine life of the school, which is concerned with carrying on those activities which the school requires for effective normal operation as a place for boys and girls to live. These activities are varied in nature. They include such items as health inspections, management of school traffic, care of school equipment and materials, and provision for free reading and play.

The clarity with which the program of work is divided into definite time periods and the detail with which the large divisions are subdivided depends on the individual teacher. The less skillful teacher will find it necessary to make rather definite period allotments, but as skill increases the school day takes on greater and greater unity. One phase of work leads naturally into another and sharp breaks are eliminated. Also, as skill is increased, less time is required for direct attention to specific habits and knowledge to insure adequate mastery. Consequently, a program of work should be made for a given teacher and a given group of pupils. The basic requirement should not be uniformity, but rather that the teacher know what he is doing and have a program sufficiently definite to assure that he does know.

In the secondary school, teachers of different subjects must give greater attention to work in various fields. They must develop a co-operative method of planning. They must be freed also from the administrative requirement of hearing pupils recite during all periods of teacher direction. The recitation period must come to be considered a time when the teacher is free to assist pupils to carry forward their work. This will require a complete revision of the attitude and method of the usual secondary school classroom.

COURSE OF STUDY MATERIALS AND INSTRUCTIONAL ORGANIZATION

Course of study materials should be prepared and organized to facilitate the desired type of instructional organization. If, for example, a flexible type of instructional organization such as is described in this chapter is desired, materials must not be presented in an organization that does not permit adjustment. Courses of study which prescribe units to be taught, or organize materials into recitation periods, or prescribe textbook pages, make impossible the development of a flexible program. Some courses of study present materials in a form different from any of these and which is especially conducive to flexibility of instructional organization. Materials are presented in such form that the teacher is permitted freedom in selecting activities and content for use in instructional units. It is recognized as well that mastery of the various abilities requires a span of grades rather than one grade only. Only two limitations are imposed in such courses, the aims of education and the scope of the work of the grade. Both are sufficiently broad to permit adjustments to individual pupil needs, abilities, and interests, and to environmental conditions.

PLANNING FOR INSTRUCTIONAL ORGANIZATION

Adequate instructional organization depends most of all on careful planning by the teacher. Even though materials may be made available which suggest desirable lines of development, and which are sufficiently flexible to permit organization to meet the needs of particular situations, the instructional organization will be poor if the teacher does not plan his work with care. Planning procedures themselves should be flexible. There is no single best way to plan, nor any single best form for plans. It is a mistake to restrict teachers to uniform planning procedures. The

CHART VII

RECORD OF UNIT OF WORK

DADE COUNTY SCHOOLS, MIAMI, FLORIDA

SCHOOL _____

TEACHER _____

GRADE _____

DATE BEGUN _____ COMPLETED _____

TITLE OF UNIT _____

SUGGESTIONS:
(a) Do no spread this sheet. Use the back of the sheet when necessary.
(b) Develop the plan to the unit progresses, making modifications as need arises.
(c) Develop your plan with care and then make it your constant guide.

OBJECTIVES FOR UNIT (State in Child's Level in Specific Terms)	ACTIVITIES, SUBJECT MATTER, AND MATERIALS THAT ARE USED	DEVELOPMENT OF UNIT (Keep a Brief Outline of the Way the Unit Develops)	CULMINATING ACTIVITIES (Plan Out Any Unit Structures)
			OUTCOMES

APPROACH
Interests That Lead to Unit:

Approach:

CONTRIBUTING PURPOSES OF THE CHILDREN AS DEVELOPED:

OBJECTIVES EMPHASIZED IN TEACHING THE VARIOUS SUBJECTS

ARITHMETIC	ART	LANGUAGE	MUSIC	PHYSICAL and HEALTH ED.	READING	SCIENCE	SOCIAL STUDIES	SPELLING	WRITING	LEADS TO OTHER UNITS

26"

397

traditional type of plan book, for example, encourages piecemeal, inadequate planning.

Planning should involve three general stages, a pre-plan, a readjustment of plans as work progresses, and an evaluation of the work after its completion to note points that need improvement and leads for further work. In each of these stages attention should be given to all elements in the learning process. Although uniform use of a specified form for plans is undesirable, most teachers find helpful a form of the type reproduced in Chart VII. It will be noted by the dimensions given on the form that it partakes more of the qualities of a work sheet than of the traditional type of plan sheet. A work sheet of this type has a number of advantages. It is large enough to provide space for recording most of the important items involved in planning and developing a unit. At the same time, it makes provision for organizing and relating these items as they are recorded. It makes provision as well for noting the abilities in the various subjects that require direct instruction. When more than one sheet is required in developing a given unit, which is frequently the case, these advantages are lessened. Even so, such a sheet is much more usable than ordinary plan books or notebooks. The sheets may be arranged conveniently in a portfolio and folded. This makes them less cumbersome and tends to facilitate their use. When so used, half of the back of the sheet may be used to keep a diary of the unit as it develops.

The success or failure of a curriculum program depends ultimately upon the ability of teachers to use in their planning the materials developed in the type of instructional organization suggested. If materials and the suggested plan of organization become a part of the teachers' plans and become a means of enriching pupil experience, the curriculum actually is improved. Consequently, the development of materials and suggestions for organizing instruction, whatever they may be, should be projected with constant reference to the way teachers can employ the suggestions in planning their day-by-day instruction.

SELECTED REFERENCES

Hollingworth, H. L., *Educational Psychology*, D. Appleton-Century Co., New York, 1933, Chapter VII.

Mead, Cyrus D. and Orth, Fred W., *The Transitional Public School*, The Macmillan Company, New York, 1934, Chapter IV.

Melvin, A. Gordon, *The Technique of Progressive Teaching*, John Day Company, New York, 1932, Chapter VII.

Rugg, Harold O. and Shumaker, Ann, *The Child-Centered School*, World Book Company, Yonkers-on-Hudson, N. Y., 1928, Chapter VI.

CHAPTER XV

THE UNIT BASIS OF ORGANIZING INSTRUCTION

There has been a decided tendency in recent curriculum programs to employ larger centers of organization for course of study materials than individual lessons.[1] These larger centers are currently referred to as *units* or *units of work*. Organization of course of study materials in units implies, of course, that instructional organization will also be in units. Unit, consequently, is a term widely used in curriculum work at the present time.

LACK OF CLARITY IN USE OF THE TERM UNIT

Although the term unit is widely employed, there is a general lack of clarity or uniformity in its use.[2] In many cases it is not defined at all and definitions that are available vary widely in fundamental respects. One element only appears to be common to most concepts. This element is the organization of instruction in such a way that the scope and time requirement are greater than in individual lessons or daily recitations. Concepts of the unit vary so widely in meaning that organization of instruction in units may imply fundamental reorganization of the curriculum or it may mean that an insignificant shuffling of subject matter has taken place. "The mere subdivision of a course into units," states Harap, "may have no further signifi-

[1] Henry Harap and Alice J. Bayne, "A Critical Survey of Public School Courses of Study Published 1929 to 1931," *Journal of Educational Research*, 26:52, September, 1932.

[2] The use of the term *unit* in accrediting work to designate the study of a particular subject for a specified number of recitation periods of a required length should not be confused with the *instructional unit* here discussed.

cance than the subdivision of a course into sections, parts, topics, or lessons." [3]   Nor can the fundamental characteristics of a particular unit organization be determined without careful analysis of course of study materials and observation of instruction.   The frequent requests of teachers and curriculum committees for titles of units indicate failure to grasp the basic concept of the particular type of unit being developed.   The title of a unit indicates little if anything about its fundamental characteristics, for units involving opposite points of view and widely different content and activities may have the same title.

The result is confusion in discussion and treatment of units. Carey, Hanna, and Meriam, in preparing a list of units of work, activities and projects, found such diverse meanings of these terms that they were unable to set up generally applicable definitions by which their selection could be made.   They state:

These chaotic conditions became most obvious when the authors attempted to formulate definitions for "units of work," "activities," "projects," "themes," etc., which would serve as criteria for selecting or rejecting the materials they discovered in print.   Indeed, they have found it impossible to so select-and-reject. . . .   These "activities," "projects," "units of work," etc., have not yet been so defined as to command general acceptance by students of education.[4]

Bruner points out the same condition:

. . . the term unit means different things to different writers.   Units differ in form, in length, in completeness, in adaptability, in richness of suggestion, and in possibilities of integration, and express different meaning in respect to the use of content and activities.[5]

Variations in meaning of the term unit probably account in part at least for the wide use of this basis of organizing instruc-

[3] Henry Harap, *How to Construct a Unit of Work,* Bulletin No. 17, Curriculum Laboratory, Western Reserve University, November 30, 1931, p. 1.
    [4] Alice E. Carey, Paul R. Hanna, and J. L. Meriam, *Catalog: Units of Work, Activities, Projects, etc, to 1932,* Bureau of Publications, Teachers College, Columbia University, 1932, p. ix.
    [5] H. B. Bruner, *The Place of Units in Course of Study Construction,* South Dakota State Department of Public Instruction, 1930, p. 3.

tion. Proponents of nearly any educational theory can find some kind of unit organization to which they can give approval. Because of this state of confusion and the popular use of the term, this chapter presents a brief analysis of various types of units.

UNITS AND SPECIAL PLANS FOR ORGANIZING INSTRUCTION

An effort is sometimes made to clarify concepts of the various types of units by identifying them with special plans for organizing instruction. Billett, for example, in dealing with the unit considers the contract plan, Dalton plan, individual instruction, laboratory plan, Morrison plan, problem method, project method, unit assignment, Winnetka plan, long unit assignment, and differentiated assignment. But after considering these plans he states that "if one sought merely to establish that no such thing exists as an orthodox problem method, differentiation of assignments, laboratory plan, system of long-unit assignments, contract plan, project method, or method of individualized instruction, he would need go no further than the literature of the field, where the evidence is written in letters so high that he who runs may read." [6] Consequently, there appears to be little hope of clarifying the concept of units by identifying various types with specialized plans for organizing instruction. A more fundamental basis of classification must be sought.

CLASSIFICATION OF UNITS

The expression *unit* implies unity or wholeness. It suggests that there is some central force or factor which binds together the particular phase of instruction to which reference is made. It is in the effectiveness of this unifying force that the merit of a particular unit as a basis for organizing instruction depends. Consequently, *source of unity* provides a basis for determining essential differences between various units.

---

[6] Roy O. Billett, *Provisions for Individual Differences, Marking, and Promotion,* National Survey of Secondary Education, Bulletin No. 17, Monograph No. 13, 1932, pp. 310–11.

All units may be classified under two major headings. In one case, the primary point of orientation may be a phase of the group culture or a segment of potential subject matter. The dominant purpose of the unit is to develop understanding of a particular body of content—expressed either in terms of facts to be mastered or generalizations to be understood—or of a given phase of the group culture, or of an aspect of the environment.

The point of view in approaching development of units of this general type is essentially as follows. Students in various subjects have found certain facts and principles in certain relationships to be especially significant in explaining individual and social development and life. It is assumed that these phases of potential subject matter possess inherent unity. Consequently, the source of unity for an instructional unit is to be found in relationships between items of potential subject matter.

This does not mean that in this type of unit the learner and his individual characteristics are ignored. After the unit has been selected he receives consideration. As the units are organized in form to be learned by the pupil, efforts are made to provide for individual differences. A variety of pupil activities is suggested that may achieve understanding of the unit. Means of motivation which will be especially effective with the particular group of children to be taught are canvassed. The unit is made as attractive as possible in all respects. But it is clear that the source of unity is external to the learner. The unit is a unit independent of the learner or any group of learners. Whether or not the learner profits from the unit depends on his mastery of it.

The second general group of units seek their primary point of orientation in the experience of the learner. It is held that subject matter that may possess unity for one person or group may be entirely lacking in this quality for other persons or groups. Needs, purposes, or interests are considered essential elements in determining whether a series of activities or body of content have real unity. Subject matter that possesses unity for a specialist or an adult student, it is contended, very probably cannot be brought to possess real unity for a child because of fundamental differences in interests, purposes, and needs. Consequently, units of this general type find their source of unity in the learner and the primary point of reference is the experience of the learner.

It does not follow, as is sometimes concluded, that subject matter is considered a non-essential in units of this type. It is recognized that a unit cannot be developed without subject matter and that the general significance and variety of subject matter required by a unit conditions materially the value of the unit. However, the initial point of orientation and the source of unity is sought in the experience of the learner and subject matter is selected to help realize ends the individual wishes to reach.

Examination of definitions of units shows how concepts of units tend to divide under these major headings. Consider the following definitions and notice the differences in emphasis on the environment, group culture, generalizations, and subject matter, on the one hand; and child experience, interest, and activities, on the other.

A unit is any division of subject matter, large or small, that, when mastered, gives an insight into, an appreciation of, or a mastery over, some aspect of life.[7]

What is a teaching unit? It is a meaningful body of subject matter so organized with appropriate learning activities as to lead to the mastery of a definite major understanding.[8]

(A unit is) a comprehensive and significant aspect of the environment, of an organized science, of an art, or of conduct, which being learned results in adaptation in personality.[9]

. . . a unit is so organized that everything that is included in the way of content, the organization itself, and the method of presenting

[7] William C. Ruediger, *Teaching Procedures*, Houghton Mifflin Co., 1932, p. 244.

[8] Zoe A. Thralls, "The Teaching Unit in Geography," *The Journal of the National Education Association*, 22:153, May, 1933.

[9] Henry C. Morrison, *The Practice of Teaching in the Secondary School*, Revised Edition, Reprinted by permission of the University of Chicago Press, 1931, pp. 24–25.

it to the class is for the purpose of making it possible for the child to grasp the big understanding or theme that is back of it.[10]

Units of work . . . means the larger learning situations which will draw upon all phases of experience and make use of all kinds of subject matter.[11]

By a unit of work we mean the various experiences and activities of a grade which center around some one interest.[12]

A unit of work is a series of worth-while experiences bound together around some central theme of child interest.[13]

. . . a unit of work is a complete experience based upon a meaningful situation in child or adult life. The unit is a fusion of mental, emotional, and sensory experience; it proceeds in a physical and social setting that resembles life, as far as possible; and it is directed toward the accomplishment of a goal that results in some improvement in life.[14]

The unit of living has been variously called an activity, a complete act, and a unit of work. It seems more logical to use the term "unit of conduct," or "unit of life." . . . The unit of life or the unit of conduct, while it suggests that separateness of a part from its whole, at the same time provides for the notion of wholeness and coherence which is suggested by the term unit.[15]

If these definitions of units are classified under the general headings described heretofore, it will be noted that those under the same heading emphasize somewhat different points of unity. This provides the basis for a more specific classification.

There are three kinds of relationships between the facts and principles in a given body of content which may be emphasized more specifically as sources of unity for subject matter units. Likewise there are three sources of unity for units that may be

[10] Bruner, *op. cit.*, p. 10.
[11] Lincoln Elementary School Staff, *Curriculum Making in an Elementary School*, Ginn and Company, 1927, p. 29.
[12] Tompsie Baxter, "Some Techniques and Principles Used in Selecting and Teaching a Unit of Work," *Teachers College Record*, 31:148, November, 1929.
[13] Katharine L. Keelor and Mayme Sweet, *Indian Life and the Dutch Colonial Settlement*, Bureau of Publications, Teachers College, Columbia University, 1931, p. 1.
[14] From *How to Construct a Unit of Work*, by Henry Harap, p. 2. By permission of the author.
[15] A. Gordon Melvin, *The Technique of Progressive Teaching*, John Day Company, 1932, pp. 45-46.

classified as experience units. These are shown in the following outline. Each is described in the succeeding discussion.

Types of Units

I. Subject Matter
- A. Topical unit
- B. Generalization unit
- C. Unit based on significant aspect of environment or culture

II. Experience
- A. Unit based on center of interest
- B. Unit based on pupil purpose
- C. Unit based on pupil need

TOPICAL UNIT

This type of unit differs only in degree from the customary topical organization of subject matter. Topics as frequently developed are short and more or less choppy. In making a topical unit topics are simply broadened to cover a larger area than previously. The same sequential relationship is maintained between facts and the same point of view is held toward the learner. Frequently, the principal difference is that what previously might have been called a chapter or part is renamed a unit.

Two questions are raised by this type of unit. First, is the source of unity upon which the unit rests fundamental? Second, does the unit involve a significant reorganization of instruction? The answer to the first question will depend upon one's viewpoint concerning the importance of logically organized subject matter. If subject matter is considered an adequate basis of instructional organization, then the topical unit will be considered sound. If considered inadequate, the topical unit will be considered unsound. French clearly brings out the issue in a discussion of units.

In what way will they (the students) now or in the future realize
that failure in this unit made a real difference? How will society be
recompensed by those who did succeed? What penalty will society
pay because some were unable to master this unit? The answer is
that the unit has none of these things in mind—it isn't intended to
make any difference. The purpose of the unit is to teach pupils some
things about botany that are needed by those who study more botany.
Anything else learned during the study of the unit was purely accidental concomitant learning unconsciously included by the teacher
and untested at the end of the study. Now we come to the crux of
the issue. Is secondary education to be devoted to a study of units
written for the purpose of getting students ready to study more units
of that subject, or is secondary education to be a period in which
adolescents undergo selected experiences which contribute to understandings and attitudes, skill and abilities of use and value in superior
living under the conditions which a complexly organized social structure
lays upon us all? [16]

Considering the second point, it is obvious that topical organization differs in no important way from the usual organization
of instruction. Texts and courses of study are simply divided
into units instead of chapters or parts. Many illustrations of
this type of unit development may be found. For example, the
following are typical of units in arithmetic:

Unit   I—Learning More about Addition and Subtraction
Unit   II—Learning More about Multiplication and Division
Unit   III—Learning to Find Parts of a Number
Unit   IV—Learning to Use the Common Measures
Unit   V—Learning to Multiply by Two- and Three-Figure
             Numbers
Unit   VI—Learning More about Solving Problems
Unit   VII—Learning to Divide by a Two-Figure Number
Unit VIII—Learning More about Long Division
Unit   IX—Learning More about Fractions
Unit   X—Getting Ready for the Fifth Grade

The units in geography in a sixth-grade course of study follow:

[16] *Curriculum Making in Current Practice,* Conference Report, School
of Education, Northwestern University, 1931, pp. 154–55.

Unit   I—The British Isles
Unit   II—France
Unit   III—Germany
Unit   IV—Three Small Countries
Unit   V—Scandinavia
Unit   VI—Iberia
Unit   VII—Italy, Switzerland, Austria
Unit VIII—Six New European Countries
Unit   IX—Japan
Unit   X—China
Unit   XI—India
Unit   XII—Southeastern Asia
Unit XIII—The Land of the Five Seas
Unit XIV—Bridge Lands of Southeastern Europe
Unit   XV—Russia
Unit   XVI—Eurasia

It is obvious that renaming the parts of a course of study or textbook can have no real significance except in that it meets the demand of the time for a book or course of study organized in units. When a new terminology arises, the term unit may be dropped as readily as chapter or part, since no fundamental reorganization of materials has occurred.

Unit organization on the topical basis has little if any significance. Perhaps upon occasion it does emphasize longer assignments and the need to see relationships from one recitation period to another. Even so, chapter or part or topic would seem to serve just as well. Consequently, unless the curriculum maker or textbook writer sees something more fundamental in unit organization than the concept underlying this type of unit, there appears to be no justification for departing from the customary topical organization of instruction.

GENERALIZATION UNIT

The generalization unit is organized to develop understanding of a particular generalization, principle, or law. The term "theme" is sometimes employed to designate the generalization which is selected as a basis for the unit. In developing such units, generalizations that seem to be most widely applicable in explaining contemporary life are usually selected. Content and activities are then chosen to illustrate the application of the generalization. For example, the generalization that men move from place to place in search of better living conditions might be chosen as a basis of a unit. In organizing the unit the teacher might select content from any period of the race's development which requires this generalization as a basis of explanation. Materials might be selected from the history of nomadic tribes, from the migration of people about Rome, from contemporary conditions in which various classes of labor move from place to place, and from other such sources. Materials in this way may be employed from a large number of the periods of history and from the histories of various peoples. Thus, instead of dealing with the history of a people chronologically or sequentially, the phase of their history which contributes to the particular generalization is employed in relation to similar materials in the histories of other peoples or periods.

This type of unit may be employed in any subject field. Special use has been made of it in the social studies. A social studies unit of this type involves an organization of subject matter quite different from the traditional one. Thus, history, which has tended to be organized chronologically, is reorganized completely around the basic generalization; geography, which has been organized largely by regions, likewise must be completely reorganized to develop units of this type.

On the other hand, there are some subjects in which the generalization type of organization is the traditional or logical type. For example, in physics the general tendency is to organize subject matter around basic principles or laws. Illustrative materials from all sources are brought together to demonstrate the general applicability of a particular physical law. The laws are customarily arranged in something of a sequential order. Consequently, organization of instruction around generalizations, principles, or laws is not a new basis of organization. It is new only in its application to the social studies.

Perhaps the contrast of this type of unit with other types of subject matter units may be made clearer if the various bases of so-called logical organization of subject matter are considered. The relationship which makes possible a logical organization of subject matter is not the same in all subject fields. There are three types of relationships that are employed. The first is the chronological, that is, working from the beginning to the present or from the present to the past, taking up all materials in terms of their time relationships. This is the sequence traditionally used in history. The second is to work from the simple to the complex. This is employed, for example, in biology, where instruction starts with the simplest form of life and gradually approaches the most complex form. The third type is the sequence between a series of laws or principles around which the knowledge in the field is organized. This, as we have pointed out above, is the basis of organization in physics. Geometry is another subject which illustrates this type of organization.

The generalization unit, then, is in all respects subject to classification as a subject matter unit. From the standpoint of developing control of a particular subject field, the generalization unit may be quite valuable in some subjects, but very much less valuable in others. If a subject matter unit is to be employed, the extension of the generalization unit to the field of social science by curriculum makers is open to question, for an organization and sequence of subject matter is thus employed which is not considered sufficiently fundamental by subject matter specialists to be established by them. That is, it would appear that if the subject matter unit is to be employed the safest guide is to use the type of subject matter unit which subject matter specialists have indicated as establishing the most fundamental and significant relationships and sequences in the subject matter of a particular field. Consequently, the generalization unit, while being a wholly appropriate type of subject matter unit for physics, might be seriously questioned when extended to the fields of history or geography.

The third type of subject matter unit is one which is organized around a widely significant aspect of the environment or culture. It is readily noted from observation of man's group and individual activities that there are certain aspects of the environment that are particularly significant. For example, the need for food, which forms a point of confluence for many activities, makes aspects of the environment, such as the markets and stores, the water supply, and the farm, of great significance to all persons. There are also certain significant forces or developments which have exerted such profound influence on life that present living can be understood only as their influence is understood—for example, such forces and developments as the westward movement, the Industrial Revolution, the Reformation, and the scientific method. The type of unit here discussed employs these significant aspects of the environment or culture as the center of unit organization.

This type of unit has significant merits not possessed by the other types of subject matter units. The basis of organization is the significance of the material in explaining contemporary life. If well selected it is almost certain that the unit may be brought to have real meaning to a majority of learners. However, it must be emphasized that such units are selected because of their general significance, not because a particular group of children, in a particular school, at a particular time, would profit, in the judgment of the teacher, from such a unit. Thus, when this type of unit is employed, potential subject matter is the primary point of reference. Units may be selected and organized in advance as they are to be taught and the same units may be taught again and again, thus permitting an inflexibility of instruction to develop unless carefully guarded against.

The greatest impetus to development of this type of unit has been afforded by the work of Henry C. Morrison. Morrison's definition of a unit is so broad as to include more than this one type of unit but much of the unit development encouraged by his work, especially in social science and general science, has been of this type. Morrison defines "the external things-to-be-learned" as *learning units,* and a serviceable learning unit as "a comprehensive and significant aspect of the environment, of an organized science, of an art, or of conduct, which being learned results in adaptation in personality." [17]

Four possible sources of unity of the "things-to-be-learned" or potential subject matter are suggested by this definition. "The things-to-be-learned" may be related (*a*) because they are associated in the environment in a significant way, *e.g.,* water mains, water supply, house connections, standpipe; (*b*) because they are associated in a significant way in an organized science, *e.g.,* addition, subtraction, fractions; (*c*) because they represent a means of expression, *e.g.,* the novel, biography, sculpture; (*d*) because they are associated in a particular type of conduct, *e.g.,* sustained application, sense of duty, leadership. The first relationship or source of unity is the one that is the basis of the classification of units we are now discussing.

This type of unit organization is the most significant and forward looking of the three types classified under the subject matter heading. Reorganization of instruction on this basis has done much to vitalize teaching. Meaningless facts, useless information, and unimportant relationships tend to be eliminated. Learning by memory is thus reduced. There is little doubt that units of this type are a distinct advance over the traditional organization of instruction.

However, examination of the way such units are selected, organized, and taught shows that consideration of the learner is a secondary matter even in this unit. "The things-to-be-learned" still receive primary attention. The usual procedure is to select the units by examination and study of the environment and of given areas of culture. Those aspects considered sufficiently significant are selected for units. The units are then arranged

[17] H. C. Morrison, *The Practice of Teaching in the Secondary School,* pp. 24–25. Reprinted by permission of the University of Chicago Press.

in courses. Having determined what to teach, the teacher then enters the classroom and turns attention to how to teach. In other words, when the teacher enters the classroom the problem becomes wholly one of method. No question is raised at this point concerning the interest or purpose of the child. It is, of course, better if he is interested, and the teacher will endeavor to find pleasant means of motivating the work, but in any event the unit is administered to the child. In fact, Morrison states that attention to subject matter which is initially unappealing is what is required. "Somebody," he states, "either parent or teacher, has to constrain and compel the pupil to the point at which this adaptation takes place." [18]

Since the basis of this type of unit is found in potential subject matter, the units that fall within a given field tend to be the same, variations being due to inadequacy of techniques. This makes it possible to organize this type of unit in advance in all its details, to teach the same units again and again, and to assign a specific amount of time for the development of a unit. It follows that units are self-contained. They are good or poor solely because of relationships between the subject matter involved. They may be well or poorly taught but that in no way influences the intrinsic value and character of the unit.

Although this type of unit organization appears to the writers to be a distinct advance over the wholly logical and topical development of subject matter, there is one point inherent in the plan which, from the point of view presented in preceding chapters, is open to question. This relates to the source of unity of this type of unit.

The issue is this: Is it possible to find a real source of unity for organizing instruction outside the experience of the learner? The fact that students of a subject matter field have found that a particular aspect of potential subject matter has general significance and involves essential relationships does increase the chances that others, as they become students in the field,

[18] H. C. Morrison, *The Practice of Teaching in the Secondary School*, p. 109. Reprinted by permission of the University of Chicago Press.

will find the material to be significant and to possess unity. But it does not necessarily follow that the aspect of the environment or of culture which is significant to a specialist or an adult will be significant to the non-specializing student or to the immature individual. Neither does it follow necessarily that the unity which the special student sees in an aspect of the environment is brought to one's realization by direct consideration of the aspect. In fact, it is entirely possible that direct consideration may be as barren in results as the piecemeal type of instructional organization which this type of unit supplants. Real unity enters when the individual or individuals dealing with the unit have an experiential background which makes the unit significant to them and causes them to hold a purpose or have a need which makes the subject matter used an integral part of experience. Lacking such a need or purpose the relationship or unity which is inevitable for the specialist in the field does not necessarily come to exist for the pupil. In brief, unity cannot be determined without consideration of the learner. Or to use Morrison's terminology, what is a *comprehensive and significant* aspect of the environment cannot be answered adequately unless considered in conjunction with the question, *for whom?* Is that aspect of the environment which is significant to the adult specializing student in a field significant to the immature student? To illustrate, might not the chronological period 1800–1830 involve real unity for a graduate student in history, whereas it would be only a patchwork of facts for an undergraduate student? Might not the Westward Movement involve real unity for a college student and not for a high-school student? Might not Pushing Back the Frontier be a suitable unit for high-school pupils and not for elementary-school pupils? But it may be said in answer to these questions, units are selected for students on particular levels. This is true and a step in the right direction, but the situation is further complicated by differences in environment and the experiential backgrounds of children. No two groups of children on the same grade level may necessarily be assumed to be equally prepared to undertake a particular unit. The result is that when teachers who are sensitive to pupil interest, needs, and abilities teach units with the same title, the content and organization in the different situations varies so greatly as to make them essentially different units. For example, the unit which Morrison outlines on the Water Supply [19] obviously is for a situation where a central water supply is provided. But in a rural area this might or might not be a significant unit, and if it were significant it would be an entirely different unit from the one outlined.

Our conclusion is this. The aspects of the environment which the specialist or adult finds of general significance are suggestive areas in which units may be located, and hence provide valuable leads for units. Units may, in fact, frequently coincide with the areas thus indicated. But the type of unity which gives meaning to a series of activities cannot be found outside the experience of the learner and consequently, units, even though within the same general area, will vary in organization and content as the experiential background, the purposes and needs, and the environment of learners vary.

UNIT BASED ON CENTER OF INTEREST

We now turn to the type of unit based on a center of interest. This type of unit falls under the general classification of experience units. Development of this type of unit may be largely attributed to Lincoln School of Teachers College, Columbia University. The account by the staff, published ten years after the opening of the school, of the procedures of curriculum making employed, gives a definition of units of work, criteria for selecting units of work, and a number of illustrative units. Units

[19] *The Water Supply*
    1. The pumping station
    2. Street mains
    3. House connections
    4. Pressure
    5. Metering
    6. Standpipe
  Ibid., p. 183.

of work are defined as "the larger learning situations which will draw upon all phases of experience and make use of all kinds of subject matter." [20] This definition, it will be noted, emphasizes the range of experience and subject matter involved as the determining characteristic of the unit. In *The Child-Centered School*, however, published a year later, Rugg and Shumaker emphasize the point that "difference in range of activities . . . is only an obvious surface distinction between the unit of work and the school subject. The true difference," they state, "is found far deeper—in the realm of child interest." [21] Definitions published at later dates by members of the Lincoln School staff also emphasize the importance of child interest. Baxter, a member of the staff, in a discussion on selecting and teaching a unit of work, published in 1929, defined a unit of work as "the various experiences and activities of a grade which center around some one interest." [22] Keelor and Sweet employ essentially the same definition in their publication of 1931. "A unit of work is a series of worth-while experiences bound together around some central theme of child interest." [23] The dominating characteristic, then, of this type of unit appears to be the relationship of activities or experiences to a central interest of the children.

Methods of selecting such units indicate how child interest is employed. Hopkins suggests three methods:

First, the experienced teacher of a given grade recognizes certain areas in which the genuine interests of children of that age are usually located. She concludes that any unit of work within these areas will probably be developed wholeheartedly by the children. During the summer she selects tentatively and prepares herself to teach some unit which she believes will fall within the range of this interest. In this process of preparation, she lists all types of different possible activities to give breadth; she plans a number of orienting experiences as approaches; she designates the subject matter most helpful in enriching

[20] Lincoln Elementary School Staff, *Curriculum Making in an Elementary School*, Ginn and Company, 1927, p. 29.
[21] Harold Rugg and Ann Shumaker, *The Child-Centered School*, World Book Co., 1928, p. 99.
[22] Baxter, *op. cit.*, p. 148.
[23] Keelor and Sweet, *op. cit.*, p. 2.

the different activities; she defines tentative objectives to be achieved; she indexes sources of materials for the pupils and for herself; she anticipates the many questions which pupils will raise and plans means of helping them obtain materials with which to make intelligent answers; she examines the unit with care to discover that richness so necessary to provide for differences in individual interests within the general unit and for individual abilities within those special interests; she records all possible opportunities for group drives and leads; she acquires a knowledge of the subject matter so necessary to enable her to give intelligent guidance to pupils; and finally, she examines the whole proposal with a most searching critical analysis to assure herself that the pupil learnings are socially and individually important both for the present and for the future, and are of greater value than some others which the unit replaces.

The teacher who uses the second method of selecting a unit may enter the classroom in the fall with no definite idea as to a unit of work for the year. She begins by accepting the interesting immediate and remote experiences of the children. The visit to the seashore during the summer suggests a study of sea life; the trip to Europe calls for water transportation; the vacation spent in the mountains creates some demand for a unit on science; the summer on the farm leads toward farm life; and, because of the already incipient tendency toward art, one individual student proposes a unit on murals. As these suggestions arise the teacher explores them to determine whether the interest of the group is genuine or cursory. She knows that her unit must be built upon incipient interests that are or will develop into real, genuine, purposeful interests. She is skeptical of cursory, temporary, capricious interests. To distinguish between the two types she gives information about a suggested unit and arouses activity toward it through readings, excursions, motion pictures, and discussions. If the enthusiasm for water transportation subsides under the sunlight of information and activity, the teacher turns to another suggested unit and repeats the process of orientation. Through a period extending from two weeks to a month, there emerges a permanent interest which the teacher capitalizes into a unit of work.

. . . .

The third method of selecting a unit differs slightly from that of the other two. The teacher may examine the previous education of a group and decide that a certain unit is necessary to give richness, area, or breadth to their experience, or to fill in what appear to be important gaps. During the summer she will plan such a unit and begin the pupil orientation immediately after the opening of school. Such planning is always in relation to the interests and educational needs of the *particular group,* and is in no sense similar to a planned-in-advance curriculum to be followed by all teachers of a given grade in a large number of schools or school systems regardless of the previous educational experiences and present interest of the learners.[24]

After the unit is selected, the children and the teacher decide what activities will be employed to satisfy their interest. As they carry out these activities new questions arise which require further activities. So long as each series of new activities leads to further questions and problems that fall in the general area of interest, the development of the unit continues. The variety and duration of activities which develop in this way are very great. Frequently the entire school year is required for one unit.

This method of development is well illustrated by Keelor and Sweet:

. . . suppose a group of children is interested in making toy sailboats, an interest rather universally evident in younger children. As a group, they take a ride on a ferryboat and see various types of boats on the river. They increase their narrow sailboat interest to ask how each boat goes, where it goes, how the ships signal to each other, and many other questions connected with boat travel. One child decides to make a steamer; another a tug. A third child makes a dock and a lighthouse. One becomes interested in the flags of various nations and their location on the boats. The group sees a book called *The Story of the Ship* with pictures of boats of all ages. This fascinates them and they begin to draw models of such historic ships as the "Santa Maria." They associate this experience with Columbus' voyage and the beliefs of his day concerning the shape of the earth. This leads to a score of other questions and stories until the interest in boats expands to include boats of all types and boats of all ages, and the people who built them. In this manner the children's first interest in making toy sailboats grows and grows with each fresh experience and each activity until in the end they have as a group gathered a most interesting fund of knowledge.[25]

[24] L. Thomas Hopkins, "Curriculum Making in a Child-Centered School," *Educational Method,* Vol. XI, No. 7 (April 1932), pp. 410-11.
[25] Keelor and Sweet, *Indian Life and the Dutch Colonial Settlement,* Bureau of Publications, Teachers College, Columbia University, 1931, pp. 2-3.

When new points cease to arise and the immediate desire for information is satisfied, a summarizing activity is planned as a conclusion to the unit. The purpose of this activity is to organize the information gained into a related whole.

This type of instructional organization has probably stimulated, in recent years, more experimentation and advance in curriculum making than any other single development. New materials and varied activities have been brought into the instructional program. The needs and interests of children have been given more adequate consideration. The importance of environmental materials and of first-hand experience have been emphasized. Consequently, this is a type of instructional organization of outstanding significance. There are, however, a number of points about this type of unit which, from an analytical point of view, might be given critical consideration. The soundness of pupil interest as a basis for instructional organization and the disregard of subject organization are frequently questioned. These issues have already been considered in a general way in the preceding discussion, and, consequently, will not be treated here. The point, from the standpoint of organizing instruction, which requires special consideration is the source of unity of this type of unit.

The source of unity is the "central theme of child interest." Just what is this central theme of child interest? Analysis of such units shows that it is an area or phase of culture within which there are activities and objects of interest to a given group of children. That is, the term "boats" suggests an area of culture which includes many objects and activities of interest to children, such as sailboats, ocean liners, taking boat rides, making boats, and stories of boats. Now the question is this: Is there within such a culture area a dynamic unifying element which relates interests and activities in a fundamental way? The writers believe that there is not and that the mere fact that activities and content employed may be classified in this area in no way assures unity of experience. To be more specific, reading about boats, taking an excursion to see boats, and drawing pictures of boats are not necessarily related in a fundamental way in the learning situation merely because all of these activities deal with boats and the children are interested in each activity.

It should be recognized that good teachers, no matter what type of instructional organization is employed, tend to inject into learning situations, experiences which give real unity to learning. The development of many units of work of the type here discussed gives evidence of such unity. But the point we are considering is whether or not the real source of unity is in the classification of a variety of objects and activities of interests under a general heading which indicates an area of culture.

The conclusion stated above is based more upon observation of public school teachers who have attempted to develop units of this type than upon reports of such units as taught by artist teachers. As this type of unit is developed in general practice, one of two things frequently occurs. First, no thread runs through the unit that gives the activities vital relationship to each other and that makes one the inevitable outgrowth of the other. The element is lacking that requires the constant integration of knowledge gained to carry the work forward, that indicates progress toward a desired end, and that gives the activities of one pupil a fundamental relationship to the activities of other pupils. Rather, the unit is apt to flow on and on more or less like the brook, activities being carried forward simply because a preceding activity has suggested them and the pupils think they would be interesting. There is frequently a tendency for aimless exploration of an area which has in it many interesting things. Like a Sunday visit to the museum, it is pleasant and worth while upon occasion, but is hardly the type of experience suitable for developing functional education. Critical consideration of the illustration presented previously from Keelor and Sweet will reveal this tendency even in it. The units of work presented in many courses of study have pronounced evidences of this characteristic.

Second, since immediate child interest tends to be emphasized, there is hardly any area of culture in which some activities or objects cannot be found in which children will not express at least a passing interest. This makes it relatively easy for a teacher to use the unit as a means of studying topics which, because of tradition, are considered good. That is, immediate child interest alone is not an adequate criterion for selection of units. The result is the development of many units that appear but little more functional than much study of logically organized subject matter. Units, for example, on Greek life, Roman life, Indians, Eskimos, Dutch life, and similar topics frequently have many of the earmarks of "well-motivated" instruction of the usual subject matter organization. Melvin emphasizes this point. He states of this type of unit as frequently reported:

. . . one may often suspect that the units do not arise from a real life situation. . . . It seems hard to believe that small children can have the judgment, the knowledge, or the fixity of purpose to enable them to choose such a unit as Indian life and carry it through in its various implications through a month or two. One suspects, in such cases, that the work carried on is the teacher's opinion of what the children want, rather than the children's choice. Any skillful teacher may persuade a group of children, in a ten-minute talk, to embark on any of half a dozen so-called units, from the study of the Eskimos to the building of a tunnel in the schoolyard. Is the unifying principle here the children's need and purpose, or is it the teacher's concept of some extensive unit of work? [26]

UNIT BASED ON PUPIL PURPOSE

In the unit based on pupil purpose a series of activities are engaged in to achieve an end or outcome which the learner considers worth while and wishes to achieve. Activities and subject matter are selected with this end in view. The entire course of the unit is planned to achieve the desired outcome. Activities are intimately related to each other, not because one suggests another, but because each takes a place in contributing to a common end. As pointed out in Chapter VIII, interest is

[26] A. Gordon Melvin, *The Technique of Progressive Teaching,* John Day Company, p. 101.

the condition out of which purposes arise. In this type of unit there is an inevitable point of culmination when the children have achieved their purpose to their present satisfaction. The unit may be long or short, depending upon the willingness of the children to work for deferred values.

Purpose as a basis for instructional organization was emphasized by Kilpatrick in his *Foundations of Method*.[27] It was made one of the determining characteristics of the project. As developed in this connection the concept of purpose was sometimes limiting in nature. Emphasis was frequently placed on objective evidences or outcomes of purpose. The tendency thus was to eliminate intellectual curiosity and creative impulses from the category of purposes. Frequently also no distinction was made as to quality of purposes; for example, in connection with clarity of perception of desired ends, variety and complexity of activities required, and persistency of effort necessitated. The result of this tendency was a rather general association of purpose with the project method and, as the popularity of projects waned, purpose received less consideration. Gradually, however, as units of work (units based on centers of interest) have developed it has been emphasized by various students of instructional organization that some force other than interest alone must be found to provide the essential unity for an instructional unit. Purpose, as a result, has again received emphasis, this time in connection with experience units.

The utility and soundness of purpose as the basis for unit organization is determined by the care with which the concept is defined. If it is conceived merely as a general term to which a variety of meanings can be ascribed, no common basis for unit organization is provided. Furthermore, if distinctions are not made as to quality of purposes, anything may be permitted to find its way into the curriculum. But with recognition of purpose as an integral part of the process of all conscious behavior, and as such, interpreted in this broad relationship rather

[27] William H. Kilpatrick, *Foundations of Method*, The Macmillan Company, 1925.

than as a mere aspect of a method, purpose takes on real meaning as a basis of unit organization. When so conceived its peculiar characteristics must be outlined in order that a basis may be established for judging what purposes provide a suitable basis for developing units. In a preceding chapter, the nature of purpose was discussed and criteria for evaluating purposes were defined. It was concluded that the type of purpose that may be described by the term *dominating* provides a suitable basis for developing the major experiential phase of the instructional program. Instruction so developed may be considered an experience unit based on purpose.

Obviously, units of this type differ with different groups of children and under varying conditions. What may be a significant purpose for one group of fourth-grade children will not necessarily be significant for another group. This point of view is sometimes interpreted to mean that units based on pupil purpose can be developed without regard to any limitations. This, however, is not the case. If the scope of the curriculum is outlined with due regard to pupil interest on the various levels, there will be no difficulty in developing such units within the limitations thus provided. For example, the limitation for the work of the seventh grade in the Virginia state curriculum is Social Provision for Co-operative Living. The environmental conditions of certain schools in the tidewater area might make a unit on Coast Guards suitable, while in the mountain region a unit on the Forest Ranger Service would be appropriate. Yet the same generalizations concerning organized provision for protection of life and property would be involved in the two units.

Illustrations of units of this type must, of course, be taken from specific situations and must be reports of the units as developed. Units reported by Mapes and Harap [28] are illustrations of this type.

[28] Charlotte Mapes and Henry Harap, *Six Activity Units in Fractions,* Bulletin No. 33, December 1, 1933; *Five Units for the Sixth Grade Applying the Arithmetic of Decimals,* Bulletin No. 36, October 15, 1934, Curriculum Laboratory, Western Reserve University.

UNIT BASED ON PUPIL NEEDS

Need has been emphasized by some students of instructional organization as a sound basis for unit development. As in the case of emphasis on purpose, stress on need has been in part a reaction from units based on centers of interest. For example, Melvin, who is perhaps the leading exponent of need as the basis of unit organization, says:

Several objections which may be levelled at these longer units make one suspect that they are really little more than a fad of organization, a device or scheme which provides a logical basis for the organization of ideas.[29]

Finding the center of interest an inadequate source of unity, vital life situations were examined to discover what element in them is accountable for the vitality and unity. Melvin concludes that this element is the need of the individual or group engaged in the activity. He developed on this basis the concept of the "unit of conduct" or "unit of life." He describes the basis of this development as follows:

I have suggested that the root and origin of the unit of life is not to be found in the *purpose*, but rather in the *need*. Consequently, the unit of conduct is to be regarded as an act which may be analyzed into the five processes of needing, purposing, planning, executing, and using or evaluating. More important than this analysis, however, is the fact that each of these processes throughout the progress of the whole unit is dominated, directed, and governed by the original need. It is the need which is the unifying principle within the unit of conduct. It is the binding force which is analogous to the force of cohesion in the granite unit of the stone wall. Thus when an individual feels the need of a window box to brighten up the front of his house, he plans for it, goes through the necessary steps to secure it, puts it in place on the house, and passes judgment upon it, all in terms of his original need. It is the original need which is the rise and the cohesive principle of a unit of living. So when the child in school feels the need of a window box for the school, he may carry out in school

[29] A. Gordon Melvin, *The Technique of Progressive Teaching,* John Day Company, p. 101.

a unit of conduct which is analogous to a unit of conduct in the world outside the school, an act which it a real unit of living because it is unified by a fundamental need.[30]

Conduct units are classified into various types. The diagram reproduced below indicates the important types.[31]

Types of Conduct Units:

	Constructive	Play	Work
Physical—	Making a Table	Swimming	Sawing Wood
Mental —	Writing a Poem	Reading a Story	Balancing Accounts

Wynne also emphasizes need as the sound basis for unit organization. He suggests that the usual concept of purpose is too limited and that "experienced need" provides for essential expansion of the concept. He does state, however, that the enlarged interpretation currently given to the concept of purpose makes it sufficiently broad to provide a basis for unit organization.

The organism whose life processes continue to function normally makes no change in his way of behaving. But whenever any disturbance occurs from within or from without, he moves in consequence of the lack which thus appears. He tends to move in the direction of restoring the normalcy that has been lost. This movement toward the restoration of a lost equilibrium is now called a purpose. But of course this is not the same thing as the conception of conscious purpose. It may reach the level of consciousness but it does not have to be conscious.

This condition of lack or loss of balance may be designated as experienced need. In point of time, this precedes the purpose even in this new sense. It is sometimes called felt need, but feeling implies consciousness and the mere loss of balance is not always conscious in the ordinary sense. It seems better designated as experienced need when experience signifies all the behavior of the organism. This seems to be the only sense in which experienced need is commonly employed. The principle of purpose referring to the movement toward a progres-

[30] A. Gordon Melvin, *The Technique of Progressive Teaching*, John Day Company, p. 46.
[31] *Ibid.*, p. 49.

sive balance or the experienced need preceding such purposeful activity thus seems to be the principle of method that is now required. Either the new conception of purpose or the conception of experienced need may be employed; either is scientifically sound. But it must be admitted without question that the principle here defined is a different conception. This new meaning of purpose is different from the older conception. The two meanings of purpose would doubtless cause considerable confusion. We should put new wine into new bottles if we wish to save either the wine or the bottles. For us, experienced need is the new bottle. However, the main consideration is not the word, but the meaning attached to it. Any expression may be used in logical discussion if we are careful to define our terms. But the use of the word purpose to express the new meaning will not likely avoid the confusion that will result from a misinterpretation that such a double meaning makes probable.[32]

The question as to the relative merits of purpose and need as a basis for unit organization is then one which involves highly theoretical distinctions. It seems clear that in both concepts emphasis is given to the initial phase of a particular aspect of behavior. Adequate description and illustration of this phase of behavior is unquestionably much more important than the term employed to designate the phase. In all probability a unit considered good by those who hold purpose as the unifying element of learning would also be considered good by those who emphasize need. The opposite would likewise be the case.

SUMMARY OF TYPES OF UNITS

Contrasts between the various types of units are presented in brief form in Chart VIII. Five points are given consideration: (1) source of unity, (2) illustrative sources for units, (3) provision for planning, (4) sequence, and (5) length. It will be observed that major differences in the first two items are found between all types of units, whereas in the last three items subject matter units differ little and experience units differ little, although the two large classifications differ radically.

[32] John P. Wynne, *The Learning-Teaching Unit,* The Farmville Herald, Farmville, Virginia, 1934, pp. 21–22.

It should have become clear from preceding chapters that unity or wholeness, considered philosophically or psychologically, is a particular characteristic of experience. Whether or not a given experience possesses this quality depends upon the dominance of a particular element. It was further shown that this element is *purpose*. Consequently, the fundamental basis of instructional organization appears to be *pupil purpose*. We might conclude that instructional units will possess unity only as it is provided by the purpose of the learner or learners. Thus the type of instructional organization described in the preceding chapter as the major experiential phase is based upon experience units which assume purpose to be the source of unity.

It should be noted, however, that additional controls of instructional organization are provided by other aspects of curriculum making. For example, in defining the scope of the curriculum by the social functions approach, the work for the respective grades is limited to areas in which pupils find many objects and activities of interest. Thus, the limitation of the "center of interest" is imposed also on instructional organization. It will be further noted that only areas are selected for centers of interest which are significant aspects of the environment or of culture. Thus, a further limitation is imposed. Consequently, although purpose appears to be the sound basis of unity for a unit of work, a good unit will be required by the method of defining scope to fall within an area which represents a center of interest of the pupils and to be of general social significance. Other requirements for effective units, it will be recalled, are presented in Chart VI.

CRITERIA FOR EVALUATING UNITS

Criteria for evaluating experience units based on purpose are suggested in the chart just mentioned and are discussed in the

Type of Unit	Source of Unity	Illustrative Sources for Units
I. Subject Matter: *A.* Topical	*A.* Sequential relationship between items of subject matter.	*A.* American Revolution, Colonial Period, invertebrates, fractions.
B. Generalization	*B.* Relationship of all materials to one generalization, principle, or law.	*B.* All bodies of the universe move in an orderly manner; the sun is the source of all energy; man's conception of truth changes; man tends to move from place to place in search of better ways of living; the volume of a gas at constant temperature varies inversely with the pressure.
C. Significant aspect of culture or environment.	*C.* Relationship of aspect of culture or environment to race development or contemporary life.	*C.* Industrial Revolution, immigration, education, crime, machine production.

VIII

PROVISION FOR PLANNING	SEQUENCE	LENGTH
A. Planning consists largely of assigning parts of the topic to be studied or pages in the text to be read. The text provides the basic organization.	*A.* A given sequence of units and material within each unit essential.	*A.* Longer than the individual assignment but otherwise may be any length. May be predetermined and uniform if desired.
B. May be planned in detail in advance. The extent to which the teacher must plan the organization is determined largely by the subject. Much more basic planning is required in social studies than in science because of the way in which texts in these fields are organized.	*B.* Sequence of units may be arranged in advance but may vary somewhat from time to time. Sequence within a unit may be varied.	*B.* Length will vary. May be approximated in advance.
C. May be planned in detail in advance. Use of a great variety of sources is required. Consequently, effectiveness is conditioned very materially by teacher plans.	*C.* Sequence of units and within units may be planned in advance but variation is possible.	*C.* Assigned proportionate time in course importance appears to merit. May be approximated in advance.

Type of Unit	Source of Unity	Illustrative Sources for Units
II. Experience: A. Center of Interest	A. Interest of children in activities and objects that may be classified under one heading.	A. Objects and activities in which children are interested; such as Indians, Eskimos, boats, trains, airplanes, games, and fire departments.
B. Pupil Purpose	B. The purpose or interest of the pupils to achieve a given end.	B. Purposes arise from interests. Interest in a fire may lead to the purpose of finding out how the fire department operates, interest in sickness to the purpose of eliminating sources of contagion, interest in new types of goods to finding out how they are made and how they may best be used.
C. Pupil Need	C. A need which the pupil recognizes.	C. Need to make purchases, to select food, to read, to keep personal accounts.

Provision for Planning	Sequence	Length
A. Continuous planning is required. Day by day developments are highly significant.	*A.* Sequence cannot be planned in advance.	*A.* Tend to extend over long periods. Sometimes an entire school year is devoted to one unit.
B. Continuous planning is required. The teacher must be thoroughly familiar with all limitations on the curriculum and the interests and abilities of the children. Plans must be highly flexible within these limits.	*B.* Sequence cannot be planned in advance, although general areas may be indicated for work in various grades and points of emphasis suggested for work in a grade.	*B.* Tend to be short for immature pupils and increase in length as maturity approaches. The time required to realize the purpose determines length. Different units may vary greatly in length.
C. Continuous planning is required. Students must be studied carefully.	*C.* Sequence cannot be planned in advance, although it may be anticipated if a group of children is well known.	*C.* Tend to be comparatively short.

preceding chapter. Criteria for evaluating other types of units obviously will be different as the basic concepts of unit organization vary. Consequently, in selecting criteria for evaluating units, care should be exercised to see that the criteria are for the type of unit it is desired to develop. Criteria are presented which have been proposed by various authorities and curriculum committees. Study of these will help to clarify concepts of various types of units.

Morrison's definition suggests two criteria for a "learning unit": 1. The unit is comprehensive. 2. The unit is significant. He explains these terms as follows:

"COMPREHENSIVE."—The term "comprehensive" means that the unit must have wide connotations in order that it may be an economical feature in the program. For example, the *Westward Movement* as a unit in American history is comprehensive because it explains so much. *The Banking Policy of Jackson* would satisfy the requirements of a unit, since it suggests an understanding or insight, but it would not serve as a feasible unit in the secondary school for the reason that it explains relatively little of our history.

It is this test of comprehensiveness which explains why it is that a unit in the early secondary school may become a full course at the end of that period, and a broad field of professional study in the university.

"SIGNIFICANT."—The unit must be not only comprehensive but significant, that is, it must be important in the field of general education. *Indirect discourse* is comprehensive but it shrinks to the immaterial in educational significance compared with *reading ability*, because it contributes little or nothing to fundamental adjustment.[33]

Melvin's discussion suggests nine criteria for a "unit of living or conduct."

1. The circumstances from which the unit of conduct arises must be a real life situation.

2. The unit of conduct must . . . be one which contributes to the growth and development of habits, skills, knowledges, procedures, and ideals which will with a high degree of probability be used by the children in the important activities of life.

[33] H. C. Morrison, *The Practice of Teaching in the Secondary School*, pp. 25–26. Reprinted by permission of the University of Chicago Press.

3. Units of conduct . . . should be of a length which makes possible the children's unified comprehension of them, and should be of a duration which is carefully planned in relation to the other work of the class.

4. Units of conduct . . . should not be based on occasional child interest, but on more deeply rooted and firm interest.

5. Units of conduct must provide activities which are appropriate to the children's level of growth, and which are of suitable difficulty.

6. Suitable units of conduct should lead in the direction of curriculum goals.

7. Units of conduct should be related to the other work of the class and to that of the school in general. . . .

8. In their progress and development, units of conduct should proceed within the limits of available and established knowledge, and in accordance with sound standards of scholarship.

9. The balanced use of all types of conduct units should be provided.[34]

In 1926 the Lincoln School staff gave eight criteria for a unit of work:

I. The unit of work must be selected from real life situations and must be considered worth while by the child because he feels that he has helped select it and because he finds in it many opportunities to satisfy his needs.

II. The unit of work must afford many opportunities for real purposing and real projects, and it will be something which the child can carry into his normal activity.

III. The unit of work must stimulate many kinds of activities and so provide for individual differences.

IV. a. The units of work must make individual growth possible.
b. The succession of units of work must provide for continuous group growth from one level to the next.

V. Each unit of work must furnish leads into other related units of work and must stimulate in the child the desire for a continued widening of his interests and understanding.

VI. Each unit of work must help meet the demands of society and must help clarify social meanings.

VII. Each unit of work must be accompanied by progress in the use of such tool subjects as contribute to that unit.

[34] A. Gordon Melvin, *The Technique of Progressive Teaching*, Chapter XI, John Day Co., Inc.

VIII. Each unit of work must lead to the development of desirable habits.[35]

Barnes and Young reporting a unit of work on architecture give the following criteria as the basis of evaluating the unit:

I. Does the material come near enough to the child for it to be real to him?

II. Does the unit give opportunities for real intellectual pursuit on the child's present mental level?

III. Does the unit stimulate many kinds of activities, thus providing for individual differences?

IV. Does the unit bring about growth from the present growth level to the next step?

V. Does the unit stimulate a desire on the part of the individual to proceed on his own initiative?

VI. Does the unit furnish a real intellectual content, thus aiding in building a cultural background? [36]

The Teachers' Guide to Child Development sets forth the following criteria for evaluating an activity. Activity is given the same meaning as unit of work.

1. Is the activity closely related to the child's life so as to lead him to want to carry it through?

2. Is it sufficiently within the range of accomplishment of the learner to insure a satisfactory degree of success?

3. Is it so varied from the previous activity as to permit the child's all-round development?

4. Does it furnish opportunities for many kinds of endeavor?

5. Does the subject matter involved present major fields of human achievement?

6. Does the activity involve an extension of present insight and abilities?

7. Does it provide an opportunity for social contacts?

8. Will it lead into other profitable activities? [37]

[35] Lincoln Elementary School Staff, *Curriculum Making in an Elementary School,* Ginn and Company, 1927, pp. 31–41.

[36] Emily A. Barnes and Bess M. Young, *Unit of Work: Children and Architecture,* Bureau of Publications, Teachers College, Columbia University, 1932, pp. 16–31.

[37] *Teachers' Guide to Child Development,* California Curriculum Commission, California State Department of Education, 1930, p. 25.

Harap gives the following criteria:

1. It should involve a variety of direct sensory experiences.
2. It should provide for some free, informal association of the pupils.
3. It should provide an opportunity for manipulative or bodily activity.
4. The parts of the unit should make a coherent whole.
5. It should provide a considerable amount of pupil activity.
6. It should be satisfying or the anticipation of the outcome should be satisfying.
7. It should provide sufficient concrete and illustrative material.
8. The unit of work should have a useful purpose in the present or future life of the pupil.
9. It should reproduce actual life situations, as far as possible.
10. It should utilize materials as they occur in life.
11. It should contain accurate information.
12. It should provide an opportunity for the pupil to originate, plan, and direct the activity, as far as possible.
13. It should provide opportunities to judge, choose, and evaluate.
14. It should be within the available time for the unit.
15. The exposition should be clear enough to make it possible for a new teacher to put the unit in practice, if she so desires.
16. It should state clearly where materials may be obtained.
17. When references are given, they should be complete and exact.[38]

Hopkins presents the following criteria as a partial list to serve as a means of evaluating units of work in connection with a project of the Society for Curriculum Study:

1. *Are there experiences under way that promote growth in habits of critical inquiry?*
    Is there experimental living and investigation—tentative choice of hypotheses—study of all pertinent issues, selection of most promising leads?
    Are there needed skills for experimentation?
    Are conclusions made in terms of consideration of all available issues and evidence?
    Is there growth in questioning and answering questions?
    Is there critical use of experts and sources?
    Is there sensitivity to important issues?

[38] *Bulletin No. 17*, Curriculum Laboratory, Western Reserve University, November 30, 1931, p. 6.

Is there concern for the welfare of the larger group?

Is there willingness and effort to relinquish disproved convictions?

Are there attitudes of openmindedness, fearlessness and sincerity?

Is there proper regard for pertinent issues from the past?

Are conclusions held tentatively?

2. *Do the activities under way offer opportunity for experience in many kinds of meaningful endeavor through physical and social media?*

Do the activities offer fullness of experience?

Do the members of the group use materials to best advantage according to their growing standards?

Is there opportunity for experience in leading and following?

Is there appropriate use of relevant tool subjects when the need and opportunity for use arises?

Is the curriculum such that formal lines are dispensed with in order to permit expression to the full?

Is there experimentation, exploration, investigation, and evaluation in various fields?

Is there co-operative group living?

Is full use made of individuals' observations as media of experience and expression?

3. *Are the activities under way such that the individual may discover his interests or tendencies?*

Is there sensitivity to problems and suggestions in the environment?

Are there some experiences which tend to identify individuals with special interests—hobbies?

Is there interchange of thought?

Are the ideas, opinions and suggestions of others considered?

Is there respect for the purposes, ideals, wishes, dreams and capacities of individuals and groups?

Is there co-operative group living?

Do individuals possess adequate skills for discovering their interests and tendencies?

Is there leadership by individuals with the ability to identify with the purposes, ideals and wishes of the individual and the group to carry these forward?

Is there adequate and timely use of experts and sources?

Is there the experimental mode of living?

4. *Do the experiences under way impel the members of the group on into increasingly challenging endeavor?*

Are learnings an intrinsic outgrowth of the learner's experience?

Are present experiences suggestive of next steps?

Are leads to further activities vigorously prosecuted?

Are previous experiences used as sources of data?

Is there experimental living?—are new leads pursued tentatively, are pertinent and comprehensive data considered, are unworthy leads thus rejected?

Does the learner choose ways and means of work within his control?

Are the learners acquiring adequate tools to pursue increasingly challenging and demanding endeavors?

5. *Are there experiences under way that promote sharing of experiences through social participation?*

Is there appreciation of the opinions and ideas of others?

Is there co-operative group living?

Is there diversity of experiences?

Is there recognition of responsibility in the group for leading and following?

Is the group developing standards of social control?

Do members of the group share in planning the life of their social group?

Do members of the group share their imaginative and play lives?

Is there sensitivity to group interests and needs?

Is there experimental living—planning, trying out leads, evaluating?

Do individuals seek assistance from the social group and give assistance when needed?

6. *Will the learners acquire increasing freedom to order their own experiences through effective assumption of responsibilities?*

Is the assistance of experts and sources sought and used?

Are more adequate tools and meanings sought and acquired?

Is there increasing ability and disposition to use controls?

Is there a desire for richer living?

Are individuals developing a perspective sufficient for awareness of significant successes and failures and facing squarely and impersonally situations and their implications?

Is there relevant use of past experience?

Is there due regard for personality values and individual abilities by all members of group? [39]

The Raleigh, North Carolina, curriculum committees set up criteria as follows:

[39] L. Thomas Hopkins, Chairman, Committee on Proposed Bulletin of Units of Work, Society for Curriculum Study, *News Bulletin No. 2,* April 1, 1933, pp. 10–11.

1. The unit of work must be selected from *real life situations;* that is, it must be related to the *present living* experience of the *children,* not of *adults.*

The activity should appeal to children's interests and should not only satisfy *present* needs, but should contribute to some of the larger needs of life, as health, citizenship, group relationship, pride in school conduct, the wise use of leisure time.

2. A unit that is worth while should be hard enough to challenge and at the same time easy enough to insure some degree of success.

Good questions to ask in this connection are, Does the activity present too many difficulties? Is it beyond the abilities of the children? An activity should be suited to the state of development of the child. To be really worth while it should require real effort on the part of the children and should call for thinking as well as for manual effort.

3. The unit of work must stimulate many kinds of activities so as to provide for individual differences.

In order to do this, the unit must have some easier possibilities than others. The teacher should so guide the work that each child will get something to do that will bring him satisfaction. It is the doing of a thing *successfully* that brings satisfaction, although *failure* for some individuals may mean *growth.*

The unit should challenge initiative and resourcefulness; should give opportunity for growth in leadership, and in independence, in ability to assume responsibility; it should stimulate the exercise of judgment on the part of the children, and the ability to plan things for themselves; it should tend to real investigation, to perseverance. An activity should have holding power.

4. A unit should lead on to other worth-while activities—make the child want to do something bigger; tend to increase appreciation of worth-while things.

A unit is not very big that does not cause the group to ask questions; it should foster an inquiring, investigating attitude. It should lead to other related units. When we leave a unit it should be with the feeling that here is a field that is interesting enough for further reading and study.

5. Is the unit practicable under school conditions? A unit should not be undertaken unless materials and helps are available for carrying it out.

6. Will the unit contribute to the child's efficiency? Will it develop good habits, desirable attitude, efficiency in some of the tool subjects, or provide opportunity for exercise of specific ethical habits, as thrift, promptness, obedience, courtesy, honesty?

The activity should bring about the right attitude of the child to the members of the group and help him to become a contributing member of the group. It should encourage co-operation. It should enrich the child's experience—make him realize the work of others in making his life comfortable and happy and what the past has contributed to his present environment.[40]

ILLUSTRATIVE MATERIALS

As has been shown, some types of unit organization make it impossible to teach the same units again and again or under different environmental conditions. Other types of units, on the other hand, may be essentially the same under any conditions. In either case, however, illustrative units are helpful to teachers and curriculum workers in developing units suitable for their own situations. There are many sources of such materials.

The Morrison "learning units" are illustrated as well as discussed in *The Practice of Teaching in the Secondary School.*[41] This source may be supplemented by a series of bulletins developed at the University of Chicago which contain *Students' Guide Sheets* for the development of certain courses.[42] The University of Virginia Department of Education has emphasized the development of this type of unit with work allocated to three levels of difficulty. A series of illustrative units are given in an issue of the *University of Virginia Record Extension Series.*[43]

There are many illustrations of "units of work," as developed at the Lincoln School. *Curriculum Making in an Elementary School*[44] by the Lincoln School staff includes a number of illus-

[40] *A Suggested List of Activities, for Grades One to Six,* Series No. 1, Raleigh Public Schools, 1928, pp. xiii-xv.
[41] *Op. cit.*
[42] See E. T. Smith, *A New Approach to European History,* University of Chicago Press, 1929; *English Instruction in the University High School,* Members of the English Department and R. L. Lyman, University of Chicago Press, 1934.
[43] W. R. Smithey, editor, "The Unit Method of Teaching," *University of Virginia Record Extension Series,* Vol. XVII, No. 7, January, 1933.
[44] *Op. cit.*

trative units. However, a more recent and adequate source of illustration is the series of Lincoln School Curriculum Studies. One or two units of work are reported per volume. These reports are carefully prepared accounts of units as actually taught in Lincoln School. The following volumes are available: Barnes and Young, *Children and Architecture;* Baxter and Young, *Ships and Navigation;* Eakright and Young, *Adventuring with Toys;* Hughes, *Carrying the Mail;* Keelor and Sweet, *Indian Life and the Dutch Colonial Settlement;* Sweeney and others, *Western Youth Meets Eastern Culture;* Wright, *A First Grade at Work.*

The California *Teachers' Guide to Child Development* includes many illustrative units. Waddell, Seeds, and White report in detail three intermediate grade units of work developed at the Elementary School of the University of California at Los Angeles.[45]

Mapes and Harap report six units of work in arithmetic in a bulletin of the Curriculum Laboratory of Western Reserve University.[46] These are good illustrations of shorter units which emphasize lifelike situations and center largely in one subject field.

McCall and Crabbs edit a series of lesson units that are published by the Bureau of Publications of Teachers College, Columbia University. Units for all grades and subjects, and of all types, are included in the series. The units are reports of work actually done in classrooms. The descriptions are in small paper-backed bulletins varying in size, most of them being from twenty-five to fifty pages in length. The cost is twenty-five cents each. Since all types of units are included it is necessary in using these bulletins to select those which illustrate the type of organization desired.

F. E. Compton & Company publish a series of units under the

[45] Charles W. Waddell, Corinne A. Seeds, and Natalie White, *Major Units in the Social Studies,* John Day Co., 1932.

[46] Charlotte Mapes and Henry Harap, *Six Activity Units in Fractions,* Bulletin No. 33, Curriculum Laboratory, Western Reserve University, December 1, 1933.

title, *Compton's Pictured Teaching-Unit Materials.* A booklet and a series of pictures are presented as helps for developing units. The booklet includes "subject matter, generalizations, objectives, approaches, and activities." Units are available on such subjects as *Coal and Iron, Switzerland, Middle Ages,* and *Land Transportation.*

In addition to sources such as the foregoing especially designed to provide illustrative units, many courses of study include illustrative units while others present units worked out in detail. An extensive list of units and sources of units may be secured from the *Catalog* prepared by Carey, Hanna, and Meriam.[47]

PLANNING FOR UNITS

All types of units require more extensive planning than does instruction organized by recitations. In subject matter units the planning may be done in advance with considerable precision and plans once developed may be employed with different groups. Consequently, in organizing this type of unit, the initial planning is of primary importance.

In developing experience units, continuous planning is of supreme importance. Careful initial planning is required for each group that is taught, and after a unit is initiated the planning must continue throughout the development of the unit. The achievements or failures of each day's work modify what is to be done the next day. Consequently, planning of experience units has two major aspects. Initial planning involves laying out the general lines along which the unit may develop and suggesting the available resources for development. Continuous planning involves developing the detailed procedures and steps to be employed from day to day, and adjusting these as demanded by the progress of the work. This kind of planning is aided by the use of a form of work sheet such as that reproduced in Chart VII and discussed in Chapter XIV.

As efforts are made to aid teachers in planning units of the

[47] *Op. cit.*

experience type, it should be held in mind that flexibility is the absolute requirement of these units, both as to planning and development. Consequently, no fixed method of planning should be required.

Effective development of a program of curriculum making which involves units of work depends to a great extent upon reports of units as they are developed in classrooms. It is from such reports that the major portion of instructional materials presented in courses of study should come. Consequently, it is important that attention be given to the method of reporting units. There are a number of items that should be given consideration in such a report. The outline that follows provides one basis for reporting.

Suggestive Outline for Reporting a Unit

I. The setting.

In order to understand how a unit develops and why certain things are done, the reader needs to know the setting in which the unit is developed. The type of school situation, the physical equipment available, major environmental factors, outstanding abilities, disabilities, and interests of the children, previous work undertaken, and other such items should be described. In so far as possible, the effort should be to lead the reader to see the important aspects of the situation with which the teacher has to work.

II. Initial planning.

This section of the report should describe how the teacher undertakes to discover the educational possibilities of the situation. Ways in which pupil interests are canvassed and evaluated should be described, and studies of the educational resources of the community and school should be reported. It should further be shown how the teacher deduced from these studies that a certain unit might be undertaken profitably by the children.

The teacher should then show in the report how preliminary plans for the work were made. This should include objectives which the unit could be expected to achieve, activities that might be employed in developing the unit, references, environmental materials, and construction materials available for use, possible ways of starting the unit, and the general line or lines of development the unit might take.

III. Starting the unit.

There are many ways of starting a unit. It may result from an unusual or unexpected incident, it may result directly from work the children have done previously at school, it may be stimulated by something that is happening in the community, or it may result from deliberate stage-setting by the teacher. In reporting a unit an effort should be made to describe accurately just how the unit started, and to give an idea of the intensity and extent of interest at that time. Methods employed to develop a general group interest should be described. There should also be given the reason the teacher believed the unit as initiated would rest on a fundamental interest of the children.

IV. Description of development of the unit.

This section of the report should contain an account of the unit in narrative form. Just how did the unit progress from day to day? What difficulties were encountered? What outstanding successes were achieved? What were the peculiar problems involved in directing the unit? What modifications in initial plans were required? What materials, references, and activities were employed? These represent the type of question that should be answered by the description of the development of the unit.

It is important that such an account be based on a carefully kept diary of the unit and that an effort be made to give an impartial picture of the work. Unless care is exercised in this regard, the description may be distorted by over-emphasis of good points and of points of minor significance.

V. Conclusion of the unit.

The conclusion of the unit may be described either as a part of the development of the unit or given emphasis under a separate heading. Concluding a unit so that it is a well-rounded, complete undertaking is very important. A direct tie-up should be made with the purposes for which the unit was initiated, and the culminating activities should represent the acme of satisfaction upon achievement of these purposes. However, not only success should be emphasized. A good conclusion of a unit of work will also recognize any failures to achieve desired outcomes, and will emphasize what was learned as a means of doing various activities in most effective ways. In brief, the conclusion should represent the general evaluation of the unit by the children. It should provide the high point of satisfaction, and at the same time give opportunity to determine how the undertaking or similar undertakings might be done more effectively.

This narrative form can be used to best advantage for reporting the conclusion, as is also true for the section on development of the unit.

VI. Report of outcomes.

It is important that the account of the unit include a list of the outcomes realized. It is desirable to list the outcomes in as specific terms as possible, and to give the evidence upon which the teacher concludes that the outcome has been achieved. Evidence may be noted from such sources as observation of pupil behavior, informal tests, and standard tests. It may also be desirable to indicate the relationship of the outcomes to the aims set up for the unit and the subject fields in which the outcomes may be classified. A major portion of this section may be presented in outline form although ample description and illustration should be included. The tests, of all types, employed may well be described and illustrated.

An illustrative outline for reporting the actual outcomes of a unit follows:

OUTCOMES OF UNIT

OUTCOME	EVIDENCE OF ACHIEVEMENT	SUBJECT TO WHICH OUTCOME RELATES	AIM TO WHICH OUTCOME RELATES
Children Co-operate much more effectively than before.	Records of development of unit show 23 special situations in which outstanding cooperative efforts were present. Only three cases are recorded in which lack of cooperation was pronounced.	All social sciences primarily	(6)* ability to work as a group more effectively
Ability to spell and use correctly the following new words: industrial, research, administration, administrative, government, etc.	Ninety per cent of the words were used by the children correctly in papers, bulletins, and pamphlets which they prepared. A test in spelling showed that the children could spell from 95 to 100 per cent of these words correctly.	Spelling	(8)* ability to spell and use new words that will be required by this unit, such as, government, administration, etc.

(Other outcomes to be listed similarly.)
* Coded to aims listed for the unit in initial planning.

VII. Bibliographies and materials.

In this section should be given the references and materials used in developing the unit. It will be found helpful to divide the references into *pupil references* and *teacher references*. Each of these lists may profitably be divided into two or three parts, *e.g., most valuable, valuable, not satisfactory*.

VIII. Leads to other units.

Finally, it will be found valuable to indicate in brief form interests that have been developed through the unit that promise to lead on to other work. Only interests that are really promising leads should be noted.

PLACE OF THE UNIT IN CURRICULUM DEVELOPMENT

We have devoted a great deal of space to the organization of instruction, types of units, and steps in planning and reporting units. This has been done because instructional organization is the crux of curriculum development. It is at this point more than any other that programs fail to achieve the purposes for which curriculum work is undertaken. Frequently, good statements of aims are given, long lists of principles are set forth, elaborate discussion of the need for "education for a new social order" is presented, but when instructional materials are finally presented and organized, tradition rules rather than the introductory statements and considerations. Consequently, it is highly important in curriculum development that the type of instructional organization adopted be compatible with the avowed philosophy of the program. It is in this stage of curriculum development, being closest to the classroom, that philosophy or point of view may really become operative.

SELECTED REFERENCES

Baxter, Tompsie, "Some Techniques and Principles Used in Selecting and Teaching a Unit of Work," *Teachers College Record*, 31:148, November, 1929.

Bruner, Herbert B., *The Place of Units in Course of Study Construction*, South Dakota State Department of Education, Pierre, South Dakota, 1930.

Carey, Alice E.; Hanna, Paul R.; and Meriam, J. L., *Catalog: Units of Work, Activities, Projects, etc., to 1932*, Bureau of Publications, Teachers College, Columbia University, New York, 1932.

Curriculum Records of the Children's School, Bureau of Publications, National College of Education, Evanston, Illinois, 1932.

Harap, Henry, *How to Construct a Unit of Work,* Bulletin No. 17, Curriculum Laboratory, Western Reserve University, Cleveland, Ohio, November 30, 1931.

Lincoln School, *Units of Work,* Bureau of Publications, Teachers College:

    Barnes and Young, *Children and Architecture,* 1932.

    Baxter and Young, *Ships and Navigation,* 1933.

    Eakright and Young, *Adventuring with Toys,* 1933.

    Keelor and Sweet, *Indian Life and the Dutch Colonial Settlement,* 1931.

    Sweeney and others, *Western Youth Meets Eastern Culture,* 1932.

    Wright, *A First Grade at Work, 1932.*

Mapes, Charlotte and Harap, Henry, *Six Activity Units in Fractions,* Bulletin No. 33, Curriculum Laboratory, Western Reserve University, Cleveland, Ohio, December 1, 1933.

Melvin, A. Gordon, *The Technique of Progressive Teaching,* John Day Company, New York, 1932, Chapters V and XI.

Morrison, Henry C., *The Practice of Teaching in the Secondary School,* Revised Edition, University of Chicago Press, Chicago, Illinois, 1931, Chapters II, XI, XII, XIII.

Rugg, Harold O. and Shumaker, Ann, *The Child-Centered School,* World Book Co., Yonkers-on-Hudson, New York, 1928, Chapters VI–X.

Teachers Guide to Child Development, California State Department of Education, Sacramento, California, 1930.

Waddell, Charles W.; Seeds, Corinne A.; and White, Natalie, *Major Units in the Social Studies,* John Day Company, New York, 1932.

Wynne, John P., *The Learning-Teaching Unit,* Farmville Herald, Farmville, Virginia, 1934.

CHAPTER XVI

THE COURSE OF STUDY

Probably no single source better reflects the basic concept of an educational program or indicates more clearly general school practice than does the course of study. Concepts regarding the functions of the various elements of the curriculum and of their relationship to each other are revealed in the form, content, and organization of published courses of study. It is the purpose here to point out the varying concepts of the function of the course of study and to show how these concepts are reflected in current practice. For the guidance of groups of teachers engaged in curriculum study and revision, certain suggestions are set forth in this chapter to be used to direct the work of committeees in the production of courses of study.

The content, organization, definitions, and stated purposes of a course of study will be determined largely by the point of view from which the curriculum is developed. In the main, there are two major concepts of the function of a course of study. A traditional concept very widely accepted is that the course of study is a means developed by a central agency of setting forth limitations within which the work of the schools shall take place. These limitations are usually expressed in terms of predetermined phases of subject matter, and of a designated time in which this subject matter is to be taught. Although such courses of study may show wide variation as to the detail with which they are worked out, fundamentally they preserve the aspect mentioned above.

Various definitions of the course of study embody this concept. For example, Monroe defines the course of study as follows:

"Course of Study" is the name given to the specifications and directions relating to a given field of instruction. These specifications and directions include in addition to the objectives to be attained (implied in "ground to be covered") directions and suggestions relating to what the teacher should do in getting his students to achieve these objectives.[1]

Herriot defines the course of study by specifying its functions:

A course of study has a two-fold fuction; first, to co-ordinate the work of the teachers of a school system, and second, to help them as individual teachers. . . . When a teacher is provided with a carefully prepared course of study, she has a detailed statement of the specific tasks assigned to her and the directions for the performance of these tasks. . . .
. . . the following two general types of material should be included: (1) specifications of the detailed objectives of the course and of the materials of instruction, and (2) directions consisting chiefly of suggestions as to learning exercises and methods of stimulating and directing learning.[2]

In describing courses of study based on the traditional concept, Bruner says:

The old type course contains little more than bare references to existing text books. Its chief aim is to dictate just what pages in the textbook should be covered during any given period of time. The methods of teaching and learning compelled by such a course are formal and inflexible.[3]

This general concept of the course of study is also evident in statements contained in published courses of study, for example:

[1] Walter S. Monroe, "Making a Course of Study," *Bureau of Educational Research, Circular No. 35,* University of Illinois, September 19, 1925, Footnote, p. 4.
[2] M. E. Herriot, "How to Make a Course of Study in Reading," *Bureau of Educational Research, Circular No. 42,* University of Illinois, January 4, 1926, pp. 4–5.
[3] H. B. Bruner, "Present Status of Curriculum," *Curriculum Making in Current Practice,* School of Education, Northwestern University, 1932, pp. 13–14.

This Course of Study is in part the old course, modified and extended by the change in textbooks.

Teachers are expected to keep within the limits, but are at liberty to use any methods or original ideas that will make the work more effective and attractive to the pupils.[4]

In the letter of transmittal in the 1926 edition of a state course of study, the following statement indicates the concept of the course of study. This statement, however, is more restrictive than the course of study which it introduces:

It is a handbook for teaching the adopted books and in my opinion teachers will get better results by following the directions contained herein. Every textbook has a certain underlying philosophy which should be understood by the teachers.[5]

In the Kentucky *Teachers' Manual and Courses of Study*, 1931, the following statutory requirement is quoted:

. . . the State Board of Education "shall prescribe and publish a public graded course of study for the common schools, specifying the order of studies, and the time to be allotted to each, which course of study shall be observed by the teacher and enforced by the trustee; . . ."[6]

The *New Course of Study for Elementary Schools of Kansas* (Arithmetic and History), 1927, states that, "It is to be kept in the schoolroom for daily use for at least five years, and at the end of each term is to be filed with the county or city superintendent . . ."[7] This course also states on the title page that it is "to be used with S——'s Arithmetics and B——'s 'The Making of Our Country.'" Under the outline for third grade arithmetic is the following statement: "The work of this grade

[4] *Course of Study, Primary Grades*, Nashville Public Schools, Nashville, Tennessee, 1928, p. 3.

[5] *Mississippi Elementary School Curriculum*, State Department of Education, 1926, p. 6.

[6] *Teachers' Manual and Courses of Study, Elementary Schools*, Kentucky State Board of Education, 1931, p. 5.

[7] *New Course of Study for the Elementary Schools of Kansas*, State Board of Education, 1927, p. 1.

is based on S——'s Primary Arithmetic and covers pages 1 to 152, inclusive, with the text in the hands of the pupil." [8] The work for the grade is further divided by months for eight months with page references to textbooks stipulated in each case.

A broader concept of the function of the course of study grows out of a different point of view regarding the nature of learning and the place of subject matter in the learning process. According to this concept, the course of study is a guide for teachers in the selection of pupil activities, the materials to be used in connection with these activities, and the manner in which they are to be organized. It is believed that the course of study should be a source book with materials and suggestions to assist the teacher in organizing instruction. It should be flexible and easily revised. It still limits the scope of the work by defining the general areas through which work should progress, but does not restrict the teacher to fifty pages of a particular textbook in a particular subject to be taught at a particular time.

Taba defines this broadened concept as follows:

Curriculum thinking should not attempt to provide exact charts for educational experiences, nor give any rigid prescriptions as to the materials to be used in connection with educational activities. Instead it should try to provide principles and materials to think with in a creative manner in dealing with educational practice. The value of curriculum planning does not so much lie in its ability to provide exact maps to be followed, as it does in furnishing those guiding the learning process with a broad and critical outlook, sensitivity to possibilities that lie in each evolving situation, and ability to see the relations that the particular experience has with as many possible general principles and implications involved in every single experience.

Planning conceived of as a mapping out of experiences and particular objectives is conducive to a static education. What is desirable is planning in the sense of developing broad and thorough knowledge as to the way certain experiences foster certain outlooks, as to how certain bodies of facts grouped in a certain way will influence thought and conduct; as to what cues towards better and fuller experience can be found in the situation at hand. An outline of major objectives, major concepts, experiences, is very helpful, but it should not serve as an

[8] *Ibid.,* p. 12.

exact map, and it should not become a substitute for a living curriculum that is based on insight into the workings of the mind and the
particular cues as to possibilities of growth that spring from the
individual character of each experience.[9]

There are various types of courses developed under this general concept. In one group comprehensive bodies of subject matter are organized into units or are presented with illustrative
units which may be used for organizing the subject matter. This
group may be illustrated by the courses of study developed for
the Long Beach City Schools. These courses depart from the
traditional type of course of study by organizing the work in
"units," definitely outlined for each grade with detailed suggestions to teachers for carrying on the work of each unit. In
some subjects the traditional subject matter lines are recognized
and followed, while in others the work is organized so as to
include a number of subjects in a given unit. For example, the
work in arithmetic begins with a definite allocation of specific
subject matter to each grade. Then follow suggested procedures
to be used by the teacher. The work for each grade is presented
in outline for each month under the general headings: Subject
Matter, Suggested Activities and Problems, Suggested Procedure,
and References. Throughout the rest of the course of study the
work is presented in subject matter units.

The courses in the Social Studies represent a departure from
the traditional plan of organization. It is stated in the introduction that: "Instead of having separate units of geography,
history, civics, economics, or sociology, these are interwoven.
No attempt has been made to preserve an equal balance between
these subjects, but each has been drawn upon to the extent that
its material could contribute to the development of individual
units and problems." [10] The work is outlined in units with
definite time allotments varying from three to eighteen weeks in

[9] Hilda Taba, *The Dynamics of Education,* Harcourt, Brace & Co.,
New York, 1932, pp. 249–50.
[10] *Social Studies Course of Study for Junior High Schools,* Long Beach
City Schools, 1927, p. 8.

length. These units are designated under general headings, such as:

7B

    Unit   I   Orientation   . . . . 4 weeks
    Unit II   Community Life . . . . . . 10 weeks
    Unit III The Westward Movement . . . . 4 weeks

The work of each of these units is then divided into a number of problems, each of which is organized into "Topics to be Developed," "References," "Activities," "How to Study," and "Correlated Reading." At the close of each unit general and specific standards of attainment are stated.

A second group tends to present specific units of work to be developed with a large selection of subject matter to be utilized in developing the unit. For example, in the curriculum bulletins of the Houston Public Schools, the scope of the curriculum is outlined according to "controlling themes" under which "units" are developed on each grade level. The foreword to the curriculum bulletins presents the point of view, as follows:

Instead of many subjects with many separate, and sometimes antagonistic, aims there are the many subjects, the aims of which are woven together to form a unified purpose to the end that there may be better individuals in a better society. . . .

The integrated curriculum is set up in units, each developing one central theme.[11]

For example, under the general theme "Interdependence," a unit entitled "Food and Shelter" with the central theme, "How man reaches out to all parts of the world in securing food, clothing, and shelter," is designated for twelve weeks in the third grade. After a description of the unit and a list of state-adopted textbooks, there follows a suggested outline of subject matter under each of the several subject fields, such as reading and literature, geography, and history.

Another group of courses of study controlled by the second

[11] *Curriculum Bulletin Number Two,* Houston Public Schools, 1933–34. p. 1.

major concept are those courses which present raw materials in the form of children's interests, possible activities and subject matter to be used in developing interests, and suggested procedures for developing these materials around centers of interest. The material of the course is organized around a common core. The usual subject fields are treated separately only in connection with the development of special abilities. The *Tentative Course of Study for Virginia Elementary Schools* is a course of this type.

Under the title "How to Use the Course of Study," the functions of the course of study are pointed out as follows:

It makes the following important provisions: it indicates the direction in which the growth of boys and girls should proceed (aims of education); it outlines the area of work for each grade (scope); and it gives suggestive raw materials for instruction (interests, activities, subject matter, teaching procedures, and methods of evaluation). The materials are arranged to facilitate ready reference. The teacher should use them in planning his work in the same way an engineer or architect uses manuals and tables. This concept of the course of study as a source book developed for the purpose of aiding teachers in planning their work is basic to effective use of the materials.[12]

This type of course, instead of setting up in advance things to be learned, is primarily a record of the experiences of teachers in what they considered desirable teaching situations brought together in such form as may be most helpful to other teachers in planning their work. Such a course of study grows continually and is limited only by the definition of the scope of the program. It contains materials and suggested procedures that have been found helpful on the various grade levels. It contemplates the continuous evaluation of the materials included with such revision as experience may suggest. It can, therefore, be adopted for no specific period of time, nor confined to any particular body of subject matter.

Thus we see that these two major concepts of the curriculum as reflected in the course of study are fundamentally differ-

[12] *Tentative Course of Study for Virginia Elementary Schools, Grades I–VII,* State Board of Education, 1934, p. 25.

ent. In the first, the course of study is designed to be the curriculum. If followed consistently, it results in a rigid, inflexible, uniform school program with uniform standards for achievement, uniform means of determining whether these standards have been met, and a thoroughly regimented administrative program. Its limitations and specifications are set up in terms of predetermined bodies of subject matter with only slight variations from time to time. In the second, the course of study is looked upon as a printed manual or guide to serve in guiding development of the curriculum. It sets forth the general direction in which the development of children should progress, the general areas through which it is believed the child's experiences will develop with greatest meaning, and suggestive materials to aid teachers in planning their work within these areas.

CHARACTERISTICS OF A GOOD COURSE OF STUDY

As an aid to the teacher in planning instruction, a course of study should have certain characteristics. Many of the characteristics of a good course of study produced under either of the major concepts discussed above will be similar. Numerous attempts have been made to set forth the qualities that should characterize a good course of study. For example, in a comprehensive treatment of 498 courses of study, Stratemeyer and Bruner found that points of strength and weakness observed in courses of study tend to group themselves around a few major headings. These are:

A. Recognition of Educational Objectives
   1. Objectives, standards of attainment
B. What to Teach: Organization of Subject Matter
   1. Content
   2. General organization
   3. Use of textbooks
C. Recognition of and Adaptation to Pupils' Needs
   1. Recognition of the individual
   2. Activities
   3. Projects and problems
   4. Use of tests and measurements

D. Adaptation to Teachers' Needs
  1. General helps for teacher
  2. Method
  3. Illustrative lessons
  4. Reference materials for teachers
  5. Reference materials for pupils
E. Course of Study Itself
  1. Mechanical make-up
  2. Course of study as a whole
F. Miscellaneous.[13]

The *North Carolina Curriculum Bulletin,* 1934, sets up seven standards or criteria for courses of study as follows:

1. A course of study should state the general objectives or aims to be accomplished.
2. It should specify *what to teach* in the way of subject matter.
3. It should specify *when to teach* it.
4. It should suggest *how to teach* the different phases of work.
5. It should provide *adjustments for individual differences* of pupils.
6. It should *provide for measurement* of results.
7. It should provide or *suggest teacher helps and references.*[14]

The form and content of courses of study recommended for teachers of Indiana are as follows:

1. *Quantity:* The Course of Study should be rich in suggestions but not too detailed.
2. *Style and Language:* The Course of Study should be within the comprehension of all teachers.
3. *Arrangement:* The materials of the courses should be arranged in learning units. Each learning unit shall be numbered and named. A brief introduction shall be written across the top of the page. This introduction shall interpret the specific objectives for the particular learning unit in terms of the general subject objectives. Each unit should be arranged in three columns as follows:

[13] Florence B. Stratemeyer and Herbert B. Bruner, *Rating Elementary School Courses of Study,* Bureau of Publications, Teachers College, Columbia University, 1926, p. 8.
[14] *Suggested Procedures for Curriculum Construction and Course of Study Building, 1934–35,* Publication No. 179, North Carolina State Superintendent of Public Instruction, 1934, pp. 104–105.

  a. The first column should state the pupil activities or materials of instruction.
     (1) The activity shall be presented as a description of things to be done and not as an outline of information to be learned.
  b. The second column should state the desirable pupil outcomes.
  c. The third column (right hand page) should offer suggestions to the teachers with respect to methods of procedure.
     (1) In each grade and subject a sample procedure should be fully developed.
4. *Differentiation:* Minimum essentials and enrichment should be indicated by "solid" and "leaded" paragraphs.
5. *References:* General helps and references should be given at the end of each unit. Specific references should be included in the procedure column.[15]

Concluding their analysis of courses of study, Stratemeyer and Bruner list the following things which every course of study should contain:

  a. Illustrative lessons of teaching procedure
  b. Standards of attainment
  c. Suggested standards for checking the results of teaching (*e.g.*, tests, scales, etc.)
  d. Type problems, projects, etc.
  e. Suggestions for the correction of specific difficulties—remedial materials
  f. Suggested drills
  g. Suggestions as to the proper use of illustrative materials, graphs, etc.
  h. Basic references for children
  i. Supplementary references for children
  j. References (for the teacher) to experiments, magazines, books treating of theory of method
  k. References (for the teacher) to subject matter and content
  l. Suggestions for teaching children how to study.[16]

In the final analysis, the concept of the nature of the curriculum and the function of the course of study will determine the

[15] Roy P. Wisehart, *Guiding Principles of Elementary Curriculum Revision for the State of Indiana,* Bulletin 107, State Department of Public Instruction, 1929, pp. 11–12.
[16] *Op. cit.,* p. 126.

contents of a course of study. If the point of view is accepted that the course of study should be a source of raw materials for the use of the teacher in planning the work of the school, the following list of items is suggestive of materials that may be included appropriately. The order in which these are named is not obligatory, but is significant in that it seems to meet a primary demand that the course of study be arranged so as to provide maximum utility. The items suggested are:

1. *A Statement of Point of View,* or the philosophy upon which the curriculum program is organized. This should be stated as far as possible in simple, non-technical language. It should include brief statements of the basic concepts of the curriculum and of the manner in which these concepts operate.

2. *A Statement of the Aims of Education.* These should be stated in such a manner that they may be referred to easily. The function they are to perform and the way in which they are to be used should be set forth explicitly.

3. *The Scope of the Curriculum.* This section of the course of study should outline clearly the general limits within which the program of instruction is to take place. It should indicate points for major emphasis at the different grade levels.

4. *Instructions in the Use of the Course of Study.* These should be explicit and sufficiently detailed to guide the teacher in the use of every section of the course of study. Suggestions for planning and developing units, including plan sheets and inventory sheets should be included. Definite help should be given in planning daily programs and in keeping proper records.

5. *Materials Organized by Grades.* These should be presented according to a uniform plan so as to facilitate easy reference to the work of any grade. All of the raw materials necessary to develop the instructional program, general cumulative inventories, suggested activities, and reference materials for both pupils and teacher should be included.

6. *Teaching Procedures.* General teaching procedures that may be appropriately employed in the several grades should be presented in sufficient detail to provide the teacher with the es-

sential concise information about a given activity. Full lists of reference materials related to each procedure dealt with should be properly catalogued and listed.

7. *Specific Subject Matter Materials.* Subject matter designed specifically for the development of special abilities should be outlined in the several subjects. Suggestions as to the proper place for emphasis in the school's program should be included.

8. *An Adequate Table of Contents.* This should be worked out with great care both as to the items it contains and the mechanical form. It should contain reference to every general item to which the teacher may wish to refer.

9. *General Reference.* Lists of publishers, lists of adopted textbooks where publication is required by law, and supplementary materials for use in special types of schools may be included here.

WHO SHOULD WRITE THE COURSE OF STUDY

The administrative provision for developing courses of study is considered in another chapter. Brief consideration is given here to ways of preparing courses of study. The production of curriculum materials may be engaged in profitably by large numbers of teachers, but the actual shaping of these materials into final form for the course of study cannot be done in this manner. This is a technical task to be performed by a small group whose training and experience especially fit them for it. The committee designated for this task may appropriately be called the editing and unifying committee. This committee should be given full authority to handle the material as they deem wise. They should be free to include or reject any materials that may have been proposed for inclusion in the course of study. They should have authority to make any editorial changes which, in their judgment, seem desirable. Sufficient time should be allowed them so that they can engage in sustained effort without interruption. Their responsibility should be to revise, reorganize, and prepare the course of study for the printer. The limitations upon their work should be the principles and procedures agreed upon for the curriculum program.

The personnel of this committee should be selected with the utmost care. It is not necessary for every subject field and every interest to be represented by a separate member of the committee. It is imperative, however, that the individuals chosen should have an intelligent grasp of the work of the school at all levels and in all fields so that no important phase of the curriculum will be overlooked. Furthermore, the ability to organize the materials of the courses consistently is necessary. If possible, several members of the committee should be capable of doing creative writing and should possess editorial ability. The ability to see each phase of the work in its proper relation to the whole and to every other phase is of paramount importance. An experienced supervisor who has engaged in the production phase of the program will be able to render valuable service as a member of this committee. A teacher experienced in co-operative planning with other teachers will work satisfactorily.

The curriculum specialist or consultant should be available for critical appraisal of the work as it proceeds. The director of the curriculum program should maintain constant contact with the work, providing general direction and guidance.

MECHANICAL MAKE-UP OF THE COURSE OF STUDY

The usefulness of a course of study depends to a considerable extent upon its mechanical make-up. If it is to be used consistently and effectively by teachers it must possess certain physical qualities. These qualities relate to its size, style, paper, ink, size and style of type, make-up, and organization. While there are no specific standards to be applied rigidly, certain general guides should be followed in planning the publication of a course of study.

The question of the form in which the course of study is to appear should be settled before the committee starts to work. A number of forms in current use should be canvassed and each studied with respect to its appropriateness for the course of study in question. These are: mimeographed and bound, mimeographed loose-leaf, printed and bound, and printed loose-leaf.

In determining which of these forms would be most appropriate for a given course of study, several things should be considered. How long will the course of study probably be used before a revision is printed? If, as is usually the case with state courses, the probability of revision and re-issue within four or five years is unlikely, then there is good reason for printing. Furthermore, if a large number of copies will be required, as in a state or large city system, it may be desirable to issue the courses in printed form. On the other hand, if a comparatively small number of copies, say a few hundred, is sufficient to meet the needs, mimeographing is more economical and practical. Mimeographed copies are less durable and are not so easily read as are printed courses. They are usually made of a quality of paper and binding that will not withstand sustained use.

Whether the course is loose-leaf or bound should be determined mainly by two considerations. If the course of study is under continuous revision, the loose-leaf plan makes it possible for all teachers to have the latest materials incorporated without inconvenience. The other principal factor is the cost. Suitable loose-leaf courses, whether mimeographed or printed, are expensive. If constructed along the usual lines these are not durable enough to withstand the wear to which they are subjected. If constructed of suitable materials, the cost, including loose-leaf binders, is from 15 to 20 per cent higher than the cost of bound copies. However, the loose-leaf form has many advantages. Chief among these is the possibility of keeping the course up-to-date by discarding materials that have proved unsuitable and adding new materials that promise to be helpful.

Current practice as to form is shown in the following summary of a recent check of ninety-three courses of study in city schools.

The overwhelming practice in cities from 30,000 to 100,000 is to mimeograph their courses of study; in the middle population group (100,-000 to 500,000), twice as many systems mimeograph their work as print it; and in the largest cities, about twice as many systems print their materials as mimeograph them.[17]

A check of 557 recent courses of study, summarized in Table XIV, shows that 186 are mimeographed and 369 are printed.

TABLE XIV

FORM IN WHICH COURSES OF STUDY APPEAR [18]

	Single Grade Single Subj.	Single Grade Sev. Subjs.	Sev. Grades One Subject	Sev. Grades Sev. Subjs.	Total
CITY ELEMENTARY COURSES					
Mimeographed	20	8	65	11	104
Printed	4	5	131	24	164
STATE ELEMENTARY COURSES					
Mimeographed	0	0	2	2	4
Printed	0	0	39	25	64
CITY HIGH SCHOOL COURSES					
Mimeographed	13	0	60	3	76
Printed	9	0	57	7	73
STATE HIGH SCHOOL COURSES					
Mimeographed	0	0	1	1	2
Printed	0	0	61	9	70
Total	46	13	416	82	557

[17] Clinton C. Trillingham, *The Organization and Administration of Curriculum Programs,* University of Southern California, 1934, p. 48.

[18] Adapted from "Recent Courses of Study for Elementary and Secondary Schools," *Circular No. 111,* United States Department of the Interior, Office of Education, Washington, D. C., July, 1933.

State courses, for both elementary and high schools, are usually printed. In city school systems, the elementary courses tend to be printed rather than mimeographed, while the high school courses show no appreciable difference as to the form in which they appear.

Table XIV also shows that generally several grades for a single subject are included in a separate course of study, for both elementary and high schools. Where the attempt has been made to develop the curriculum on other than traditional subject matter lines, the course of study for several grades and several subjects is included in a single volume. The point of view from which the curriculum is developed should determine the procedure to be followed.

The mechanical make-up of the course of study should be such as to facilitate its efficient use. The committee should give careful consideration to the size of the book, the paper, the size and style of type, and other mechanical features. The following suggestions may be helpful in developing specifications for the mechanical make-up of courses of study.

The cover of the course of study should be of sixty-five pound antique cover stock or other paper of approximately this weight, of a color that will not soil easily. The binding should be glued on the backbone of the book; flexible glue should be used. For books up to sixty-four pages wire stitching may be used but sewing in sixteen page forms is preferable. On a larger book wire stitching is to be avoided, since a wire stitched book of more than sixty-four pages will not stay open. For a larger book sewing in sixteen page forms is the only satisfactory type of binding. A book approximately seven by eleven inches will stay open more easily than a smaller book. If the course is to be loose-leaf, it may be considered desirable to have the book approximately eight by eleven so that additional materials and suggestions written on ordinary loose-leaf paper may be incorporated. The paper should be of good quality and should meet standard specifications as to weight, color, and texture. A seventy pound basis white eggshell paper makes an attractive, useful book. A slightly thinner paper, such as fifty pound machine finish, is also desirable. The style of type is an important detail in the physical make-up of the course of study. An artistic and pleasing type style, with proper variety to designate subheads, etc., easily read both because of clearness and size, contributes much to the usefulness of a course of study. Ten point on a twelve base or nine point on an eleven base may be used effectively. Type in the tables should not exceed at any time six point caps on an eight point base.

A uniform style for the composition of the course of study should be adopted at the beginning and should be followed at every stage of the writing. This will simplify the work of editing and will reduce the probability of errors and omissions. A single style book may be adopted for guidance, or a set of specifications may be made up to suit the tastes of the committee.

Finally, the course of study should be a model of good composition. Unfortunately, this is not always the case. A recent check of a random selection of courses of study reveals an inexcusable number of errors in grammar and in the selection of words. This condition is apparently the result of the lack of sufficient time for committees to review their own work critically after having labored with the selection of materials and their organization for printing. The course of study, however, is the chief objective evidence of the work of curriculum revision, and, hence, should represent the best efforts of those who are commissioned to produce it.

SELECTED REFERENCES

Bruner, Herbert B., "Present Status of the Curriculum," *Curriculum Making in Current Practice,* School of Education, Northwestern University, Evanston, Illinois, 1932.

Herriot, M. E., "How to Make a Course of Study in Reading," *Bureau of Educational Research, Circular 42,* University of Illinois, Urbana, Illinois, January 4, 1926.

Monroe, Walter S., "Making a Course of Study," *Bureau of Educational Research, Circular 35,* University of Illinois, Urbana, Illinois, September 19, 1925.

Oakland, *Handbook for Course of Study Committees,* Course of Studies Series No. 100, Oakland, California, 1928.

Stratemeyer, Florence B. and Bruner, Herbert B., *Rating Elementary School Courses of Study,* Bureau of Publications, Teachers College, Columbia University, New York, 1926.

Trillingham, Clinton C., *The Organization and Administration of Curriculum Programs,* University of Southern California, Los Angeles, California, 1934.

CHAPTER XVII

ADMINISTRATIVE CONSIDERATIONS IN CURRICULUM DEVELOPMENT

Preceding chapters have indicated that a curriculum program should entail fundamental reorganization of instruction, requiring the organized co-operation of administrators, supervisors, teachers, specialists, and lay groups. Such a curriculum program to improve instruction may not be inaugurated in a haphazard manner. It involves more than a re-shuffling of courses or a re-listing of topics. If the program is to achieve fundamental reorganization, certain definite procedures must be followed. It is the purpose of this chapter to indicate some of the major aspects of a curriculum program and to suggest procedures or guides that will facilitate the planning and the promotion of the program. The procedures suggested are in accord with the broad concept of the curriculum presented in previous chapters.

In determining the procedures of any program of curriculum making, sound principles of administration should be applied. These principles are essentially the same as are found in any administrative organization. Since it is contrary to sound administrative practice to lay down arbitrary requirements or regulations, flexibility should characterize administrative procedures. However, the organization for carrying on a curriculum program should be so set up that the line of authority is clear, responsibilities are fixed, duties are defined, and the usual administrative relationships observed.

Procedures to be followed in carrying on a curriculum program will be determined to a great extent by the scope of the program to be undertaken. The program should be comprehensive in scope, that is, it should embrace every division in the school system. Whether radical reconstruction or gradual evolution of a new curriculum is the aim, the implication for those planning the organization of a curriculum program is the same; namely, that the organization should be such that the resulting curriculum will provide for the continuous growth of children. Failure to observe this general guide tends to result in inconsistent curriculum changes, and in a serious lack of articulation between the divisions within a school system. The ideal curriculum organization would be one so organized that continuous comprehensive revision activity in all fields and all divisions of the school system might be present whenever considered necessary. Such an ideal has elements of practicability as is evidenced by the fact that certain large school systems [1] have administrative organizations based on the theory that revision activity may be present in practically all fields at all times.

Certain administrative procedures to be adopted in a curriculum program will be materially influenced by the concept held of what constitutes curriculum making. Procedures set up for the preparation of courses of study to distribute to the teachers within a given system differ fundamentally from procedures that will result in the provision in organized form of all types of guidance for all teachers in the system to the end that the curriculum as it actually develops will achieve optimum educational outcomes. Until recent years, as pointed out in the preceding chapter, the idea has tended to predominate that curriculum making is primarily, if not solely, course of study making. Curriculum procedures, therefore, have been developed to build new curricula and to revise old curricula. The typical administrative organization of a curriculum program has been one of special committees, usually small, with an assigned task of preparing or revising courses of study for general use. The program has been one of short duration, six to eighteen months usually having been considered sufficient to accomplish the task. This procedure of curriculum making rests upon the concept that curriculum and course of study are synonymous terms, a

[1] For example, Los Angeles, California, and Rochester, New York.

concept which is gradually being replaced by one broader and more comprehensive.

In planning a curriculum program provision should be made for three general types of participation: wide participation by all teachers, supervisors, and administrators in the given school system; intensive participation by small selected professional groups; and general participation by representative lay groups working on certain aspects of the program. Accepting the broad concept of the curriculum, every teacher in a school system is a curriculum maker. Since the social concept of the curriculum implies the desirability of participation by laymen, it is evident that the development of the curriculum should also involve the interest and co-operation of representative lay groups. An effective curriculum program, then, should provide for extensive participation by all teachers and representative lay groups. In addition there are many tasks in curriculum making which require the undivided attention of selected groups of persons for definite periods of time.

Such a program of curriculum study and revision as is here indicated calls for a variety of procedures and an extensive administrative organization. It is not the purpose of this chapter to set up the administrative organization necessary to carry out the program, or to indicate the specific delegation of responsibility, but to suggest general procedures that seem advisable. It should be emphasized that every effort should be made to develop a type of administrative organization which will not pass out of existence the moment the intensive phases of the program are completed. If sporadic efforts at curriculum making are to be avoided and the improvement of classroom instruction through curriculum development is to be a continuous process, the observance of this general guide is extremely important.

TEACHER PARTICIPATION

If the success of a curriculum program is to be measured by the changes that are achieved in the conduct of boys and girls by reason of improvements accomplished in the instructional program, it becomes evident that early in the program the entire teacher-group within the system must become sensitized to the need for the improvement of instruction. Provision should be made for the stimulation and guidance of the professional reading and study of teachers. Procedures for classroom exploration and experimentation should be provided. Illustrative instructional materials should be made available. Opportunities should be provided for wide participation in the discussion of curriculum problems. In other words, the entire teacher-group should be brought into close contact with the program in its early stages and should be kept constantly informed of the progress of the program. In a well-conceived and organized program of curriculum revision the entire teacher-group will know why the program is being projected, what the purposes of the program are, and the means proposed for accomplishing these purposes. Only through a thorough understanding of the curriculum program and of all its implications can the teacher-group give the intelligent co-operation that will result in improved classroom instruction. Therefore, every available means should be used to sensitize the teacher-group to the need for curriculum change and to keep the group informed of developments in order that their interest may be maintained and their continued co-operation secured.

Failure to sensitize the teacher-group to the needs for curriculum change and failure to keep the entire group in contact with the developments of the program have resulted in the production of courses of study which were little used except by the few teachers who worked on them. The original tendency in the type of programs designed solely to develop courses of study was to have the work done by a small group of persons, the active participants in the curriculum programs often being only twenty-five to fifty people. The results of such programs were unsatisfactory, not necessarily because the new materials were not well selected and well written, but because these materials were not generally used. Because of this condition emphasis began to be placed upon large committees and upon wide teacher participation in course of study making. It was maintained that one of the best ways to give teachers a knowledge of what is in the course of study and an interest in its effective use is to give them a part in its production.

Several hundred teachers, or even all the teachers in a system, were encouraged to participate in developing the curriculum through participation in producing the course of study. For example, Lynchburg, Virginia, used its entire staff of 260 teachers in curriculum work. Little Rock, Arkansas, in its program also utilized its entire staff of 450 teachers.[2] The purpose of the encouragement of such wide participation in course of study making has not necessarily been to produce better courses of study, but rather to insure their use once they were produced. Often the size of large unwieldy groups of teachers working on the final phases of a program has made impossible the production of courses of study of high quality. This does not mean, however, that all teachers cannot and should not participate in a curriculum program. It simply means, as is pointed out in Chapter XVI, that the actual production of high grade courses of study is a technical task which should be delegated to small groups of trained persons.

This dual type of participation by teachers may be provided for in a curriculum program that has for its purpose the improvement of instruction. Since every teacher is looked upon as a curriculum maker, it is assumed that he should be continuously preparing curriculum materials for his own use. Contributions from technical studies by specialists and from the general experience of teachers must be selected and organized in such form that they can be employed easily by teachers. The course of study is merely a means of selecting from the materials so prepared what may be valuable for teachers generally and making it available to them. It is highly desirable that in so far as possible courses of study evolve from materials and procedures found

[2] Clinton C. Trillingham, *The Organization and Administration of Curriculum Programs,* University of Southern California, 1934, p. 40.

valuable in actual classroom situations of the school system for which the courses are being prepared. Thus, although teachers in general may not advantageously try to write courses of study, the materials which they develop in their classrooms for their own guidance in developing the curriculum for their classes may be employed to advantage by the committee in preparing the course of study. Obviously, then, it is neither feasible nor desirable to develop classroom teachers into specialists in curriculum procedures or in writing courses of study. Rather, the effort should be to increase the ability of teachers to employ the various sources of guidance available for their help in developing the curriculum.

An example of general participation is seen in the Virginia state program, where 10,000 teachers participated in the first phase of their program, which had for its aim the study of the need for curriculum revision and of ways of accomplishing desired changes in the work of the schools. During the second year or phase of the program, practically an equal number of teachers, working under guidance provided by small selected committees, made definite efforts to improve the work in their respective classrooms. Similarly, during the first year of the Arkansas program, more than 7,000 teachers and all teacher training institutions in the State participated in a study of the instructional needs of the State. In addition, more than 3,000 members of the State Congress of Parents and Teachers pursued essentially the same type of study.

It is evident that such wide participation calls for careful planning and direction as well as for the production of numerous types of guidance materials. Opportunities must, therefore, be provided for small groups to do intensive, prolonged work under the direction of capable curriculum specialists. For this purpose, curriculum laboratories have been established by institutions of higher learning in many states. In these laboratories selected groups of people work on specific problems. It is here that plans are made, and bulletins and other materials are produced for the guidance of each phase of the program as it develops.

As a program progresses to the point of production, special committees working in these laboratories organize, edit, and finally publish the materials of instruction that have been tried out in classroom situations. The adequate guidance for a program furnished by following this procedure may be illustrated by what certain states are doing in their programs. In the Virginia state program a series of bulletins was prepared to guide each phase of the work. One bulletin [3] sets forth the purposes of the program and the administrative organization to carry it forward. Another bulletin [4] proposes questions and outlines procedures and materials for study. A third bulletin [5] outlines procedures for producing new instructional materials. A fourth bulletin [6] presents the proposed scope of the curriculum and makes suggestions for initiation of work within the limitations for the several grades. In addition to these bulletins for guidance, experimental editions of courses of study were issued and tried out in selected schools. On the basis of this experience, the courses of study were revised and made available to all teachers. Along with the installation of the courses of study, a further effort is being made to develop a more adequate understanding of the scope of the curriculum and the aims of education, and to secure more adequate instructional materials.

Similarly, in Arkansas, bulletins prepared by selected groups have been used to direct the work of each of the first two years of their program; a study bulletin [7] to guide the first or study phase and a procedures bulletin [8] to guide the second or production phase. Eleven thousand study bulletins were used in carry-

[3] *Organization for Virginia State Curriculum Program,* Bulletin State Board of Education, March, 1932.

[4] *Study Course for Virginia State Curriculum Program,* Bulletin State Board of Education, January, 1932.

[5] *Procedures for Virginia State Curriculum Program,* Bulletin State Board of Education, November, 1932.

[6] *Illustrative Materials from Tentative Course of Study for Virginia Elementary Schools,* Bulletin State Board of Education, September, 1933.

[7] *Study Program,* The Arkansas Co-operative Program to Improve Instruction, Bulletin No. I, State Department of Education, 1933.

[8] *Procedures in Production of Curriculum Materials,* The Arkansas Co-operative Program to Improve Instruction, Bulletin No. II, State Department of Education, 1934.

ing out the first phase. In Mississippi a bulletin [9] prepared for the guidance of the first phase of the State's proposed five-year program, provides materials to aid the teachers of the State in orienting themselves to the program through participation in study and discussion groups. Texas has published a *Handbook for Curriculum Study* [10] to guide the first or "study for orientation" phase of their work. Other bulletins for guidance are to be developed as the program progresses.

From the foregoing discussion of the two general types of teacher participation requisite to an effective curriculum program, it is evident that while the functions to be performed by all classroom teachers and by small selected groups of persons are interrelated and interdependent, each group, nevertheless, has its own peculiar functions.

LAY PARTICIPATION

Since education of its members is one of the important functions of society, the participation of laymen is implied in any fundamental reorganization of the instructional program. In our society the layman has certain rights and obligations in the direction of the instruction of future citizens of the democracy. He should be informed about the aims and purposes of the schools and should know the extent to which they are serving the needs of the society that maintains them. While professional educators must bear the responsibility for developing the technical aspects of the curriculum, sound procedure requires that a definite place be made for the layman in a program of curriculum revision.

The lay public has been considered to a certain extent in the development of the school program. However, this consideration has been primarily in the direction of stimulating adequate financial support in order to carry on the work of the schools.

[9] *Study Program,* Mississippi Program for the Improvement of Instruction, Bulletin No. 1, State Department of Education, October, 1934.

[10] *Handbook for Curriculum Study,* Bulletin State Department of Education, September, 1934, Austin, Texas.

This has involved the development of a type of publicity which had as its object the informing of the general public as to the work of the schools so that favorable aspects of the school program could be duly impressed upon the taxpayer. However important this kind of publicity may be, it does not encourage the type of participation demanded by the broader concept of the curriculum and its development. The problem is more than one of publicity. It involves the securing of co-operative effort on the part of representative citizens. Such co-operative effort involves careful study of various aspects of the work of the schools, with emphasis entirely different from that of merely "selling the schools to the public." Farley supports this point of view as follows:

In order to participate effectively they must be aware of the desirable social goals and of the educational activities undertaken to achieve them. A sound program of educational interpretation lays the basis for sympathetic appreciation and intelligent co-operation. Through such a program, citizens may envisage the schools as a means of working together for the future of their children and the future of the nation.[11]

The necessity of bringing lay groups to a full appreciation of the purposes and scope of the school's program has been widely recommended by educational leaders. For example, the importance of lay participation in the development of the curriculum is emphasized by the National Education Association, as follows: "The curriculum revision program which fails to carry editors, civic leaders, and other intelligent laymen along with it, will encounter active opposition or lukewarm support."[12] Lay participation is not recommended, however, merely as a means of forestalling possible opposition to curriculum revision. It is rather a means of securing from the layman constructive suggestions for improving the work of the schools.

It is difficult to ascertain the extent or the character of lay participation. Trillingham states that:

[11] Belmont Farley, *School Publicity*, Stanford University Press, 1934, p. 2.
[12] *Research Bulletins*, Nos. 4 and 5, Vol. III, National Education Association, September and November, 1925, p. 121.

School systems utilize the following curriculum publicity agencies in order of frequency of mention: the press; the parent-teacher association; pamphlets, bulletins, letters; school papers; civic clubs; and the radio. Six cities provide no curriculum publicity. General practice is in agreement with the specialists that the public must be informed of the curriculum work being done. The necessity for such publicity, with its very slight cost, makes it imperative that school administrators care for this phase of the work.[13]

Curriculum programs in two thirds of the cities have not involved the participation of community lay members. Every school system that attempts to maintain a modern program would do well to utilize the advisory services of selected laymen. This should serve to make the educational offering more practical and to increase general community understanding of the work being done.[14]

A further indication of the extent to which the lay public contributes to the development of the curriculum is shown by Lide in the National Survey of Secondary Education, who finds that:

The most common use of such agencies is simply through consulting members of the community individually. Business men are interviewed concerning the commercial curriculum and men in industries concerning vocational curriculums in seven and five centers, respectively. Alumnae, board members, and professional men were also indicated in a few cases. On the whole lay agencies seem to be consulted very little.[15]

Commenting on some of the difficulties involved, Lide further states:

As one school points out, it is rather difficult to get in touch with individuals who have a general idea of the problems of group instruction and who, at the same time, have broader contacts with vocational life. A most extensive use of laymen, however, was reported in the development of the curriculum at Saginaw, Michigan, where the respondent reports it as the "most valuable thing we did." Both questionnaire and conferences were used in a survey of the community and of such establishments as the Manufacturers' Association, Board of Commerce, Wholesale-Retail Dealers' Association, and Employment

[13] *Op. cit.*, p. 153.
[14] *Ibid.*, p. 155.
[15] Edwin S. Lide, *Procedures in Curriculum Making*, National Survey of Secondary Education, Bulletin No. 17, Monograph No. 18, 1932, p. 27.

Managers' Association. Each of these organizations furnished a committee to co-operate with the school committee.[16]

The extent of lay participation in city school systems has been
limited. In a questionnaire study of curriculum programs in
thirty-four city school systems, David found that:

> When the reorganization of the curriculum began, some educators
> connected with the movement contended that certain groups of lay-
> men might make worth-while contributions to the revised courses
> of study. This suggestion was not widely accepted. Only eight
> reports indicated that the assistance of these agencies outside the
> school were sought, and some of those which were called on were closely
> related to the public schools.[17]

Examples of recent attempts to procure wider participation in
curriculum construction by lay groups contain valuable suggestions. For example, the state program of curriculum revision
in North Carolina devotes a section in its procedures bulletin
to the participation of lay groups. The extent to which this
phase is emphasized is reflected in the following statements:

> Of primary importance was the attempt to acquaint the general public
> with the undertaking. Each state-wide lay organization, through its
> duly appointed representative, was invited to attend a meeting at the
> State Capitol in Raleigh.[18]

Sixty-three organizations were included in the invitation, most
of which were represented.

> About three hundred individuals attended the meeting, representing
> the organized life of the State. . . . Many of these organizations
> have appointed committees which are now at work. At another
> state-wide meeting which will be held early in the fall these organiza-
> tions will make known their wishes and recommendations through
> proper committees or spokesmen.[19]

[16] *Ibid.*, pp. 27–28.
[17] Flavius L. David, *The Selection and Organization of Personnel for
Curriculum Revision*, Curriculum Laboratory Bulletin No. 30, Western Reserve University, October 1, 1932, p. 30.
[18] *Suggested Procedures for Curriculum Construction and Course of
Study Building, 1934–35*, Publication No. 179, State Superintendent of Public Instruction, Raleigh, North Carolina, 1934, p. 8.
[19] *Ibid.*, p. 9.

This bulletin contains a section entitled "Suggested Guide for Lay Organizations Studying the Curriculum." After a general statement regarding the proposed revision program, a number of quotations are proposed for consideration. Thus opportunity is afforded for parents and other interested laymen to express their views regarding the work of the schools.

One of the essential steps in lay participation is to provide adequate opportunity for study. This does not mean that the layman should be expected to study all of the technical aspects of curriculum revision. Provision should be made, however, for laymen to study such important matters as the aims of education, needs for education, characteristics of present educational program, and major aspects of proposed plans for improvement. Recent attempts to provide such study materials for laymen have yielded wholesome results. For example, in Virginia, after a professional committee had prepared a tentative statement of the aims of education for the schools of Virginia, one hundred selected laymen, representing various organized groups, were invited to sit in conference and review the aims with the committee. These laymen were requested to study the aims critically in light of certain instructions which were furnished them, and to make suggestions concerning them.

As a result of this conference, approximately fifteen hundred individuals were requested to review the statement of aims. Each person was asked to study the aims critically and suggest any modification which he considered desirable. He was asked to delete any statement which he considered undesirable and add any which might have been omitted. The responses were numerous and gave evidence of a sincere attempt to contribute to the program. The replies were tabulated and were utilized by the Aims Committee in making a revised report.

As a special phase of this program, the aims were submitted to the editors of the various newspapers of the State with requests for criticism and suggestion. A number of constructive criticisms were made and the statements of aims were modified accordingly. This procedure had a most salutary effect, when, more than two years later, new courses of study containing many departures from traditional practice had been produced and were installed in the schools. The intelligent support of parents and other laymen greatly simplified the problem of securing effective use of the new courses of study.

During the initial year of the Arkansas state program for the improvement of instruction through curriculum revision, teachers engaged in intensive study of the present educational program and of the needs of the schools in the light of social demands. Members of parent-teacher organizations were invited to participate in the discussions. The result was a definite demand for a similar study course for members of the parent-teacher associations in order to acquaint the patrons with the needs of the schools and with the fundamental problems involved in revising the school program. Special bulletins designed to give parents an intelligent grasp of the fundamental concepts of the curriculum and of the procedures developed by teachers for revision were given wide circulation and were used as the basis of discussions.

In Mississippi the teachers entered into a year of study in order to be better prepared to enter upon a program of revision. Study materials were prepared and placed in the hands of study groups in each county in the State. In each of these groups laymen were present and participated in the discussions. In addition, special program outlines dealing with aspects of the curriculum were prepared by parent-teacher association committees as a basis for meetings. In Mississippi, as in Virginia, a lay advisory committee was set up as a definite part of the organization for carrying on the curriculum program.

RESULTS OF LAY PARTICIPATION

A number of desirable results of lay participation may be observed. In the first place, it tends to reduce noticeably the number of unfounded criticisms by laymen of teachers and of the work of the schools. Moreover, it tends to break down a defensive attitude on the part of teachers who often look upon suggestions from laymen as meddling in affairs that are primarily the concern of the teacher. Another important result of lay participation is that laymen have made constructive suggestions for improvement of the work of the schools, the need of which teachers had failed to see, or having seen, were reluctant to propose for adoption. It has also served as an outlet through which the public could give expression to its opinions and its wishes regarding the work of the schools. Open and free discussion of all aspects of the work of the schools also makes possible a better control over the efforts of groups with special interests who endeavor to use the schools as a means of propaganda.

Due to the intelligent co-operation of parents who have had a part in developing the curriculum, instructional conditions have been greatly improved in many instances. An interesting example is seen in the opinions expressed by more than two hundred teachers in one school system who used new curriculum materials in the production of which laymen had participated somewhat extensively. Among these expressions that contain valuable suggestions, are the following:

My pupils, usually uninterested in school because of home influences, have shown real interest this year. For the first time in my four years' experience with them their school activities have carried over into the homes.

Homes have been ransacked for material. Parents have made special trips to bring materials that couldn't be brought on the bus.

My patrons have been much interested in the unit work. They have visited our room and have given us all sorts of help. I believe nearly all of them are in favor of the new curriculum.

The results of lay participation indicate strong possibilities for adult education. Participation in planning the work for the schools inevitably results in increased participation in carrying on the school program. Parents become interested in the things their children are doing in the school. They see the direct and immediate relation between the school work and their own problems in the home and community. This suggests an opportunity to tie up definitely the program of adult education with the work of the schools. It should result in the development of a co-ordinated program of education including all the educative agencies in the community.

The results of failure to recognize lay groups in the development of curriculum programs are observable in a number of instances. In certain school systems curriculum revisions involving somewhat radical departure from traditional lines have been made by groups of teachers without enlisting the co-operation of lay groups. When courses of study were ready for installation in the schools, non-progressive teachers in the system found it easy to arouse opposition and prejudice on the part of a public which had had no opportunity to become informed as to the meaning and purposes of the program. Thus, courses of study containing excellent instructional materials, the results of careful work on the part of progressive teachers, have been relegated to disuse because the public had no basis for judging their merits.

The participation of laymen in curriculum revision cannot be left to chance. Without proper guidance it can be harmful instead of helpful. It should be planned as definitely and as carefully as any other phase of the curriculum program. It should be included in the program with full expectation that a positive contribution to the curriculum will result. The administrative organization should include laymen at every point where the work is not strictly of a professional or technical nature.

GENERAL GUIDES TO ADMINISTRATIVE PROCEDURES

A general guide to be followed in developing procedures for curriculum revision requires the use of the existing administrative organization as far as possible. In other words, in a curriculum program which has as its purpose the continuous improvement of classroom instruction, a type of organization should be developed which will function as a regular part of the educational program of the school system. In a state system, the state department of education should undertake the direction of the program; in a city system, the superintendent should assume the direction or delegate this authority to a member of his staff. Relationships with localities within states and with individual schools within city systems should be established through regular administrative officers. Localities and individual schools should be encouraged to develop organizations that can carry forward curriculum work on a permanent basis. Teacher training institutions should be used as centers for intensive study and experimentation, and to aid local and state groups with materials and consultative service. In brief, responsibilities and duties should be assigned to those persons who might be expected to bear the responsibility as a regular part of the administrative program. For example, the person responsible for instruction or for the in-service training of teachers frequently assumes direction of a state program. In Virginia, the Director of the Division of Instruction assumed this responsibility, while in Arkansas, Georgia, and Mississippi, this responsibility has been assumed by state directors of teacher training. In city systems, some member of the regular educational staff usually directs the program. Supervisors and principals often assume this responsibility in the smaller cities, while assistant superintendents and curriculum directors frequently assume it in cities over 100,000.[20]

An enterprise involving the co-operation of so many individuals must be so planned that certain major tasks will be designated for general consideration at specified times. These should be set up as steps or points of emphasis considered as tasks to be achieved during the intensive phases of the curriculum program. Illustrations of this type of procedure are found in certain recent curriculum programs; for example, a state curriculum program suggests the following points of emphasis:

First Year: A study of the needs of the child and society as a basis for improving instruction.
Second Year: A continuation of the study of such needs and the development of appropriate instructional materials.

[20] Trillingham, *op. cit.*, p. 104.

Third Year: A further development and try-out in the classroom of instructional materials produced during the second year.

Fourth Year: Selection and organization of these materials for publication in a state course of study which will be used to guide teachers in their efforts to improve instruction continuously.[21]

The proposed plan of curriculum revision for Texas provides for: (1) study for orientation; (2) production of materials of instruction; (3) the trying out of courses in selected schools; and (4) the installation of courses and the setting up of a permanent curriculum organization.[22] The proposed work to be done during summer sessions of state institutions of higher learning is significant. During one summer it is proposed that the senior colleges of the state offer a course in procedures and technique of production. During the next summer students in seminar courses in the State University will study the materials submitted by the various committees and arrange them in form for mimeographing or printing. The following summer a course of special concern to superintendents, principals, and supervisors, dealing with the installation of courses, is to be offered in the University and the senior colleges. Also, during the final summer of the proposed intensive phase of the program seminar students in the University will work over the materials previously tried out in selected schools and arrange them in form for publication.

The steps or points of emphasis outlined in the Mississippi state program are illustrative of typical procedures involved in a comprehensive program on a state-wide basis:

The first year will be spent on study, analysis, and discussion of our present program and of our educational needs. Attention will also be given to possible methods of improvement. Study and dis-

[21] *Procedures in Production of Curriculum Materials,* Arkansas Co-operative Program to Improve Instruction, Bulletin No. II, State Department of Education, 1934, p. 7.

[22] *Handbook for Curriculum Study, op. cit.*

cussion groups will be organized throughout the State. Every effort will be made to assure such groups a profitable period of study. Materials are presented in this bulletin which suggest general areas and procedures for study. Members of the State Department and of the higher institutions of learning, will provide counsel and guidance. The central state committees will be at work during this time preparing materials for guidance of the second years' work.

During the second year, the teachers of the State will be encouraged to make exploration into new materials and new procedures. These materials will be appraised and organized by state committees.

The work of exploration and expansion will be continued during the third year and, at the same time, materials previously collected will be put into the hands of selected teachers to be tried in practical classroom situations.

A further extension of the use of new materials by all teachers will be encouraged in the fourth year. Provisions will be made for the continuous revision of the instructional materials.

During the fifth year, materials which have been selected from the work of the preceding years as being of special value to all teachers in the state, will be made available on a state-wide basis and teachers will be aided in their use.[23]

The steps or points of emphasis followed in a curriculum program at Bessemer, Alabama, are suggestive of procedures that may be employed by small city systems. Arrangements were made with the Division of Field Studies of the College of Education of the University of Alabama whereby various members of the faculty would meet monthly with the Bessemer public school faculty during the three-year period devoted to the intensive phases of the program. Thus expert advice was secured from specialists at nominal expense. All the teachers in the Bessemer public schools participated in the program. The outline of activities engaged in suggests the steps or points emphasized in the program.

1930–31:
1. Orientation through a series of lectures.
2. Direction of the incidental collection of materials.
3. Unification and co-ordination of all work.

[23] *Study Program, op. cit.,* pp. 8–9.

1931–32:

1. Lectures on special topics.
2. Survey of various aspects of education in Bessemer.
3. Examination of present curriculum practices; collection and evaluation of curriculum material.

1932–33:

1. General discussion by selected leaders on curriculum reorganization and adjustment.
2. Survey results and materials made available to all workers.
3. Preparation, testing, and revision of materials.
4. Unification and co-ordination of all work.
5. General review, revision, and adoption of tentative curriculum.[24]

These suggested steps are for the intensive phases of the program only and do not imply that the program is completed when these things are done. In fact, the publication of new materials of instruction and new procedures is only the basis for the real improvement of classroom instruction. This implies, of course, that the administrative organization of the curriculum program has been set up in such a way that it may continue to function indefinitely. In other words, this type program may be characterized as a continuous, co-operative, comprehensive enterprise, calling for wide participation as well as work by special groups, and involving an inaugural period of intense activity during which a permanent administrative organization is developed to carry on the work after the intensive phases of the program are completed.

Certain general guides for planning a curriculum program are inherent in this concept of the curriculum and curriculum making. These guides are:

1. Sound principles of general administration should be applied at all times. This suggests that the administrative organization must be flexible, the line of authority must be clear, responsibility must be fixed, duties must be defined, and the usual administrative relationships observed.

2. The curriculum program should provide for a comprehensive change in the instructional program; that is, the administra-

[24] Lide, *op. cit.*, p. 22.

tive organization should extend throughout every school division in the school system.

3. The curriculum program should provide for three types of participation: extensive participation by all teachers, supervisors, and administrators; intensive participation by small selected special groups during certain aspects of the program; and general participation by representative lay groups working on certain aspects of the program.

4. In determining who shall perform given tasks in a curriculum program, it should be recognized that it is neither feasible nor desirable to develop classroom teachers into specialists in curriculum procedures or in writing courses of study. Such tasks as studying the need for curriculum revision, exploring new teaching materials and procedures, and the like, are the peculiar functions of large groups of teachers and in many cases the function of all teachers in a system. Such specialized tasks as determining the aims and scope of the program, defining terms in order to clarify and co-ordinate thinking, preparing materials for the guidance of the various phases of the program, appraising and organizing the new materials and new procedures developed by classroom teachers of the system, and writing courses of study, are some of the peculiar functions of selected small groups.

5. The curriculum program should provide early for the sensitizing of the teacher-group and lay groups to the need for curriculum revision, and, as the program progresses, provision should be made whereby these groups may be kept in constant contact with the program.

6. The curriculum program should provide for the guidance of the workers on each phase of the program. This implies the preparation of bulletins, materials, and the like by small selected groups or committees.

7. A type of administrative organization should be employed which will function as a regular part of the educational program of the school system, and which will insure the continuance of the curriculum program after the intensive phases of the work

are completed. In state programs, the administrative organization from the state department through the local units to the individual schools should be so set up that it will not pass out of existence the moment the intensive phases of the program are completed. In city systems, the implications are the same for the units within the system.

8. The curriculum program should provide for a relatively long inaugural period of rather intense activity which will culminate in a continuous program.

SELECTED REFERENCES

Arkansas Co-operative Program to Improve Instruction, *Study Program*, Bulletin No. I, State Department of Education, Little Rock, Arkansas, 1933.

David, Flavius L., *The Selection and Organization of Personnel for Curriculum Revision*, Curriculum Laboratory, Bulletin No. 30, Western Reserve University, Cleveland, Ohio, October 1, 1932.

Farley, Belmont, *School Publicity*, Stanford University Press, Stanford University, California, 1934.

Lide, Edwin S., *Procedures in Curriculum Making*, National Survey of Secondary Education, Bulletin No. 17, Monograph No. 18, Government Printing Office, Washington, D. C., 1932.

Mississippi Program for the Improvement of Instruction, *Study Program*, Bulletin No. 1, State Department of Education, Jackson, Mississippi, October, 1934.

North Carolina, *Suggested Procedures for Curriculum Construction and Course of Study Building, 1934–35*, Publication No. 179, State Superintendent of Public Instruction, Raleigh, North Carolina, 1934.

Texas, *Handbook for Curriculum Study*, Bulletin State Department of Education, Austin, Texas, September, 1934.

Trillingham, Clinton C., *The Organization and Administration of Curriculum Programs*, University of Southern California, Los Angeles, California, 1934.

Virginia, *Organization for Virginia State Curriculum Program*, Bulletin State Board of Education, Richmond, Virginia, March, 1932.

Virginia, *Procedures for Virginia State Curriculum Program*, Bulletin State Board of Education, Richmond, Virginia, November, 1932.

Virginia, *Study Course for Virginia State Curriculum Program*, Bulletin State Board of Education, Richmond, Virginia, January, 1932.

CHAPTER XVIII

ADMINISTRATIVE ORGANIZATION IN CURRICULUM DEVELOPMENT

In the preceding chapter, certain general guides for planning a curriculum program were suggested. It is the purpose in this chapter, by applying these guides; first, to consider the agency or agencies to which the various tasks connected with a curriculum program should be assigned and to show how these agencies may be marshalled into an effective organization; and second, to consider specific administrative procedures which may be employed by these agencies.

THE AGENCIES RESPONSIBLE FOR DIFFERENT ASPECTS OF CURRICULUM PROGRAM DEVELOPMENT

In formulating an organization to carry forward a curriculum program, responsibility for the different aspects must be delegated to those agencies best qualified to perform the task or tasks involved. As pointed out in previous chapters, the agencies having a part in curriculum programs may be grouped as follows: (1) professional agencies within the school system, (2) professional agencies from without the system, and (3) lay groups.

Current practice, both in state and city programs, indicates wide variation in assignment of responsibility. The three agencies reported to be responsible most frequently for certain elements of curriculum programs are presented in Tables XV and XVI.[1] It will be observed from Table XV that in only six

[1] Lide determined by questionnaire the agency responsible in 162 cities and nine states for twenty-two separate elements of the curriculum pro-

of the twenty-one elements mentioned is a single agency designated in more than 50 per cent of the city programs studied.
This variation is even more pronounced in the material presented
in Table XVI where in no instance is a single agency designated
in as many as 50 per cent of the cases studied. Lide [2] points
out that only a little more than one-fourth of the cities reported
using the services of a department of research and a department
of supervision, while only one-tenth utilized the services of a
department of teacher training or of curriculum. As the cities
increase in size the number of agencies utilized increases. This
may be accounted for by the fact that in the larger school systems more agencies are employed to carry on the regular program and, consequently, the services of a greater number of
agencies are available for use in a curriculum program.

In state curriculum programs the practice varies much less
than in city programs. This may be due to the fact that there
is less variation in the size and type of administrative organization of state school systems. Also, because of the wide territory covered and the large number of local units involved, a
state program cannot be as flexible as a program in a smaller
unit.

As pointed out in the previous chapter, the administrative
organization of the curriculum program should coincide as nearly
as possible with the administrative organization for carrying
on the work of a given school unit. Thus individuals who com-
prise the regular administrative unit should be assigned responsibilities in a curriculum program that are related most closely
to their usual duties. According to this general guide the superintendent of schools as the administrative head of the school
system should be responsible for the initiation, for securing the

gram, while Trillingham ascertained in a similar manner the agency responsible in ninety-three city systems for thirty separate elements. The
cities in Lide's study ranged from less than 10,000 to more than 100,000 in
population; those included in Trillingham's study ranged from 30,000 to
over 500,000, over half the cities having over 100,000 population.

[2] Edwin S. Lide, *Procedures in Curriculum Making*, National Survey of
Secondary Education, Bulletin No. 17, Monograph No. 18, 1932, pp. 24–25.

authorization by the board of education, and for the general administration and supervision of the curriculum program. If he delegates the direction of the program to another person, he should reserve the privilege of setting up certain requirements, of offering suggestions, and of approving or disapproving the work of the person charged with the direction of the curriculum program.

Studies of practice reveal that, whether the school system is large or small, the superintendent initiates the program. In an analysis of curriculum practice in thirty-four selected cities, David[3] found that the responsibility for the initial step rested almost solely upon the superintendent. Trillingham,[4] in a similar study of curriculum programs in ninety-three cities, found that, while the superintendent must necessarily assume certain duties, there is a distinct tendency to delegate the responsibility for directing curriculum programs in all cities, irrespective of size. More than half of the cities included in the study report that the superintendent reserves the right to approve the work of the person in charge and to offer suggestions to him. In a comparatively small number of cities, the superintendent apparently grants full authority to the person in charge of the program. In 10 per cent of the cities studied the superintendent himself assumes charge of the direction of the curriculum program.

General practice seems to indicate, therefore, that the superintendent of schools is responsible for the general administration and supervision of the curriculum program. However, the work of directing the program should be delegated to some qualified member of the educational staff who can give his attention wholly to it.

There is one important aspect of a curriculum program for which the superintendent must accept full responsibility. Since

[3] Flavius L. David, *The Selection and Organization of Personnel for Curriculum Revision,* Bulletin No. 30, Curriculum Laboratory, Western Reserve University, October 1, 1932, pp. 7–8.
[4] Clinton C. Trillingham, *The Organization and Administration of Curriculum Programs,* University of Southern California, 1934, pp. 30–31.

TABLE XV

AGENCIES REPORTED TO BE RESPONSIBLE MOST FREQUENTLY FOR VARIOUS ELEMENTS IN CURRICULUM MAKING IN NINE STATE AND 162 CITY PROGRAMS [5]

Element		Agency Designated by		
		Largest Number	Secondest Largest Number	Third Largest Number
Formulating general plans	Cities	Superintendent 31	Principal 20	Central Committee 17
	States	Central or Executive Committee 6	Director of Program 1	
Formulating guiding principles	Cities	Superintendent 22	Principal 20	Central Committee 20
	States	Central or Executive Committee 5	Production Committee 1	Special Committee 1 / Director of Program 1
Formulating general aims	Cities	Central Committee 23	Principal 21	Superintendent 19
	States	Central or Executive Committee 7	Production Committee 1	Special Committee 1
Training teachers for revision	Cities	Principal 13	Central Committee 8	Department Heads 7
	States			
Investigating community characteristics	Cities	Principal 13	Central Committee 11	Special Committee 10
	States	Production Committees 2		
Investigating needs of pupils	Cities	Principal 23	Teachers 11	Special Committee 10
	States			
Revising program of studies	Cities	Principal 37	Superintendent 17	Special Committee 9
	States	Central or Executive Committee 5	Special Committee 2	Production Committee 1
Revising content in subject fields	Cities	Subject Committee 35	Teachers 13	Principal 12
	States	Production Committee 6	Central or Executive Committee 1	Special Committee 1
Suggesting teaching procedures	Cities	Subject Committee 23	Principal 15	Teachers 9 / Director of Program 1 / State Officials 1
	States	Production Committee 5	Special Committee 1	

[5] The number of respondents mentioning each agency is shown in the column following that which contains the type of respondent. Adapted from Edwin S. Lide, "Plans for Curriculum-Making in Secondary Schools," *School Review*, 40:754, December, 1932; and *Procedures in Curriculum Making*, National Survey of Secondary Education, Bulletin No. 17, Monograph No. 18, 1932.

Function	Area	1st choice	2nd choice	3rd choice
Correlating work of special departments	Cities	Principal 21	Central Committee 11	Superintendent 9
	States	Central or Executive Committee 2	Special Committee 2	State Officials 1 / Director of Program 1
Co-ordinating work of separate grades	Cities	Principal 18	Central Committee 16	Department Heads 7
	States	Central or Executive Committee 2	Special Committee 2	State Officials 1 / Director of Program 1
Determining time allotments	Cities	Principal 28	Central Committee 15	Superintendent 13
	States	Central or Executive Committee 8	Production Committee 1	
Determining minimum standards	Cities	Principal 19	Central Committee 13	Superintendent 11
	States	Central or Executive Committee 3	Production Committee 3	State Officials 1
Organizing and conducting experimental classes	Cities	Teachers 14	Principal 10	Research Department 5
	States	Central or Executive Committee 2	Production Committee 1	Special Committee 1
Trying out courses before adoption	Cities	Teachers 19	Principal 9	Central Committee 5
	States	Central or Executive Committee 1	Production Committee 1	Special Committee 1
Editing for expression and form	Cities	Principal 13	Superintendent 7	Special Committee 6
	States	Director of Program 2	Central or Executive Committee 1	Production Committee 1
Editing for content	Cities	Principal 12	Special Committee 11	Supervisors 10
	States	Production Committee 3	Special Committee 2	Central Executive Committee 1 / Director of Program 1
Training teachers in use of revised courses	Cities	Principal 16	Administrative and Supervisory Heads 16	Department Heads 11
	States	Special Committee 2	Central or Executive Committee 2	State Officials 1
Selecting textbooks	Cities	Special Committee 16	Special Committee 14	Department Heads 14
	States	Production Committee 1	Production Committee 2	Special Committee 1
Appraising results	Cities	Principal 27	Research Department 12	Department Heads 12
	States	Special Committee 1	State Officials 1	
Providing continuous revision	Cities	Superintendent 15	Principal 10	Central Committee 9
	States	State Officials 3	Central or Executive Committee 1	Production Committee 1

TABLE XVI

AGENCIES REPORTED TO BE RESPONSIBLE MOST FREQUENTLY FOR VARIOUS ELEMENTS OF CURRICULUM MAKING IN NINETY-THREE CITY PROGRAMS [6]

Element	Largest Number		Second Largest Number		Third Largest Number	
Plans curriculum program	Assistant Superintendent	36	Supervisors	32	Director of Curriculum	23
Direct charge of program	Assistant Superintendent	28	Supervisors	22	Director of Curriculum	19
Chairman of council or central committee	Assistant Superintendent	16	Supervisors	10	Director of Curriculum	8
In charge of committee work	Supervisors	27	Assistant Superintendent	19	Director of Curriculum	16
Recommends committee members	Supervisors	35	Assistant Superintendent	32	Principals	29
Makes committee assignments	Assistant Superintendent	31	Supervisors	19	Director of Curriculum	13
Consultant to committees	Assistant Superintendent	32	Supervisors	27	Principals	16
Stimulates teacher interest	Supervisors	39	Principals	37	Assistant Superintendent	28
Determines educational objectives	Supervisors	42	Teachers	33	Assistant Superintendent } Principles	30
Determines subject aims and objectives	Supervisors	42	Teachers	38	Principals	31
Determines curricula or program of studies	Principals	32	Assistant Superintendent	31	Supervisors	30
Determines time allotment and grade placement	Supervisors	39	Principals	34	Assistant Superintendent	29
Determines subject content, work units	Supervisors	45	Teachers	44	Principals	27

[6] Adapted from Trillingham, *The Organization and Administration of Curriculum Programs*, p. 103.

492

Activity						
Suggests methods and procedures	Supervisors	41	Teachers	36	Principals	29
Suggests pupil activities and experiences	Teachers	46	Supervisors	43	Principals	32
Examines and selects textbooks	Teachers	45	Supervisors	42	Principals	39
Examines and selects practice materials and supplies	Supervisors	41	Principals	33	Teachers	28
Makes objective tests	Teachers	36	Supervisors	31	Director of Research	25
Prepares service bulletins	Supervisors	30	Director of Curriculum	17	Assistant Superintendent	17
Prepares bibliographies	Supervisors	26	Director of Curriculum	14	Teachers	14
Prepares diagnostic and remedial exercises	Supervisors	31	Director of Research	18	Teachers	18
Writes courses of study	Supervisors	36	Teachers	33	Principals	19
Edits courses of study	Assistant Superintendent	28	Supervisors	25	Director of Curriculum	19
Installs courses of study in schools	Supervisors	32	Principals	29	Assistant Superintendent	28
Conducts experimental work and research	Supervisors	31	Assistant Superintendent	22	Principals	21
Has charge of testing and research	Director of Research	29	Assistant Superintendent	17	Supervisors	15
Interprets curriculum test results	Director of Research	26	Supervisors	23	Assistant Superintendent	18
Analyzes and evaluates curriculum studies	Supervisors	27	Assistant Superintendent	21	Director of Research	19
Checks for statutory requirements	Assistant Superintendent	33	Supervisors	16	Director of Curriculum	15
Publicity of curriculum program	Assistant Superintendent	30	Director of Curriculum	18	Supervisors	13

the board of education is the regularly constituted legislative body of the public school system, the superintendent should submit the plans and policies of the curriculum program to it for authorization and approval. The board of education should also consider and pass on ways and means of financing the curriculum work as suggested by the superintendent.

Both practice and the opinions of specialists indicate that the superintendent should initiate and recommend the various phases of curriculum work to the board of education, which in turn should approve them. Such a procedure not only insures the legality of every phase of the work, but tends to engender in the members of the board and the citizens whom they represent a co-operative attitude toward the curriculum program.

SELECTION OF DIRECTOR

The selection of the director of a curriculum program is of primary importance. In general practice the superintendent of schools selects the director. Various educational staff members may be chosen to direct curriculum programs. The National Survey of Secondary Education revealed thirteen different individuals or agencies having direction of curriculum programs in cities: [7] Of the 154 cities studied, twenty or more selected, in the order named, superintendent, principal, assistant or deputy superintendent, or general committee. Only ten of the systems employed a director of curriculum and in only eight was the direction under the division of research. Similarly, David [8] found the superintendent of schools, the assistant superintendent, and the director of research the most favored officials to direct curriculum programs.

While the chief state school official retains general supervision of a state curriculum program, active responsibility for directing the work is usually delegated to a member of the state depart-

[7] Lide, *op. cit.*, p. 23.
[8] *Op. cit.*, pp. 8, 10.

ment of education or to a professor at the state university.[9]
If a type of organization is to be developed which will function
as a regular part of the educational program of the school system
and insure the continuous improvement of instruction, the director of the program should either be chosen from the regular
staff of the state department of education, or should be immediately and permanently added to it. It should be pointed out
here that the direction of a curriculum program is essentially
an administrative task. In addition to other professional qualifications, therefore, the director should possess the abilities of
a good administrator.

Sound administrative procedure requires that the direction of
a program be the sole responsibility of the individual designated
as director. He should be subordinate only to the superintendent
or to the executive committee which, in some organizations, ap-
points the director.[10] All curriculum workers should work under
the director. He should not be obliged to accept advice from
anyone except those to whom he is directly responsible. It
should be definitely understood that the function of advisory
committees is to counsel with, and not to dictate to, the director
of the program.

While the specific duties of the director of a curriculum program will vary in different situations, certain duties usually
performed by this official may be indicated. The curriculum director often assumes responsibility for: (1) developing and pro-
posing, for the approval of the superintendent, an organization
for curriculum work; (2) recommending for appointment the
personnel of the organization; (3) assisting in the organization of
committees; (4) securing services of consultants; (5) scheduling
activities of committees and checking on their progress; (6)
supervising the preparation of bulletins necessary for the success-

[9] Lide (*op. cit.*, pp. 24–25), shows that in six states active direction of
the curriculum program is delegated to a member of the state department
of education, and in five states to a professor at the state university.

[10] Where executive committees exist the superintendent of schools is
usually chairman of the committee and, therefore, the line of authority is
virtually the same in either type organization.

ful conduct of the program, and arranging for their distribution; (7) arranging for meetings with consultants; (8) assembling materials from committees and supervising the reviewing and editing of these materials; (9) supervising the printing of materials; (10) advising with the superintendent upon the appointment of advisory committees of educators and laymen; (11) preparing and circulating bibliographies for the use of committees; and (12) developing a plan for securing the effective use of courses of study as they are completed.

SPECIALISTS AND CONSULTANTS

In developing a curriculum program, it is highly desirable to secure the counsel and assistance of general consultants and other curriculum specialists. Curriculum specialists coming from outside the system and possessing broad perspective of the whole program are in a position to contribute technical advice as consultants to the staff, and general professional stimulation to teacher groups. The general consultants should be selected by the director of the curriculum program, and should become members of his staff. Their relationship should be entirely advisory. They should have no administrative function and no direct authority in connection with the program. Some of the duties commonly assigned general curriculum consultants are: (1) giving advice upon policies and procedures for curriculum work; (2) aiding the director in developing an organization, in planning the program, and in checking on its progress; (3) assisting in the preparation of curriculum bulletins, bibliographies, and study materials; (4) assisting in securing other special assistants who may be required; (5) aiding the director in guiding the work of the various committees; and (6) aiding the director in preparing the materials of instruction for inclusion in courses of study. The amount of time required of curriculum consultants will vary. It is probably wise, therefore, to have the consultant or consultants subject to call whenever their services are needed rather than to have them conform to a regular schedule.

COMMITTEE ORGANIZATION

In order to organize the agencies having a part in a curriculum program for effective work, it is necessary to form different types of committees and assign them specific duties. Before attempting to set up committees, however, it is necessary to set forth clearly the major aspects of the program to be undertaken. An analysis of the functions of the proposed program will reveal to the administrator the nature of the tasks to be performed. Some of these tasks can best be performed by committees. The administrator should have before him, therefore, an outline of each phase of the program that is being projected before determining what committees are necessary and the personnel of each committee.

An analysis of practice reveals five general types of committees. They are: (1) administrative committees; (2) production committees, or those which have charge of gathering and arranging the materials of instruction; (3) editing and reviewing committees; (4) special problems committees, or those which deal with special curriculum problems not directly connected with the production of materials of instruction, such as, use of library, equipment of the schoolroom, and grading and grouping; and (5) advisory committees.

The number and size of committees will vary with the basic point of view underlying the curriculum program. Where the point of view is taken that the best way for teachers to acquire an intelligent attitude toward teaching is for them to participate in making the courses of study,[11] the number and size of committees will be relatively large. On the other hand, where the point of view is taken that this may be achieved most effectively by wide participation of teachers in the study of the need for curriculum revision, in the exploration of new materials and procedures, in trying out materials of instruction produced by others, and in producing materials for their own use,[12] the number and size of

[11] As in the Denver program.
[12] As in the Virginia program.

committees will be relatively small. Potentially, all teachers participate in both types of programs, the difference lies in the manner of participation.

Committees usually deal with such phases of the curriculum as, the formulation of statements of the principles, aims, and procedures which are to be followed in the preparation of the courses of study; production of materials of instruction; review and unification of materials submitted by production committees; and the editing of materials for publication. For example, the Central State Curriculum Organization for Virginia consists of the following committees: Principles, Aims, and Procedures Committee; State Production Committees; State Reviewing and Unifying Committee; and Editing Committee. The State Administrative Organization for Arkansas includes the following state central committees: Platform and Principles Committee, Aims Committee, Scope Committee, Adaptations Committee, Research and Information Committee, Advisory Committee, and State Production Committee. The duties of these committees are as follows:

1. *Platform and Principles:* Formulate an educational platform for Arkansas, and state the principles to be observed in developing the curriculum.

2. *Aims:* Formulate the general aims which, at present, appear to be the most desirable goals for the public schools in Arkansas.

3. *Scope:* Suggest the scope of the work of the various grades.

4. *Adaptations:* Suggest adaptations in instructional materials necessary to meet the needs of significant groups.

5. *Research and Information:* Carry on research in curriculum materials and procedures with special reference to the state program. See that teachers and lay groups are generally informed as to the nature, purpose, and progress of the state curriculum program.

6. *Advisory:* Advise with the State Commissioner as to general policies and procedures and make recommendations. Suggest to production committees materials of value that may be secured from industrial and commercial organizations. Inform interested groups in

the State about the purposes and progress of the curriculum program.

7. *State Production:* Receive and consider all curriculum materials produced in the various regions of the state. Through laboratory procedures select and organize these materials for publication as tentative courses of study for the grades of the public schools of Arkansas.[13]

The Mississippi organization provides for four state committees as follows:

1. The Principles and Definitions Committee shall determine the philosophic background that is to be the basis of the program and develop a common terminology.

2. The Aims Committee shall determine the desired outcomes of the educational program.

3. The Procedures Committee shall have the task of putting the curriculum revision program into operation and of adjusting same to the conditions of the State.

4. The Research Committee shall provide necessary materials and facts to adapt correctly the program to the needs of the State.[14]

In order for the curriculum program to develop effectively, answers to certain questions must be determined early. For instance, production committees cannot proceed with their work until the principles, aims, scope, definitions, and procedures are rather definitely agreed upon. Therefore, committees to perform these functions should be appointed at the beginning of the program. These committees should be composed of a relatively small number of the most capable persons in the entire school system.

Central production committees should be organized in elementary and secondary schools in each of the fields into which the principles, aims, scope, and procedures committees decide the work of the school should be divided. The chairmen of these committees should be outstanding teachers in their respective fields. In state programs, where regional organizations are

[13] *Procedures in Production of Curriculum Materials,* The Arkansas Cooperative Program to Improve Instruction, Bulletin No. II, 1934, pp. 13–15.

[14] *Study Program,* Mississippi Program for the Improvement of Instruction, State Department of Education, 1934, p. 12.

functioning, the membership of the central committees should be composed of the several chairmen of regional production committees together with other outstanding teachers. Two reasons may be given for this method of forming the membership of these state production committees: (1) the chairmen of regional production committees should be in touch with the best work going on in the several regions and, hence, should be able to make the most significant contribution to state courses of study, and (2) planning and executing the work of production for the state production committees should be of great value to these chairmen in planning and executing the work of production in their respective local regions.

The materials produced by production committees should be carefully reviewed and, as far as possible, unified. That is, in the courses of study produced proper relationships should be established between various fields and grades. This may be the work of a separate committee, usually designated as a reviewing and unifying committee. This committee should be composed of a comparatively small number of the most capable classroom teachers and supervisors available within the system.

The courses of study, as well as study bulletins and other materials, must be carefully edited with respect to form and style before publication. Therefore, an editor or editorial committee is needed. This person or committee should be appointed by the director at the very beginning of the program. It is a mistake to wait until the materials are produced before appointing the editorial committee. Much time and energy may be saved if the editorial committee can set up at the beginning of the program certain rules of form and style to be observed by all production committees.

In developing a curriculum program, counsel and guidance should be secured from both laymen and professional groups. In some programs two advisory committees, one composed of laymen and one of educational leaders, have been appointed by the superintendent to assist him or the director in outlining the general plans for the curriculum program. The superintendent acts as chairman of both these committees. It should be clearly understood that the relationship of these committees to the curriculum organization is advisory only. They are to advise with the superintendent or director as to general policies and procedures, to make recommendations to him concerning policies and procedures, to present for consideration the viewpoint of lay and professional groups concerning the curriculum, to suggest materials of value to production committees that may be secured from industrial and commercial organizations, and to inform interested groups about the purposes and progress of the curriculum program.

SIZE OF COMMITTEES

Questions every administrator must answer are: What size committee can perform a particular task most effectively? Are there any general principles to indicate what size committee functions most satisfactorily? Cocking[15] points out a general tendency to reduce the size of committees, and states that it is doubtful if an efficient committee should consist of fewer than three or more than nine persons. Hopkins[16] considers the use of too many and too large committees a defect in many curriculum programs. He recognizes, however, that the size of committees should vary according to function. For example, the aims committee should include members from all the school divisions in order that the varying points of view may be considered; while the production committees should be composed of smaller groups. Comparatively large advisory committees may function effectively.

Some of the disadvantages of large committees are: lack of a definite feeling of responsibility on the part of individual members, difficulty of arranging suitable time and place for meeting, and the difficulty of securing final agreement on policies and

[15] Walter D. Cocking, *Administrative Procedures in Curriculum Making for Public Schools,* Teachers College, Columbia University Contributions to Education No. 329, 1928, p. 89.
[16] L. Thomas Hopkins, *Curriculum Principles and Practices,* Benjamin H. Sanborn and Company, 1929, pp. 325–32.

procedures. Practice has revealed that small committees, care-fully selected, are able in most cases to complete a task more satisfactorily than large committees. The type and the number of elements involved in the task assigned will often indicate the size of committee that will function best in a given situation.

The foregoing discussion suggests three controlling principles for determining the size of curriculum committees. The committee should be so constituted as to allow the fixing of responsibility; the personnel of the committee should be limited to those thoroughly competent to perform the desired task; and, there should be a sufficient number of members on the committee to bring out varying points of view but not too large a number to prevent final agreement.

COMMITTEE PERSONNEL

The membership of the various committees should next be determined. There seems to be only one safe general guide for the selection of the individuals chosen to perform the tasks assigned to committees. Other considerations should be secondary to the provision of a committee personnel peculiarly qualified to perform a particular task.

The selection of the personnel of the committees should be a co-operative enterprise. Since it is impossible for the director to know all who are best qualified in a system, it is desirable that nominations of teachers and others come from the principals and supervisors who know them best. The consensus of many estimates of the ability of the workers should be obtained. In one system a careful appraisal of candidates by five officials, in the order named, principal, supervisor, director of elementary education, assistant superintendent, and the superintendent, was made before the final selections were made and approved.[17] Such practice is not universal, however. Even in systems where careful ratings and other objective data are available, the nominations of curriculum workers should come in most cases from

[17] David, *op. cit.*, p. 9.

those close to teachers. The final selection, however, should be the responsibility of the director. In large school systems, a division of personnel under the direction of a supervisor may be created for this purpose; in others, the director himself should assume this responsibility. In either case the personnel selected must always be subject to the approval of the director of the program.

The major bases used for the selection of curriculum workers are: (1) strong teaching ability, (2) special interest in curriculum work, and (3) college training which includes curriculum study. Trillingham says that a "preponderance of evidence indicates that strong teaching ability is a safer basis for securing general fitness for curriculum work than is special interest in such work." He concludes: "A combination of the two factors should produce the best type of person for the job." [18] As previously indicated, however, the peculiar fitness of a person should be the final deciding factor in selecting curriculum workers.

FINANCIAL PROVISION

Sound administrative procedure requires that the work of curriculum revision be planned in advance and that adequate financial provision be made for it. If possible, this provision should extend over the entire time for which the curriculum program is projected. It should be administered as a part of the regular educational budget.

Due to the wide variation in the character and scope of curriculum programs, and in local conditions, it is not possible to set up specific guides for determining the probable cost of a program in a given situation. However, information as to total cost and the various items calling for financial provision in a number of curriculum programs should be helpful to the administrator in preparing his budget.

Trillingham [19] found that American cities spent school money

[18] *Op. cit.*, p. 33.
[19] *Ibid.*, pp. 133–134.

for curriculum supplies and services in the following order of frequency: general curriculum supplies, production of courses of study, professional libraries, clerical help, services of specialists, teachers' substitutes, salary of directors, experimental work, extra pay for teachers, and curriculum publicity. His study further reveals that in 1931–1932 the cost of curriculum activities in American cities ranged from $30.00 to $70,000, the median being $3,000; and that the total cost of curriculum programs per city for the five years previous to 1933 ranged from no cost to $140,000.

State curriculum programs also require financial provisions for the items named above, although the amounts vary widely. An additional item, however, is of major importance. It is necessary from time to time for committees whose members reside in various parts of the state to come together for conference. This requires expenses for travel and for maintenance while the committees are in session. Furthermore, consultants and specialists will be required to visit various local centers. This requires additional provision for travel. An added problem in financing a state curriculum program lies in the fact that plans must be made far enough in advance so that they can be included in the budget proposed to the legislature.

SECURING GENERAL INTEREST AND CO-OPERATION

Whether a curriculum program is projected on the basis of wide participation or is more restricted in conception, it is necessary to make definite provision for enlisting general interest and co-operation in the program. In Chapter XVII the importance of wide participation of teachers and laymen has been emphasized. Specific suggestions are made here for securing the interest and co-operation of teachers.

General practice shows a number of ways for stimulating interest and securing co-operation of teachers: general faculty meetings, meetings of special teacher groups, special recognition for significant achievement, additional remuneration for curriculum work, the development of professional study courses that apply particularly to the curriculum, circulation of bulletins designed especially to stimulate interest, publication of articles concerned with curriculum problems, and the use of radio.

Logically, the faculty meeting under the direction of the superintendent or his designated representative should be a primary means of stimulating interest of teachers in a proposed curriculum program. Unfortunately, however, the typical faculty meeting consists largely in routine announcements of an administrative nature, and is dull and uninteresting. On the other hand, a carefully planned meeting in which supervisors, principals, and teachers participate freely has been most effective in stimulating an active interest in a proposed curriculum program. If a regularly scheduled faculty meeting is used for this purpose, the teachers should be informed in advance of the nature of the meeting. An occasional visiting speaker may be provided to good advantage. In every meeting opportunity should be given to any teacher or group of teachers to contribute suggestions regarding the proposed program.

Smaller teacher groups may be used effectively when specific problems relating to the proposed program are up for discussion. In many school systems teachers are required or encouraged to participate in professional study courses. Provisions for such work vary widely from a suggested list of professional books that teachers are encouraged to read, to a definitely outlined course of reading and study with meetings for recitation and discussion. In many cases extension courses from universities are suggested and occasionally required of faculty groups. As pointed out previously, in some state and city programs special study course bulletins have been provided for the use of teacher groups. Also bulletins containing information regarding such significant problems as: pupil achievement, retardation, elimination, and non-promotion, have been used effectively to stimulate a consciousness of need for revision. It should be noted that the stimulation of interest and co-operation should be in direct charge of the person responsible for the direction of the program.

PROVIDING CONDITIONS FOR WORK

The success of any curriculum program will depend to a large extent upon the provision of conditions under which the work is to be done. A number of factors influencing the conditions encountered in state and city curriculum programs must be taken into account.

The question of releasing teachers from their regular duties in order to participate in curriculum revision must be settled early in the program. This requires provision in the budget as well as adjustments in the administrative and instructional program. Here again, the general point of view accepted will determine the course to pursue in a given curriculum program. If courses of study are to be revised in a comparatively short time by a selected group of teachers, then those responsible for the work must be relieved of their regular duties for such time as may be necessary for revising the courses of study. If, on the other hand, a long-time program involving general participation is adopted there is little need, except in rare cases, for teachers to be relieved from their regular duties. Similarly, the question of additional remuneration for curriculum work will be determined.

Whatever the type of program, it is essential that adequate provision be made for suitable meeting places for workers and committees. These should be comfortable and should be so located that the workers will be protected from interruption and other annoyances. The provision of meeting places should not be left to a chance arrangement at the time of meeting. Time and place of meetings should be regularly scheduled in advance.

It is of utmost importance that competent clerical assistance be provided for curriculum workers. Lack of this provision will materially limit the effectiveness of the work of the individuals and committees. The amount of clerical assistance necessary will vary greatly at different stages of the program. The director will find it necessary, therefore, to have an available supply which can be called upon as need may require. In order to prevent the indiscriminate use of the clerical force and the needless expenditure of funds for clerical assistance, it will be necessary for the director to provide that only such work will be done as has been approved by some designated authority.

Provision of adequate materials for the use of curriculum workers is of major importance. The usual materials and supplies should be easily available in such quantities as may be needed. The major responsibility for materials has to do with the provision of library and reference materials. Universities, colleges, and teacher training institutions, when accessible, may provide general library facilities. In addition to the general professional libraries where they are available, special reference materials must be secured and made accessible to curriculum workers. Full advantage should be taken of usable free materials. Recent textbooks in addition to adopted texts should be provided when possible. In some programs it has been found desirable to provide the services of a professional librarian to assist the curriculum workers in the use of materials.

PRODUCING MATERIALS OF INSTRUCTION

The production of new materials of instruction may be carried on by teachers working individually or co-operating in groups. It is essential, however, that in either case the materials be developed in classroom situations. Materials produced by individual teachers or local groups should be written up in uniform style and submitted to reviewing committees to be used as a basis for developing tentative courses of study. In this manner, teachers generally are given an opportunity to improve the curriculum in their own classrooms, and the resulting new courses of study are based on a wider range of teacher experience. The exact steps to be taken in production will vary with different types of situations and with the training and experience of teachers. However, the following steps involved in a general plan for production of new instructional materials in a state program are suggestive: "(1) know the program; (2) study scope of the curriculum; (3) make a suggestive list of aims; (4) prepare inventories; (5) collect suitable materials; (6) select and initiate a unit of work; (7) make adaptations required by the situation; (8) develop the unit; (9) evaluate and report the unit; and (10) develop other units if time permits." [20]

A further illustration of steps proposed for producing curriculum materials is found in Chart IX.

TRY-OUT AND EVALUATION OF NEW MATERIALS OF INSTRUCTION AND PROCEDURES

There should be a preliminary appraisal of all new curriculum materials and procedures. This requires that the new materials be collected and organized in "try-out" courses of study. These should be carefully edited and mimeographed so that they can be placed in the hands of teachers selected for trying them out. Instructions for their use should be full and explicit. Teachers should be supplied with forms for evaluating materials and reporting the results of their try-out. The try-out methods employed most frequently are: the use of tentative materials in a given course, subject, or grade, in the classroom by all teachers; criticism by teachers of the outlines but without classroom try-out; and testing of the results of instruction in the new materials in organized experimental classes.

Two points are to be especially observed in a try-out program. First, care should be taken to see that all materials in the try-out course of study are used by a sufficient number of teachers to make their combined evaluation significant. This does not mean that the teacher must devote his attention exclusively to the try-out materials but rather that he will select from the new materials those which appear most desirable for his particular situation. Second, teachers who are trying out the new materials should receive careful supervision. In school systems

[20] *Procedures in Production of Curriculum Materials*, The Arkansas Cooperative Program to Improve Instruction, Bulletin No. II, 1934, pp. 19-28.

CHART IX

STEPS BY WHICH IT IS PROPOSED THAT CURRICULUM MATERIAL BE PRODUCED [21]

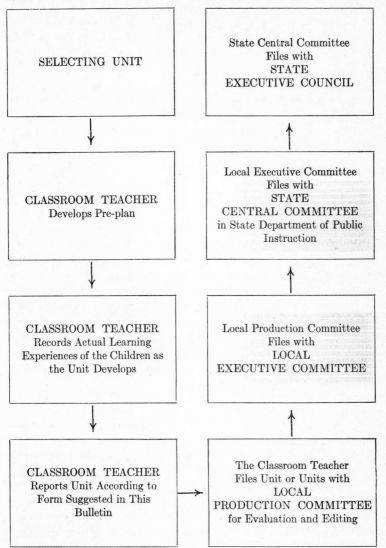

[21] North Carolina, *Suggested Procedures for Curriculum Construction and Course of Study Building*, 1934–1935, State Superintendent of Public Instruction, p. 24.

where supervisors of instruction are provided, they should assume this responsibility under the general direction of the person in charge of the curriculum program. Where supervisors are not provided in the regular instructional organization, special assistants to the director should be provided for this purpose.

Evaluation of the results of a curriculum program involves a number of seemingly intangible elements. It is a process that begins early in the program and continues after the intensive phase has been completed. Any evaluation of a curriculum program should take into account the purposes stated at the outset of the program. While specific techniques for this purpose have not been developed, it may be helpful to point out some of the results that have been observed in certain curriculum programs.

The principal results of curriculum programs, according to Cocking's study, are: "stimulation of the professional staff, increased interest on the part of pupils in school work, improved morale and co-operation, and better methods of teaching." [22] Lide's [23] survey of 139 systems revealed that most of the appraisal of curriculum programs is of an informal nature, conducted by the administrative and supervisory staff. Less than fifty schools make formal special appraisal through the use of questionnaires, standardized tests, or specially prepared tests.

In Denver, [24] 750 classroom teachers co-operated in the appraisal of thirty-four of the new courses of study, and a thorough program of testing was used in measuring pupil achievement under the new courses. Two methods of attack were involved in the appraisal: (1) the securing of teacher judgments, and (2) the use of Denver curriculum tests and certain standardized tests. Teacher judgments were secured through the use of a printed appraisal form applicable to all subjects. This was

[22] *Op. cit.*, p. 98.
[23] *Op. cit.*, p. 51.
[24] A. K. Loomis, "Recent Developments in Curriculum-Making in Denver," *Progressive Education*, 6:262–264, September, October, November, 1929.

supplemented by a mimeographed form for each subject. Since the new courses of study place major emphasis upon attitudes and undertakings which give significance and purpose to the more easily measurable knowledges and skills, the curriculum tests and the standardized tests were used in order to determine whether emphasis upon these more intangible objectives means less efficient work in the skill and knowledge objectives. In Indiana [25] widespread reaction of classroom teachers to the tentative course of study was secured. For the purpose of securing the reaction of various groups to each course of study, a booklet was sent to city, town, and county school districts over the state. A general explanation of each of twelve major phases of each course of study is given in the booklet and space provided for suggested evaluation.

INSTALLATION

The installation of new courses of study is a phase of the curriculum program that requires careful consideration. As in other aspects of a curriculum program, the nature of the work of installation will be conditioned by the type of program or the point of view from which the program has been developed. If writing new courses of study has been the chief purpose of the program, the period of installation will be brief and the procedures employed largely formal. It will consist, for the most part, in the distribution of the courses of study and the announcement of general regulations regarding their use. If, on the other hand, the curriculum program is more comprehensive in purpose and scope, the process of installation will of necessity require a longer period of time and will include every aspect of the instructional program.

It is suggested that a program of installation should provide: (a) that installation of new courses be optional, (b) that it be gradual, (c) that it be carefully supervised, and (d) that it provide for the training of teachers in the use of new materials.

[25] Lide, *op. cit.*, p. 73.

PROVISION FOR CONTINUATION

If we assume, as is generally agreed, that curriculum revision should be a continuous process, then provision should be made for continuing the work after the intensive phases of the program have been completed. Provision in the administrative organization for continuous study and revision may be best accomplished by establishing a permanent curriculum department in the school system with a curriculum director. Several states have provided for this continuity by selecting some person in the regular organization, such as director of teacher training or director of instruction, as director of the continuing curriculum program. Lide [26] found that it is the policy of most schools in cities to assign responsibility for continuous revision to the same committee which assumed responsibility for general revision. The responsibility for continuing the work on the curriculum in the larger cities is usually assigned to the research and curriculum departments, while in the smaller cities this responsibility generally rests upon the superintendent and principal.

In accord with the administrative guides set up in the preceding chapter, the improvement of instruction through continuous curriculum revision should be organized as a regular part of the instructional program of the school system.

EXAMPLES OF EFFECTIVE ORGANIZATION

In planning a curriculum program organization it is helpful to consider examples of the major phases of effective organizations set up by individual school systems to carry on curriculum programs. For this reason, certain phases of both city and state administrative organizations have been selected for presentation.

The administrative organization utilized in a city of over 300,000 population is presented in a recent study by Lide. The summary reproduced herewith indicates the work done by the

[26] *Ibid.*, p. 52.

two most important committees and by a co-operating higher
institution.

GENERAL SUMMARY OF THE WORK OF SECONDARY-SCHOOL REVISION,
ROCHESTER, N. Y., 1927–1931

Central committee under chairmanship of deputy superintendent.	Survey of work of the schools. Study of needs revealed. Establishment of organization for revision. Gathering of literature on curriculum building.
University of Rochester co-operating extension course. Members of class were available for faculty meeting presentation in schools desiring service. Faculty and principals' meetings:	Study of curriculum theory and practice.
Subject committees	Analysis of objectives. Selection and arrangement of content to meet objectives. Decisions as to form of curriculum. Development of tentative course.
Central committee	Supplying all teachers with materials for classroom tryout. Providing for acquaintance of teachers and principals with new materials. Definite establishment of certain experimental classes and situations. Provision for teacher comment and criticism. Provision for expert counsel.
Subject committees	Rerevision in the light of a semester's experience. Development of a second edition of the courses embodying valid suggestions and criticisms.

Central committee	Provision for second classroom try-out.
	Analysis of entire curriculum (all subjects and grades) to eliminate overlapping and poor-grade placement, to determine relative load for ability ranges, to effect horizontal and vertical co-ordination.
	Testing program.
	Study of textbooks.
Subject committees	Final additions and changes as result of second tryout.
Central committee	Editing for printing (delegated to one member).
	Co-operation with press, and with local organizations for publicity and understanding.[27]

It will be noted that co-ordination and articulation are provided through general junior and senior high school committees, through special articulation committees in English and social studies, and through a special co-ordination committee for elementary schools; that the entire program is based on a careful survey of the work of the schools, and that an extensive effort is made to secure criticism resulting from actual try-out of materials of instruction in the classroom. Failure to provide a permanent organization through which desired changes may be made after final adoption is contrary to the generally accepted principle that curriculum revision should be continuous.

Another city's curriculum organization is presented by Trillingham.[28] This organization is for a city of approximately 75,000. The membership and functions of the various committees is indicated in the study. The following points should be noted: co-ordination and articulation are provided through a general elementary curriculum committee, a general secondary curriculum committee, and a superintendent's curriculum council; on each

[27] *Ibid.,* pp. 17, 20–21.
[28] Pasadena's Curriculum Organization. *Op. cit.,* p. 198.

of these committees are representatives of every point of view in the system; and the line of responsibility is direct from elementary and secondary subject matter committees to elementary and secondary curriculum committees, to the superintendent's curriculum council, and finally to the superintendent. Adequate co-ordination should be present since each committee is composed of five persons, three working in the grades being revised and two in the same field at other levels.

The method of procedure used in carrying on a state curriculum program is indicated by the following outline of the plan of committee organization.

COMMITTEE ORGANIZATION FOR THE ELEMENTARY
CURRICULUM
REVISION FOR SOUTH DAKOTA [29]

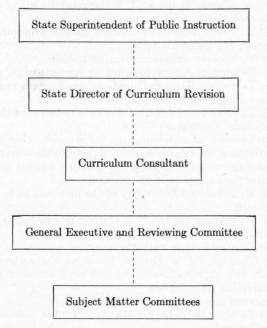

[29] The plan of committee organization indicates the provision for organization of the subject matter content of the curriculum.

The duties of the various committees are as follows:

A. General Executive Committee:

    (1) To study and interpret in the light of the educational needs of South Dakota the various approaches to curriculum construction.

    (2) To collect, rate, and organize the general aims of education.

    (3) To collect, rate, and organize the general aims of elementary and secondary education.

    (4) To formulate guiding principles for elementary and secondary education.

    (5) To serve as advisor to all subject-matter committees in determining grade placements and time allotments.

    (6) To review the work of each subject-matter committee and transmit it to the State superintendent for approval.

    (7) To suggest the form and organization of the course of study.

B. Subject-Matter Committees:

    (1) To collect, define, rate, and organize the specific aims of the school subjects in the light of the general aims of education; (a) for each grade, (b) for each subject.

    (2) To select, define, and organize guiding principles; (a) for each grade, (b) for each subject.

    (3) To appoint sub-committees as needed.

    (4) To appoint special contributing committees.

    (5) To prepare forms and questionnaires for gathering materials and data from contributing schools.

    (6) To make use of scientific studies in determining the selection of curriculum content.

    (7) To assist in correlating the subject with other subjects in the curriculum by submitting brief reports to the director of curriculum construction concerning the activities selected by the committee for the various units of instruction.

    (8) To include a bibliography of the materials to be used with the subject.

    (9) To develop illustrative and type lessons for experimental purposes.

    (10) To provide for a testing program.

    (11) Transmit to the General Executive Committees the productions with all recommendations and helps necessary to successfully carry out the program.

C. Adaptation Committee:

    (1) To adapt the courses of study to the rural, consolidated, and the small school.

    (2) To provide methods and materials for these schools.

D. Publicity Committee:
    (1) To give accurate and interesting publicity to the curriculum construction work in the daily papers, college bulletins, and the S. D. E. A. Journal.

E. Standard Materials Committee:
    (1) To select a list of the outstanding textbooks in each field.
    (2) To select a list of outstanding reference material for each subject.
    (3) To select a list of purposeful teaching material, such as: (a) Maps, paper-tests, etc., (b) laboratory equipment, and (c) supplementary texts.[30]

One committee not generally included in curriculum program organizations was used in South Dakota—the Standard Materials Committee. This committee represents an attempt to supply the need for some agency within each system to select books, materials, and supplies in accordance with curriculum requirements. Emphasizing the need for such an agency, Cocking says:

More and more school officials are coming to recognize that books and supplies are integral parts of curriculum making. Those books and those supplies should be selected which will best serve to aid in the interpretation and carrying out of the courses of study. The work of curriculum making is not completed in any unit until there is specified a list of books both for teachers and pupils which seems to give most promise for aid in carrying out the work. In the same way supplies should be selected solely upon the basis of their function in helping to carry out the work in a particular course.[31]

This suggests that there should be some agency in the permanent curriculum organization responsible for the selection and purchase of books, materials, and supplies in accordance with curriculum needs. The report of the survey of the Los Angeles City Schools emphasizes this need:

Curriculum revision must give consideration to textbooks available, supplementary texts, library books, teaching aids, and instructional supplies. These elements determine what is taught in the classroom as

---

[30] Mina M. Langvick, *Current Practices in the State Courses of Study,* United States Office of Education Bulletin No. 4, 1931, p. 49.
[31] *Op. cit.,* p. 62.

much as or more than the course of study itself. The determination of the selection of these materials should be closely related to the Curriculum Division. These services are now distributed among the various Superintendents and the Acting Co-ordinating Director.[32]

The administrative organization of the Virginia state curriculum program is presented in Charts X and XI as an illustration of an organization designed to carry forward a co-operative endeavor to improve classroom instruction on a state-wide basis. The state curriculum program organization in Virginia was set up to achieve the following major purposes:

1. To improve classroom instruction in Virginia by encouraging teachers, through study of their own curriculum problems, to provide children with richer and more purposeful experience in the classroom.
2. To aid teachers in developing division courses of study especially adapted to their own needs.
3. To develop State courses of study.
In order that these major objectives may be achieved, the State Program proposes to:
1. Provide the services of specialists to the division and State production committees.
2. Provide materials for use in curriculum construction.
3. Organize curriculum centers around the State teacher training institutions for the purpose of offering courses in curriculum construction and of providing expert advice to the divisions on their curriculum work.[33]

The foregoing purposes should be kept in mind when studying the Virginia organization.

The organization to carry forward the Virginia program, then, is developed "(1) to secure the best talent and materials from the entire State for the development of a State Course of Study, (2) to provide expert guidance and assistance to divisions in developing their own courses of study, and (3) to make possible a gradual evolution into a type of organization which will

---

[32] Osman R. Hull and Willard S. Ford, *Survey of the Los Angeles City Schools,* 1934, p. 27.
[33] *Organization for Virginia State Curriculum Program,* Bulletin State Board of Education, March, 1932, p. 6.

CHART X

A CENTRAL STATE CURRICULUM ORGANIZATION IN VIRGINIA [34]

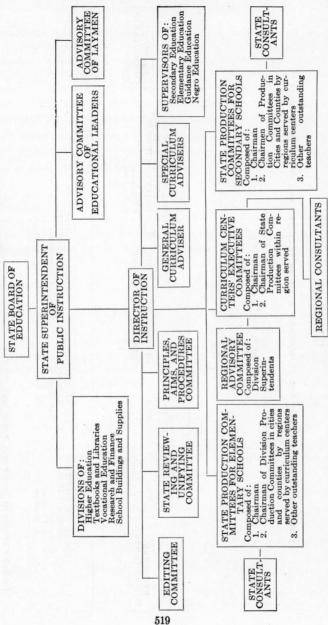

[34] *Organization for Virginia State Curriculum Program,* Bulletin, State Board of Education, March, 1932, p. 17.

CHART XI

A SUGGESTED ORGANIZATION FOR CURRICULUM WORK IN COUNTIES AND CITIES IN VIRGINIA [35]

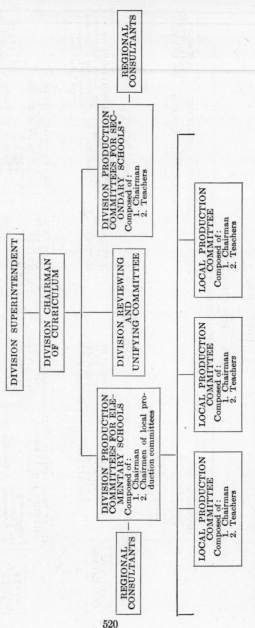

* Includes grades in junior and senior high schools.

[35] *Organization for Virginia State Curriculum Program,* Bulletin, State Board of Education, March, 1932, p. 13.

520

achieve the ultimate ideal of the State Department in connection with curriculum work." [36]

To achieve these purposes two organizations were necessary; one for general state work, and the other for work in local school divisions.[37] The relationship of agencies within these organizations are presented graphically in Charts X and XI respectively.

ADMINISTRATIVE ORGANIZATION MUST BE DEVELOPED FOR A PARTICULAR SCHOOL SYSTEM

Suggestions such as the foregoing will be found helpful in projecting an administrative organization for curriculum development. In the final analysis, however, each school system will find it necessary to develop an organization fitted to its particular needs and resources. In undertaking this, consideration should be given, first to the purposes to be realized, next to the requirements of sound practice in administration, and finally to suggestions that may be derived from practices in other school systems.

SELECTED REFERENCES

Arkansas, *Procedures in Production of Curriculum Materials,* The Arkansas Co-operative Program to Improve Instruction, Bulletin No. II, State Department of Education, Little Rock, Arkansas, 1934.

Cocking, Walter D., *Administrative Procedures in Curriculum Making for Public Schools,* Contributions to Education No. 329, Bureau of Publications, Teachers College, Columbia University, New York, 1928.

David, Flavius L., *The Selection and Organization of Personnel for Curriculum Revision,* Bulletin No. 30, Curriculum Laboratory, School of Education, Western Reserve University, Cleveland, Ohio, 1932.

Langvick, Mina M., *Current Practices in the State Courses of Study,* United States Office of Education Bulletin No. 4, Washington, D. C., 1931.

[36] *Ibid.,* p. 11.
[37] In Virginia a "division" is comprised of one or more counties.

Lide, Edwin S., *Procedures in Curriculum Making*, National Survey
of Secondary Education, Bulletin No. 17, Monograph No. 18,
Government Printing Office, Washington, D. C., 1932.

Mississippi, *Study Program*, Mississippi Program for the Improvement
of Instruction, State Department of Education, Jackson, Mississippi, 1934.

Trillingham, Clinton C., *The Organization and Administration of Curriculum Programs*, University of Southern California, Los Angeles,
California, 1934.

Virginia, *Organization for Virginia State Curriculum Program*, Bulletin,
State Board of Education, Richmond, Virginia, March, 1932.

BIBLIOGRAPHY

The selected references for the several chapters represent a minimum bibliography on the general problems of curriculum development. A comprehensive bibliography is herewith presented to aid in more intensive study of curriculum problems and in the prosecution of the various tasks of curriculum making. A table of contents of the bibliography to facilitate ready reference follows:

GENERAL REFERENCES

General Works on Education Relating to the Curriculum

Bagley, William C., *Education and Emergent Man*, Thomas Nelson and Sons, New York, 1934.

Bagley, William C., *Education, Crime and Social Progress*, The Macmillan Co., New York, 1931.

Boas, George, *Our New Ways of Thinking*, Harper and Brothers, New York, 1930.

Bode, Boyd H., *Fundamentals of Education*, The Macmillan Co., New York, 1921.

Bode, Boyd H., *Modern Educational Theories*, The Macmillan Co., New York, 1927.

Bonser, Frederick G., *Life Needs and Education*, Bureau of Publications, Teachers College, Columbia University, New York, 1932.

Boyd, William, and Mackenzie, M. M., Editors, *Towards a New Education*, Alfred A. Knopf, New York, 1930.

Brewer, John M., *Education as Guidance*, The Macmillan Co., New York, 1932.

Briggs, Thomas H., *The Great Investment*, Inglis Lecture, Harvard University Press, Cambridge, Mass., 1930.

Briggs, Thomas H., *Secondary Education*, The Macmillan Co., New York, 1933.

Chapman, J. C., and Counts, George S., *Principles of Education*, Houghton Mifflin Co., Boston, 1924.

Childs, John L., *Education and the Philosophy of Experimentalism*, The Century Co., New York, 1931.

Cobb, Stanwood, *The New Leaven; Progressive Education and Its Effect Upon the Child and Society*, John Day Co., New York, 1928.

Committee of the Progressive Education Association on Social and Economic Problems, *A Call to the Teachers of the Nation*, John Day Co., New York, 1933.

Counts, George S., *The American Road to Culture*, John Day Co., New York, 1930.

Counts, George S., *Secondary Education and Industrialism*, Inglis Lecture, Harvard University Press, Cambridge, Mass., 1929.

Counts, George S., *The Social Foundations of Education*, Part IX: Report of the Commission on the Social Studies, American Historical Association, Charles Scribner's Sons, New York, 1934.

Cox, Philip W. L., and Long, Forrest, E., *Principles of Secondary Education*, D. C. Heath & Co., Boston, 1932.

Demiashkevich, Michael, *An Introduction to the Philosophy of Education*, American Book Company, New York, 1935.

Dewey, John, *Democracy and Education*, The Macmillan Co., New York, 1916.

Dewey, John, *My Pedagogic Creed*, The Progressive Education Association, Washington, D. C., 1929.

Dewey, John, *The School and Society*, Revised Edition, University of Chicago Press, Chicago, 1915.

Dewey, John, *The Way Out of Educational Confusion*, Inglis Lecture, Harvard University Press, Cambridge, Mass., 1931.

Dewey, John, and Dewey, Evelyn, *Schools of Tomorrow*, E. P. Dutton & Co., New York, 1915.

Eurich, A. C., *The Changing Educational World, 1905–1930*, University of Minnesota Press, Minneapolis, Minn., 1931.

Ferrière, Adolphe, *The Activity School*, John Day Co., New York, 1928.

Finney, Ross L., *A Sociological Philosophy of Education*, The Macmillan Co., New York, 1928.

Gray, William S., Editor, *General Education: Its Nature, Scope, and Essential Elements*, University of Chicago Press, Chicago, 1934.

Gray, William S., Editor, *The Junior College Curriculum*, University of Chicago Press, Chicago, 1929.

Harap, Henry, *Economic Life and the Curriculum*, The Macmillan Co., New York, 1927.

Harap, Henry, *The Education of the Consumer: A Study in Curriculum Materials*, The Macmillan Co., New York, 1924.

Hart, Joseph K., *A Social Interpretation of Education*, Henry Holt & Co., New York, 1929.

Hartshorne, Hugh, *Character in Human Relations*, Charles Scribner's Sons, New York, 1932.

Hissong, Clyde, *The Activity Movement*, Warwick & York, Baltimore, Md., 1932.

Horne, Herman Harrell, *Democratic Philosophy of Education*, The Macmillan Co., New York, 1932.

Johnson, Marietta Louise, *Youth in a World of Men*, John Day Co., New York, 1929.

Johnston, John B., *The Liberal College in Changing Society*, The Century Co., New York, 1930.

Judd, Charles H., *Problems of Education in the United States*, Recent Social Trends Monographs, McGraw-Hill Book Co., New York, 1933.

Judd, Charles H., *Education and Social Progress*, Harcourt, Brace & Co., New York, 1934.

Kelly, Robert Lincoln, Editor, *The Effective College*, Association of American Colleges, 11 Fifth Ave., New York, 1928.

Kilpatrick, William H., *Education and the Social Crisis*, Liveright, Inc., New York, 1932.

Kilpatrick, William H., *Education for a Changing Civilization*, The Macmillan Co., New York, 1926.

Kilpatrick, William H. and others, *The Educational Frontier*, The Century Co., New York, 1933.

Kinneman, John A., *Society and Education*, The Macmillan Co., New York, 1932.

Kotinsky, Ruth, *Adult Education and the Social Scene*, D. Appleton-Century Co., New York, 1933.

Lindeman, Eduard C., *Social Education*, The New Republic, New York, 1933.

Martin, Everett Dean, *The Meaning of a Liberal Education*, W. W. Norton & Co., New York, 1926.

Mead, Cyrus D., and Orth, Fred W., *The Transitional Public School*, The Macmillan Co., New York, 1934.

Meriam, J. L., *Child Life and the Curriculum*, World Book Co., Yonkers-on-Hudson, N. Y., 1920.

Morrison, Henry C., *Basic Principles in Education*, Houghton Mifflin Co., Boston, 1934.

Morrison, Henry C., *The Evolving Common School*, Inglis Lecture, Harvard University Press, Cambridge, Mass., 1933.

National Education Association, "Creating a Curriculum for Adolescent Youth," *Research Bulletin*, January, 1928.

National Education Association, "Keeping Pace with the Advancing Curriculum," *Research Bulletin*, September and October, 1925.

National Education Association, "Modern Social and Educational Trends," *Research Bulletin*, November, 1934.

National Education Association, "Vitalizing the High School Curriculum," *Research Bulletin*, September, 1929.

National Education Association, *Department of Superintendence Tenth Yearbook*, "Character Education," Washington, D. C., 1932

Pierce, Bessie Louise, *Citizens' Organizations and the Civic Training of Youth*, Part III, Report of the Commission on the Social Studies, American Historical Association, Charles Scribner's Sons, New York, 1933.

Pinkevitch, Albert P., *The New Education in the Soviet Republic*, John Day Co., New York, 1929.

Reisner, Edward H., *Nationalism and Education Since 1789*, The Macmillan Co., New York, 1922.

Robinson, James Harvey, *The Humanizing of Knowledge,* Revised Edition, George H. Doran Co., Garden City, N. Y., 1926.

Rugg, Harold O., *Culture and Education in America,* Harcourt, Brace & Co., New York, 1931.

Rugg, Harold O., *The Great Technology,* John Day Co., New York, 1933.

Russell, Bertrand, *Education and the Good Life,* Boni & Liveright, New York, 1926.

Russell, Bertrand, *Education and the Modern World,* W. W. Norton & Co., New York, 1932.

Scott, J. F., *The Menace of Nationalism in Education,* The Macmillan Co., New York, 1927.

Stowe, A. R., Monroe, *Modernizing the College,* Alfred A. Knopf, New York, 1926.

Taba, Hilda, *The Dynamics of Education,* Harcourt, Brace and Co., New York, 1932.

Tuttle, Harold S., *A Social Basis of Education,* Thomas Y. Crowell Co., New York, 1934.

West, Andrew F., *American General Education; A Short Study of its Present Condition and Needs,* Princeton University Press, Princeton, N. J., 1932.

White House Conference, *The Home and the Child: Housing, Furnishing, Management, and Clothing,* The Century Co., New York, 1931.

Whitehead, A. N., *The Aims of Education and Other Essays,* The Macmillan Co., New York, 1929.

Wilkins, Ernest H., *The College and Society, Proposals for Changes in the American Plan of Higher Education,* The Century Co., New York, 1932.

Problems of School Administration Relating to the Curriculum

Armentrout, W. D., *A Comparison of Time Allotments of Subjects in Elementary Training Schools and Elementary Public Schools,* Bulletin No. 4, Colorado State Teachers College, Greeley, Col., 1927.

Bair, Frederick H., *The Social Understandings of the Superintendent of Schools,* Contributions to Education No. 625, Bureau of Publications, Teachers College, Columbia University, New York, 1933.

Bibliography, Grade Placement, Curriculum Laboratory, School of Education, Western Reserve University, Cleveland, Ohio.

Bibliography, Time Allotment, Curriculum Laboratory, School of Education, Western Reserve University, Cleveland, Ohio.

Billett, Roy O., *Provisions for Individual Differences, Marking, and Promotion*, National Survey of Secondary Education, Bulletin No. 17, Monograph No. 13, Government Printing Office, Washington, D. C., 1932.

Brammell, P. Roy, *Articulation of High School and College*, National Survey of Secondary Education, Bulletin No. 17, Monograph No. 10, Government Printing Office, Washington, D. C., 1932.

Broady, Knute O.; Platt, Earl T.; and Bell, Millard D., *Practical Procedures for Enriching the Curriculums of Small Schools*, University of Nebraska Publication No. 84, Educational Monographs No. 2, Lincoln, Neb., 1931.

Caswell, Hollis L., *Program Making in Small Elementary Schools*, Field Studies No. 1, Revised Edition, Division of Surveys and Field Studies, George Peabody College for Teachers, Nashville, Tenn., 1932.

Caswell, Hollis L., *Non-Promotion in Elementary Schools*, Field Study No. 4, Division of Surveys and Field Studies, George Peabody College for Teachers, Nashville, Tenn., 1933.

Courtis, Stuart Appleton, *Why Children Succeed*, Courtis Standard Tests, 1807 East Grand Bend, Detroit, Mich., 1925.

Covert, T., *Time Allotments in Selected Consolidated Schools*, United States Department of the Interior, Office of Education, Rural School Leaflet No. 46, Government Printing Office, Washington, D. C., 1930.

Cox, Philip W. L., and Langfitt, R. Emerson, *High School Administration and Supervision*, American Book Company, New York, 1934.

Farley, Belmont, *School Publicity*, School Economy Series No. 6, Stanford University Press, Stanford University, Cal., 1934.

French, Will, *Promotional Plans in the High School*, Contributions to Education No. 587, Bureau of Publications, Teachers College, Columbia University, New York, 1933.

Harrington, Harold L., *Program Making for Junior High Schools*, The Macmillan Co., New York, 1930.

Irwin, Elizabeth A., and Marks, L. A., *Fitting the School to the Child; An Experiment in Public Education*, The Macmillan Co., New York, 1924.

Kefauver, Grayson N.; Noll, Victor H.; and Drake, C. Elwood, *The Horizontal Organization of Secondary Education*, National Survey of Secondary Education, Bulletin No. 17, Monograph No. 2, Government Printing Office, Washington, D. C., 1932.

Loomis, A. K.; Lide, Edwin S.; and Johnson, B. Lamar, *The Program of Studies*, National Survey of Secondary Education, Bulletin No.

17, Monograph No. 19, Government Printing Office, Washington, D. C., 1932.

Mann, C. H., *How Schools Use Their Time*, Contributions to Education No. 333, Bureau of Publications, Teachers College, Columbia University, New York, 1928.

Mort, Paul R., *The Individual Pupil*, American Book Company, New York, 1928.

National Education Association, *Department of Classroom Teachers Eighth Yearbook*, "Teacher and Public: A Handbook of Interpretation for Teachers," Washington, D. C., February, 1934.

National Education Association, *Department of Superintendence Seventh Yearbook*, "The Articulation of the Units of American Education," Washington, D. C., 1929.

National Education Association, *Department of Superintendence Ninth Yearbook*, "Five Unifying Factors in American Education," Washington, D. C., 1931.

Newlon, Jesse H.; Bruner, Herbert B.; and others, *The Curricula of the Schools*, Report of the Survey of the Schools of Chicago, Illinois, Volume III, Bureau of Publications, Teachers College, Columbia University, New York, 1932.

Proctor, William Martin, *The Six-Four-Four Plan of School Organization in Pasadena, California*, The Board of Education, Pasadena, Cal., 1933.

Puckett, Roswell C., *Making a High School Schedule of Recitations*, Longmans, Green & Co., New York, 1931.

Richardson, M. W., *Making a High School Program*, World Book Co., Yonkers-on-Hudson, N. Y., 1921.

Rosenstengel, William Everett, *Criteria for Selecting Curricula for the Public Junior Colleges*, Doctor's Thesis, University of Missouri, Columbia, Mo., 1931.

Report of the Carnegie Foundation for the Advancement of Teaching, Recommendations of the Commission of Seven, *State Higher Education in California*, California State Printing Office, Sacramento, Cal., June 24, 1932.

Stewart, H. H., *A Comparative Study of the Concentration and Regular Plans of Organization in the Senior High School*, Contributions to Education No. 600, Bureau of Publications, Teachers College, Columbia University, New York, 1934.

Waller, J. Flint, *Public Relations for the Public Schools: A Manual Based on a Study of Good Practice*, MacCrellish and Quigley Co., Trenton, N. J., 1933.

Washburne, Carleton W., *Adjusting the School to the Child; Practical First Steps*, World Book Co., Yonkers-on-Hudson, N. Y., 1932.

Textbooks on the Curriculum

Bobbitt, Franklin, *The Curriculum*, Houghton Mifflin Co., Boston, 1918.

Bobbitt, Franklin, *How to Make a Curriculum*, Houghton Mifflin Co., Boston, 1924.

Bonser, Frederick G., *The Elementary School Curriculum*, The Macmillan Co., New York, 1920.

Briggs, Thomas H., *Curriculum Problems*, The Macmillan Co., New York, 1926.

Charters, W. W., *Curriculum Construction*, The Macmillan Co., New York, 1923.

Clement, John Addison, *Curriculum Making in Secondary Schools*, Henry Holt & Co., New York, 1923.

Cox, Philip W. L., *Curriculum-Adjustment in the Secondary School*, J. B. Lippincott Co., Philadelphia, 1925.

Cox, Philip W. L., *The Junior High School and Its Curriculum*, Charles Scribner's Sons, New York, 1929.

Davis, Calvin O., *Our Evolving High School Curriculum*, World Book Co., Yonkers-on-Hudson, N. Y., 1927.

Harap, Henry, *The Technique of Curriculum Making*, The Macmillan Co., New York, 1928.

Hines, Harlan C., *Junior High School Curricula*, The Macmillan Co., New York, 1924.

Hopkins, L. Thomas, *Curriculum Principles and Practices*, Benjamin H. Sanborn & Co., Chicago, 1929.

McMurry, Charles A., *How to Organize the Curriculum*, The Macmillan Co., New York, 1923.

Uhl, Willis L., *Secondary School Curricula*, The Macmillan Co., New York, 1927.

Williams, Lester A., *The Making of High School Curricula*, Ginn & Co., Boston, 1928.

History and Status of the Curriculum

American Educational Research Association, *Review of Educational Research, The Curriculum*, National Education Association, Washington, D. C., April, 1934.

Bagley, William C., and Kyte, George C., *The California Curriculum Study*, University of California Printing Office, Berkeley, Cal., 1926.

Caliver, Ambrose, *Secondary Education for Negroes*, National Survey of Secondary Education, Bulletin No. 17, Monograph No. 7, Government Printing Office, Washington, D. C., 1932.

Clements, J. A., *Progressive Trends in the External Organization and in the Curriculum Content of Our Schools,* University of Illinois Bulletin No. 54, Urbana, Ill., February 24, 1931.

Conference Report, *Curriculum Making in Current Practice,* Northwestern University, Evanston, Ill., 1932.

Counts, George S., *The Senior High School Curriculum,* Supplementary Educational Monographs No. 29, University of Chicago Press, Chicago, 1926.

Ferriss, Emery N.; Gaumnitz, W. H.; and Brammell, P. Roy, *The Smaller Secondary Schools,* National Survey of Secondary Education, Bulletin No. 17, Monograph No. 6, Government Printing Office, Washington, D. C., 1932.

Gilbert, Charles B., *What Children Study and Why,* Silver, Burdett & Co., New York, 1913.

Glass, James M., *Curriculum Practices in the Junior High School and Grades 5 and 6,* Supplementary Educational Monographs No. 25, University of Chicago Press, Chicago, 1924.

Gray, William S., Editor, *Recent Trends in American College Education, Part I: Reorganization of the Junior College,* University of Chicago Press, Chicago, 1931.

Hudelson, Earl, Editor, *Problems of College Education; Studies in Administration, Student Personnel, Curriculum, and Instruction,* University of Minnesota Press, Minneapolis, Minn., 1928.

Johnson, B. Lamar, *The Secondary School Library,* National Survey of Secondary Education, Bulletin No. 17, Monograph No. 17, Government Printing Office, Washington, D. C., 1932.

Kefauver, Grayson N.; Noll, Victor H.; and Drake, C. Elwood, *Part-Time Secondary Schools,* National Survey of Secondary Education, Bulletin No. 17, Monograph No. 3, Government Printing Office, Washington, D. C., 1932.

Kefauver, Grayson N.; Noll, Victor H.; and Drake, C. Elwood, *The Secondary School Population,* National Survey of Secondary Education, Bulletin No. 17, Monograph No. 4, Government Printing Office, Washington, D. C., 1932.

Koos, Leonard V., "How to Use the Findings of the National Survey of Secondary Education," *North Central Association Quarterly,* Ann Arbor Press, Ann Arbor, Mich., 8:347–355, January, 1934.

Koos, Leonard V., and Staff, *Summary,* National Survey of Secondary Education, Bulletin No. 17, Monograph No. 1, Government Printing Office, Washington, D. C., 1932.

Monroe, Walter S., and Herriott, M. E., *Reconstruction of the Secondary School Curriculum: Its Meaning and Trends,* Bureau of Educational Research, Bulletin No. 41, University of Illinois, Urbana, Ill., 1928.

National Education Association, "Facts on the Public School Curriculum," *Research Bulletin,* November, 1923.

National Education Association, *Department of Superintendence Second Yearbook,* "The Elementary School Curriculum," Washington, D. C., 1924.

National Education Association, *Department of Superintendence Third Yearbook,* "Research in Constructing the Elementary School Curriculum," Washington, D. C., 1925.

National Education Association, *Department of Superintendence Fourth Yearbook,* "The Nation at Work on the Public School Curriculum," Washington, D. C., 1926.

National Education Association, *Department of Superintendence Fifth Yearbook,* "The Junior High School Curriculum," Washington, D. C., 1927.

National Education Association, *Department of Superintendence Sixth Yearbook,* "The Development of the High School Curriculum," Washington, D. C., 1928.

National Society for the Study of Education, Twenty-Sixth Yearbook, Part I, "Curriculum Making: Past and Present," Public School Publishing Co., Bloomington, Ill., 1927.

National Society for the Study of Education, Twenty-Sixth Yearbook, Part II, "The Foundations of Curriculum-Making," Public School Publishing Co., Bloomington, Ill., 1927.

National Society for the Study of Education, Thirtieth Yearbook, Part I, "The Status of Rural Education," Public School Publishing Co., Bloomington, Ill., 1931.

National Society for the Study of Education, Thirty-First Yearbook, Part II, "Changes and Experiments in Liberal-Arts Education," Public School Publishing Co., Bloomington, Ill., 1932.

National Society for the Study of Education, Thirty-Third Yearbook, Part II, "The Activity Movement," Public School Publishing Co., Bloomington, Ill., 1934.

North Central Association of Colleges and Secondary Schools, *High School Curriculum Reorganization,* The North Central Association of Colleges and Secondary Schools, Ann Arbor, Mich., 1933.

Reavis, William C., *Programs of Guidance,* National Survey of Secondary Education, Bulletin No. 17, Monograph No. 14, Government Printing Office, Washington, D. C., 1932.

Reavis, William C., and Van Dyke, George E., *Nonathletic Extracurriculum Activities,* National Survey of Secondary Education,

Bulletin No. 17, Monograph No. 26, Government Printing Office, Washington, D. C., 1932.

Rooney, John Robert, *Curricular Offerings of Catholic Secondary Schools: An Examination of 283 Institutions*, Catholic University of America, Educational Research Monograph, Volume 6, No. 4, The Catholic Education Press, Washington, D. C., 1931.

Soper, Wayne, W., and Coxe, Warren W., *Trends in Secondary Education*, Bulletin No. 961, University of the State of New York, Albany, N. Y., 1930.

Spaulding, Francis T.; Frederick, O. I.; and Koos, Leonard V., *The Reorganization of Secondary Education*, National Survey of Secondary Education, Bulletin No. 17, Monograph No. 5, Government Printing Office, Washington, D. C., 1932.

ADMINISTRATIVE ASPECTS OF CURRICULUM MAKING

Adams, Fay, *The Initiation of an Activity Program into a Public School*, Contributions to Education No. 598, Bureau of Publications, Teachers College, Columbia University, New York, 1934.

Arkansas, *Procedures in Production of Curriculum Materials*, The Arkansas Co-operative Program to Improve Instruction, Bulletin No. II, State Department of Education, Little Rock Ark., 1934.

Arkansas, *Study Program*, Parent Co-operation in the Arkansas Co-operative Program to Improve Instruction, Arkansas Congress of Parents and Teachers, Little Rock, Ark., 1934.

Arkansas, *Study Program*, The Arkansas Co-operative Program to Improve Instruction, Bulletin No. I, State Department of Education, Little Rock, Ark., 1933.

Bibliography: Procedures in Curriculum Revision, Curriculum Laboratory, School of Education, Western Reserve University, Cleveland, Ohio.

Bobbitt, Franklin, *Curriculum Making in Los Angeles*, Supplementary Educational Monographs No. 20, University of Chicago, Chicago, 1922.

Cocking, Walter D., *Administrative Procedures in Curriculum Making for Public Schools*, Contributions to Education No. 329, Bureau of Publications, Teachers College, Columbia University, New York, 1928.

David, Flavius L., *The Selection and Organization of Personnel for Curriculum Revision*, Bulletin No. 30, Curriculum Laboratory, School of Education, Western Reserve University, Cleveland, Ohio, October 1, 1932.

Denver, *The Denver Program of Curriculum Revision,* Monograph No. 12, Denver Public Schools, Denver, Col., 1927.

Flanders, Jesse K., *Legislative Control of the Elementary Curriculum,* Contributions to Education No. 195, Bureau of Publications, Teachers College, Columbia University, New York, 1925.

Florida, *The Florida Program of Curriculum Revision—General Plans and Organization,* Curriculum Bulletin No. 1, State Department of Public Instruction, Tallahassee, Fla., November 1, 1931.

Hamilton, Otto T., *The Courts and the Curriculum,* Contributions to Education No. 250, Bureau of Publications, Teachers College, Columbia University, New York, 1927.

Holloway, William J., *Participation in Curriculum Making as a Means of Supervision of Rural Schools,* Contributions to Education No. 301, Bureau of Publications, Teachers College, New York, 1928.

Houston, Texas, Independent School District, *Curriculum Revision and Development in Houston, Texas, 1924-30,* Part II, Board of Education, Houston, Tex., 1930.

Keesecker, Ward W., *Legal and Regulatory Provisions Affecting Secondary Education,* National Survey of Secondary Education, Bulletin No. 17, Monograph No. 9, Government Printing Office, Washington, D. C., 1932.

Lide, Edwin S., *Procedures in Curriculum Making,* National Survey of Secondary Education, Bulletin No. 17, Monograph No. 18, Government Printing Office, Washington, D. C., 1932.

Mississippi, *Study Program,* Mississippi Program for the Improvement of Instruction, Bulletin No. 1, State Department of Education, Jackson, Miss., October, 1934.

Monroe, Walter S.; Hindman, Darwin A.; and Lundin, Roy S., *Two Illustrations of Curriculum Construction,* Bureau of Educational Research, Bulletin No. 39, University of Illinois, Urbana, Ill., February 28, 1928.

North Carolina, *Suggested Procedures for Curriculum Construction and Course of Study Building, 1934-35,* Publication No. 179, State Superintendent of Public Instruction, Raleigh, N. C., 1934.

South Dakota, *Preliminary Reports on Approaches to and Theories Regarding Curriculum Construction, General Aims and Guiding Principles of Education for the State of South Dakota,* Bulletin No. 1, State Department of Education, Pierre, S. D., 1930.

St. Louis Public Schools, *Introduction of the Suggested Courses of Study,* Curriculum Service Bulletin No. 1, Board of Education, St. Louis, Mo., 1926.

Texas, *Handbook for Curriculum Study,* Bulletin State Department of Education, Austin, Tex., 1934.

Tidwell, Clyde J., *State Control of Textbooks,* Contributions to Education No. 299, Bureau of Publications, Teachers College, Columbia University, New York, 1928.

Trillingham, C. C., *The Organization and Administration of Curriculum Programs,* Southern California Education Monographs, 1933–1934, Series No. 4, University of Southern California Press, Los Angeles, Cal., 1934.

Virginia, *Procedures for Virginia State Curriculum Program,* Bulletin No. 3, State Board of Education, Richmond, Va., November, 1932.

Virginia, *Organization for Virginia State Curriculum Program,* Bulletin No. 5, State Board of Education, Richmond, Va., March, 1932.

Virginia, *Study Course for Virginia State Curriculum Program,* Bulletin No. 4, State Board of Education, Richmond, Va., January, 1932.

Wisehart, Roy P., *Guiding Principles of Elementary Curriculum Revision for the State of Indiana,* Bulletin No. 107, Department of Public Instruction, Indianapolis, Ind., 1929.

AIMS

Bibliography (Annotated) of Investigations of Curriculum Objectives, Curriculum Laboratory, School of Education, Western Reserve University, Cleveland, Ohio.

Beach, Walter Greenwood, *Social Aims in a Changing World,* Stanford University Press, Stanford University, Cal., 1932.

Bobbitt, Franklin, *Curriculum Investigations,* Supplementary Educational Monographs, No. 31, Chapters I–XI, University of Chicago Press, Chicago, 1926.

Campbell, Doak S., *A Critical Study of the Stated Purposes of the Junior College,* Contribution to Education No. 70, George Peabody College for Teachers, Nashville, Tenn., 1930.

Carmichael, Albert Maxwell, *Moral Situations of Six-Year Old Children As a Basis for Curriculum Construction,* Studies in Education, Volume IV, No. 6, University of Iowa, Iowa City, Ia., 1927.

Charters, W. W., and Waples, Douglas, *The Commonwealth Teacher-Training Study,* The University of Chicago Press, Chicago, 1929.

Commission on Reorganization of Secondary Education, *Cardinal Principles of Secondary Education,* Bureau of Education, Bulletin No. 35, Washington, D. C., 1918.

Hanus, Paul H., *Educational Aims and Educational Values,* The Macmillan Co., New York, 1899.

National Educational Association, "What Are the Major Objectives of Education," *Research Bulletin,* March, 1931.

Rowland, W. T., *Aims of Public Education in the United States,* Contribution to Education No. 117, George Peabody College for Teachers, Nashville, Tenn., 1933.

Snedden, David S., *Foundations of Curricula; Sociological Analyses,* Bureau of Publications, Teachers College, Columbia University, New York, 1927.

Snedden, David S., *Sociological Determination of Objectives in Education,* J. B. Lippincott Co., Philadelphia, 1921.

St. Louis Public Schools, *General and Divisional Aims,* Curriculum Bulletin No. 1, Board of Education, St. Louis, Missouri, 1926.

Strong, E. K. and Uhrbrock, R. S., *Job Analysis and the Curriculum, With Special Reference to the Training of Printing Executives,* Williams and Wilkins, New York, 1923.

CURRICULUM FOR ATYPICAL CHILDREN

Cowen, Phillip A. and Mathews, E. R., *Special Class Curriculum Study,* Bulletin No. 944, University of the State of New York, Albany, N. Y., 1930.

Crayton, Sherman G., *A Proposed Program for the Care and Education of Kentucky's Handicapped Children, Based Upon Current Practice and Philosophy Within the State and Throughout the United States,* Bulletin of the Bureau of School Service, Vol. VII, No. 1, University of Kentucky, Lexington, Ky., 1934.

Dransfield, J. Edgar, *Administration of Enrichment to Superior Children in the Typical Classroom,* Contributions to Education No. 558, Bureau of Publications, Teachers College, Columbia University, New York, 1933.

Featherstone, W. B., *The Curriculum of the Special Class, Its Underlying Principles,* Contributions to Education No. 544, Bureau of Publications, Teachers College, New York, 1932.

First Assistants in the High Schools of the City of New York, *Educating Superior Students,* American Book Co., New York, 1935.

Hilleboe, Guy L., *Finding and Teaching Atypical Children,* Contributions to Education No. 423, Bureau of Publications, Teachers College, Columbia University, New York, 1930.

Merry, Ralph V., *Problems in the Education of Visually Handicapped Children,* Harvard University Press, Cambridge, Mass., 1933.

National Society for the Study of Education, Twenty-third Yearbook, Part I, "The Education of Gifted Children," Public School Publishing Co., Bloomington, Ill., 1924.

National Society for the Study of Education, Twenty-fourth Yearbook,

Part II, "Adapting the Schools to Individual Differences," Public School Publishing Co., Bloomington, Ill., 1925.

New York State, *Organization of Special Classes for Subnormal Children*, University of the State of New York, Albany, N. Y.

Osburn, Worth J., and Rohan, Ben J., *Enriching the Curriculum for Gifted Children*, The Macmillan Co., New York, 1931.

Wallin, J. E. Wallace, *The Education of Handicapped Children*, Houghton Mifflin Co., Boston, 1924.

Whipple, Helen Davis, *Making Citizens of the Mentally Limited; A Curriculum for the Special Class*, Public School Publishing Company, Bloomington, Ill., 1927.

SOCIAL AND ECONOMIC FOUNDATIONS OF CURRICULUM MAKING

Adams, James Truslow, *The Epic of America*, Little, Brown and Co., Boston, 1931.

Adams, James Truslow, *The March of Democracy*, two volumes, Charles Scribner's Sons, New York, 1932–33.

Adams, James Truslow, *Our Business Civilization*, Boni Brothers, New York, 1930.

Allen, Frederick L., *Only Yesterday*, Harper and Brothers, New York, 1931.

Angell, Sir Norman, *From Chaos to Control*, The Century Co., New York, 1933.

Beard, Charles A., *America Faces the Future*, Houghton Mifflin Co., Boston, 1932.

Beard, Charles A., and Beard, Mary, *The Rise of American Civilization*, The Macmillan Co., New York, 1927.

Beard, Charles A., and Smith, G. H. E., *The Idea of National Interest*, The Macmillan Co., New York, 1934.

Blackmar, Frank W., *History of Human Society*, Charles Scribner's Sons, New York, 1926.

Boas, Franz, *Anthropology and Modern Life*, W. W. Norton & Co., New York, 1932.

Bogardus, Emory, *Fundamentals of Social Psychology*, The Century Co., New York, 1931.

Bowman, Isaiah, *The Pioneer Fringe*, American Geographical Society, New York, 1931.

Brant, Irving, *Dollars and Sense: Questions and Answers in Finance*, John Day Co., New York, 1933.

Breckinridge, Sophonishba P., *Women in the Twentieth Century*, McGraw-Hill Book Co., New York, 1933.

Brinkmann, Carl, *Recent Theories of Citizenship in Its Relation To Government*, Yale University Press, New Haven, Conn., 1927.

Carter, Mary Duncan, *The Story of Money*, Farrar & Rinehart, New York, 1932.

Catlin, George E. G., *A Preface to Action*, The Macmillan Co., New York, 1934.

Chapin, F. Stuart, *Cultural Change*, The Century Co., New York, 1928.

Chapman, John Jay, *New Horizons in American Life*, Columbia University Press, New York, 1932.

Charters, W. W., Chairman, *Motion Pictures and Youth*, The Payne Fund Studies, The Macmillan Co., New York, 1933.

Chase, Stuart, *The Economy of Abundance*, The Macmillan Co., New York, 1934.

Chase, Stuart, *Men and Machines*, The Macmillan Co., New York, 1929.

Chase, Stuart, *The Tragedy of Waste*, Grosset & Dunlap, New York, 1929.

Chase, Stuart, and Schlink, J. F., *Your Money's Worth*, The Macmillan Co., New York, 1931.

Committee on Commerce—United States Senate, *Investigations of So-Called "Rackets,"* Government Printing Office, Washington, D. C., 1933.

Committee on Commerce—United States Senate, *Crime and Crime Control*, Government Printing Office, Washington, D. C., 1934.

Committee on Recent Economic Changes, *Recent Economic Changes in the United States*, two volumes, McGraw-Hill Book Co., New York, 1929.

Counts, George S., *The Soviet Challenge to America*, John Day Co., New York, 1931.

Davis, Jerome, *Contemporary Social Movements*, The Century Co., New York, 1930.

Dewey, John, *Individualism, Old and New*, Minton, Balch and Co., New York, 1930.

Dewey, John, *Philosophy and Civilization*, Minton, Balch and Co., New York, 1931.

Ellwood, Charles A., *Man's Social Destiny in the Light of Science*, Cokesbury Press, 810 Broadway, Nashville, Tenn., 1929.

Embree, Edwin R., *Brown America*, The Viking Press, New York, 1931.

Engelbrecht, H. C. and Hanighen, F. C., *Merchants of Death*, Dodd, Mead and Co., New York, 1934.

Epstein, Abraham, *Insecurity; a Challenge to America*, Harrison Smith and Robert Haas, New York, 1933.

Everett, Samuel, *Democracy Faces the Future*, Columbia University Press, New York, 1935.

Fiske, George W., *The Changing Family*, Harper and Brothers, New York, 1928.

Foreman, Clark, *The New Internationalism*, W. W. Norton & Co., New York, 1934.

Forman, Henry James, *Our Movie Made Children*, The Macmillan Co., New York, 1933.

Frankl, Paul T., *Machine-Made Leisure*, Harper and Brothers, New York, 1932.

Gibbons, Herbert A., *Nationalism and Internationalism*, Frederick A. Stokes Co., New York, 1930.

Gilfillan, Lauren W., *I Went to Pit College*, The Viking Press, New York, 1934.

Gruening, Ernest H., *The Public Pays*, The Vanguard Press, New York, 1931.

Henderson, Fred, *The Economic Consequences of Power Production*, John Day Co., New York, 1933.

Henderson, Fred, *Foundations for the World's New Age of Plenty*, Victor Gollanez, Ltd., 14 Henrietta St., Bloomsbury, London, 1933.

Hepner, Harry W., *Human Relations in Changing Industry*, Prentice-Hall, Inc., New York, 1934.

Hertzler, Joyce O., *Social Progress*, The Century Co., New York, 1928.

Hindus, Maurice G., *The Great Offensive*, Harrison Smith and Robert Haas, New York, 1933.

Hockett, John A., *A Determination of the Major Social Problems of American Life*, Contributions to Education No. 281, Bureau of Publications, Teachers College, Columbia University, New York, 1927.

Johnson, Charles S., *The Negro in American Civilization*, Henry Holt and Co., New York, 1930.

Johnson, Charles S., *Shadow of the Plantation*, University of Chicago Press, Chicago, 1934.

Josephson, Matthew, *Robber Barons*, Harcourt, Brace and Co., New York, 1934.

Kallet, Arthur, and Schlink, F. J., *100,000,000 Guinea Pigs*, The Vanguard Press, New York, 1933.

Kandel, Isaac L., *The Dilemma of Democracy*, Inglis Lecture, Harvard University Press, Cambridge, Mass., 1934.

Knox, Raymond C., *Religion and the American Dream*, Columbia University Press, New York, 1934.

Landis, Benson Y., *The Third American Revolution*, Association Press, 347 Madison Ave., New York, 1933.

Leech, Harper, *The Paradox of Plenty*, McGraw-Hill Book Co., New York, 1932.

Leven, Maurice; Moulton, H. G.; and Warburton, C., *America's Capacity to Consume*, Brookings Institution, Washington, D. C., 1934.

Lies, Eugene T., *The New Leisure Challenges the Schools*, National Recreation Association, 315 Fourth Avenue, New York, 1933.

Lindquist, Ruth, *The Family in the Present Social Order*, University of North Carolina Press, Chapel Hill, N. C., 1931.

Lippert, Julius, *The Evolution of Culture*, The Macmillan Co., New York, 1931.

Lippmann, Walter, *Public Opinion*, The Macmillan Co., New York, 1922.

Lundberg, George A.; Komarovsky, Mirra; and McInerny, M. A., *Leisure: A Suburban Study*, Columbia University Press, New York, 1934.

Lynd, Robert S., and Lynd, Helen Merrell, *Middletown*, Harcourt, Brace and Co., New York, 1929.

MacIver, Robert M., Chairman, *Economic Reconstruction*, Report of the Columbia University Commission on Economic Reconstruction, Columbia University Press, New York, 1934.

MacIver, Robert M., *Society: Its Structure and Changes*, Ray Long and Richard Smith, Inc., New York, 1931.

Martin, Prestonia M., *Prohibiting Poverty*, The Author, 115 W. 16th Street, New York, 1933.

McCarthy, James R., *New Pioneers*, Bobbs-Merrill Co., Indianapolis, Ind., 1934.

Minehan, Thomas, *Boy and Girl Tramps of America*, Farrar and Rinehart, New York, 1934.

Mumford, Lewis, *Technics and Civilization*, Harcourt, Brace and Co., New York, 1934.

National Recreation Association, *Leisure Hours of 5,000 People: A Report of a Study of Leisure Time Activities and Desires*, National Recreation Association, 315 Fourth Avenue, New York, 1934.

Nourse, Edwin G. and others, *America's Capacity to Produce*, The Brookings Institution, Washington, D. C., 1934.

Odegard, Peter H., *The American Public Mind*, Columbia University Press, New York, 1930.

Odum, Howard W., *Man's Quest for Social Guidance*, Henry Holt & Co., New York, 1927.

Ogburn, William F., *Social Changes*, University of Chicago Press, Chicago, 1927.

Ortega y Gasset, José, *The Revolt of the Masses*, W. W. Norton & Co., New York, 1932.

Orton, William A., *America in Search of Culture*, Little, Brown & Co., Boston, 1933.

Overstreet, H. A., *We Move in New Directions*, W. W. Norton & Co., New York, 1933.

Page, Kirby, Editor, *A New Economic Order*, Harcourt, Brace and Co., New York, 1930.

Phillips, M. C., *Skin Deep*, Vanguard, New York, 1935.

Pitkin, Walter B., *Capitalism Carries On*, Whittlesey House, New York, 1935.

Rich, Margaret E., *Family Life Today*, Houghton Mifflin Co., New York, 1928.

Ripley, William Z., *Main Street and Wall Street*, Little, Brown & Co., Boston, 1927.

Roosevelt, Franklin Delano, *Looking Forward*, John Day Co., New York, 1933.

Rorty, James, *Our Master's Voice: Advertizing*, John Day Co., New York, 1934.

Rost, O. Fred, *Distribution Today*, McGraw-Hill Book Co., New York, 1933.

Shaw, Charles Gray, *Trends of Civilization and Culture*, American Book Co., New York, 1932.

Siegfried, André, *America Comes of Age: A French Analysis*, Harcourt Brace and Co., New York, 1927.

Soule, George, *The Coming American Revolution*, The Macmillan Co., New York, 1934.

Steffens, Lincoln, *Autobiography of Lincoln Steffens*, Harcourt, Brace and Co., New York, 1931.

Steiner, Jesse Frederick, *Americans at Play*, Recent Social Trends Monographs, McGraw-Hill Book Co., New York, 1933.

Steiner, Jesse Frederick, *The American Community in Action, Case Studies of American Communities*, Henry Holt & Co., New York, 1928.

Thomas, Norman, *The Choice Before Us: Mankind at the Crossroads*, The Macmillan Co., New York, 1934.

Tugwell, Rexford Guy, *The Battle for Democracy*, Columbia University Press, New York, 1935.

Tugwell, Rexford Guy, *The Industrial Discipline and the Governmental Arts*, Columbia University Press, New York, 1933.

Tugwell, Rexford Guy, and Keyserling, Leon H., Editors, *Redirecting Education*, Volume I, *The United States*, Columbia University Press, New York, 1934.

Veblen, Thorstein, *The Engineers and the Price System*, The Viking Press, New York, 1933.

Wallace, Henry A., *New Frontiers*, Reynal and Hitchcock, New York, 1934.

Wallas, Graham, *Our Social Heritage*, Yale University Press, New Haven, Conn., 1921.

Weatherford, Willis D., and Johnson, Charles S., *Race Relations*, D. C. Heath & Co., Boston, 1934.

Weatherly, Ulysses G., *Social Progress*, J. B. Lippincott Co., Philadelphia, 1926.

Woll, Matthew and Walling, W. E., *Our Next Step: A National Economic Policy*, Harper and Brothers, New York, 1934.

Wormser, I. Maurice, *Frankenstein Incorporated*, McGraw-Hill Book Co., New York, 1931.

Pamphlets

Numerous pamphlets dealing with the social and economic foundations of curriculum making are available. They are inexpensive and often contain much pertinent material. Some sources of pamphlets and a few titles obtainable from each follow.

American Library Association, Chicago, Illinois:
Ogburn, W. F., *Living with Machines*, 1933.
Douglas, Paul H., *Collapse or Cycle?* 1933.

Day and Hour Series, University of Minnesota Press, Minneapolis, Minnesota:
Haggerty, M. E., *Children of the Depression*, 1933.
Moulton, H. G., *International Economic Recovery*, 1933.
Murchie, R. W., *Land Settlement as a Relief Measure*, 1933.

Foreign Policy Association, New York:
Wallace, Henry A., *America Must Choose*, 1934.

John Day Pamphlets, The, John Day Company, New York:
Beard, Charles A., *The Myth of Rugged American Individualism*, 1933.
Chase, Stuart, *The Promise of Power*, 1933.
Chase, Stuart, *Technocracy: An Interpretation*, 1933.
Committee of the Progressive Education Association on Social and Economic Problems, *A Call to the Teachers of the Nation*, 1933.
Counts, George S., *Dare the School Build a New Social Order?* 1933.
Lippmann, Walter, *A New Social Order*, 1933.
Melvin, A. Gordon, *Education for a New Era: A Call to Leadership*, 1933.

League for Industrial Democracy, New York:
  Chase, Stuart, *Poor Old Competition*, 1932.
  Chase, Stuart, *Waste and the Machine Age*, 1931.
  Epstein, Abraham, *Old Age Security*, 1930.
  Laidler, Harry W., *How America Lives*, 1932.

Modern Problems Series, American Education Press, Inc., Columbus, Ohio:
  Bagley, William C., *Crime: Its Prevalence, Causes, and Costs*, 1932.
  Clark, Harold F., *Recent Economic Changes and Their Meaning*, 1933.
  Leech, Harper, *Plenty: Can Man Have It Without Sharing It?* 1933.
  Stanley, G. N., and Sayre, H. M., *Economic Planning: Can Depressions Be Abolished?* 1933.
  Wolff, Gertrude, *Modern Economic Systems: Socialism, Communism, Fascism, Capitalism.*

National Crisis Series, Bureau of Publications, Teachers College, Columbia University, New York:
  Everett, Samuel, and Marshall, Leon C., *Uncle Sam's Relation to Industry and Railroads*, 1934.
  Mendenhall, James E., and Marshall, Leon C., *Our Government's Relation to Money, Banking, and Securities*, 1934.

University of Chicago Press, Chicago, Illinois:
  Burke, Thomas E., *A Hundred Years of the Labor Movement*, 1932.
  Lewis, John L., *Wages and Hours*, 1932.
  Morrison, Frank, *The Closed and Open Shop*, 1932.

THE NATURE OF THE INDIVIDUAL AND THE LEARNING PROCESS

Allport, Floyd H., *Social Psychology*, Houghton Mifflin Co., Boston, 1924.
American Educational Research Association, *Review of Educational Research, Psychology of the School Subjects*, National Education Association, Washington, D. C., December, 1931.
American Educational Research Association, *Review of Educational Research, Psychology of Learning, General Methods of Teaching and Supervision*, National Education Association, Washington, D. C., October, 1933.
Bode, Boyd H., *Conflicting Psychologies of Learning*, D. C. Heath & Co., Boston, 1929.
Book, W. F., *Economy and Technique of Learning*, D. C. Heath & Co., Boston, 1932.
Burnham, W. H., *The Normal Mind*, D. Appleton & Co., New York, 1924.

Burnham, W. H., *The Wholesome Personality: A Contribution to Mental Hygiene*, D. Appleton & Co., New York, 1932.

Cameron, E. H., *Psychology and Recent Movements in Education*, University of Illinois Bulletin No. 54, Urbana, Ill., 1931.

Charters, W. W., *The Teaching of Ideals*, The Macmillan Co., New York, 1927.

Dewey, John, *The Child and the Curriculum*, University of Chicago Press, Chicago, 1902.

Dewey, John, *Human Nature and Conduct*, Henry Holt & Co., New York, 1922.

Dewey, John, *Interest and Effort in Education*, Houghton Mifflin Co., Boston, 1913.

Fletcher, John M., *Psychology in Education*, Doubleday Doran and Co., Garden City, N. Y., 1934.

Fryer, Douglas, *The Measurement of Interests in Relation to Human Adjustment*, Henry Holt & Co., New York, 1931.

Glover, Katherine, and Dewey, Evelyn, *Children of the New Day*, D. Appleton-Century Co., New York, 1934.

Hollingworth, H. L., *Educational Psychology*, D. Appleton Co., New York, 1933.

Lichtenstein, Arthur, *Can Attitudes Be Taught?* Johns Hopkins University Studies in Education, No. 21, Johns Hopkins Press, Baltimore, Md., 1934.

National Education Association, *Department of Classroom Teachers Second Yearbook*, "The Child and His Teacher," Washington, D. C., 1927.

Ogden, Robert M., and Freeman, F. S., *Psychology and Education*, Harcourt, Brace and Co., New York, 1932.

Pressey, Sidney L., *Psychology and the New Education*, Harper and Brothers, New York, 1933.

Ragsdale, Clarence E., *Modern Psychologies and Education*, The Macmillan Co., New York, 1932.

Raup, Robert B., *Complacency: The Foundation of Human Behavior*, The Macmillan Co., New York, 1925.

Robinson, James Harvey, *The Mind in the Making*, Harper and Brothers, New York, 1921.

Symonds, Percival M., *Psychological Diagnosis in Social Adjustment*, American Book Co., New York, 1934.

Thorndike, Edward L., and Gates, A. I., *Elementary Principles of Education*, The Macmillan Co., New York, 1929.

Thorndike, Edward L., *Human Learning*, Century Co., New York, 1931.

Troland, Leonard T., *The Fundamentals of Human Motivation*, D. Van Nostrand Co., New York, 1928.

ORGANIZING INSTRUCTION

American Educational Research Association, *Review of Educational Research, Special Methods in the Elementary School*, National Education Association, Washington, D. C., October, 1931.

American Educational Research Association, *Review of Educational Research, Special Methods on the High School Level*, National Education Association, Washington, D. C., February, 1932.

Arkansas, *Tentative Units for High School Level in Social Science, English, Home Economics, and Natural Science*, The Arkansas Cooperative Program to Improve Instruction, Supplementary Bulletin, Curriculum Laboratory, College of Education, University of Arkansas, Fayetteville, Ark., 1934.

Baker, Clara B., Chairman, *Curriculum Records of the Children's School*, Bureau of Publications, National College of Education, Evanston, Ill., 1932.

Bibliography: The Unit of Work, Curriculum Laboratory, School of Education, Western Reserve University, Cleveland, Ohio.

Bibliography of Experimental Curricula, Curriculum Laboratory, School of Education, Western Reserve University, Cleveland.

Borgeson, F. C., *Elementary School Life Activities*, two volumes, A. S. Barnes & Co., New York, 1931.

Bourne, W. R., *A Method of Evaluating Secondary School Units*, Contribution to Education No. 16, George Peabody College for Teachers, Nashville, Tenn., 1925.

Bruner, H. B., *The Place of Units in Course of Study Construction*, South Dakota Curriculum Revision Program, Bulletin No. 2, State Department of Education, Pierre, South Dakota, 1930.

California Curriculum Commission, *Teachers' Guide to Child Development*, Bulletin No. 26, United States Office of Education, Washington, D. C., 1930.

Carey, Alice E.; Hanna, Paul R.; and Meriam, Junius L., *Catalog of Units of Work, Activities, Projects, Themes, etc., to 1932*, Bureau of Publications, Teachers College, Columbia University, New York, 1932.

Charters, W. W., *The Stephens College Program for the Education of Women*, Bulletin No. 4, Stephens College, Columbia, Mo., December, 1933.

Clouser, Lucy W.; Robinson, Wilma J.; and Neely, D. L., *Educative Experiences through Activity Units*, Lyons & Carnahan, Chicago, 1932.

Clouser, Lucy W., and Millikan, C. E., *Kindergarten-Primary Activities Based on Community Life*, The Macmillan Co., New York, 1929.

Coleman, Satis N., *A Children's Symphony*, Bureau of Publications, Teachers College, Columbia University, New York, 1931.

Collings, Ellsworth, *An Experiment with a Project Curriculum*, The Macmillan Co., New York, 1923.

Compton, *Pictured Teaching-Unit Materials*, F. E. Compton & Co., Chicago.

Criteria of a Unit of Work, Curriculum Laboratory, School of Education, Western Reserve University, Cleveland, Ohio.

Curtis, Nell C., *Boats (Adventures in Boat Making)*, Rand McNally & Co., Chicago, 1927.

Docking, Doris E., *The Hudson River Valley*, A Horace Mann Teaching Unit, Bureau of Publications, Teachers College, Columbia University, New York, 1932.

Durost, Walter Nelson, *Children's Collecting Activities Related to Social Factors*, Contributions to Education No. 535, Bureau of Publications, Teachers College, Columbia University, New York, 1932.

Functional Organization of Formal Subjects, Curriculum Laboratory, School of Education, Western Reserve University, Cleveland, Ohio.

Garrison, N. L., *The Technique and Administration of Teaching*, American Book Co., New York, 1933.

Gustin, Margaret, and Hayes, Margaret L., *Activities in the Public School*, University of North Carolina Press, Chapel Hill, N. C., 1934.

Harap, Henry, *How to Construct a Unit of Work*, Bulletin No. 17, Curriculum Laboratory, School of Education, Western Reserve University, Cleveland, Ohio, November 30, 1931.

Heaton, Kenneth L., *Character Emphasis in Education*, University of Chicago Press, Chicago, 1933.

Hosic, J. F., and Chase, S. E., *Brief Guide to the Project Method*, World Book Co., Yonkers-on-Hudson, N. Y., 1924.

Houston, *The Scope of the Curriculum, Kindergarten and Grades One and Two*, Curriculum Bulletin No. 1, Houston Public Schools, Houston, Tex., 1933.

Houston, *The Scope of the Curriculum, Grades Three, Four, and Five*, Curriculum Bulletin No. 2, Houston Public Schools, Houston, Tex., 1933.

Houston, *The Scope of the Curriculum, Grades Six, Seven, and Eight*, Curriculum Bulletin No. 3, Houston Public Schools, Houston, Tex., 1933.

Keelor, Katherine L., *Curriculum Studies in the Second Grade*, Bureau of Publications, Teachers College, Columbia University, New York, 1925.

Keelor, Katherine L., *Working with Electricity*, The Macmillan Co., New York, 1929.

Kilpatrick, William H., *Foundations of Method*, The Macmillan Co., New York, 1925.

Knudsen, Charles W., *Evaluation and Improvement of Teaching*, Doubleday, Doran & Co., Garden City, N. Y., 1932.

Lane, Robert H., *A Teacher's Guide Book to the Activity Program*, The Macmillan Co., New York, 1932.

Lewis, Mary, *An Adventure with Children*, The Macmillan Co., New York, 1928.

Lincoln Elementary School Staff, *Curriculum Making in an Elementary School*, Ginn & Co., Boston, Mass., 1927.

Lincoln School, *Units of Work*, Bureau of Publications, Teachers College, Columbia University, New York:

  Barnes, Emily Ann, and Young, Bess M., *Children and Architecture*, 1932.

  Baxter, Tompsie, and Young, Bess M., *Ships and Navigation*, 1933.

  Eakright, Jessie B., and Young, Bess M., *Adventuring with Toys*, *Activities of a Fourth Grade*, 1933.

  Hughes, Avah W., *Carrying the Mail—A Second Grade's Experiences*, 1933.

  Keelor, Katherine L., and Sweet, Mayme, *Indian Life and the Dutch Colonial Settlement—Third Grade*, 1931.

  Sweeney, F. G.; Barry, E. F.; Schoelkopf, A. E., *Western Youth Meets Eastern Culture*, 1932.

  Wright, Lula E., *A First Grade at Work*, 1932.

Mapes, Charlotte, and Harap, Henry, *Making Household Preparations*, Bulletin No. 36, Curriculum Laboratory, School of Education, Western Reserve University, Cleveland, Ohio, October 15, 1934.

Mapes, Charlotte, and Harap, Henry, *Six Activity Units in Fractions*, Bulletin No. 33, Curriculum Laboratory, School of Education, Western Reserve University, Cleveland, Ohio, December 1, 1933.

McCall, William A., Editor, *Teachers' Lesson Unit Series*, Bureau of Publications, Teachers College, Columbia University, New York, 1931–1934.

Melvin, A. Gordon, *The Technique of Progressive Teaching*, John Day Co., New York, 1932.

Monroe, W. S., *Directing Learning in the High School*, Doubleday, Doran & Co., Garden City, N. Y., 1927.

Morrison, Henry C., *The Practice of Teaching in the Secondary School*, Revised Edition, University of Chicago Press, Chicago, 1931.

Mossman, Lois Coffey, *Principles of Teaching and Learning in the Elementary School*, Houghton Mifflin Co., Boston, 1929.

National Education Association, *Department of Classroom Teachers Fourth Yearbook*, "Creative Teaching and Professional Problems," Washington, D. C., 1929.

National Education Association, *Department of Classroom Teachers Fifth Yearbook*, "Teaching as a Creative Art," Washington, D. C., 1930.

National Education Association, *Department of Classroom Teachers Seventh Yearbook*, "The Classroom Teacher and Character Education," Washington, D. C., 1932.

Porter, Martha Peck, *The Teacher in the New School*, World Book Co., Yonkers-on-Hudson, N. Y., 1930.

Pratt, Caroline, and Stanton, Jessie, *Before Books*, Greenberg Publishing Co., New York, 1926.

Pratt, Caroline, and Wright, Lula E., *Experimental Practice in the City and Country School*, E. P. Dutton & Co., New York, 1924.

Retan, George A., *Management and Teaching Technique in the Elementary School*, Prentice-Hall, New York, 1933.

Reynolds, R. G., and Harden, M., *The Horace Mann Plan for Teaching Children*, Bureau of Publications, Teachers College, Columbia University, New York, 1932.

Ruediger, William C., *Teaching Procedures*, Houghton Mifflin Co., Boston, 1932.

Rugg, Harold O., and Shumaker, Ann, *The Child-Centered School*, World Book Co., Yonkers-on-Hudson, N. Y., 1928.

Salisbury, Ethel I., *An Activity Curriculum*, Harr-Wagner, Chicago, 1924.

Stevens, Marion P., *The Activities Curriculum in the Primary Grades*, D. C. Heath & Co., Boston, 1931.

Stormzand, Martin J., and McKee, Jane W., *The Progressive Primary Teacher*, Houghton Mifflin Co., Boston, 1928.

Stott, Lelia V., *Adventuring with Twelve-Year-Olds* (Caroline Pratt, Editor), Greenberg Publishing Co., New York, 1927.

University of Virginia, *The Evolution of the Unit Method of Teaching*, Secondary Education in Virginia, Record Extension Series, Extension Division, University of Virginia, Charlottesville, Va., 1934.

Waddell, Charles W.; Seeds, Corinne; and White, Natalie, *Major Units in the Social Studies*, John Day Co., New York, 1932.

Waples, Douglas, *Procedures in High-School Teaching*, The Macmillan Co., New York, 1924.

Waples, Douglas, and Stone, C. A., *The Teaching Unit: A Type Study*, D. Appleton & Co., New York, 1929.

Wells, Margaret E., *A Project Curriculum*, J. B. Lippincott Co., Philadelphia, 1921.

SELECTING LEARNING EQUIPMENT AND SUPPLIES

Bibliography of Learning Equipment and Supplies for All Subjects, Curriculum Laboratory, School of Education, Western Reserve University, Cleveland, Ohio.

Brown, Henry E., and Bird, Joy, *Motion Pictures and Lantern Slides for Elementary Visual Education*, Bureau of Publications, Teachers College, Columbia University, New York, 1931.

Fowlkes, John Guy, *Evaluating School Textbooks*, Silver Burdett & Co., New York, 1923.

Franzen, R. H., and Knight, F. B., *Textbook Selection*, Warwick & York, Baltimore, Md., 1922.

Fuller, Florence D., *Scientific Evaluation of Textbooks*, Houghton Mifflin Co., Boston, 1928.

Jensen, Frank A., *Current Procedure in Selecting Textbooks*, J. B. Lippincott Co., Philadelphia, 1931.

Knox, Rose B., *School Activities and Equipment*, Houghton Mifflin Co., Boston, 1927.

Long, Frank N., *Desirable Physical Facilities for an Activity Program*, Contributions to Education No. 593, Teachers College, Columbia University, New York, 1933.

Maxwell, Charles R., *The Selection of Textbooks*, Houghton Mifflin Co., Boston, 1921.

National Society for the Study of Education, Nineteenth Yearbook, Part I, "New Materials of Instruction," Public School Publishing Co., Bloomington, Ill., 1920.

National Society for the Study of Education, Twentieth Yearbook, Part I, "New Materials of Instruction," Public School Publishing Co., Bloomington, Ill., 1921.

National Society for the Study of Education, Thirtieth Yearbook, Part II, "The Textbook in American Education," Public School Publishing Co., Bloomington, Ill., 1931.

Steele, R. M., "Equipment Apparatus Supplies Needed for Classroom Instruction," National Education Association, Department of Superintendence *Official Report*, Washington, D. C., 1930.

Stevens, Marion Paine, *Primary Equipment*, Ethical Culture School, 33 Central Park West, New York, 1931.

Taylor, Robert B., *Principles of School Supply Management*, Bureau of Publications, Teachers College, Columbia University, New York, 1926.

Windes, E. E., Compiler, *Government Publications Useful to Teachers*, United States Office of Education Bulletin No. 23, Government Printing Office, Washington, D. C., 1924.

Wood, Benjamin D., and Freeman, F. N., *Motion Pictures in the Classroom*, Houghton Mifflin Co., Boston, 1929.

Wynne, John P., and Holton, Samuel M., Jr., *Source Materials on the Learning-Teaching Unit*, Farmville Herald Co., Farmville, Va., 1934.

CONSTRUCTION AND EVALUATION OF COURSES OF STUDY

Bibliography: How to Appraise a Course of Study, Curriculum Laboratory, School of Education, Western Reserve University, Cleveland, Ohio.

Harap, Henry, "A Critique of Public School Courses of Study, 1928–1929," *Journal of Educational Research*, 21:109–19, February, 1930.

Harap, Henry, and Bayne, Alice J., "A Critical Survey of Public School Courses of Study Published 1929 to 1931," *Journal of Educational Research*, 26:46–55, 105–09, September and October, 1932.

Langvick, Mina M., *Current Practices in the Construction of State Courses of Study*, United States Office of Education Bulletin No. 4, Government Printing Office, Washington, D. C., 1931.

Monroe, Walter S., "Making a Course of Study," *Educational Research Circular* No. 35, University of Illinois, Urbana, Ill., September 19, 1925.

Oakland Public Schools, *Handbook for Course of Study Committees*, Board of Education, Oakland, California, June, 1928.

Reinoehl, Charles M., *Analytical Survey of State Courses of Study for Rural Elementary Schools*, United States Office of Education Bulletin No. 42, Government Printing Office, Washington, D. C., 1922.

Stratemeyer, Florence B., and Bruner, Herbert B., *Rating Elementary School Courses of Study*, Bureau of Publications, Teachers College, Columbia University, New York, 1926.

United States Office of Education, *Characteristic Features of Recent Superior State Courses of Study*, Rural School Leaflet No. 41, Government Printing Printing Office, Washington, D. C., 1926.

Outstanding Courses of Study

In securing courses of study it is advisable to obtain price lists from those states and cities having outstanding courses. The following states and cities are suggested as among those having recently developed such courses.

State

Alabama, State Board of Education, Montgomery
Florida, Board of Public Instruction, Tallahassee
Idaho, State Board of Education, Boise
Iowa, Department of Public Instruction, Des Moines
Minnesota, State Board of Education, St. Paul
Missouri, State Department of Education, Jefferson City
New Jersey, State Board of Education, Trenton
South Dakota, Department of Public Education, Pierre
Virginia, State Board of Education, Richmond
West Virginia, State Board of Education, Charleston

City and County

Ann Arbor, Michigan, Office of Superintendent
Baltimore County, Baltimore, Maryland, Office of Superintendent
Cleveland Heights, Ohio, Office of Superintendent
Dayton, Ohio, Office of Superintendent
Denver, Colorado, Office of Superintendent
Forth Worth, Texas, Office of Superintendent
Grand Rapids, Michigan, Office of Superintendent
Houston, Texas, Office of Superintendent
Long Beach, California, Office of Superintendent
Los Angeles County, Los Angeles, California, Office of Superintendent
Muncie, Indiana, Office of Superintendent
Pasadena, California, Office of Superintendent
Raleigh, North Carolina, Office of Superintendent
Sacramento, California, Office of Superintendent
San Antonio, Texas, Office of Superintendent
Seattle, Washington, Office of Superintendent
St. Louis, Missouri, Office of Superintendent

Lists of Courses of Study

Bruner, Herbert B., *Outstanding Courses of Study*, News Bulletin, Society for Curriculum Study, Western Reserve University, Cleveland, Ohio, January 15, 1935.
United States Office of Education, *Recent Courses of Study for Elemen-*

tary and Secondary Schools, Government Printing Office, Washington, D. C., 1933.

ART

Classroom Teacher, The; Volume IV, "Primary Art"; Volume VII, "Art for Intermediate Grades"; Volume XI, "Junior High School Art"; The Classroom Teacher, Inc., Chicago, 1927–28.

Craven, Thomas, *Men of Art,* Simon and Schuster, New York, 1931.

Crossman, A. W., *Changing Conceptions in Art Education,* Master's Thesis, Ohio State University, Columbus, Ohio, 1931.

Dewey, John, *Art as Experience,* Minton, Balch and Co., New York, 1934.

Dewey, John, and others, *Art and Education,* The Barnes Foundation Press, Merion, Pa., 1929.

Dobbs, Ella Victoria, *First Steps in Art and Handwork,* The Macmillan Co., New York, 1932.

Dobbs, Ella Victoria, *Primary Handwork,* The Macmillan Co., New York, 1914.

Eng, Helga, *Psychology of Children's Drawings from the First Stroke to the Coloured Drawing,* Harcourt, Brace and Co., New York, 1931.

Farnum, Royal B., *Education Through Pictures,* The Art Extension Press, Inc., Westport, Conn., 1931.

Federal Board for Vocational Education, *Teaching of Art Related to the Home,* Home Economics Series No. 13, Bulletin No. 156, Government Printing Office, Washington, D. C., 1931.

Federated Council on Art Education, *Report of the Committee on Elementary School Art,* American Federation of Arts, Barr Building, Farragut Square, Washington, D. C., 1926.

Federated Council on Art Education, *Report of the President,* American Federation of Arts, Barr Building, Farragut Square, Washington, D. C., 1926.

Geddes, Norman Bel, *Horizons,* Little, Brown and Co., Boston, 1932.

Glace, Margaret F. Schaeffer, *Art in the Integrated Program,* Master's Thesis, George Peabody College, Nashville, Tenn., 1934.

Holmes, Sir Charles John, *A Grammar of the Arts,* The Macmillan Co., New York, 1932.

Keppel, Frederick P., and Duffus, R. L., *The Arts in American Life,* Recent Social Trends Monographs, McGraw-Hill Book Co., New York, 1933.

Kirby, C. Valentine, *The Business of Teaching and Supervising the Arts,* Abbott Educational Co., 1603 Michigan Avenue, Chicago, 1927.

Klar, W. H.; Winslow, L. L.; and Kirby, C. V., *Art Education in Principle and Practice*, Milton Bradley Co., Springfield, Mass., 1933.

Mathias, Margaret E., *Art in the Elementary School*, Charles Scribner's Sons, New York, 1929.

Mathias, Margaret E., *The Beginnings of Art in the Public Schools*, Charles Scribner's Sons, New York, 1924.

Mathias, Margaret E., *The Teaching of Art*, Charles Scribner's Sons, New York, 1932.

Mellinger, Bonnie E., *Children's Interests in Pictures*, Contributions to Education No. 516, Bureau of Publications, Teachers College, Columbia University, New York, 1932.

Mendenhall, James E., and Mendenhall, Marcia E., *The Influence of Familiarity Upon Children's Preferences for Pictures and Poems*, Bureau of Publications, Teachers College, Columbia University, New York, 1933.

Mumford, Lewis, *Sticks and Stones: A Study of American Architecture and Civilization*, Boni and Liveright, New York, 1924.

Nyquist, Frederick V., *Art Education in Elementary Schools*, Warwick & York, Baltimore, Md., 1929.

Opdyke, George H., *Art and Nature Appreciation*, The Macmillan Co., New York, 1932.

Pelikan, Alfred G., *The Art of the Child*, Bruce Publishing Co., Milwaukee, Wis., 1931.

Perry, Evadna K., *Art Adventures with Discarded Materials*, Wetzel Publishing Co., Inc., 336 S. Broadway, Los Angeles, Cal., 1933.

Pierce, Anne E., and Hilpert, Robert, *Instruction in Music and Art*, National Survey of Secondary Education, Bulletin No. 17, Monograph No. 25, Government Printing Office, Washington, D. C., 1932.

Rank, Otto, *Art and Artists: Creative Urge and Personality Development*, Alfred A. Knopf, New York, 1932.

Richards, Charles R., *Art In Industry*, Report National Society for Vocational Education, The Macmillan Co., New York, 1922.

Tannahill, Sallie B., *Fine Arts for Public School Administrators*, Bureau of Publications, Teachers College, Columbia University, New York, 1932.

Todd, Jessie, and Gale, Ann Van Nice, *Enjoyment and Use of Art in the Elementary School*, University of Chicago Press, Chicago, 1933.

United States Office of Education, *Art Education in the United States*, Bulletin No. 38, Government Printing Office, Washington, D. C., 1925.

Wall, Ernest A., *Aesthetic Sense and Education*, Doctor's Thesis, New York University, New York, 1931.

Whitford, W. G., *An Introduction to Art Education*, D. Appleton & Co., New York, 1929.

Winslow, Leon L., *The Organization and Teaching of Art*, Warwick & York, Baltimore, Md., 1928.

COMMERCIAL EDUCATION

Blackstone, E. G., collector, *Research Studies in Commercial Education*, Iowa Research Conference on Commercial Education, University of Iowa, Iowa City, Iowa, 1926.

California State Department of Education, *Aims and Desired Outcomes of Typewriting Instruction in California Secondary Schools*, Bulletin No. 8, State Department of Education, Sacramento, Cal., 1933.

Charters, W. W., and Whitley, Isadore B., *Analysis of Secretarial Duties and Traits*, Williams and Wilkins Co., Baltimore, Md., 1924.

Commercial Education Leaflets, Government Printing Office, Washington, D. C.

Connor, W. L., and Jones, L. L., *A Scientific Study in Curriculum Making for Junior Courses in Business Education*, Gregg Publishing Co., New York, 1929.

Eastern Commercial Teachers Association, Second Yearbook, "Curriculum Making in Business Education," Eastern Commercial Teachers Association, 155 W. 65th St., New York, 1929.

Iowa University Research Studies in Commercial Education, University of Iowa Studies in Education, Volume 8, No. 3, University of Iowa, Iowa City, Ia., 1932.

Kitson, Harry D., *Commercial Education in Secondary Schools*, Ginn and Co., Boston, 1929.

Nichols, Frederick G., *Commercial Education in the High School*, D. Appleton-Century Co., New York, 1933.

Nichols, Frederick G., and others, *A New Conception of Office Practice Based on an Investigation of Actual Office Requirements*, Harvard University Press, Cambridge, Mass., 1927.

Wisconsin State-Wide Commercial Education Survey, Bulletin No. 158, State Teachers College, Whitewater, Wis., 1931.

Woodring, Maxie N., and Harold, Gilbert, *Enriched Teaching of Commercial Subjects in the High School*, Bureau of Publications, Teachers College, Columbia University, New York, 1930.

FOREIGN LANGUAGES

American Classical League, *The Classical Investigation*, Part I, General Report, Princeton University Press, Princeton, N. J., 1924.

Bagster-Collins, E. W., and others, *Studies in Modern Language Teaching*, Publications of the American and Canadian Committees on Modern Languages, Volume XVII, The Macmillan Co., New York, 1930.

Baker, Florence M., *The Teaching of French*, Houghton Mifflin Co., Boston, 1931.

Buchanan, Milton A., compiler, *A Graded Spanish Word Book*, Publications of the American and Canadian Committees on Modern Languages, Volume III, University of Toronto Press, Toronto, Canada, 1927.

Buchanan, Milton A., and MacPhee, E. D., *An Annotated Bibliography of Modern Language Methodology*, Publications of the American and Canadian Committees on Modern Languages, Volume VIII, University of Toronto Press, Toronto, Canada, 1928.

Buswell, G. T., *A Laboratory Study of the Reading of Modern Foreign Languages*, Publications of the American and Canadian Committees on Modern Languages, Volume II, The Macmillan Co., New York, 1927.

Cheydleur, Frederic D., compiler and editor, *French Idiom List*, Publications of the American and Canadian Committees on Modern Languages, Volume XVI, The Macmillan Co., New York, 1929.

Cole, Robert D., *Modern Foreign Languages and Their Teaching*, D. Appleton & Co., New York, 1931.

Coleman, Algernon, *Experiments and Studies in Modern Language Teaching*, Compiled for the Committee on Modern Language Teaching, University of Chicago Press, Chicago, 1934.

Coleman, Algernon, *The Teaching of Modern Foreign Languages in the United States*, Publications of the American and Canadian Committees on Modern Languages, Volume XII, The Macmillan Co., New York, 1929.

Eddy, Helen M., *Instruction in Foreign Languages*, National Survey of Secondary Education, Bulletin No. 17, Monograph No. 24, Government Printing Office, Washington, D. C., 1932.

Fife, Robert Herndon, *A Summary of Reports on the Modern Foreign Languages*, Issued by the Modern Foreign Language Study and the Canadian Committee on Modern Languages, with an Index to the Reports, The Macmillan Co., New York, 1931.

Gray, Mason De Witt, *The Teaching of Latin*, D. Appleton & Co., New York, 1929.

Handschin, Charles H., *Methods of Teaching Modern Languages*, World Book Co., Yonkers-on-Hudson, N. Y., 1923.

Hauch, Edward F., compiler, *German Idiom List*, Publications of the American and Canadian Committees on Modern Languages, Volume X, The Macmillan Co., New York, 1929.

Henmon, V. A. C., *Achievement Tests in the Modern Foreign Languages*, Publications of the American and Canadian Committees on Modern Lauguages, Volume V, The Macmillan Co., New York, 1929.

Henmon, V. A. C., and others, *Prognosis Tests in the Modern Foreign Languages*, Publications of the American and Canadian Committees on Modern Languages, Volume XIV, The Macmillan Co., New York, 1929.

Huse, Howard R., *The Psychology of Foreign Language Study*, University of North Carolina Press, Chapel Hill, N. C., 1931.

Keniston, Hayward, compiler, *Spanish Idiom List*, Publications of the American and Canadian Committees on Modern Languages, Volume XI, The Macmillan Co., New York, 1929.

Modern Language Association, *Report of Committee of Twelve*, D. C. Heath & Co., Boston, 1910.

Modern Language Instruction in Canada, Publications of the American and Canadian Committees on Modern Languages, Volumes VI and VII, University of Toronto Press, Toronto, Canada.

Morgan, B. Q., edited and arranged by, *German Frequency Word Book*, Publications of the American and Canadian Committees on Modern Languages, Volume IX, The Macmillan Co., New York, 1928.

O'Shea, M. V., *The Reading of Modern Foreign Language*, United States Office of Education, Bulletin No. 16, Government Printing Office, Washington, D. C., 1927.

Purin, C. M., *The Training of Teachers of the Modern Foreign Languages*, Publications of the American and Canadian Committees on Modern Languages, Volume XIII, The Macmillan Co., New York, 1929.

Vander Beke, George E., compiler, *French Word Book*, Publications of the American and Canadian Committees on Modern Languages, Volume XV, The Macmillan Co., New York, 1929.

West, Michael, *Language in Education*, Longmans, Green & Co., New York, 1929.

Wheeler, C. A., and others, compilers, *Enrollment in the Foreign Languages in Secondary Schools and Colleges of the United States*, Publications of the American and Canadian Committees on Modern Languages, Volume IV, The Macmillan Co., New York, 1928.

Wood, Ben D., *New York Experiments with New-Type Modern Lan-*

guage Tests, Publications of the American and Canadian Committees on Modern Languages, Volume I, The Macmillan Co., New York, 1927.

Woodring, Maxie N., and Sabin, Frances E., *Enriched Teaching of Latin in the High School*, Bureau of Publications, Teachers College, Columbia University, New York, 1930.

HEALTH AND PHYSICAL EDUCATION

American Child Health Association, *Principles and Practices of Health Education*, American Child Health Association, 450 Seventh Ave., New York, 1930.

American Child Health Association, School Health Research Monographs:

Number   I: Health Education Tests
Number   II: Physical Measures of Growth and Nutrition
Number III: Public Health Aspects of Dental Decay in Children
Number   IV: Influence of Social and Economic Factors on the Health of the School Child
Number   V: An Evaluation of School Health Procedures

American Physical Education Association, Committee on Dancing, *Dancing in the Elementary Schools*, A. S. Barnes & Co., Inc., New York, 1933.

Bache, Louise F., *Health Education in An American City: An Account of a Five-Year Program in Syracuse, New York*, Doubleday, Doran & Co., Garden City, N. Y., 1934.

Brammell, P. Roy, *Health Work and Physical Education*, National Survey of Secondary Education, Bulletin No. 17, Monograph No. 28, Government Printing Office, Washington, D. C., 1932.

Brammell, P. Roy, *Intramural and Interscholastic Athletics*, National Survey of Secondary Education, Bulletin No. 17, Monograph No. 27, Government Printing Office, Washington, D. C., 1932.

Brock, George Delangacy, *Health Through Projects*, A. S. Barnes & Co., New York, 1931.

Cairns, Laura, *A Scientific Basis for Health Instruction in Public Schools*, University of California, Berkeley, Cal., 1930.

Caldwell, Otis W.; Skinner, C. E.; and Tietz, J. W., *Biological Foundations of Education*, Ginn and Co., Boston, 1931.

Davis, Elwood C., *Methods and Techniques Used in Surveying Health and Physical Education in City Schools*, Contributions to Education No. 515, Bureau of Publications, Teachers College, Columbia University, New York, 1932.

Gillett, Lucy H., and Rice, Penelope B., *Influence of Education on the Food Habits of Some New York City Families*, New York Association for Improving the Condition of the Poor, 105 East 22nd St., New York, 1931.

Horrigan, Olive K., *Creative Activities in Physical Education*, A. S. Barnes & Co., New York, 1929.

Hussey, Marguerite M., *Principles and Methods of Teaching Health* Doctor's Thesis, New York University, New York, 1930.

Kerr, James, *The Fundamentals of School Health*, The Macmillan Co., New York, 1927.

Laton, Anita Duncan, *The Psychology of Learning Applied to Health Education Through Biology*, Contributions to Education No. 344, Bureau of Publications, Teachers College, Columbia University, New York, 1929.

LaSalle, Dorothy, *Play Activities for Elementary Schools—Grades One to Eight*, A. S. Barnes & Co., New York, 1926.

Lee, Joseph, *Play in Education*, The Macmillan Co., New York, 1915.

Lloyd, Frank S., *Safety in Physical Education in Secondary Schools*, National Bureau of Casualty and Surety Underwriters, New York, 1933.

Lowman, Charles; Colestock, C.; and Cooper, H., *Corrective Physical Education for Groups*, A. S. Barnes & Co., New York, 1928.

Lehman, Harvey C., "Play Activities of Persons of Different Ages," Chapter XIV, *Curriculum Investigations*, University of Chicago Press, Chicago, 1926.

Lehman, Harvey C., and Witty, P. A., *The Psychology of Play Activities*, A. S. Barnes & Co., New York, 1927.

Matthias, Eugen, *The Deeper Meaning of Physical Education*, A. S. Barnes & Co., New York, 1929.

Nash, Jay B., *The Administration of Physical Education, with Special Reference to Public Schools*, A. S. Barnes & Co., New York, 1931.

Nash, Jay B., editor, *Character Education Through Physical Education*, A. S. Barnes & Co., New York, 1932.

Objectives of a Course of Study in Health for High School Girls, Curriculum Laboratory, School of Education, Western Reserve University, Cleveland, Ohio.

Rathbone, Josephine L., *Corrective Physical Education*, W. B. Saunders Co., Philadelphia, 1934.

Rathbone, Josephine L., and others, *Foundations of Health*, Houghton Mifflin Co., Boston, 1932.

Rhoton, Paul, *Health Misconceptions of Prospective Teachers*, Pennsylvania State Studies in Education No 5, Pennsylvania State College, State College, Pa., 1932.

Rogers, F. R., *Educational Objectives of Physical Activity*, A. S. Barnes & Co., New York, 1929.

Spencer, Mary Elizabeth, *Health Education for Teachers: A Critical Study of the Pre-Service Preparation of Classroom Teachers for the School Health Program*, Contributions to Education No. 589, Bureau of Publications, Teachers College, Columbia University, New York, 1933.

Stafford, George T., *Preventive and Corrective Physical Education*, A. S. Barnes & Co., New York, 1928.

White House Conference on Child Health and Protection, Committee on the School Child, *School Health Program*, The Century Co., New York, 1930.

Williams, Jesse F., *Principles of Physical Education*, W. B. Saunders Co., Philadelphia, 1927.

Williams, Jesse F., and Brownell, C. L., *Administration of Health and Physical Education*, W. B. Saunders Co., Philadelphia, 1934.

Williams, Jesse F., and Brownell, C. L., *Health and Physical Education for Public School Administrators*, Bureau of Publications, Teachers College, Columbia University, New York, 1930.

Wood, T. D., and Cassidy, R. F., *The New Physical Education*, The Macmillan Co., New York, 1927.

Woodring, Maxie N., and Schwendener, Norma, *Enriched Teaching of Physical Education in the High School*, Bureau of Publications, Teachers College, Columbia University, New York, 1929.

World Federation of Education Association, *School Health Programs from Many Lands*, American Child Health Association, 450 Seventh Avenue, New York, 1928.

HOME ECONOMICS

Amidon, Edna P., and McKibbon, H. B., *The Teaching of Science Related to the Home*, Federal Board for Vocational Education, Bulletin No. 158, Government Printing Office, Washington, D. C., 1931.

Bauer, Catherine, *Modern Housing*, Houghton Mifflin Co., Boston, 1934.

Brodshang, Melvin, *Buildings and Equipment for Home Economics in Secondary Schools*, Contributions to Education No. 502, Bureau of Publications, Teachers College, Columbia University, New York, 1932.

Dyer, Annie R., *Administration of Home Economics in City Schools*, Contributions to Education No. 318, Bureau of Publications, Teachers College, Columbia University, New York, 1928.

Dyer, Annie R., *The Placement of Home Economics Content in Junior and Senior High Schools,* Home Economics Curriculum Study No. 1, Bureau of Publications, Teachers College, Columbia University, New York, 1927.

Judy, Helen E., *Trends and Needs in Home Management,* Contributions to Education No. 365, Bureau of Publications, Teachers College, Columbia University, New York, 1929.

Lindquist, Ruth, *The Family in the Present Social Order,* University of North Carolina Press, Chapel Hill, N. C., 1931.

Phillips, Velma, *Evidence of the Need of Education for Efficient Purchasing, Contributions to Education* No. 447, Bureau of Publication, Teachers College, Columbia University, New York, 1931.

President's Conference on Home Building and Home Ownership, *Household Management and Kitchens,* National Capital Press, Washington, D. C., 1932.

Russell, R. D.; McFarland, Muriel; and Williamson, Mary, *Summary of Studies in Home Economics,* State Board for Vocational Education, Boise, Idaho, 1932.

Williamson, Maude, and Lyle, Mary Stewart, *Homemaking Education in the High School,* D. Appleton-Century Co., New York, 1934.

Wilson, Mary A., *A Study of Homemaking Activities of Girls in Rural Mississippi,* Bulletin No. 65, State Board for Vocational Education, Jackson, Miss., 1931.

Winchell, Cora Marguerite, *Home Economics for Public School Administrators,* Bureau of Publications, Teachers College, Columbia University, New York, 1931.

INDUSTRIAL ARTS

Bawden, William T., and others, *Industrial Arts in Modern Education,* Manual Arts Conference of the Mississippi Valley, The Manual Arts Press, Peoria, Ill., 1934.

Bennett, Charles A., *The Manual Arts,* The Manual Arts Press, Peoria, Ill., 1917.

Bonser, Frederick G., *Industrial Arts for Public School Administrators,* Bureau of Publications, Teachers College, Columbia University, New York, 1930.

Bonser, Frederick G., and Mossman, Lois C., *Industrial Arts for Elementary Schools,* The Macmillan Co., New York, 1923.

Ericson, E. E., *Teaching Problems in Industrial Arts,* The Manual Arts Press, Peoria, Ill., 1930.

Friese, J. F., *Exploring the Manual Arts*, The Century Co., New York, 1926.

Mays, Arthur B., Editor, *Education* (Special Industrial Arts Number) Volume 52, No. 10, June, 1932.

Mays, Arthur B., *The Problem of Industrial Education*, The Century Co., New York, 1927.

Schweickhard, Dean M., *Industrial Arts in Education*, The Manual Arts Press, Peoria, Ill., 1929.

Selvidge, R. W., and Fryklund, V. C., *Principles of Trade and Industrial Teaching*, The Manual Arts Press, Peoria, Ill., 1930.

Smith, Fred C., *Curriculum Problems in Industrial Education*, Doctor's Dissertation, Graduate School of Education, Harvard University, Harvard University Press, Cambridge, Mass., 1930.

Smith, Homer J., *Industrial Education: Administration and Supervision*, The Century Co., New York, 1927.

Snedden, David, and others, *Reconstruction of Industrial Arts Courses*, Bureau of Publications, Teachers College, Columbia University, New York, 1927.

Sotzin, Herbert Allen, *An Industrial Arts Curriculum for Grades Four to Twelve Inclusive*, University of Cincinnati, Cincinnati, Ohio, 1930.

Struck, F. Theodore, *Methods and Teaching Problems in Industrial Education*, John Wiley and Sons, New York, 1929.

Vaughn, S. J., and Mays, A. B., *Content and Methods of the Industrial Arts*, The Century Co., New York, 1924.

Warner, William E., *Policies in Industrial Arts Education*, Ohio State University Press, Columbus, Ohio, 1928.

LANGUAGE ARTS

English Language and Literature

Aiken, Janet Ruth, *New Plan of English Grammar*, Columbia University Bookstore, New York, 1933.

Bamberger, Florence E., and Broening, Angela M., *A Guide to Children's Literature*, Johns Hopkins Press, Baltimore, Md., 1931.

Barnes, Walter, *Certain Aspects of the Language Activities of Children in the Seventh, Eighth, and Ninth Grades*, Doctor's Thesis, New York University, New York, 1930.

Betts, E. A., and Bontrager, O. R., *Research Studies in Elementary School Language No. 1*, University of Iowa Studies in Education, Volume IX, No. 2, University of Iowa, Iowa City, Ia., 1934.

Benst, Nora, *Graded List of Books for Children*, American Library Association, Chicago, 1930.

Blaisdell, Thomas C., *Ways to Teach English*, Doubleday, Doran & Co., Garden City, N. Y., 1930.

Bobbitt, Sarah A., "Shortcomings in the Written English of Adults," Chapter XII, *Curriculum Investigations*, University of Chicago Press, Chicago, 1926.

Bolenius, Emma M., *Teaching Literature in the Grammar Grades and High School*, Houghton Mifflin Co., Boston, 1915.

Bolenius, Emma M., *The Teaching of Oral English*, J. B. Lippincott Co., Philadelphia, 1914.

Broening, Angela M., *Developing Appreciation through Teaching Literature*, Johns Hopkins University Studies in Education, No. 13, Johns Hopkins Press, Baltimore, Md., 1929.

Cavins, L. V., *Standardization of American Poetry for School Purposes*. University of Chicago Press, Chicago, 1928.

Chubb, P., *Teaching of English in the Elementary and the Secondary School*, Revised Edition, The Macmillan Co., New York, 1929.

Coleman, J. H., *Written Composition Interests of Junior and Senior High School Pupils*, Contributions to Education No. 494, Bureau of Publications, Teachers College, Columbia University, New York, 1931.

Cook, Elizabeth Christine, *Reading the Novel*, Little, Brown and Co., Boston, 1933.

Coryell, Nancy Gillmore, *An Evaluation of Extensive and Intensive Teaching of Literature*, Contributions to Education No. 275, Bureau of Publications, Teachers College, Columbia University, New York, 1927.

Craig, Virginia J., *The Teaching of High School English*, Longmans, Green & Co., New York, 1930.

Crow, Charles S., *Evaluation of English Literature in the High School*, Contributions to Education No. 141, Bureau of Publications, Teachers College, Columbia University, New York, 1926.

Dalgliesh, Alice, *First Experiences with Literature*, Charles Scribner's Sons, New York, 1932.

Davis, Helen I., *Practical English Projects for the High School*, Isaac Pitman and Sons, New York, 1931.

Drew, Elizabeth A., *Discovering Poetry*, W. W. Norton & Co., Inc., New York, 1933.

Driggs, Howard R., *Our Living Language*, The University Publishing Co., Chicago, 1920.

Dudley, Louise, *The Study of Literature*, Houghton Mifflin Co., Boston, 1928.

Dyer, Clara A., "The Placement of Poems in the Grades," Chapter XV, *Curriculum Investigations*, University of Chicago Press, Chicago, 1926.

Frawley, Honora Margaret, *Certain Procedures of Studying Poetry in the Fifth Grade*, Contributions to Education No. 539, Bureau of Publications, Teachers College, Columbia University, New York, 1932.

Fries, C. C., *The Teaching of the English Language*, Thomas Nelson and Sons, New York, 1927.

Fries, C. C., and others, *The Teaching of Literature*, Silver, Burdett & Co., New York, 1926.

Greene, Harry Andrew, *A Criterion for the Course of Study in the Mechanics of Written Composition*, University of Iowa Studies in Education, Volume VIII, No. 4, University of Iowa, Iowa City, Ia., 1933.

Gruen, Ferdinand Bernard, *English Grammar in American High Schools Since 1900*, Catholic University of America, Washington, D. C., 1934.

Hartman, Gertrude, and Shumaker, Ann, Editors, *Creative Expression*, John Day Co., New York, 1932.

Hitchcock, Alfred M., *Bread Loaf Talks on Teaching Composition*, Henry Holt & Co., New York, 1927.

Hosic, James Fleming, Chairman, *Reorganization of English in Secondary Schools*, Report by the National Joint Committee on English Representing the Commission on the Reorganization of Secondary Education of the National Education Association and the National Council of Teachers of English, Bureau of Education, Bulletin No. 2, Government Printing Office, Washington, D. C., 1917.

Huber, Miriam Blanton; Bruner, H. B.; and Curry, C. M., *Children's Interests in Poetry*, Rand, McNally & Co., Chicago, 1927.

Irion, Theo. W. H., *Comprehension Difficulties of Ninth Grade Students in Literature*, Contributions to Education No. 189, Bureau of Publications, Teachers College, Columbia University, New York, 1925.

Jespersen, Otto, *Growth and Structure of the English Language*, D. Appleton-Century Co., New York, 1923.

LaBrant, Lou Le Vanche, *Diagnostic Tests and Remedial Measures for the Teaching of English in the High School*, Kansas Studies in Education, Volume I, No. 10, University of Kansas, Lawrence, Kan., 1928.

Leonard, J. Paul, *The Course of Study in Secondary School English*, Proceedings of the Eighteenth Annual Meeting of the Department of Secondary School Principals of the National Education Association at Cleveland, Ohio, National Education Association, Washington, D. C., 1934.

Leonard, J. Paul, *The Use of Practice Exercises in the Teaching of Capitalization and Punctuation*, Contributions to Education No. 372, Bureau of Publications, Teachers College, Columbia University, New York, 1930.

Leonard, Sterling A., *Current English Usage*, English Monographs No. 1, The National Council of Teachers of English, Chicago, 1932.

Leonard, Sterling A., *English Composition as a Social Problem*, Houghton Mifflin Co., Boston, 1917.

Leonard, Sterling A., *Essential Principles of Teaching Reading and Literature in the Intermediate Grades and the High School*, J. B. Lippincott Co., Philadelphia, 1922.

Lewin, William, *Photoplay Appreciation in American High Schools*, English Monographs No. 2, The National Council of Teachers of English, D. Appleton-Century Co., New York, 1934.

Lyman, R. L., *The Enrichment of the English Curriculum*, Supplementary Educational Monographs No. 39, University of Chicago Press, Chicago, 1932.

Lyman, R. L., *Summary of Investigations Relating to Grammar, Language, and Composition*, Supplementary Educational Monographs No. 36, University of Chicago Press, Chicago, 1929.

Lynch, Cecile J., and Beard, S. A., *Books for Youth*, Brooklyn Public Library, Brooklyn, N. Y., December, 1931.

McKee, Paul G., *Language in the Elementary School*, Houghton Mifflin Co., Boston, 1934.

Mearns, Hughes, *Creative Power*, Doubleday, Doran & Co., Garden City, N. Y., 1929.

Mearns, Hughes, *Creative Youth*, Doubleday, Doran & Co., Garden City, N. Y., 1925.

Mirrielees, Lucia Bush, *Teaching Composition in High School*, Harcourt, Brace and Co., New York, 1931.

Moore, Annie E., *Literature Old and New for Children*, Houghton Mifflin Co., Boston, 1934.

National Council of Teachers of English, *Books for Home Reading for High Schools*, National Council of Teachers of English, 211 W. 68th Street, Chicago, 1930.

National Council of Teachers of English, *Leisure Reading*, National Council Teachers of English, 211 W. 68th Street, Chicago, 1932.

National Society for the Study of Education, Twenty-Second Yearbook, Part I, "English Composition: Its Aims, Methods, and Measurement," Public School Publishing Co., Bloomington, Ill., 1923.

Opdycke, Oliver, *In the Service of Youth,* Isaac Pitman and Sons, New York, 1928.

O'Rourke, L. J., *Rebuilding the English-Usage Curriculum to Insure Greater Mastery of Essentials,* Psychological Institute, 3506 Patterson St., N. W., Washington, D. C., 1934.

Paschall, Alma, *Creative Expression,* Harper and Brothers, New York, 1933.

Pendleton, Charles S., *The Content of High School English,* George Peabody College for Teachers, Nashville, Tenn., 1929.

Pendleton, Charles S., *The Social Objectives of School English,* The Author, George Peabody College for Teachers, Nashville, Tenn., 1924.

Pooley, Robert C., *Grammar and Usage in Textbooks on English,* Bureau of Educational Research, Bulletin No. 14, University of Wisconsin, Madison, Wis., 1933.

Rivlin, Harry N., *Functional Grammar,* Contributions to Education No. 435, Bureau of Publications, Teachers College, Columbia University, New York, 1930.

Robbins, Phyllis, *An Approach to Composition through Psychology,* Harvard Studies in Education, Harvard University Press, Cambridge, Mass., 1929.

Seely, Howard Francis, *Enjoying Poetry in School,* Johnson Publishing Co., Richmond, Va., 1931.

Seely, Howard Francis, *On Teaching English,* American Book Co., New York, 1933.

Shuttleworth, Frank K., *A Critical Study of Two Lists of Best Books for Children,* Genetic Psychology Monographs, Clark University Press, Worcester, Mass., 1932.

Smith, Dora V., *Instruction in English,* National Survey of Secondary Education, Bulletin No. 17, Monograph No. 20, Government Printing Office, Washington, D. C., 1932.

Smith, Johnie Rutland, *An Analytical Study of the Factors Involved in Learning to Appreciate Literature,* Bulletin No. 10, Bureau of Co-operative Research, School of Education, Indiana University, Bloomington, Ind., 1933.

Smith, Milton, *A Guide to Play Selection,* D. Appleton-Century Co., New York, 1934.

Steeves, Harrison Ross, *Literary Aims and Art,* Silver, Burdett & Co., New York, 1927.

Stormzand, M. J., and O'Shea, M. V., *How Much English Grammar?* Warwick & York, Baltimore, Md., 1924.

Terman, Lewis M., and Lima, Margaret, *Children's Reading; A Guide for Parents and Teachers,* D. Appleton Co., New York, 1926.

Thomas, Charles Swain, *The Teaching of English in the Secondary School*, Houghton Mifflin Co., Boston, 1927.

Trommer, Caroline J., and Regan, Teresa A., *Directing Language Power in the Elementary School Child Through Story, Dramatization, and Poetry*, The Macmillan Co., New York, 1933.

Troxell, Eleanor, *Language and Literature in the Kindergarten and Primary Grades*, Charles Scribner's Sons, New York, 1927.

Ward, Charles H., *What is English?* Scott, Foresman & Co., Chicago, 1925.

Washburne, Carleton; Weedon, Vivian; and Wilkinson, Mary S., *The Right Book for the Right Child*, John Day Co., New York, 1933.

Webster, Edward H., and Smith, Dora V., *Teaching English in the Junior High School*, World Book Co., Yonkers-on-Hudson, N. Y., 1927.

Wisconsin English Teachers' Association, *Report on English Usage as a Teaching Problem*, The Association, Milwaukee, Wis., 1933.

Woodring, Maxie N.; Jewett, Ida A.; and Benson, Rachel T., *The Enriched Teaching of English*, Bureau of Publications, Teachers College, Columbia University, New York, 1934.

Young, Nell J., and Memmott, Frederick W., *Methods in Elementary English*, D. Appleton & Co., New York, 1923.

Handwriting

Freeman, Frank N., *The Teaching of Handwriting*, Houghton Mifflin Co., Boston, 1914.

Freeman, Frank N., and Dougherty, Mary L., *How to Teach Handwriting*, Houghton Mifflin Co., Boston, 1923.

Voorhis, Thelma G., *The Relative Merits of Cursive and Manuscript Writing*, Bureau of Publications, Teachers College, Columbia University, New York, 1931.

Wise, Marjorie, *On the Technique of Manuscript Handwriting*, Charles Scribner's Sons, New York, 1924.

Reading

Anderson, C. J., and Davidson, I., *Reading Objectives*, Laurel Book Co., Chicago, 1925.

Baker, Harry J., and Leland, Bernice, *In Behalf of Non-Readers*, Public School Publishing Co., Bloomington, Ill., 1934.

Buswell, G. T., *Fundamental Reading Habits: A Study of Development*, University of Chicago Press, Chicago, 1922.

Dunn, Fannie Wyche, *Interest Factors in Primary Reading Material*,

Contributions to Education No. 113, Bureau of Publications, Teachers College, Columbia University, New York, 1921.

Gates, Arthur I., *The Improvement of Reading*, Revised Edition, The Macmillan Co., New York, 1934.

Gates, Arthur I., *Interest and Ability in Reading*, The Macmillan Co., New York, 1930.

Gates, Arthur I., *New Methods in Primary Reading*, The Macmillan Co., New York, 1928.

Gray, William S., *Summary of Investigations Relating to Reading*, University of Chicago Press, Chicago, Supplements for 1924–29.

Gray, William S., and Munroe, Ruth, *The Reading Interests and Habits of Adults*, The Macmillan Co., New York, 1929.

Gray, William S., and others, *Remedial Cases in Reading: Their Diagnosis and Treatment*, Supplementary Educational Monographs No. 22, University of Chicago Press, Chicago, 1922.

Gray, William S., and Whipple, Gertrude, *Improving Instruction in Reading: An Experimental Study*, University of Chicago Press, Chicago, 1933.

Harris, Julia M.; Donovan, H. L.; and Alexander, T., *Supervision and Teaching of Reading*, Johnson Publishing Co., Richmond, Va., 1927.

Herriott, M. E., *How to Make a Course of Study in Reading*, Educational Research Circular No. 42, Bureau of Educational Research, University of Illinois, Urbana, Ill., 1926.

Jordan, Arthur M., *Children's Interests in Reading*, University of North Carolina Press, Chapel Hill, N. C., 1926.

Judd, C. H., and Buswell, G. T., *Silent Reading: A Study of the Various Types*, Supplementary Educational Monographs No. 23, University of Chicago Press, Chicago, 1922.

Ladd, Margaret Rhoads, *The Relation of Social, Economic and Personal Characteristics to Reading Ability*, Contributions to Education No. 582, Bureau of Publications, Teachers College, Columbia University, New York, 1933.

Lindsay, Edward Y., *An Etymological Study of the Ten Thousand Words in Thorndike's Teacher's Word Book*, Volume 12, No. 65, Indiana University, Bloomington, Ind., 1925.

McKee, Paul, *Reading and Literature in the Elementary School*, Houghton Mifflin Co., Boston, 1934.

Monroe, Marion, *Children Who Cannot Read: the Analysis of Reading Disabilities and the Use of Diagnostic Tests in the Instruction of Retarded Readers*, University of Chicago Press, Chicago, 1932.

Moore, Annie E., *Literature Old and New for Children*, Houghton Mifflin Co., Boston, 1934.

National Society for the Study of Education, Twentieth Yearbook,

Part II, "Report of the Society's Committee on Silent Reading," Public School Publishing Co., Bloomington, Ill., 1921.

National Society for the Study of Education, Twenty-Fourth Yearbook, Part I, "Report of the National Committee on Reading," Public School Publishing Co., Bloomington, Ill., 1925.

Paul, Vera Alice, *Present Trends of Thought on Oral Reading,* University of Iowa Extension Bulletin No. 299, University of Iowa, Iowa City, Ia., 1932.

Pennell, M. E., and Cusack, A. M., *How to Teach Reading,* Houghton Mifflin Co., Boston, 1923.

Sangren, P. V., *Improvement of Reading Through Tests,* Bulletin No. 1, Western State Teachers College, Kalamazoo, Mich., 1932.

Storm, Grace E., and Smith, Nila B., *Reading Activities in the Primary Grades,* Ginn & Co., Boston, 1930.

Terman, Lewis M., and Lima, Margaret, *Children's Reading: A Guide for Parents and Teachers,* D. Appleton & Co., New York, 1926.

Thorndike, Edward Lee, *The Teacher's Word Book,* Bureau of Publications, Teachers College, Columbia University, New York, 1921.

Uhl, Willis L., *The Materials of Reading,* Silver, Burdett & Co., New York, 1924.

Uhl, Willis L., *Scientific Determination of the Content of the Elementary School Course in Reading,* University of Wisconsin, Madison, Wis., 1921.

United States Office of Education Bulletin No. 2, *The Activity Program and the Teaching of Reading,* Government Printing Office, Washington, D. C., 1931.

White House Conference on Child Health and Protection, *Children's Reading: A Study of Voluntary Reading of Boys and Girls in the United States,* The Century Co., New York, 1932.

Yoakam, G. A., *Reading and Study,* The Macmillan Co., New York, 1928.

Zirbes, Laura, *Comparative Studies of Current Practice in Reading, with Techniques for the Improvement of Teaching,* Contributions to Education No. 316, Bureau of Publications, Teachers College, Columbia University, New York, 1928.

Spelling

Breed, Frederick S., *How to Teach Spelling,* F. A. Owen Publishing Co., Dansville, N. Y., 1930.

Coleman, W. H., *A Critique of Spelling Vocabulary Investigation,* Education Series, No. 12, Colorado State Teachers College, Greeley, Colo., 1931.

Cook, Walter W., *The Measurement of General Spelling Ability Involving Controlled Comparisons between Techniques*, University of Iowa Studies in Education, Volume 6, No. 6, University of Iowa, Iowa City, Ia., 1932.

Foran, Thomas G., *The Psychology and Teaching of Spelling*, Catholic Education Press, Washington, D. C., 1934.

Foran, Thomas G., and Rock, Robert T., *An Annotated Bibliography of Studies Relating to Spelling*, Supplement No. 1, Educational Research Bulletin, Volume 5, No. 1, Catholic University of America, Catholic Education Press, Washington, D. C., 1930.

King, Luella M., *Learning and Applying Spelling Rules in Grades Three to Eight*, Contributions to Education No. 517, Bureau of Publications, Teachers College, Columbia University, New York, 1932.

Mendenhall, James E., *An Analysis of Spelling Errors: A Study of Factors Associated with Word Difficulty*, Bureau of Publications, Teachers College, Columbia University, New York, 1930.

Miller, Helen; Courtis, S. A.; and Watters, Garnette, *Creative Teaching in the Field of Spelling*, Wallace Publishing Co., Des Moines, Ia., 1931.

Sartorious, Ina C., *Generalization in Spelling*, Contributions to Education No. 472, Bureau of Publications, Teachers College, Columbia University, New York, 1931.

Selzer, Charles A., *Lateral Dominance and Visual Fusion; Their Application to Difficulties in Reading, Writing, Spelling and Speech*, Harvard Monographs in Education, No. 12, Harvard University Press, Cambridge, Mass., 1933.

Thompson, Robert S., *Effectiveness of Modern Spelling Instruction*, Contributions to Education, No. 436, Bureau of Publications, Teachers College, Columbia University, New York, 1930.

Thorndike, Edward Lee, *The Teacher's Word Book*, Bureau of Publications, Teachers College, Columbia University, New York, 1921.

Wickey, Rose, and Lambader, May B., *The Teaching of Spelling*, Webster Publishing Co., St. Louis, Mo., 1932.

Zyve, Claire, *An Experimental Study of Spelling Methods*, Contributions to Education No. 466, Bureau of Publications, Teachers College, Columbia University, New York, 1931.

MATHEMATICS

Blackhurst, James Herbert, *Principles and Methods of Junior High School Mathematics*, The Century Co., New York, 1928.

Blom, Sister Mary Callixta, *Educational Objectives in Arithmetic*, Catholic Education Press, Washington, D. C., 1925.

Bowden, A. O., *Consumers Uses of Arithmetic*, Contributions to Education No. 340, Bureau of Publications, Teachers College, Columbia University, New York, 1929.

Breslich, Ernst R., *The Administration of Mathematics in Secondary Schools*, University of Chicago Press, Chicago, 1933.

Breslich, Ernst R., *Problems in Teaching Secondary-School Mathematics*, University of Chicago Press, Chicago, 1931.

Breslich, Ernst R., "The Teaching of Mathematics in Secondary Schools," Volume I, *Technique*, University of Chicago Press, Chicago, 1930.

Brownell, William A., *The Development of Children's Number Ideas in the Primary Grades*, Supplementary Educational Monographs No. 35, University of Chicago Press, Chicago, 1928.

Brownell, William A., *The Effect of Unfamiliar Settings on Problem Solving*, Duke University Research Studies in Education, No. 1, Duke University Press, Durham, N. C., 1931.

Brueckner, Leo J., *Diagnostic and Remedial Teaching in Arithmetic*, John C. Winston Co., Philadelphia, 1930.

Buswell, G. T., and John, Lenore, *Diagnostic Studies in Arithmetic*, Supplementary Educational Monographs No. 30, University of Chicago Press, Chicago, 1926.

Buswell, G. T., and John, Lenore, *The Vocabulary of Arithmetic*, Supplementary Educational Monographs No. 38, University of Chicago Press, Chicago, 1931.

Buswell, G. T., and Judd, C. H., *Summary of Educational Investigations Relating to Arithmetic*, Supplementary Educational Monographs No. 27, University of Chicago Press, Chicago, 1925.

Caldwell, A. G., *Arithmetic Activities*, Board of Education, Cleveland, Ohio, 1931.

Congdon, Allen R., *Training in High School Mathematics Essential for Success in Certain College Subjects*, Contributions to Education No. 403, Bureau of Publications, Teachers College, Columbia University, New York, 1930.

Grossnickle, Foster E., *The Teaching of Arithmetic in the Elementary School*, Edwards Brothers, Inc., Ann Arbor, Mich., 1934.

Guiler, Walter S., *Objectives and Activities in Arithmetic*, Rand McNally & Co., Chicago, 1926.

Hanna, Paul R., *Arithmetic Problem Solving*, Bureau of Publications, Teachers College, Columbia University, New York, 1929.

Hassler, Jasper Ole, and Smith, R. R., *Teaching of Secondary Mathematics*, The Macmillan Co., New York, 1930.

Herriott, M. E., *How to Make a Course of Study in Arithmetic*, Bureau of Educational Research, Circular No. 37, University of Illinois, Urbana, Ill.

Judd, Charles H., *Psychological Analysis of the Fundamentals of Arithmetic*, Supplementary Educational Monograph No. 32, University of Chicago Press, Chicago, 1927.

Klapper, Paul, *The Teaching of Arithmetic*, D. Appleton-Century Co., New York, 1934.

Knight, F. B., and Behrens, Minnie S., *The Learning of the One Hundred Addition Combinations and the One Hundred Subtraction Combinations*, Longmans, Green & Co., New York, 1928.

Lide, Edwin S., *Instruction in Mathematics*, National Survey of Secondary Education, Bulletin No. 17, Monograph No. 23, Government Printing Office, Washington, D. C., 1932.

McCormick, Clarence, *The Teaching of General Mathematics in the Secondary Schools of the United States: A Study of the Development and Present Status of General Mathematics*, Contributions to Education No. 386, Bureau of Publications, Teachers College, Columbia University, New York, 1929.

National Committee on Mathematical Requirements, *The Reorganization of Mathematics in Secondary Education* (1923), Houghton Mifflin Co., Boston, 1927.

National Council of Teachers of Mathematics, Bureau of Publications, Teachers College, Columbia University, New York:

First Yearbook, "A General Survey of Progress in the Last Twenty-Five Years," 1926.

Second Yearbook, "Curriculum Problems in Teaching Mathematics," 1927.

Third Yearbook, "Selected Topics in the Teaching of Mathematics," 1928.

Fourth Yearbook, "Significant Changes and Trends in the Teaching of Mathematics Throughout the World Since 1910," 1929.

Fifth Yearbook, "The Teaching of Geometry," 1930.

Sixth Yearbook, "Mathematics in Modern Life," 1931.

Seventh Yearbook, "The Teaching of Algebra," 1932.

Eighth Yearbook, "The Teaching of Mathematics in the Secondary School," 1933.

Ninth Yearbook, "Relational and Functional Thinking in Mathematics," 1934.

Tenth Yearbook, "The Teaching of Arithmetic," 1935.

National Society for the Study of Education, Twenty-Ninth Yearbook, "Report of the Society's Committee on Arithmetic," Public School Publishing Company, Bloomington, Ill., 1930.

Neulen, Leon N., *Problem Solving in Arithmetic*, Contributions to Education No. 483, Bureau of Publications, Teachers College, Columbia University, New York, 1931.

Osburn, W. J., *Corrective Arithmetic*, Houghton Mifflin Co., Boston, 1924.

Overman, James R., *An Experimental Study of Certain Factors Affecting Transfer of Training in Arithmetic*, Educational Psychology Monographs No. 29, Warwick & York, Baltimore, Md., 1931.

Perry, Winona M., *A Study in the Psychology of Learning in Geometry*, Contributions to Education No. 179, Bureau of Publications, Teachers College, Columbia University, New York, 1925.

Reeve, William D., *A Diagnostic Study of the Teaching Problems in High-School Mathematics*, Ginn and Co., Boston, 1926.

Robertson, Minns Sledge, *Oral Problem Solving in the Elementary School*, Contribution to Education No. 20, George Peabody College for Teachers, Nashville, Tenn., 1925.

Scarf, Robert C., "The Mathematic Used in Popular Science," Chapter XIII, *Curriculum Investigations*, University of Chicago Press, Chicago, 1926.

Schaaf, William L., *Mathematics for Junior High School Teachers*, Johnson Publishing Co., Richmond, Va., 1931.

Schorling, Raleigh, *A Tentative List of Objectives in the Teaching of Junior High School Mathematics with Investigations for the Determining of Their Validity*, George Wahr, Inc., Ann Arbor, Mich., 1925.

Smith, David Eugene, and Reeve, William D., *The Teaching of Junior High School Mathematics*, Ginn and Co., Boston, 1927.

Thorndike, Edward L., *Psychology of Arithmetic*, The Macmillan Co., New York, 1922.

Thorndike, Edward L., and others, *The Psychology of Algebra*, The Macmillan Co., New York, 1923.

Wheat, Harry Grove, *The Relative Merits of Conventional and Imaginative Types of Problems in Arithmetic*, Contributions to Education No. 359, Bureau of Publications, Teachers College, Columbia University, New York, 1929.

Wilson, G. M., *What Arithmetic Shall We Teach?* Houghton Mifflin Co., Boston, 1926.

Woodring, Maxie N., and Sanford, Vera, *Enriched Teaching of Mathematics in the High School*, Bureau of Publications, Teachers College, Columbia University, New York, 1928.

MUSIC

Adler, Mortimer J., *Music Appreciation: An Experimental Approach to Its Measurement*, Archives of Psychology, No. 110, Bureau of Publications, Teachers College, Columbia University, New York, 1929.

Beattie, John W.; McConathy, Osbourne; and Morgan, R. V., *Music in the Junior High School*, Silver, Burdett & Co., New York, 1930.

Coleman, Satis N., *A Children's Symphony*, Bureau of Publications, Teachers College, Columbia University, New York, 1931.

Coleman, Satis N., *Creative Music for Children*, G. P. Putnam's Sons, New York, 1922.

Dykema, Peter W., *Music for Public School Administrators*, Bureau of Publications, Teachers College, Columbia University, New York, 1931.

Gehrkens, Karl W., *An Introduction to School Music Teaching*, C. C. Birchard & Co., Boston, 1929.

Gehrkens, Karl W., *Music in the Grade Schools*, C. C. Birchard & Co., Boston, 1934.

Hubbard, George E., *Music Teaching in the Elementary Grades: for Grades One to Six Inclusive*, American Book Co., New York, 1934.

McKinney, H. D., and Anderson, W. R., *Discovering Music*, American Book Co., New York, 1934.

Mohler, Louis, *Teaching Music from an Appreciative Basis: the Fundamentals of Musical Development*, C. C. Birchard & Co., Boston, 1927.

Mursell, James L., *Human Values in Music Education*, Silver, Burdett & Co., New York, 1934.

Mursell, James L., *Principles of Musical Education*, The Macmillan Co., New York, 1927.

Mursell, James L., and Glenn, Mabelle, *The Psychology of School Music Teaching*, Silver, Burdett & Co., New York, 1931.

Pierce, Anne E., and Hilpert, Robert S., *Instruction in Music and Art*, National Survey of Secondary Education, Bulletin No. 17, Monograph No. 25, Government Printing Office, Washington, D. C., 1932.

Progressive Education Association, *Creative Expression: the Development of Children in Art, Music, Literature and Dramatics*, edited by Gertrude Hartman and Ann Shumaker, John Day Co., New York, 1932.

Seashore, Carl Emil, *The Psychology of Musical Talent*, Silver, Burdett & Co., New York, 1919.

Thorn, Alice G., *Music for Young Children*, Charles Scribner's Sons, New York, 1929.

Zanzig, Augustus D., *Music in American Life,* Oxford University Press, London, England, 1932.

SCIENCE

Adams, Mary, Editor, *Science in the Changing World,* The Century Co., New York, 1933.
Beauchamp, Wilbur L., *Instruction in Science,* National Survey of Secondary Education, Bulletin No. 17, Monograph No. 22, Government Printing Office, Washington, D. C., 1932.
Craig, Gerald S., *Certain Techniques Used in Developing a Course of Study in Science for the Horace Mann Elementary School,* Contributions to Education No. 276, Bureau of Publications, Teachers College, Columbia University, New York, 1927.
Curtis, Francis D., *Digest of Investigations in the Teaching of Science in the Elementary and Secondary Schools,* P. Blakiston's Son & Co., Philadelphia, 1926.
Curtis, Francis D., *A Synthesis and Evaluation of Subject-Matter Topics in General Science,* Ginn and Co., Boston, 1929.
Downing, Elliot R., *An Introduction to the Teaching of Science,* University of Chicago Press, Chicago, 1934.
Ellwood, Charles Abram, *Man's Social Destiny in the Light of Science,* Cole Lecture, Cokesbury Press, Nashville, Tenn., 1929.
Finley, Charles W., *Biology in Secondary Schools and the Training of Biology Teachers,* Contributions to Education No. 199, Bureau of Publications, Teachers College, Columbia University, New York, 1926.
Fitzpatrick, Frederick Linder, *Biology for Public School Administrators,* Bureau of Publications, Teachers College, Columbia University, New York, 1934.
Frank, J. O., *How to Teach General Science,* P. Blakiston's Son & Co., Philadelphia, 1926.
Frank, J. O., and White, H. K., *High School Science Terminology— Chemistry and Physics,* J. O. Frank & Sons, 159 W. Irving St., Oshkosh, Wis., 1930.
Hunter, George W., *Science Teaching at the Junior and Senior High School Levels,* American Book Co., New York, 1934.
Hurd, A. W., *Coöperative Experimentation in Materials and Methods in Secondary School Physics,* Bureau of Publications, Teachers College, Columbia University, New York, 1933.
Hurd, A. W., *An Experiment in the Use of a Teaching Unit in Science,* Institute of School Experimentation, Bureau of Publications, Teachers College, Columbia University, New York, 1933.

Huxley, Julian S., *A Scientist among the Soviets,* Harper and Brothers, New York, 1932.

Johnson, Palmer O., *Curricula Problems in Science at the College Level,* University of Minnesota Press, Minneapolis, Minn., 1930.

Maxwell, Paul Ammon, *Cultural Natural Science for the Junior High School—Objectives and Procedures,* Williams and Wilkins Co., Baltimore, Md., 1932.

Millikan, Robert A., *Science and the New Civilization,* Charles Scribner's Sons, New York, 1930.

National Society for the Study of Education, Thirty-First Yearbook, Part I, "A Program for Teaching Science," Public School Publishing Co., Bloomington, Ill., 1932.

Parker, Bertha M., *An Introductory Course in Science in the Intermediate Grades,* Publications of the Laboratory Schools of the University of Chicago, No. 3, University of Chicago Press, Chicago, 1931.

Peters, Charles C., and Himes, H. E., "What Biology Functions Most Largely in Giving Pleasures of Recognition?" *National Society for the Study of Educational Sociology, Second Yearbook,* Bureau of Publications, Teachers College, Columbia University, New York, 1929.

Pollock, C. A., *Children's Interests as a Basis of What to Teach in General Science,* Ohio State University, Columbus, Ohio, 1924.

Rulon, Phillip Justin, *The Sound Motion Picture in Science Teaching,* Harvard Studies in Education, Harvard University Press, Cambridge, Mass., 1933.

Russell, Bertrand, *The Scientific Outlook,* W. W. Norton & Co., Inc., New York, 1931.

Slavson, S. R., and Speer, Robert K., *Science in the New Education as Applied to the Elementary School,* Prentice-Hall, Inc., New York, 1934.

Thomson, Sir J. Arthur, *Riddles of Science,* Liveright, Inc., New York, 1932.

Trafton, G. H., *The Teaching of Science in the Elementary School,* Houghton Mifflin Co., Boston, 1918.

Twiss, George Ransom, *A Textbook in the Principles of Science Teaching,* Revised Edition, The Macmillan Co., New York, 1927.

United States Bureau of Education, Bulletin No. 26, *Reorganization of Science in Secondary Schools,* Government Printing Office, Washington, D. C., 1920.

Veblen, Thorstein, *The Place of Science in Modern Civilization and Other Essays,* The Viking Press, New York, 1919.

Whitehead, Alfred North, *Science and the Modern World,* The Macmillan Co., New York, 1925.

Woodring, Maxie N.; Oakes, Mervin E.; and Brown, H. Emmett, *Enriched Teaching of Science in the High School,* Bureau of Publications, Teachers College, Columbia University, New York, 1928.

SOCIAL STUDIES

Bamesberger, V. C., *An Appraisal of a Social Studies Course in Terms of the Effect upon the Achievement, Activities, and Interests of Pupils,* Contributions to Education No. 328, Bureau of Publications, Teachers College, Columbia University, New York, 1928.

Barnes, Harry Elmer, *The New History and Social Studies,* The Century Co., New York, 1925.

Beard, Charles A., *A Charter for the Social Sciences in the Schools;* Part I: Report of the Commission on the Social Studies, American Historical Association, Charles Scribner's Sons, New York, 1932.

Beard, Charles A., *The Nature of the Social Sciences,* Part VII: Report of the Commission on the Social Studies, American Historical Association, Charles Scribner's Sons, New York, 1934.

Biddle, William W., *Propaganda and Education,* Contributions to Education No. 531, Bureau of Publications, Teachers College, Columbia University, New York, 1932.

Billings, Neal, *A Determination of Generalizations Basic to the Social Studies Curriculum,* Warwick & York, Baltimore, Md., 1929.

Bowman, Isaiah, *Geography in Relation to the Social Sciences,* Part V: Report of the Commission on the Social Studies, American Historical Association, Charles Scribner's Sons, New York, 1934.

Bye, E. C., *A Bibliography of the Teaching of the Social Studies,* Revised Edition, H. W. Wilson Co., New York, 1933.

Chicago University, *Introductory General Course in the Social Sciences, No. I, Syllabus and Selected Readings,* University of Chicago Press, Chicago, 1932.

Chicago University, *Second Year Course in the Social Sciences, No. II, Syllabus and Selected Readings,* University of Chicago Press, Chicago, 1932.

Commission on the Social Studies, American Historical Association, *Conclusions and Recommendations,* Charles Scribner's Sons, New York, 1934.

Dawson, Edgar, and others, *Teaching the Social Studies,* The Macmillan Co., New York, 1927.

Dunn, F. W., and Bathurst, E. G., *Social Studies for Rural Schools: Agriculture in World Civilization,* Institute of School Experimentation, Bureau of Publications, Teachers College, Columbia University, New York, 1932.

Fairbanks, H. W., *Real Geography and Its Place in the Schools,* Harr Wagner & Co., 149 Montgomery Street, San Francisco, 1927.

Fancler, Della G., and Crawford, C. C., *Teaching the Social Studies,* C. C. Crawford, University of Southern California, Los Angeles, 1932.

Gee, W., Editor, *Research in the Social Sciences,* The Macmillan Co., New York, 1929.

Hatch, R. W., *Training in Citizenship,* Charles Scribner's Sons, New York, 1926.

Helseth, Inga Olla, *Children's Thinking: A Study of the Thinking Done by a Group of Grade Children When Encouraged to Ask Questions about United States History,* Bureau of Publications, Teachers College, Columbia University, New York, 1926.

Herriott, M. E., *How to Make Courses of Study in the Social Studies,* Educational Research Circular No. 46, Bureau of Educational Research, University of Illinois, Urbana, Ill., 1926.

Hockett, John A., *Determination of the Major Social Problems of American Life,* Contributions to Education No. 281, Bureau of Publications, Teachers College, Columbia University, New York, 1927.

Hockett, John A., "Some Ways Out of Social Studies Confusion," *Social Studies Leaflet,* 9:1–3, Southern California Social Science Association, Los Angeles, April, 1935.

Hunter, Earle L., *A Sociological Analysis of Certain Types of Patriotism,* The Author, 69 Tiemann Place, New York, 1932.

Johnson, Henry, *An Introduction to the History of the Social Sciences in Schools,* Part II: Report of the Commission on the Social Studies, American Historical Association, Charles Scribner's Sons, New York, 1932.

Kelty, Mary G., *Teaching American History in the Middle Grades of the Elementary School,* Ginn and Co., Boston, 1928.

Kimball, R. S., and others, *Current-Events Instruction,* Houghton Mifflin Co., Boston, 1929.

Kimmel, William G., *Instruction in the Social Studies,* National Survey of Secondary Education, Bulletin No. 17, Monograph No. 21, Government Printing Office, Washington, D. C., 1932.

Kimmel, William G., *The Management of the Reading Program in the Social Studies,* National Council for the Social Studies, McKinley Publishing Co., Philadelphia, 1929.

Klapper, Paul, *The Teaching of History*, D. Appleton & Co., New York, 1926.

Knowlton, Daniel C., *History and the Other Social Studies in the Junior High School*, Charles Scribner's Sons, New York, 1926.

Knowlton, Daniel C., *Making History Graphic*, Charles Scribner's Sons, New York, 1925.

Lacey, Joy M., *Social Studies Concepts of Children in the First Three Grades*, Contributions to Education No. 548, Bureau of Publications, Teachers College, Columbia University, New York, 1932.

Lee, Baldwin, *Issues in the Social Studies*, Lincoln School Social Science Monographs No. 3, Bureau of Publications, Teachers College, Columbia University, New York, 1928.

Logasa, Hannah, Compiler, *Historical Fiction Suitable for Junior and Senior High Schools*, National Council for the Social Studies, McKinley Publishing Co., Philadelphia, 1927.

Mahan, Thomas J., *An Analysis of the Characteristics of Citizenship*, Contributions to Education No. 315, Bureau of Publications, Teachers College, Columbia University, New York, 1928.

Martz, Charles E., and Kinneman, John A., *Social Science for Teachers*, Houghton Mifflin Co., Boston, 1923.

Mathews, C. O., *The Grade Placement of Curriculum Materials in the Social Studies*, Contributions to Education No. 241, Bureau of Publications, Teachers College, Columbia University, New York, 1926.

Meltzer, Hyman, *Children's Social Concepts; A Study of Their Nature and Development*, Contributions to Education No. 192, Bureau of Publications, Teachers College, Columbia University, New York, 1925.

Merriam, Charles E., *Civic Education in the United States*, Part VI: Report of the Commission on the Social Studies, American Historical Association, Charles Scribner's Sons, New York, 1934.

Merriam, Charles E., *The Making of Citizens: A Comparative Study of Methods of Civic Training*, University of Chicago Press, Chicago, 1931.

Miller, George J., Editor, *Geography: How to Teach It*, Geographic Education Series, McKnight and McKnight Co., Bloomington, Ill., 1934.

Moore, Clyde B., and Wilcox, Lillian A., *The Teaching of Geography*, American Book Co., New York, 1932.

National Council for the Social Studies, First Yearbook, "Some Aspects of the Social Sciences in the Schools," McKinley Publishing Co., Philadelphia, 1931.

National Council for the Social Studies, Second Yearbook, "Classroom and Administrative Problems in the Teaching of the Social Sciences," McKinley Publishing Co., Philadelphia, 1932.

National Council for the Social Studies, Third Yearbook, "Supervision in the Social Studies," McKinley Publishing Co., Philadelphia, 1933.

National Council for the Social Studies, Fourth Yearbook, "The Social-Studies Curriculum," McKinley Publishing Co., Philadelphia, 1934.

National Council of Geography Teachers, *An Elective Course in Senior High School Geography,* A. J. Nystrom & Co., Chicago, 1929.

National Society for the Study of Education, Twenty-Second Yearbook, Part II, "The Social Studies in the Elementary and Secondary School," Public School Publishing Co., Bloomington, Ill., 1923.

National Society for the Study of Education, Thirty-Second Yearbook, "The Teaching of Geography," Public School Publishing Co., Bloomington, Ill., 1933.

Penningroth, Paul W., *A Study of Public Opinion on International Relations in Certain Communities,* Florida Grower Press, Tampa, Fla., 1932.

Peters, Charles C., *Objectives and Procedures in Civic Education,* Longmans, Green & Co., New York, 1930.

Pierce, Bessie Louise, *Civic Attitudes in American School Textbooks,* University of Chicago Press, Chicago, 1930.

Procedures and Sources in Curriculum Making for the Social Studies in the Elementary Grade, Curriculum Laboratory, School of Education, Western Reserve University, Cleveland, Ohio.

Progressive Education, Entire issue devoted to the Social Studies, Volume II, No. 4, Progressive Education Association, 716 Jackson Place, Washington D. C., October–November–December, 1925.

Progressive Education, Entire issue devoted to the Social Studies, Volume XI, Nos. 1 & 2, Progressive Education Association, 716 Jackson Place, Washington, D. C., January–February, 1934.

Reed, Mary, and Wright, Lula E., *The Beginnings of the Social Sciences,* Charles Scribner's Sons, New York, 1932.

Reeder, Edwin H., *Geography for Public School Administrators,* Bureau of Publications, Teachers College, Columbia University, New York, 1931.

Reeder, Rudolph R., *Training Youth for the New Social Order,* Antioch Press, Yellow Springs, Ohio, 1933.

Ridgley, Douglas C., *Geographic Principles, Their Application to the Elementary School,* Houghton Mifflin Co., Boston, 1925.

Ridgley, Douglas C., *A Study of Children's Learning about Places,* Clark University Press, Worcester, Mass., 1928.

580   BIBLIOGRAPHY

Rugg, Earle U., *Curriculum Studies in the Social Sciences and Citizenship,* Colorado State Teachers College, Greeley, Col., 1928.

Rugg, Harold O., and Hockett, J., *Objective Studies in Map Location,* Bureau of Publications, Teachers College, Columbia University, New York, 1925.

Shaffer, Laurance F., *Children's Interpretations of Cartoons,* Contributions to Education No. 429, Bureau of Publications, Teachers College, Columbia University, New York, 1930.

Storm, Grace E., *Social Studies in the Primary Grades,* Lyons and Carnahan, New York, 1931.

Swindler, R. E., *Social Studies Instruction in the Secondary Schools,* Prentice-Hall, Inc., New York, 1933.

Thralls, Z. A., and Reeder, E. H., *Geography in the Elementary School,* Rand McNally & Co., Chicago, 1931.

Tryon, R. M., *The Teaching of History in Junior and Senior High Schools,* Ginn and Co., Boston, 1921.

Van Wagenen, Marvin J., *Historical Information and Judgment in Pupils of Elementary Schools,* Contributions to Education No. 101, Bureau of Publications, Teachers College, Columbia University, New York, 1919.

Wilson, F. H., and Wilson, H. E., *Bibliography of American Biography, Selected and Annotated for Secondary Schools,* National Council for the Social Studies, McKinley Publishing Co., Philadelphia, 1930.

Wilson, H. E., *The Fusion of Social Studies in Junior High Schools: A Critical Analysis,* Harvard Studies in Education, Harvard University Press, Cambridge Mass., 1933.

INDEX

Abbott, A., study of pupils' preferences of classics, 218
Abilities
involving specific habits and motor skills, list, 138–139
of individual pupils vary, 327–328
to be taught, criteria for choosing, 390–391, 392–393
variability of, within grades, 324–326
Accreditment, 59–61
Achievement, variability within grades, 324–327
Achievement tests
development of, 57
summary of results on the Stanford, in reading, 326
Activities (see also Teacher activities)
a variety desirable, 233–234
aims as directive force of teacher, 123
available for educational use, 235–239
classifications of, 235–239
curriculum development and pupil, 239–246
determining appropriateness of, 234–235
emphasis on overt physical, 231–232, 233
for construction or production of material objects, 238
for creative expression, 238–239
for recreation, 239
levels of, complexity of, 229
need for evaluation of, 246–247
occur on various levels, 230
of individuals tend to cluster around major centers, 173–174
organization of, dependent upon method of defining scope, 240
play and recreational, 219
relation to aims of education, 234–235

relation to learning, 230–233
relation to purpose, 234, 385–386
required to discharge social functions, 175
suggested by social functions approach, 243–246
to facilitate mastery of skills, 237
to organize and present information, 237
to secure information, 236–237
underemphasis of intellectual, 232
unit of work organization of, 240–243
various interpretations of meaning, 226–229
Activity analysis
as developed by Bobbitt, 151–152
of adult practices, 258–259
Activity curricula
confusion in meaning of, 228–229
discovered in courses of study, 40
Adams, J. T., on breaking down of education, 29
Administration, relation to curriculum development, 76–78
Administrative organization in curriculum development
agencies responsible for different aspects of program, 487–494
committee organization, 497–503
duties of committees, 498–501
examples of effective, 512–521
financial provision, 503–504
for particular school system, 521
personnel of committees, 502–503
securing specialists and consultants, 496
selection of director, 494–496
size of committees, 501–502
type to be employed, 468
types of committees, 498–501
Administrative procedures in curriculum development
general guides to, 480–486